MARRIAGES
of Some
VIRGINIA RESIDENTS

1607 - 1800

MARRIAGES
of Some
VIRGINIA RESIDENTS
1607 - 1800

By Dorothy Ford Wulfeck

VOLUME IV
Surnames T - Z

CLEARFIELD

NOTICE

This work is a reproduction of the original mimeographed edition. In spite of the uneven type image of the original, our printer has made very effort to produce as sharp a reprint as possible.

Reprinted, seven volumes in four,
for Clearfield Company by
Genealogical Publishing Company
Baltimore, Maryland
2009

ISBN, Volume IV: 978-0-8063-5419-4
ISBN, four-volume set: 978-0-8063-5420-0

Made in the United States of America

Originally published in seven volumes:
Volume 1 (surnames A-B), 1961
Volume 2 (surnames C-E), 1963
Volume 3 (surnames F-H), 1963
Volume 4 (surnames I-Me), 1964
Volume 5 (surnames Mi-Q), 1966
Volume 6 (surnames R-S), 1967
Volume 7 (surnames T-Z), 1967

Reprinted, seven volumes in two,
by Genealogical Publishing Co., Inc.
Baltimore, Maryland, 1986

Reprinted, seven volumes in three,
for Clearfield Company by
Genealogical Publishing Co., Inc.
Baltimore, Maryland, 2003

CONTENTS

FOREWORD

"Marriages of Some Virginia Residents, 1607-1800," is a series of books designed to cover a wider scope of information than other compilations limited to the Returns of Ministers, Parish Registers, or records of marriages in Court Houses. In each instance such marriages occurred within the boundaries of the Old Dominion.

The references and records in these volumes relate to three different classes of people:

1. Those who were married before settling in Virginia. References to these are of special aid to searchers tracing their ancestors back to the immigrant, as information given aids them in knowing the Colony in which to continue their search.
2. Those who were married in Virginia.
3. Those who married after removing from Virginia to another Colony or State. These are needed to assist in one of the most difficult problems in genealogy: identification of the native Colony of ancestors who died in Indiana, Illinois, Kentucky, Tennessee, Missouri, the Carolinas, Georgia, or elsewhere. This third class is a boon to compilers of a genealogy, guiding them to the various new areas to which descendants migrated.

COMPILATION TECHNIQUES

There has been no attempt to modernise the spelling. "Cook" is recorded as "Kuke," "McInteer" as "Manadear," preserving the phonetic spelling used by clerks, ministers or descendants.

Many items are a composite of data found in all references cited. Not all data were found in each reference. Some references to the same marriage presented vast differences as to dates, places, and, occasionally, as to names. References are cited separately for these. It is expected that current searchers can use these differences as clues for resolving the facts.

SCOPE OF RESEARCH

The search for Virginia marriages was begun as a personal hobby of the compiler and reached such vast proportions that the files contain over 150,000 cards. Three main ideas have been followed in accumulating information:

1. To identify the native Colony of settlers moving into southern and western areas.
2. To assemble information from family Bibles, traditions and personal knowledge as to marriages for which no official records exist. Migrants to the unpopulated areas took their Bibles with them and many county histories, published between 1850 and 1900, give statements of marriages before 1800. People of advanced years gave information from

their knowledge of the names of their grandparents, or even of their great-grandparents. These volumes can, in some measure, fill in the records so unfortunately destroyed in Virginia.

3. To prove "by inference" as many marriages as possible from abstracts of wills, deeds, court suits and records from Orphans' Courts.

MARRIAGES OF RECORD

Thousands of proven marriages are recorded in these volumes, as it is necessary to have all records easily available to know when this wide research has added something NEW to the facts.

HOW TO SECURE PROOF

The compiler of these volumes assumes no responsibility for the accuracy of the statements made. The information, in many instances, has been taken from lineages, histories, and listings made by people of varying ability and interest, sometimes based on family traditions. However, two to five statements from as many different sources are brought together into one paragraph, from which the current searcher may gather valuable clues leading to the irrefutable proof of the marriage. It is possible to secure photostats or certified copies of marriage bonds and records, and of DAR lineages, from their original sources.

BIBLIOGRAPHY

The listing of a book here means that these volumes include references from it, but it does not mean that all marriage information from that book has been compiled. Some rare books were used only for a brief period of time in a distant library — public or private.

Albemarle	"Albemarle County in Virginia," by Rev. Woods. 1932.
Am. Hist.	"The American Historical Magazine." Published by Peabody Normal College Nashville, Tenn. 1896-
Bagby	"King and Queen County, Virginia," by Rev. Alfred Bagby. 1809.
Ball	"Ball Family Records," by Rev. William Ball Wright. 1908.
Barton	Barton's "Colonial Decisions," Vol. I, Sir John Randolph's Reports. Cases decided between 1728 and 1743, as given in Tyler's Quarterly Historical Magazine. Vol. I, pp. 60-67, 115-126.
Baskerville	"Additional Baskerville Genealogy;" a Supplement to "Genealogy of the Baskerville Family," 1912, by P. Hamilton Baskerville. 1917.
Bath	"Annals of Bath County, Virginia," by Oren F. Morton. 1917.
Bell	"Cumberland Parish, Lunenburg County," by Landon C. Bell. 1930.
Biog. Enc. Ky.	Biographical Encyclopedia of Kentucky. 1878.
Blisland Parish	"Vestry Book of Blisland Parish, New Kent and James City Counties, 1721-1786," by C. G. Chamberlayne. 1935.
Boddie-Hist. of Boddie-HSF	"Historical Southern Families," by John B. Boddie.
Boddie-Isle or Isle of Wight	"Seventeenth Century Isle of Wight County, Virginia," by John B. Boddie. 1959.

Boddie-Southside or Boddie-SVF — "Southside Virginia Families," by John B. Boddie.

Boogher — "Gleanings of Virginia History," by William Fletcher Boogher. 1903.

Brockman or Br * * — "The Brockman Scrapbook," by W. E. Brockman. 1952.

Calhoun — "Calhoun, Hamilton, Baskin and Related Families," by L. D. McPherson. 1957.

Cameron — Rev. John Cameron's "Little Black Book," a register of marriages.

Caroline — "A History of Caroline County, Virginia, from its Formation in 1727 to 1924," by Marshall Wingfield. 1924.

Carrington — See Halifax

Carson — "Carson Family History," by F. Tom Carson. 1958.

Charles Parish — "Charles Parish, York County, Virginia, History and Registers," by Landon C. Bell. 1932.

Christ Church — "The Parish Register of Christ Church, Middlesex County, Virginia, 1653-1812," published by the National Society of Colonial Dames of America in the State of Virginia. 1897.

Collins — "History and Genealogy of the Collins Family of Caroline County, Virginia, and Related Families, 1569-1954," by Herbert Ridgeway Collins. 1954.

Colonial or Colonial Families — "Colonial Families of the Southern States of America," by Stella Pickett Hardy. 2nd edition, 1958.

Cowherd — "Cowherd Genealogy," by Edythe Cowherd Newton. 1962.

Crozier-Spts. — "Spotsylvania County Records, 1721-1800," by William A. Crozier. 1955.

Cumberland — "History of Cumberland County, Kentucky," by J. W. Wells. 1947

** Burns — See Walker

Curd — "Edward Curd of Henrico County, Virginia, and Some of His Descendants." Typescript owned by Mrs. W. B. Walker, Lexington, Ky.

Custer — "The Rev. Alexander Miller of Virginia," by Milo Custer.

Dameron — "The Dameron-Damron Genealogy," by Helen Foster Snow. 1954.

Dames or Squires — "Squires and Dames of Old Virginia," by Evelyn Kinder Donaldson. 1950.

DAR — Lineage Books of the Daughters of the American Revolution.

DAR Mag. — Daughters of the American Revolution Magazine.

Darnall — "The Darnall, Darnell Families," Vol. I, by H. C. Smith, M. D. 1955.

Dinkins — "The Dinkins and Springs Families," by Capt. James Dinkins. 1908.

Douglas Reg. — "The Douglas Register," edited by W. Jones. 1928.

Draper Mss. — Manuscripts of Dr. Lyman C. Draper, in Wisconsin Historical Society, Madison, Wisc.

Duke — "Henry Duke, Councilor, His Descendants and Connections," by Walter Garland Duke. 1949.

East Tenn. — "The East Tennessee Historical Society's Publications." 1929-

Emison Supp. — Supplement (1962) to "The Emison Families Revised," (1954) by James Wade Emison.

Fairfax — "An Historic Sketch of the Two Fairfax Families of Virginia," by Thomas K. Cartmell. A reprint from his "History of Frederick County, Virginia."

Farmer — "Descendants of Thomas Farmer Who Came to Virginia in 1616," by Ellery Farmer. 1956.

Field	"Field Genealogy," by Frederick Clifton Pierce. 1901.
Fleet	"Virginia Colonial Abstracts," by Beverley Fleet. Reference indicates volume.
Free	"The Old Free State: A Contribution to the History of Lunenburg County and Southside Virginia," by Landon C. Bell. Vols. I and II. 1927.
Fulton	"History of Fulton County, Illinois." 1878.
Germanna	"The Germanna Record," Official Publication of the Memorial Foundation of the Germanna Colonies in Virginia, Inc. Vol. I, published July, 1961.
Gillmore	"Gillmore-Carter and Allied Families," by Helen Gilmore Smith Thomas and Dolly Reed Gilmore Barmann. 1962.
Gordon Mss.	Manuscripts in files of Maj. M. K. Gordon.
Green or T. M. Green	"Historic Families of Kentucky," by Thomas Marshall Green. 1889.
Gwin	"History of the Gwin Family," by Jesse Blaine Gwin. 1961.
Habersham	"Historical Collections of the Joseph Habersham Chapter, DAR." 1910.
Halifax or Carrington	"A History of Halifax County, Virginia," by Wirt Johnson Carrington. 1924.
Harllee	"Kinfolks," a Genealogical and Biographical Record, by William Curry Harllee. 1935.
Hartford	The Hartford (Connecticut) Times Genealogy Page.
Hayden	"Virginia Genealogies," by Horace Edwin Hayden. 1891.
Hening	"Personal Names in Hening's Statutes at Large of Virginia and Shepherd's Continuation," by J. J. Casey. 1933.
Henrico	"The Vestry Book of Henrico Parish, 1730-1773," by R. A. Brock. 1874.

Hines — Manuscript Collections of Hines Vol. 1-18, Virginia Archives.

Hinshaw or H — "Encyclopedia of American Quaker Genealogy," by William Wade Hinshaw.

Hist. of Louisa or Louisa — "History of Louisa County, Virginia," by Malcolm H. Harris. 1936.

Hist. of Shelby Co. — "History of Shelby County, Kentucky," by George L. Willis, Sr. 1929.

Huguenot — "The Huguenot," a publication by the Huguenot Society of the Founders of Manakin in the Colony of Virginia.

Hume or Kennedy — "Early American History: Hume and Allied Families," by William Everett Brockman. 1926.

Jett — "Minor Sketches of Major Folk," by Dora C. Jett. 1928.

Johnson — "The Ancestry of Grafton Johnson," by Damaris Knobe. 1924.

Joliffe — "Historical, Genealogical and Biographical Account of the Joliffe Family of Virginia," by William Joliffe. 1893.

Jones or Jones Gene. — "Captain Roger Jones of London and Virginia," by Judge L. H. Jones. 1891.

KCG — Manuscript records from the files of the late Kathryn Cox Gottschalk, Washington, D. C.

Kegley — "Kegley's Virginia Frontier," by Frederick Bittle Kegley. 1938.

Kennedy — See Hume.

Ky. Bible Records — "Kentucky Bible Records," Kentucky Records Research Committee. Kentucky DAR. 1962.

Ky. Cem. — "Kentucky Cemetery Records," by Kentucky Society, Daughters of the American Revolution.

Ky. Reg. — "The Register," published quarterly by Kentucky Historical Society.

Kingston Parish Reg.	"The Vestry Book of Kingston Parish, Mathews County, Virginia, 1679-1796," transcribed by C. G. Chamberlayne. 1929.
King William	"King William County, Virginia," by Elizabeth Hawes Ryland. 1955.
LNCo or LNCoAntiquary	"The Lower Norfolk County, Virginia, Antiquary," edited by E. W. James. 1895-1906.
Lofland	"History of the Family Lofland in America, and Related Families," by Jewell Lofland Crow. 1956.
Lord-Supplement	"Ahnentafels," by Charles M. Lord, 2800 Erie St., S. E., Washington 20, D. C.
Louisa	See Hist. of Louisa
Lucas	"Lucas Genealogy," by Annabelle Kemp. 1964.
Lynchburg	"A History of Lynchburg's Pioneer Quakers and their Meeting House, 1754-1936," by Douglas Summers Brown. 1936.
McClung	"Genealogy of the McClung Family."
McCullough or Yesterday	"Yesterday When It Is Past: For Edward," by Rose Chambers Goode McCullough. 1957.
McGhee	"Virginia Pension Abstracts," by Lucy Kate McGhee. 1953-
Major	"The Majors of Virginia and Their Connections," by Julian N. Major, Sr. 1937.
Meade	"Andrew Meade of Ireland and Virginia," by P. Hamilton Baskerville. 1921.
Miller Mss.	Manuscript in office of the late Mrs. Glen Earle Miller, Ridley Park, Penna.
Mss.	Manuscript records of I. A. G. Compendium (from Genealogical Book Company, in possession of Mrs. B. M. Hines).
Morton	"A History of Rockbridge County, Virginia," by C. F. Morton. 1920.
Moss	"A Genealogical Record of the Moss Family in America: John Moss, Sr., Line," by Columbus Joseph Moss, 1631 Hodges St., Lake Charles, La. 1964.

Nash	"Nashes of Ireland: Richard and Alexander of Eastern Shore and Their Allied Families, 1200-1956," by Anna Catherine Smith Pabst. 1963.
NNHist.Mag. or NNHM	"Northern Neck of Virginia Historical Magazine," published by Northern Neck Historical Society. 1951.
Nugent	"Cavaliers and Pioneers," by Kate Nugent. 1934.
Old King Wm.	"Old King William: Homes and Families," by Peyton Neale Clarke. 1897.
Opal Combs	From the files of Opal Harsch Combs, 9022 S. E. Clay, Portland 16, Ore.
OPR	Overwharton Parish Register, Stafford County.
Orange III	"Orange County, Virginia, Families," Vol. III, by W. E. Brockman. 1959.
Page	"Genealogy of the Page Family in Virginia," by Richard Channing Moore Page, M. D. 2nd Edition. 1893.
Perrin 1882	"History of Kentucky, Containing Bourbon and Surrounding Counties," by William Henry Perrin. 1882.
Perrin or Perrin-Simpson	"History of Kentucky," (including the families of Simpson County) by William Henry Perrin. 1886.
Poscud	"Three Courageous Women and Their Kin. A Pescud Genealogy," by Elizabeth Hogg Ironmonger. 1965.
Peyton	"History of Augusta County, Virginia." 1953.
Pharr	"Pharrs and Farrs," by Henry Newton Pharr. 1955.
Pocahontas	"Pocahontas and Her Descendants," by Wyndham Robertson. Reprint 1956.
Puckett	"The Roots and Some of the Branches of the Puckett Family Tree," by Christine South Gee. 1958.

Roames	"The Roams, Roames Family and Allied Families," by H. C. Smith, M. D.
Rhodes	"The Rhodes Family in America," by Howard J. Rhodes. 1959.
Rixey	"The Rixey Genealogy," by Randolph Picton Rixey. 1933.
St. Mark's or Slaughter	"A History of St. Mark's Parish, Culpeper County, Virginia," by Rev. Philip Slaughter. 1877.
St. Paul's	"St. Paul's Parish Register. A typescript copy. Los Angeles Public Library.
St. Peter's	"The Vestry Book and Register of St. Peter's Parish, New Kent and James City Counties, Virginia, 1684-1786," transcribed and edited by C. G. Chamberlayne. 1937.
Sale	"Root and Branch of the Sale Tree in America," by Dorothea Sale Goodman. 1939.
Sangamon	"History of Sangamon County, Illinois."
Scarborough	"Southern Kith and Kin," Vol. IV, by Jewel Davis Scarborough. 1958.
Seaton	"The Seaton Family," by Oren Andrew Seaton. 1906.
Shelby	See History of Shelby Co.
Simpson Co.	See Perrin
Slaughter	See St. Mark's
Squires	See Dames
Stoddard or Stoddard-Sudduth	"Stoddard-Sudduth Papers," by Mary Sudduth Stoddard. No date, but after 1956.
Surry	"Colonial Surry," by John B. Boddie. 1959.
T	"Tyler's Quarterly Historical and Genealogical Magazine," edited by Lyon G. Tyler.
Talbot	"Genealogical Sketch of Certain of the American Descendants of Mathew Talbot, Gentleman," by Robert Howe Fletcher, Jr. 1956.

Taylor	"Southern Taylor Families, 1507-1830, by Dr. Albert Eugene Casey. 1958.
Tompkins	"Rockbridge County, Virginia," by Edmund Pendleton Tompkins. 1952.
Utterback	"The Utterback Family, 1620-1938," by William I. Utterback. 1937.
V	"The Virginia Magazine of History and Biography," a quarterly by the Virginia Historical Society. 1893-
Va. Gaz.	"The Virginia Gazette," published in Williamsburg, Virginia. Weekly Genealogy Feature.
Valentine	"Edward Pleasants Valentine Papers." 1929.
Venable	"Some Venables of England and America," by Henrietta B. Brown. 1961.
Virginia Cousins	"Virginia Cousins," by G. Brown.
Va. Gen.	"The Virginia Genealogist," a quarterly published by John Frederick Dorman, Box 4883, Washington, D. C.
W	"The William and Mary Quarterly," published by William and Mary College.
Waddell	"Annals of Augusta County, Virginia, from 1725 to 1871," by Joseph A. Waddell. 1902.
Walker	"Dr. Thomas Walker Family History Records," Vol. I, by Annie Walker Burns, P. O. Box 6183, Apex Station, Washington, D. C. 1950.
Wayland	"Virginia Valley Records," by John W. Wayland. 1930.
Wilcoxson	"Wilcoxson and Allied Families," by Dorothy Ford Wulfeck. 1958.
Wilford	"Wilford-Williford Family Treks Into America," by Eurie Pearl Wilford Neel. 1959.

Winston or Winston of Va.	"Winston of Virginia and Allied Families," by Clayton Torrence. 1927.
Woodford	"History of Woodford County, Kentucky."
Woodley	"The Woodleys of Isle of Wight County, Virginia," by James Francis Crocker. 1914.
Yesterday	See McCullough
Young Chart	"Memorial and Family Tree of Michael Cadet Young," compiled and arranged by Col. Calvin Duvall Cowles. Washington, D. C. 1895.
** Prewitt	"The Wolfe-Hawkins-Sheets-Yates-Wheeler and Allied Families," by Lela Wolfe Prewitt. 1964.

T

TABB

____ m. Abram Keen.
____ m. Mary Sclater, dau. of James, whose will, prov. 17 Aug., 1724. 4W(1)138.
Anna m. John Nash, Jr.
Diana m. John Robinson.
Dorothy m. George Dudley.
Edward, b. 1719; d. 1782; m. 11 Nov., 1749, Lucy Todd. 25V314.
Edward Lowry, b. 6 Jan., 1769, son of John and Mary (Mallory); m. 31 Jan., 1791 (or 3 Feb.), Elizabeth Blair Burwell, b. 19 June, 1774, dau. of Col. John Lewis Burwell and his wife, Anne (Spotswood). Mecklenburg Co. Mar Bond; 26W(1)202; McCullough, pp. 220, 282.
Elizabeth m. George Burtenhead.
Elizabeth m. John Patterson.
Elizabeth m. George H. Baskerville.
Euphany m. Matthew T. Maury.
Henry, d. 17 Jan., 1822, son of John and Mary (Parsons); m. 3 Oct., 1799, Diana Moore, d. July, 1824. 7W(1)47.
Humphrey Toy m. 24 Nov., 1756, Mary Peyton in Kingston Parish, Mathews Co. (formerly Gloucester). 15T263; 42V67.
Humphrey Frances Toy m. George Fitzhugh (1st wife).
John, Col. of Elizabeth City Co., son of Thomas and Elizabeth (Moss) Heyward, m. (1) Mary Sclater, dau. of Rev. James of Charles Parish, York Co. 7W(1)19, 46.
John, b. 15 Nov., 1728, son of Thomas and Mary (Armistead); m. Mary Parsons; res. Elizabeth City Co. 7W(1)47.
John, son of Thomas and (2) Rebecca (Booker) of Amelia Co., m. 17 Feb., 1770, Frances Peyton, dau. of Sir John. She d. 12 April, 1828. 7W(1)49.
Johnson, b. 11 Nov., 1759, son of John; m. Dorothy Harwood. 7W(1)47.
Lucy m. ____ Cary.
Margaret m. George Walton.
Margaret m. Abraham Keen.
Martha m. Rev. Armistead Smith.
Martha m. Joseph Mayo.
Martha (____) m. Edmond Sweeney.
Martha Peyton m. William B. Giles.
Mary m. Westwood Armistead.
Mary m. Col. John Mayo.
Mary m. Robert Bolling.
Mary m. William G. Goode.
Mary m. Starkey Armistead.
Mary (____) m. Richard Swepson (or Swepston).
Mary Marshall m. Robert Bolling (2nd wife).
Pauline m. George Wythe Booth.
Philip, b. 6 Nov., 1750; d. 25 Feb., 1822, tombstone at Toddsbury, son of Edward and Lucy (Todd); m. 7 Dec., 1780, Mary Mason Booth,

TABB (cont.)

dau. of Nathaniel Wythe Booth and his wife, Elizabeth. 25V314.

Priscilla m. Robert Armistead.

Rachel m. ___ Tivash.

Ruth m. John Newman.

Sarah m. Littleton Kendall.

Sarah m. Westwood Armistead.

Susanna m. Capt. John Kearney.

Thomas m. 27 Dec., 1790, Elizabeth Teackle, dau. of Caleb, dec'd. Northampton Co. Mar. Bond.

Thomas, son of Thomas, m. Mary Armistead, dau. of Anthony. Their son, Thomas, b. 18 Dec., 1730. 7W(1)46-7; Bell, p. 287.

Thomas m. 27 Sept., 1735, Amelia Co., Rebecca Booker, dau. of Col. Edward; mentioned in will of Frances (Booker) Stokes, 1752, Amelia Co. 16T258-9; Bell, p. 114.

Thomas, will prov. 16 Oct., 1717, son of Thomas; m. Elizabeth (Moss) Heyward, widow of Henry of York Co., who d. 1712, and dau. of Edward Moss of York Co., whose will, prov. 1716. 2W(1)167; 7W(1)46. She was given as Elizabeth (Moss) Howard. 6T49-50.

Thomas of Amelia Co., son of John and Martha (Hand), m. (1) Elizabeth Mayo, dau. of Joseph of Henrico Co.; m. (2) 1735, Rebecca Booker. 7W(1)48.

TABERER

___ prob. m. Capt. Robert Spencer (1st wife).

___ m. ___ Copeland.

Christian m. (1) William Oudelant; m. (2) Robert Jordan.

Christian m. William Outland.

Elizabeth m. ___ Copeland.

Mary m. William Webb.

Thomas m. bef. 1696, Elizabeth Williams, legatee of estate of Thomas Taberer. Was she widow or married daughter? Boddie-Isle, p. 629.

Thomas m. (1) ___ ___; m. (2) Margaret (___) Wood, widow of John; res. 1672, Surry Co. Boddie-Hist.IV:71.

TABOR

Rhoda m. R. Edwards.

TACKET

Lidia m. William Daghaty.

Mary m. Isaac Burgan.

Rachel m. Charles Friend.

TACKETE

Nimrod m. 15 March, 1787, Ann Howard by Rev. John Alderson, Jr. Rockingham Co. or Greenbrier Co. Ministers' Returns.

TACKETT

Bartley m. 14 July, 1791, Sarah Wren. Prince George Co. Cameron.

Elizabeth m. Thomas Briscoe.

Keziah m. John Young.

Lewis m. 14 Nov., 1789, Sukey Sumpter, dau. of Edmund. Sur. William Sumpter. Charlotte Co. Mar. Bond.

Sarah m. Major St. John.

TADFORD

Alexander m. 6 Sept., 1787, Mary McCampbell by Rev. John Brown. Rockbridge Co. Ministers' Returns.

TAFF

Anne m. Thomas Brooke.

Elizabeth m. Isaac Palmer.

Mary m. Reuben Alderson.

Thomas m. bef. 1750, Mary Frizell, dau. of Francisco. Proven by will of Francisco Frizell, dated 23 Jan., 1732, and Court Record, 9 Nov., 1750, both in Lancaster Co.

Thomas m. bef. Oct., 1737, Eliza (____) Fendla, widow of John, whose estate sett., Oct., 1737, Lancaster Co., proves it.

TAILOR

Moses m. 23 Jan., 1767, Obedience Smith, both in this parish. Douglas Reg., p. 9.

TAIT(-E)

Betsy m. Edward Travis (1st wife).

James m. Rebecca Hudson, dau. of Charles and Susan (Patrick) of Prince Edward Co.; rem. to Wilkes Co., Ga. 26T178.

Sarah m. Rev. James Madison.

William, Maj., m. Ann (____) Metcalf, widow of William, who d. 1726. 6T280.

TALBERT (See TALBOT)

Charles m. 26 Nov., 1798, Fanny Coleman. Halifax Co. Mar. Record.

E. m. Thomas Milam.

Martha m. William Woodall.

Matthew m. Mary (Heale) Dale, b. 1728, dau. of Nicholas and Ann (____) Heale. Boddie-Hist.V:23.

TALBOT

____ believed m. bef. 1802, Elizabeth Cock, dau. of George, whose will, filed 1802, Campbell Co., named dau. Elizabeth Talbot.

Anne Williston m. Col. Triplett.

Charles, d. 1779, Bedford Co.; m. Drusilla ____. Bell, p. 288.
Charles, b. 1723, Md., son of Mathew and (1) Mary (Williston); m. 3 Aug., 1747, in Va., Drusilla Gwin. Talbot, pp. 23-4.

David G. m. 1791, Patsey Jennings by Rev. John Chappell, Methodist. Lunenburg Co. Ministers' Returns.

Edmund, b. 28 March, 1767, Bedford Co.; d. 1858; m. (1) 1787, Mary Harvey, d. 1807, dau. of John of Washington Co., Ga.; m. (2) ca 1807, ____ (Cauthorn) McCulloch. 9W(1)258; Bell, p. 293.

Elizabeth m. George Walker.

Hail m. Elizabeth Irvine, dau. of David and Jane (Kyle) of Bedford Co.; rem. to Mo. 3 Ky. Reg. 91.

Isham, b. 3 Nov., 1738, Bedford Co., son of Mathew and (2) Jane Clayton; m. Elizabeth Davis. Talbot, p. 32.

James, b. 7 Nov., 1733, Bedford Co.; will prov. there, 1777; m. 1759, Elizabeth Smith. Talbot, p. 30.

James m. Jane Quarles, dau. of John (d. 1789) and Sarah (Winston) (b. 1748). 38V361-2.

John, b. 13 July, 1735, Va., son of Mathew and (1) Mary (Williston); m. (1) Sarah Anthony of Bedford Co.; m. (2) Mary Mosely, dau. of Col. William of Princess Anne Co. Talbot, p. 30. Mar. (2) Phoebe Moseley of Henrico Co.; rem. 1784, to Wilkes Co., Ga. Bell, p. 289.

Martha m. Barnabas Arthur.

Mary m. William Triplett.

TALBOT (cont.)

Mary m. Plummer Thurston.

Mary (____) m. John Dyke, Jr.

Mathew m. (1) in Md. Mary Williston; m. 23 May, 1737, Bedford Co. Jane Clayton, probably a widow. Some references say "Anne" Williston. 9W(1)257; Bell, p. 290; Mss. of M. K. Gordon; DAR No. 28 908.

Mathew, son of John and (2) Mary (Mosely), m. Elizabeth Munger. Talbot, pp. 30-1.

Mathew, b. 27 Nov., 1729, Bristol Parish, Va.; d. ca 1812, Wilkes Co., Ga., son of Mathew and (1) Mary (Williston); m. Mary (Hale) Day, b. 1728; d. 1785, dau. of Nicholas and widow of Thomas Day. 9W(1)257; Bell, p. 291; Talbot, pp. 32-3.

Patsy m. John Owen.

Phoebe m. Col. David Cresswell.

Thomas, son of John and (2) Mary (Mosely), m. Elisabeth Cresswell, dau. of the Rev. James and Elizabeth (Garlington). Talbot, p. 30.

Williston, Lieut., b. 1751, Bedford Co.; d. 1830, Campbell Co.; m. (1) Elizabeth Cocke. DAR No. 41 876.

TALBOTT

Benjamin m. Mary Whaley, dau. of James (d. ca 1782, Loudoun Co.). 10W(2)344.

Catherine (____) Moss m. John Muse.

Harry, b. England; m. Barbara Whaley, dau. of James (d. ca 1782, Loudoun Co.). 10W(2)344.

TALBUTT

Mary m. Thomas Williamson.

Penelope m. John Smith.

Sarah m. Shadrack Talbutt.

Shadrack m. 19 Sept., 1751, Sarah Talbutt. Norfolk Co. Mar. Record.

William m. bef. 1676/7, Mary Sharp, dau. of John. Proven by will of William Talbutt, that date, Rappahannock Co.

TALER

N. m. John Polley.

TALFORD

James m. 22 Jan., 1789, Jean McCorkery by Rev. John Brown in Augusta Co.

Samuel m. 13 April, 1786, Elizabeth Call by Rev. John Brown in Augusta Co.

TALIAFERRO

____ m. ____ Walker and had dau. Lucy Taliaferro and son, Christopher. Jones Gene., p. 43.

____ m. Judge William Nelson.

____ of "Blenheim" m. Jane Brockenbrough (2nd husband). 5V448.

____ m. Daniel Call.

____ m. Carter Nicholas.

____ m. William Browne.

____, a dau., m. ____ Wilkinson.

____ m. William P. Harris.

____ m. bef. 1799, Betty Thornton, dau. of John. Proven by Court Suit of that date. 11W(2)115.

____, a dau., m. ____ Wedderburn.

____ m. ____ Wishart, dau. of John (d. ca 1774). Proven by Chancery

TALIAFERRO (cont.)

Suit, 1800. 11W(2)118.

____, a dau., m. ____ Stubbs.

____ m. Francis Taliaferro.

____, a dau., m. ____ McCandish.

Agatha m. ____ Kennon.

Alice D. m. James A. Thom.

Ann m. Nicholas Taliaferro.

Ann m. William Fitzhugh.

Ann Hay m. ____ Brooke.

Ann Hay m. Lawrence Battaile.

Ann Hay m. Richard Brooke (1st wife).

Anne m. Carter Nicholas.

Anne m. Daniel Ellott (2nd wife).

Anne m. Jonathan McCrary.

Anne (____) m. Edward Evans.

Anne Hubbard m. Charles Thornton.

Baldwin, son of Lawrence and Sarah (Dade), m. 1797, Anne Spottswood. 11T18. Mar. 14 March, 1797. St. Mark's, p. 79.

Benjamin, b. 1750; d. 1821, son of Zachariah and Mary (Boutwell); served in Rev. War; m. (1) Martha Meriwether; m. (2) ____ Cox. 11T19.

Benjamin, son of Dr. John (1733-1821) and Mary (Hardin), m. Ada Snow. 11T20.

Benjamin Franklin, b. 9 June, 1770, son of Charles and Isabella (Mc Cullough); m. Mildred Franklin. 11T20.

Burton, son of Zachariah (1730-1811) and Mary (Boutwell), m. (1) Sarah Gilmer; m. (2) Lucy Carter. 11T19.

Catharine m. Rice Hooe.

Catherine m. John Taylor.

Catherine m. Col. John Battaile.

Caty T. m. William Rucker.

Charles, son of Col. John (1656-1720) and Sarah (Smith), m. bef. May, 1714, Ann Kemp, b. 13 Aug., 1694, dau. of Richard, will prov. 1714, Essex Co. She m. (2) Edward Evans. 11T13; 21T189; 26T107.

Charles, d. 1734, son of Robert and Kathryn (Grymes); m. Mary Carter. 21T189. His mother was Sarah Grymes. 11T12.

Charles, b. 29 March, 1761, son of Charles and Isabella (McCullough); m. Mary Loving. 11T19.

Charles, b. 17 July, 1735, son of Capt. Richard and Rose (Berryman); m. 1757, Isabella McCullough. 11T19.

Eliza m. Samuel Hildrup.

Elizabeth m. Col. William Taliaferro.

Elizabeth m. ____ Moseley.

Elizabeth m. Thomas Stribling.

Elizabeth m. Benjamin Hume (1st wife).

Elizabeth m. Levy Prewet (or Pruitte).

Elizabeth m. William Stewart.

Elizabeth m. Zachary Hawkins.

Elizabeth m. John Catlett.

Elizabeth m. (1) Col. William Taliaferro; m. (2) Capt. Benjamin Hume.

Elizabeth m. Judge Samuel Call.

TALIAFERRO (cont.)

Elizabeth m. George Wythe (2nd wife).

Elizabeth m. John Catlett III.

Elizabeth (____) m. Moseley Batteley.

Frances m. Wilson Penn.

Frances m. Kenelm Cheseldine.

Frances m. Moses Penn.

Francis, b. 1700; d. 1758, son of Lawrence and Alice (Thornton); m. 1730, Elizabeth Hay, b. 1700; d. 1750. 11T13, 14.

Francis, d. 1710, son of Robert and Sarah (Grymes); m. bef. 1691, Elizabeth Catlett, d. ca 1716, dau. of Col. John. Proven by Deed, 1691, Essex Co. 11T12; 21T188; 20W(1)268.

Francis, b. 1743; d. 1815; will prov. Spotsylvania Co., son of Francis and Elizabeth (Hay); m. after 1764, Jane (or Jane Champe) Taliaferro, his cousin, dau. of Col. John Taliaferro, Sr., of King George Co. and Ann (Champe). 11T14, 18; 44V350-1; 20W(1)271; 7W(2)273; 13W(2) 270.

Francis m. Letitia Hughes, dau. of Stephen (d. 1793). Albemarle, p. 232

Francis Whitaker, son of Francis and Jane (Taliaferro), m. bef. 1797, his cousin, Jane Taliaferro of "Blenheim." 11T15; 9W(2)311.

George of Orange Co. m. 1767, Sarah (Taliaferro) Conway, widow of Francis and dau. of Col. John and Sarah (____) Taliaferro of Williamsburg. 11T26.

Hardin m. Elijah Lingo.

Hay, b. 1775; d. 1834, son of Lawrence and (2) Sarah (Dade); m. 18 March, 1797, his cousin, Susannah "Sukey" Conway, dau. of Catlett and Susannah (Fitzhugh). (Mar. 16 March, 1797, in Col. F. Taylor's Diary.) 11T17; 2W(2)134-5; 7W(2)276; Orange Co. Mar. Record.

Hay, b. 1740; d. 1825, son of Francis and Elizabeth (Hay) of Spotsylvania Co.; m. 5 April, 1791, his cousin, Lucy Mary (Taliaferro) Thurston, widow of William Plummer Thurston and dau. of Col. William and Mary (Battaile) Taliaferro. 11T14; 26V301; 30V68; 50V274; 13W (2)270; Orange Co. Mar. Record; announced in the Virginia Herald, 21 April, 1791.

Hay, son of William and Margretta (Aylett), m. 1800, Mary Tutt of Spotsylvania and Culpeper counties; rem. to Ky. 37V173.

Hay, b. 17 March, 1790; d. aged 85; m. Lucy (Taliaferro) Thornton, dau. of Col. William. 20W(1)271.

Hay of Orange Co., son of John and Jane (Bankhead), m. Mildred Taylor. 9W(2)311.

Hay of "Piedmont," son of Richard (b. 1747) and Jane (Bankhead), m. Mildred Taylor. 11T27.

Jael m. (1) ____ Williams; m. (2) Richard Johnson.

James, b. 12 April, 1779, son of Charles and Isabella (McCullough); m. (1) Lucy Rice; m. (2) Susan Brockman. 11T20.

James, son of Richard (b. 1747) and Jane (Bankhead), m. Mary Dick. She m. (2) Sir John Peyton, d. 1790. 11T27. James was son of John and Jane (Bankhead). 9W(2)312.

James Bankhead, son of Robert and Anne Hubbard (Taylor), m. Harriet Mayo. 11T27.

James Garnett, son of John and Elizabeth (Garnett), m. 1787, Wilhelmina Wishart. 11T16.

TALIAFERRO (cont.)

Jane m. Francis Whitaker Taliaferro.

Jane Champe m. Samuel Washington (1st wife).

Joan m. ____ Lukey.

John, b. 1765; d. 1809, son of Charles and Isabella (McCullough); m. Elizabeth Loving. 11T19.

John m. 30 June, 1737, Frances Robinson. Christ Church, p. 170.

John m. 12 March, 1795, Alice Leckie at home of Capt. Henry Taliaferro by Rev. John Woodville. St. Mark's Parish.

John, b. 31 July, 1753, son of Col. William and (1) Mary (Battaile); m. 12 May, 1772, Ann (or Amy) Stockdell, dau. of Capt. John and Mary (____) of Orange Co. Orange Co. Mar. Record; 11T18; 41V357; 29V502; 4W(1)50; 1W(2)147, 151.

John, b. 1768 at "Hays," King George Co.; d. 12 Aug., 1852, near Fredericksburg, son of John and Elizabeth (Garnett) of Essex and King George counties; m. Lucy Thornton Hooe. 11T16; 42V79.

John of King George Co., b. 1745; d. 1790, son of Francis and Elizabeth (Hay); m. (1) Elizabeth "Betty" Garnett, b. 6 June, 1750, dau. of James and (3) Mary (Rouzie) Garnett Jones; m. (2) 24 Jan., 1774, St. Paul's Parish, Stafford Co., Lucy Alexander. 11T15; 30T47; 33V29; 42V79; 13W(2)270.

John, Dr. and Capt. in Rev. War, b. 7 April, 1733; d. 7 April, 1821, son of Capt. Richard and Rose (Berryman); m. ca 1755, Mary Hardin, dau. of Henry and Judith (Lynch). 11T20.

John, Sr., Col., b. Essex Co.; m. ca 1745, Ann Champe, dau. of Col. John and Jane (____) of King George Co.; res. "Dissington." 30T47; 39V29.

John, d. 3 May, 1744; m. 22 Dec., 1708, Mary Catlett, dau. of Col. John, Jr., and Elizabeth (Gaines). Family Register. 1W(2)145-6. Mar. bef. 31 Dec., 1708. Proven by Court Record in Essex Co. He, son of John and Sarah (Smith), m. 1718. 35V415.

John, "The Ranger," Col., b. 1656; d. 1720, son of Robert and Sarah (Grymes); m. ca 1682, Sarah Smith, dau. of Maj. Lawrence of Gloucester Co.; res. Essex Co. Court Record, 25 March, 1693, Essex Co.; 11T13; 21T188; 23V68; 28V316; 35V415; 41V181; 6W(1)43; 20W(1)269-70; Louisa, p. 412.

John, Jr., of "Dissington," King George Co., d. 1805; m. Elizabeth "Betty" Thornton, dau. of Col. John and Mildred (Gregory). Proven by Chancery Suit, 1799. 11T18; 39V29; 11W(2)117. He, son of Col. John and Ann (Champe), d. bef. 1788. 30T47; 44V350; 4W(1)162.

John Narborne, son of Robert and Anne Hubbard (Taylor), m. Frances Mary Southgate. 11T27.

Judith m. Shadrack Franklin.

Judith m. Rhodan A. Greene.

Katherine m. John Stubbs.

Kemp, son of Charles and Anne (Kemp), m. Mary Thornton. 11T13.

Lawrence, b. 8 Sept., 1721; d. 1748, son of Col. John, Jr., of Spotsylvania Co. and Mary (Catlett); m. Susannah Power, dau. of Maj. Henry. 11T14; 35V415; 1W(1)144; 7W(1)129; 1W(2)145-6.

Lawrence, b. 3 Dec., 1734, Spotsylvania Co.; d. 8 April, 1798, Orange Co., son of Francis and Elizabeth (Hay); m. (1) bef. 1764, Mary Jackson, dau. of Robert, whose will of that date, Spotsylvania Co.,

TALIAFERRO (cont.)

names, "my dau. Mary, now the wife of Lawrence Taliaferro." WBD, p. 103; DAR No. 27 164. He m. (2) 3 Feb., 1774, St. Paul's Parish, Stafford Co., Sarah Dade, b. 20 Jan., 1747, dau. of Baldwin and (2) Verlinda (____). 16T171; 13W(2)270; DAR No. 65 455.

Lawrence, b. 1683; d. 1726, Essex Co., son of Col. John and Sarah (Smith); m. bef. 11 Oct., 1706, Sarah Thornton, b. 17 Dec., 1680, a twin, dau. of Francis and (1) Alice (Savage). Proven by Deed, 31 Aug., 1706, Richmond Co., and Court Record, 11 Oct., 1706, Essex Co. 11T13; 20W(1)270.

Lucy m. William Champe Willis.

Lucy m. (1) Charles Carter; m. (2) Col. William Jones.

Lucy m. (1) ____ Thornton; m. (2) Hay Taliaferro.

Lucy m. John Lawrence Jones.

Lucy m. Col. Charles Lewis.

Lucy Mary m. (1) William Plummer Thurston; m. (2) Hay Taliaferro.

Martha m. William Hunter.

Martha m. Col. Thomas Hunter (1st wife).

Martha m. Thomas Turner.

Mary m. Robert Reynolds.

Mary m. Judge William Nelson.

Mary m. ____ Mercer.

Mary m. Thomas Turner.

Mary m. Francis Thornton.

Mary m. Joseph Jones.

Mary Berryman m. ____ Wortham.

Mary Holden m. ____ Keith.

Mary Turner m. John Thornton Woodford.

Matilda m. William Helm.

Mildred m. William Strother.

Mollie Brook m. Col. Catesby Jones (1st wife).

Nancy m. Thompson Watkins.

Nicholas, Lieut., b. 30 Oct., 1757; d. 1812, son of Col. William and Mary (Battaile); served in Rev. War; m. (1) 3 Nov., 1781, by Rev. James Stevenson, Ann(-e) Champe Taliaferro, b. 7 April, 1756; d. 3 Feb., 1798, dau. of John and Elizabeth (Thornton); res. Culpeper Co.; rem. 1796, to Bracken Co., Ky. Orange Co. Mar. Record; 44V351. Ann was dau. of Col. John and Ann (Champe). 11T14, 18; 30T47; 41V 357.

Peter, b. 12 Feb., 1740, son of Capt. Richard and Rose (Berryman); m. Ann(-e) Hackley, dau. of John (d. 1760) and Judith (Ball) of King George Co. 11T20; 30T269; 48V269.

Richard, b. 1762, Fredericksburg, Va.; d. 1836, Clermont Co., Ohio; m. (2) Rebecca Riddle. DAR No. 47 843.

Richard, b. 1756; d. 1781, son of Dr. John and Mary (Hardin); served in Rev. War; m. Dorcas Perkins. 11T20.

Richard, son of Richard (b. 1747) and Jane (Bankhead), m. ____ Gilmer. 11T27.

Richard, b. 1759; d. 15 April, 1806, son of Charles and Isabella (Mc Cullough); Capt. in Rev. War; m. 18 July, 1780, Mildred Powell, dau. of Lucas. She was living, 1833, aged 74, in Pickens Co., Ala. 11T 19.

TALIAFERRO (cont.)

Richard, Col., b. 1705; d. 3 July, 1779, son of Francis and Elizabeth (Catlett); m. Elizabeth Eggleston; res. James City Co. 11T13; 9W(1) 128; 20W(1)269.

Richard, Col., son of Richard (1705-1779) and Ann (Eggleston), m. Rebecca Cocke, dau. of Richard of Surry Co. 11T13; 5V74; 20W(1)269.

Richard, b. 1706; d. 1748, son of John and Sarah (Smith); m. 10 June, 1726, Rose Berryman, dau. of Benjamin and Elizabeth (Newton) of Westmoreland Co. Court Record, 25 March, 1727, Essex Co.; St. Paul's Parish, Stafford Co.; 11T19. He was son of Zacariah and res. "Blenheim," Caroline Co. 29T242.

Robert, b. 1667; d. 1728, son of Robert and Sarah (Grymes); m. 1682, Sarah Catlett, b. 1666; d. 1726, dau. of Col. John and Elizabeth (Underwood). Proven by Deed, 1687, and Court Record, 25 March, 1692, Essex Co. 11T12; 20W(1)267.

Robert, son of John and Jane (Bankhead), m. Ann Taylor, dau. of Col. James of Orange Co. She m. (2) John Todd. 29V372; 9W(2)312.

Robert, son of Richard (b. 1747) and Jane (Bankhead), m. Anne Hubbard Taylor. 11T27.

Robert, res. 1636, Gloucester Co.; m. ____ Grymes, dau. of Rev. Charles. 27V185; Old King Wm., p. 101. Robert, d. ca 1677; m. Katherine Grymes, dau. of Rev. Charles (d. 1677) and Katherine (____). "To correct earlier lineage." 21T183.

Robert, b. ca 1625, England; d. 1687, Va.; m. ca 1653, Sarah Grymes, dau. of Rev. Charles. 11T12; 35V415.

Robert, d. 1728, son of Col. John and Sarah (Smith); m. bef. 1 Jan., 1726/7, Elizabeth Mathews, dau. of Capt. Samuel and Katherine (Tunstall). She m. (2) Moseley (or Moses) Battaley. Court Record, 1726/7, Essex Co.; 11T13; 45V97; 5W(1)277.

Robert H. m. Elizabeth (Thornton) Wilkinson. 5V74.

Roderick, b. 16 May, 1777, son of Charles and Isabella (McCullough); m. ____ Price. 11T20.

Rose Berryman m. Joseph Loving.

Sally m. Robert G. Leckie.

Sarah m. (1) Francis Conway; m. (2) George Taylor.

Sarah m. John Lewis (1st wife).

Sarah m. Lieut. John McKinney.

Sarah m. Anthony Thornton (1st wife).

Sarah m. Col. Thomas Turner (2nd wife).

Sarah m. Daniel Harvey (or Harvie).

Sarah m. Capt. William Dangerfield.

Sarah m. William Wilkinson.

Sarah m. James Taylor (2nd wife).

Sarah m. (1) Capt. Francis Dade; m. (2) Capt. William Dade.

Sarah m. Richard Brooke (2nd wife).

Sarah m. William Brooke.

Sarah (____) m. Samuel Sallis.

Sarah Bohethland m. William Loving.

Walker, son of William (b. 1707) and Anne (Walker), m. (1) Sarah "Sally" Turner, dau. of Thomas and Mary (Taliaferro); m. (2) Elizabeth Hartwell. 11T28; 21V107.

Warner T. m. Fanny Booth, dau. of George Wythe and Lucy (Jones). 2W

TALIAFERRO (cont.)
(1)234.
Warren, son of Zachariah (1730-1811) and Mary (Boutwell), m. Nancy Gilmer. 11T19.
William, d. 1760, son of Col. John and Sarah (Smith); m. Katherine Hay. 11T13.
William, Capt., b. 17 Jan., 1707, son of Francis and Elizabeth (Catlett) m. Anne Walker, b. 17 Jan., 1707/8; res. Essex Co. 11T13; 20W(1)269.
William, Col., b. 1718; served in Rev. War; m. bef. 1777, Elizabeth Holden, d. bef. 1803, sis. of George of Gloucester Co., whose will, 1777, Williamsburg, Va., proves it. Court Suit, 1803. 11T15; 5W (1)176; 11W(2)123.
William, Col., b. 9 Aug., 1726, at "Snow Creek," Spotsylvania Co.; d. 21 April, 1798, Orange Co., son of Col. John and Mary (Catlett); m. (1) 4 Oct., 1751, by Rev. Musgrove Dawson to Mary Battaile, b. 18 Sept., 1731; d. 9 Nov., 1757, dau. of Capt. Nicholas and ____ (Thornton) of Caroline Co.; m. (2) 5 Dec., 1758, by Rev. Musgrove Dawson to Elizabeth Taliaferro, b. 4 Oct., 1741; d. about age 90, dau. of Francis and Elizabeth (Hay) of "Epsom," Spotsylvania Co. She m. (2) Capt. Benjamin Hume. 11T14; 35V415; 41V357; 20W(1)271; 1W(2)45-6; 7W(2)274; 8W(2)213; 13W(2)270.
Zachariah, b. 1767; d. 1823, son of Charles and Isabella (McCullough); m. Sallie Warmuck. 11T19.
Zachariah, b. 1739, Va.; d. 1811, So. Car., son of Capt. Richard and Rose (Berryman); m. Mary Boutwell. 11T19; DAR No. 79 251.
TALLEY
Betsey m. Thomas Nash.
Carter m. 17 Dec., 1788, Pattey Gauldin by James Hurt. Campbell Co. Mar. Record.
George m. 24 Dec., 1793, Sally Cole. Louisa, p. 261. (Also given as Tally and as Sept., 1793.)
Nancy m. Joseph D. Gibson.
William m. Feb., 1791, Lydia Cole. Louisa, p. 266.
TALLMAN
Ann m. John Harrison.
TALLY
John m. 22 Dec., 1796, Sally Dizmang by Rev. John Neblett, Methodist. Lunenburg Co. Ministers' Returns.
Mary m. John Gibson.
Michael m. 1793, Barbara Cole, both in Louisa. Douglas Reg., p. 27.
Reuben m. 7 Oct., 1773, Martha Dyer, both of Louisa. Douglas Reg., p. 14.
Sally m. James Gibson.
Story m. 10 Nov., 1784, Ann Hagert (or Harger). Douglas Reg., p. 119.
William m. March, 1791, Lydia Cole, both of Louisa. Douglas Reg., p. 27.
TALMAN
Henry m. bef. 1733, Ann Eliza Ballard. Bell, p. 174.
TALOR
____ m. bef. Aug., 1765, Mary Stephens, dau. of William, whose will of that date, Orange Co., mentions "my daughter Mary Talor."
Giles m. 6 July, 1786, Sine Stokes by Rev. Thomas Crymes, Baptist.

TALOR (cont.)
Lunenburg Co. Ministers' Returns.

TAMIAN
Margaret m. William Ward.

TANDDY
John m. 8 Nov., 1797, Betsy Bickley by Rev. William Cooke. Louisa, p. 271.

TANDY
____, a dau., m. ____ Holman.
Achilles, b. 1758; d. 1820, Fayette Co., Ky., son of William; served in Rev. War; m. ca 1787, Nancy Ferguson. 14T118.
Ann m. Edward Waller.
Frances m. Thomas Burris (or Burruss).
Frances m. Joseph Lipscomb.
Frances m. Will. Bush.
Henry, b. 6 March, 1741; d. 1 July, 1809; m. 18 Nov., 1763, Ann Mills, d. 14 Dec., 1810, Orange Co. 15T40. He, son of Roger and Sarah (Quarles). 14T120; Brockman, p. 54.
Henry, Jr., b. 1660, son of Henry of Old Rappahannock Co.; m. bef. 1685, Priscilla (____) Watson, widow of John. Proven by Court Suit, 5 Aug., 1685, Rappahannock Co., and Court Record, 25 March, 1693, Essex Co. Brockman, p. 53.
Henry, Jr., b. 15 Sept., 1772, son of Henry and Ann (Mills) of Orange Co.; m. 28 Nov., 1796, Elizabeth Adams. Orange Co. Mar. Record; 14T120; 27V345.
Henry III, b. ca 1686; d. 1741, son of Henry, Jr., and Priscilla (____); m. ca 1717, Frances (____) Crittenden, widow of Henry; rem. Essex Co. to King and Queen Co. 14T116; Brockman, p. 53.
Jane m. Maj. John Allen.
John, b. 9 Dec., 1751, Caroline Co., son of William; m. (1) Judith ____; m. (2) bef. 1791, ____ Rowland; rem. to Ky. 14T118.
Lucy Quarles m. Maj. Thomas Hughes.
Martha m. John Parker.
Martha m. William Dix.
Mary m. John Morton.
Nancy m. James Perry.
Roger of King and Queen Co., son of Henry and Priscilla (____); m. bef. 1728, Sarah Quarles, dau. of Roger (d. 1751, Caroline Co.); res. Spotsylvania Co. and Caroline Co. 14T117; Brockman, pp. 53-4.
Sarah m. Claiborne Graves.
William, will prov. 1794; m. Jane Quarles; res. Fredericksville Parish, Va. Brockman, p. 54.

TANKARD
Azariah m. 3 Feb., 1764, Rachel Pettitt, dau. of William, dec'd. Northampton Co. Mar. Record.
Elizabeth m. Charles Floyd.
John m. 10 Jan., 1791, Lilla Downing. Northampton Co. Mar. Record.
Margaret m. William Joyne.
Nancy m. Revel Watson.
Patience m. James Heath.

TANKERSLEY
George m. 29 Sept., 1779, Elizabeth Garrison. Henry Co. Mar. Record.

TANKERSLEY (cont.)

John, b. 1760; m. in Port Royal, Va., Frances Muse, d. 1846, dau. of Richard and Margaret (Payne) of Westmoreland Co. 53V312-3.

John, Jr., m. 2 Feb., 1778, Sarah Foster. Sur. John Tankersley. Charlotte Co. Mar. Bond.

Mary m. Joseph Murdock.

Richard m. 1800, Nancy Leech. Morton, p. 533. Mar. Nancy Lusk. Morton, p. 499.

TANKERY

Ezra m. 1797, Hannah Mitchell. Rockbridge Co. Morton, p. 511.

TANKRED

____ m. bef. 1707, Sarah Smart, dau. of William. 4V422.

TANNEHILL

Anne m. Cuthbert Harrison (3rd wife).

Josiah, b. 7 June, 1753, Montgomery Co., Md.; d. March, 1811, Baton Rouge, La.; served in Rev. War from Md. and Va.; m. 27 April, 1786, Pittsburgh, Pa., Margaret Wilkins, b. ca 1767; d. 21 Dec., 1839, Louisville, Ky., dau. of John. Pension W8777.

TANNER

____ m. bef. 1773, Lucy Ellington, dau. of David, whose will of that date, Amelia Co., mentions "daughter Lucy Tanner."

Christopher m. Elizabeth Aylor, prob. in Madison Co. Hartford B-6095 (6), 6 Feb., 1954. Signed N. E. N. Ans. 3 April, 1954. Signed C. W. R.

Elizabeth m. William Osborne.

Elizabeth m. Arnold Cain.

Elizabeth m. Jonias Cliborne.

Frances m. Capt. Henry Holcombe.

Frances m. Peter Feild Archer.

Joseph, d. bef. 1677; m. Mary ____. She m. (2) bef. April, 1679, Gilbert Platt. 49V176.

Maria m. Christopher Zimmerman.

Martha m. Edward Stewart.

Mary m. George McKenney.

Mary m. William Lygon.

Mary m. Darby Enroughty.

Mary m. William Powell.

Mary (____) m. Gilbert Platt.

Mary Page m. William Tazewell.

Patsy m. Peter Willson.

Paul, d. 5 Aug., 1800, Fairfax Co.; served in the cavalry in Rev. War; m. Dec., 1784, Mary Ann Walker. Pension W26510.

Sarah m. Peter Jones.

Sarah (____) m. Samuel Pulton.

Thomas, b. 9 May, 1763, Mecklenburg Co.; d. there, 29 Oct., 1839; m. 5 Feb., 1795, Dinwiddie Co., Elizabeth Murphy, b. 20 June, 1774, dau. of William and Elizabeth (____); res. 1832, Mecklenburg Co. Pension R10391 (not allowed).

TAPP

____ m. Mary Jett, dau. of John, whose will, 1763-1771, Culpeper Co., proves it.

TAPSCOT(-T)

____ m. bef. 1769, Mary Shearman, dau. of Martin, whose will of that date, Lancaster Co., names "daughter Mary Tapscott." It was prob. Henry Tapscott, whose will, 1777, names wife, Mary, and a witness was Joseph Shearman.

Ann m. Charles Rogers.

Ann (____) m. Benjamin George, Jr.

Dorcas m. Jeduthun George.

James m. 8 Nov., 1774, Elizabeth Davis. Northumberland Co. Mar. Record.

Rawleigh m. 1783, Ann Sherman. 8W(1)209.

Susanna m. Nicholas Lawson George.

TARENT

Leo m. bef. Jan., 1714/5, Mary Brooks, heir of Samuel Thacker. Proven by Deed of that date, Essex Co.

TARLETON

Judith m. John Woodson.

Judith m. Charles Fleming.

TARLTON

Elizabeth m. Stephen Hughes.

Hannah m. George Webb, Jr.

Sallie m. ____ Hughes.

TARPIN

John m. 8 March, 1798, Elizabeth Carter. Halifax Co. Mar. Record.

TARPLEY

Betty m. L. R. Peachy.

Elizabeth m. Leroy Peachey.

Elizabeth m. David Miller.

Fanny m. Raleigh Chinn.

John, son of John and Mary (____), m. Ann Glascock, dau. of Thomas and Ann (Nicholls). Boddie-Hist. IV:47.

Lucy m. Lodowick Jones.

TARRANT

Lewis m. 26 Feb., 1797, Elizabeth Redd. Caroline Co. Mar. Record.

TARRENT

Leonard m. bef. 8 April, 1714, Mary Brooke, dau. of Robert. Proven by Court Record of that date, Essex Co.

Mary m. Rev. Robert Rose.

TARRY

George, b. 12 June, 1740; d. 1814, "Ivy Hill," Mecklenburg Co.; m. there, 7 Dec., 1790, Sarah Taylor. Bell, p. 114.

Gracy m. Gideon Flournoy.

Mary Booker m. Rev. James Craig.

Rebecca m. Chilton Masters.

Robert m. 10 June, 1793, Nancy Smith, dau. of Peartree Smith. Sur. Joseph Townes. Mecklenburg Co. Mar. Bond.

Samuel m. Mary Booker. Bell, p. 112.

TART

John m. 24 Oct., 1787, Mary Taylor. Norfolk Co. Mar. Record.

John m. 9 March, 1790, Mary (____) Smith. Norfolk Co. Mar. Record.

Robert m. 17 Dec., 1787, Esther Wilson. Norfolk Co. Mar. Record.

TARTER

Peter m. 6 June, 1787, Elizabeth Moore, dau. of Frederick. Montgomery Co. Mar. Record.

TARTT

Nancy m. Willis Tucker.

TARVER

____ m. Elizabeth Lowe. She m. (2) Absalom Harris. DAR No. 27 189.

____ believed m. bef. 1778, Mary Davis, dau. of Thomas, whose will, dated 1778, Southampton Co., names "daughter Mary Tarver."

Elizabeth m. (1) ____ Jordan; m. (2) Absalom Harris.

Elizabeth (Lowe) m. Absolom Harris.

Thomas m. Sarah Little. 20V431.

Thomas m. ____ (____) Bailey, widow of Anselm. Proven by his will, 1711. Boddie-SVFII:24.

TASE

Jane m. Samuel Estell.

TASKER

Frances Ann m. Robert Carter.

TASSAKER

Mary m. Capt. Chandler Fowke.

TATAM

Thomas m. 1794, Nanky (____) Evins. Orange Co. Mar. Record.

TATE

____ m. Matthew Harris.

____ m. Rev. James Madison.

Ann m. James Anthony.

Cisiah m. Nathan Tate.

Daniel m. 1789, Botetourt Co., Comfort Knox. Kegley, p. 481.

Darcus m. John Campbell.

Edward m. 1786, Botetourt Co., Sarah McMillin. Kegley, p. 481.

Elizabeth m. Enos Tate.

Elizabeth m. Andrew Steele.

Enos m. 12 Oct., 1772, Louisa Co., Elizabeth Graves, dau. of Rice and Jane (____). 19T244. Mar. Elizabeth Groom. Louisa, p. 256. Mar. 9 Sept., 1772, Elizabeth Tate. Louisa, p. 255.

James, killed in Battle of Guilford, Rev. War; m. Sallie Hall, b. 19 Dec., 1751, dau. of Edward and Eleanor (Stuart) of Augusta Co. She m. (2) Hugh Fulton and moved west. Boddie-Hist.V:93; Waddell, pp. 311-368.

Jesse m. Micajah Anthony.

John m. 12 Nov., 1799, Sally Poindexter. Louisa Co. Mar. Record.

Joseph m. 1783, Botetourt Co., Mary Lloyd, dau. of or consent of Thomas. Kegley, p. 481.

Lucy m. Joseph Nelson.

Margaret m. William Tate.

Mary m. ____ Snelson.

Mary m. Anderson Parish.

Mary m. Samuel Wallace.

Mary m. Charles Perkins.

Nancy m. Samuel McGhee.

Nancy m. Samuel Hill.

Nathan m. 13 May, 1786, Cisiah Tate. Louisa, p. 260.

TATE (cont.)

Nathaniel m. 8 Oct., 1788, Frances Gentry, dau. of George (d. 1818). Albemarle, p. 205; Louisa, p. 259.

Peggy m. Battaile Muse.

Robert m. 21 Dec., 1780, Susanna Bibb, both of Louisa. Douglas Reg., p. 20; Louisa, p. 280.

Robert m. Margaret McClung, dau. of John and Elizabeth (Alexander). Morton, p. 503.

Samuel m. 1785, Elizabeth Alexander. Morton, p. 533. Mar. 1 Feb., 1785 by Rev. John Brown. Rockbridge Co. Ministers' Returns.

Sarah m. ____ Street.

Sarah m. Charles Daniel.

Sarah m. Lieut. James Callaway.

Sarah m. Rev. James Madison.

Sarah (____) m. (2) Hugh Fulton.

Sarah H. m. Mark Anthony.

Susan m. Will. Arnold.

Susan L. m. Col. William Starke.

Thomas m. ca 1780, ____ Campbell. Rockbridge Co. Records. Morton, p. 533.

Uphans m. Anthony Winston (1st wife).

Will. m. 25 Dec., 1779, Margaret Tate, both of Louisa. Douglas Reg., p. 19.

TATEM

Ann Godfrey m. Francis Wright.

John m. 7 Nov., 1743, Anne Wright. Sur. Samuel Boush. Norfolk Co. Mar. Bond. She, dau. of Stephen Wright. LNCo 3:79.

Lydia m. John Trimble.

Mirium m. James Egerton.

Nathaniel m. 13 Dec., 1743, Prudence Wilson, dau. of James, Sr. LNCo 3:79.

Nathaniel m. 22 Feb., 1785, Elizabeth Wright. Norfolk Co. Mar. Record.

Nathaniel m. 12 Feb., 1755, Dinah Nash. Norfolk Co. Mar. Record. Mar. 12 Jan., 1755. LNCo 3:125.

TATHAM

Mary Ann m. James Anderson.

TATHUM

John m. 1796, Botetourt Co., Mary Helmintoller. Kegley, p. 482.

TATOM

Abel, b. ca 1747; d. 1798, Lincoln Co., Ga., son of John, Sr., and (1) Ann (Wright); m. Milly Harris, b. ca 1755; d. 1832, Monroe Co., Ga. Scarborough, p. 363.

Charity m. James Robertson.

Henrietta m. John Fullilove.

Isaac, b. ca 1773, Norfolk Co.; d. 1805, Lincoln Co., Ga., son of Abel and Milly (Harris); m. ca 1794, Mary Jane Stinson, b. 1777; d. 1806, dau. of Alexander and Jane (Baker). Scarborough, p. 365.

John, Sr., b. ca 1720, Norfolk Co.; d. 1793, Wilkes Co., Ga., son of Capt. Nathaniel; m. (1) 7 Nov., 1743, Norfolk Co., Ann Wright, b. ca 1725, dau. of Capt. Stephen Wright. May have married (2) 30 March, 1774, Norfolk Co., Alsey Smith; m. prob. (3) Sarah ____,

TATOM (cont.)

named in his will, 1793, Wilkes Co., Ga. Scarborough, p. 355.

TATUM

___ m. bef. July, 1786, Mary Crenshaw, dau. of Thomas, whose will of that date, Lunenburg Co., proves it.

___ m. bef. June, 1724, Bridget Scott, dau. of John, whose will of that date, Prince George Co., proves it.

___ believed m. bef. 1724, Emelia Scott, dau. of John, Sr., whose will of that date, Prince George Co., names "daughter Emelia Tatum."

Christopher, patent, 1728, Prince George Co., d. 16 Jan., 1750, Surry Co.; m. Bridgett Scott, dau. of John and Emelia (Boyce) of Prince George Co. Boddie-SVF 1:101.

Crafton m. 1794, Susanna Fullilove by Rev. James Shelburne, Baptist. Lunenburg Co. Ministers' Returns.

Frances m. George Rives.

Henry, son of Josiah; served in Rev. War; m. 1778, Dorothea Claiborne, dau. of Daniel and Mary (Maury) of Dinwiddie Co. Old King Wm., pp. 54, 103.

Isham m. 19 Oct., 1780, Rachel Garrett. Christ Church, p. 202.

John, will dated 1754, Surry Co.; m. Mary Eppes, dau. of Daniel (d. 1753). Boddie-SVF 1:103.

Mary m. Thomas Young, Jr.

Molly m. Daniel Lefoe.

Nathaniel m. Emelia Scott, dau. of John (d. 1724, Prince George Co.) and Emelia (Boyce). SVF 1:101-3.

Peter, will dated 1751; m. Sarah Heath, dau. of William (d. ca 1746, Surry Co.) Boddie-HSV 5:27.

Robert m. 30 Jan., 1773, Amy Gee, dau. of Charles. Sussex Co. Mar. Record.

Sally m. Elam Lewis.

Susanna m. John Hailey.

William m. 11 March, 1784, Mary Crenshaw by Rev. Thomas Crymes, Baptist. Lunenburg Co. Ministers' Returns.

TAVERNER

John m. Rebecca Travers. 25V279.

TAVERNOR

Elizabeth m. John Mathews.

George m. 2 Jan., 1739/40, Elizabeth Bishop. St. Paul's.

TAWNEY

Caty m. John Loftrich.

Elizabeth m. John Williams.

George m. 1 Feb., 1798, Catey Staley. Wythe Co. Mar. Record.

John m. 7 May, 1799, Polly Price. Sur. James Steward. Botetourt Co. Mar. Bond.

TAYLER

Ann m. Edward Eastham.

James, Capt., m. bef. 1685, Elizabeth (___) Brown Morgan, widow 1st of William Brown, 2nd of Evan Morgan. Essex Co. Order Book 1, p. 124. Taylor, p. 278.

James, Dr., m. bef. 1654, Elizabeth Underwood, b. ca 1632, sis. of Col. William (d. 1673); divorced. She m. (2) Francis Slaughter;

TAYLER (cont.)
m. (3) Col. John Catlett; m. (4) Rev. Amory Butler. Taylor, p. 278.

TAYLOE

Ann m. John Wormely.
Anne Corbin m. Maj. Thomas Lomax.
Anne Corbin m. Mann Page, Jr., (2nd wife).
Betty m. Richard Corbin.
Catherine m. Col. Landon Carter.
Eleanor m. Ralph Wormley.
Elizabeth m. Col. Edward Lloyd IV.
Jane m. Col. Robert Beverley.
John, b. 28 May, 1721; d. 18 April, 1779; m. 11 July, 1747, Rebecca Plater, b. 8 Aug., 1731; d. 22 Jan., 1787, dau. of Hon. George Plater, Esq., of Md. Bible Record. 14T245; Page, p. 81.
John, Col., m. bef. 1715, Elizabeth (Gwyn) Lyde (or Loyd), widow of Stephen and dau. of David Gwyn. Court Record, 1715, Essex Co.; 35 V205.
John III, Col., of "Mount Airy," Richmond Co., b. Sept., 1771; m. 4 Oct., 1792, Anne Ogle, dau. of Benjamin of Md. 2T80; 6T4; 14T249. She, dau. of Gov. Samuel Ogle of Maryland and Anne (Tasker), his wife. 25V191.
Joseph of Lancaster Co. m. bef. 22 May, 1710, Barbara Billington, dau. of Luke (will, 1672, Rappahannock Co.). 2W(2)119; Taylor, pp. 74-5.
Mary m. Mann Page.
Rebecca m. Francis Lightfoot Lee.
Sarah "Sally" m. Col. William Augustine Washington.
William, Col., m. bef. 1687, Ann Corbin, b. 9 Feb., 1664, Middlesex Co., dau. of Henry. 17V369-75; 29V381.
William, Col., m. Elizabeth Kingsmill, dau. of Richard. She m. (2) ____ Bacon. 2W(1)81; Winston, p. 378.
William II of "Mount Airy," son of Hon. John III, m. his cousin, Henrietta Oglo, dau. of Hon. Benjamin Tasker Oglo. 25V192.

TAYLOR

____ m. William Williams.
____ m. Notley Williams.
____ m. Peter Thornton.
____ m. bef. 1703, Ann James, dau. of David, whose will of that date, Northampton Co., proves it.
____ m. bef. May, 1758, Elizabeth Jones, sis. of John, whose will of that date, Orange Co., mentions "my loving sister Elizabeth Taylor" and names Zachary Taylor as an executor.
____, b. Va.; m. Sarah Major, b. 18 Dec., 1740, dau. of Samuel I and Elizabeth (Jones) of Middlesex and Culpeper counties; rem. to Ky. Major, p. 53.
____ believed m. bef. 1803, Sally Carter, dau. of Thomas, whose will, dated 1 Aug., 1803, Russell Co., names daughter Sally Taylor.
____ (____) m. Col. Edward Moseley.
____ m. Edmond Baysey (or Basye).
____ m. James Patton Preston.
____ m. bef. 1678, Elizabeth (____) Persons, widow of Loughon, father of Ann Persons. Inventory of estate of Loughon Persons, York Co., 23 April, 1678. Book 6, p. 43. Given as Lawn Peirson and Daniel

TAYLOR (cont.)

Taylor given as marrying the relict. Taylor, p. 63.

___ m. bef. 1682, Mary Flower, sis. of George, whose will, dated 7 Oct., 1682, Lancaster Co., proves it.

___ m. Benjamin Edwards.

___ m. Archer Green.

___ m. Lurania Young, b. ca 1669, dau. of Robert of Rappahannock Co. She m. (2) ___ Featress (?Fentress); m. (3) Thomas Hudson; m. (4) Robert Miller. Taylor, p. 283.

___ m. bef. 1722, Urslee Sanders, dau. of Philip, whose will, 1722, Westmoreland Co., proves it.

___ m. Thomas Underwood.

___ m. William Thomas Underwood (2nd wife).

___ m. bef. 20 Nov., 1797, Annie Booker, dau. of Richard. Halifax, p. 116.

___ m. bef. Feb., 1730, Penelope Goodwyn, dau. of Thomas, whose will of that date, Surry Co., proves it. See 8W(1) Supplement, p. 141.

___ m. Elizabeth (Kavanaugh) Conner, dau. of Philemon Kavanaugh, whose will, 1744, Orange Co., proves it.

___ m. William Browne.

___ m. John Pendleton.

___ m. Simon Sallard.

___ m. William Hall.

___ m. ___ Dameron and had son, Joseph Dameron.

___ m. (1) ___ Stringer; m. (2) Edward Moseley.

___ m. Sarah Strother and became parents of Gen. "Dick" Taylor. 2W(1) 134.

___, d. bef. 1791; m. Anne Pollard, dau. of Joseph, whose will, 1791, Goochland Co., proves it. She, b. 22 Feb., 1732. Bagby, p. 346.

___ m. Anne Pendleton, dau. of James and granddau. of Henry and Mary (Taylor) Pendleton. Slaughter, p. 148.

___ m. Mary Neill, dau. of John and Anne (Hollingsworth). Joliffe, p. 184.

___ m. bef. 1778, Mary Moorman, dau. of Charles, Jr., whose will, prov. that date, Louisa Co., names "daughter Mary Taylor." Her mother was Mary Venable. Albemarle, p. 286.

___, Capt., m. ca 1790, ___ ___ of Campbell Co. Rockbridge Co. Morton, p. 535.

Abigail m. John Harvey.

Abraham m. 3 Nov., 1660/1, Debora Kechine. Northampton Co. Mar. Record.

Adam m. 18 April, 1791, Mary Caston by Alexander Ross. Montgomery Co. Mar. Record.

Agnes m. William Kersey.

Alexander m. 23 Feb., 1797, Sally Hix by Rev. John Neblett, Methodist. Lunenburg Co. Ministers' Returns.

Alexander, son of Robert, m. Mildred C. Lindsay. St. Mark's, p. 173.

Alexander m. 24 Feb., 1757, Hannah Brooke. OPR.

Alexander m. 28 April, 1763, Elizabeth Sparrow. Norfolk Co. Mar. Record.

Aley m. John Thurston.

Alice m. Joseph Perkins.

TAYLOR (cont.)

Alice m. Washington Berry.
Alice m. Anthony Winston.
Amos m. 21 Jan., 1796, Mildred Fenton. Frederick Co. Mar. Record.
Ana m. George Ball.
Andrew m. (1) Elizabeth Wilson (NOT Sarah); m. (2) Ann Wilson. DAR Mag., Sept., 1933, p. 576. Ann Wilson was his cousin and their son, Nathaniel, was born 1772. Rockbridge Co. Morton, p. 534.
Ann m. (1) Robert Taliaferro; m. (2) John Todd.
Ann m. Edward Eastham.
Ann m. Robert Scott.
Ann m. William Brown.
Ann m. John Doss.
Ann m. Richard Gabriel.
Ann Catherine m. Samuel Ball.
Anna m. George Ball, Jr.
Anne m. William Garrett.
Anne m. James Patton Preston.
Anne m. Chatwin Cowning.
Anne m. William Spratley.
Anne m. Samuel Ball.
Anne m. John Washington Berry.
Anne m. Miles Cary.
Anne Corbin m. Mann Page (2nd wife).
Anne Hubbard m. Robert Taliaferro.
Archer m. 23 June, 1779, Judith Markham. 5V334.
Archibald m. 7 March, 1758, Louisa Richard. Sur. Nathaniel Fife. Norfolk Co. Mar. Bond.
Barbara m. Job Combs.
Barbara m. ___ Stuart.
Barbara m. James Moore.
Bartho. m. ___ Stringer, dau. of Col. John. 5V330.
Bartholomew, b. ca 1762; enl. in Rev. War from Caroline Co.; res. 1791, King and Queen Co.; m. Frances Loving, b. ca 1770; widow res. 1855, Caroline Co. Pension W3473.
Benjamin m. 30 Nov., 1789, Catherine Weaver. Fauquier Co. Mar. License. Taylor, p. 185.
Benjamin m. 19 May, 1790, Ann Harner. Frederick Co. Mar. Record.
Benjamin m. 1 June, 1797, Sarah Hastings. Frederick Co. Mar. Record.
Benjamin, b. 1760; d. 1814, Richmond, Va., son of George (b. 1711) and Rachel (Gibson); m. Susan Courtney, b. 1772; d. 1855. DAR No. 28 714.
Berryman m. 17 Dec., 1787, Nancy Grant. Halifax Co. Mar. Record.
Betsey m. Dr. Thomas Hinde.
Betsy m. John Nottingham.
Betsy m. Daniel Benston.
Betsy m. David Dortch.
Betsy m. Francis Lawson.
Betty m. Kendal Richerson.
Betty m. William Johnston.
Betty (___) m. (2) William Johnston.
Brunelia, a dau., m. ___ Lunsford.

TAYLOR (cont.)

Bushrod m. 29 Jan., 1801, Patsy Stubblefield. Frederick Co. Mar. Record.

Caroline m. Benjamin Grayson.

Catharine m. ____ Penn.

Catharine m. William Chimp.

Catherine m. ____ Bruce.

Catherine m. Nicholas Tillinghost.

Catherine m. Moses Penn.

Catherine (____) m. (2) William Sydnor.

Charlotte m. Samuel Smith McCroskey.

Comfort m. ____ Warrington.

Crisy m. Lewis Caudle.

Daniel, b. 13 Aug., 1761, Cumberland Co.; d. 25 Nov., 1835, Grainger Co., Tenn., son of James and Ann (____); m. Jean (or Jane) Rowland, b. ca 1764. Pension W6232.

Daniel m. 19 Jan., 1764, Sarah Carver. St. Paul's.

Daniel, son of William and Martha (Waller), m. 24 May, 1792, Eliza Hinton. Free II:364.

Daniel of York Co. m. bef. 1699, Mary (____) Day, widow of Edward. Deed of that date, York Co., proves it.

Daniel m. 23 July, 1795, Rebecca Johnson by Rev. John Neblett, Methodist. Lunenburg Co. Ministers' Returns.

Daniel m. Sarah (Pinkethman) Eaton, widow of William Eaton and dau. of William Pinkethman. 6T121.

Daniel m. Ann Laird, b. 1778, Botetourt Co.; d. 1854, dau. of H. H. Laird. Rockbridge Co. Morton, p. 497.

Daniel, b. ca 1705, Va.; d. 29 Sept., 1742, King William Co., Minister of St. John's Parish, King William Co., 1729-1742, son of Rev. Daniel Taylor, Minister of Blisland Parish, New Kent and James City counties; m. Alice Littlepage, b. 14 Jan., 1707/8; d. 1787, dau. of Richard of New Kent Co. 32V219; 50V266; 14W(2)48, 248; Hayden, p. 396; Taylor, p. 17; Winston, p. 412.

Daniel (or David), Capt., m. Mary Merritt, d. bef. 1719, sis. of William. She m. (2) John King. Proven by Court Suits, 16 July, 1719, and 18 Sept., 1695, Elizabeth City Co. Taylor, pp. 8, 9.

David m. 8 May, 1778, Rebecca Dortch, dau. of David and Lucy (Russell). Boddie-HSF IV:14.

David m. 8 Jan., 1793, Mary Payne. Halifax Co. Mar. Record.

Dicey m. Archer Lester.

Edmund, son of John and Catharine (Pendleton), m. Anne Lewis. St. Mark's, p. 172.

Edmund m. 23 Feb., 1797, Eloisa Thurston. Frederick Co. Mar. Record.

Edmund m. 10 Aug., 1758, Sarah Calthorpe. Southampton Co. 22V423.

Edmund m. 1 April, 1775, Millicant Shelton, dau. of Daniel, who was Surety. Pittsylvania Co. Mar. Bond.

Edward C., d. 24 Aug., 1829; served in Rev. War from King William Co.; m. 13 March, 1788, Joanna Now, widow; res. 1843, Woodford Co., Ky. Pension W8778.

Eli m. 4 May, 1799, Elizabeth Dudley. Christ Church, p. 303.

Elisha m. 1795, Delia Walker. Orange Co. Mar. Record.

Elisha m. 15 Nov., 1794, Elizabeth Yates. Halifax Co. Mar. Record.

TAYLOR (cont.)

Eliza m. Anthony Sydnor.
Elizabeth m. William Smith.
Elizabeth m. John Pendleton.
Elizabeth m. Andrew G. Capell.
Elizabeth m. James Basye.
Elizabeth m. Nicholas Rhoades.
Elizabeth m. ____ Edwards.
Elizabeth m. Andrew Glassell.
Elizabeth m. Capt. Thomas Minor.
Elizabeth m. George Reid.
Elizabeth m. (1) James Morgan; m. (2) Henry Mauzy.
Elizabeth m. (1) ____ Lewis; m. (2) ____ Bullock.
Elizabeth m. James Ford.
Elizabeth m. James Orford.
Elizabeth m. Phil. Johnson.
Elizabeth m. Henry Duke.
Elizabeth m. John Chambless.
Elizabeth m. ____ Sutton.
Elizabeth m. ____ Flowers.
Elizabeth m. Peter Hogg.
Elizabeth m. ____ Smith.
Elizabeth m. ____ Watson.
Elizabeth m. Ambrose Walden.
Elizabeth m. William Whittington.
Elizabeth m. Charles Ratcliff.
Elizabeth m. Miles Cary.
Elizabeth m. ____ Strickland.
Elizabeth m. Charles Miles.
Elizabeth m. James Nool(-l).
Elizabeth m. Joseph Grant.
Elizabeth m. Samuel Landrum.
Elizabeth m. John Dameron.
Elizabeth m. Levi Pitts.
Elizabeth m. Thomas Hicks.
Elizabeth m. Miles Cary, Jr.
Elizabeth m. ____ Peterson.
Elizabeth m. Col. John Carter.
Elizabeth m. Col. William Call.
Elizabeth m. Peter Blow.
Elizabeth m. Leven Dorsey.
Elizabeth m. Thomas Cofer.
Elizabeth (____) m. Robert Jones.
Elizabeth (____) m. Tobias Horton.
Elizabeth Lee m. Robert Edmonds.
Erasmus, b. 5 Sept., 1715; d. Dec., 1794, son of James and Martha (Thompson); m. 13 Oct., 1749, Jane Moore, b. 22 Dec., 1728; d. Sept., 1812. 30V387; 34V269-72. Jane Moore, dau. of John and (1) ____ (____). 52V62-3.
Estor m. ____ Pilsher.
Esther m. John Stephenson (2nd wife).
Ethelred, d. 1716, Surry Co.; m. bet. 1696 and 1702, Elizabeth (Duke)

TAYLOR (cont.)

Mason, widow of James Mason of Surry Co., whose will, 1696, and inventory, 1702, prove it. She was dau. of Col. Duke. 7T282; 24T 230; 22V446. She was dau. of Col. Henry Duke of James City Co. and Henrietta Maria (____). Duke, p. 76.

Ethelrod, d. 1755, Southampton Co.; res. Surry Co. and Isle of Wight Co., Va., and Northampton Co., No. Car.; m. Patience ____ (prob. Kinchen). 23V105. Mar. Patience Kinchen, will prov. 1766, South-
* ampton Co. Duke, p. 77.

Eve m. Solomon Ewell.

Evelina m. George Morton.

Fanny m. Edward Lawrence.

Fanny m. William Dandridge Claiborne (prob. 3rd wife).

Fanny m. Samuel Sublett.

Frances m. William Cotton.

Frances m. William Stone.

Frances m. Solomon Walker.

Frances m. James Basham.

Frances m. Hugh Crutcher.

Frances m. Garland Burnley.

Frances m. Ambrose Madison.

Frances m. ____ Greenhill.

Frances m. ____ Craddock.

Frances m. William Clarke.

Frances m. Capt. John Madison.

Francis m. 1788, Elizabeth Thompson. Orange Co. Mar. Record.

Francis m. bef. 1681, Elizabeth Snead, dau. of Charles. Deed, 4 Jan., 1681/2, Rappahannock Co., proves it.

Francis m. Judith Field, dau. of Lieut. Henry Field, who d. ca 1778, Culpeper Co. Field II:1104.

Francis, son of James and (1) Alice (Thornton) Catlett, m. Ann Craddock. Taylor, p. 133.

Frederick m. 16 Jan., 1792, ____ Womble. Isle of Wight Co. Mar. Record.

George, Col., b. 10 Feb., 1711; d. 4 Nov., 1792, Orange Co., son of Col. James II and Martha (Thompson); m. 28 Feb., 1738, Rachel Gibson, b. 4 May, 1717; d. 19 Feb., 1761, dau. of Jonathan. Ky. Reg. 18:53:28. George, b. 1711, Orange or Caroline Co.; d. 1792, Orange Co.; Member of Committee of Safety of Orange Co.; m. 1738, Rachel Gibson, b. 1717; d. 1761. DAR No. 28 714; DAR No. 28 907; DAR No. 41 194; DAR No. 41 799; DAR No. 79 868; DAR No. 85 400. He m. (2) Sarah "Sally" (Taliaferro) Conway, b. 8 Oct., 1727; d. 17 Jan., 1784, widow of Capt. Francis and dau. of Charles and Sarah (____) Taliaferro. 21T192; 2W(2)135.

George from County Armagh, Ireland, to Rockbridge Co., 1760, m. ____ Paul, dau. of Capt. Audley Paul. Morton, p. 274.

George m. 4 Feb., 1797, Betsy Leatherman. Shelby Co., Ky. Mar. Record.

George, Capt., m. bef. 25 March, 1693, Martha Tomlin, sis. of Robert. Proven by Court Record of that date, Essex Co.

George, Capt., m. bef. 1 Feb., 1683, Martha (Brasseur) Mosely, widow of William and dau. of Robert Brasseur of Nansemond Co. Boddie-HSF

*Ethelred m. (1) June, 1782, Martha Tyus; m. (2) 13 Feb., 1790, Elizabeth Ridley. 23V436.

TAYLOR (cont.)

IV:146-7; Court Record, 25 March, 1693, Essex Co.

George m. 28 Jan., 1791, Elizabeth Garret, dau. of Thomas. Northampton Co. Mar. Record.

George m. 20 Aug., 1799, Sarah Dalby. Northampton Co. Mar. Record.

George m. 1787, Ann Stanton. Orange Co. Mar. Record.

George m. Elizabeth Dowell, dau. of Thomas, prob. in Albemarle Co. Orange III:39.

Griffin m. 10 Sept., 1789, Molly Cannon. Frederick Co. Mar. Record.

Griffin m. 1 Jan., 1824, Rhoda Kingore. Frederick Co. Mar. Record.

Griselda m. John Colyar (or Collier).

Hannah m. John Basye.

Hannah m. Nicholas Battaile.

Harriet m. Catlett Conway.

Henrietta Maria m. John Hardiman.

Henrietta Maria m. Francis Hardyman (1st wife).

Henry m. Rebecca Tyson. 24V103. Henry, son of Henry and Temperance (Peterson) of Southampton Co., m. Rebecca Tyron. She m. (2) Richard Barham. Duke, p. 77. (?Error)

Henry, d. 1781, Southampton Co., son of Ethelred and Patience (Kinchen); m. 25 Dec., 1758, Brunswick Co., Temperance Peterson, dau. of John. Mar. Record; Duke, p. 77.

Henry m. 1743, Charlotte Anderson, dau. of Rev. Charles. 6T263; 4W(1)127.

Henry, Sr., d. 1770, Loudoun Co., son of John (d. 1748, Fairfax Co.); m. Susanne Whiteley. 7W(2)219; Taylor, p. 190.

Henry m. ____ (Anderson) Stith, widow of John and dau. of Rev. Charles Anderson of Charles City Co. She m. (3) Ellyson Armistead. Taylor, p. 195.

Hester m. Thomas Morgan.

Hezekiah m. 10 Nov., 1792, Sarah (____) Wildair. Norfolk Co. Mar. Record.

Hubbard, Col., b. 2 Aug., 1760; d. 1845; m. 27 July, 1782, Clarissa Minor, b. 1782; d. 1842, dau. of Thomas and Alice (Thomas) of Spotsylvania Co.; rem. to Fayette Co., Ky., and, in 1790, to Clark Co., Ky. 29V372; 9W(1)59.

Isabella m. Samuel Hopkins.

Isabella m. Samuel Paxton.

Isabella Pendleton m. Capt. Samuel Hopkins.

Jacob m. 20 Feb., 1786, Nancy Webb, dau. of William. Wit. William Webb. Montgomery Co. Mar. Record.

James m. 1775, Delilah Stanton. Orange Co. Mar. Record.

James, res. Richmond Co.; rem. to Westmoreland Co. bef. 1694; m. bef. Feb., 1694, ____ (____) Browne, widow of Evan. Proven by Court Record of that date, Richmond Co.

James m. 5 Aug., 1800, Rachel Raeburn. Sur. John Raeburn and Thomas Taylor. Botetourt Co. Mar. Bond.

James m. 15 April, 1761, Alcie Smith. Norfolk Co. Mar. Record.

James m. 9 July, 1800, Elizabeth Parten. Sur. William White. Charlotte Co. Mar. Bond.

James m. 16 Dec., 1784, Nancy Wooten. Sur. Thomas Harris. Buckingham Co. Mar. Bond.

TAYLOR (cont.)

James m. 1794, Helen Triplett. Fauquier Co. Taylor, p. 185.

James of Cumberland Co., d. ca 1773; m. Elizabeth Hughes, dau. of John of Amelia Co. Proven by will of James Taylor.

James, b. 1738; d. 1807, son of George and (1) Rachel (Gibson); res. Orange Co.; served in Rev. War; m. his cousin, Ann Pendleton. DAR No. 28 907.

James m. Frances Brockman, dau. of William and Elizabeth (Mason) of Albemarle Co. Orange III:107.

James, Col., b. 27 Dec., 1732, Caroline Co.; d. there, 12 March, 1814; m. Ann (-e) Hubbard. 25V81; 34V366-7; 1W(1)56; 34 Ky. Reg. 103; DAR No. 75 738. He, son of James and Alice (Thornton) Catlett Taylor, m. (2) Sarah Taliaferro; m. (3) Elizabeth Conway. St. Mark's, p. 173; Taylor, p. 133. James III m. Elizabeth (Fitzhugh) Conway, widow of Francis, Jr., and dau. of John and Alice (Thornton) Fitzhugh. 11T26.

James m. Sarah Newton. 30V87.

James of Northumberland Co. m. ca 1650, Alice Gascoyne, dau. of Thomas. 11T29.

James m. 16 Jan., 1774, Susanna Ragin. Northampton Co. Mar. Record.

James, Gen., b. 19 April, 1769, Caroline Co.; d. 2 Nov., 1848, son of Col. James and Ann (Hubbard); m. 15 Nov., 1795, Keturah (Moss) Leitch, widow of David; rem. to Newport, Ky. 29V372; 34 Ky. Reg. 104-6.

James, son of John (d. 1712, Lancaster Co.) and Ann (Vesey); m. Dorcas Waters (or Walters); sett. 1742, Prince William Co.; rem. to Prince William Co., and bef. 1762, to So. Car. 11T30-1; 6W(2)333; Taylor, pp. 73-4. Dorcas Walters was a cousin of John Contanceau, whose will, prov. 1719, Northumberland Co. 35V217. See Order Book, 1729-37, p. 481. Northumberland Co.

James, b. 30 March, 1703; d. 1 March, 1784; m. (1) bef. 25 March, 1727, Alice (Thornton) Catlett, widow of Lawrence Catlett and dau. of Col. Francis Thornton of Caroline Co.; m. (2) Elizabeth (McGrath) Lewis; m. (3) ____ (____) Gregory. Taylor, p. 133. James, of Orange Co., was son of Col. James. 30V387; 4W(1)158; Essex Co. Records, 1727; 34 Ky. Reg. 103.

James, b. County Armagh, Ireland; to Rockbridge Co., 1760; d. 1801; m. 1768, Ann "Annie" Paul, b. 1758; d. 1828, dau. of Capt. Audley Paul. She m. (2) William McCorkle. Morton, pp. 274, 280, 518, 534. James, b. bef. 1760, Ireland; d. 1839, Tenn. DAR No. 65 518.

James m. Mary Moorman, b. 5 Feb., 1751, dau. of Charles and Mary (Adams). Boddie-HSF IV:22. Mar. 26 Sept., 1771. Louisa Co. Mar. Record.

James, son of John and Catharine (Pendleton), m. Anne Pollard. St. Mark's, p. 172.

James m. 6 June, 1772, Elizabeth Bunch. Louisa Co. Mar. Record.

James m. 5 May, 1788, M. Wooding. Halifax Co. Mar. Record.

James m. 29 Dec., 1794, Elizabeth Williams. Henry Co. Mar. Record.

James, b. 1721; d. 1815, Grainger Co., Tenn.; res. 1761, Cumberland Co., Va., and 1764, Henry Co.; m. 1755, Ann "Nancy" Owen, b. 1738, dau. of George and Elener (____) of Cumberland Co. 35V79. James, b. 1731, son of William and Mary (____); rem. 1797, to Grainger Co.,

TAYLOR (cont.)

Tenn. 12T219.

James m. ca 1800, Catharine McClure. Rockbridge Co. Morton, p. 534.

James m. 1778, Ann Tellery. Botetourt Co. Kegley, p. 480.

James m. Mary Gregory, dau. of John and Elizabeth (____). She m. (2) by April, 1711, Rowland Thomas. Rhodes, p. 391. James, b. 1635, Carlisle, Eng.; to Virginia ca 1665; d. 1698, Caroline Co.; m. (1) in England, Frances ____, d. 1680; m. (2) 1682, Mary Gregory. 34 Ky. Reg. 103; Ky. Reg. 18:53:29. Mar. 10 Aug., 1682, Mary Gregory. James d. 30 April, 1698, King and Queen Co. 34V269-72; Winston, p. 217. John Gregory was of Sittenbourne Parish in 1665. 5V162.

James, b. ca 1757; d. 15 March, 1823; res. 1816, Madison Co.; m. 26 Dec., 1789, Orange Co., Sarah Hunt, b. ca 1770; d. 20 Oct., 1839. Orange Co. Mar. Record; Pension W19431.

James served in Rev. War from Fairfax Co.; m. 6 Feb., 1790, at Richmond, Va., Dorothy Miller, b. 9 Aug., 1773. Pension R10411.

James, Jr., Col., b. 14 March, 1674; d. 23 June (or Jan.), 1729/30, son of James, the immigrant; m. 23 Feb., 1699, Martha Thompson, b. 1679; d. 19 Nov., 1762. 30V387; 32V17; 34V269; 34 Ky. Reg. 103, 269-72; Taylor, pp. 132-3, 280; Winston, pp. 216, 217. "His wife is stated in some accounts to have been the daughter of William Thompson and granddaughter of Sir Roger Thompson. No. Sir Roger Thompson was over in Virginia and much more probable is the account in the little chart prepared by President Madison, where she is said to be Martha, daughter of Roger Thompson." 32V17. Res. Caroline and Orange counties. 4V463.

James, Jr., m. 22 Dec., 1795, Frances "Fanny" C. Moore. Orange Co. Mar. Record; St. Mark's, p. 78; 26V404.

Jane m. James McDonald.

Jane m. Martin Pettus.

Jane m. Charles P. Howard.

Jane m. Melton Durham.

Jaune m. John Smither.

Jean m. Absalom Williams.

Jesse m. 1795, Fauquier Co., Sarah Embrey. Taylor, p. 185.

Jesse m. 31 Jan., 1793, Mary Jacquelin Smith. Frederick Co. Mar. Record.

John, will dated 7 Jan., 1805; prov. 11 March, 1806, Southampton Co., son of Ethelred and Patience (Kinchen); m. (1) Hannah Tompkins, d. 1775; m. (2) 5 Aug., 1783, Sarah (Williamson) Ruffin, dau. of Col. Thomas Williamson, whose will, dated 24 June, 1787, Southampton Co. 23V324; Duke, p. 78.

John m. 2 May, 1786, Elizabeth Moore, spinster. Sur. Minetree Orrell. York Co. Mar. Bond.

John m. 2 June, 1761, Elizabeth (____) Blakey, widow. Sur. John Yarrington. Middlesex Co. Mar. Bond; 7W(1)190.

John of Richmond Co. m. 21 May, 1747, Rebecca Plator, dau. of George of St. Mary's Co., Md. Sur. Richard Corbin. Middlesex Co. Mar. Bond; 25V191.

John m. 3 Oct., 1796, Elizabeth Davis. Frederick Co. Mar. Record.

John m. bef. 7 June, 1714, Elizabeth (____) Lyde, widow of Stephen. Proven by Court Record of that date, Essex Co.

TAYLOR (cont.)

John, son of Henry, m. 3 March, 1783, Southampton Co., Martha Peterson. 24V102.

John of Caroline Co., b. 19 Dec., 1753; served in Rev. War; m. ca 1783, Lucy Penn. 46V285. John, Col., b. 1749; d. 1824; m. 1781. DAR No. 31 155.

John m. 22 Nov., 1790, Catherine Taliaferro Buckner. Fauquier Co. Mar. License. Taylor, p. 185.

John m. 1796, Polly Deleas. Fauquier Co. Taylor, p. 185.

John m. 7 Jan., 1778, Catherine Moore. Northampton Co. Mar. Record.

John m. 19 Aug., 1724, Mary Moss. St. Paul's.

John m. 27 Feb., 1726/7, Mary Ancrum. St. Paul's.

John m. 13 Dec., 1776, Verlinda Dunahoo. St. Paul's.

John m. 1795, Elizabeth Pierson. Orange Co. Mar. Record.

John m. 6 Oct., 1762, Ann Rogers. Sur. John Yarrington. Middlesex Co. Mar. Bond.

John, b. 1752, Fauquier Co.; d. 12 April, 1835, was a Baptist minister; m. 1782, Elizabeth Kavanaugh, dau. of Philemon and Nancy (Cave) Kavanaugh. Dict. of Amer. Biog. Orange Co. Mar. Record.

John m. 8 Nov., 1755, Elizabeth Summers. OPR.

John m. 1782, Mary Jarrell. Orange Co. Mar. Record.

John m. 9 Aug., 1787, Elizabeth Smith by James Kenney. Campbell Co. Mar. Record.

John m. 28 May, 1766, Sarah Tucker. Norfolk Co. Mar. Record. She, b. 13 Oct., 1747, dau. of Robert and Joanna (Corbin). 4V361.

John, b. 17 July, 1727; d. 26 Oct., 1787, son of John and Catherine (Pendleton); m. Betsy Lynn (or Lyne). St. Mark's, p. 172; Taylor, p. 133.

John, Capt., d. 6 Aug., 1825, son of Erasmus and Jane (Moore); m. 6 Sept., 1786, Anne Gilbert, b. 13 June, 1769; d. Dec., 1823; res. 1788, Orange Co., when son, John Moore Taylor, was born. 34V269-72; St. Mark's, p. 173.

John, Capt., m. 7 Jan., 1790, Sally Garner. Announced in the Virginia Herald. 30V68, 69.

John of Newport News, received patent, 1724; came to Virginia, 1623, in the "Bonnybesse;" m. bef. 1633, Rebecca Rabenning. 1V192.

John, b. 18 Nov., 1696; d. 22 March, 1780, son of James, who d. 1698; res. King and Queen and Caroline counties; m. 14 Feb., 1716, Catherine Pendleton, b. 8 Dec., 1699; d. 26 July, 1774, dau. of Philip and Isabella (Hart). 39V282; 24W(1)256; St. Mark's, p. 172; Slaughter, p. 148; Winston, pp. 196, 217. Isabella (Hart). Taylor, p. 133.

John m. Martha (or Margaret) Slaughter, dau. of Francis, Jr., and Elizabeth (Underwood) Taylor Slaughter Catlett Butler. Taylor, p. 278.

John, d. 1702; to Virginia in 1648; res. Northumberland Co.; m. ca 1649/50, Alcie Gascoyne (or Gaskins), d. 1702, dau. of Thomas, who d. 1629. 11T30; 35V213; Wayland, p. 313.

John, d. 1713, son of John (d. 1652, Lancaster Co.) and Alice (Gaskins or Gascoine); m. Ann Veazey (Vezey, Vesey), dau. of George of Suffolk Co., England, to Virginia ca 1654. 11T30; 35V214; Taylor, p. 74; Wayland, p. 313.

John Foster m. 9 Oct., 1755, Elizabeth Woodhal, both of this parish.

TAYLOR (cont.)

Douglas Reg., p. 2.

John Young, b. 11 July, 1765, Va.; d. 6 Oct., 1845, Greensburg, Ky., son of Richard of Lancaster Co.; m. 22 Nov., 1790, Fauquier Co., Catherine Taliaferro Buckner, dau. of Aylett, who made Deed of Gift to John Young Taylor, 1802. 47V83.

Jonathan, b. 3 Dec., 1742, Orange Co.; d. 1804, Basin Spring, Clark Co., Ky., son of Col. George and Rachel (Gibson); Lieut. in Rev. War; m. Jan., 1764, Ann Berry, b. 1749; d. 1808, dau. of Col. William and Mary (Pryor). 25V82; Ky. Reg. 18:53:28; DAR No. 41 194; DAR No. 79 868.

Jonathan m. 1777, Mary Kelly. Botetourt Co. Kegley, p. 480.

Joseph m. bef. 1762, Elizabeth Fishback, dau. of Harman. Proven by Deed of that date, Culpeper Co. Joseph, son of Benjamin of Prince William Co., m. (2) prob. ____ Gascoyne. 11T31.

Joseph m. 27 Aug., 1770, Sarah Moseley, dau. of Richard. Cumberland Co. Mar. Record.

Joshua m. 11 May, 1775, Martha Sturgis, dau. of William, dec'd. Northampton Co. Mar. Record.

Judith m. Richard Taylor.

Judith (____) m. (2) Richard Taylor.

Katherine m. Edward Holloway, Jr.

Kinchen, d. 1771, Southampton Co., son of Ethelred and Patience (Kinchen); m. 16 Jan., 1760, Elizabeth Ridley Brown, dau. of Jesse. 23V323. Mar. 1768. Duke, p. 78.

Lazarus, d. ca 1677, son of John (d. 1652, Lancaster Co.) and Alice (Gaskins); m. Mary Vesey (or Maria Veazey), dau. of George and Joan (____) of Lancaster Co.; rem. from Lancaster Co. to Prince William Co. bef. 1755. (Some confusion in dates.) 11T30; 27T136; 35V214; Taylor, p. 74.

Leanna m. Peter Lehugh.

Leonard, b. 22 Dec., 1757, New Kent Co.; d. 14 Sept., 1841, Ky.; served in Rev. War; rem. to Mercer Co., Ky.; m. Sarah Blagrave, d. 1 July, 1848. Hartford B-7311(1), L Jan., 1955. Signed N. D.

Lettice m. James Campbell.

Lucy m. James Eubank.

Lucy m. Alexander Balmain.

Lucy m. C. P. Howard.

Margaret m. Richard Howson.

Margaret m. (1) George Dameron; m. (2) ____ Winter (or Thomas Winters).

Maria m. John Page.

Marian (____) m. Caleb Ward.

Martha m. Phillips Pettus.

Martha m. William Douglas.

Martha m. Bernard Gaines.

Martha m. ____ Miller.

Martha m. Thomas Chew.

Martha m. James Pitman.

Martha m. Thomas Woodlief.

Martha m. Henry Sandifer.

Martha m. Edmund Wells.

TAYLOR (cont.)

Martha m. William Robinson Taylor.
Martha Todd m. Peter Thornton.
Mary m. George Watwood.
Mary m. John McNaughton.
Mary m. James Bryan.
Mary m. John Prichet.
Mary m. Batte Peterson.
Mary m. ____ Everett.
Mary m. ____ Penn.
Mary m. ____ Holloway.
Mary m. ____ Fargeson.
Mary m. ____ Waite.
Mary m. ____ Worley.
Mary m. Reuben Settle.
Mary m. Thomas Barbour.
Mary m. ____ Masterson.
Mary m. Samuel Brooking.
Mary m. ____ Pendleton.
Mary m. ____ Butler.
Mary m. James Pendleton.
Mary m. ____ Peterson.
Mary m. Edward Watkins.
Mary m. ____ Sousberry.
Mary m. Christopher Chambliss.
Mary m. Joseph Hudnall.
Mary m. James Butler.
Mary m. Samuell Owen.
Mary m. Henry Pendleton.
Mary m. Thomas McCormack.
Mary m. (1) Henry Pendleton; m. (2) Edward Watkins.
Mary m. James Parrish.
Mary m. John Tart.
Mary Ann m. ____ Club.
Mary Dues m. David Kirby (2nd wife).
Mary Geohegan m. Jno. Glynn.
Mary Mason m. Benjamin Edwards Browne.
Mathew m. 7 Nov., 1776, Sally Cram, both of this parish. Douglas Reg., p. 17.
Matilda m. William Moore.
Michael m. William Coombs.
Mildred m. Hay Taliaferro.
Mildred m. Richard Thomas III.
Mildred m. Joseph McCoy.
Milly m. William Morton.
Molly m. Benjamin Hawkins.
More m. William Johnson.
Moses m. Mary Burbury, dau. of Malachi, vestryman of Wicomico Church at an early date. 35V217.
Nancy m. John Eaves.
Nancy m. Richard Boyse.
Nancy m. Zadock Benston.

TAYLOR (cont.)

Nancy m. John Gore.

Nancy m. William Smith.

Nancy m. Reuben Dowell.

Nancy m. John Day.

Nancy m. ___ Fitzhugh.

Nancy m. ___ Johnson.

Nanny m. ___ Birchell.

Nathaniel, b. 1772; d. 1816, son of Andrew and Ann (Wilson); m. 1791, Mary Patton. Rockbridge Co. Morton, p. 534.

Nathaniel, d. 1804, Jefferson Co., Va.-W. Va.; m. Mary (or Nancy) Wright, sis. of John. 34V151.

Nimrod m. 4 Dec., 1781, Mary Lotz. Fauquier Co. Mar. License. Served in Rev. War. DAR No. 365 753.

Orphy (____) m. Thomas Wright.

Parmenas, b. 4 April, 1753, Prince William Co.; d. 28 Feb., 1827, Jefferson Co., Tenn., son of William and Hannah (Bradford); m. 1779, Betty White, b. ca 1760, No. Car.; d. 1838, Jefferson Co., Tenn., dau. of Col. William. 27T138.

Patsey m. Robert DePriest.

Patsey m. John Buckner.

Patty m. John Willmore.

Peggy m. Dickey Board.

Peter, b. 1745, Orange Co.; d. 1812, Madison Co., Ky.; m. Nancy Crossthwaite, b. 1765; d. 1835. DAR No. 79 484.

Peter m. 31 Jan., 1768, Margaret Wallace. Norfolk Co. Mar. Record.

Philip, son of John and Catharine (Pendleton), m. Mary Walker. St. Mark's, p. 172.

Polly m. Ellis G. Blake.

Polly m. James Pettigrew.

Polly m. William Henley.

Rachel m. ___ Teague.

Rachel m. William Blake.

Rachel m. John Roberts.

Raleigh m. 10 Sept., 1792, Elizabeth Waddell. Fauquier Co. Mar. Record.

Raney m. Henry Slaughter.

Rebecca m. Henry Green.

Rebecca m. Pleasant Mitchell.

Reuben, b. 1757, Orange Co.; d. Ky.; served as Captain in Rev. War; m. 1782, Rebecca Moore, dau. of William and Mary (Throckmorton) of Va. Orange Co. Mar. Record; DAR No. 85 400. He was son of George and Rachel (Gibson). 26V197.

Reuben Thornton, b. 4 May, 1779, Caroline Co.; d. 27 May, 1864, Clark Co., Ky., son of Col. James; m. Mary T. Thornton, b. 9 Nov., 1783, Caroline Co.; d. 15 April, 1839; both bur. Clark Co., Ky. 29V372; Ky. Con., p. 127.

Richard m. 9 Oct., 1719, Honor Pepper. Middlesex Co. Christ Church, p. 163.

Richard, Commander, b. 1749, Orange Co.; d. 1825, Oldham Co., Ky.; m. Dec., 1771, Catherine Davis. King George Co. Mar. Record; DAR No. 41 799.

TAYLOR (cont.)

Richard, Col. in Rev. War, b. 3 April, 1744; d. 19 Jan., 1829, son of Zachary and Elizabeth (Lee); m. 20 Aug., 1779, Sarah Dabney Strother, b. 11 Dec., 1760; d. 13 Dec., 1822, dau. of William and Sarah (Bayley) Pannill Strother. 11T129. He, b. 1741, Orange Co.; d. 1829, Jefferson Co., Ky.; m. Sarah Strother. DAR No. 28 907.

Richard, b. ca 1769; d. 1805, son of Richard Squire Taylor and ____ (Meaux); m. 23 Dec., 1789, Elizabeth Temple, b. 17 Oct., 1769; d. 31 Jan., 1841, dau. of Benjamin and Mollie (Baylor) of King William Co. Marriage proven by will of Benjamin Temple, dated 23 March, 1800, King William Co. 14W(2)51, 55; King William, p. 69.

Richard, will prov. 1774, Lancaster Co.; m. 1759, Judith (____) Taylor, widow of Argyle, whose est. sett. proves it. He was son of Benjamin of Lancaster, Prince William and Fauquier counties. 45V82.

Richard m. 13 Oct., 1773, Lucy (____) Gregory. Charles City Co. Mar. Record.

Richard m. 4 Jan., 1773, Hannah Varnon, dau. of Jonathan. Sur. Benjamin Parrott. Charlotte Co. Mar. Bond.

Richard m. ____ Baxter, dau. of Nathaniel, whose will, prov. 1677, Old Rappahannock Co. See record of est. sett. of Richard Taylor, 4 Dec., 1684.

Richard m. ____ (Lawrence) Sanders, widow of Henry and dau. of John Lawrence, whose will, 1696, Nansemond Co. Boddie-Isle, p. 497.

Robert m. 11 April, 1662, Elizabeth Welsh. Middlesex Co. Christ Church, p. 11.

Robert, b. 29 April, 1763; d. 3 July, 1845, son of Erasmus and Jane (Moore); m. 1784, his cousin, Frances Pendleton, b. 18 Sept., 1767; d. 20 Oct., 1831, dau. of Edmund, Jr., and Mildred (Pollard). 41V 85-6; St. Mark's, p. 173. He was son of Zachary and Elizabeth (Lee). 46V232.

Robert of Norfolk m. Sept., 1771, Sally Barraud, dau. of Daniel, merchant of Norfolk. Announced in The Virginia Gazette. 8W(1)190.

Robert m. 1795, Agnes McCroskey. Rockbridge Co. Morton, p. 534.

Robert m. bef. 1747, Elizabeth Stone, dau. of William and Elizabeth (____), whose Deed of Gift, 15 March, 1747/8, Amelia Co., proves it. Res. 1772, No. Car., when Power of Attorney was given to sell estate in Amelia Co. Taylor, p. 6; Amelia Co. Deed Book 3, p. 31.

Robert m. (1) Mary (___); divorced, Elizabeth City Co. Court, 18 Jan., 1699/70; m. (2) 10 Feb., 1701, Elizabeth Hudson. Elizabeth City Co. Mar. License. Mar. (3) Martha Daniel, dau. of Darby. 5W(1)57; Taylor, pp. 8, 10.

Robert m. 17 Dec., 1789, Elizabeth Ward by H. J. Burgess. Surry Co. Ministers' Returns.

Robert m. bef. 1689, ____ (____) Vincent, relict and extrx. of Dorothous Vincent. Proven by Deed, 18 Nov., 1689, Elizabeth City Co. Taylor, p. 10.

Rose m. John MacCloud.

Ruth m. John Scandland.

Ruth m. William Layne.

Sally m. Thomas Hanshaw.

Sally m. George Hunt.

Sally m. John Elliott.

TAYLOR(cont.)

Sally m. William Tolley.
Samuel m. 1793, Catharine Walker. Rockbridge Co. Morton, p. 534.
Sarah m. Francis Hardiman.
Sarah m. Jacob Roberts.
Sarah m. (1) John Hardyman; m. (2) Francis Hardyman.
Sarah m. James Garnett.
Sarah m. Joseph Hudnall.
Sarah m. ___ Pope.
Sarah m. ___ Jasper.
Sarah m. John Walker.
Sarah m. George Tarry.
Sarah m. James Heron.
Sarah m. James Denson.
Sarah m. ___ Lisles.
Sarah m. James Coleman.
Sarah m. Zachariah Rose.
Sarah m. Robert Powell.
Susanna m. Dr. Augustine Smith.
Susanna m. (1) Kemp Hurst; m. (2) Onisophorous Harvey.
Susannah m. Thomas Heaton.
Susannah m. ___ Robertson.
Tabitha m. Thomas Wild.
Tabitha m. ___ Wild.
Tabitha m. Rice Noell.
Thomas, killed by a falling ree ca 1749; will prov. Augusta Co.; m. Elizabeth Paxton, dau. of Thomas. Rockbridge Co. Morton, p. 535; Kegley, p. 157.
Thomas, served as Colonel in Rev. War; b. 1743, Va.; d. 1833, Columbia, So. Car.; m. 1767, Anna Wyche. DAR No. 79 563.
Thomas m. 29 May, 1774, Milley Barker, both of Goochland. Douglas Reg., p. 15.
Thomas, est. sett., 1755, Lancaster Co.; m. Eva Ball, dau. of James. She m. (2) Solomon Ewell. 35V215.
Thomas m. bef. 1689, Frances (___) Perrine, relict of Sebastian, by whom she had a son, Sebastian Perrine, Jr., a minor in 1689. Proven by Court Suit, 18 Nov., 1689, Elizabeth City Co.
Thomas, bro. of Lazarus of Lancaster Co., m. ___ Hemolt of that county. Taylor, p. 74.
Thomas m. 1794, Katy Gore. Fauquier Co. Taylor, p. 185.
Thomas, son of John (d. 1652, Lancaster Co.) and Alice (Gaskins), m. Elizabeth Thorriott, dau. of William and granddaughter of Dominick of Lancaster Co. Proven by Deed Book 9, pp. 189, 382; Order Book 1699-1713; 11T30; 35V214.
Thomas m. 28 Oct., 1800, Martha C. Hamblin. Mecklenburg Co. Cameron.
Thomasine m. Ellis Gill.
Timothy, b. 1761, Bucks Co., Penna.; d. 1838, Loudoun Co.; served in Rev. War; m. 1780, Achsah Johnson, b. 1749; d. 1826. DAR No. 68 415.
Ursley m. Jeremiah Doss.
Walter m. bef. 3 March, 1672/3, Mary Harris, dau. of Richard of Lawne's Creek Parish. Marriage Gift, Surry Co., of that date,

TAYLOR (cont.)

proves the marriage.

William m. 11 Feb., 1773, Henrietta Dunton, dau. of Stephen. Northampton Co. Mar. Record.

William m. 21 Nov., 1780, Sarah Wheeler. Northampton Co. Mar. Record.

William m. 21 July, 1792, N. Collins. Halifax Co. Mar. Record.

William, merchant at Holt's, New Kent Co., m. Nancy Booker, only dau. of Col. Richard of Amelia Co. Reported in The Virginia Gazette, 5 March, 1772. 9W(1)239.

William m. 5 Dec., 1696, Judith Arthur. Henrico, p. 226.

William m. Mary Waters. Proven by Order Book, Northumberland Co., 1709, when John Waters is shown to be grandfather of their orphans: Pheby, William, Mary, Elizabeth and John Taylor. 35V212.

William m. 5 Sept., 1790, Mary Watterson, dau. of Henry. Botetourt Co. Kegley, p. 596.

William, representative in Assembly for Lunenburg Co., b. 1732, New Kent Co.; d. 1820, Lunenburg Co., son of Rev. Daniel and Alice (Littlepage); m. ca 19 March, 1767, Martha "Patty" Waller, eldest dau. of Judge Benjamin Waller of Williamsburg, Va. Announced in The Virginia Gazette, 19 March, 1767. Free II:362. William, b. 1739; d. 11 Sept., 1820; m. Martha Waller, b. 28 Nov., 1747, dau. of Benjamin and Martha (Hall). 50V267; 59V352; 8W(1)27; 14W(2)49.

William m. 5 July, 1796, Nancy Lancaster. Isle of Wight Co. Mar. Record.

William m. 9 March, 1799, Mary Walls by William Pettus Martin. Campbell Co. Mar. Record.

William m. 1778, Susannah Drummond. Fauquier Co. Taylor, p. 185.

William m. ____ (____) Glasscock, widow of George. Proven by Court Record, York Co., 24 March, 1701.

William m. Mary (____) Halbert, mother of Elizabeth, Joel and William Halbert. Proven by wills of William Taylor, 1733, and Mary Taylor, 1737, both of Essex Co.

William m. 13 May, 1775, Priscilla Segar. Middlesex Co. Christ Church, p. 201.

William m. 1781, Margaret Timmons. Botetourt Co. Kegley, p. 480.

William m. 12 Feb., 1795, Caty Alsup by Rev. John Alderson, Jr. Rockingham or Greenbrier Co. Ministers' Returns.

William m. 1792, Jean Cuffey. Rockbridge Co. Morton, p. 535.

William from County Armagh, Ireland, to Rockbridge Co., 1760; m. Janet Paul, said to be sis. of John Paul Jones, who was born John Paul and took the Jones name of his foster parent. Morton, p. 274.

William m. 7 July, 1796, Fanny Fowler by Rev. John Lasley. Louisa Co. Ministers' Returns.

William m. 1789, Elizabeth Walker. Orange Co. Mar. Record.

William m. Patience Kinchen. Boddie-Isle, p. 232; 23V105.

William m. Elizabeth (Teackle) Melchops, dau. of Rev. Thomas Teackle. 22V84.

William, d. ca 1655; m. bet. 26 Sept., 1638 (date of a Patent), and 4 April, 1642 (date of a Deed, James City Co.), Elizabeth Kingsmill, dau. of Richard of James City Co. She was a patentee in 1638. She m. (2) Hon. Nathaniel Bacon. 17V369-75. He is given as Col. William Tayloe. 2W(1)81.

TAYLOR (cont.)

William m. 8 Oct., 1730, Elizabeth Henderson. Richmond Co. Farnham Parish Register.

William Berry, b. 26 Feb., 1768; d. 2 Feb., 1836 (Bible Record); . . . (Record incomplete).

William Robinson m. 17 March, 1790, Martha Taylor. Norfolk Co. Mar. Record.

Zachary, b. 17 April, 1707; d. 1768; m. (1) Elizabeth Lee, dau. of Hancock and Sarah (Allerton); m. (2) ___ (___) Blackburn. He was son of James and Martha (Thompson). Taylor, pp. 133-4.

Zachary of Orange Co. m. Elizabeth (___) Jones, widow of Swann (d. bef. 1742). 23W(1)269.

TAYNER

Mary m. Thomas Robinson.

TAZEWELL

Anne m. John Niverson (or Nivision).

Elizabeth m. Dr. Samuel Griffin.

Gertrude m. John Stratton.

Henry of Brunswick Co. m. 13 Jan., 1774, Dorothy Elizabeth Waller, b. 2 Jan., 1754; d. 13 May, 1777, dau. of Benjamin and Martha (Hall) of Williamsburg, Va. Announced in The Virginia Gazette, 13 Jan., 1774. 59V352; Free II:363.

John, Judge, m. Sarah Bolling, b. 16 June, 1748, dau. of John and Elizabeth (Blair). 22V217.

Littleton, son of John and Sarah (Bolling), m. Catherine (Boush) Nevison. Pocahontas, p. 36.

Littleton m. 13 Feb., 1753, Mary Gray, b. 10 Feb., 1733/4, dau. of Joseph and Sarah (Simmons). 5V201; 30V65, 294. Mar. 13 Feb., 1753. 30V65. Mar. 12 Feb., 1753. Sur. Ben Ruffin of Surry Co. Southampton Co. Mar. Bond.

William, d. 1840, son of John and Sarah (Bolling); m. Mary Page Tanner. Pocahontas, p. 36.

William m. 10 June, 1723, Sophia Harmanson. Northampton Co. Mar. Record.

TEACKLE

Abel Upshur m. 7 July, 1790, Rachel Gascoyne. Northampton Co. Mar. Record.

Ann m. Hillery Stringer.

Caleb m. 14 Dec., 1771, Elizabeth Harmanson, dau. of George. Northampton Co. Mar. Record. Caleb, son of Thomas (1711-1769) and Elizabeth (Curtis). Old King Wm., p. 104.

Catherine m. Charles Smith.

Elizabeth m. (1) ___ Melchops; m. (2) William Taylor.

Elizabeth m. Thomas Tabb.

Elizabeth m. Isaac Smith.

John of Craddock, b. 2 Sept., 1673; d. 3 Dec., 1721, Yorktown, Va., son of Thomas and (2) Margaret (Nelson); m. 2 Nov., 1710, Susannah Upshur, dau. of Arthur and Sarah (Brown). Old King Wm., p. 103.

John m. 17 Dec., 1783, Anne Upshur, dau. of Thomas. Northampton Co. Mar. Record.

John, b. 12 Jan., 1762; d. 18 Feb., 1811, son of Thomas and Elizabeth (Upshur); m. 18 Dec., 1783, Ann Stockley, dau. of Thomas of

TEACKLE (cont.)
"Brownsville." Old King Wm., p. 104.
Katherine m. Charles Smith.
Katherine m. John Robins.
Margaret m. Thomas Littleton Savage.
Margaret m. George Hack.
Margaret Catherine m. Col. Edward Robins (1st wife).
Sarah m. John Boisnard.
Sarah m. Bowdoin Kendall.
Severn, b. 25 Oct., 1756, son of Thomas (1711-69) and Elizabeth (Curtis); served in Rev. War; m. Lucretia Edmondson. Old King Wm., p. 104. His mother was Elizabeth Custis. 21V433.
Susannah m. Col. John Robins.
Susannah m. Daniel Gore.
Thomas, b. 11 Nov., 1711, son of John and Susannah (____); m. 9 Nov., 1732, Elizabeth Custis, b. 27 Aug., 1718, dau. of Thomas and Ann (____). Family Papers. 21V432. He d. 20 July, 1769; m. Elizabeth Curtis, dau. of John of the Eastern Shore. Old King Wm., p. 103.
Thomas, b. 1763, son of Thomas and Elizabeth (Upshur); m. Catherine Stockley. Old King Wm., p. 104.
Thomas, d. 15 April, 1784, son of Thomas and Elizabeth (Curtis) m. Elizabeth Upshur, d. 14 Jan., 1782, dau. of Abel and Rachel (Revell). Old King Wm., p. 104.
Thomas, b. 1624, Gloucestershire, Eng.; d. 1695, Minister in Hungars Parish, Va., 1665-1695; m. (1) 1658, Isabella (____) Douglass, widow of Lieut.-Col. Edward Douglass; m. (2) 1682, Margaret Nelson, sis. of John Nelson of New England and dau. of Robert and Mary (Temple) of London, Eng. 22V84; Old King Wm., p. 103; Hartford B-8373, 29 Oct., 1955. Signed S. E. T.

TEAFORD
James m. 4 Nov., 1786, Mary McCaskry, dau. of John who gave consent. Rockbridge Co. Ministers' Returns.

TEAGARDEN
Bazel m. 21 Oct., 1797, Ann Todd. Shelby Co., Ky. Mar. Record.

TEAGUE
____ m. bef. 1760, Rachel Taylor, dau. of Samuel, whose will of that date, Frederick Co., proves it.
Elizabeth m. William Lock.
John m. 6 Aug., 1795, Polly Harris. Shelby Co., Ky. Mar. Record.
Thomas m. 21 Feb., 1767, Keziah Scott, dau. of Henry. Northampton Co. Mar. Record.

TEAGY
Sarah m. John Messick.

TEAL
Elizabeth m. John McCullough.

TEAS
____ m. Martha Steele, dau. of David (d. 1747). Rockbridge Co. Morton, p. 531.

TEBBS
Judith m. Robert Young.
William, b. 1732, Prince William Co.; d. there, 1813; m. (2) Victoria Haislip. DAR No. 27 046.

TEDFORD

Alexander m. 1797, Elizabeth McClung. Morton, p. 535.
Alexander m. 1787, Mary McCampbell. Rockbridge Co. Morton, p. 535.
Geannet (or Janet) m. James McKee.
James m. 1797, Agnes Dickson. Rockbridge Co. Morton, p. 535.
James m. 1789, Jane McCroskey. Rockbridge Co. Morton, p. 535.
James m. 4 Nov., 1785, Mary McCoskry by Rev. John Brown. Rockbridge Co. Ministers' Returns. Given as McCroskey. Morton, p. 535.
Jane m. James L. McKee (1st wife).
John m. Mary Paxton, dau. of Thomas and (1) Elizabeth (McClung). Rockbridge Co. Morton, p. 518.
Joseph, b. 1763, Va.; d. 1825, Maryville, Tenn.; served as private under Capt. John Tedford and Capt. David Gray in Virginia troops; m. 1793, Mary "Polly" McNutt, b. 1769; d. 1857. DAR No. 165 153.
Martha m. James Alexander.
Mary m. Samuel Dickson.
Samuel m. 13 April, 1786, Eliza Cull by Rev. John Brown. Rockbridge Co. Ministers' Returns.
Sarah m. Elihu Barclay.
William m. 1798, Rebecca McClung. Rockbridge Co. Morton, p. 535.

TEEL

Elizabeth m. Edward Sanders.

TEGANFUS

Jacob m. 13 Aug., 1776, Christenah Brilian by Rev. John Alderson, Jr. Rockingham Co. or Greenbrier Co. Ministers' Returns.

TELFAIR

Sarah (____) m. Noah Prichard.

TELFORD

____ m. Agnes Dickson, dau. of James (d. 1797). Rockbridge Co. Morton, p. 482.
Alexander m. 6 Sept., 1787, Mary McCampbell by Rev. John Brown. Her mother was Ann (____) McCampbell. Rockbridge Co. Ministers' Returns.
Andrew m. 1777, Priscilla Robertson. Rockbridge Co. Morton, p. 535.
John m. 12 March, 1793, Catharine Runkle, dau. of Lewis (d. 1805, Augusta Co.) 31T271.
John m. 6 Dec., 1780, Margaret King, both of Louisa. Douglas Reg., p. 20.
Martha m. James Alexander.
Mary m. James Weir.
Samuel m. 13 April, 1786, Elizabeth Cull. May Cull, mother of Elizabeth, gave consent. Mar. by Rev. John Brown. Rockbridge Co. Ministers' Returns.
Sarah m. Elihu Barclay.

TELLER

Lilly m. William Williams.

TELLERY

Ann m. James Taylor.

TELLIS

Elizabeth m. Henry Oldakers.

TEMBLE

Margaret m. Edward Riddick.

TEMBTE

Henning, physician, b. 1700; d. 1771, Halifax Co., No. Car.; m. ca 1730, Elizabeth Sherwood, b. ca 1708; d. bef. 1750, dau. of Daniel of Talbot Co., Md.; res. 1744, Nansemond Co., Va.; rem. 1765 to No. Car. 65V89.

Margaret m. Edward Riddick.

TEMPEST

Barbara (Needham) m. Christopher DeGraffenreid.

TEMPLE

Anne (____) m. Francis Clay.

Benjamin, Col., of "Presque Isle," son of Joseph and Ann (Arnold), will dated 23 March, 1800; m. Mary "Mollie" Brooke Baylor. 25V322; Old King Wm., p. 69.

Elizabeth m. Richard Taylor.

Elizabeth m. Thomas Tenney.

Eppes m. 1 March, 1792, Elizabeth Peebles. Prince George Co. Cameron.

Fanny m. Andrew Broaddus.

Frances m. Humphrey Walker.

John m. 1775, Mary Ann Canterbury. Orange Co. Mar. Record.

John m. 1790, Jenny Wardlaw. Rockbridge Co. Morton, p. 535.

Joseph of "Presque Isle" m. Ann Arnold, dau. of Benjamin, who lived in King William Co. in 1704. 25V322; 32V256; Old King Wm., p. 50.

Joshua m. 11 Feb., 1792, Martha Williams. Prince George Co. Cameron.

Liston, d. bef. 1804, son of Joseph; m. Agnes Elliott. Old King Wm., p. 50.

Lucy m. Timothy Chandler.

Mary m. Dr. George Williamson.

Nancy m. Eppes Temple.

Peter, Capt., d. 1694-5, son of Rev. Peter Temple of York Parish; m. 1693, Anne (Bray) Booth, d. 1711, widow of Robert Booth, Jr., and dau. of Col. James Bray. She m. (3) Mungo Ingles. 14T182; 2W(1)234.

Peter, Rev., of York Parish, m. Mary (____) Ludlow, widow of Thomas (d. 1660); rem. with her three children to England. 1T236; 2W(1) 5, 15.

Robert, b. 1774; d. Dec., 1836, son of Col. Benjamin and Mary (Baylor); m. 6 Feb., 1799, Elizabeth M. Skyren, b. Aug., 1779, King William Co.; d. 1862; res. Chesterfield Co. 54V162; 14W(2)55.

Samuel, Capt., m. Fanny Rodd. Caroline, p. 399.

William m. Catherine "Kitty" Tompkins, dau. of William (1736-1772) and Ann Cosby of Caroline Co. 10W(2)232.

TEMPLEMAN

Mary m. Daniel Muse.

Samuel m. Sibella Pierce, dau. of Capt. Joseph and Sarah (Ransdell). 6W(1)27.

TEMPLETON

____ m. bef. 1792, Margaret Cloyd, dau. of David, whose will, filed that year, Rockbridge Co., names dau., Margaret Templeton, and grandsons, David and James Templeton. Morton, p. 479; Kegley, p. 502.

David m. 1791, Mary McClure. Rockbridge Co. Morton, p. 535.

James m. 1787, Botetourt Co., Lucy Billups. Kegley, p. 540; DAR Mag., April, 1930, p. 522.

TEMPLETON (cont.)
James m. 1792, Elizabeth Edmondson. Rockbridge Co. Morton, p. 555.
John m. Margaret Cloyd, dau. of David. Kegley, p. 502.
TENANT
Nancy m. Charles Cochran.
TENCH
James m. 1 June, 1786, Sarah Williams. Prince George Co. Cameron.
Sukey m. Abraham Johnston.
TENDALL
Thomas m. 31 Dec., 1793, Patsey Wall. Halifax Co. Mar. Record.
TENEY
Prisey m. Charles Cross.
TENKLE
Dolly m. Abraham Huffman.
TENNANT
Elizabeth m. Elijah West.
John m. 27 June, 1729/30, Dorothy Paul. Spotsylvania Co. Mar. Record.
Lewis m. 18 Dec., 1799, Sally Clark. Caroline Co. Mar. Record.
Nancy m. Charles Colhorn.
TENNEY
Thomas m. 17 May, 1788, Elizabeth Temple. Prince George Co. Cameron.
TENNILL
Joseph m. 15 Aug., 1794, Mary P. Hicks. Sur. David Hicks. Albemarle Co. Mar. Bond.
TENNISON
Sarah m. Evan Lewis.
TENOE
Thomas m. 21 May, 1774, Judith Belfare. Christ Church, p. 201.
TENOR
Stephen m. 17 Dec., 1744, Ann Rhodes, dau. of John, who gave consent. Sur. Robert Price. Middlesex Co. Mar. Bond.
TERHUNE
Stephen m. 21 Jan., 1800, Mary Montfort. Shelby Co., Ky. Mar. Record.
TERMAN
Willy m. Hopewell Wood.
TERREL
Beckie m. Nicholas Hunter Merriwether.
Jesse m. 5 Dec., 1797, N. Strange. Halifax Co. Mar. Record.
Mary m. Garrett Minor.
TERRELL (TERRIL, TERRILL)
____ m. David Lewis (1st wife).
Abigail m. Col. Richard Durrette.
Abigail m. Col. William Durrett (1st wife).
Ann m. Col. Zachary Lewis.
Ann m. ____ Moore.
Ann m. Joseph Towles.
Anna m. Charles Lynch, Jr.
Barbara m. Capt. Aaron Fontaine.
Becky m. Nicholas Merriwether.
Betsy m. Nathaniel Welch.

TERRELL (cont.)

Charles, b. 2 Aug., 1748; d. 1828, son of Henry and (2) Sarah (Woodson); m. Ann Tyler, dau. of William and Elizabeth (Keeling). 14T59. Charles m. Susie Tyler; res. Caroline Co. 12T245.

Charles L. m. 1789, Sally Lynch by James Kenney. Campbell Co. Mar. Record.

Chiles m. 1783, Margaret (Douglass) Meriwether, widow of Nicholas. Albemarle, p. 326.

Christopher m. 26 Dec., 1798, Mary Collins by Rev. Archer Woody. Caroline Co. Ministers' Returns. Christopher d. 1826; Mary, dau. of John and Mary (Carr). Collins, p. 21.

David, b. Va., son of William and Frances (Wingfield); m. Mary Ann Mounger. 60V315.

David m. 25 Sept., 1788, Molly Anthony. Lynchburg, p. 157.

E. m. John Rawlins.

Edmund m. 24 Nov., 1760, Peggy Willis. Orange Co. Mar. Record. Edmund, b. 21 March, 1740; d. 1784, Culpeper Co.; m. 1760, Margaret Willis, b. 1741; d. 1812, dau. of John and Elizabeth (Plunkett) of Orange Co.; res. Culpeper Co. 31V178; Albemarle, p. 326; Orange III:100; Rhodes, p. 405; DAR No. 69 000.

Eliza m. Joseph Andrews.

Eliza m. Frederick Harris.

Eliza m. Josiah Young.

Elizabeth m. Nathaniel Welch.

Elizabeth m. John Chandler.

Elizabeth m. Achilles Douglas.

Elizabeth m. Isaac Johnson.

Elizabeth m. Zachariah Moorman (1st wife).

Elizabeth m. John Rawlins.

Elizabeth m. John Rollins.

Elizabeth m. William Wilkins.

Elizabeth m. Thomas Wingfield.

Fanny m. Thomas Booker.

Frances m. Charles C. Lacy.

George m. 1795, Polly Wolf. Orange Co. Mar. Record.

George, b. 28 June, 1758; d. 1818, son of Henry and (2) Sarah (Woodson); m. 21 Dec., 1776, Elizabeth Tyler, dau. of William and (3) Elizabeth (Keeling); res. Caroline Co. 58V194-5.

Hannah m. Israel Burnley.

Henry, b. 1735; d. 1812, Ky., son of Henry and (1) Ann (Chiles); m. 1776, Mary Tyler, b. 1743, dau. of William of Caroline Co.; rem. 1787, to Ky. 14T57; Lynchburg, p. 123.

Henry, son of William, dec'd., of Hanover Co., m. 3 da 4 mo 1744, Sarah Woodson, dau. of Tarleton of Henrico Co. Society of Friends, Henrico Co. Henry m. (1) Anna Chiles; m. (2) Sarah (Woodson), dau. of Tarleton (will, 1761, Chesterfield Co., proves it) and Ursula (Fleming). 58V195; 9W(1)256; Br, p. 389; Lynchburg, p. 123.

James m. 1793, Rebecca Chambers. Orange Co. Mar. Record.

James Hunter m. Susan Vibert; res. Music Hall. Albemarle, p. 326.

Jane m. Joseph Bishop.

Jemima m. Jacob Cole.

Joel, b. Va., son of William and Frances (Wingfield); m. 25 Nov., 1780,

TERRELL (cont.)

Lucy Ragland, dau. of Samuel. Louisa Co. Mar. Record; 60V315.

Joel, d. 1773; res. 1734, Hanover Co.; m. his cousin, Ann(-a) Lewis, b. 1733, dau. of David and ___ (Terrell). She d. 1835, Rutherford Co., No. Car.; m. (2) Stephen Willis. Albemarle, pp. 255, 325; Jones Geno., p. 189.

John m. 1794, Caty Miller. Orange Co. Mar. Record.

John, will dated 18 Jan., 1803, son of Robert; m. Ann Towles, b. 19 Jan., 1739, dau. of John and Margaret (Daniel). 13T25.

Joseph, son of Timothy of New Kent Co., m. 29 Sept., 1767, Elizabeth Mills, b. 26 Jan., 1747; d. 22 Nov., 1853, prob. dau. of Charles and Ann (___). 15T43.

Judith m. George Tyler.

Lucy m. Tristam Coggshall.

Martha m. John Daniel (2nd wife).

Martha J. m. Dabney Minor (2nd wife).

Mary m. ___ Hudson.

Mary m. John Wood.

Mary m. Francis Robinson.

Mary m. John Richardson.

Mary m. Richard Swift.

Mary m. Edward Lynch.

Mary m. Richard Sims.

Mary m. Jno. Marston.

Mary Overton m. Col. Garrett Minor.

Mildred m. Jesse Wood.

Mildred (___) m. Jesse Wood.

Neff m. John Rawlins.

Oliver m. 1789, Susannah Mallory. Orange Co. Mar. Record.

Peter, d. 1794/5; m. Mary Wingfield, b. 15 Oct., 1747, dau. of John and Frances Oliver (Buck). 60V311.

Rebecca m. Charles Christian.

Reuben m. 14 May, 1771, Mary Walker. Orange Co. Mar. Record.

Richard m. 5 Oct., 1792, Lucy Carr. Douglas Reg., p. 127. Richard M., d. 1802, son of Richmond and Anne (Overton); m. Lucy Maria Carr, b. 7 March, 1768; d. 1803, dau. of Dabney and Martha (Jefferson); rem. to Ky. Boddie-HSF V:131; Louisa, p. 414; DAR No. 75 112.

Richmond m. Anne "Nancy" Overton, b. 1725; d. 1790, dau. of Capt. James and Elizabeth (Garland); res. Louisa Co. Boddie-HSF V:131; Louisa, p. 396.

Richmond, son of Richmond and Ann (Overton), m. Sally Overton. Louisa, p. 414.

Richmond m. 8 April, 1782, Essella (or Cecilia) Darracott. Louisa Co. Mar. Record; Douglas Reg., p. 22.

Robert m. 1798, Ann Mallory. Orange Co. Mar. Record. He, son of John and Ann (Towles); she, dau. of Uriel. 13T26.

Robert m. Judith Stokeley, b. 13 April, 1735; rem. to Lincoln Co., Ky. 13T29.

Rosannah m. Thomas Tylor.

Samuel m. 1799, Amey Pettus, dau. of Thomas and (1) Mary (Henderson). 29T147.

Sarah m. (1) Joseph Towles; m. (2) ___ Murray.

TERRELL (cont.)

Sarah m. Henry Thurman.
Sarah m. Benjamin Arthur.
Sarah m. James Newton.
Sarah m. John Scott III.
Sarah m. Augustine Cornelius.
Thomas m. 20 Oct., 1780, Sarah Shelton, dau. of David. Louisa Co. Mar. Record. He, b. Va., son of William and Frances (Wingfield). 60V315.
Timothy m. 1798, Miriam Murdaugh Hunnicutt, b. 21 Sept., 1777, dau. of James and Rebecca (Pretlow). 27W(1)42.
Timothy m. Elizabeth Foster; res. New Kent Co. A son, Robert, b. 1697. 31V177.
Virginia m. Dr. Frank Carr.
William, mar. contract, July, 1749, Charles City Co., with Mary Collier. 22V436.
William, b. 1757, Halifax Co.; d. there, 1829; m. 1785, Martha Patterson, b. 1758; d. 1831. DAR No. 65 267; DAR No. 66 163.
William, b. 11 Feb., 1732; d. 6 Aug., 1812, son of Joel and Sarah Elizabeth (Oxford); served in Rev. War; m. 1756, Frances Wingfield, b. 30 Dec., 1736; d. 20 Nov., 1802, dau. of Thomas and Sarah (Garland); rem. to Wilkes Co., Ga. 60V315.
William, son of Richmond and Anne (Overton), m. Martha "Patsy" Winston, dau. of William and Polly (Overton). Boddie-HSF V:131; Louisa, p. 414.
William m. 26 Nov., 1780, Ann Daniel. Orange Co. Mar. Record; Douglas Reg., p. 20.
William, Jr., m. 1793, Jane Morton. Orange Co. Mar. Record.
Zachariah m. 1771, Millie Walker. Orange Co. Mar. Record.

TERRETT

Francis of Richmond Co. m. bef. 5 Oct., 1717, Catherine, dau. of Eleanor Kemp. Proven by Court Record of that date, Essex Co.
George Hunter, Capt., b. 1778; d. 1843, son of Capt. William Henry and Amelia (Hunter); served in War of 1812; m. Hannah Butler Ashton, b. 1785; d. 1860, dau. of Henry and Jane (Alexander). Orange III: 88, 91.
William Henry, b. 1752; d. 1826, son of William Henry and Margaret (Pearson); m. 25 July, 1775, Amelia Hunter, b. 1756; d. 1830, dau. of Dr. John and Elizabeth (Chapman). Orange III:88.
William Henry, b. 19 April, 1707, England; m. 27 Jan., 1735, Margaret Pearson, b. 5 March, 1720; will dated, 1798, dau. of Simon of Stafford Co. (will, 1755); res. Fairfax Co. Margaret m. (2) John West, Jr. 23V216; 32V309; Orange III:88, 90, 92.

TERREY

William m. 21 April, 1689, Elizabeth Cooper. Christ Church, p. 37.

TERRY

____ m. Michael Prewitt (3rd wife).
____ m. June, 1786, Lucy Lax. Sur. Elisha Lax. Buckingham Co. Mar. Bond.
____ believed m. bef. 1762, Judith Crawford, dau. of David, whose will, filed 1762, Amherst Co., names "daughter Judith Terry."
Andrew m. 14 Dec., 1714, Elizabeth Moxon. Christ Church, p. 83.

TERRY (cont.)

Ann m. Thomas Nuckols.
Anna m. John Sims.
Barbara m. Nathan Smith.
Catherine m. Richard Dudgeon.
Charles m. 7 Jan., 1783, Judah Terry by Rev. Lazarus Dodson. Pittsylvania Co. Mar. Record.
Christian m. David Crawford.
Drusillar m. Robin Harris Walton.
E. m. Peter Green.
Elizabeth m. Thomas Smith.
Elizabeth m. William Walton.
Emanuel m. 14 Oct., 1784, Elizabeth Thomson, both in Louisa. Douglas Reg., p. 23.
Frances m. John Smith (prob. Jr.)
Frances m. John White, Jr.
Frances m. James Branch.
Henrietta m. William Nichols (or Nuckols).
James m. 25 Jan., 1790, Anna Smith, dau. of John. Sur. Thomas Smith. Louisa Co. Mar. Bond.
James m. 23 March, 1797, Polly Smith by Rev. William Cooke. Louisa Co. Ministers' Returns.
James, d. after 1790, Richmond Co., No. Car.; m. Elizabeth Leake, b. Va., dau. of Richard of Henrico Co. Harlee 1:151.
Jane m. David Bullock.
Jemima m. Ezekiel Boucher.
Jery m. March, 1795, Winney Holt. Halifax Co. Mar. Record.
Joannah m. James Goodwin.
Joe Coleman, Col., m. his cousin, Elizabeth Dickerson Green, dau. of Berryman and Nancy (Terry). Halifax, p. 185.
John m. 1795, Lucy Oaks. Orange Co. Mar. Record.
John m. Mary Quarles, b. ca 1762, dau. of Solomon and Dorothy (Waller). She m. (2) Dec., 1793, John Reins. 52V279.
John m. 3 Dec., 1782, Sarah Hodnett by Rev. Lazarus Dodson. Pittsylvania Co. Ministers' Returns.
John m. 1781, Botetourt Co., Esther Brown. Kegley, p. 539.
John Sandwich m. 1 Sept., 1784, Mary Ellis, spinster. Sur. William Ellis. York Co. Mar. Bond.
Joseph m. 21 Nov., 1783, S. Hill. Halifax Co. Mar. Record.
Judah m. Charles Terry.
Keeble m. 5 Nov., 1787, S. Terry. Halifax Co. Mar. Record.
Keziah m. ____ Murphy.
Livinia m. ____ King.
Lucy m. William Williams.
Mary m. Thomas Brown.
Mary m. Henry Womack.
Mary m. William Ryburn.
Mary m. William Gibson.
Mills m. Sarah LaMarr. A son, Thomas, b. 1791, near Richmond, Va. Ky. Bible Records 2:81.
Nancy m. Cosby Dickinson.
Nancy m. Capt. Berryman Green (2nd wife).

TERRY (cont.)

Nathaniel, d. 21 April, 1780; m. bef. 1760, Sarah Royall; res. Halifax Co. 7T201; 33V323.

Nathaniel m. 24 Nov., 1795, Franky Watts. Sur. David Watts. Albemarle Co. Mar. Bond.

Patsy m. Bannister Wade.

Patsy m. Martin Dunn.

Polly m. James Thompson.

Rebecca m. Nathaniel Dickerson.

S. m. Keeble Terry.

S. m. R. Goodwin.

Samuel m. 1799, Amey Pettus, dau. of Thomas and Mary (Henderson). 29T147.

Sarah m. Richard Thomason.

Sarah m. James Hunt.

Stephen m. 14 Dec., 1782, Mildred Bagby, dau. of John. Louisa, p. 265.

Stephen m. 14 Dec., 1793, Sarah Davis. Louisa, p. 266.

Susanna m. Thomas Brown.

Thomas m. 22 April, 1784, Mary Thomason by Rev. Lazarus Dodson. Pittsylvania Co. Ministers' Returns.

Thomas m. 17 Jan., 1797, Sarah Hendrick. Lynchburg, p. 157.

William m. 15 June, 1794, Sarah Crank by Rev. William Cooke. Louisa Co. Ministers' Returns.

William m. Polly (Watlington) Thompson, widow of William and dau. of Armistead Watlington. Halifax, p. 345.

William, b. 1736; d. 1776; served in Rev. War from Va.; m. Nancy Raiford. DAR No. 41 209.

William m. Susannah Thompson, dau. of William (will, 1780). Halifax, p. 340.

TETER

Catherine Margaret m. Rev. John Mitchell.

George, b. 1740, Rowan Co., No. Car.; d. 1798, Pendleton Co.; m. 1763, Anna Margaret Henkel, b. 1745; d. 1805. DAR No. 51 865.

TEVIS

Nancy m. Thomas Jewell.

TEW

John of Westmoreland Co. m. Grace (____) Baldridge, widow of Maj. Thomas. 4W(1)42.

*Restitua m. John Hallowes.

THACH

Elizabeth m. Jesse Berry.

THACKER

Alice m. William Gough.

Andrew m. 11 Jan., 1799, Sally Martin by Rev. Richard Pope. Louisa Co. Ministers' Returns.

Ann m. Henry Washington.

Anne m. Rev. Adam Dickie.

Anne m. Henry Washington (1st wife).

Archelaus m. 31 July, 1781, Ann Chace, both of Louisa. Douglas Reg., p. 21.

Benjamin m. 5 Nov., 1767, Neffeny Emmerson, both in this parish. Douglas Reg., p. 10.

Chickeley m. 3 March, 1729/30, Hannah Clowder. Spotsylvania Co. Mar.

THACKER (cont.)

Record.

Daniel m. 25 Oct., 1786, Lucy Humphrey. Louisa, p. 258.

Edward m. 31 Oct., 1789, Priscilla Yarbrough. Caroline Co. Mar. Record.

Edwin of Middlesex Co., m. 12 Aug., 1694, Frances Daingerfield, dau. of Anne Walker and (2) John Daingerfield. Essex Co. Mar. Record; 13T99.

Elizabeth m. John Vivion, Jr.

Elizabeth m. John Vivion (or Vivian).

Elizabeth m. John Thacker.

Ezekiel m. 20 March, 1794, Anne Wood. Sur. Henry Wood. Albemarle Co. Mar. Bond.

Frances m. Thomas Vivion (1st wife).

Frances m. James Bray.

Frances m. Lewis Burwell.

Henry m. 1662, Eltonhead Conway, d. 28 Oct., 1689, dau. of Edwin and Martha (Eltonhead) Conway; res. Middlesex Co. She m. (2) bef. 1678, William Stanard. 33V408; 8W(1)97; 5W(2)174; NNHist.Mag. 5:1:427.

Henry of Middlesex Co. m. bef. 6 March, 1727, Mary Elizabeth Clowder, dau. of Jeremiah. Proven by Deed of that date, Spotsylvania Co.

Henry, Jr., b. 9 Aug., 1663, son of Henry and Eltonhead (Conway); m. bef. 25 March, 1693, Elizabeth Payne, d. 22 May, 1714, Middlesex Co., dau. of John, Jr., and Ann (Walker). Marriage proven by Court Record, 1693, Essex Co. 5V431; 5W(2)174.

Joel m. 13 Jan., 1792, Greensville Co., Rebecca Lanier, dau. of Thomas and Mary (____) Lanier. Boddie-SVF I:301.

John m. 5 Nov., 1758, Elizabeth Thacker, both of this parish. Douglas Reg., p. 4.

Lettice m. Thomas Todd.

M. Ann m. Adam Dickie.

Martha m. Rice Curtis.

Martha m. Thomas Hickman.

Mary (____) m. Rev. John Bagge.

Matilda m. John Willis.

Nancy m. Overton Lowry.

Reuben m. 11 July, 1786, Frances Holland. Louisa, p. 259.

Samuel m. bef. 25 March, 1693, Mary (____) Keeling, widow of Edward. Proven by Court Record of that date, Essex Co.

Sarah m. Leonard Hill.

Susan m. John Denton.

Will. m. 3 Dec., 1784, Elizabeth Smith by Rev. William Douglas; both in Louisa. Douglas Reg., p. 23.

THACKSTON

David m. 16 March, 1777, Sarah Shepherd, both of this parish. Douglas Reg., p. 18.

Elizabeth m. Nathaniel Davis.

Elizabeth m. Nicholas Love.

THACTSON

James m. 20 Sept., 1753, Elizabeth Clark, both of this parish. Douglas Reg., p. 1.

THANY

Anne m. George Dameron.

THARBAUGH

Mary m. Andrew Haffner.

THARP

____ m. Charles Jones.

Fanny m. William Porter.

Nancy m. James Bailey.

Terry m. 19 March, 1788, Susanna Totty, dau. of Abner. Sur. William Tharp. Charlotte Co. Mar. Bond.

THATCHER

____ believed m. bef. 1749, Leanna Flower, dau. of George, whose will, dated 27 Oct., 1749, Lancaster Co., mentions "daughter Leanna Thatcher."

____ m. John Doane.

____ m. William Clapham.

____ m. bef. 1717, Elizabeth Underwood, dau. of William, whose will of that date, Richmond Co., proves it.

James believed m. Judith (____) Schophill. His will, dated 1745, prov. 1755, named wife Judith, but no children. Will of Judith Thatcher, prov. June, 1755, named her Schophill children. Lancaster Co. Records.

THAXTON

Betsy m. Jeremiah Johnson.

Elizabeth m. ____ Johnston.

Lucy m. ____ Overby.

Lucy m. Absolum Overby.

Martha m. ____ DeGraffenreid.

Martha m. Vacent DeGraffenreed.

Nancy m. Anthony Fullerlove.

Nancy m. Thomas Chavus.

THELABALL

Courtney m. John Williams.

Elizabeth m. Thomas Langley.

James m. bef. 1648, Elizabeth Mason, dau. of Francis and Alice (____). 4V84; LNCo. 3:141.

Joyce (____) m. John Wishard.

Margaret m. William Langley.

THELKELD

Mary m. Nathaniel Burrus.

THEOBALD

Thomas m. 18 Sept., 1797, Patience Pendergrass. Shelby Co., Ky. Mar. Record.

THERRIOTT (THERIOTT, THERRIATT, etc.)

Ann m. Peter Montague.

Dominick "Dominic" m. bef. Jan., 1652/3, Joan (____) Lee, widow of Henry. Proven by Court Record of that date, Lancaster Co.

Elizabeth m. Thomas Taylor.

Hannah m. Henry Towles.

Mary m. Thomas Salmon.

THILMAN

Jane m. James Doswell.

THILMAN (cont.)

Paul m. 27 Jan., 1689, Margaret (___) Price, widow of Robert. Christ Church, p. 37.
Paul m. 17 April, 1723, Jane George. Christ Church, p. 164.
Paul m. Barbara Overton Winston. Winston, p. 44.
Paul m. 16 Dec., 1730, Elizabeth Vivion. Christ Church, p. 167.
Paul m. ca 1697, Sarah Perrott. 5V166.
Sarah m. John Soanes.
Sarah m. Edmond Hamerton.

THOM

Alexander m. Elizabeth Triplett, b. ca 1751, dau. of John and Lucy (Abbett) of Culpeper Co. 55V289.
James A. m. 31 Dec., 1797, Alice D. Taliaferro by Rev. John Woodville. Culpeper Co. Ministers' Returns.

THOMAS

___ ___ m. Ann Moore, dau. of Col. Francis. Farmer, p. 61.
___ m. 19 Nov., 1797 (?Orange Co.), Ambrose Macon. St. Mark's, p. 79.
___ believed m. bef. 1775, Mary Reese, dau. of Joseph, whose will, dated 1775, Southampton Co., names "daughter Mary Thomas." Will Bk. III, p. 248.
___ m. bef. 4 Oct., 1766, Amy (or Anna) Evans, dau. of John, whose will was prov. 9 Nov., 1766, Loudoun Co. Will Bk. A, p. 180.
___ m. Henry Pendleton.
___ m. bef. May, 1778, Elizabeth Woolfolk, dau. of Joseph, whose will of that date, Orange Co., proves it.
___ m. Mary Pendleton. She m. (2) Col. Thomas Barbour. DAR No. 28 765.
Agnes m. Thomas Merry.
Alice m. Capt. Thomas Minor.
Allen m. 6 Sept., 1798, Eliz. Fowler. Caroline Co. Mar. Record.
Amy m. George Moorehead.
Angelany m. John Bailey.
Ann m. Henry Pendleton IV.
Ann m. Wiley Ward.
Ann m. Richard Blow, Jr.
Ann m. Joseph Butler.
Anne m. John Parsons.
Anne m. Thomas Griffin.
Anne m. James Exum.
Anthony Buckner m. 20 April, 1755, Amy Powell. St. Paul's.
Arthur m. 26 Oct., 1711, Mary Saunders. Christ Church, p. 82.
Augustine m. 1 Dec., 1778, Deborah Fulkerson. Henry Co. Mar. Record.
Barsheba m. George Cants.
Benjamin m. between Oct., 1774 and Oct., 1775, in King George Co., Caty Handall. Mar. Record in Fee Book.
Benjamin m. 13 June, 1769, Rebekah Hurst, both in this parish. Douglas Reg., p. 11.
Benjamin m. 15 Nov., 1792, Elizabeth Young. Petersburg. Cameron.
Betsy m. Thomas Cottrell.
Betsy m. Thomas Powell.
Bridget m. John Dixon.

THOMAS

Bryant m. 27 July, 1790, Dolly Strange. Halifax Co. Mar. Record.
Carver m. Susan Watts, dau. of David, who d. 1817. Albemarle, p. 340.
Catherine m. Innes Baxter Brent.
Catherine m. Daniel Thomas.
Catherine m. Ambrose Barbour.
Catherine m. David Ross.
Catherine (____) m. William Young.
Charles m. 9 May, 1723, Susanna Davis. Christ Church, p. 164.
Charles m. 24 Jan., 1786, Sally Adams. Louisa, p. 259.
Charles, Mayor of Norfolk, 1770 and 1773, m. Frances Hutchings, dau. of Col. John and Amy (Godfrey). 15T380.
Charles L. m. Margaret Lewis, dau. of Nicholas and Mary (Walker). Albemarle, p. 253.
Daniel m. 7 Sept., 1775, Sally Welday, both of this parish. Douglas Reg., p. 16.
Daniel, b. 1706/7, son of Hugh; m. in Westmoreland Co. his cousin, Catherine Thomas, dau. of James; res. Fairfax Co. Boogher, p. 285.
David m. Patsy Parker, dau. of Harry and Josie (Thomas) Parker, who rem. from Va. to Mason Co., Ky. Harry d. 1823, Lewis Co., Ky. Hartford B-8445, 25 Nov., 1955. Signed C. B. S.
David of Loudoun Co., b. 27 June, 1726; d. 1796; m. Ruth Rogers, b. 1727; d. 1794; owned land in Penna. at his death. Rixey, p. 374.
Dorothy m. Thomas East.
E. m. Ann Chiles, b. 1772, Va.; d. 31 July, 1855, Frankfort, Ky., dau. of Walter of Spotsylvania Co. From obituary. Stoddard, p. 251.
Edith m. George Smith.
Edward m. Hannah Hughes, dau. of William and Mary (____). Albemarle, p. 232.
Edward m. bef. 17 Dec., 1698, Catherine Williamson, dau. of Henry. Proven by court records of that date, Essex Co.
Edward m. ____ Slaughter, dau. of Col. Francis and Ann (Lightfoot); rem. to Nelson Co., Ky. 21V310.
Edward, son of Edward and ____ (Slaughter), m. Susannah Beale, dau. of Walter of Kentucky. 21V310.
Edward P. m. Ann Chiles, dau. of Walter and Phebe (Carr). 8W(1)106.
Eleanor Metcalfe m. Samuel Mitchell.
Elijah m. 25 Dec., 1792, Polley Owen. Halifax Co. Mar. Record.
Eliza m. Samuel Daniel.
Elizabeth m. Joseph Brame.
Elizabeth m. John Wood.
Elizabeth m. John Smith.
Elizabeth m. Giles Dewberry.
Elizabeth m. Moses Willis (1st wife).
Elizabeth m. Samuel Pugh.
Elizabeth m. (1) John Boddie; m. (2) Col. John Dawson.
Elizabeth m. Hugh Tulloch.
Ellinor M. m. Samuel Mitchell.
Ellis, Jr., son of Ellis, Sr. (will prov. 1760, Winchester, Va.), m. Phoebe Van Meter, b. ca 1760, dau. of Henry and Martha (Moore); rem. to Ohio Co., thence to Tyler Co. Lucas, p. 416.
Evan, Jr., m. bef. 1741, Albenah Ross, dau. of Alexander and Cath-

THOMAS (cont.)

erine (Chambers). Joliffe, p. 71.

Ezekiel, b. ca 1776, near Raleigh, Va.; d. 1843, Richmond, Miss., age 67; bur. Keyes Graveyard; m. Nancy Jane Caruthers, d. ca 1841. Hartford B-9006(1), 21 April, 1956. Signed M. S. C.

Frances m. Abner Beckham.

Franky m. Augustine Woolfolk.

George m. 17 Nov., 1796, Mary Marr. Frederick Co. Mar. Record.

George of Hanover Co. m. 7 Aug., 1758, Dorothy Elliott. Sur. Henry Whiting. Middlesex Co. Mar. Bond.

Giles, b. 1763; d. 1842; bur. Blacksburg, Va.; served in Rev. War from Maryland; m. 1786, Ann Wheeler. DAR No. 27 956; DAR No. 158 197; DAR No. 165 195.

Harrison m. 23 March, 1793, Elizabeth Downing. Northampton Co. Mar. Record.

Henry, will prov. 1772, Southampton Co.; m. (1) Mary Blow, dau. of Col. Richard (Sussex Co. Bk. 4, p. 231); m. (2) Martha (____) Jarrel, widow of Col. Thomas. Boddie-HSF IV:63.

Henry m. 7 Aug., 1798, Sally Nelson. Halifax Co. Mar. Record.

Isaac m. Harriet Watkins, dau. of John, who d. 1838 and had served in Rev. War from Rockbridge Co. Morton, p. 404.

Jacob m. 25 June, 1792, Hannah Farley. Halifax Co. Mar. Record.

James m. 20 Sept., 1794, Lucy Glasby (?Gillespie). Sur. Nathan Glasby. Albemarle Co. Mar. Bond.

James m. 30 Jan., 1795, Mourning Mangum. Isle of Wight Co. Mar. Record.

James, b. 1751, Va.; d. 1826, Ga.; m. bef. 1779, Mary Wright Lowens, dau. of John (est. sett., 1779); rem. to Ga. ca 1787. 57V85; Hume, p. 172.

James II, son of Richard and Mildred (Taylor), m. 1781, Elizabeth Pendleton, dau. of Henry IV and Ann (Thomas). Farmer, p. 64.

Jane m. Feanly McCoy.

Jane m. Thomas King.

Jane m. Capt. William Scott.

Jane m. Christopher Watkins.

Jane m. Thomas Stribling.

Jane m. (1) John Collier; m. (2) John Lother.

Jeremiah, b. 1737, Charles City Co.; d. 1806, Harper's Ferry, W. Va.; m. 1760, Mary Harper, b. 1738; d. 1822. DAR No. 51 505.

Jesse of Cumberland Co. m. 15 Feb., 1781, Jane Bowles of Goochland Co. Douglas Reg., p. 21.

Joanna m. Harry Parker.

Joel m. 6 Sept., 1787, Agnes Owen. Halifax Co. Mar. Record.

John, b. 1757, Albemarle Co.; d. there, 1847; m. (1) Frances Henderson. DAR No. 47 832.

John m. Winefred Dameron, dau. of Lazarus and Elizabeth (Smith). Dameron Genealogy, p. 2 of section on Moses Dameron; Chart A.

John, d. 1847; rem. from Amherst Co. to Albemarle Co.; m. (1) Frances Henderson, dau. of John; m. (2) Frances Lewis, dau. of Charles, Jr. Albemarle, p. 327; Dameron, Section 3, Supplement, p. 23.

John, b. 1757, Albemarle Co.; d. there, 1847; m. Frances Lewis. DAR No. 66 220; DAR No. 68 750.

THOMAS (cont.)

John m. 4 Dec., 1793, Sally Younger. Halifax Co. Mar. Record.

John m. 19 Feb., 1762, Mary Thomas. St. Paul's.

John, b. 1698, England; d. 1796, Leesburg, Va.; m. (2) Hannah Meade. DAR No. 66 615.

John m. 10 Aug., 1741, Jemima Derrick. St. Paul's.

John m. 11 Feb., 1737/8, Eliza Oagely. Sur. John Drury. Norfolk Co. Mar. Bond.

John m. Oct., 1768, Jane Green. King George Co. Mar. Record.

John m. bef. 6 April, 1693, Susannah Portis (?Porteus) Frizzell, dau. of John, who made Deed of Gift to Susannah Thomas, widow of John Frizzell. Boddie-Isle, p. 609.

John m. 1796, Peggy Christmas by Rev. Martin Walton. Louisa Co. Ministers' Returns.

John of Nansemond Co. m. Mary Lawrence. Boddie-Isle, p. 258. She was dau. of John, whose will was prov. 1696, Nansemond Co., and was 2nd wife of John Thomas. Proven by a Deed of 1704. Boddie-Isle, p. 495.

John m. bef. 1756, Sarah Crosthwait, sis. of Timothy, whose will, prov. 26 Aug., 1756, Orange Co. Br, pp. 430-1.

John m. bef. 1794, Frances Tyus, dau. of Lewis, Sr., whose will of that date, Greensville Co., proves it.

John, b. ca 1664, son of Hugh of Charles Co., Md.; m. (2) ca 1718, Elizabeth Spencer, dau. of Nicholas; res. Stafford Co. and Fairfax Co. Boogher, p. 286.

John m. 23 Sept., 1774, Betty Wornom. Northumberland Co. Mar. Record.

Jordan m. 1 April, 1791, Mary Hancock. Isle of Wight Co. Mar. Record.

Joseph m. Sarah Pendleton, b. ca 1720, dau. of Philip and Elizabeth (Pollard). 43V278.

Josie m. Harry Parker.

Kezia m. James Williamson.

Lewis m. 28 Aug., 1795, Elizabeth Lane. Sur. Hendley Travillion. Albemarle Co. Mar. Bond.

Lucy m. Col. James Lewis (1st wife).

Lydia m. John Hodges.

Margaret m. Thomas McKinsey.

Margaret m. Edmund Owen.

Margaret M. m. (1) Julius Clarkson; m. (2) Robert Cashmere.

Martha m. ____ Goolsby.

Martha m. Robert Moore, Jr.

Mary m. Ambrose Clark.

Mary m. John Newton.

Mary m. Aaron Mardus.

Mary m. John Ancrum.

Mary m. Edmund King.

Mary m. Winslow Parker.

Mary m. (1) Anthony Simmons; m. (2) John Roberts.

Mary m. Will. Daniel.

Mary m. Thomas Barbour.

Mary (____) m. John Frazier.

Mary Pendleton m. Col. Thomas Barbour.

Massey m. 28 Nov., 1731, Mary Price. St. Paul's.

THOMAS (cont.)

Massey, Jr., m. 1787, Martha Pendleton, b. ca 1766; d. 1824, dau. of Henry and Martha (Curtis). 43V279.

Micajah, b. 13 Feb., 1725; m. 7 Oct., 1753, Mourning (____) Crudup. Boddie-Isle, p. 259.

Micajah m. 5 June, 1776, Elizabeth Crafford. Sur. Carter Crafford. Surry Co. Mar. Bond.

Michael m. 1 Dec., 1792, Elizabeth Staiton. Sur. Ralph Thomas and John Carroll. Albemarle Co. Mar. Bond.

Mildred m. Rev. Philip Pendleton.

Mildred (____) m. John Holloday.

Miriam m. James Mathews, Jr.

Nancy m. Thomas Reafield.

Nancy m. Green Hill (1st wife).

Nancy m. Lewis Thomason.

Nathan m. 23 Oct., 1790, Mary (____) Ward. Norfolk Co. Mar. Record.

Nathan m. 18 Dec., 1774, Mary Jones, both in Goochland. Douglas Reg., p. 15.

Nathaniel m. 7 May, 1793, Sarah Price, dau. of William and Sarah (____). Sur. Samuel Price. Charlotte Co. Mar. Bond.

Obediah m. 30 Dec., 1794, Rebecha Posey. Halifax Co. Mar. Record.

Patience (____) m. William Shelton, Jr.

Peter m. ____ Sims, dau. of George, whose will, 1763, Brunswick Co. Scarborough IV:130.

Phebe m. Joseph Phillips.

Polly m. Josiah Davis.

Polly m. Robert Snelson.

Price m. 7 Nov., 1779, Mary Monroe. St. Paul's.

Priscilla m. James Butler, Jr.

Rachel m. Lieut. Robert Denny.

Ralph m. Lucy Brown, dau. of Andrew, who d. 1804. Albemarle, pp. 153-4.

Reuben m. 1787, Ann Spencer. Orange Co. Mar. Record.

Richard, d. 1790; m. 24 Aug., 1753, Mildred Taylor, b. 11 Dec., 1724; d. after 1790, dau. of James and Martha (Thompson). Taylor, p. 133. Res. Orange Co., where mar. is recorded. 4W(1)59. He was son of James. 30V387; Farmer, p. 64; Taylor, p. 133.

Richard, b. ca 1680; d. 1748, son of John and Elizabeth (____); m. Isabella Pendleton, dau. of Philip and Isabella (Hurt). 39V282; 24W(1)256; Slaughter, p. 148; Winston, p. 196.

Robert m. 10 June, 1679, Ancoretta Wells. Christ Church, p. 18.

Robert, d. Fairfax Co.; m. bef. 1759, ____ Ramey. 10W(2)345.

Robert m. 1793, Dolley Smoth. Orange Co. Mar. Record.

Robert m. 7 Aug., 1793, Polly Smith, dau. of Joseph, who gave consent. Sur. William Smith. Orange Co. Mar. Bond.

Robert m. 9 April, 1757, Anne Moore. Orange Co. Mar. Record.

Roberts m. 11 Aug., 1781, Sarah Lawson. Halifax Co. Mar. Record.

Roland m. 5 April, 1757, Jane Thurston. Orange Co. Mar. Record.

Rowland of Caroline Co. m. bef. 1711, Mary (Gregory) Taylor, widow of James, Jr., and dau. of John and Elizabeth (____) Gregory. Rhodes, p. 391; Winston, p. 241.

Salley m. John Willis.

THOMAS (cont.)

Sallie P. m. Lieut. William Buckner.

Sally m. Will. Jones.

Sally m. Thomas Moore.

Sally m. John Nelson.

Samuel m. 23 April, 1797, Patsey Inge by Rev. John Neblett, Methodist. Lunenburg Co. Ministers' Returns.

Samuel m. 1 Sept., 1780, Katherine Carrell. Eliza Carrell writes consent for her dau., Katherine. Surry Co. Mar. Record.

Sarah m. (1) Thomas Powell; m. (2) Thomas Moore.

Sarah m. John Gray.

Sarah m. Lovel White.

Sarah m. Allen deGraffenreid.

Sarah m. Augustus McGhee.

Sarah Kenyon m. James Frazer (2nd wife).

Sarah P. m. Capt. Wm. Buckner.

Sophia m. Peter Parrish.

Susanah m. George Dameron.

Susanna m. William Saunders.

Susanna m. John Worsley.

Susannah m. ____ Stephens.

Susannah m. Philip Shepherd.

Thomas m. 1 Sept., 1765, Rebekah Lookadoe, both in Maniken Town. Douglas Reg., p. 8.

Thomas m. bef. 13 May, 1653, Elizabeth Knott, dau. of James, whose will rec., Nansemond Co., 1653. Book 1, p. 51. 4V425.

Thomas m. bef. Nov., 1715, Sarah Salmon, dau. of Middleton. Proven by Court Record of that date, Northumberland Co.

William m. 4 April, 1795, Polly Smith. Northampton Co. Mar. Record.

William m. 13 Dec., 1785, Mary White. St. Paul's.

William m. 22 Dec., 1724, Thomison Hamm. St. Paul's.

William m. 1778, Elizabeth Woolfolk. Orange Co. Mar. Record.

William m. 25 Dec., 1752, Jane Johnson. St. Paul's.

William m. 8 Jan., 1798, Hannah Chissher. Halifax Co. Mar. Record.

William m. 3 July, 1794, Frances Crowder. Halifax Co. Mar. Record.

William m. 30 Dec., 1794, Mary Cyphers. Shelby Co., Ky. Mar. Record.

William m. 17 Oct., 1797, Patsy Woodall by William Baskett, minister. Louisa Co. Ministers' Returns.

William, will dated 17 Jan., 1719; m. (1) 1697, Elizabeth Bramley (Surry Co. Order Bk., 1691-1700, p. 187); m. (2) Priscilla (Browne) Blunt, widow of Thomas and dau. of Col. William Browne. Her will dated 15 March, 1732. Boddie-HSF IV:62.

William m. bef. 1692, Hannah Goodall, dau. of ____ and Ann (____). Proven by Court Suit, 1737. Barton's Decisions, Vol. II, p. 180.

William m. 26 Dec., 1754, Rebekah Upton. Douglas Reg., p. 1.

William m. Nancy Parker, dau. of Harry (d. 1823, Lewis Co., Ky.). He had rem. from Virginia to Mason Co., Ky. Hartford B-8445, 26 Nov., 1955. Signed C. B. S.

William m. Elizabeth Hill, dau. of Nicholas and (2) Sylvester (Bennett). Boddie-Isle, p. 279.

William, son of Ellis, Sr., of Frederick Co., served in Rev. War; m.

THOMAS (cont.)

Elizabeth Van Meter, b. ca 1762, dau. of Henry and Martha (Moore); res. Monongahelia Co. Lucas, p. 417.

William, Jr., will prov. 1723, son of William and Elizabeth (Bramley); m. Elizabeth Catlett, dau. of Col. William and Elizabeth (Thompson). Boddie-HSF IV:63.

Winifred m. James Reveer.

Zachariah, b. 1767, prob. Ireland; m. 8 Aug., 1794, Mary Chloeantha Young in Franklin Co.; res. Botetourt Co. Gillmore, p. 24.

THOMASON

____ m. bef. 1742, Mary Pollard, a granddau. of William Fleming, whose will of that date, Hanover Co., proves the marriage.

Anthony m. Ann Bibb, b. ca 1733; d. 1798, dau. of Henry and Eleanor (Fleming); rem. to Woodford Co., Ky. 34 Ky. Reg. 98.

Byares m. 15 April, 1784, Sarah White, both in Louisa. Douglas Reg., p. 23. Given as Byars. Louisa, p. 280.

Delilah m. George Smith.

Elizabeth m. James Shelton.

Elizabeth m. Emanuel Terry.

Fannie m. John Wright.

John m. 23 Dec., 1780, Frances Cook, sis. of Wm. Louisa, pp. 264, 280.

John m. 6 May, 1799, Elizabeth Nuckols. Louisa, p. 266.

Lewis m. 3 Jan., 1796, Nancy Thomas. Louisa, p. 262.

Mary m. Thomas Terry.

Milly m. Benjamin Coopwood.

Nancy m. Patrick Ryan.

Nathaniel m. 28 Dec., 1773, Martha Wood. Louisa, p. 255.

Richard m. 25 April, 1786, Sarah Terry, both of Louisa. Douglas Reg., p. 24.

Sarah m. John Bibb.

Thomas m. 19 Nov., 1770, Elizabeth Weldie, both of Goochland. Douglas Reg., p. 12.

THOMASSON

Anderson m. 4 May, 1785, Ann Clopton Anderson. Louisa Co. Mar. Record.

Ann L. m. John Slaughter.

Christiana m. John Timberlake.

Elias m. 28 July, 1774, Mary Harris. Louisa Co. Mar. Record.

Elizabeth m. Nelson Foster.

Elizabeth m. Emanuel Terry.

George m. Mary Pollard, b. 1706, granddau. of William Fleming and dau. of Richard Pollard. 34 Ky. Reg. 98.

Henrietta m. David Shelton.

Mary m. William Daniel.

Mary m. Nathaniel Anderson.

Poindexter, d. 1 Sept., 1833; m. 1 March, 1792/3, Sarah Dupuy, b. 1762; d. 23 Aug., 1851. H 6:140.

Richard m. 23 April, 1786, Sarah Terry. Louisa, p. 260.

Samuel m. 14 Dec., 1783, Lydia McGhee. Louisa, p. 272.

Sarah m. William Woodall.

THOMISON

Richard m. 3 June, 1724, Elizabeth Oxford. St. Paul's.

THOMPKINS

James m. 1 Sept., 1789, Polly Hurt. Halifax Co. Mar. Record.

John m. 25 Feb., 1747, Anne Custis by Rev. Barlow. Bible Record. Boogher, p. 328.

Robert m. Frances Marshall, b. 1774, dau. of William (b. Caroline Co.) and Ann (McLeod). 39V268.

Sarah m. John Philips.

Will. in Hanover Co. m. 26 Dec., 1786, Mary Meekie in Louisa Co. Douglas Reg., p. 24.

THOMPSON

____ m. Edward Watkins.

____, a dau., m. ____ Woodson.

____ m. bef. 1792, ____ (____) Spotswood, widow of Joh . 11W(2)111.

____ believed m. bef. 1786, Rosannah Davies, dau. of Hugh, whose will, filed 1786, Rockbridge Co., names "daughter Rosannah Thompson."

____ m. Mary Herbert Claiborne. 1V321.

____ m. by 1785, Rebecca Gay. Rockbridge Co. Morton, p. 536.

____ m. bef. 1794, Drucilla Thorpe, dau. of John, Sr., whose est. sett., 1794, Southampton Co., proves it.

____ m. bef. 18 Dec., 1773, Ann Mason. H 6:115.

____ m. Mary Bond, dau. of Robert, whose will, dated 1723/4, Spotsylvania Co. Will Bk. A, p. 14.

Alexander m. 16 Dec., 1762, Mary Ross. Norfolk Co. Mar. Record.

Alice Corbin m. John Hawkins.

Andrew m. 2 Jan., 1787, Mary Rose. St. Paul's.

Ann m. (1) John Slaughter; m. (2) Philip Grafton.

Ann m. Francis Thornton.

Ann m. ____ Neilson.

Ann m. William Simpson.

Ann m. William Brooking.

Ann (____) m. Nicholas Muse.

Anne (____) m. (2) William Whiteside.

Anne Cocke m. Joel Madera.

Annie m. Thomas Boman.

Anthony m. ____ Bibb, dau. of Henry and Eleanor (Fleming). Louisa, p. 288.

Archibald, son of William (1722-1798), m. Rebecca Perry, dau. of George of Abb's Valley. Hartford B-8010(2), 16 July, 1955. Signed T. J. C.

Asa m. Ann Quarles, dau. of Roger (b. 1720) and Mary (Goodloe). 38 V361-3.

Becky m. Frederick Lane.

Betsey m. John Stevens.

Catharine m. Isaac Coles (2nd wife).

Charles m. 1737, Elizabeth Nelson, b. 1720, dau. of Edward and Mary (Garland). 27T37.

Charles, b. 1743; d. 1836; m. 19 Nov., 1778, Louisa Co., Ann Jerdone, b. 1763; d. 1794, dau. of Francis and Sarah (Macon). 62V209; Louisa, p. 372.

THOMPSON (cont.)

Charles, b. 27 March, 1773; d. 9 April, 1844, son of William and Frances Jackson (Mills); m. 14 Dec., 1800, in Louisa Co., Ann Pettus Graves, b. 13 May, 1781; d. 24 July, 1858, dau. of Thomas and Isabel (Bartlett). 19T185.

Charles Raphael m. Ann Fauntleroy. Res. Westmoreland Co., 1804, when son, Charles Raphael, was born 19 Nov., son d. 10 Jan., 1877, Fayette Co., Ky. Ky. Cem., p. 158.

Christopher m. 8 May, 1762, Margaret (___) Ritch. Norfolk Co. Mar. Record.

Clara m. James Twyman.

Clifton m. 22 Feb., 1788, Mary Ragland. Louisa, p. 260.

David m. 23 Nov., 1784, Elizabeth Brockman, dau. of Samuel and (1) Mary (Bell). Orange Co. Mar. Record; Orange III:109.

David m. 17 Aug., 1785, Nancy Coadie, dau. of William. Wit. William Coadie. Montgomery Co. Mar. Bond.

David m. 27 Nov., 1779, Eleanor Thomson, dau. of Waddy. Louisa Co. Mar. Record.

Eleanor m. Samuel Watkins.

Eliza m. Thomas Swann.

Elizabeth m. John B. Johnson.

Elizabeth m. Benjamin Beachboard.

Elizabeth m. Edwin Conway II.

Elizabeth m. Francis Taylor.

Elizabeth m. Peter Presly, Sr.

Elizabeth m. Michael Crowbarger.

Elizabeth m. William Catlett.

Elizabeth m. James Riley.

Elizabeth m. George Clay.

Fanney m. Johnson Wood.

Frances m. Nathaniel Mills.

Frances m. ___ Woodson.

Francis m. 18 May, 1786, Rebeckah Harvie in Petersburg, Va. Cameron.

Hannah m. Peyton Walker.

Hannah m. Roger Lawson.

Helen m. John Johnston.

Henry m. 7 Aug., 1788, Jenny Campbell by Rev. William Graham. Rockbridge Co. Ministers' Returns.

Henry m. 30 Dec., 1791, Lucy Giles. Isle of Wight Co. Mar. Record.

Isaac m. 26 Jan., 1763, Prudence Scott. Norfolk Co. Mar. Record.

Isaac m. 13 June, 1786, Mary Duff by Rev. Samuel Carrick. Rockbridge Co. Ministers' Returns.

Isham, son of Robert, m. Mary Ann Oliver and had a dau., b. 1762. Free II:370.

Jacob m. 26 May, 1795, Sukey Morris. Northampton Co. Mar. Record.

James m. 25 April, 1786, Polly Terry. Halifax Co. Mar. Record.

James m. 24 Dec., 1785, Sarah Newall. Prince George Co. Cameron.

Jane m. Caleb Baker.

Jane m. James Watkins, Jr.

Jena m. James Sloan.

Joana m. Benjamin Waller.

Joel m. 1798, Sarah Thompson. Orange Co. Mar. Record.

THOMPSON (cont.)

John m. 10 Nov., 1796, Kesiah Franklin by William Flowers. Campbell Co. Mar. Record.

John m. 24 March, 1796, Margaret Davidson by Rev. William Mahon. Campbell Co. Ministers' Returns.

John, minister, m. (1) 1742, Butler (Brayne) Spotswood, widow of Gov. Spotswood; m. (2) ____ Rootes. 31V59; St. Mark's, pp. 39, 174. Mar. Elizabeth Rootes, dau. of Philip. 4V208.

John, will dated 1698, m. Elizabeth (____) Salway, widow of John, whose will, dated 1678. Surry, p. 70.

John m. 8 May, 1799, Elizabeth Nucholls by William Cooke. Louisa Co. Ministers' Returns.

John, b. 1757, Albemarle Co.; d. 1833, Mercer Co., Ky.; m. Susan Burton. DAR No. 65 864.

John m. 17 March, 1794, Rebecca Scurlock. Halifax Co. Mar. Record.

John, son of William (1722-1798), m. Louisa Bowen, dau. of Lieut. Rees and Louisa (____). Hartford B-8010(2), 16 July, 1955. Signed T. J. C.

John m. 5 Sept., 1786, Martha Langford, spinster. Sur. Thomas Langford. Albemarle Co. Mar. Bond.

John m. 30 Sept., 1793, Rebeckah Whitlow. Halifax Co. Mar. Record.

John m. 1787, Catrene Steele. Rockbridge Co. Morton, p. 536.

John, son of Rev. John and (2) ____ Rootes, m. 1784, Elizabeth Howison, dau. of Dr. Howison of Culpeper; rem. to Ky., 1793; afterwards Judge in Louisiana. St. Mark's, p. 176.

John m. 1798, Margaret McCormick. Rockbridge Co. Morton, p. 536.

John m. Margaret Jones, dau. of Matthew and Mary (Lee) of York Co. 11T34.

John m. 19 Sept., 1779, Jane Shelladay, dau. of George. Wit. George Shelladay and James McCorkle. Montgomery Co. Mar. Bond.

John m. 1781, Botetourt Co., Winifred Breckey. Kegley, p. 430.

John m. 21 March, 1785, Sarah Strong. Sur. John Strong. Goochland Co. Mar. Bond. 8W(1)94.

John m. prob. 1795, Polly Gooch by Richard Pope. Louisa Co. Ministers' Returns.

John m. 9 Dec., 1786, Rebecca Edwards Powell, dau. of Lucas. 30T64.

John of Middlesex Co. m. 13 April, 1727, Catherine Twyman, b. 19 April, 1702, dau. of George and Catherine (Montague). Wilcoxson, p. 415.

Joseph, b. 1703; d. 1764; m. Sarah Claiborne, b. 1713; d. 1777; rem. to Goochland Co. 58V238.

Joseph m. 15 Nov., 1790, Polly Ferguson. Halifax Co. Mar. Record.

Joseph m. 17 Nov., 1798, Anna Owen. Halifax Co. Mar. Record.

Josiah m. 21 Aug., 1755, Mary Swann. Sur. Thompson Swann. Cumberland Co. Mar. Bond.

Joyce m. Elisha Leake (1st wife).

Judith m. William Poindexter.

Katherine m. ____ Paine.

Leweasia m. Robert Hughey.

Lucy m. William Pulley.

Lucy m. Thomas Richardson.

Lucy m. Charles Boswell.

THOMPSON (cont.)

M. m. Haynes Morgan.
Margaret m. Thomas Gilmore.
Margaret m. Isaiah Vansant.
Margaret m. ____ Hall.
Margaret m. Samuel Paxton.
Margaret m. William Loyall.
Margaret m. William Christie.
Martha m. Lawrence Smith.
Martha m. James Taylor, Jr.
Martha m. Daniel Javen.
Martha m. James Watkins.
Mary m. Thomas Brown.
Mary m. Haynes Morgan.
Mary m. William Blain.
Mary m. Thomas Booth.
Mary m. James Poindexter.
Mary m. John Davidson.
Mary m. James Miles.
Mary m. John Adams.
Mary m. (1) James Day; m. (2) John Johnson; m. (3) Reuben Gladhill.
Mary m. Robert Martin, Jr.
Mary m. Thomas Lewis.
Mary m. Samuel Weir (or Wier).
Mary m. Robert Turner.
Mary m. William Shields.
Mary m. James Curtis.
Mary m. Thomas Moore.
Mary m. Charles Wilkins.
Mary m. Booth Armistead.
Mary m. James Armstrong.
Mary m. (1) Robert Booth; m. (2) Capt. Graves Packe (1st wife).
Mary m. William Cason.
Mary m. Thomas Vahane.
Mary m. Capt. William Tucker.
Mary (____) m. James Shearn.
Mary (____) m. Daniel Underhill.
Mary A. (____) m. William Bibb.
Mary Elizabeth m. John Chambers.
Mary Marshall m. Thomas Watkins.
Mary Shaw m. George Hatch.
Meriday m. 16 Jan., 1794, Elizabeth Langdon, dau. of Samuel. Botetourt Co. Kegley, p. 597.
Mildred m. Christopher Robertson.
Mildred m. George Weedon Gray.
Mildred m. James Scott.
Molly (____) m. William Wright.
Nancy m. Tandy Demsey.
Nancy m. Peter Robinson.
Nancy m. David Sheeres.
Nancy m. William Ward.
Nancy m. Josiah Gentry.

THOMPSON (cont.)

Oliver m. 2 June, 1789, Polly Anderson Norris, dau. of John, Jr. Sur. Robert Watson. Charlotte Co. Mar. Bond.

Patsy m. John Baytop Scott (2nd wife).

Patsy m. John Painter.

Philip Rootes, Member of Congress, son of Rev. John and (2) ___ Rootes, m. (1) ___ Davenport, dau. of Burkett, vestryman of St. Mark's; m. (2) Sarah Slaughter, b. 28 Feb., 1777, dau. of Robert. 22V208; St. Mark's, pp. 39, 175.

Phoebe m. John Greathouse.

Polly m. Pleasant Smith.

Rachel m. Alexander Berryhill.

Rachel m. John Michael.

Raphael, son of Raphael and Susanna (___) of St. Mary's Co., Md., m. 2 Jan., 1798, at "Mars Hill," Richmond Co., Anne Fauntleroy, dau. of Griffin Murdock and Ann (Belfield) Fauntleroy. Jones, p. 173.

Rebecca m. Lieut. Col. Nathaniel Cocke.

Rebecca m. William ?Clinch.

Rebecca m. John Simonds.

Rebecca m. William McPheeters.

Rebecca m. ___ Cocke.

Rebeccah m. Charles Morgan.

Rhodes (or Rodes) m. 13 Oct., 1778, Sally Vivion, dau. of John III and Jane (Smith); rem. to Ky. 47V62; 5W(2)177.

Richard m. 3 March, 1789, Mary Moore. Halifax Co. Mar. Record.

Richard m. Ursula Byshe. She m. (2) Col. John Mottrom; m. (3) George Colclough. 4W(1)171.

Richard m. 19 Nov., 1799, Mary McGhee by R. O. Ferguson. Louisa Co. Ministers' Returns.

Robert, son of Drury, m. 27 Oct., 1779, Sarah Watkins, dau. of James. Sur. William Watkins. Charlotte Co. Mar. Bond.

Robert m. 11 Jan., 1790, Mary Anderson. Louisa, p. 266.

Robert m. 21 Feb., 1783, Lucy Hunter. Louisa Co. Mar. Record.

Robert m. 19 Feb., 1660, Margaret (___) Welch, widow of Jno. Christ Church, p. 11.

Robert m. 1 Sept., 1742, Catharine Tomlinson. OPR.

Rodes m. 1778, Sally Vivian. Orange Co. Mar. Record.

Roger, Capt. in Rev. War, m. Sallie Light; res. 1776, Albemarle Co. DAR No. 41 809.

Sally m. Maness Moore.

Sally m. James Eubank.

Samuel, will dated 1779, Amelia Co.; m. Anne Jennings. 55V97. She, dau. of Capt. William and Mary Jane (Pulliam). 55V179.

Samuel m. after April, 1678, Elizabeth (___) Salway, widow of John. 43V203.

Samuel m. 15 May, 1799, Polly Baird. Shelby Co., Ky. Mar. Record.

Samuel m. ___ Staige, dau. of Rev. Theodosius Staige, in Orange Co. Charles Parish, p. 27.

Samuel m. 27 Aug., 1797, Nancy Lucas. Sur. John Lucas. Kegley, p. 59

Samuel m. bef. 7 Sept., 1682, Mary Marriott, b. 1663, dau. of Maj. William. Surry Co. Book II, pp. 323, 331; 51V200.

Samuel Thompson, Capt. in the British Navy, m. 1769, Elizabeth Blair,

THOMPSON (cont.)
dau. of Hon. John and Mary (Monro). Announced in The Virginia Gazette, 16 March, 1769. 32V386; 5W(1)280; 8W(1)187.
Sarah m. James S. John.
Sarah m. Charles Strong.
Sarah m. Bradley Kimbrough.
Sarah m. John Rannolds.
Sarah m. Thomas Willoughby.
Sarah m. Augustine McGeehee.
Sarah m. Samuel Henry.
Sarah m. Dennis Mehorner.
Sarah m. John Coates.
Sarah K. m. Charles Strong.
Stith, b. 19 June, 1782, son of William F. and Margaret (Darvill); m. ___ Warwick. 9T209.
Susan m. (1) David Rodes (2nd wife); m. (2) James Kerr.
Susan m. Jesse Davenport.
Susanna m. Peter Tinsley.
Susannah m. William Terry.
Temperance m. John Jennings.
Thomas m. 15 May, 1784, Nancy Pleasants. Sur. Isaac Younghusband. Henrico Co. Mar. Bond.
Thomas m. Penelope (___) Spence, widow of Patrick (d. 1694). 15T269.
Thomas m. 17 Sept., 1682, Eliza Hill. Christ Church, p. 21.
Thomas m. 15 Aug., 1754, Sophia Kinner. Sur. Richard Kelsick. Norfolk Co. Mar. Bond.
Ursula (___) m. (2) Col. John Mottrom; m. (3) Major George Colclough.
Waddy from Louisa Co., 1766; d. 1801; m. (1) Elizabeth Anderson, dau. of Nelson of Hanover Co.; m. (2) Mary (Lewis) Cobb, widow of Samuel and dau. of Robert Lewis. She d. 1813. Albemarle, p. 329. Res. Albemarle Co. 20V219. Mar. 8 Aug., 1787, Elizabeth Anderson. Louisa, p. 280.
Walter m. 2 Dec., 1784, Wilmoth Shields by Rev. David Barr. Pittsylvania Co. Ministers' Returns.
Will m. Ellen Montague, dau. of Peter. N.W.Hist.Mag. 5:1:419. Mar. bef. 1659. Proven by will of Peter Montague, dated 27 March, 1659, Lancaster Co. (Also William.)
William m. Mary Patton, dau. of Col. James, whose will, prov. Nov., 1755, Augusta Co. Waddell, p. 113. Was William b. 1722; d. 9 July, 1798, Tazewell Co.? Hartford B-8010(1), 16 July, 1955. Signed T. J. C.
William, son of John (d. ca 1791) and Margaret (Davidson), m. Jane Shilladay, dau. of George and Esther (Baker). 51V397.
William m. 7 Aug., 1786, Henrietta Williams, dau. of John. Sur. Matthew J. Williams. Charlotte Co. Mar. Bond.
William, b. 1722; d. 1798; m. (1) prob. ___ Buchanan; m. (2) in Penna., Lydia Ward. Res. Tazewell Co. Names of children given in this reference. Hartford B-8010(2), 16 July, 1955. Signed T. J. C.
William m. 1790, Botetourt Co., Temperance Breckey, dau. of Jarred (given as Brickley). Kegley, p. 481.
William m. 26 Dec., 1787, Mary Meekie. Louisa, p. 280.
William m. 12 March, 1794, Dotthien Stockton. Henry Co. Mar. Record.

THOMPSON (cont.)

William m. 17 Jan., 1787, Frances Rives. Prince George Co. Cameron.

William m. 29 Jan., 1771, Frances Mills, prob. dau. of Charles and Ann (____). 15T43.

William m. Bessie Ann Garland, dau. of Edward and Jane (Jennings). She m. (2) William Sydnor and had 1st Sydnor child, 1769. 4T45; 20W(1)222.

William m. bef. 1744 (date of birth of a son in Albemarle Parish), Hannah Bell; rem. from Sussex Co. to Chatham Co., No. Car., ca 1750. Boddie-Isle, pp. 302-3.

William, b. ca 1679-82; d. 1732, Surry Co., son of Rev. William and Katherine (Treat); m. bef. 10 Aug., 1708, Martha Moseley, dau. of Col. William of Essex Co. and Hannah (Hawkins); res. Essex Co. and Surry Co. Boddie-Hist. IV:145-6.

William, Rev. of New Haven, Conn., m. 29 Nov., 1665, Boston, Mass., Katherine Treat (or Trott), bapt. 29 June, 1637, Wethersfield, Conn., dau. of Richard and Alice (Gaylord); rem. to Surry Co. Boddie-Hist. IV:144-5.

William m. 1798, Sally Caruthers. Rockbridge Co. Morton, p. 478.

William m. 28 July, 1787, Polley Worthington. Halifax Co. Mar. Record.

William m. Polly Watlington, dau. of Armistead. She m. (2) William Terry. Halifax, p. 345.

William m. Catharine Mayo, dau. of James and Mary (Hughes). Albemarle, p. 270.

William m. 8 Nov., 1792, Anna Mullins. Sur. John Mullins. Albemarle Co. Mar. Bond.

William m. 12 Oct., 1799, Nancy Vaughan by Rev. John Neblett, Methodist. Lunenburg Co. Ministers' Returns.

William of Colchester m. 3 Aug., 1785, Ann(-e) Washington, b. 10 Nov., 1768, dau. of Robert. 23V100; 33V156; St. Paul's.

William m. 26 Dec., 1765, Jane Holland. St. Paul's.

William m. 24 Feb., 1681/2, Grace Elwood. Christ Church, p. 20.

William m. 1785, Acquila Breeding. Orange Co. Mar. Record.

William m. 10 Sept., 1788, Lucy Herbert Cocke. Sussex Co. Cameron.

William m. Feb., 1772, King George Co., Sarah Carter. 31V59.

William, son of Rev. John and (1) Butler (Brayne) Spotswood Thompson, m. Sally Carter, dau. of Charles and (2) ____ Byrd. St. Mark's, pp. 39, 175.

William F. m. bef. 1765 (date of birth of 1st child), Margaret Darvill. 9T208.

William Mills m. Harriet Broadus, dau. of Maj. William and Martha (Slaughter) Jones. 21V428.

William P. m. Mary Zemee, b. ca 1777; d. 11 April, 1852, age 75, dau. of Anthony and Sophia (____) of Lancaster, Penna. Her tombstone in St. John's Churchyard. Henrico, p. 513.

William T. m. 1795, Jeane McNeale. Orange Co. Mar. Record.

THOMSON

____ m. Rev. Richard Sankey.

____ believed m. bef. 1772, Susannah Kirby, dau. of John of Pittsylvania Co., whose will of that date names "daughter Susannah Thomson."

____ m. bef. Dec., 1784, Judith (____) Spence, widow of Patrick, whose est. sett., that date, Westmoreland Co., proves it.

THOMSON (cont.)

Agnes m. Charles Johnson.
Ann m. George Mason.
Ann Lewis m. John Slaughter.
Anne m. Philip Webber.
Anthony m. Ann Bibb, dau. of Benjamin and Mary (___) of Hanover Co.; rem. to Woodford Co., Ky., 1785, from Louisa Co. 3 Ky. Reg. 96.
Byars m. 15 April, 1784, Sarah White. Louisa, p. 258.
Charles m. 19 Nov., 1778, Anne Jerdone, dau. of Sarah. Louisa Co. Mar. Record.
Clifton m. 26 Feb., 1788, Mary Raglane, both of Louisa. Douglas Reg., p. 25. (Also given as Ragland.)
David m. 14 Nov., 1797, Elizabeth Thomson by James Mitchell. Campbell Co. Mar. Record.
David m. 25 Oct., 1799, Susanna Skelton. Rockingham Co. Wayland, p. 11.
David m. 30 Nov., 1779, Eleanor Thomson, both of Louisa. Douglas Reg., p. 19. (Given elsewhere as Ellen.)
David m. 30 Jan., 1788, Anna Cary. Louisa, p. 260.
Edward m. 4 Dec., 1723, Alice Smith. St. Paul's.
Edward m. 15 March, 1785, Ann Anderson. Louisa Co. Mar. Record.
Eleanor m. David Thomson.
Elizabeth m. ___ Langford.
Elizabeth m. David Thomson.
Elizabeth m. John Selvie.
Elizabeth m. Emmanuel Terry.
Elizabeth m. Jeremiah Johnson.
Esther m. ___ Phair.
Hannah m. Charles Johnson.
Hannah m. ___ Epperson.
Henrietta m. David Shelton.
Isaac m. 22 Sept., 1792, Leah Stevens. Northampton Co. Mar. Record.
James m. 10 Aug., 1724, Elizabeth Armour. St. Paul's.
James m. 6 July, 1783, Tempe Moon. Louisa, p. 280. Given as Tempe Mooney. Douglas Reg., p. 23.
Jane m. ___ Mitchell.
Jane m. Richard Drake.
Jane Sophonsiba m. Maj. John Lewis (1st wife).
Jean m. ___ Crenshaw.
Johanna believed m. ___ Canon. Named as mother of James Canon in Deed, 27 April, 1728, Spotsylvania Co.
John, b. ca 1716; d. 1791, son of John of Ireland, N. Y., Delaware, Penna., Va., and No. Car.; m. Margaret Davidson; res. Prince Edward Co., Bedford Co. and Campbell Co. 51V396-7.
John m. bef. June, 1756, Sarah Crosthwait, sis. of Timothy, whose will of that date, Orange Co., proves it.
John m. 31 March, 1789, Sally Ragland. Louisa, p. 280. Given as Ragline. Douglas Reg., p. 25.
Josiah. (See Josiah Thompson.)
Joyce m. Elisha Leake (1st wife).
Judith m. ___ Mallory.
Lucy m. Alex Anderson.

THOMSON (cont.)

Margaret m. John Shields.
Mary m. ____ Davis.
Mary m. Robert Pully.
Matthew m. Sarah Wyatt. She m. (2) Augustine McGehee. 20T63.
Mildred m. Clayborn (or Clayburn, Claiborn) Gooch.
Molly m. John Brown.
Nathaniel, son of Anthony and Ann (Bibb), m. 27 Oct., 1795, Frances Major, b. 1768; d. 1838, dau. of John and Elizabeth (Rodd); res. Woodford Co., Ky. 3 Ky. Reg. 96.
Polly m. James Poindexter.
Rachel m. Isaac Stevens.
Sally m. John Christopher Horn.
Samuel m. 16 Dec., 1794, Nancy Cole. Louisa, p. 266.
Sarah m. Richard Sankey.
Sarah m. James Gregory.
Sarah m. Edward Couch.
Sarah m. ____ Brown.
Susanna m. Philip Shepherd.
Susanna m. Thomas Tinsley.
Susannah m. John Covington.
Susannah m. ____ Statham.
Unity m. Rhodes Smith.
Waddy m. 8 Aug., 1787, Elizabeth Anderson in Louisa. Douglas Reg., p. 24; Louisa, p. 259.
Washington m. 26 Oct., 1785, Jean Scott in Amelia Co. 51V401.
William m. 20 Dec., 1781, Frances Quarles in Spotsylvania Co. Douglas Reg., p. 21.
William m. 8 Dec., 1792, Nancy Blakely. Petersburg. Cameron.
William m. 16 Sept., 1786, Frances Hoomes, spinster. Sur. David Wood. Albemarle Co. Mar. Bond.
William, Capt. in Rev. War, b. 1727, Va.; m. Anna Rhodes. DAR No. 27 317.
William m. 17 April, 1786, Unity Hix. Louisa, p. 260.

THORN (?THOM)

Al m. Dec., 1770, Sarah Triplett. King George Co. Mar. Record.

THORNBERRY

James Wigginton m. his cousin, Sarah Wigginton, dau. of John (d. 1825) and Elizabeth (Botts) of Culpeper Co.; rem. to Ky. 33T253.
John m. 14 Dec., 1749, Elizabeth Bolling. St. Paul's.
Mary m. William Horton.
Samuel m. 20 April, 1744, Mary Kidwell. St. Paul's.
Samuel m. Mary Wigginton, b. bef. 1766; d. bef. 1817, dau. of James and Sarah (Botts). 33T252; Rhodes, p. 372.
William m. 10 July, 1746, Elizabeth O'Daneal. OPR.
William m. bef. 1694, Christian (____) Robinson, widow of Thomas. Proven by Court Suit, that date, Richmond Co. 35V417.

THORNE

Frances (____) m. Thomas Carter.

THORNHILL

____ m. bef. 15 Feb., 1773, Elizabeth Walker, dau. of David, Sr., whose will of that date, Goochland Co., proves it.

THORNHILL (cont.)

Bryant m. between 1766 and 1772, Leanna Nash, dau. of Mrs. Betty Nash, whose will, 1766, and est. sett., 1772, Culpeper Co., prove it.

Elizabeth m. ____ North.

Jesse, b. 13 Oct., 1763; d. 5 Jan., 1837, son of Thomas, the immigrant; m. Elizabeth Stevens, b. May, 1766; d. 12 June, 1845, dau. of Thomas and Elizabeth (Taylor). 48V169.

Margaret (____) m. Dennis Conyers.

Nancy m. John Stevens.

THORNLEY

Aaron m. April, 1772, Caty Dobyns. King George Co. Mar. Record.

THORNTON

____, Col., m. Mary Alexander. She m. (2) Gen. Thomas Posey. Free II:338.

____, a dau., m. ____ Woodford.

____ m. Capt. William Sanford.

____, a dau., m. ____ Buckner.

____ m. Jane Boswell, dau. of Maj. Thomas. 8W(1)54.

____ m. James Taylor.

____ m. Capt. John Catesby Cocke.

____ m. 1772, Mary Rootes, dau. of Philip. Proven by Court Suit, 1806. 11W(2)127.

____, a dau., m. ____ Washington.

____ m. Catharine Yates. Jett, p. 121.

____ m. Lucy Taliaferro, dau. of Col. William. She m. (2) Hay Taliaferro. 20W(1)271.

____ m. Capt. John Cocke.

Agatha m. Christopher Chinn.

Alice m. Lawrence Catlett.

Alice m. (1) ____ Catlett; m. (2) James Taylor.

Alice m. Lawrence Taliaferro.

Alice m. Capt. Presley Thornton.

Alice m. John Fitzhugh.

Ann m. Thomas West.

Ann m. Samuel Timson (1st wife).

Ann m. Edward Eastham.

Ann m. Seth Spencer.

Anne (____) m. (2) ____ Bickerton.

Annie m. John Ogilby.

Anthony of St. Paul's Parish, Stafford Co., b. 1695; d. 1757, son of Francis and Alice (Savage); m. Winifred Presley, dau. of Col. Peter (d. 1750) and Winifred (Griffin) of Northumberland Co. A son was born in 1721. 16V149; 32V63; 34V192; 4W(1)93; 8W(1)2; 23W(1)185; 9W(2)177.

Anthony, b. 1 Feb., 1748; d. 1 Dec., 1828, son of Anthony; m. 8 May, 1772, Mary Rootes, d. 21 Dec., 1828, dau. of Philip and Mildred (Reade) of King and Queen Co.; res. Caroline Co.; rem. to Ky. 4V 208; 25W(1)128.

Anthony of "Ormesley," Caroline Co., son of Anthony, m. (1) Sarah Taliaferro; m. (2) 5 Jan., 1764, St. Paul's Parish, Susannah Fitzhugh. 5W(1)58.

Betsy m. ____ Dunbar.

THORNTON (cont.)

Betty m. John Taliaferro.
Betty m. ____ Taliaferro.
Boswell m. Lucy Battaile. 4V209.
Caleb m. 1791, Patsy Ford. Orange Co. Mar. Record.
Charles m. his cousin, Anne Hubbard Taliaferro, dau. of Robert and Anne Hubbard (Taylor). 11T27.
Charles, son of Anthony, m. (1) Mary Jones, dau. of William of Essex Co.; m. (2) Sarah Fitzhugh, dau. of John of "Bel Air," Stafford Co.; res. Caroline Co. and ca 1812, Oldham Co., Ky. 3T181.
Coats m. 1787, Mary King. Rockbridge Co. Morton, p. 536.
Dorothy m. Lewelling Jones.
Dozier, b. 1755, Lunenburg Co.; d. 1843, Franklin Co., Ga.; m. Lucy Hill. DAR No. 68 734.
Elizabeth m. Edward Carter.
Elizabeth m. John Poindexter.
Elizabeth m. John Taliaferro, Jr.
Elizabeth m. (1) Thomas Meriwether; m. (2) Dr. Thomas Walker.
Elizabeth m. Joseph Pollard.
Elizabeth m. Presley Thornton.
Elizabeth m. John Ford.
Elizabeth m. James Starke.
Elizabeth m. William M. Nance.
Elizabeth m. John Lewis (2nd wife).
Elizabeth m. (1) William Wilkinson; m. (2) Robert H. Taliaferro.
Elizabeth m. Edward Carter.
Elizabeth (Carter) m. Landon Carter.
Elizabeth Gregory m. Robert Dunbar.
Frances "Fannie" m. (1) Dr. Horace Buckner; m. (2) Col. William Strother Jones.
Frances m. Dr. ____ Harris.
Frances m. Willoughby Randolph.
Francis, b. 1762, Gloucester Co.; d. there, 1819; m. 1800, Maria Meacham. DAR No. 89 193.
Francis m. 26 Dec., 1782, Elizabeth Hackney. Christ Church, p. 203.
Francis m. 2 April, 1747, Sarah Fitzhugh. St. Paul's. He, son of Anthony of "Society Hill," King George Co. 5W(1)58.
Francis of Spotsylvania Co., b. 1760, son of Francis and Anne (Thompson); m. Sally Innes, dau. of Judge Harry Innes of Ky. A dau., b. 1793. 3T185; St. Mark's, p. 174; Old King Wm., p. 106.
Francis, d. 1749, son of Francis and Mary (Taliaferro); m. 1736, (3 Sept. or 3 Nov.), Frances Gregory, dau. of Roger and Mildred (Washington). 11T26-7; 5V163; 4W(1)158; 2W(2)134; St. Mark's, p. 177; Old King Wm., pp. 58, 105; Crozier, p. 150.
Francis, b. 5 Nov., 1651; d. 1726, son of William, Sr.; m. (1) bef. 1678, Alice Savage, dau. of Capt. Anthony of Gloucester; m. (2) Jane (____) Harvey, widow of John of Stafford Co. 12T51; 4W(1)90-1; Gillman, p. 76; Old King Wm., p. 105.
Francis, son of Francis and Frances (Gregory), m. 1759, Ann(-e) Thompson, dau. of Rev. John and Butler (Brayne) Spotswood Thompson. Will of Rev. John Thompson, 1771, Culpeper Co., mentions "son-in-law Francis Thornton and my daughter Ann." Will of Francis Thornton was

THORNTON (cont.)

proved, 3 April, 1795. 5W(1)59; Old King Wm., p. 106; St. Mark's, p. 39. She was "daughter of Lady Spottswood." 11T27.

Francis, Jr., b. 1682; d. 1752; m. 1703, Mary Taliaferro, dau. of Col. John and Sarah (Smith). 11T13.

Franky m. Thomas Bryant.

George, b. 18 Nov., 1752, Caroline Co.; d. 30 Aug., 1853, aged nearly 101 years, son of Anthony; served in Rev. War; m. 9 June, 1774, Margaret Stanley. 3T182.

George m. 9 Oct., 1773, Mary Alexander. St. Paul's. He, son of Francis; she, dau. of John. 5W(1)59-60, 141.

Henry Fitzhugh, physician, b. 14 July, 1763 (or 1765), son of Anthony and Susannah (____); m. 22 Sept., 1785, Ann Rose Fitzhugh, dau. of John of "Bel Air." 3T184; 21V204.

Howard, son of Col. William, m. Charlotte Norris of Charlestown, W. Va. 5W(1)60.

James m. Sarah Bailey Hawkins, dau. of Capt. Moses (d. 1777) and Susannah (Strother). 11T127.

James m. 26 Sept., 1800, Jemima Seat. Halifax Co. Mar. Record.

James Bankhead, b. 1770; d. 29 March, 1843, Caroline Co., son of Peter; m. Mildred Rootes Thornton, dau. of Col. Anthony. 25W(1)125.

Jane Clacke m. Josiah Venable.

Jesse m. 1784, Ann Bohen. Orange Co. Mar. Record.

John of Orange Co. m. Jemima Longworth, dau. of William of Westmoreland Co. 31V262.

John m. 13 Dec., 1761, Behethland Gilson Berryman. St. Paul's. She, b. 23 March, 1744, dau. of Gilson and Hannah (Berryman). 9W(2)175.

John m. Susan Kenner. 5W(1)200.

John, will 1687, Isle of Wight Co.; m. Willmouth (____) Sims, whose sons, Richard and Robert Sims, are mentioned in John Thornton's will.

John m. between 20 Oct., 1777, and 20 Oct., 1778, Catherine Yates. Gloucester Co. Mar. Record.

John, b. 4 March, 1775 (Family Bible), son of Anthony; m. (1) 17 Sept., 1795, Sarah Fitzhugh, dau. of George and Mary (Digges) of Fauquier Co.; m. (2) Mildred Washington Dade; m. (3) 22 Oct., 1812, Jane Loughlin. 3T184-5. John, b. 4 March, 1771; m. 17 Sept., 1795, Sarah Fitzhugh, b. 22 July, 1779; d. 25 Feb., 1810; m. (2) 22 Oct., 1812, Jane Loughlin; m. (3) ____ Dade. 21V204.

John, Col., son of Francis and Frances (Gregory), served in Rev. War; m. Jane Washington, dau. of Augustine. 11T27; 5W(1)197; Biog.Enc. Ky., p. 336.

John, Col., son of Francis, Jr., and Mary (Taliaferro), m. 28 Oct., 1740, Mildred Gregory, dau. of Roger and Mildred (Washington). Spotsylvania Co. Mar. Record; 11T27; 5V163; 4W(1)161; 2W(2)134; Caroline, p. 186; Old King Wm., p. 58.

John m. 28 Aug., 1777, Susannah Pace, dau. of W. Pace. Sur. Stephen Coleman. Pittsylvania Co. Mar. Bond.

John m. Anna Maria (Jones) Scarburgh; b. 1685; d. 1760; tombstone at Travis' Point, widow 1st of Capt. William Timson, 2nd of William Barber, 3rd of Edmund Scarburgh and dau. of Rev. Rowland Jones. 4V318; 2W(1)80; 5W(1)193.

John Wyatt, b. 14 Oct., 1775, bro. of Dr. Richard T.; m. Betsy Vawter.

THORNTON (cont.)

Halifax, p. 250.

Joshua m. 19 June, 1787, Nancy Wilkins. Norfolk Co. Mar. Record.

Judith Presley m. Maj. Aylett Buckner.

Lucy m. John Lewis (1st wife).

Lucy m. Isham Richardson.

Lucy m. John Brooke.

Luke, son of Rev. Thomas, m. 27 June, 1799, in Orange Co., Lucy Sleet. Announced in The Virginia Herald, 19 July, 1799. Lucy, b. 1780, a twin of Martha, daus. of James and Ann (Ford) Sleet. 30V69; Gillmore, p. 96. (Also given as Sarah Sleet.)

Margaret m. William Strother.

Margaret m. Anthony Strother (1st wife).

Mary m. Kemp Taliaferro.

Mary m. Gen. William Woodford.

Mary m. (1) William Champe; m. (2) Churchill Jones.

Mary m. Maj. Gen. Everard Meade (1st wife).

Mary m. Richard Locke.

Mary m. ____ Woodford.

Mary Gallihue m. Lieut. Alexander Keith.

Mary T. m. Reuben Thornton Taylor.

Mildred m. Col. Samuel Washington (2nd wife).

Mildred m. Charles Washington.

Mildred m. (1) Nicholas Meriwether; m. (2) Dr. Thomas Walker (1st wife).

Mildred m. Lieut. Abraham Maury.

Mildred Rootes m. James Bankead Thornton.

Mordecai, Capt., m. Mary Reade, dau. of Thomas and Lucy (Gwynne). 9W(2)312.

Nancy m. ____ Branch.

Peter, of "Rose Hill," Caroline Co., son of Anthony; m. Ellen Bankhead. 5W(1)58.

Peter, b. 1774; d. Sept., 1833, Caroline Co.; m. ____ Taylor. 25W(1) 125.

Peter Presley, b. 10 Aug., 1750; d. ca 1781, son of Col. Presley; m. May, 1771, Sally Throckmorton, dau. of Maj. Robert of Gloucester Co. Marriage notice in The Virginia Gazette. 22V203; 5W(1)198; 8W(1)189.

Peter Presley, b. 12 Nov., 1765, Brunswick Co.; d. 6 Aug., 1856, son of William; m. 9 March, 1792, Elizabeth McCulloch, b. 25 Feb., 1771, Amherst Co.; d. 19 Sept., 1851. 5W(1)59.

Peter Presley, son of William and Jane (Clack), m. Oct., 1795, Susanna Stith. Harllee III:2802.

Peter Presley, will dated 1815; m. 1 Dec., 1784, Va., Mary Crawley (or Croley). Children: Zachariah, Bolen, Moses, William, Presley, Elizabeth Nance, Sarah Barnett, Jane Wilson, Fanny Oakes, Barbary Jones, Susannah Watts and Roland Thornton. Pittsylvania Co. Mar. Record. Hartford Times B-8923(1), 4 June, 1955. Signed B. T. A.

Presley, Col., m. (1) Elizabeth ____; m. (2) Charlotte Belson, an English lady, adopted dau. of Col. Jno. Tayloe of "Mt. Airy." 4W(1)164.

Presley m. 26 March, 1784, his cousin, Elizabeth Thornton, dau. of Francis and Sarah (Fitzhugh). 5W(1)58; St. Paul's.

Presley, Capt., m. 19 Oct., 1785, Alice Thornton. St. Paul's. He, b. 1760, Caroline Co.; d. 1811, Hendersonville, Ky., son of Anthony;

THORNTON (cont.)
served in Rev. War; m. Alice Thornton, b. 1759; d. 10 Nov., 1811, dau. of Col. Francis of "Society Hill" and Sarah (Fitzhugh). 3T183-4; 5W(1)58; DAR No. 27 266.
Prudence m. John Adams.
Prudence m. Col. Samuel Pryor.
Prudence m. Capt. John Starke.
Reuben, b. 28 March, 1756, son of William and Jane (Clack); m. 1784, Prudence (Jones) Ward, widow of Henry. Harllee III:2802.
Reuben of Caroline Co., son of Anthony, m. Mildred Grymes, d. 1822, dau. of Benjamin and Priscilla (Rootes). She m. (2) Peter Dudley. 3T183; 28V188.
Reuben of Caroline Co., d. 1768, son of Francis, Jr., and Mary (Taliaferro); m. 29 April, 1743, Elizabeth (Gregory) Willis, widow of Henry, Jr., of Spotsylvania Co., and dau. of Roger and Mildred (Washington) Gregory. Elizabeth m. (3) Dr. Thomas Walker of Albemarle Co.; m. (4) Dr. Alcock of the British Army. 11T27; 4W(1)159; Old King Wm., p. 58.
Rowland, d. bef. May, 1701; m. Elizabeth Fleming, dau. of Capt. Alexander. Proven by Court Suit, 1714. 23T206. Mar. bef. 1692. Proven by Deed of that date, Richmond Co. 4W(1)90; Gillmore, p. 76.
Rowland of Richmond Co., b. 1 Aug., 1685; will dated 21 Sept., 1741, son of Francis and Alice (Savage); m. bef. 24 March, 1715/6, Elizabeth Catlett, dau. of Col. John, Jr., of Essex Co. Marriage proven by Court Record, 1715/6, Essex Co. 23T206; 4W(1)93.
Sally m. Thomas Lewis.
Sarah m. ____ Slaughter.
Sarah m. Thomas Slaughter.
Sarah m. Col. Lawrence Taliaferro.
Sarah m. Samuel Timson.
Sarah m. Carr Chapman.
Sterling m. Winifred Thornton, dau. of Peter and Ellen (Bankhead). 5W(1)58.
Sterling m. 30 Oct., 1769, Ann Cary. Kingston Parish, Matthews Co. 7W(1)183.
Sterling Clack, b. 12 Aug., 1753, Gloucester Co.; d. 1790, son of William and Jane (Clack); m. 17 March, 1777, Amelia Co., Mary (Jones) Jones, widow of Branch Jones and dau. of Maj. Peter and Dorothy (____) Jones. Harllee III:2801.
Stuart, son of Col. William, m. Adelaide Stuart of Fairfax Co. 5W(1) 60.
Sydney, son of James, m. 27 Dec., 1830, Patsy (Petty) Sleet, widow of Weedon Sleet and dau. of George Petty. Gillmore, pp. 95-6.
Thomas m. 25 July, 1708, Agatha Curtis. Christ Church, p. 81.
Thomas m. Mary (____) Thorpe, widow of William (d. 1724). Proven by Court Record, 1731, Surry Co., when they signed the account settlement of estate of William Thorpe.
Thomas Griffin of Caroline Co., b. 11 June, 1775, son of Anthony; m. Oct. 1795 or 6, Ann Harrison Fitzhugh, dau. of William and Sarah (Digges) of Fauquier Co. 3T184; 21V204.
William m. 16 Feb., 1774, Sarah Goodrich, dau. of Edward. Sur. John Clack. Brunswick Co. Mar. Bond. He, b. 14 April, 1751, son of

THORNTON (cont.)

William and Jane (Clack); she, dau. of Edward Goodrich. Harllee III:2801, 2806.

William m. 11 May, 1775, Martha Stuart. St. Paul's. He was a colonel and son of Francis; she, dau. of John. 5W(1)59-60.

William m. 26 April, 1757, Elizabeth Fitzhugh. St. Paul's. William d. 1779; will prov. in King George Co. 5W(1)198.

William m. between Oct. 1785, and May 1786, Patsey Owen by Rev. James Shelburne, Baptist. Lunenburg Co. Ministers' Returns.

William, b. 20 Dec., 1717; d. ca 1790, son of Francis and Ann (Sterling); m. 25 June, 1738, Jane Clack, b. 9 Jan., 1721, Gloucester Co., dau. of James and Mary (Sterling) of Brunswick Co. 46V176; 4W(1) 158; Harllee III:2804-5.

Winifred m. Col. Daniel McCarty.

Winifred m. William Bernard (1st wife).

Winifred m. Capt. John Catesby Cocke.

Winifred m. ____ Bernard.

Winifred m. Sterling Thornton.

THORNWELL

____ m. 5 Dec., 1757, Lucy Coleman, both in this parish. Douglas Reg., p. 3.

THOROUGHGOOD (THOROGOOD, THOROWGOOD)

____ m. ____ Mason, dau. of Col. Lemuel. 5V182.

____ m. bef. 1 April, 1709, Mary (____) Moseley, widow of William. 26V415.

____ (____) m. William Christian (2nd wife).

Adam, Col., d. 1719, son of Lieut. Col. Adam and Frances (Yeardley); m. Mary Mosely. Am.Hist. I:346.

Adam, Lieut. Col., son of Capt. Adam and Sarah (Offley), m. Frances Yeardley, dau. of Col. Argall; res. Norfolk Co. 4W(1)170; Am.Hist. I:346.

Adam, Capt., b. 1603; will prov. 27 April, 1640, son of William and Ann (Edwards) of Norwich, England; m. Sarah Offley of London. She m. (2) Capt. John Gookin; m. (3) Col. Francis Yeardley. 17T109; 31T87-8; 5V330, 435; Am.Hist. I:345.

Amey m. Tully Moseley.

Ann m. Job Chandler.

Argall m. Elizabeth Keeling. 8W(1)275; LNCo. 1:127.

Elizabeth m. (1) Simon Overzee; m. (2) Maj. George Colclough; m. (3) Col. Isaac Allerton.

Elizabeth m. James Nimmo.

Elizabeth m. Cornelius Calvert II.

Elizabeth m. Capt. John Michael.

Elizabeth (____) m. (2) William Hunter; m. (3) Dr. Christopher Wright (2nd wife).

Frances m. John Wanehouse Thorowgood.

James m. bef. 1800, Susannah Thorowgood, dau. of John of Princess Anne Co., whose will, prov. 1803, Williamsburg, Va., proves it.

John of Princess Anne Co., d. 1757; m. Elizabeth Mason. 29V506.

John m. 13 Oct., 1743, Margaret Walke, dau. of Anthony. 28V175.

John of Princess Anne Co. m. bef. 4 Feb., 1718, Pembrook Fowler, dau. of George. Proven by Deed of that date, Princess Anne Co. 26V414.

THOROUGHGOOD (cont.)

John, Lieut. Col., m. bef. 6 May, 1702, Margaret Lawson, dau. of Col. Anthony. Proven by Court Record of that date, Princess Anne Co. 5V152; 26V416; LNCo. I:48.

John Wanehouse m. 30 Oct., 1798, Frances Thorowgood by Rev. Anthony Walke. Princess Anne Co. Ministers' Returns.

Margaret m. Thomas Walke.

Mary m. John Mackey.

Mary (____) m. Stephen Wright.

Mary Ann m. Thomas Walke.

Sarah m. Simon Oversee (1st wife).

Sarah (____) m. (2) Capt. John Gookin; m. (3) Col. Francis Yeardley.

Susannah m. James Thorowgood.

Thomas m. 10 Feb., 1724, Mary Trevethan, dau. of Sampson. Sur. Robert Thorowgood. Princess Anne Co. Mar. Bond.

THORP

____ m. bef. 1758, Elizabeth (____) Webb, widow of Moses. Proven by Deed, 1758, Lancaster Co.

Elizabeth (____) m. Maj. Otho Thorpe.

Elizabeth T. m. Benjamin J. Walton.

Joel of New Haven, Conn., m. Priscilla Armistead, b. Nov., 1783, dau. of William; res. Edenton, No. Car. (Mar. in Va. or No. Car.?) 8W (1)65.

Mark m. Nov., 1769, Susannah Stewart. King George Co. Mar. Record.

Mary Collia m. Joshua Ford.

Parmela m. Thomas Crump.

Tomsey m. John Boothe.

THORPE

____ believed m. bef. 1796, Sarah (____) Seward, mother of Edwin, whose will of that date, Southampton Co., names "mother Sarah Thorpe."

Cecelah (or Celia) m. Michael David.

Drucilla m. ____ Thompson.

Elizabeth m. William Jones.

Frances (____) m. John Annesley.

John m. bef. 1792, Mary Reese, dau. of John, Sr., whose will of that date, Southampton Co., proves it.

Lewis m. 13 Nov., 1771, Elizabeth Simmons, dau. of Benjamin. Southampton Co. 33V42.

Mary m. William Howard.

Mary m. William Hord.

Mary m. (1) Edward Harris; m. (2) Owen Myrick.

Mary (____) m. Thomas Thornton.

Mildred m. ____ Spence.

Olive m. ____ Reese.

Otho, Maj. of York Co., d. 1686-7, London, Eng.; m. (1) 1660, Elizabeth (____) Thorp, widow of Richard; m. (2) Dorothy (____) Fenn, d. 27 Oct., 1665, widow of Samuel; m. (3) Frances ____. 4V134-5.

Peggy m. Lander Veatch.

Sarah m. ____ Harris.

Sophia m. Capt. Nathan Reid.

Thomas, Maj., d. 7 Oct., 1693, aged 48; m. bef. 1686/7, Katharine Sea-

THORPE (cont.)

ton, d. 6 June, 1695, aged 43, dau. of Francis of Northampton Co., England; both bur. Bruton Churchyard, Williamsburg, Va. She m. (2) James Whaley. There was a mar. sett. in 1695 and she left property to him but it is possible that she died before the marriage could be performed.

THOURON

John m. 26 March, 1791, Ann Smith. Norfolk Co. Mar. Record.

THRAILKILL

Mary (____) m. Benjamin Doggett.

THRELKELD

Ann "Nancy" m. Capt. John Fox.

Daniel, b. ca 1772, Va.; d. 25 March, 1851, Boone Co., Ind.; m. 20 April, 1795, Betsey Branson, d. 1797; res. Mercer Co., Ky. Hartford C-1086(1), 20 Nov., 1957. Signed M. M. T.

Elijah m. 14 Nov., 1781, Elizabeth Cook. Henry Co. Mar. Record.

Elijah m. June, 1772, Mary (Bronough) Waugh, widow of Joseph and dau. of David Bronough (will dated 13 Dec., 1773). 23V312.

Henry m. 2 Nov., 1748, Mary Hinson. OPR.

Moses m. 25 Aug., 1800, Elizabeth Weakley. Shelby Co., Ky. Mar. Record.

Sarah m. William Rogus, Jr.

THRESH

Clement m. bef. 1656, ____ (____) Harris, mother of Ann who was mentioned in will of Clement Thresh as "daughter-in-law, not yet 13 years old," (Step-daughter). 5V282.

THRIFT

Delilah m. Vincent Walker.

Joannah m. Robert Dixon.

Mary m. Richard Downton.

THROCKMORTON

____ m. bef. 1798, Catherine Roberson, dau. of John (d. bef. 1798). Proven by a Deed, 30 May, 1798, Spotsylvania Co.

____ m. Mary Langbourn, dau. of ____ and Susanna (Smith). 5W(1)39.

____ m. bef. 1778, Ann Redford. 32V58.

Albion (or Albine), a Baptist preacher, b. ca 1761; d. Clark Co., Ky., son of Capt. Gabriel and Judith (Edmondson); m. Mary Webb, dau. of Capt. James, Jr., and Mary (Smith). 7T189, 272; 42V62; 26W(1)67; Wilcoxson, p. 414.

Ann m. John Rogers, Jr.

Dorothy m. James Webb.

Elizabeth m. ____ Davis.

Elizabeth m. Sir Thomas Dale.

Elizabeth m. John Perrin.

Fanny m. William Madison.

Frances m. William Debnam.

Gabriel, b. 1665, Gloucester Co.; d. July, 1737, son of John and Frances (Mason); m. 1690, Frances Cooke, dau. of Hon. Mordecai and Frances (Ironmonger). Wilcoxson, p. 414.

Gabriel, Capt., b. 16 Aug., 1735; d. bef. 1791, son of Capt. Mordecai and Mary (Reade); m. Judith Edmundson, dau. of Thomas of Essex Co. and Dorothy (Todd). 7T187, 272; 42V60, 62; Wilcoxson, p. 414.

THROCKMORTON (cont.)

Hannah m. ____ Fairfax.

John, b. ca 163?; d. ca 1680; m. Frances Mason, dau. of Edward and Elizabeth (Locke). Wilcoxson, p. 414.

John m. bet. 20 Oct., 1777, and 20 Oct., 1778, Susanna Hughes. Gloucester Co. Mar. Record.

John, b. bef. 1748, son of Robert and Mary (Lewis); m. (1) Elizabeth Cooke, dau. of John; m. (2) Rebecca Richardson, dau. of William. 13 Ky. Reg. 80.

Julius m. 22 Dec., 1791, Rachel Cole. Halifax Co. Mar. Record.

Lucy m. Maj. Robert Throckmorton.

Mary m. Maj. William Moore.

Mary m. Thomas Throckmorton.

Mordecai, b. ca 1695; d. 1768, son of Gabriel and Frances (Cooke); res. Gloucester Co. and King and Queen Co.; m. Mary Reade, dau. of Thomas and Lucy (Gwyn). 32V290; 10W(2)25; Wilcoxson, p. 414.

Richard m. 15 Jan., 1791, Salley Dunkley. Halifax Co. Mar. Record.

Robert m. 8 April, 1788, Betty Hack. Halifax Co. Mar. Record.

Robert, Col., m. bef. 1776, Sarah (____) Cooke. Proven by will of her son, Mordecai Cooke, Jr., of Gloucester Co., dated 1769; prov. 1776, Williamsburg, Va.

Robert, Maj., of Culpeper Co., b. bef. 1748, son of Col. Robert of Ware Parish; m. Lucy Throckmorton, dau. of Capt. Mordecai. 42V61; 13 Ky. Reg. 80.

Robert, son of Gabriel and Frances (Cooke), m. (1) Mary Lewis, d. 1748, dau. of John and Elizabeth (Warner); m. (2) Sarah Smith, dau. of Augustin. 16T128; 13 Ky. Reg. 37:80.

Sally m. Peter Presley Thornton.

Thomas m. 15 Feb., 1797, Susanna Morton. Sur. William Hill. Charlotte Co. Mar. Bond.

Thomas, b. 1739; d. 27 April, 1826, son of Capt. Mordecai; m. (1) Mary Throckmorton, b. bef. 1748, dau. of Col. Robert of Ware Parish and Mary (Lewis); m. (2) Mary Anne Hooe, b. 7 Nov., 1756, King George Co., dau. of Maj. John and Anne (Fowke). 14T24; 42V60; 13 Ky. Reg. 80.

Warner m. Mary Langborne, dau. of William, b. 1723, and Susanna (Smith). 15T431; Old King Wm., p. 18.

William, son of Capt. Mordecai, m. 15 March, 1787, Elizabeth Phillips. Sur. Harwood Burt, Jr. York Co. Mar. Bond. She may have been his 2nd wife. 42V61.

William m. 9 Jan., 1788, N. Nash. Halifax Co. Mar. Record.

William Todd, b. ca 1767; d. 1812, Frederick Co., son of Capt. Gabriel and Judith (Edmondson); m. ca 1785, Mary Dixon, dau. of Roger and Lucy (Rootes) of Fredericksburg, Va. 42V62.

THROGMORTON

____ m. Dorothy Roade. 32V290.

Mordecai m. 11 Dec., 1773, Mary Peyton in Kingston Parish, Matthews Co. 7W(1)183.

Sally m. William Guill.

THROP

____ m. bef. 1710, Mary Lewis, dau. of Daniel and Susan (Bennett) and granddau. of Richard Bennett, whose est. sett. of that date proves

THROP (cont.)
the marriage. Boddie-Isle, p. 296.

THROPP
Elizabeth m. Robert Scott.

THRUSTON
Elizabeth m. Thomas Whiting (2nd wife).

THURMAN
Ann m. Benjamin Schoolfield.
Baze m. 20 Nov., 1791, Margaret Osbourne. Sur. John Osbourne. Bedford Co. Mar. Bond.
Benjamin in Albemarle Co. bef. 1790 m. Nancy Carr, dau. of Gideon. Albemarle, p. 330.
Henry m. 15 Jan., 1795, Sarah Terrell. Sur. Joseph Thurman. Consent of Edward Terrell. Bedford Co. Mar. Record.
Joseph m. 15 Dec., 1792, Nancy Franklin. Sur. John Porter. Consent of Mary Ann Franklin, mother of Nancy. Bedford Co. Mar. Record.
Lydda m. Alexander Mayhew.
Richard m. 24 Nov., 1794, Elizabeth Rynor. Sur. George Rynor. Bedford Co. Mar. Bond.
Sally m. John Schoolfield.
Susanna m. Joseph Smith.

THURMAND
William m. 4 Dec., 1787, Martha Gooch, spinster. Sur. Nathan Dedman. Albemarle Co. Mar. Bond.

THURMER
Robert m. 17 Oct., 1756, Catherine Westerhouse, dau. of William. Northampton Co. Mar. Record.

THURMOND
____ m. Sarah Goolsby, dau. of William (d. 1819). Albemarle, p. 211.
Ann m. Alexander Moss.
Benjamin m. 11 Jan., 1758, Susannah Moss, both in this parish. Douglas Reg., p. 3.
Benjamin m. Nancy Carr, dau. of Gideon; res. by 1790, Albemarle Co. Hartford C-637, 20 July, 1957. Signed M. R. C.
Mary m. Philip Thurmond.
Mary m. Jacob Davis.
Nancy m. William Thurmond.
Philip, d. 9 June, 1841; m. Mary "Polly" Thurmond, dau. of Benjamin and Susanna (Moss). Moss, p. 1.
Philip m. 1764, Judith Tucker, both in Albemarle. Douglas Reg., p. 7.
Sally m. Edward Ware, Jr.
Sarah m. Austin (?Augustine) Sandidge.
William m. 10 April, 1766, Mackie Norvil, both in this parish. Douglas Reg., p. 9.
William m. 10 Jan., 1787, Mary Dickerson, spinster. Sur. Richard Thurmond. Albemarle Co. Mar. Bond.
William m. Martha Gooch, dau. of William (d. 1796). Albemarle, p. 209.
William, b. 1769, Va.; d. 28 Aug., 1841, Ga.; m. his cousin, Nancy Thurmond, dau. of Benjamin and Susanna (Moss). Moss, p. 2.

THURMOR
Anna Katharina m. Edmund Glanville.

THURSTAIN
Abner m. 25 Jan., 1782, Elizabeth Williams, dau. of Peter, dec'd. Northampton Co. Mar. Record.

THURSTANE
Sarah m. William Profit.

THURSTON
___ m. 18 April, 1797, Caty Reynolds. Caroline Co. Mar. Record.
Ann m. David Clowder.
Batchelder m. 16 March, 1786, Peggy Daniel. Christ Church, p. 205.
Buckner, b. 9 Feb., 1764, son of Col. Charles Minn Thurston and Mary (Buckner); m. March, 1795, Jannett January, dau. of Peter of Ky. 4W(1)181.
Charles, b. 3 Aug., 1765, son of Col. Charles Minn Thurston and (1) Mary (Buckner); m. 20 Jan., 1796, Frances (Clark) O'Fallon, widow of Dr. James and dau. of John Clark of Ky. 4W(1)182.
Charles Minn (or Mynn), Col., b. 6 Nov., 1738, Gloucester Co.; d. 1812, La., son of Col. John and Sarah (Minn); m. (1) 1760, Mary Buckner, d. 18 Aug., 1765, dau. of Col. Samuel of Gloucester Co.; m. (2) Ann Alexander of Gloucester Co. 4W(1)181; 7W(1)58; DAR No. 28 438; DAR No. 66 179. (Often recorded as Thruston.)
Edward m. (1) 28 Oct., 1666, at Martin's Hundred, Va., Anne Loveing, dau. of Thomas; m. (2) 3 Sept., 1671, Susanna Perry, dau. of Nicholas. 4W(1)117.
Edward, Jr., m. 31 Aug., 1706, Elizabeth Housden, dau. of Rev. Thomas Housden of Nansemond Co. Family Record. 4W(1)180.
Eleanor Mynn m. Henry Daingerfield.
Elizabeth m. Cornelius Calvert.
Elizabeth m. Col. Thomas Whiting.
Elizabeth m. William Daingerfield.
Elizabeth m. Richard Allin.
Elizabeth m. John Ashley.
Elizabeth m. Humphrey Watkins.
Elizabeth m. John Blake.
Elizabeth m. William Kidd.
Eloisa m. Edmund Taylor.
Frances m. Col. William Hubbard.
Frances m. Frederick Conrad.
Frances m. James Lee.
Henry m. 23 Feb., 1769, Elizabeth Brame. Christ Church, p. 198.
Jane m. Roland Thomas.
John, Col., b. 21 Oct., 1709; d. 20 Feb., 1766, Gloucester Co.; m. 6 Dec., 1737, Sarah (Mynn) Dalton Haynes, b. 15 Sept., 1716, widow 1st of William Dalton (or Dolton), 2nd of Herbert Haynes and dau. of Capt. Robert, Jr., and Sarah (Cary) Mynn. Family Bible; 40V80; 4W (1)181; 5W(1)120; Boddie-HSF IV:87; Court Record, 1733, Spotsylvania Co.
John m. 18 May, 1772, Patty Witherspoon, both in Goochland. Douglas Reg., p. 13.
John m. 13 Oct., 1773, Aley Taylor, dau. of James. Sur. Henry Kay. Charlotte Co. Mar. Bond.
John m. 27 Feb., 1783, Elizabeth Stamper. Christ Church, p. 208.
John, b. 2 Dec., 1668, son of Edward and (1) Anne (Loveing); m. 23

THURSTON (cont.)

Sept., 1690, Ellinor (____) Cary, widow of John. 4W(1)117.

John m. 13 Oct., 1782, Elizabeth Thurston Whiting, dau. of Col. Thomas of Gloucester. 4W(1)181.

John m. in Pittsylvania Co. Susannah Pace. Family Mss. of Noble H. Pace.

John m. bef. 29 Aug., 1745, Ann Wiatt, dau. of Francis, whose est. sett., Spotsylvania Co., proves it.

John L. m. 25 Dec., 1793, Susanna Whiting by Mr. John Hughs. Family Bible Record. 32V131; 5W(1)120.

Lucy (____) m. Hay Taliaferro.

M. m. Michael Prewit.

Marcia m. Garland Hurt.

Mary m. Michael Prewitt.

Mary m. John Netherland.

Mary m. Col. Charles Magill.

Mary m. Hugh Walker.

Mary Buckner m. Thomas January.

Massey m. Stephen Jones.

Nanny m. Mosely Daniel.

Plummer m. bef. 4 July, 1779, Mary Talbot, dau. of Charles, whose will prov. 1779, Bedford Co. Bell, p. 289.

Reuben m. 24 Dec., 1772, Marianne Lawry, both in Goochland. Douglas Reg., p. 12.

Robert m. 3 June, 1742, Gustant Daniell. Sur. Richard Allen. Middlesex Co. Mar. Bond. She was Constant Daniel, dau. of William and Frances (Boseley). 12T206.

Robert m. 26 Oct., 1765, Margaret Jones. Sur. John George. Middlesex Co. Mar. Bond.

Sally m. John Daniel.

Samuel m. 9 March, (?)1781, Sarah Stamper Coats. Christ Church, p. 171.

Sarah m. George Floerdew Norton.

Sarah m. John Thornton.

Sarah m. James Lewis.

Susanna m. ____ Robertson.

Susanna m. David Gutherie.

William m. 12 Sept., 1763, Jean Jones, both in this parish. Douglas Reg., p. 7.

William m. 13 Nov., 1728, Frances Kidd. Christ Church, p. 166.

William m. 29 April, 1729, Elizabeth Franks. Christ Church, p. 166.

William Plummer m. 11 June, 1773, Lucy Mary Taliaferro. Orange Co. Mar. Record. He d. 16 March, 1789; she, b. 13 Dec., 1755, dau. of Col. William and Mary (Battaile) of Spotsylvania Co.; m. (2) 1791, Hay Taliaferro of Orange Co. 11T14; 41V357; 50V274; 4W(1)60; 13W(2)270.

THWEAT(-T)

____ m. Dycie Farmer. Bell, p. 208.

Anna m. Ward Hudson.

Archibald m. Lucy Eppes, dau. of Francis (d. 1808) and Elizabeth (Wayles). 6T266-7.

Betsey m. William Britton.

THWEATT (cont.)
Betsy m. Abram Green.
Betty m. Nathaniel Dunn.
David m. 19 Dec., 1782, Rebecca (____) Jones. Sussex Co. Mar. Record.
Drury m. 16 March, 1784, Solah Smith, dau. of Isham. Sur. Peter Cain. Sussex Co. Mar. Bond.
Elizabeth m. ____ Burchett.
James m. 24 Nov., 1701, Mrs. Judith Soane. Henrico, p. 227. James m. 24 Oct., 1702, Henrico Co., Judith Soane, dau. of William (d.1714); res. Prince George Co. Boddie-HSF V:89.
James m. ca 1722, prob. in Prince George Co., Sarah Sturdivant. 61V 483. He was of Dinwiddie Co. and had a son, b. ca 1749. Habersham I:347-8.
James, Jr., b. 1751; d. 14 Sept., 1814, Hancock Co., Ga., son of James and Sarah (Sturdivant); m. 3 April, 1777, Elizabeth Peterson, dau. of John of Va. Habersham I:348.
John, b. ca 1745, Dinwiddie Co., son of James and Sarah (Sturdivant); m. Rebecca Peterson, dau. of James of Va. Habersham I:347.
John m. Elizabeth Soane, dau. of William (d. 1714, Henrico Co.) Boddie-HSF V:88.
Judith m. James Goodwin.
Martha m. John Peterson.
Miles, d. 1766/7, Prince George Co., prob. son of James and Judith (Soane); m. Sarah Green. Boddie-HSF V:89.
Patty m. William Collier.
Peter m. 28 July, 1787, Lucretia Parish. Dinwiddie Co. Cameron.
Rebecca m. John Grigg.
Richard N. m. Mary Eppes, dau. of Francis (d. 1808) and Elizabeth (Wayles). 6T266-7.
Sarah m. John Mitchell.
Susan m. Theophilus Field.
Tabitha m. John Hamilton.
Thomas m. 15 Nov., 1792, Susannah Barksdale. Halifax Co. Mar. Record.

THWEATTS
William m. 10 Feb., 1775, Jane Parham, dau. of Ephraim. Sur. James Thweatts. Sussex Co. Mar. Bond.

TIBBOTH
Richard, Capt. of the ship "Mary and Anne," m. bef. 16 July, 1686, Mary Bridger, dau. of Col. Joseph, whose est. sett. proves it. 7W (1)243. His mother was Hester (Pitt) Bridger. Boddie-Isle, p. 426.

TIBBS
____ m. Nancy Miller, dau. of Simon, whose will, prov. 1805, Culpeper Co., proves it. 12T241.
John m. 16 Dec., 1778, Penelope Buxton. Sur. William Watkins. Northumberland Co. Mar. Bond.
William m. 1777, Molly Williams. Northumberland Co. Mar. Record.

TIBET
Nancy m. Thomas Kooling.

TICE
William m. 6 Oct., 1786, Tabitha McCann. Frederick Co. Mar. Record.

TICER
William m. 15 Dec., 1754, Aggy Hutt. OPR.
TIDBALL
Josiah m. Lucy Gwynn Page, b. ca 1779, dau. of Mann and Mary (Tayloe) of Spotsylvania Co. Page, p. 81.
TIDBURY
John m. 25 Jan., 1682, Elizabeth Ball. Christ Church, p. 22.
TIDCOCK
Elizabeth m. James Hartley.
TIDWELL
___ m. Reuben Lindsey (2nd wife).
TIGHT
Elizabeth m. William Hamock.
TIGNALL
___ m. Matthew Jones.
TIGNOIR
Mabel m. ___ Hill.
TIGNOR
Aquila m. 29 Aug., 1765, Ann Lucas, both of this parish. Douglas Reg., p. 8.
Caty m. Gilbert Nokes.
Mabell (___) m. William Luck.
Mary m. Thomas Hughlett.
Philip m. Sarah Bonnis, dau. of John and Sarah (___). Proven by Court Record, 25 Sept., 1699, Northumberland Co. Dameron, Part I, p. 13.
Priscilla m. Jonathan Johnson.
Thomas m. 27 Oct., 1737, Sarah Stiff. Christ Church, p. 170.
William m. 17 Sept., 1794, Frances Covington. Caroline Co. Mar. Record.
William, Jr., of Fairfield Parish, Northumberland Co., m. 18 July, 1682, Dorothy Hill. Christ Church, p. 21.
TIGWELL
William m. 20 April, 1708, Priscilla Snelling. Christ Church, p. 81.
TILDEN
John Bell, Lieut., b. 1761, Philadelphia, Penna.; d. 1838, Stephen City, Va.; m. Jane Chambers. DAR No. 66 434.
TILFORD
Nancy m. James McCoun.
TILLAS
John m. 14 May, 1788, Sarah Moorlan. Lynchburg, p. 157.
TILLER
Daniel m. 28 Dec., 1798, Rebecca Camall. Caroline Co. Mar. Record. (Also given as Daniel Tyler and Rebecca Campbell.)
Daniel m. 25 Dec., 1793, Agnes Williams by Rev. Martin Walton. Louisa Co. Ministers' Returns.
George m. 28 July, 1799, Lucy Mills. Caroline Co. Mar. Record.
Jane m. John Baxter.
Nancie m. Thomas Pugh.
Robert m. 26 Dec., 1799, Dice Rice by Rev. William Baskett. Louisa Co. Ministers' Returns.
William m. bef. Sept., 1715, Catherine Brown, dau. of Charles, Sr., whose Deed of Gift of that date, Essex Co., proves it.

TILLERY

Rebecca m. William Price.

TILLEY

Agnes m. Samuel Mitchel.

Thomas m. 22 Nov., 1719, Phebo Syddorn. Christ Church, p. 163.

TILLINGHOST

Nicholas m. bef. 1769, Catherine Taylor, dau. of Thomas Teackle Taylor, whose will, dated 1769, Newport Co., R. I., showed he owned land in Va. Will on file in Accomac Co. Will Book 1772-

TILLMAN

Elizabeth m. Curtis Hardee.

Elizabeth m. William Harrison.

John m. 23 May, 1758, Mary Simmons. Sur. John Daniel. Brunswick Co. Mar. Bond.

Richard m. bef. 1770, Anne Randle, dau. of William, whose will of that date, Brunswick Co., proves it. Boddie-HSF V:57.

Roger m. bef. 1717, Susanna (____) Parham. 34V153.

TILLY

Nancy m. Daniel Hedden.

Nelly m. Dickey Graves.

TILMAN

Edna m. Lewis Willis.

Elizabeth m. William Walton.

Thomas m. Susan Moon, dau. of William (d. 1800). Albemarle, p. 282.

TILNEY

____ m. bef. 1747, Bettie Harmanson Stringer, dau. of Jacob and Elishe (Harmanson). 37V381.

Ann m. Richard Drumond.

Jonathan m. 2 June, 1742, Sarah Marshall. Northampton Co. Mar. Record.

Margaret m. John Moore.

Sarah (____) m. Robert James.

Susannah m. Michael Dixon.

TILSON

Jenny m. Joseph Cole.

TIMBERLAKE

____ m. Warner Minor

____ m. Mary Bowie, dau. of John and Judith (Catlett). Caroline, p. 388.

Elizabeth m. John Smith.

Elizabeth m. Sam Bever.

Elizabeth m. Samuel Noell.

Francis m. 9 March, 1730, Judith Lawson. Lancaster Co. Mar. Record.

Hannah Thacker m. Dr. George Lorimer.

James, purser in U. S. Navy, m. Peggy O'Neal, dau. of an Irish hotel-keeper in Washington. She m. (1) John H. Eaton, Secretary of War under Pres. Jackson. Albemarle, p. 331.

Jane m. John Catlett Bowie (1st wife).

John m. 20 May, 1778, Susanna Christian, dau. of Gideon who gave consent. Charles City Co. Mar. Record.

John m. Elizabeth Nelson, b. 1767, dau. of James and Keziah (Harris). 27T38.

TIMBERLAKE (cont.)

John m. 12 April, 1772, Christiana Thomasson. Louisa Co. Mar. Record.
Joseph m. 9 Dec., 1718, Joanna Hackney. Christ Church, p. 163.
Louisa m. William Wortenbaker.
Lucy m. William Bullock.
Lucy Duke m. Henry Lacy.
M. m. John Bradford.
Mary m. William Chaney.
Mildred m. Thomas East.
Nelly m. Thomas Bustin.
Philip m. 9 Oct., 1791, Elizabeth Johnson by Joseph Drury. Campbell Co. Mar. Record.
Richard m. (2) Mary (Mundon) Smith. 33V405.
Sarah m. Capt. John Hathaway.
Sarah m. Thomas Butler.
Sarah m. Abraham Estes.
William m. 11 Feb., 1786, Elizabeth Turnbull. Petersburg, Va. Cameron.
Winofred m. William Sharpe.

TIMBERLICK

Elizabeth m. Sam Bever.
Richard m. 22 Dec., 1759, Mary Curd, both in this parish. Douglas Reg., p. 5.
Sarah m. James Parish.
Sarah m. Abraham Estis.

TIMBERLIN

Joseph m. 11 Dec., 1711, Elizabeth Grey. Christ Church, p. 82.

TIMMONS

Collings m. 1790, Nancy Payne by Rev. Joshua Lawrence. Princess Anne Co. LNCo. 2:73.
Michael m. 18 May, 1799, Mary Sabra. Northampton Co. Mar. Record.
Thomas m. 14 May, 1749, Susanna Owens. St. Paul's.

TIMMS

Mary m. William Robertson.

TIMONS

Mary m. Batson Whitehurst.

TIMSON

Ann m. Samuel Major.
Anne m. (1) Robert Crawley; m. (2) William Sanders.
Anne Thornton m. Samuel Major.
Elizabeth m. Nathaniel Crawley.
Elizabeth (____) m. (2) John Ferguson.
John, son of John (will prov. 21 June, 1742), m. Sarah (?)Jackson. 5W(1)5.
Mary m. Thomas Sherlock.
Mary m. Thomas Barber.
Nancy m. Scervant Jones.
Priscilla m. William Henley.
Samuel m. (1) Ann Thornton, dau. of Thomas and Ann (____) of Gloucester Co. (Family Bible Record). She, b. 11 Sept., 1739; d. 28 Feb., 1763 (Tombstone and Bible Record). 5W(1)4.
Samuel, will prov. 1782, son of John and Sarah (Coke) Hoge Timson; m. (1) Sarah Thornton, d. 28 Feb., 1763, in 21st year of her age, dau.

TIMSON (cont.)

of Thomas and Ann (___) Thornton of Gloucester Co.; m. (2) Mary ___. 22W(1)220; 5W(2)202. (See Samuel Timson above.)

Samuel m. bef. July, 1777, Mary (___) Valentine, widow of Joseph, whose est. sett. of that date, York Co., proves it.

Sarah m. Peter Powell.

William m. bef. 1740, ___ Hyde, dau. of Samuel, whose est. sett. of that date, York Co., proves it.

William, Capt., will, 1719, York Co., son of Samuel and Mary (Juxon); m. Anna Maria Jones. 5W(1)3-4; 5W(2)201.

TINCHER

Elizabeth m. Robert Hews.

Margaret m. William Oharra.

Mary m. Samuel Kincaide.

Robert m. 28 Feb., 1787/8, Nancy Dickson by Rev. John Alderson, Jr. Rockingham Co. or Greenbrier Co. Ministers' Returns.

Sarah m. Samuel Peepels.

TINDALL

John m. Elizabeth Shelton, dau. of Samuel (d. 1793). Albemarle, p. 313.

TINDAR

James m. 1785, Molly Shadrach. Orange Co. Mar. Record.

TINDER

Anthony m. 1797, Lucy Robinson. Orange Co. Mar. Record.

Jesse m. 1786, Alcapear Abell. Orange Co. Mar. Record.

Margaret m. John Abel.

TING

Hannah (or Ann) m. Ensign Thomas Savage.

TINSLEY

___ m. John Pendleton.

___ m. Richard Pendleton.

___ m. ___ Ragland, dau. of John and Anne (Beaufort). Halifax, p. 240.

Anne Ragland m. Sgt. John Dabney Davis.

Betsey m. John Rucker.

David m. 6 April, 1776, Elizabeth Walton. Louisa Co. Mar. Record.

Elizabeth m. Henry Willy.

Elizabeth m. William Meeks.

Elizabeth m. William Pendleton.

Frances m. Joel Yager.

Isaac m. bef. 18 Jan., 1742/3, Margaret Rucker, dau. of Peter. Proven by Court Record of that date, Essex Co.

John m. 19 Aug., 1791, Ann Washington. Sur. Thomas Quarles. Albemarle Co. Mar. Bond. John m. 1791, Ann (Quarles) Washington, widow of Henry of King George Co. and dau. of James, Sheriff, 1783. Albemarle, p. 299.

John m. Martha Ragland, dau. of John and Susanna (Pettus). Louisa, p. 408.

Margaret m. William Molin.

Mary m. John Pendleton.

Mary m. Richard Pendleton.

Mary m. David Johnson.

TINSLEY (cont.)
Peter m. Susanna Thompson, dau. of William and Bessie Ann (Garland). 4T45.
Tabitha m. John Morton.
Thomas of Hanover Co. m. 1726, Frances Bickley, dau. of Joseph and Sarah (____). 5W(1)126. Thomas m. 1778, Frances Bickley, dau. of Joseph. Louisa, p. 289.
Thomas, b. 1755, Hanover Co.; d. there, 1822; m. Susanna Thomson. DAR No. 32 416.
Thomas m. 12 Feb., 1779, Tabitha Spencer, spinster, dau. of Ahimas, who was surety. Charlotte Co. Mar. Bond.
Thomas, d. ca 1700; m. Elizabeth Randolf. 41V346.
William m. 30 April, 1789, Dolly Estis. Caroline Co. Mar. Record.
William, b. 1735, Hanover Co.; d. there, 1800; m. 1761, Jane Goose, b. 1743; d. 1790. DAR No. 32 725.

TIPLADY
Rebecca m. Peter Goodwin.

TIPPETT
Mary m. William Coppedge.

TIPPITT
Lavina m. George Roberts.

TIPTON
John, Col., d. 1813, son of Jonathan; m. (1) 1753, Mary Butler, d. 8 June, 1776, Shenandoah Co., dau. of Thomas; rem. from Md. to Shenandoah Co., Va.; rem. to No. Car., Oct., 1782; m. (2) Martha (____) Moore, widow of James of Shenandoah Co. East Tenn. 1:69, 75.
Mary m. John McGuire.

TISDALE
John m. 1 Dec., 1789, Charlotte Johnson by Rev. James Shelburne, Baptist. Lunenburg Co. Ministers' Returns.
Patsy m. Thomas Gooch.
Robert m. 14 Jan., 1799, Sally Beadles. Louisa Co. Mar. Record.
Shirley m. 24 Dec., 1770, Ursula Ragland. Louisa Co. Mar. Record.
William m. 29 Jan., 1789, Jenny Buzentine by Rev. Thomas Crymes, Baptist. Lunenburg Co. Ministers' Returns.
William m. 20 Nov., 1793, Polly Morris. Louisa, p. 260. Mar. by Rev. Richard Pope. Louisa Co. Ministers' Returns.

TISHER
Polly m. William Holt.

TITMARSH
Richard m. 15 June, 1793, Sarah Braser. Prince George Co. Cameron.

TITUS
____ m. James Howard.

TIVASH
____ m. Rachel Tabb, b. 1 Feb., 1734, dau. of Thomas. 7W(1)47.

TOAKE (or TUKE)
Dorothy m. John Harvey.

TOBEN
Thomas m. 27 July, 1740/1, Elizabeth Straughan. Northumberland Co. Mar. Record.

TOBERTSON
Tabitha m. John Webster.

TOBIAS

Christopher m. 23 Sept., 1798, Rebecca Edmunds by Rev. Anthony Walke. Princess Anne Co. Ministers' Returns.

TOBY

Mary m. John Nelson.

TOD

John in Cumberland Co. m. 9 March, 1764, Mary Williams in this parish. Douglas Reg., p. 8.

TODD

____ m. bef. 1788, ____ Mallory, dau. of John of Isle of Wight, whose will, dated 1788, prov. 1789, Williamsburg, Va., names "grandchild William Todd."

____ m. Rev. James Moore.

____ m. Jonathan Hide.

____ (____) m. James Madison.

Andrew, physician, m. ____ Holt; rem. to Ky. Louisa, p. 234.

Andrew m. 4 May, 1785, Mary Todd. Louisa Co. Mar. Record.

Ann m. Dazel Teagarden.

Ann m. John Cooke.

Ann m. Richard Todd.

Anne m. Dudley Brown.

Anne m. John Cooke.

Barbara m. (1) ____ Reynolds; m. (2) John Jones.

Bernard, son of Thomas and Elizabeth (Waring), m. prob. Elizabeth Pollard, dau. of William of Hanover Co. 25V307.

Bernard of Charlotte Co. m. Elizabeth Pollard, dau. of Peter Thornton Pollard and ____ (Anderson). Bagley, p. 348.

Catherine m. James Ware, Jr.

Charles, Col., m. 7 May, 1805, Betsy M. (Pierce) Burke, widow of Thomas. 33T119.

Christopher, b. 2 April, 1690; d. 26 March, 1743 (tombstone at Toddsbury), son of Thomas; m. between 20 Jan., 1718, and 13 Sept., 1721, Elizabeth Mason, dau. of Lemuel. Proven by a Deed, 13 Sept., 1721, Princess Anne Co. 25V312. The mother of Christopher Todd was Elizabeth (Bernard). 25V91. Christopher was of Gloucester Co. Elizabeth Mason, b. 1701; d. 1764. Duke, p. 44; Winston, p. 99.

Clarissa "Clary" m. James Collins (2nd wife).

Dolly Payne m. James Madison, Jr.

Dorothy m. Thomas Edmundson.

Elizabeth m. Benjamin Hubbard.

Elizabeth m. (1) Henry Seaton; m. (2) Col. Augustine Moore.

Elizabeth m. James Barbour II (1st wife).

Elizabeth m. (1) George Seaton; m. (2) Augustine Moore. (See above. More searchers say HENRY Seaton.)

Elizabeth m. Rev. Daniel McCalla.

Frances m. Robert North.

Hannah m. Robert Stuart.

Hannah m. Thomas Edmonson.

Hannah m. Elijah Smith.

Harry, son of Thomas, m. bef. 1774, Aphia ____, sis. of wife of Walker Tomlin. She may have been a Meriwether. 35V306-7.

Hayward m. 7 Sept., 1746, Sarah Rosser. OPR. He, b. ca 1725; will

TODD (cont.)

dated 24 June, 1754, Stafford Co., son of Richard and Lucy (Ellitt). 28T22.

Isabella m. John Madison.

James m. 12 March, 1791, Franca Cotton. Prince George Co. Cameron.

James, b. ca 1670; d. 9 May, 1709; m. (1) Elizabeth ___; m. (2) Penelope Scudamore. Winston, p. 98.

Jane "Jenny" m. Thomas Crawford.

Jane m. Capt. John Scott.

John, Col., b. Penna., res. Va.; rem. to Ky. in 1770's; m. ___ Hawkins. Biog. Enc. Ky., p. 183.

John m. 1794, Agnes Todd. Rockbridge Co. Morton, p. 536.

John m. Ann (Taylor) Taliaferro, widow of Robert and dau. of Col. James Taylor. 29V372.

Lucy m. Edward Tabb.

Lucy m. John Martin.

Lucy m. (1) ___ O'Brien; m. (2) John Baylor.

Mallory, Capt., m. Angelina Mallory, sis. of Martha (Mallory) Bridges, whose will, 1789, Williamsburg, Va., mentioned "my sister Angelina Todd," and appointed as exec. "my brother-in-law Capt. Mallory Todd."

Mallory m. 25 April, 1778, Anne Robinson. Sur. Thomas Everard. York Co. Mar. Bond.

Margaret m. John Carter (3rd wife).

Margaret m. James Moore.

Maria m. Waller Bullock.

Mary m. Joshua Wynne.

Mary m. John Bickerton.

Mary m. Andrew Todd.

Mary m. John Murray.

Mary m. John Wyatt.

Owen m. Jane Paxton, dau. of Thomas and (1) Isabella (Quate). Rockbridge Co. Morton, p. 520.

Philip, b. 1681-88; d. bef. 1740, son of Thomas; m. Ann(-e) Day, dau. of Edward of Somerset Co., Md. 29V364, 366; Winston, p. 99.

Richard m. 19 Sept., 1780, Mary Lankford, dau. of Ban. Sur. Joseph Aiken. Pittsylvania Co. Mar. Bond.

Richard m. 31 Dec., 1781, Ann Todd. Louisa, p. 264.

Richard, will dated 1736/7, Stafford Co., prob. son of Samuel; m. bef. 29 Sept., 1734, Lucy Ellitt, sis. of Charles, Jr. Stafford Co. Book M, p. 165; 28T22.

Richard, son of William, m. Elizabeth Richards; res. King and Queen Co., 1765, when a son was born. 25V308; Biog. Enc. Ky., p. 195.

Richard, b. 1748/9; d. May, 1824, Spotsylvania Co., son of Hayward and Sarah (Rosser); m. (1) 1775, King George Co., Elizabeth Davis, dau. of Samuel; m. (2) in Spotsylvania Co., Margaret "Peggy" ___. 28T23. Mar. between Oct., 1774, and Oct., 1775. King George Co. Mar. Record.

Samuel of Rockbridge Co. m. Charity Dabney, dau. of James and Judith (Anderson). Louisa, p. 307.

Sarah m. John Houston.

Sarah m. Elisha Purrington.

Thomas, b. 1765, King and Queen Co.; d. 1826, Frankfort, Ky., son of

TODD (cont.)

Richard; m. (1) Elizabeth Harris; m. (2) Lucy (Payne) Washington. He was a Justice of the U. S. Supreme Court. 25V310; DAR No. 65 862.

Thomas, Capt., of Gloucester Co. and Baltimore Co., Md., b. 1619; d. 1677; m. Anna Gorsuch, dau. of Rev. John. 26V95; Winston, p. 98.

Thomas m. 7 June, 1728, Lettice Thacker. Christ Church, p. 166.

Thomas, b. 1660; d. 16 Jan., 1724/5 (Tombstone at Toddsbury, Gloucester Co.); m. Elizabeth Bernard, dau. of William and Lucy (Higginson). 25V87-8; Winston, pp. 98, 116.

Thomas, b. ca 1710; m. ca 1744, Elizabeth Waring, b. 14 Jan., 1720, dau. of Col. Thomas and Elizabeth (Gouldman) of Essex Co.; res. King and Queen Co. 25V304; Bagley, p. 66; Old King Wm., p. 77.

William m. bef. 11 April, 1693, Elizabeth ____, admx. of Thomas Foster. Proven by Court Record of that date, Essex Co.

William m. 7 Feb., 1774, Jane Shelton, dau. of Crispon. Sur. John Griggory. Pittsylvania Co. Mar. Bond.

William, son of Richard and Elizabeth (____) of Pittsylvania Co., m. 29 Jan., 1770, Phebe Ferguson; rem. 28 March, 1771, from Halifax Co. to Pittsylvania Co. DAR Mag. Query 13033. Halifax Co. Mar. Record.

William, b. 12 Feb., 1727/8, St. Paul's Parish, Stafford Co., son of Richard and Lucy (Ellitt); m. 23 Oct., 1751 or 1752, Margaret Cocklin. OPR; 28T23.

William of King and Queen Co., grandson of Thomas, the immigrant, m. Anna Gorsuch, niece of the poet, Richard Lovelace. 33V193.

William, b. 1681-88; d. 1736-45, son of Thomas and Elizabeth (Bernard); m. ca 1709, Martha Vicaris. 25V91; Winston, p. 99.

TOFEL

John m. 28 Aug., 1799, Nancy Williams. Sur. Francis Foster. Norfolk Co. Mar. Bond.

TOKESY

Joanna m. Robert Higginson.

TOLBART

Margaret m. Thomas Bird.

TOLBEN

Mary m. Eddie Holebrook.

TOLBERT

Sarah m. Robert Wilson.

TOLBUT(-T)

Isaac m. 14 Jan., 1755, Elizabeth Langley. Norfolk Co. Mar. Record.

TOLEMAN

Elizabeth m. Isaac Dunton.

William m. 9 June, 1792, Polly Heath. Northampton Co. Mar. Record.

TOLER

Absalom, son of Joseph and Frances (____), m. Elizabeth Linthicum. Hartford B-8763(2), 18 Feb., 1956. Signed B. T. A.

Adam m. 14 Jan., 1789, Mary Pottie by Rev. Charles Hopkins. Louisa Co. Ministers' Returns. Adam m. Mary (Jerdone) Pottie, b. 1754; d. 1837, widow of George Pottie and dau. of Frances and Sarah (Macon) Jerdone. 62V209; Louisa, pp. 233, 255, 372.

Barnabas, son of William (will prov. 1799, Pittsylvania Co.), m. Sally

TOLER (cont.)
Hackworth. Hartford B-9306(2), 21 July, 1956. Signed B. T. A.
Cornelius m. Catherine Good. Hartford B-9306(2), 21 July, 1956. Signed B. T. A.
Frances m. (1) ___ Oakes; m. (2) William Dixon.
Godfrey m. 27 Sept., 1799, Charity Barnes. Caroline Co. Mar. Record.
Henry m. ca 1787, Cynthia Southall, dau. of Col. Turner and Martha (Vanderwall) Southall. 45V287.
Jesse m. 26 Oct., 1787, Phillis Yates. Halifax Co. Mar. Record.
Jesse m. 27 Oct., 1797, Polly Toler by Rev. William Cooke. Louisa Co. Ministers' Returns.
John m. Sally Arthur. John, son of William (will prov. 1799, Pittsylvania Co.). Hartford B-9306(2), 21 July, 1956. Signed B. T. A.
Joseph, son of William (will prov. 1799, Pittsylvania Co.), m. Frances ___. Hartford B-9306(2), 21 July, 1956. Signed B. T. A.
Lucy m. ___ Bowles.
Mary m. Littleberry Dixon.
Nancy m. Landford Dove.
Nancy m. John Polley.
Nancy (___) m. John Leonard Walton.
Polly m. Jesse Toler.
Samuel m. 29 Nov., 1793, Sally Winston. Sur. Henry Toler. Henrico Co. Mar. Bond.
William of Goochland Co. m. Hannah Brockman, dau. of John and Mary (Collins). Orange III:108.

TOLLE
Sarah m. Alexander Hoseck.

TOLLEY
Isom, b. ca 1754, Va.; m. in Ky. Isabel Whitesides; rem. to St. Clair Co., Ill., thence to Morgan Co. and, in 1823, to Sangamon Co. Sangamon, p. 717.
Nancy m. ___ Stricklin.
William m. 1800, Sally Taylor. Rockbridge Co. Morton, p. 536.

TOLLIVER
William m. 27 Feb., 1770, Mary Hopper, both of this parish. Douglas Reg., p. 11.

TOLMARK
James m. 17 May, 1792, Mary Clark. St. Paul's.

TOLSON
Ann m. Isaac Dunnaway.
Benjamin, Jr., m. 31 Dec., 1751, Hannah Maccothough (?MacCollough). OPR.
Judith m. Simon Stacey.

TOMBS
Emanuel m. 13 Sept., 1791, Elizabeth Genkins. Halifax Co. Mar. Record.
John m. 23 April, 1792, Sally Graves. Sur. Richard Graves. Albemarle Co. Mar. Bond.
Nancey m. John Woodall.
Sally m. Davis Paylor.

TOMER
John m. Constance Wythe, dau. of Thomas. 2W(1)69.

TOMER (cont.)

John m. Hope Booth, d. 19 Jan., 1686, dau. of William and Margaret (___). 2W(1)11.

TOMKIES

Edward of Hanover Co. m. Mary Christian, dau. of Turner and (3) Polly (Dancy). 8W(1)128.

Mary m. Robert Yates.

Mildred (___) m. Humphrey Brooke (2nd wife).

TOMKINS

John m. 19 Feb., 1747, Ann (___) Custis. Northampton Co. Mar. Record.

Mary m. R. Brown.

William m. 10 April, 1795, Sarah Shores (Baptists). Fluvanna, p. 19.

William m. 25 Dec., 1786, Mary Michie. Louisa, p. 260.

TOMLIN

___ m. Susan (Grayson) Wood, widow of Isaac and dau. of William Grayson (d. 1829). Albemarle, p. 214.

Arthur m. 9 Feb., 1796, Polly Sykes. Isle of Wight Co. Mar. Record.

Elizabeth (___) m. William Daingerfield.

Jane m. Abram Litle.

John m. 19 Dec., 1797, Charlotte Holland. Isle of Wight Co. Mar. Record.

Martha m. Capt. George Taylor.

Martha m. Francis Gouldman.

Martha m. (1) Edward Gouldman; m. (2) William Winston.

Robert m. bef. 1669, Rebekah Fox, dau. of David, whose will of that date, Lancaster Co., proves it. See Court Record, 25 March, 1693, Essex Co., also.

Robert, d. 1689, son of Robert, the elder; m. Hester (or Esther) Walker, dau. of Col. John. 5V162.

Sally m. Elijah Brockman.

Sarah m. Levi Westray.

Walker m. ___ ___, a sis. of Aphia ___, who m. Harry Todd. 25V 306-7.

Walter m. Richmond Co. Sarah Fauntleroy. Sur. LeRoy Peachy. (Date illegible.) 5W(1)19.

William, d. 1708; m. bef. 29 Dec., 1704, Elizabeth Bathurst, sis. of Lawrence, whose will of that date, Essex Co., proves it. She was dau. of Lancelot Bathurst (will prov. 11 Feb., 1705/6, Essex Co.). She m. (2) bef. Feb., 1709/10, William Daingerfield, on which date they administered the estate of William Tomlin, dec'd. 11T173; 8W (1)99; Jones Gene., p. 149.

William, son of Robert of Old Rappahannock Co., m. Anne (Robinson) Hazlewood; res. Essex Co. 5V161.

TOMLINSON

Amye (or Amey) m. John Williams.

Catharine m. Robert Thompson.

Elizabeth m. ___ Cook.

George m. 1785, Elizabeth White. Orange Co. Mar. Record.

John m. 1780, Mildred White. Orange Co. Mar. Record.

Martha m. Benjamin Edmondson.

Mary m. ___ Collier.

TOMLINSON (cont.)

Mary m. Thomas Wooten.
Mary m. John Wyatt.
Phoebe m. Charles Cross.
Sally m. Frederick Moss.
Sarah m. Overstreet Wyatt.
Sary m. ____ Wiatt.
William m. 26 Nov., 1784, Anne Redd. Norfolk Co. Mar. Record.

TOMPKINS

____ m. bef. Nov., 1785, Ann Dickerson, dau. of Griffeth, whose will of that date, Louisa Co., proves it.
Agnes m. Nicholas Hamner.
Bailey, b. 1778; d. 29 March, 1848; m. Frances Redd, b. 1781; d. 25 March, 1868, dau. of William and Franky (Tyler). 14T58.
Bennett, b. 5 June, 1769; d. 13 Aug., 1813, son of Robert and Ann (Dickenson); m. Matilda Redd, b. 16 May, 1773; d. 8 June, 1812. 10W(2)36.
Bennett m. 24 Dec., 1793, Elizabeth Redd, b. 16 May, 1773; d. 18 June, 1812, dau. of William and Elizabeth (Keeling). 14T58.
Catharine m. James Minor.
Catharine m. Robert Massenburgh.
Catherine m. William Temple.
Catherine m. Richard Tompkins.
Christopher m. Ann Fleet. A son, b. 27 Sept., 1781. Old King Wm., p. 124.
Christopher, Lieut., d. 13 March, 1780 or 1789 (indistinct on Pension Record); m. Martha (____) Dameron, widow of Ommafores. Dameron 51-g.
Christopher, b. Oct., 1705, Gloucester Co.; d. 16 March, 1778/9, Caroline Co.; m. Joyce Reade, b. 6 March, 1701, Gwynne's Island; d. 8 Aug., 1771, Caroline Co., prob. dau. of Thomas and Lucy (Gwynne) of Gloucester Co. 32V290; 10W(2)25-6, 222-3; 13W(2)224; Louisa, p. 392.
Custis m. William W. Wilson.
Frank, son of Christopher (1705-1779) and Joyce (Reade), m. Frances Quarles. 10W(2)27. She, dau. of Roger (b. 1720) and Mary (Goodloe) of Caroline Co. 38V361-2; 10W(2)232.
Giles m. 24 May, 1736, Valentine Chiles. Spotsylvania Co. Mar. Record. 19T438.
Hannah m. John Taylor (1st wife).
Humphrey, d. 1679; m. 22 Dec., 1649, Hannah (Bennett) Turner, widow of Abraham and dau. of Samuel Bennett of Elizabeth City Co. 10W(2)25.
John, b. 19 June, 1718; d. 21 Aug., 1757; m. 25 Feb., 1747, by Rev. Barlow, to Anne Custis. Family Bible. 34V371.
Martha m. William Staples.
Martha m. Edward Armistead.
Mary m. William Sandefur.
Mary Overton m. Lancelot Minor.
Richard, b. 1765; d. 25 Dec., 1832, son of William and Ann (Cosby); m. his cousin, Catherine R. Tompkins, b. 1771; d. 1815, dau. of Robert and Ann (Dickinson). 10W(2)38; Duke, pp. 302-3.
Richard m. ____ Cosby, dau. of David and Mary Garland (Overton). Caroline, p. 448.
Robert Reade, b. ca 1730; d. 7 Jan., 1795, son of Christopher and Joyce

TOMPKINS (cont.)

(Reade); m. 1760, Ann Dickinson, b. ca 1741; d. 1819, dau. of Griffith and Ann (Cosby) of Louisa Co. 10W(2)27, 28; Duke, p. 327; Louisa, p. 310.

Samuel m. bef. 1680, ___ (___) Clark, widow of John. Proven by Deed of that date, York Co. 13T38.

William, b. 30 Dec., 1765; d. 1 March, 1834, son of Benjamin and Elizabeth (Goodloe); m. Sarah Shores, dau. of Thomas. 10W(2)26.

William, b. 1736; d. 24 Feb., 1772, Caroline Co., son of Christopher and Joyce (Reade); m. Ann "Nancy" Overton Cosby, b. ca 1745-8; d. 24 Feb., 1772, dau. of David and Mary Garland (Overton). 10W(2)27, 28; Boddie-HSF V:30; Duke, p. 302; Louisa, p. 392.

TOMPLIN

Molley m. John Smith.

TOMS

Edward m. 13 July, 1779, Elizabeth Ford. Amelia Co. Mar. Record.

TOMSON

John m. 13 April, 1727, Catherine Twyman. Christ Church, p. 163.

John m. 9 Jan., 1727, Susanna George. Christ Church, p. 165.

Joseph m. 15 June, 1787, Susannah Garrot. Sur. Stephen Garrot, father of Susannah. Buckingham Co. Mar. Bond.

Margaret m. David Mordah.

Mary m. Henry Knight.

William m. 9 May, 1723, Mary Symes. Christ Church, p. 164.

William m. 24 April, 1718, Mary Sibley. Christ Church, p. 162.

TONEY

Anne m. William Spurlock.

Betsey m. Thomas Moss.

William m. 22 Aug., 1782, Leah Gatlift by Rev. John Alderson, Jr. Rockingham Co. or Greenbrier Co. Ministers' Returns.

TONGATE

Jeremiah m. 3 March, 1751, Elizabeth Waus (or Wans). Reference missing.

TONSTALL

Edward m. bef. 21 Nov., 1636, Martha (___) Greenhill, widow of Nicholas. 5V459.

TONY

Agnes m. John Gill.

Alex. m. 16 March, 1777, Ann Ashline, both of this parish. Douglas Reg., p. 18.

Ann m. Anselm Alford.

Charles m. 1 Feb., 1761, Ann Steventon, both in this parish. Douglas Reg., p. 5.

Mary m. Charles Rice.

Mary m. Richard Clark.

Nannie m. Abraham Stratton.

Sherwood m. 7 Feb., 1765, Lory England, both of this parish. Douglas Reg., p. 8.

Tabitha m. William Depriest.

TOOK(-E)

Dorcas (___) m. John Lundy.

Dorothy m. John Harvey.

TOOK (cont.)

Joan m. John Scott.
Mary m. Edmond Bellson.
Mary m. John Collings.

TOOKER

____ (____) m. Nicholas Wilson (1st wife).

TOOL

John m. 23 Dec., 1788, Sarah (____) Moran. Sur. William Moran. Albemarle Co. Mar. Bond.
Judith m. Thomas Daniel.
Mary m. Joseph Wingfield.
Richard m. 20 Aug., 1792, Ann Power, spinster. Sur. Richard C. Walter. York Co. Mar. Bond.
Sarah m. Richard Hernden.

TOOLE

Sarah m. Archer Davise.

TOOLEY

Ann m. John Martin.
Elizabeth m. James Gentry.
Harbert m. Feb., 1786, Prudence Butt by Rev. Joshua Lawrence, Baptist. Princess Anne Co. Ministers' Returns.
Judith m. Archelaus Gilliam.
Judith m. John Gabbert.
Mary m. John Gilliam.
Nancy m. Thomas Eubanks.
Sarah m. Edmund New.
Sarah m. Bartlett Miller.

TOOLS

Nancy m. Michael Reynolds.

TOOLY

James in Buckingham Co. m. 20 Dec., 1767, Elizabeth Maddox in this parish. Douglas Reg., p. 10.

TOOMBES

Sally m. Davis Baylor.

TOOMBS

Ann Dawson m. John Spearman.
Dicey m. Obediah Owen.
Elizabeth m. Thomas Fears.
Euland m. Asa Ireland.
Nancy m. William Roberts.

TOONE

James m. Anne (____) Dew, widow of Andrew (d. bef. 1661, Old Rappahannock Co.). She m. (3) Dominick Rice. Anne was mother of Andrew and Thomas Dew. Proven by will of James Toone, dated 1676, and of his widow, dated 1677, both in Old Rappahannock Co. 5V287.
James m. 9 April, 1770, Milly Daniel, dau. of William. Sur. Will Taylor. Mecklenburg Co. Mar. Bond.
Nancy m. John Fentress.
Polly m. Freeman Walker.
Thomas m. 22 June, 1797, Susanna McClenahan by Rev. Anthony Walke. Princess Anne Co. Ministers' Returns.

TOOT

Adam m. 6 March, 1796, Sally King. Halifax Co. Mar. Record.

TOPPING

Peggy m. Stephen Bonwell.

Sarah (____) m. (2) John Anderson; m. (3) Peter (or Jeter) Vines.

TORBET

John m. Mary Paxton, dau. of Thomas and (2) Martha (White). Rockbridge Co. Morton, p. 521.

TORIAN

Andrew m. 29 March, 1785, Anne Blackwell. Halifax Co. Mar. Record.

Andrew m. 1 Feb., 1773, S. Comer. Halifax Co. Mar. Record.

George m. 4 Sept., 1799, Nancy Hall. Halifax Co. Mar. Record.

George m. 6 Dec., 1794, Sarah Ragland. Halifax Co. Mar. Record.

Peter m. 1 Dec., 1789, Susanna Palmer. Halifax Co. Mar. Record.

Polly m. Thomas Torian.

Salley m. John McCarty.

Sally m. Frederick Botts.

Thomas m. 17 Jan., 1793, Polly Torian. Halifax Co. Mar. Record.

TORKESY

Joanna m. Robert Higginson.

TORKSEY

Phillip m. 31 July, 1683, Mary French. Christ Church, p. 22.

TORNES

Mary m. Eli Peterson.

TOSELEY

Elizabeth m. Thomas Clarke.

TOSH

James m. 1787, Anne Broadwater. Botetourt Co. Kegley, p. 540.

Mary m. Peter Evans.

Nancy m. Stephen Ferrill.

TOTTY

Abner m. 21 Nov., 1793, Mary White, dau. of Sarah Matthews. Sur. William Totty. Charlotte Co. Mar. Bond.

Archelous (?Archibald) m. 5 Dec., 1791, Liddy Stow, dau. of Susanna. Sur. James St. John. Charlotte Co. Mar. Bond.

Benjamin m. 26 March, 1788, Mary Blankenship. Chesterfield Co. Cameron.

Margaret m. Drury Disleman.

Robert m. 10 Jan., 1793, Sandal Andrews. Chesterfield Co. Cameron.

Susanna m. Terry Tharp.

Thomas m. 23 Aug., 1770, Mary Mann. Sur. Burwell Vaiden. Charlotte Co. Mar. Bond.

TOUL

Mary m. George Stone.

William m. 15 Oct., 1722, Mary Porter. St. Paul's.

TOULSON

Molly m. Shapleigh Waddy.

TOUNSLEY

Mary m. James Messeck.

TOURMAN

Frances m. Jo. Golson.

Thomas m. 20 Oct., 1778, Elizabeth Mitchell in Goochland Co. Douglas

TOURMAN (cont.)
Reg., p. 18. She was widow of Thomas Mitchell. 4W(1)197.

TOUSLER
Mary Ann m. John Sutler.

TOUSLEY
Frances m. Joel Yager.

TOWELL
Margaret m. Jacob Stover.
Mark m. bef. 1794, Ann Hunton, dau. of Thomas, whose will of that date, Lancaster Co., proves it.

TOWLER
Edith m. Cornelius Beasley.
Mary m. William Whitefield.
Sally m. William Rowe.

TOWLES
____ m. Capt. Philip Slaughter (2nd wife).
Ann m. Russell Hill.
Ann m. Adam Snyder.
Ann m. John Terrill.
Catherine m. Abraham Eddins.
Elizabeth m. Capt. Philip Slaughter.
Elizabeth m. Hugh Marston.
Frances m. Richard Vawter.
Frances m. Edmund Willis.
Henry m. Lucy James, b. after 1763, dau. of John and Anne (Strother). 11T119.
Henry, b. 1738; d. 1799, son of Stockley; m. 1760, Judith Haynes. NNHist.Mag. 5:1:441.
Henry, Maj., d. 10 Jan., 1829, son of Joseph and Ann (Terrill); m. 27 July, 1776, Elizabeth Wetherall; widow received Rev. War pension. 13T28; NNHist.Mag. 5:1:446.
Henry, aged 32 in 1684; m. 1668, Ann Stockeley; res. Accomac Co. NN Hist.Mag. 5:1:440; Orange III:94.
Henry, b. 1670; m. bef. 1711, Hannah Therriott (or Therriat), dau. of William. Deed, 1711, Lancaster Co. 35V215; NNHist.Mag. 5:1:441.
Jane m. James Sims.
Jane m. Isaac Medley.
John, b. 5 April, 1712, son of Stokeley and Ann (Vallott); m. 9 Oct., 1735, Margaret Daniel, dau. of James and Margaret (Vivion). 3T30; 12T217; 13T25; Christ Church, p. 169; NNHist.Mag. 5:1:447.
Joseph, b. 23 Feb., 1728, son of Stokeley and Ann (Vallott); d. bef. 13 Feb., 1786; will dated 1770; m. Sarah Terrell, dau. of Robert. (Given as Ann Terrell by one compiler.) NNHist.Mag. 5:1:441.
Joseph, Jr., Capt. in Rev. War, son of Joseph and Sarah (Terrill), m. 15 Feb., 1786, Mary Wetherall. 13T28. He, son of Stockley and Jane (____); rem. to Green Co., Ky. NNHist.Mag. 5:1:446.
Lucy m. Robert Garnett.
Mary m. Richard Sims.
Mary m. Benjamin Spicer.
Mary m. John Clark.
Mary m. Thomas Sparks.
Molly m. Archibald Dick, Jr.

TOWLES (cont.)

Oliver, Col., of Campbell Co., m. 1794, Agatha Lewis, b. 1774; d. 1843, dau. of Col. William and Anne (Montgomery). Peyton, p. 291.

Oliver, Lieut. Col., b. 1 Sept., 1736; d. 1825, Lynchburg, Va., son of John and Margaret (Daniel) of Middlesex Co.; served in Rev. War; m. bef. 1769, Mary (Chew) Smith, widow of John of "Rickahock" and dau. of Larkin Chew of Spotsylvania Co. 3T30; 13T30; DAR No. 79 246.

Sarah m. William Rowe.

Sarah m. Charles Leland.

Stockeley (many spellings), b. 1740; m. 1773, Elizabeth Porteus Downman, b. 21 Feb., 1752, dau. of Robert and Elizabeth (Porteus). 16T 189; NNHist.Mag. 5:1:446.

Stockeley, b. 1695, Accomac Co.; d. 1757, Culpeper Co., son of Henry and Ann (Stockeley); m. (1) 21 Oct., 1708, Ann Vallott, in Christ Church, Middlesex Co., b. 31 July, 1693, dau. of Claude and Ann (Jenkinson); m. (2) Jane (Sparks) Wharton, widow of Thomas and dau. of John Sparks. 13T24; 20T250; NNHist.Mag. 5:1:445; Orange III:94.

Stockley, b. 1711; d. 1765; m. 26 July, 1736, Lancaster Co., Elizabeth Martin. NNHist.Mag. 5:1:441.

Thomas, served in Rev. War, m. Mary Smith, dau. of John and Mary (Chew). 3T30.

Thomas m. Keturah George. NNHist.Mag. 5:1:447.

TOWNES

____ m. Ann Godwin, dau. of Jonathan and Anne (____). Boddie-Isle, p. 466.

____ believed m. bef. Jan., 1774, Obedience Allen, dau. of Samuel, whose will of that date, Goochland Co., names "daughter Obedience Townes."

Alena m. John Dickie.

Ann "Nancy" m. Charles Jones.

Elizabeth m. Blackman Ligon.

Elizabeth F. m. John T. Leigh.

Halcut, b. Amelia Co.; d. age 35, son of William; m. (1) ____ Coleman. 21V195.

Joel m. 2 March, 1778, Franky Gains, dau. of Richard who was surety. Charlotte Co. Mar. Bond.

Joel m. 29 July, 1780, Mary McPearson. Halifax Co. Mar. Record.

Joseph m. 16 Jan., 1800, Susanna Cralle. Lunenburg Co. Cameron.

Lucretia m. Frank Robinson.

Lucretia m. James Akin.

Molly m. William Pride.

N. m. Daniel Dismukes.

Priscilla Allen m. Zachariah Greenhill Leigh.

Rebecca Clark m. William Moseley.

Richard m. 23 Jan., 1753, Elizabeth Burk. Sur. Henry Thacker. Middlesex Co. Mar. Bond.

Salley m. Spencer Griffin.

Samuel Allen, son of William, m. 1799, Rachel Stokes of Fredericksburg, Va.; rem. to Greenville, So. Car. 21V196.

Stephen m. 2 Oct., 1777, Lucy Watkins. Halifax Co. Mar. Record.

Thomas m. 14 Aug., 1780, Sally Wade. Halifax Co. Mar. Record.

William, d. 1774, aged 63, son of James of Henrico Co.; m. Obedience

TOWNES (cont.)

Allen, dau. of Samuel; res. Amelia Co. 21V195.

TOWNLEY

___ m. bef. 8 March, 1777, Sarah Mann, dau. of Joseph, whose will of that date, Essex Co., proves it.

Alice m. John Grymes.

Elizabeth m. Richard Moody.

Lawrence, Col., m. Sarah Warner, dau. of Col. Augustine, Sr. (d. 1674, age 63), and Mary (___). 22T262; 23V395; 27V185; Old King Wm., p. 74. Sarah, dau. of Augustine (1610-1674) of Elizabeth City Co. 13 Ky. Reg. 80.

Mann m. Ann Clarkson, dau. of Peter and Ann (___) (d. 1822, age 87). Albemarle, p. 166.

Robert m. 29 Dec., 1781, Jane Anderson of King and Queen Co. Christ Church, p. 203.

TOWNS

Levinia m. David Abernathy.

Lucretia m. (1) ___ Robertson; m. (2) Tscharner DeGraffenreid (4th wife).

Mazy m. Zachariah Branscomb.

TOWNSEN

Joshua m. 19 June, 1784, Elizabeth Caperton by Rev. John Alderson, Jr. Rockingham Co. or Greenbrier Co. Ministers' Returns.

TOWNSEND

Daniel m. 13 Dec., 1799, Jencey Townsend by Rev. Matthew Dance. Lunenburg Co. Ministers' Returns.

Elizabeth m. Jonathan White.

Frances m. Rice Hooe (2nd wife).

Frances m. William Sandeford.

Jencey m. Daniel Townsend.

Jerusha m. James Alexander.

Light m. 1 June, 1796, Betsy Duhroon. Shelby Co., Ky. Mar. Record.

Littleton m. Sally (Polk) Lurton, b. 13 March, 1766, widow of Jacob Lurton and dau. of Capt. William and Sabra (Bradford) Polk. DAR Answer 1296.

Mary m. John Washington.

Richard m. 4 Dec., 1783, Fanny Jordan by Rev. James Shelburn, Baptist. Lunenburg Co. Ministers' Returns.

William m. 18 Jan., 1794, Amey Booth by Rev. John Neblett, Methodist. Lunenburg Co. Ministers' Returns.

TOWNSHEND

Frances m. (1) Francis Dade, Jr.; m. (2) Capt. John Withers; m. (3) Col. Rice Hooe.

Frances m. Col. Griffin Stith.

Frances m. Thornton Washington (2nd wife).

Griffin m. George Pickerin, Jr.

Mary m. Capt. John Washington.

Robert, Col., b. 1640; d. 1675; m. Mary Langhorne, d. 1685. 16T160.

TOYE

Humphrey Ann Frances m. Henry Whiting.

TRABUE

___ m. ___ Dupuy, dau. of Bartholomew and Susanne (La Villon). Dam-

TRABUE (cont.)

eron Pt. II, p. 27a.

____ m. Olimp Dupuy, dau. of John James Dupuy (will prov. 1775, Cumberland Co.). Huguenot 6:163-7.

Anthony m. Magdalene Flournoy. 9W(1)275.

Anthony, Jr., b. ca 1702, son of Anthony and Magdelaine (Flournoy); m. ____ Vermoil, dau. of Moyse. 17 Ky. Reg. 50:49.

Antoine, Gent., m. 1699, in Holland, Magdalene Flournoy, dau. of Jacob and Martha (Morel). She m. (2) Pierre Chastain. Huguenot 7:228.

Caroline m. George Smith.

Daniel m. 21 Aug., 1786, Elizabeth Farrar. Sur. Will Farrar. Goochland Co. Mar. Bond.

Daniel, Capt. in Rev. War, b. 31 March, 1760; d. 1840, son of John James Trabue and Olympe (Dupuy); m. Mary Haskins, dau. of Col. Robert and Elizabeth (Hill); rem. to Woodford Co., Ky. 17 Ky. Reg. 50:55; Woodford Co., p. 40.

Edward, Col. in Rev. War, b. 1762, Chesterfield Co.; d. 6 July, 1814, Woodford Co., Ky., son of John James Trabue and Olympe (Dupuy); m. (1) ca 1786, Martha Haskins, d. ca 1794, dau. of Col. Robert and Elizabeth (Hill); m. (2) 1797, Jane E. Clay, b. 1 Jan., 1776; d. 8 June, 1845, dau. of Rev. Eleazer of Chesterfield Co. 17 Ky. Reg. 50:56-7; Woodford Co., p. 40.

Elizabeth m. Fenleson R. Willson.

James, b. 29 Jan., 1745, Chesterfield Co.; d. 23 Dec., 1803, son of John James Trabue and Olympe (Dupuy); served in Rev. War; m. 1782, Jane E. Porter, b. ca 1756, Va.; d. 17 March, 1833, Ky., dau. of Robert. 17 Ky. Reg. 50:52.

Jane m. Joseph Minter.

John, Col. in Rev. War, b. 17 March, 1754; d. 1788, at Logan's Fort, Ky., son of John James Trabue and Olympe (duPuy); m. Margaret Pierce. 17 Ky. Reg. 50:53.

John James, b. 1722, Chesterfield Co.; d. 1803, Ky.; m. 1744, Olympe duPuy, b. 12 Nov., 1729; d. 1822, Woodford Co., Ky., dau. of John James duPuy and Susanna (Levilain). DAR No. 68 065; DAR No. 79 499; 17 Ky. Reg. 50:49, 51. (The last reference states that the will of John James Trabue was probated, 1777, in Cumberland Co.)

Judith m. John Major, Jr.

Judith m. Stephen Watkins.

Magdalene m. Peter Guerrant.

Magdelene m. Edward Clay.

Martha "Patsy" m. Josiah Woolridge.

Mary m. Lewis Sublett (1st wife).

Stephen, b. 2 Feb., 1756; d. 24 Nov., 1833, son of John James Trabue and Olympe (Dupuy); m. 24 July, 1788, Jane Haskins, b. 12 Oct., 1767; d. 15 Sept., 1833, dau. of Col. Robert and Elizabeth (Hill). 4V452; 17 Ky. Reg. 50:57.

Susanna m. Thomas Major.

TRACEY

Daniel m. 22 May, 1799, Fanny Butt. Sur. John Randall. Norfolk Co. Mar. Bond.

Joyce m. Capt. Nathaniel Powell.

TRACY

____ m. Capt. Nathaniel Powell.

John m. 10 Dec., 1800, Catharine Fought. Shelby Co., Ky. Mar. Record

John of Washington Parish m. 7 Aug., 1740, Anne Caplee. St. Paul's.

Timothy m. 19 Feb., 1692/3, Rebecca Goodrich. Christ Church, p. 53.

TRAINHAM

Sam. m. 25 March, 1782, Mary Ogilsvy, both of Orange. Douglas Reg., p. 22.

TRAMMEL

John m. 17 April, 1799, Ellen Parris. Shelby Co., Ky. Mar. Record.

Nelley m. William Yates.

TRANUM

Clemens m. 7 Jan., 1787, Alizabeath Melone by Rev. Thomas Crymes, Baptist. Lunenburg Co. Ministers' Returns.

TRANT

George Richards m. Mary E. Walker, dau. of Thomas and Fannie (Hill). Old King Wm., p. 79.

TRAUHAM (?TRANHAM)

John m. 14 June, 1796, Mary Daniel. Caroline Co. Mar. Record.

TRAVELLER

Alice (____) m. (2) William Burdett.

TRAVERS

____ m. bef. 1711, Hannah Ball, dau. of Joseph, whose will of that date, Lancaster Co., proves it.

Elizabeth m. (1) Col. John Carter, Jr.; m. (2) Col. Christopher Wormeley.

Elizabeth m. John Cooke.

Elizabeth m. John Cave.

Elizabeth m. Lewis Elzey.

Letitia m. James Grigsby.

Million m. Joseph Waugh.

Million m. William Downman.

Raleigh m. Hannah Ball, dau. of Col. Joseph and 1st wife; res. Stafford Co. She m. (2) Simon Pearson. 20T85; 21V376; NNHM 5:1:429.

Rebecca m. (1) John Tavener; m. (2) Capt. Charles Colston.

Winifred m. Robert Wormeley Carter.

Winifred m. Daniel Hornby (or Hornsby).

TRAVERSE

Eliza (____) m. William Smelt.

Elizabeth m. William Smelt.

Sarah m. Peter Daniel.

TRAVILION

Edmond m. 27 Jan., 1794, Susannah Carr. Sur. Gideon Carr. Albemarle Co. Mar. Bond.

TRAVILLIAN

Thomas m. 11 Dec., 1787, Mary Carr, spinster. Sur. Mekins Carr. Albemarle Co. Mar. Bond.

TRAVIS

Betsy m. William I. Cooke.

Catherine m. Jesse Cole.

Champion m. 28 Nov., 1772, Elizabeth Boush. Norfolk Co. Mar. Bond. She, dau. of Capt. Francis of Norfolk Co. 5W(1)16.

TRAVIS (cont.)

Edward m. bef. 1637, ____ Johnson, dau. of John; res. 1624, Jamestown, Va. She m. (2) John Brodnax. 5W(1)16.

Edward of Jamestown, son of Edward Champion and Susannah (Hutchings), m. (1) Betsy Taite, d. 1773. Mar. announced in The Virginia Gazette, 26 March, 1772. He m. (2) Clara Waller, dau. of Benjamin. 5W(1)16; 9W(1)239.

Edward Champion, Col., member of the Convention of 1775 and 1776 for Jamestown, Va.; will prov. 20 Sept., 1779, York Co.; m. Susannah Hutchings, d. 28 Oct., 1761, age 32, dau. of Col. Joseph of Norfolk. 5W(1)16. She, dau. of Col. John and Amy (Godfrey). 15T380. He m. Susanna Hutchings Armistead. 1W(1)27.

James m. 10 Nov., 1792, Sally Dunton. Northampton Co. Mar. Record.

John m. 28 June, 1722, Margaret Hubert. St. Paul's.

Joseph H., son of Edward and (2) Clara (Waller), m. Patsy (Waller) Williams, widow of Montague Williams and dau. of John Waller of "Enfield." 5W(1)16.

Samuel, son of Col. Champion and Elizabeth (Boush), m. Elizabeth Bright of Hampton, Va. 5W(1)16.

Susan m. Edmund Ruffin.

Susanna m. ____ Armistead.

TRAWELL

Jane m. Phillip Johnson.

TRAYLOR

Buckner m. 12 Jan., 1789, Mary Handy. Chesterfield Co. Cameron.

Edward m. ca 1663, Martha Randolph. 43V261.

Michael m. William Combs.

Polly m. William Sands.

Thomas m. 13 July, 1786, Phebe Ferguson. Halifax Co. Mar. Record.

TRAYNHAM

Benjamin m. 14 Nov., 1791, Betsey Palmer. Halifax Co. Mar. Record.

Dorathea m. William Williams.

John m. 14 June, 1796, Mary Daniel. Caroline Co. Mar. Record.

John m. 11 Dec., 1799, Fanny Richeson. Caroline Co. Mar. Record.

TRAYNUM

Reuben m. 2 Jan., 1783, Judith Overton by Rev. Thomas Johnston. Charlotte Co. Ministers' Returns.

William m. 10 May, 1793, Milly Redmon. Sur. Matthews Williams. Charlotte Co. Mar. Bond.

TREACLE

Dorothy m. John Driver.

TREAT

Katherine m. Rev. William Thompson.

TREE

Mary m. John Wyatt.

TREGANY

Henry of Philadelphia, Penna., m. bef. 1712, Elizabeth Wilson, dau. of William, whose will of that date, Elizabeth City Co., proves it.

TREGAR

Anne m. William Crismund.

TREMBLE

May m. John Wyatt.

TRENAR

Mary m. Joseph Cooke.

TRENCHER

Isaac m. 6 Dec., 1785, Margaret McColmick by Rev. John Brown. Augusta Co. Ministers' Returns.

TRENT

____ believed m. bef. 1801, Lucy Daniel, dau. of Peter, whose will, prov. 1801, Campbell Co., names "daughter Lucy Trent."

Alexander, Jr., m. 27 Sept., 1750, Frances Scott, spinster. Sur. John Dobie. Cumberland Co. Mar. Bond. Douglas Reg., pp. 27-32.

Alexander m. 1 Jan., 1753, Elizabeth Woodson, dau. of Stephen, dec'd. Consent given by Charles Bates, guardian. Sur. John Woodson. Goochland Co. Mar. Bond. He, b. 3 March, 1729; d. 27 Feb., 1793; res. Cumberland Co. 39V163.

Anne m. John James.

Betsy m. Samuel Baker.

Elizabeth m. John Archer.

Frances m. William Gay (1st wife).

Henry m. Edith Harris, dau. of Thomas. She m. (2) ____ Osborne; m. (3) ____ Patrick. 4V249.

Henry m. Jan., 1797, Nancy Reynolds by Charles Cobbs. Campbell Co. Mar. Record.

Henry, b. 1642; will prov. 5 April, 1701, Henrico Co.; m. Elizabeth Sherman, b. 1656, dau. of Henry, whose will, prov. 1 Oct., 1695, proves the marriage.

John, Col. of Cumberland Co., m. Elizabeth Montgomery Lewis, b. 1777; d. 1837, dau. of Col. William and Anne (Montgomery). Peyton, p. 291. He, son of Alexander and Elizabeth (Woodson). 39V164.

Obedience (____) m. ____ Turpin.

Patty m. Dudley Callaway.

Peterfield mar. contract, 2 March, 1770, Chesterfield Co., with Angelica Wilkinson, dau. of Edward and ____ (Epes). 25W(1)112.

Priscilla m. John Wilson.

Priscilla m. Josiah Daniel.

Stephen Woodson, b. 20 Jan., 1769; d. 1844, son of Alexander and Elizabeth (Woodson); m. Elizabeth Bassett Coupland; res. "Auburn," Cumberland Co. 34V91; 39V164.

TREVELIEN

Elizabeth m. Stephen Jones.

TREVETHAN

Mary m. Thomas Thorowgood.

William m. Dinah ____, extrx. of Capt. Robert Thoroughgood, dec'd., and admr. of estate of Lemuel Wilson, dec'd., her 2nd husband. Princess Anne Co. Court Record, 12 Jan., 1713. 26V415.

TREZEVANT

John Timothy, physician, b. 1758, Charleston, So. Car.; d. 1818, Va.; m. (2) Estelle ____. DAR No. 51 709.

TRIBBEY-WILLIAMS

Margaret m. Capt. James McIlhany.

TRIBBLE

____ m. bef. 1721, Dinah Meadors, dau. of John, whose will, 1721, Essex Co., proves it.

TRIBBLE (cont.)

Andrew, minister, b. 1741; d. 1822, son of George and Betsy (Clark); m. Sally Burruss, b. 1753; d. 1830, dau. of Thomas and Frances (Tandy). 14T119; Orange III:132.

Elizabeth m. Richard Johnston.

George m. 5 Jan., 1792, Mary Owen. Halifax Co. Mar. Record.

George, Sr., served in Rev. War; m. Betty (or Betsy) Clark, dau. of Jonathan and Elizabeth (Wilson). 14T119; Orange III:132.

Peter m. 4 May, 1793, Mary Pruitt. Halifax Co. Mar. Record.

Prissila m. Joseph Owen.

TRIBLE

Jany m. Abraham Martin.

Mary m. Lewis Jordan.

TRIBUE

David m. 7 May, 1760, Mary Sallee, both in Maniken Town. Douglas Reg., p. 5.

TRICE

Anderson m. Martha Sandidge. Louisa, p. 267.

Edward m. 13 Feb., 1783, Ann Jeffries of King and Queen Co. Christ Church, p. 203.

Frances m. John Sargent.

James m. 22 Feb., 1787, Polly Smith, both of Louisa. Douglas Reg., p. 24.

John m. 9 Sept., 1783, Patty Smith. Sur. Nathan Smith. Louisa Co. Mar. Bond.

Joseph m. 21 Aug., 1794, Elizabeth Anderson. Louisa, p. 262.

Martha m. Byrd Rogers (2nd wife).

Mary m. Byrd Rogers (1st wife).

William m. 16 Aug., 1790, Ann Nelson. Louisa Co. Mar. Record.

William in Amherst m. 13 Dec., 1768, Molly Rice in this parish. Douglas Reg., p. 11.

William m. 9 May, 1786, Mary Watkins. Louisa Co. Mar. Record.

William of Amherst Co. m. Molly (____) Green, widow of Forester Green, Jr., dec'd. Sur. Charles Rice. Goochland Co. Mar. Bond. 7W(1)104.

TRIDGE

Alice m. Thomas Kidd.

TRIGG

____ m. Preston Breckenridge. 27V158.

Abraham, son of Daniel, m. (1) 14 Dec., 1705, Elizabeth Queen; m. (2) 11 Jan., 1710, Judith Clarke. Christ Church, pp. 80, 82; 27V164.

Abraham from Cornwall, England, 1725, to Spotsylvania Co., m. Dosia Johnson. DAR Query, Dec., 1948.

Alanson m. 1796, Lucy Quarles, dau. of John (d. 1789) and Sarah (Winston) (b. 1748). 38V361-2.

Alice m. Thomas Kidd.

Daniel m. 15 Nov., 1799, Sally Abbott. Spotsylvania Co. Mar. Record.

Daniel, Capt. in Rev. War, b. 14 Aug., 1749, son of William; m. (1) Ann Smith; m. (2) Lucy Booker. 27V324.

Isabella m. Charles Lewis.

James m. Elizabeth Montague (1st husband). 27V324.

John m. 30 March, 1797, Susanna Collier of Gloucester. Christ Church, p. 302.

TRIGG (cont.)

Judith m. Henry Burk.

Mary m. Thomas Hatfield.

Mary m. Roger Quarles.

Nancy m. (1) Thomas Foster; m. (2) James Laughlin.

Nancy m. Arthur Moseley.

Sarah m. Henry Bassett.

Stephen m. 1795, Botetourt Co., Polly Hardy. Kegley, p. 482.

Stephen, killed at Battle of Blue Lick, 19 Aug., 1782; m. Mary Christian, dau. of Israel (in Augusta Co. by 1740) and Elizabeth (Stark). 27V324; Waddell, p. 124.

Stephen, b. 1771, Bedford Co.; d. 1834, son of Col. John and Dinah (Ayers); m. 1790, Elizabeth Clark, b. 1772; d. 1822, dau. of Robert and Susannah (Henderson). DAR No. 79 960.

William, Col., son of Abraham and Dosia (Johnson), m. bef. 1758, Jane Smith. A dau., b. 1758, Berkeley Co. DAR Query, Dec., 1948.

William m. 1788, Botetourt Co., Susanna Smith, dau. of or consent of Frances Smith. Kegley, p. 481.

TRIGGER

Mary m. William King.

William m. 1 Feb., 1786, Sarah Levy. St. Paul's.

TRIMBLE

____ m. bef. 1803, Margaret Delaney, dau. of John and Frances (Durrett). 35V88.

Agnes m. David Steel.

Alexander, b. 15 Feb., 1762, Augusta Co.; d. there, 1816-7; m. 1793, Martha Grigsby, d. after 1866. Rockbridge Co. Morton, p. 437; Waddell, p. 179.

David m. 28 Aug., 1781, Lucy Lacy by Rev. John Alderson, Jr. Rockingham Co. or Greenbrier Co. Ministers' Returns.

Isaac m. 14 June, 1787, Mary Graham by Rev. John Brown. Arthur Graham, father of Mary, gave consent. Rockbridge Co. Ministers' Returns.

James, Capt., b. 1756, Augusta Co.; d. 1804, Ky., son of John and Mary (____) Moffett Trimble; served in Rev. War; m. (2) ca 1780, Jane Allen, b. 15 March, 1753, dau. of James and Margaret (____) of Augusta Co.; rem. 1783, to Woodford Co., Ky. 33V79; Boogher, p. 309; Old King Wm., p. 25; Waddell, pp. 153, 179.

James, d. ca 1776; to America from Armagh, Ireland; m. Sarah Kersey; res. bef. 1745, Augusta Co. Rockbridge Co. Morton, p. 537; Waddell, p. 179.

Jane m. William McClure.

John m. 18 Feb., 1768, Susanna Woods, b. 1752, dau. of Archibald and Isabel (Goss); rem. to So. Car. bef. July, 1769. 51V370; 52V49.

John, d. 1764 in an Indian massacre; from Armagh, Ireland, to Augusta Co. in early 1740's; m. Mary (____) Moffett, widow of John. Waddell, p. 179.

John, son of James and Sarah (Kersey), m. ca 1780, Mary McClure, d. 1783. Rockbridge Co. Morton, p. 537.

John m. 10 April, 1786, Rachel Ridgway. Frederick Co. Mar. Record.

John m. 21 May, 1785, Lydia Tatom. Norfolk Co. Mar. Record.

John m. Mary Alexander, b. 1760, dau. of Archibald and (2) Jane (Mc Clure). Rockbridge Co. Morton, p. 470.

TRIMBLE (cont.)

John m. 16 April, 1791, Elizabeth Wigley. Norfolk Co. Mar. Record.
Mary m. McCord Bready.
Mary m. Lewis Jordan.
Mary (____) m. Lewis Jorden.
Polly m. Capt. John McKinney.
Rachel m. Joseph Caruthers.
Sarah m. Samuel Steele.
Thomas m. 5 Nov., 1785, Abigail Gatliff by Rev. John Alderson, Jr. Rockingham Co. or Greenbrier Co. Ministers' Returns.
William, b. 1760, Augusta Co.; m. 19 April, 1787, Mary Fleming by Rev. John Alderson, Jr., in Greenbrier Co.; rem. 1792, to Ky.; Pension W8791, for service in Rev. War from Virginia; res. 1833, Pulaski Co., Ky. Wayland, p. 159.

TRIMMER

Elizabeth (____) m. ____ Pollard.

TRIPLETT

____ m. Susanna Botts, dau. of Joshua, whose est. sett., 1818, Culpeper Co., proves it.
____ m. Jane (Harrison) Linton, b. 9 Dec., 1726; d. 3 April, 1759, widow of ____ Linton and dau. of Burr Harrison. Family Bible. 23V331.
____, Col., m. Anne Williston Talbot, dau. of John and (2) Mary Mosely. Talbot, p. 31.
____ (____) m. ____ French.
Ann m. Elias Hord.
Benedite m. Lawrence Triplett.
Betsey m. Edmund Denney.
Daniel, b. 15 Oct., 1763, Culpeper Co.; d. 27 Sept., 1845, Shenandoah Co., son of John and Lucy (Abbott); served in Rev. War; m. 3 Feb., 1791, Culpeper Co., Susannah Botts, b. 9 June, 1774, Prince William Co.; d. 1859, Warren Co., dau. of Joshua and Frances (Gaines). 31T 50.
Daniel m. Nov., 1776, Elizabeth Richards. King George Co. Mar. Record. He, d. May, 1818, son of Francis; she, d. 24 Sept., 1826, Norfolk, Va., dau. of John. 21W(1)118-9.
Elizabeth m. Alexander Thom.
Elizabeth Hedgman m. Capt. Thomas Triplett.
Francis, Col., b. ca 1730, prob. in Prince William Co.; will prov. 1795, Fauquier Co., son of Francis of Fairfax Co. (will prov. 1758); m. bef. 17 March, 1758, Benedicta Hedgman Sennett, dau. of Robert of Charles Co., Md.; res. Prince William Co. and Fauquier Co. 11T 37, 40; 21W(1)116-7.
Hedgman, b. 1753-63, son of John and Lucy (Abbett) of Culpeper Co.; m. Nancy Popham; rem. to Franklin Co., Ky. 55V289.
Hedgman, b. 1755; d. 1826, son of Col. Francis and Benedicta Hedgman (Sennett) of Fauquier Co.; m. 1788, Mary Marshall McClanahan, dau. of Rev. William and Mary (Marshall). 11T40; DAR No. 31 136.
Helen m. James Taylor.
Isabella m. William Harrison.
James m. bef. Oct., 1801, Nancy Massie, dau. of Thomas, whose will, prov. that date, Fauquier Co., and will of Mollie Massie, widow of Thomas, prove it.

TRIPLETT (cont.)

James m. Sept., 1769, Jenny Pearce. King George Co. Mar. Record.

John, inv. 1790, Culpeper Co., son of William; m. ____ Popham, dau. of George. 21W(1)119.

John m. Sarah Harrison, dau. of William. She m. (2) John Manly. 23V331.

Lawrence m. 1786, his cousin, Benedite Triplett, dau. of Col. Francis and Benedicta Hodgman (Sennott) of Fauquier Co. 11T40.

Mary m. George Hibbill (?Hill).

Sarah m. Al. Thorn (?Thom).

Thomas m. Sarah Dade, dau. of Townshend (1707-1781) and Parthenia (Alexander) Massey Dade of Fairfax Co. 16T165.

Thomas m. his cousin, Elizabeth Hedgman Triplett, dau. of Col. Francis and Benedicta Hedgman (Sennett) of Fauquier Co. 11T40.

William, will prov. 3 Dec., 1738, King George Co., son of Francis Triplett, the immigrant; m. Isabella Miller, will prov. 1760, King George Co., dau. of Capt. Symon Miller of Old Rappahannock Co., whose will, prov. 1684, proves the marriage. 12T239; 21W(1)36-7.

William m. 12 Dec., 1785, Elizabeth Moorehead. Fauquier Co. Mar. Record.

William, b. prob. 1760's, son of John and Lucy (Abbott) of Culpeper Co.; m. Mary Talbot; rem. to Wilkes Co., Ga. 55V289.

TRIPPE

Jemima m. William Stallworth.

TRIPPELS

Johna m. Alexander Howard.

TRONE

Elizabeth m. Henry Horn.

TROTMAN

Samuel m. 7 Oct., 1783, Catherine Barnet, both of Louisa. Douglas Reg., p. 23.

TROTTER

Ann m. Charles Woodson, Jr.

Elizabeth m. Maj. Maurice Langhorne.

Elizabeth m. John Walker.

Elizabeth m. William Scott.

James, Col., b. 1753; d. 1826, Ky.; m. Margaret Downey. DAR No. 31 432.

Mary m. James McCown.

Mary m. Thomas Hardaway.

Nancy m. Charles Woodson, Jr.

Sarah m. James Campbell.

Thomas m. bef. April, 1768, Ann Pleasants, dau. of Dorothy and sis. of Joseph. Proven by Deed of that date, Goochland Co.

TROUT

Catherine m. John Brush.

Christian m. 1795, Elizabeth Geerhart. Rockbridge Co. Morton, pp. 487, 537.

Michael m. Elizabeth Baer, dau. of John and Catherine (Miller). Wayland, p. 384.

Mira m. Lieut. Col. Samuel Shreve.

TROWE

David m. 9 Sept., 1788, Mary Williams. Louisa, p. 260.

TROWER

Anne m. William Costin.
Anne m. Caleb Vangover.
Elizabeth m. William Brewer.
James of Richmond City m. 19 June, 1787, Alice Christian, dau. of Gideon, who gave consent. Charles City Co. Mar. Record. 23V87.
John m. 19 Dec., 1793, Nancy Robinson. Sur. John Robinson. Albemarle Co. Mar. Bond.
John m. 11 June, 1791, Sarah Smith, dau. of Richard. Northampton Co. Mar. Record.
Nancy m. Southy Spady.
Polly m. John Cox.
Robert m. 31 Oct., 1795, Nelly Costin. Northampton Co. Mar. Record.
Samuel m. 19 June, 1787, Alice Christian, dau. of Gideon. Charles City Co. Mar. Record. 8W(1)194.

TROWERBOUGH

Adam m. 3 Dec., 1799, Catherine Pence. Rockingham Co. Wayland, p. 11.

TROXAL

Abraham, d. 1812; m. 1794, Anna E. Hoylman. Rockbridge Co. Morton, p. 537.

TRUAX

Obediah m. 17 Oct., 1797, Nelly Sturgeon. Shelby Co., Ky. Mar. Record.

TRUBLOOD

Caleb m. 19 Feb., 1763, Mourning Morriott. Hinshaw 6:116.

TRUBY

John m. Jane Hatchett, dau. of William (will 1784, Amelia Co.) and Margaret (Remay). Free II:282.
Rebecca m. John Cutright.

TRUE

____ (____) m. Edward Kelly.
Martin m. 8 Dec., 1791, Mary Hill. Halifax Co. Mar. Record.
Martin m. 26 Nov., 1797, Frances Burges. Spotsylvania Co. Mar. Record.
Martin m. bef. 19 April, 1748, Sarah Martin, dau. of Henry, whose will of that date, Spotsylvania Co., proves it.
Mary m. William Berry.
Sarah (____) m. Edmund Bryant.

TRUEHEART

____ m. bef. 1770, Mary Shelton, sis. of Joseph (d. Sept., 1784). 11 W(2)110.
Mary m. Joseph Curd (2nd wife).

TRUEMAN

____ m. Elizabeth Farmer, dau. of Mark and Amy (Bowman). Farmer, p. 16.
Catherine m. ____ Murfie.
Mary m. ____ Williams.

TRUITT

Solomon m. 24 April, 1751, Frances (____) Smith. Northampton Co. Mar. Record.

TRULY
Sarah m. Samuel Brown.
TRUMAN
Ann m. ____ Warriner.
Isham m. 8 Sept., 1779, Mary Gibbons. Sur. William Evans. Surry Co. Mar. Bond.
Mary m. John Redd.
Mary m. William Haley.
Richard, will dated 3 Nov., 1772, Henrico Co.; m. Mary Woodson, dau. of Richard. 25W(1)286.
TRUMBO
____ m. Elizabeth ____, prob. Lair; named as dau. in will of Catherine Lair, 9 July, 1799, Rockingham Co. Wayland, p. 416.
Dorotha m. Charles Beggs.
Jacob m. 6 Feb., 1797, Polly Hughes. Rockingham Co. Wayland, p. 8.
TRUSLOW
Benjamin m. 12 March, 1786, Keziah Mannard. St. Paul's.
Thomas m. 19 Jan., 1789, Zilpah Skinner. St. Paul's.
TRUSSELL
Elizabeth (____) m. Henry Hutson.
Jane (____) m. John Harding.
Jane (____) m. Henry Harding.
TRUST(?)
Tillie m. Caesar Johnson.
TRUSTY
William m. bef. 1746, Elizabeth Musick, dau. of George, whose will, 1754, and Deed of Gift, 1746, Spotsylvania Co., prove it.
TSCHARNER
Regina m. Christopher DeGraffenreid.
TSCHEFELI
Sally m. Peter Gottie.
TUBBLE
Dianna m. Thomas Woosley.
TUCK
Cary m. 1 April, 1790, Nancy Standley. Halifax Co. Mar. Record.
Edward m. 6 Dec., 1791, Luck Standley. Halifax Co. Mar. Record.
John m. 10 Nov., 1791, Edey Standley. Halifax Co. Mar. Record.
John m. Mary Powell, dau. of Edward (will, 1766). Halifax, p. 328.
Josiah m. 22 Dec., 1790, Tabitha Harris. Halifax Co. Mar. Record.
Lucy m. William Chapman.
Mary m. Thomas Watkins.
Moses m. 13 Aug., 1784, Susannah Nash by Rev. David Blair. Pittsylvania Co. Ministers' Returns.
Ned, b. Ireland; served in Rev. War; m. ____ Winfrey. A son, John C. Tuck, b. ca 1800, Halifax Co. Perrin, 1886, Simpson Co., p. 712.
Sally m. Moses Chapman.
Susannah m. Thomas Malone.
Vashty m. James Weaver.
William m. 22 Aug., 1797, Hannah Irby. Halifax Co. Mar. Record.
TUCKER
____ m. bef. July, 1749, Judith Wales, dau. of John, whose est. sett., 9 July, 1749, Lancaster Co., proves it.

TUCKER (cont.)

____ m. John Woodson.

____ m. Sarah Nance, dau. of William, whose will, 1801, Halifax Co., proves it.

____ m. Margaret Herbert, dau. of Thomas (will, 1749, Norfolk Co.). 8W(1)148.

____ m. Frances Houston. She m. (2) Thomas Nelson. 33V188.

Alice m. Arthur Allen.

Alphia m. Henry Stokeley.

Ann m. Peter Reaves.

Ann Green m. William Ragsdale.

Anne Frances Bland m. Judge John Coalter.

Anthony m. Rosea (____) Curle, widow of Joshua. 7W(1)21. Anthony, will prov. 1759; m. (1) Mary Curlo, dau. of Pasco and Sarah (____). 15W(2)133. Anthony m. by 1728, Mary (Curle) Jenkins, widow of Capt. Henry Jenkins and dau. of Pasco and Sarah (____). 7W(1)185; 9W(1) 125-6.

Caroline H. m. Daniel Norton.

Courtney m. ____ Bowdoin.

Courtney (____) m. Jacob Walker.

David m. 24 Nov., 1759, Athalia Kezia (____) Hunt. Sur. Thomas Goodwyn. Sussex Co. Mar. Bond. He, son of Capt. Joseph and Patsy (Colson); m. Athaliah Kessia (Wright) Hunt, widow of Thomas Hunt. McCullough, p. 110.

Dorothy m. (1) Capt. Bryan Smith; m. (2) Hugh Owen.

Elijah m. 3 Dec., 1789, Betsy Barley. Halifax Co. Mar. Record.

Eliza. m. Jno. Colwell.

Elizabeth m. Henry Sparrow.

Elizabeth m. William Winfiold.

Elizabeth m. Peter Winfield, Jr.

Elizabeth m. Rev. Wright Tucker (1st wife).

Elizabeth m. John Gosee.

Fanny m. ____ Coleman.

Frances m. David Kerr.

Frances m. Saunders Calvert.

Frances (____) m. Thomas Nelson.

James, Capt., m. 30 Sept., 1792, Anne McCawley. Princess Anne Co. LNCo.2:22.

Jane (____) m. John Pleasants.

Joanna m. Gawin Corbin.

Joel m. 17 Oct., 1799, Usley Chappell. Halifax Co. Mar. Record.

John m. 5 Dec., 1778, Amherst Co., Rhoda Powell, dau. of Richard, Sr. 30T67.

John m. 18 July, 1782, Frances Pigg, King and Queen Co. Christ Church, p. 208.

John of Westmoreland Co. m. Rose ____. 33V302.

Joseph m. 20 Feb., 1733/4, Rosamond Carroll of Brunswick Parish. St. Paul's.

Joseph, Capt. of the English Navy, from Bermuda to America prior to 1760; m. Patsy Colson, said to be dau. of an officer in the Portuguese Navy. McCullough, pp. 106, 109.

Joseph, b. ca 1710, son of Robert and Martha (____); m. Lucretia

TUCKER (cont.)

Wynn(-e), dau. of Maj. Robert, whose will dated 1754, Sussex Co., proves the marriage. 12T175; Boddie-HSF V:297.

Judith m. Philip Thurmond.

Judith (____) m. Peter Cain.

Lice m. 24 Jan., 1788, Asaula Pettipool by Rev. Thomas Crymes, Baptist. Lunenburg Co. Ministers' Returns.

Louisa m. James Old.

Louisa m. Christopher Irvin(-e).

Margaret (____) m. Joseph Croshaw (4th wife).

Maria D. m. (1) ____ Craik; m. (2) Capt. Charles Ewell.

Martha m. James Keats.

Martha m. George M. Rucker.

Martha m. John Morgan, Sr.

Martha m. Benjamin Bell.

Martha m. Thomas Newton.

Mary m. John Woodson, Jr.

Mary m. Michael McHenry.

Mary m. Jno. Fryby.

Mary m. Robert Johns.

Mary m. Walter Coles.

Mary m. Thomas Martin.

Mathew m. 22 Jan., 1748/9, Lucretia Childers of Albemarle Co. Diary of Rev. Robert Rose.

Merriman m. 1 Feb., 1796, Anna Overstreet, dau. of William, by Rev. John Chappell. Charlotte Co. Ministers' Returns.

Milley m. ____ Clay.

Nancy m. Ephraim Winfield.

Nanny m. Littleberry Sullivant.

Obadiah m. 11 Dec., 1769, Elizabeth Kent, both of Albemarle. Douglas Reg., p. 11.

Patsey m. Thomas Vaughan.

Patsy m. Aaron Moore.

Patsy m. Thomas Newton.

Polly m. Fred Leonard.

Rachel m. Larken Langford.

Rebecca m. Victor Buckhannon.

Robert m. 12 Nov., 1787, Sarah Smith. Sur. Edward Elam. Mecklenburg Co. Mar. Bond. Mar. 27 Nov., 1787, by Rev. Thomas Crymes, Baptist. Lunenburg Co. Ministers' Returns.

Robert m. 17 May, 1739, Joanna Corbin, dau. of Gawin and Martha (____), by Rev. William Phillips in King and Queen Co. 23T123. He d. 1 July, 1737. Announced in The Virginia Gazette. Her mother was Martha (Bassett) Corbin. 29V521. Given as Corwin. 4V361, 362.

Robert m. 1 Jan., 1782, Martha Shelton. Sur. Joseph Aiken. Pittsylvania Co. Mar. Bond.

Robert, b. 8 Sept., 1739, Prince George Co.; m. Mary Green, b. 24 April, 1741, dau. of Peter. Boddie-HSF V:297.

Robert of Prince George Co. m. 2 Sept., 1772, Mary Ann Parham. Sur. Stith Parham of Sussex Co. Sussex Co. Mar. Bond. Boddie-HSF V:121.

Robert m. 13 Feb., 1786, Sarah Parham. Prince George Co. Cameron.

Robert m. Elizabeth (prob. Parham), dau. of Thomas, whose will, 1716,

TUCKER (cont.)

names "daughter Elizabeth Tucker." Boddie-Isle V:296.

Rose (____) m. (2) Dr. Thomas Gerard (2nd wife); m. (3) John Newton.

S. m. George Carrington.

St. George, Judge, b. 10 July, 1752, Bermuda; d. 10 Nov., 1827 or 1828, Nelson Co.; m. (1) 3 Sept., 1778, Frances (Bland) Randolph, widow of John Randolph of "Mattoax," Chesterfield Co., and dau. of Theoderick Bland of "Cawsons," Prince George Co.; m. (2) 8 Oct., 1791, Lelia (Skipwith) Carter, widow of George Carter of "Corotoman," and dau. of Sir Peyton Skipwith, baronet. 29V154; 2W(1)202; 8W(1)154. Court Record, 1778, Chesterfield Co., proves the 1st marriage.

Sarah m. John Taylor.

Sarah m. Samuel Freeman.

Sarah m. ____ Cooke.

Sarah m. Charles Ellis, Jr. (2nd wife).

Stephen m. 8 April, 1782, Frances Wells Glascock by Rev. James Shelburne, Baptist. Lunenburg Co. Ministers' Returns.

William m. 12 Jan., 1798, Margaret Scanland (or Scandlon). Caroline Co. Mar. Record.

William, Capt., m. Mary Thompson. 1V189.

Willis m. 15 Sept., 1792, Nancy Tartt. Norfolk Co. Mar. Record.

Wright, minister, b. 22 Nov., 1760, son of David and Athaliah Kessia (Wright); m. (1) ca 1779, Elizabeth Tucker; m. (2) 5 March, 1784, Brunswick Co., Elizabeth Williams, dau. of Charles. McCullough, p. 110.

TUCKWELL

Nancy m. Anthony Sebrok.

TUEL

John m. 22 March, 1771, Mary Mason, dau. of Isaac, dec'd. Sussex Co. Mar. Record.

TUELL

James m. 1 April, 1734, Eliza Baxa. Sur. William Box. Norfolk Co. Mar. Bond.

Tabitha m. William Mason.

TUGELL

Henery m. 31 Oct., 1710, Elizabeth Browne. Christ Church, p. 82.

Judith m. William Balding.

TUGGLE

Anna m. ____ Bondvine.

Frances m. William Kidd.

Frances m. William Mansfeild.

Griffin m. 10 Jan., 1779, Frances Berry. Christ Church, p. 171.

Henry m. 1751, Hollender Conolly, both in Goochland. Douglas Reg., pp. 26-32.

Jane m. John Lee.

John m. 18 Nov., 1779, Elizabeth Harrison. Henry Tuggle gave consent to son's marriage and Frances Overstreet consented to her daughter's marriage. 7W(1)199.

John m. 29 July, 1770, Ann Cawley, both in Goochland. Douglas Reg., p. 12.

Joshua m. 26 Dec., 1780, Elizabeth Pace, both of Goochland. Douglas

TUGGLE (cont.)

Reg., p. 20. Amherst Co. Mar. Record.

Lodowick, Gent., m. 1 Oct., 1765, Dorothy Lee, spinster. Wit. John Stringer. Middlesex Co. Mar. Record. She, b. 31 March, 1749, dau of George and Mary (Buford). 49V76; 7W(1)192.

Mary m. William Mallery.

Mary m. George Hauks.

Nicholas m. 16 Feb., 1777, Susanna Abbot. Christ Church, p. 201.

Nicholas m. Susanna Mickelborough, b. after 1746, dau. of Henry and Susanna (Daniel). 13T195.

Rachel m. John Chowning.

Sally m. Asher Bray.

William m. 25 Sept., 1765, Ann Nash, both in this parish. Douglas Reg., p. 8.

TUGLE

Elizabeth m. Henry Ball.

Henry m. 30 March, 1722, Mary Godbee. Christ Church, p. 164.

John m. 8 Oct., 1725, Catharine Kelly. Christ Church, p. 165.

Molly m. Robert Cairden.

TUGWELL

Ann m. Nicholas Rice.

Henry m. 26 Aug., 1692, Mary Baskett. Christ Church, p. 53.

Lucretia m. Joseph Goare.

Martha m. George Chowning.

TUKE

Catherine m. Peter Lee.

TUKKER

Polly m. Manoah Sullivan, Jr.

TULEY

Judith m. John Gabbert.

TULLIS

Martha m. Jason Moreland.

TULLOCH

Hugh m. 20 Aug., 1786, Elizabeth Thomas. Petersburg. Cameron.

Jane m. Robert Goodwin.

Thomas m. Barbara Garland. Louisa, p. 326.

TULLY

Israel of Fleming Co., Ky., m. Frances Young, b. 20 Nov., 1773, Va.; d. 2 May, 1813, dau. of Leonard and Mary Ann (Higgins). Cowherd, pp. 330-1.

James m. Agnes Kirby, b. 1765, Va., dau. of David (d. 1811, Warren Co., Ky.). Gillmore, p. 102.

TUMMONS

Margaret m. William Taylor.

TUNBRIDGE

Catherine m. William Nash.

Vicey m. John Platt.

TUNE

Betsey m. Jesse Sampson.

James m. 18 Feb., 1796, Rebeckah Conley. Halifax Co. Mar. Record.

Nancy m. William Conley.

Thomas m. 19 Sept., 1786, Milley King. Halifax Co. Mar. Record.

TUNING

Unice m. George Shepherd.

TUNNEL

Elizabeth m. William Sacheverd.

Francis m. 9 Nov., 1740, Margaret Sinclair. OPR.

TUNNELL

John m. 18 Feb., 1763, Sarah Martin. St. Paul's.

John m. 13 Feb., 1774, Elizabeth Long. St. Paul's.

Mildred m. Woodford Kelly.

Stephen, b. 1753, Spotsylvania Co.; d. 1828, Tompkinsville, Ky., son of William and Lady Ann (Howard); m. Kezia Money. Ball, p. 306.

William, d. 18 Dec., 1787, prob. in Loudoun Co.; bur. in Fairfax Co., son of Guilaum Tonnelier (or Tunnell); m. in England, Lady Ann Howard of Yorkshire, d. 18 Feb., 1814; came to Va. ca 1736. Ball, p, 305.

William, b. 1751, Spotsylvania Co.; d. 16 Aug., 1814, near Robertsville, Tenn., son of William and Lady Ann (Howard); m. Mary Maysey (as spelled in the Family Bible). Ball, p. 306.

TUNSTALL

____ m. Catherine Brooke, sis. of William, whose will, 1804, Williamsburg, Va., proves it.

Catherine m. Samuel Mathews.

Caty m. John Chandler.

Edmund of King and Queen Co., d. 1691; m. Catherine Long (or Katherine Longe), dau. of John and Katherine (Morris) Pettis Long. 21T 241; 26T120. Given as Edward and her second husband as Capt. Richard Wyatt. Gillmore, p. 97.

Elizabeth m. Hamblin Gunn.

Hannah m. George Brooke.

Mary m. Thomas Fox.

Richard, Col., m. Ann Hill, dau. of Leonard (d. 1729, Essex Co.). 16T27.

Richard m. bef. 12 May, 1728, Ann (____) Walker, widow of James. Proven by Court Record of that date, Essex Co.

Richard m. Catherine Brooke, d. 1827, dau. of George. 20V215.

TURBERBILLE

Richard Lee m. Henrietta Lee, dau. of Richard Henry Lee and Anna (Gascoyne) Pinkard Lee. She m. (2) Rev. William Maffit. 11T29.

TURBERVILLE

____ m. Gowry Waugh.

____ m. Walter Shropshire.

Edward m. (2) Sarah (____) Willis Wood Hudson, widow 1st of William Willis, 2nd of Henry Wood, 3rd of Rush Hudson. Orange III:98.

Gawin Corbin m. 5 April, 1792, Mary Daingerfield. 32V135.

George, Capt., m. 16 May, 1727, Lettice Fitzhugh, dau. of Hon. William and Ann (Lee). 7W(1)96.

George m. 1718, Frances Ashton, b. 1699; d. 24 April, 1720, in her 21st year (tombstone), dau. of Henry and (1) Elizabeth (Hardidge). 7W(1)95, 116; 14W(2)162.

George m. Martha Lee (1st husband). 30V20.

George m. (1) 1 June, 1769, Martha Corbin; m. (2) Ann ____. 30V309, 312.

TURBERVILLE (cont.)
George Lee m. 4 Jan., 1782, Betty Tayloe Corbin. Her grandfather, Richard Corbin, gave consent. 30V313; 7W(1)193.
John, Col., m. Martha Corbin, dau. of Col. John of Portobago. 5W(1) 281.
Lettice Corbin m. Catesby Jones.
Martha Felicia m. Robert Beale.
TUREMAN
Charles, d. bef. 1782; m. Margaret Crutcher, dau. of Thomas of Caroline Co., whose will, dated 1782, prov. 1786, Williamsburg, Va., proves it. She m. (2) John Saunders, d. 1803. 27T284.
Ignatius m. 3 June, 1731, Mary Pace. Christ Church, p. 167.
Mary m. Joel Lewis (1st wife).
TURK
Elizabeth m. William Gleaves.
TURLEY
____ m. John Turley.
Henrietta Maria m. James Waugh.
John m. Aug., 1783, ____ Turley by Rev. Lazarus Dodson. Pittsylvania Co. Mar. Record.
John m. 18 March, 1783, Susanna Squires. Fauquier Co. Mar. Record.
Ruth m. John Baylis.
TURLEYFIELD
John m. 23 Dec., 1799, Rebecca Josie Parham by Rev. William Ellis, Baptist. Lunenburg Co. Ministers' Returns.
TURLONG
____ m. Ann (____) Wharton, mother of Samuel Wharton, whose will, dated 22 Oct., 1738, Spotsylvania Co., proves it.
TURMOND
Mary m. Ezekiel Morris.
TURNBULL
Ann m. Francis Osborne.
Elizabeth m. William Timberlake.
James m. 11 April, 1799, Mrs. Ann Armstrong. Sur. David McAllester. Norfolk Co. Mar. Bond.
Mary m. Armistead Burwell.
Robert m. Elizabeth Kemper, b. 1738, Germantown, Va.; d. 7 March, 1811, Ohio, dau. of John and Alice (Utterback). Germanna Colonies 2:83; Utterback, p. 35.
Robert m. bef. 1796, Hannah (____) Minor, mother of Peter Minor. Proven by a Deed, 27 Jan., 1796, Spotsylvania Co.
TURNER
____ m. bef. 1778, ____ Dickinson, dau. of John, whose will of that date, Essex Co., proves it.
____ m. Ruth Farmer, dau. of Thomas. Farmer, p. 15.
____ m. Mary Bush, dau. of James (will, 1801, Russell Co.). 35V194.
____ m. bef. 1767, Mary Johnson, dau. of Samuel, whose will of that date, Southampton Co., names "daughter Mary Turner."
____ m. bef. 1792, Molly Dabney, dau. of Cornelius, whose will of that date mentions "daughter Molly Turner."
____ believed m. bef. 1795, Charlotte Harris, dau. of Edmund, whose will of that date, Southampton Co., named "my child Charlotte Tur-

TURNER (cont.)

ner."

Abner m. 1800, Chaste Esther Love, dau. of Lieut. Col. David Love; rem. from Isle of Wight Co. to Ga. DAR Query 13610, Nov., 1930.

Abraham m. 11 Dec., 1644, prob. York Co., Hannah Bennett, dau. of Samuel of Elizabeth City Co. She m. (2) 1649, Humphrey Tompkins. 5V93; 10W(2)25.

Ann m. Person Turner.

Ann m. Obediah Martin.

Ann m. (1) John Wren; m. (2) Alexander Hansford.

Bartholomew m. 1763, Mary Johnson, both in this parish. Douglas Reg., p. 7.

Benjamin m. Elizabeth Clack, dau. of John. Harllee III:2775.

Benjamin m. 22 Dec., 1777, Rebecca Grantham, dau. of Thomas. Surry Co. Mar. Record.

Betty m. Henry Dawson.

Charles m. 12 Aug., 1691, Mary Cox. St. Peter's, p. 416.

Clary m. John McAlester.

D. m. 1796, E. Pendleton of Caroline Co. St. Mark's, p. 78.

Daniel m. 17 Feb., 1770, Catharine Montague. Christ Church, p. 304.

Daniel, b. 1775; m. 5 Feb., 1796, Sarah Pendleton, b. 1781; d. 1815, dau. of Edmund, Jr., and Mildred (Pollard). 41V85-6.

E. m. John Hancock.

Edmund m. 29 Dec., 1792, E. Richardson. Halifax Co. Mar. Record.

Elizabeth m. Robert Harris.

Elizabeth m. Robert Sturdivant.

Elizabeth m. Joseph Reynolds.

Elizabeth m. Joseph Morehead.

Elizabeth m. Joseph Wyatt.

Elizabeth m. Charles Cocke.

Elizabeth m. John Morris.

Elizabeth m. Capt. Jethro Sumner.

Esther m. Robert Page.

Fleming of Buckingham Co. m. Jane Clark, dau. of John and Mary (Towles). 13T35.

Frances m. Hackly Warren.

George m. 14 June, 1786, Lurany Russell. Petersburg, Cameron.

George m. 7 Nov., 1799, Susannah Adams. Halifax Co. Mar. Record.

George m. 6 July, 1795, Polly Rowlett. Sur. William Rowlett. Charlotte Co. Mar. Bond.

George, son of Charles (d. 1789), m. 14 Feb., 1798, Ann Maupin. Sur. Robert Turner. She, dau. of Gabriel and Ann (____). Albemarle Co. Mar. Bond; Albemarle, p. 333; Huguenot 7:258.

Hanna (____) m. Humphry Tompkins.

Hannah m. Richard Martin.

Harden m. 21 Dec., 1798, Patsey Crenshaw by Rev. Reuben Ford. Louisa Co. Ministers' Returns.

Harry, Maj., d. 1751, son of Col. Thomas and Martha (Taliaferro); m. bef. 1747, Elizabeth Smith, dau. of Nicholas. Proven by Deed of that date, King George Co. She m. (2) Bowler Cocke, Jr. 19T107; 4V446; 21V106; 25W(1)171-2.

Hen m. 9 March, 1701, Elizabeth City Co., Sydwell Minson. 5W(1)57.

TURNER (cont.)

Henry m. 6 Jan., 1708/9, Mary Baker. St. Peter's, p. 416.

Henry m. 14 Jan., 1784, Martha (____) Wood. Norfolk Co. Mar. Record.

Henry m. 24 Nov., 1794, Polly Kimball. Isle of Wight Co. Mar. Record.

Henry m. bef. 1756, Susanna Johnson. Douglas Reg. shows a son born on that date.

Henry Smith, b. 1770; d. 18 July, 1834, son of Thomas; m. (1) Lucy Hopkins; m. (2) 1796, Catherine Blackburn, dau. of Col. Richard and Alice (Elzey); res. Westmoreland Co. and "Wheatland," Jefferson Co., Ky. 4W(1)266. Catherine was dau. of Col. Thomas of Prince William Co. 21V211.

Hezechia m. bef. Dec., 1692, ____ (____) Hugill, widow of Michael. Proven by Land Grant, that date, Richmond Co.

Isham m. 11 Dec., 1797, Fanney Wall. Halifax Co. Mar. Record.

Jacob m. bef. 1794, Patience Boykin, dau. of John, Sr., whose will of that date, Southampton Co., names "daughter Patience, wife of Jacob Turner."

Jacob m. bef. 1778, Priscilla ____ (prob. Blunt), dau. of Priscilla Blunt, whose will of that date, Southampton Co., names "daughter Priscilla Turner."

James m. 27 Feb., 1792, Mary Gooch. Louisa Co. Mar. Record.

James m. 30 March, 1789, Patty M. Cosby. Sur. James Watkins. Patty's father, Samuel Cosby, gave consent. Goochland Co. Mar. Bond.

James m. 27 June, 1780, Sarah Irby. Halifax Co. Mar. Record.

James m. 17 Feb., 1763, M. McMahaney. Halifax Co. Mar. Record.

James m. Hannah Green, dau. of Thomas and Elizabeth (Filmer). 5T136.

James of Amherst Co. m. Rebecca Hamner, dau. of William. Albemarle, p. 333.

James m. bef. 30 Jan., 1733, Kerenhappuch Norman, dau. of Isaac, whose Deed of Gift of that date, Spotsylvania Co., proves it.

James m. 29 Sept., 1775, Martha Rowe. Christ Church, p. 201.

James m. 3 March, 1757, Mary Matthews. OPR.

Jane m. William Storke Jett.

Jennett m. Cordy Clifton.

John m. 13 Aug., 1789, Sarah Carpenter by Rev. John Waller. Louisa Co. Ministers' Returns.

John m. 1790, Fanny Davis. Caroline Co. Mar. Record.

John m. 2 Oct., 1741, Sarah Derrick. St. Paul's.

John m. 2 Sept., 1769, Martha Derrick. St. Paul's.

John m. 1790, Sarah Fitzgerrell. Orange Co. Mar. Record.

John m. 2 July, 1788, Henrietta Johnson. Halifax Co. Mar. Record.

John m. 6 June, 1791, Mary Lawrence. Isle of Wight Co. Mar. Record.

John m. 23 April, 1790, Sally Pitts, dau. of John. Northampton Co. Mar. Record.

John m. bef. Feb., 1714, Priscilla Shippey, legatee of James Jones. Proven by Court Record of that date, Northumberland Co.

John m. Mildred Suddarth, dau. of James, Sr., and Patience (Sumter). Stoddard, p. 201.

Joseph m. bef. 1795, Nancy Peterson, dau. of Batte, whose will of that date, Greensville Co., proves it.

Joshua, b. 1 March, 1741, Charles Co., Md.; d. 27 March, 1825, Henry Co., Ky., son of Edward and Eleanor (____); m. (1) in Md. ____ ____;

TURNER (cont.)

m. (2) 3 Dec., 1792, Culpeper Co., by Rev. John Prickett to Mary Ann (Maddox) Corly, widow of Aqrilla and dau. of Notley Maddox and Susannah (Burch); rem. to Ky., 1813-1816. The widow d. 25 Jan., 1856, Henry Co., Ky. 19 Ky. Reg. 55:15.

Keziah m. James Moseley.

Keziah m. Thomas Elliott.

Letty m. William Martin (or Martain).

Lewis, b. 1 Oct., 1774, Henrico Co.; m. Sarah Martin, b. 15 Feb., 1776. DAR Query K-148. Nov. 1948.

Lewis Elzey, b. 14 Sept., 1754; m. Theo. Payne. Stoddard, p. 221.

Margret m. Edward Delridge.

Martha m. James McMullon.

Martin m. 24 Dec., 1798, Sally Stanfield. Halifax Co. Mar. Record.

Mary m. Charles Morehead.

Mary m. Turner Dixon.

Mary m. Jesse Dailey.

Mary m. Capt. Augustine Leftwich, Jr.

Mary m. Edward Harris.

Mary m. Arthur Brown.

Mary m. John Wall.

Mary m. Alexander Stuart.

Mathew m. 23 Aug., 1792, Elizabeth Saunders. Isle of Wight Co. Mar. Record.

Matthew m. 24 Feb., 1798, Mary Ingram. Lunenburg Co. Cameron.

Meshack m. 6 Feb., 1760, Rebecca Roberson. Halifax Co. Mar. Record.

Mildred m. Austin Peay.

Mildred m. James Smith.

N. m. Peter Vaughan.

Nancy m. Bartholomew Stovall.

Nancy m. Moses Mayhew.

Nancy m. George Goodrich.

Nancy m. Samuel Drinkwater.

Nancy m. Revel Savage.

Olive m. George Foster.

Pass m. bef. 1786, Ann Fulgham, dau. of Mary, whose will of that date, Southampton Co., names "daughter Ann Turner," and appoints as an extr., "son-in-law Pass Turner."

Patience m. Burwell Brown.

Patsy m. Archer Applewhaite.

Peggy m. Charles Gelding.

Peggy m. John Jacob.

Person m. 9 Sept., 1797, Ann Turner, dau. of John and Priscilla (Blunt). Boddie-SVF I:71.

Phebe m. ____ Newsum.

Pleasant m. 11 Oct., 1781, Agnes Woodson. Sur. Archer Pledge. Goochland Co. Mar. Bond.

Pleasant m. bef. Oct., 1790, Agatha Woodson, dau. of Joseph; res. 1790, Halifax Co. Proven by Deed of that date, Goochland Co.

Polly (____) m. John Rose.

Priscilla m. Timothy Rives.

Rebeckah m. Joel Frazier.

TURNER (cont.)

Reuben m. 1 Oct., 1793, Nancy Jones, spinster, dau. of Thomas. Sur. Thomas Jones. Albemarle Co. Mar. Bond.

Reuben m. 17 June, 1793, Elizabeth Pendleton, b. 24 Oct., 1776, dau. of Edmund, Jr., and Mildred (Pollard). 41V85-6.

Reuben m. Susan Hamner, dau. of William (d. 1785). Albemarle, p. 215.

Revel m. 26 Aug., 1790, Betsey Parker. Northampton Co. Mar. Record.

Rhoda m. Peter Butler.

Rhoda m. Simon Gooch.

Rhoda m. Liner Gooch.

Richard m. 24 Sept., 1725, Helena Carter. St. Paul's.

Robert m. 1787, Mary Thompson. Rockbridge Co. Morton, p. 537.

Sally m. Walker Taliaferro (1st wife).

Sally m. William Hatchett.

Sally m. James Heath.

Sally m. Augustine Denton.

Sarah m. Sgt. Christopher Long.

Sarah m. John Jones.

Sarah m. Edward Dixon.

Sarah m. John Watkins.

Sarah m. John Norris.

Sarah m. Jonathan Matthews.

Sarah (____) m. Thomas Fisher.

Sarah (____) m. John Milbee.

Sophia m. Theophilus Turner.

Stoakley m. 25 Nov., 1794, Susannah Vaughan. Halifax Co. Mar. Record.

Susanna m. Byrd B. Link.

Susanna m. Thomas Dowty.

Teackle m. 13 July, 1790, Nancy Sandford. Northampton Co. Mar. Record.

Teackle m. 5 Feb., 1798, Peggy Mapp. Northampton Co. Mar. Record.

Theodosha m. John Murphy, Jr.

Theophilus m. 22 Jan., 1759, Sophia Turner, dau. of Edward. Northampton Co. Mar. Record.

Thomas m. 13 Sept., 1748, Eleanor Radcliffe. OPR.

Thomas m. 1787, Catey Brown. Orange Co. Mar. Record.

Thomas m. bef. 7 Nov., 1749, Mary Taliaferro, granddau. of Charles, Sr., of Caroline Co. Proven by Deed of that date, Spotsylvania Co. She was dau. of Col. John and Sarah (____); he d. 1747, intestate, son of Thomas and Martha (Taliaferro). 11T26; 21V106-7.

Thomas, Col., of "Walsingham" and "Smith's Mount," will prov. 30 Oct., 1787, Westmoreland Co., son of Harry and Elizabeth (Smith); m. Jane Fauntleroy, b. 15 Aug., 1749, dau. of William of "Naylor's Hole," Richmond Co., and ____ (Murdock). 21V108; 9W(1)174; Jones Gene., p. 181.

Thomas m. 7 April, 1798, Unity Smith. Sur. Nathan Smith. Louisa Co. Mar. Bond.

Thomas, Col., of "Kinloch," Fauquier Co., b. 3 April, 1772; d. 30 Jan., 1839; m. 2 Oct., 1798, at "Shirley," Elizabeth Carter, b. 2 Oct., 1782; d. May, 1866, dau. of Col. Robert of "Eastern View," Fauquier Co. 21V212.

TURNER (cont.)

Thomas, Col., will dated 19 Feb., 1757, King George Co.; m. bef. 25 March, 1715, Martha Taliaferro, dau. of Richard of Richmond Co. and Sarah (____); m. (2) Sarah Taliaferro, dau. of Richard. Court Record, 1715, Essex Co. 19T107; 21T189; 20V439; 21V106-7.

William m. 20 April, 1726, Dorothy Whitlock. St. Peter's, p. 417.

William m. 4 Oct., 1798, Nancy Legrand. Halifax Co. Mar. Record.

William m. Sarah Ellzey, dau. of Lewis, whose will, 1780, Fairfax Co. Stoddard, p. 220.

Wilson m. 3 May, 1797, Polly Hurt. Caroline Co. Mar. Record.

TURNLEY

Ann m. Benjamin Johnson.

Betsey m. Moses Perry.

Elizabeth m. George Graham.

Francis m. 1791, Susanna Watts. Orange Co. Mar. Record.

John m. Mary Handy; res. Botetourt Co. In 1786, she moved to Jefferson Co., Tenn. DAR Query 12 959.

TURNOR

Elizabeth m. Edward Moore.

TURPEN

Aaron m. 18 June, 1786, Jane Barns by Rev. John Alderson, Jr. Rockingham Co. or Greenbrier Co. Ministers' Returns.

Martin m. 8 March, 1785, Nancy Fleming by Rev. John Alderson, Jr. Rockingham Co. or Greenbrier Co. Ministers' Returns.

Moses m. 27 Nov., 1781, Magdelia Black by Rev. John Alderson, Jr. Rockingham Co. or Greenbrier Co. Ministers' Returns.

TURPIN

George m. 1798, Frances "Fanny" (Shipp) Sullenger, widow of Thomas of Caroline Co., Va., and Woodford Co., Ky., and dau. of Thomas Shipp. 28T230.

Henry m. bef. 1768, Ann Williamson, dau. of George and Frances (Davis). Hines, Vol. 18.

James m. 12 Nov., 1794, Polly Smith. Halifax Co. Mar. Record.

John m. 8 March, 1797, E. Carter. Halifax Co. Mar. Record.

John m. 27 Oct., 1789, Sally Gascoyne. Northampton Co. Mar. Record.

Mary m. Robert Goode.

Matthew m. 1686, Henrico Co., Sarah Hatcher. 5V99-100. She, dau. of Ed. Henrico, p. 225.

Obedience m. Col. John Harris, Sr.

Philip, son of Thomas (1708-1790) and Mary (Jefferson), m. Caroline Rose. 25W(1)111.

Polly m. James Powell.

Sarah m. Joseph Farrar.

Solomon m. 18 March, 1788, Mary West by Rev. John Alderson, Jr. Rockingham Co. or Greenbrier Co. Ministers' Returns.

Thomas m. Obedience Cocke. A dau. was born in 1720. McCullough, p. 276.

Thomas, son of Thomas (1708-1790) and Mary (Jefferson), m. Martha Ward Gaines. 25W(1)111.

Thomas m. Mary (Langhorne) Callard, b. 30 Nov., 1746, widow of Joseph Callard and dau. of Maj. Maurice and Elizabeth (Trotter) Langhorne. She m. (3) Col. James Calloway. 13T263.

TURPIN (cont.)

Thomas of Goochland Co., b. 9 May, 1708; d. 20 June, 1790, Powhatan Co., son of Thomas and Obedience (Branch) Cocke Trent Turpin; m. Mary Jefferson, dau. of Thomas and Mary (Field). 6T268; 4V249; 25W(1)110; Free II:292.

William m. 23 June, 1773, Sary Harris, dau. of William. Cumberland Co. Mar. Record. He, son of Thomas and Mary (Jefferson); she, dau. of William (will prov. 1794, Powhatan Co.). 25W(1)111; Louisa, p. 333.

TURPINE

Cecily m. Abram Perkins.

Thomas m. 9 April, 1767, Martha Ward Gaines, in Maniken Town. Douglas Reg., p. 9.

TURTON

Charlotte (____) m. Willis Simmons.

TUTHILL

Anna m. John Cleves Symmes.

TUTT

____ m. after 1776, ____ Minor, dau. of Thomas (will prov. 1776, Spotsylvania Co.) and Alice (Thomas). 9W(1)59.

____ m. Sarah Covington, dau. of Thomas, whose will, prov. 1767, Culpeper Co., proves it.

____ m. bef. 1717, Mary Underwood, dau. of William, whose will of that date, Richmond Co., proves it.

Archibald m. 18 Nov., 1789, Caty Pendleton of Culpeper. St. Mark's, p. 77. He d. 1827; m. Catherine Bowie Pendleton, dau. of James, Jr., and Catherine (Bowie) of Culpeper Co. 39V285; Rixey, pp. 245-6; Slaughter, p. 149.

Benjamin, d. 1817; m. Elizabeth Pendleton, dau. of Nathaniel and Elizabeth (Clayton) Anderson Pendleton; res. "The Retreat," Culpeper Co. 40V295; Slaughter, p. 154.

Mary m. Hay Taliaferro.

Mildred m. Thomas Norman (1st wife).

Richard m. Mary Underwood, dau. of Capt. William (will, 1717, Richmond Co.). 2T288.

Richard m. 7 Oct., 1731, Elizabeth Johnson. Spotsylvania Co. Mar. Record.

Richard J. m. Margaret "Peggy" (Miskell) Garnett, b. 4 Feb., 1762; d. 1 Feb., 1824, widow of Thomas Garnett and dau. of William and Elizabeth (Samford). Boddie-HSF IV:49.

TUTWILER

____, a dau., m. ____ McClough.

Elizabeth m. ____ Brock.

Fanny m. John Keesner.

Mary m. ____ Whitesel.

TWEEDEL

William m. 1 Jan., 1789, Sarah Johnson. Halifax Co. Mar. Record.

TWEEDY

Joseph m. 22 Sept., 1791, Elizabeth Franklin by Menoah Lesley. Campbell Co. Mar. Record.

Mary m. John Cocke.

Nancy m. Thomas Rosser.

TWENTYMAN

Benjamin of Orange Co., age 70, m. 26 Jan., 1790, Mrs. Betty Nulty, age 50. Announced in The Virginia Herald and the Fredericksburg Advertiser.

Benoni m. 1790, Elizabeth Nutly. Orange Co. Mar. Record.

Betsy m. Lawrence Gillock.

Polly m. Benjamin Bragg.

TWIFORD

Director m. Moses Watson.

Elizabeth m. John Moor.

Joice m. Amos Lockwood.

William m. 24 April, 1794, Ann Griffy. License signed by James Newell, Esq. Wythe Co. Mar. Record.

TWISDALE

____ m. bef. Oct., 1712, Sarah Williams, dau. of John, whose will of that date mentions "daughter Sarah Twisdale."

TWISDELL

John m. bef. 19 Oct., 1711/2, Sarah Williams, dau. of John. Proven by Court Record of that date, Essex Co.

TWITTY

Betty m. William Clack.

TWITWILER

John m. 21 Nov., 1796, Mary Strough. Rockingham Co. Wayland, p. 8.

TWOMEY

Nancy Annis m. John Stephens.

TWYFORD

William m. 13 Oct., 1797, Caty Slimp. Wythe Co. Mar. Record.

TWYMAN

Agatha m. Robert Dearing.

Agatha m. John Warwick.

Betty m. William Johnson Wood.

Catherine m. John Thompson (or Tomson).

Catherine m. Phillipp Warwick.

Elizabeth m. William J. Wood.

Elizabeth Montague m. (1) Col. Alex Willis; m. (2) Col. Joshua Fry.

George m. 16 July, 1724, Agatha Buford. Christ Church, p. 164. George, Jr., b. 1698; d. 1734, son of George and Catherine (Montague). Agatha, b. 13 Aug., 1705, dau. of Thomas and Elizabeth (____). They res. in Spotsylvania Co. Cowherd, p. 267; Wilcoxson, p. 415.

George, b. 1676; d. 1703; m. Catherine Montague, b. 1678, dau. of Peter. Cowherd, p. 267; Wilcoxson, p. 398.

George III, b. 19 March, 1731; d. 1822, son of George, Jr., and Agatha (Buford); m. 1754, Mary Walker, dau. of John; res. Albemarle Co. Cowherd, p. 267; Wilcoxson, p. 415.

James, son of George III and Mary (Walker), m. (1) Theresa James; m. (2) Clara Thompson. Wilcoxson, p. 415.

Joseph m. 26 Sept., 1794, Lucy Rodes. Sur. Horsley Goodman. Albemarle Co. Mar. Bond. He, son of George III and Mary (Walker). Wilcoxson, p. 415. Lucy was dau. of David (d. 1794). Albemarle, p. 306.

Mary m. James Bristow.

TWYMAN (cont.)
Reuben Cowherd, Capt. in Rev. War, b. 1758, Culpeper Co.; d. 1839, Woodford Co., Ky., son of William, Sr., and Winnifred (Cowherd); rem. to Ky., 1783; m. 10 Oct., 1788, Bourbon Co., Ky., Margaret Griffin, b. 1763-5; d. 1835. 18 Ky. Reg. 53:96; Cowherd, pp. 268-9; Woodford Co., p. 55.
Ruth m. David Watts, Jr.
Samuel, d. 1822/3, son of George III and Mary (Walker); m. April, 1782, Frances Rogers, d. 1837/8, dau. of Giles of Albemarle Co.; res. Orange Co. Wilcoxson, p. 415.
Sarah m. ____ Sanford.
Sarah m. Richard Sanford.
William, Sr., b. 27 May, 1727; d. 1810, son of George III and Mary (Walker); served in Rev. War; m. ca 1753, Winnifred Cowherd, b. ca 1729, dau. of James and Elizabeth (Lacy). Cowherd, p. 267; Woodford Co., p. 55.
William, Jr., b. 1754; d. 1843, son of William, Sr., and Winnifred (Cowherd); m. Elizabeth Garnett, dau. of James (will prov. 1765, Essex Co.). Cowherd, p. 267.

TYCE
Huldah m. Edward Thatcher.

TYE
____ (____) m. John Coggin (2nd wife).

TYLER
____ m. Mary Randolph, dau. of John of Prince William Co. (will dated 11 Sept., 1789). 26V312.
Able m. 28 Nov., 1798, Charlotte Nevil. Shelby Co., Ky. Mar. Record.
Ann m. Charles Terrell.
Ann m. (1) Capt. Peter A. Sturges; m. (2) James Denny; m. (3) Michael Humble.
Ann m. John Badget.
Anne (____) m. Martin Gardiner.
Anne Contesse m. Judge James Semple (1st wife).
Betty m. Andrew Williamson.
Catherine m. John Corrie (1st wife).
Catherine m. Charles Baird.
Charles, of Cameron Parish, Loudoun Co., d. ca 1768, son of John and Susanna (Monroe) Linton Tyler; m. Ann Moore, will dated 1769, dau. of William Moore, whose will, prov. 1769, names "daughter Anne Tyler." Res. Loudoun Co. 21W(1)23.
Charles, son of Henry and Eleanor (Middleton), m. Ann Moore. A dau., Jane Tyler, b. ca 1782. Ann m. (2) Alexander Lithgow. Rhodes, p. 396.
Christian m. Andrew Monroe.
Edith m. Rev. Thomas Robinson.
Edward, b. 17 Jan., 1767; d. 23 March, 1840, son of Edward and Ann (Langley); m. (1) 28 Dec., 1788, Nancy Hughes. 30T40-1. He m. 12 Nov., 1817, Elizabeth (Young) Hitt, b. 4 Nov., 1767, Va.; d. after 1848, Ky., widow of Joel Hitt and dau. of Leonard and Mary Ann (Higgins) Young. Cowherd, p. 330.
Edward, b. 18 Jan., 1718/9; d. 20 May, 1802, Jefferson Co., Ky., son of Edward and Elizabeth (Duvall) of Prince Georges Co., Md.; m. ca

TYLER (cont.)

1750, prob. in Frederick Co., Va., Ann "Nancy" Langley, d. 31 July, 1820, aged 88. 30T40.

Eleanor m. Matthew Harrison.

Elizabeth m. George Terrell.

Elizabeth m. John Greenhow (2nd wife).

Elizabeth m. Samuel Blackwell.

Elizabeth m. ___ Korbey.

Elizabeth Lowe m. (1) Henry Bowcock; m. (2) John Palmer.

Frances m. Richard Gatewood, Jr.

Frances m. Robert Cole.

Francis m. 17 May, 1744, Anne Strother. OPR. She, b. 1723, dau. of William and Margaret (Watts); res. Culpeper Co. and, in 1761, in Augusta Co. 11T120.

Franky m. William Rodd.

Franky m. (1) Richard Gatewood, Jr.; m. (2) Robert Cole.

George, Capt., in Rev. War, b. 1755; d. 1833, son of William and Elizabeth (Keeling); m. Judith Terrell, b. 6 Feb., 1750, dau. of Henry and (2) Sarah (Woodson). 14T58-9.

Hannah m. James Anderson.

Henry of Bruton Parish, will, 1729, York Co., son of Henry; m. (1) Elizabeth Chiles, dau. of Lieut. Col. Walter Chiles (d. bef. 1672); m. (2) Edith Hardaway, dau. of John and Frances (___). She m. (2) ___ Pierce of York Co. 1W(1)84; 8W(1)105; Boddie-HSF V:198; Taylor, p. 189.

Henry m. 1738, Alice Strother, b. 1719, dau. of William (d. 1732, King George Co.) and Margaret (Watts). 11T120; 23W(1)143; 15 Ky. Reg. 45:93.

Jane (___) m. William Woffendale.

Joanna m. Dr. Kenneth McKenzie.

Joanna m. Wood Bouldine.

John, will prov. 1758, son of Richard; m. (1) Elizabeth ___; m. (2) Anne Graves, b. 16 Nov., 1718, dau. of Alexander and Mary (___) Stapleton. 14T52.

John, b. Prince William Co.; d. there, 1792; m. Seagnora Brown. DAR No. 31 432.

John m. 13 Feb., 1782, Sarah Valentine. Sur. James Valentine. Henrico Co. Mar. Bond.

John, son of Capt. Charles and Ann (Moore), m. ___ Muschett of Md.; res. Loudoun Co. 21W(1)23.

John, b. ca 1715; d. 1773, son of John of James City Co.; m. Anne Contesse, dau. of Dr. Louis Contesse, a French Huguenot physician of Williamsburg, Va. 6T262; 10T201; 14T110.

John m. Eleanor Strother, dau. of Benjamin (1712-1789) and Mary (Mason) Fitzhugh Strother. 11T119.

John, Gov. of Va., b. 1747; d. 1813; Capt. in Rev. War; m. Mary Marat Armistead, b. 1761; d. 1797, dau. of Robert and Ann (Shields) Inglis Armistead. 10T20; 7W(1)22; DAR No. 47 465.

John m. 7 Aug., 1799, Mildred Stone by Rev. Martin Walton. Louisa Co. Ministers' Returns.

Judith m. Robert Goodwin.

Lewis m. 29 Dec., 1772, Mary Barradall Palmer, dau. of John Palmer,

TYLER (cont.)

Esq., dec'd. Sur. Richard M. Booker. Charlotte Co. Mar. Bond.

Margaret m. William Waugh.

Margaret m. William Washington.

Maria Henry m. John Boswell Seawell.

Mary m. James Boughan.

Mary m. William Irby, Jr.

Mary m. Rev. William Preston.

Mary m. Henry Terrell.

Mary m. John Irby.

Mary m. James Hatton.

Nancy m. Samuel Fielder.

Pleasants m. 20 Jan., 1796, Anne Valentine, dau. of James. Sur. James Valentine. Henrico Co. Mar. Bond.

Priscialla m. Capt. Abner Dunn.

Rachel m. Stith Hardyman.

Richard m. bef. 25 March, 1693, ____ Baxter, dau. of Nathaniel Baxter, dec'd. Proven by Court Record of that date, Essex Co.

Richard, d. 1803-4, prob. son of William of Caroline Co.; m. by 1772, his cousin, Catherine Gatewood, d. 1816, dau. of Richard, Jr., and Franky (Tyler); res. Caroline Co. 14T57.

Richard, Jr., of Essex Co., b. ca 1685; d. 1761; m. (1) 1722, Catherine Williamson, dau. of Henry and (2) Catherine (Weeks); m. (2) Ann ____. 14T48, 49.

Richard, Jr., m. bef. 25 March, 1725, Catherine (____) Montague, widow of Thomas. Proven by Court Record of that date, Essex Co.

Richard Keeling, b. 27 Oct., 1760; d. bef. 15 Aug., 1832, son of William and Elizabeth (Keeling); m. 1 July, 1790, Mary Cluverius Duke, b. 3 Aug., 1767; d. bef. 1846, dau. of John and Elizabeth (Burnley); rem. 1818 to Tenn. and later to Ky. 14T58; Duke, p. 96.

Robert, Capt., b. 19 Aug., 1751, Cross Creek then in Frederick Co.; d. 6 April, 1815, Tyler's Station, Shelby Co., Ky., son of Edward and Ann (Langley); m. ca 1772, his cousin, Margaret Tyler, b. 15 March, 1755, Va.; d. 15 Oct., 1840, Shelby Co., Ky., dau. of Robert and Eleanor (Bradley). 30T40-2.

Robert, Jr., m. 18 Feb., 1794, Sarah Pritchett. Shelby Co., Ky. Mar. Record.

Samuel, Chancellor, m. Elizabeth Johnson, dau. of James Bray Johnson and Rebecca (Cocke). 4V325; 21W(1)263.

Susanna m. John Phillips.

Susie m. Charles Terrell.

Thomas m. 5 Jan., 1787, Elizabeth Settle. St. Paul's.

William, b. ca 1725; d. 1794, son of William; m. Elizabeth Keeling, dau. of Richard; res. 1771, Caroline Co. 14T57-8; Duke, p. 96. She was his 3rd wife. 58V194-5.

William, prob. son of William and Margaret (Pratt), m. 1755, Esther Jones, dau. of James (will, 1744, King George Co.) and Hester (____). 5T255.

William of Westmoreland Co. m. Esther (____) Jones, widow of James. Her will prov. May, 1770. 4W(1)274.

William, son of Charles (d. ca 1723) of Westmoreland Co., m. Margaret Pratt, dau. of John, Jr., of King George Co. 5T255.

TYLER (cont.)
William, b. 23 June, 1755; d. 23 Sept., 1836, age 80; tombstone in Jefferson Co., Ky., son of Edward and Ann (Langley); m. Sarah Williams, d. 3 Sept., 1834, age 67. 30T40.

TYLEY
Judith m. Archer Gilliam.
Mary m. John Dunston.

TYLOR
Absolom m. 1796, Frances Smith. Orange Co. Mar. Record.
Thomas m. 31 Jan., 1787, Rosanah Terrell, spinster. Sur. Joseph Terrell. Albemarle Co. Mar. Bond.

TYNES
Benjamin m. 1784, Susannah (____) Bridger, widow of James (will, 1782). Boddie-Isle, p. 431.
Isaac m. 2 Oct., 1788, M. Cheatham. Halifax Co. Mar. Record.
Robert m. 28 Dec., 1797, Patsy Gibbs. Isle of Wight Co. Mar. Record.
Sarah m. Arthur Washington.

TYNGEY
____ m. bef. 21 Jan., 1668/9, Elizabeth (____) Knott Man. Proven by Court Record of that date and of May, 1667, Northumberland Co.

TYRA (?TYREE)
Jonathan m. 21 Oct., 1786, Usby (?Ursley) Gowing. Sur. Shedrick Battles. Albemarle Co. Mar. Bond.

TYRE
Thomas m. 28 Nov., 1738, Catherine Jones. Christ Church, p. 170.

TYREE
Winny m. Jesse Middlebrook.

TYRIE
Frances (____) m. Jno. Harris.
William m. 16 May, 1776, Elisabeth Price, both of Dunmore of Rev. John Alderson, Jr. Wayland, p. 154.

TYRREL
Beckie m. Nicholas Hunter Merriwether.

TYRRIE
Ann m. William Day.

TYRRELL
Blacky mar. contract, 8 Dec., 1698, with Sarah Jones, spinster. Boddie-Isle, p. 636.

TYSON
John m. 14 Dec., 1787, Mary Widgeon. Northampton Co. Mar. Record.
Nancy m. Jonathan Fitchett.
Nathaniel m. 13 June, 1764, Judith Wilkins, dau. of John. Northampton Co. Mar. Record. He, d. Sept., 1792; she, dau. of Hon. John Wilkins (d. 1775). 37V374.
Rebecca m. (1) Henry Taylor; m. (2) Richard Barham.

TYUS
Amey m. Hugh Hall.
Elizabeth Mary m. John Hunt.
Frances m. John Thomas.
Hannah m. Green Wynne.
Pamelia m. James Howle.
Polly m. Joshua C. Lundy.

TYUS (cont.)

Thomas was not 14 in 1663, but was of age in 1673. He m. Amy (____) Holdsworth Scarboro, widow 1st of Walter Holdsworth of Charles City Co., 2nd of William Scarboro (d. ca 1679). Boddie-SVF I:385.

U

UMBLES

Ann m. Charles Bebb (or Bibb).

UMBRECKHOUSE

Jacob m. 27 Nov., 1787, Patsy Dismukes. Caroline Co. Mar. Record.

Patty m. Thomas Donahoe.

UNDERHILL

Betsey m. Arthur Roberts.

Daniel m. 27 May, 1761, Mary (____) Thompson. Northampton Co. Mar. Record.

Elizabeth m. Henry Harrison.

John, Capt., will prov. 24 Oct., 1672; m. 1660, Mary (____) Bassett Felgate, widow 1st of William Bassett, 2nd of William Fellgate of London (d. York Co., Va.). She m. (4) Dr. Isaac Clopton. 2W(1)85; 5W(1)80.

Mary m. Josiah Harrison.

Mary m. Benjamin Gary.

Rachel m. William Major.

Sally m. John Badger.

Thomas m. 14 Nov., 1767, Susanna Evans, dau. of Arthur, dec'd. Northampton Co. Mar. Record.

William m. 7 Oct., 1786, Mary Ann Caroline Meachum. Sussex Co. Cameron.

UNDERWOOD

____ m. James Williamson.

____ m. bef. 1798, Mary Faulconer, dau. of Samuel, who made Deed of Gift to his daughter, Mary Faulconer, 2 June, 1798, Spotsylvania Co.

____ m. bef. 1757, Elizabeth Joyner, dau. of William, whose will, dated 25 Oct., 1757, Southampton Co., named as a legatee "daughter Elizabeth Underwood."

____ m. John Dandridge.

____ m. bef. 1776, Margaret Marsh, dau. of John, whose will of that date, Culpeper Co., names "daughter Margaret Underwood."

____ m. bef. 1772, Elender (____) Stubblefield, widow of Capt. Thomas Stubblefield, whose est. div. of that date, Culpeper Co., proves it.

Ann m. Dr. James Williamson.

Ann m. John Curd.

Ann m. John Pope.

Ann (____) m. William Richardson.

Dianah m. Thomas Brumwell.

Elizabeth m. ____ Thatcher.

Elizabeth m. John Shorter.

Elizabeth m. (1) Dr. James Taylor; m. (2) Francis Slaughter; m. (3) Col. John Catlett; m. (4) Rev. Amory Butler.

Fanny m. John Lee.

UNDERWOOD (cont.)

Frances m. Richard Neale.

George m. 25 Dec., 1768, Elizabeth Curd, dau. of Richard[2] and Sarah (Downer). Douglas Reg., p. 11; 22V317; Curd, p. 4.

Gideon m. 1791, Mary Dohony. Orange Co. Mar. Record.

Hannah m. William Lewis.

John m. bef. 24 July, 1646, Dorothy (____) Cay(n)hooe(-hoes), widow of William. Proven by York Co. records, Book 2, 1645-48, p. 49.

John m. Frances Rogers, dau. of George and Frances (Pollard); res. Goochland Co., 1791, when son, Hon. Joseph Rogers Underwood, was born. Biog. Enc. Ky., p. 271.

John m. Molly Muse, dau. of James (d. 1784) and (1) Susannah (____) of Westmoreland Co. 53V316.

Margaret (____) m. (2) John Upton; m. (3) Thomas Lucas (2nd wife).

Mary m. ____ Tutt.

Mary m. James Williamson.

Mary m. (1) Richard Tutt; m. (2) John Fox.

Nathan m. 11 April, 1797, Betsy Wright. Shelby Co., Ky. Mar. Record.

Sarah m. Maj. William Pierce (or Peirce).

Thomas m. (2) ____ Taylor. Grandson, b. 1791, Goochland Co. Biog. Enc. Ky., p. 271.

Thomas m. Jane Pollard, b. 26 May, 1744, dau. of Joseph. She m. (1) ____ Dandridge. Bagby, pp. 346, 347.

Thomas of Goochland Co. m. ca 1792, Elizabeth Southall, dau. of Col. Turner and Martha (Vanderwall). 45V287.

William m. after 1758, Ellen (Hackley) Doniphan Stubblefield, widow 1st of Robert Doniphan, Jr., 2nd of Thomas Stubblefield, and dau. of James and Elizabeth (Shippey) Hackley of King George Co. 26T279.

William, Sr., m. bef. Dec., 1691, ____ Butler, sis. of Amory Butler, given as Ammaree in the Deed of that date, Richmond Co., which states the marriage.

William Thomas, England to America late 1600's, m. (2) ____ Taylor. Great-grandson, b. 1791, Goochland Co. Biog. Enc. Ky., p. 271.

UPDEGRAVE

Susanna m. Benjamin Melton.

UPSHAW

Anne m. ____ Davis.

Cordelia m. Thomas Hopkins.

Elizabeth (____) m. John Christian.

Forrest m. bef. 25 March, 1753, Anne (____) Hunt, widow of John, Sr. Proven by Court Record of that date, Essex Co.

Hanna m. Capt. Thomas Jones.

Hannah m. Daniel Sullivan, Jr.

James m. bef. 1 July, 1753, Succa (____) Streshley, widow of William. Proven by Court Record of that date, Essex Co.

John, b. 2 July, 1715, Essex Co.; d. there, 23 July, 1801, son of Capt. William; m. bef. 31 Dec., 1765, Mary Lafon, b. 1744, Essex Co.; d. 1807, dau. of Nicholas. Mar. proven by Court Record, 31 Dec., 1765, Essex Co. 18W(2)80. They moved to Ky. by 1786. Woodford Co., p. 36.

Margaret m. Col. Samuel Hipkins.

Maria m. Capt. Nicholas Lafon.

UPSHAW (cont.)
Susanna m. William Brooking.
William m. bef. 16 Dec., 1716, Hannah (____) Carber, widow of James. Proven by Court Record of that date, Essex Co.
William, Jr., will prov. 1760, Essex Co.; m. 1733-35, Tamazen Sthreshley, dau. of Capt. Thomas. 18W(2)78-9.

UPSHUR
____ m. Edmund Bayly.
Abell m. 15 Nov., 1779, Elizabeth Gore, dau. of David, dec'd. Northampton Co. Mar. Record.
Anne m. John Teackle.
Elizabeth m. Littleton Dennis.
Elizabeth m. Thomas Teackle.
John m. 23 July, 1794, Rosey Robins. Northampton Co. Mar. Record.
John m. 17 March, 1781, Margaret (____) Michael, widow of William. Northampton Co. Mar. Record.
Martha m. Francis William Buckner.
Mary m. Cave Jones.
Rachel m. Edmund Bayly.
Sally m. Peter Hack.
Sarah m. Henry Gascoigne.
Susanna m. Edward Robins (2nd wife).
Susannah m. John Teackle.
Thomas m. 29 Jan., 1761, Anne Stockley, ward of Nathaniel and Mary Beavans. Northampton Co. Mar. Record.

UPTEGRAVES
Molly m. Humphrey Wells.

UPTIGROVE
Hannah m. Elisha Collins.

UPTON
John, Lieut. Col., d. 1652, Isle of Wight Co.; m. Margaret (____) Underwood, widow of William. 7T190; Boddie-Isle, p. 92; Boddie-HSF IV:148.
Margaret m. John Finey.
Margaret (____) m. Capt. Thomas Lucas.
Rebekah m. William Thomas.
Sarah m. William Pierce.

URQUHART
James m. 4 Aug., 1787, Penelope Malory by Rev. John Buchanan of Henrico Parish. Henrico, p. 231.
Jno. m. 18 Nov., 1787, Lucy Lepetit by Rev. John Buchanan of Henrico Parish. Henrico, p. 231.

USHER
Ann Jenny m. Loftus Pullin.
James m. 1788, Catherine Whitesides. Bath, p. 131.
Margaret m. William Steuart.

USSERY
John m. 23 Dec., 1797, Nancy Green by Rev. John Neblett, Methodist. Lunenburg Co. Ministers' Returns.
Mary m. Sherwood Callaham.
Nancy m. John Christopher.
William m. 21 Dec., 1797, Sally Williams by Rev. John Jones, Methodist

USSERY (cont.)
Lunenburg Co. Ministers' Returns.

UTIE
Mary Ann m. Gov. Richard Bennett.

UTLEY
John m. 23 Dec., 1772, Nancy Clarkson, both in Goochland. Douglas Reg., p. 13.
William m. 13 Dec., 1766, Mary Ragline, both in this parish. Douglas Reg., p. 9.

UTTERBACK
Alice m. John Kemper.
Anne m. George Willingham.
Benjamin, b. 17 Jan., 1754, Prince William Co.; d. March, 1842, Morgan Co., Ind., son of Harmon; served in Rev. War; m. 15 Nov., 1780, Elizabeth Snelling, b. ca 1760, Fauquier Co.; d. 1810, Woodford Co., Ky.; res. 1797-1822, Woodford Co., Ky. Utterback, p. 43.
Charles, b. 8 May, 1769, Fauquier Co.; d. 14 Feb., 1843, Anderson Co., Ky., son of Henry and Agnes (Brumback); m. 7 Sept., 1789, Jemima Nelson, b. 1770, Fauquier Co.; d. Anderson Co., Ky., dau. of John and Sarah (Whitson); rem. to Ky. ca 1805. Utterback, p. 45.
Christina m. Peter Wommack.
Elizabeth m. George Norman.
Hankinson Adam, b. ca 1770, Culpeper Co.; d. 1825, Boone Co., Ky., son of Joseph; m. ca 1791, Catherine Pence, a Quaker woman, b. ca 1771, Va.; d. ca 1840, Boone Co., Ky. Utterback, p. 48.
Henry, b. ca 1751, Bromfield Parish, Culpeper Co.; d. 1805, Montgomery Co., Ky.; m. ca 1796 in Ky. Tabitha McDowell of Va. parents. Utterback, p. 41.
John, b. 1740, Germantown, Prince William Co.; d. ca 1833; Fauquier Co., son of Henry and Anna (____); m. 1764, Anna Catherine ____, b. Fauquier Co. Utterback, p. 38.
Mary m. Alexander Scott.
Nimrod, b. 10 May, 1768, Fauquier Co.; d. 7 Oct., 1823, Woodford Co., Ky., son of Jacob and Anna Elizabeth (Martin) of Frederick Co.; m. 6 Oct., 1796, Quinnie Perry, b. 22 July, 1776, Frederick Co.; d. 30 Aug., 1858, Keokuk Co., Iowa. She res. Johnson Co., Ind., with small children. Utterback, pp. 61-2.
Priscilla m. John Pitts.
Selly m. Thomas Norman.
Susannah m. John Perry.
William, b. ca 1776, Fauquier Co., son of John and Anna Catherine (____); m. 4 July, 1799, Mary "Polly" O'Bannon, b. ca 1777, dau. of P. H. and Josephine (Miller). Utterback, p. 47.

UTZ
Abram m. 1 Nov., 1795, Sarah Snyder, dau. of Adam and Ann (Towles). 13T28-9.
Rachel m. Joshua Wayland.

UZZEL(-L)
Julia m. Thomas Carroll.
Mary m. John Davis.
Patsey m. Josiah Wills.
Thomas m. 13 Nov., 1795, Polly James. Isle of Wight Co. Mar. Record.

UZZLE

Rebecca m. Isaiah Heath.

V

VADEN

____ m. Mary Meekins, dau. of Thomas (d. 1721). Barton I:15.

Henry m. 1768, Susan Green, dau. of Abram and Elizabeth (Cowles). 5T137.

Herod m. 13 Nov., 1785, Susannah Smith. Sur. Grief Talley. Amelia Co. Mar. Bond.

VADING

____ m. bef. 1787, Elizabeth Vaughan, sis. of Rabley Vaughan of King William Co., whose will, prov. 1787, Williamsburg, Va., proves it.

VAHANE

Thomas m. 10 Jan., 1683, Mary Thompson. Christ Church, p. 22.

VAIDEN

John m. 1 Feb., 1787, Jennie Moss. Sur. Augustine Eastern. Goochland Co. Mar. Bond.

Micajah of New Kent Co. m. Nancy Edwards, b. King William Co.; d. 25 May, 1835, dau. of Ambrose and (1) Wealthean (Butler). Old King Wm., p. 178.

VAIL

Rebecca m. Job Jeffries (2nd wife).

VAINT

William m. 27 Aug., 1723, Catherine Reddish. St. Paul's.

VALENTINE

Anne m. Stanhope Vaughan.

Anne m. Pleasants Tyler.

Edward m. 17 July, 1791, Princess Anne Co., Elizabeth Singleton. LN Co. 2:21.

Elizabeth m. Richard Croshaw Graves.

Elizabeth m. William Montague.

Elizabeth Jones m. Isam Lester.

George m. 13 Nov., 1787, Dinah Sparrow. Norfolk Co. Mar. Record.

Jacob m. 29 Sept., 1762, Josiah (?) Laughlin. Middlesex Co. 7W(1)19

Jacob m. bef. March, 1792, Fanny Moore, dau. of James (d. 1787). Proven by Deed, 1792, Princess Anne Co.

James m. 11 Dec., ____, Anne Owens. Petersburg. Cameron.

James m. bef. Jan., 1667, Mary Midland, dau. of George (d. bef. 1667) Proven by Deed of that date, King William Co.

Mary (____) m. Samuel Timson.

Sarah m. John Tyler.

Sarah m. Mathew Godfrey.

VALLANDIGHAM

Lewis served in Rev. War from Va., m. Elizabeth Bruce; rem. to Scott Co., Ky., 1780-85. A son was born, 1794. Perrin, 1886, Simpson Co., p. 712.

VALLENTINE

John m. Mary Midland, eldest dau. of George, dec'd. See Deed, 9 Jan. 1667. Boddie-Isle, p. 550.

VALLINES
Elizabeth m. Thomas Hurst (2nd wife).
VALLOTT
Ann m. Stockeley Towles.
Ann (____) m. Angell Jacobus.
Catherine m. Samuell Batchelder.
Claude, age 35 in 1684, m. Ann Jenkinson; res. 1708, Middlesex Co., where dau. married. Ann m. (2) Angell Jacobus; m. (3) Philip Calvert. 13T24; Orange III:94.
VAN BUSKIRK
Isaac, b. 1760, Loudoun Co.; d. 1843, Monroe Co., Ind.; m. Jerusha Little. DAR No. 51 818.
VANCE
____ m. Jacob Warwick.
Catherine m. Henry Spitzer.
David, Capt., b. ca 1748, Frederick Co.; m. Priscilla Brank; rem. to Burk Co., No. Car. Hartford C-1655(6), 10 May, 1958. Signed R. Z. H. He d. 1813, No. Car., from where he served in Rev. War. DAR No. 32 229.
Elizabeth m. David Young.
Elizabeth m. William Davidson.
Elizabeth m. Joseph Edwards.
Hugh, will 1756; m. Lydia (Ridley) Portlock, widow of Charles Portlock (will, 1752) and dau. of Capt. Nathaniel and Elizabeth (Day). Boddie-Isle, p. 203.
John m. 11 July, 1800, Barren Co., Ky., Sally Perkins, b. 23 Oct., 1768, dau. of Joel and Ann (Bailey) of Albemarle Co. 30T287.
John m. 4 Dec., 1795, Jane Green. Rockingham Co. Wayland, p. 7.
Margaret m. Leonard George.
Mary m. Robert Boggs.
Sally m. James McAllister.
William m. 15 April, 1777, Barbara Crider by Rev. John Alderson, Jr. Rockingham Co. or Greenbrier Co. Ministers' Returns.
VANCIL
Samuel, b. ca 1768; d. 1828, Sangamon Co., Ill., son of John of Patrick Co.; m. (1) ca 1795, Patrick Co., Mary Peckelheimer, d. 1822; m. (2) ____ (____) Wakefield; res. Montgomery Co. then to Ky. and lived in Logan Co. and Lincoln Co., then moved to Warren Co., Ohio, and to Franklin Co., Ind., and settled in Sangamon Co., Ill., in 1818. Sangamon, p. 735.
VAN CLEAVE
Aaron m. 4 March, 1794, Elizabeth Van Cleave. Shelby Co., Ky. Mar. Record.
Benjamine m. 30 Dec., 1800, Sarah Kearns. Shelby Co., Ky. Mar. Record.
Elizabeth m. Aaron Van Cleave.
Eunes m. John Van Cleave.
Jane m. Adam Weble.
Jane m. Nathan Chapman.
John m. 22 Sept., 1794, Eunes Van Cleave. Shelby Co., Ky. Mar. Record.
John m. 8 Nov., 1794, Mariah Kernes. Shelby Co., Ky. Mar. Record.

VAN CLEVE (cont.)
Ralph (female) m. Benjamin Daugherty.
VAN CLIEF
Ann m. Joseph Payne.
VANDAGESTEEL
Priscilla m. ____ Hay.
VANDEGROT
Martha m. Edward West.
VANDERHEYDEN
Ariana m. (1) James Frisby; m. (2) Thomas Bordley; m. (3) Edmund Jennings.
VANDERWALL
Martha m. Turner Southall.
Nathaniel m. 1734, Martha Pleasants, dau. of Joseph and Martha (Cocke) res. Henrico Co. 45V280. Given as Vandewall. 13T66; 4V327.
VANDEVERTER
Jacob m. 3 Feb., 1777, Elizabeth Bibl(?) by Rev. John Alderson, Jr. Rockingham Co. or Greenbrier Co. Ministers' Returns.
VANDEVOR
Eleanor m. John Scott.
VANDEWALL
Mary m. William Lewis.
VAN DIKE
Chalmers Delilah m. George Walton.
VANGOVER
____ m. bef. 1713, ____Lawry, sis. of James, whose will of that date, Lancaster Co., proves it.
Caleb m. 16 June, 1796, Anne Trower. Princess Anne Co. LNCo. 2:24.
VANHAN
William m. 25 Dec., 1715, Mary Wake. Christ Church, p. 83.
VANHOLT
Joseph m. 27 Feb., 1798, Elizabeth Whitehurst by Rev. Anthony Walke. Princess Anne Co. Ministers' Returns.
VANHOOK
Anna m. ____ Jones.
Jacob, b. 1761, Orange Co., No. Car.; rem. to Va., 1807, where he died pensioned in Halifax Co. for service in Rev. War; m. Lucretia ____. DAR No. 28 576.
Mary m. Capt. James Fulkerson.
VAN HORN
Clara m. Samuel Sale.
VANLANDINGHAM
____, a dau., m. ____ Clowes.
VAN METER
____ m. Thomas Swan.
____ m. Thomas Shepard.
Absolom, b. ca 1751; d. Mason Co., 1803, son of Henry and Martha (Moore); m. in Greene Co., Penna., his cousin, Priscilla Van Meter. Lucas, p. 412.
Ann m. Abel Seymour.
Catherine m. George McCulloch.
Elizabeth m. William Thomas.

VAN METER (cont.)

Garrett, Col., b. 1732, N. Y.; d. 1788, Point Pleasant, Va.; served in Rev. War from Hampshire Co.; m. 1757, Ann (Markee) Sibley. DAR No. 51 892. He, b. Feb., 1734, N. Y., son of Isaac and Ann (Wynkoop); rem. to Va., 1744. 34 Ky. Reg. 38.

Hannah m. Thomas McFerran.

Henry, b. 1767, son of Henry, Sr., and Margaret (Moore); m. Christina Van Sickles, sis. of Capt. Anthony; rem. ca 1800 to Mason Co. Lucas, p. 418.

Isaac m. ca 1717, Mooreland Manor, Penna., Anne (or Annah or Annetgie) Wynkoop, dau. of Garrit and Jacomytge (Fakker); rem. 1744 to Hardy Co.; killed and scalped by Indians, 1757. 34 Ky. Reg. 37.

Isaac, b. 10 Dec., 1757, son of Garrett; m. Bettie Inskeep; res. Frederick Co. 34 Ky. Reg. 38.

Isaac, b. 1750; d. 1798, son of Henry and Hannah (Pyle); served in Rev. War; m. Hester Ann Peck, b. 1760; d. 1835, dau. of Jacob and Lydia (Borden); res. Pattonsburg, Va. 11W(2)328; 13W(2)276.

Jacob, b. Somerset Co., N. J.; d. 16 Nov., 1798, Hardin Co., Ky.; served in Rev. War; m. 1741, Frederick Co., Letitia Strode (or Stroud), b. 30 Aug., 1725; d. 25 Dec., 1799; rem. 1769 to S. W. Penna., now Greene Co.; in 1779 to Hardin Co., Ky. DAR Mag., April, 1930, p. 521.

Jacob, Col., b. 18 May, 1764, Va., son of Garrett; m. 1791, Tabitha Inskeep, dau. of Joseph and Hannah (McCullock). 34 Ky. Reg. 38.

Joanna m. Jacob Lancaster.

John, will, 1745, Frederick Co.; m. (1) Sarah Bodine; m. (2) Margaret Miller. He had a dau., b. 1715. Hartford B-9407(6), 18 Aug., 1956. Signed M. M. H.

Katherine m. Jacob Holzapfel.

Margaret m. Samuel Haycraft.

Mary "Patsie" m. Capt. Anthony Van Sickes.

Mary m. (1) David Henton; m. (2) William Chenoweth.

Phoebe m. Ellis Thomas, Jr.

Priscilla m. Absolom Van Meter.

Rebecca m. Abraham Hite.

Rebecca m. Edward Rawlings.

Ruth m. Capt. Samuel Gill.

Sarah m. ____ Rickman.

VAN NORTH

Margaret m. William Brown.

VANORDAL

Laney m. Nicholus Kerns.

VANOSDALE

Cornelius m. 1785, Jane Wilson. Bath, p. 132.

VANS

Agatha m. James Curtis.

Constance m. ____ Daniel.

Elizabeth m. ____ Curtis.

VANSANDT

Elizabeth m. William Maxwell.

Joshua m. 1794, Mary Morris. Rockbridge Co. Morton, p. 537.

VANSANT

Elijah m. 1789, Botetourt Co., Elinor Nelson. Kegley, p. 481.

Isaiah m. 1783, Botetourt Co., Margaret Thompson. Kegley, p. 481.

VANSE

Vincent m. bef. 1692, Anne Sharp, dau. of John. Barton I:39.

VAN SICKES

Anthony, Capt., b. 1771; d. 29 April, 1815, Meigs Co., Ohio; enl. in War of 1812 from Mason Co.; m. (1) 29 April, 1799, Mary "Patsie" Van Meter, b. ca 1771, dau. of Henry and Martha (Moore); m. (2) 6 June, 1811, Zelpla Hubbill in Meigs Co., Ohio. She m. (2) Rev. Eli Stedman. Lucas, p. 420.

Christina m. Henry Van Meter.

VANSTAVERN

Nicholas m. 31 March, 1788, Catey Howard, spinster. Sur. George Howard. Albemarle Co. Mar. Bond.

VARNON

Hannah m. Richard Taylor.

VASOR

____ m. Fanny Chastain, dau. of John, Sr. (will prov. 1807, Bedford Co.). Huguenot 6:162-3.

VASS

____ m. bef. 8 Aug., 1763, Mary Curtis, dau. of Rice, whose will of that date, Spotsylvania Co., proves it.

Ann m. ?Peter Brooks.

Catharine m. Thomas Montague.

Catherine m. ____ Jones.

James, merchant of Falmouth, m. 12 Oct., 1799 in Prince William Co., Susanna Brooke of that county. Announced in The Virginia Herald, 18 Oct., 1799. 13V223, 224; 14V107; 20V100; 30V69.

John m. Rachel Pendleton, b. 1690's, dau. of Philip and Isabella (Hurt 39V282; 24W(1)256; Farmer, p. 65; Slaughter, p. 148; Winston, p. 196 He m. bef. 25 March, 1713. Proven by Court Record of that date, Essex Co.

Katherine m. ?Henry Hudson.

Martha m. William Jack.

Mary m. Baker De Graffenreid.

Philip m. 28 Dec., 1780, Sarah Mead. Louisa Co. Mar. Record.

Vincent m. 29 Aug., 1783, Elizabeth Mannin, both in Orange. Douglas Reg., p. 48. Given as Manning. 26V197.

Vincent m. bef. 25 March, 1693, Anne Sharp, dau. of John, dec'd. Proven by Court Record of that date, Essex Co.

Vincent of Essex Co. m. 22 Aug., 1757, Jane (____) Mountague. Sur. Jno. Montague. Middlesex Co. Mar. Bond. Court Record, 31 Dec., 1757, Essex Co., indicates she was widow of Thomas Montague.

VASSAR

Mary m. Theophilus Scott.

VASSER

____ believed m. bef. 1795, Tabitha Vick, dau. of James, whose will of that date, Southampton Co., names "daughter Tabitha Vasser."

George m. 2 March, 1791, Salley Hunt. Halifax Co. Mar. Record.

Peter m. 5 Feb., 1799, Polly Vasser. Halifax Co. Mar. Record.

Polly m. Peter Vasser.

VASSER (cont.)

William m. 8 Dec., 1797, Tabitha White. Halifax Co. Mar. Record.

VAUDEVILLE

Marks m. 17 Oct., 1789, Susanna Lewis by Rev. John Buchanan in Henrico Parish. Henrico, p. 291.

VAUGHAN

____ m. bef. 1779, Rebecca Burn, dau. of David, whose will, dated 1779, Southampton Co., names "daughter Rebecca Vaughan."

____ m. Mary Bacon. She m. (2) Edwin Stark. 4W(1)271.

____ m. Elizabeth Shields, dau. of James (d. 1727). 5W(1)117.

____ m. Dr. Andrew Kean (1st wife).

Betsey m. William Poltney.

Chancy m. 7 Feb., 1793, Elizabeth Martin. Halifax Co. Mar. Record.

Craddock m. Feb., 1793, Mary Williamson. Sur. Frederick James. Cumberland Co. Mar. Bond.

Dorothy m. Thomas Hunt.

Edmund m. 6 March, 1775, Sally Michaux. Sur. John Woodson. Cumberland Co. Mar. Bond.

Elizabeth m. Nathaniel Preston.

Elizabeth m. ____ Vading.

Elizabeth m. William Haynes.

Elizabeth m. William Rives.

Ephraim m. 17 April, ____, Parthena Ridout. Dinwiddie Co. Cameron.

Erman Elliott m. William Le Grand.

Frances m. John McFarquhar.

Frances A. m. Fred Jones.

Frankey m. Moses Palmer.

Frederick m. 5 Feb., 1781, N. Bowlware. Halifax Co. Mar. Record.

James m. 27 Feb., 1783, Judith Hopkins, both of Goochland. Douglas Reg., p. 22.

James m. 20 Jan., 1777, Mary Harris, both of this parish. Douglas Reg., p. 17.

James m. 27 Feb., 1757, Amelia Brumfield, both in this parish. Douglas Reg., p. 3.

James m. 15 Dec., 1785, Sarah LeGrand. Halifax Co. Mar. Record.

Jane m. Daniel Stone.

John m. 5 Nov., 1686, Sarah Poindexter. St. Peter's, p. 417.

John m. 9 June, 1794, Betty Mullins. Sur. William Mullins. Charlotte Co. Mar. Bond.

John m. 2 March, 1787, Anne Stanfield. Halifax Co. Mar. Record.

John m. 3 Feb., 1754, Mary Barnes. Douglas Reg., p. 1.

Joseph m. 1798, Nancy Turner. Orange Co. Mar. Record.

Kitty m. Dr. Andrew Kean.

Lewis m. 23 Oct., 1787, Mary Lee. Caroline Co. Mar. Record.

Lily m. Coleman Pitts.

Littleberry m. 22 May, 1774, Julianna Brown, both in Henrico. Douglas Reg., p. 15.

M. m. William Martin.

Major m. Anne "Nancy" Lanier, dau. of Sampson and Elizabeth (Chamberlin). 3T135.

Martha m. John Blackwell.

Martha m. William Jackson.

VAUGHAN (cont.)

Mary m. Jesse Brooks.
Mary m. Larkin Sandidge.
Mary m. James Morriss.
Mary (____) m. Seth Purkeson.
Mildred m. Benoni Smith.
Molly m. ____ Christian.
Molly m. Edward Freeman.
Nancy m. William Thompson.
Nancy m. Richard Brooks.
Nancy m. Jeremiah Childrey (or Childress).
Nancy (____) m. (2) Vivion Daniel (2nd wife); m. (3) Shelton C. Watkins.
Obedience m. John Mitchell.
Patrick m. 21 April, 1783, Mary Smith. Sur. Elijah Brumfield. Goochland Co. Mar. Bond.
Patsey m. John Dickie.
Patsy m. Anthony Haydon.
Patty m. William Vaughan.
Peggy m. William Page.
Peter m. 10 Nov., 1798, N. Turner. Halifax Co. Mar. Record.
Peter m. 28 Aug., 1784, Elizabeth Raines. Prince George Co. Cameron
Peter m. 31 Aug., 1797, Sarah Beazley by Rev. John Woodville. St. Mark's Parish.
Peter m. 18 Oct., 1786, Mary Godwyn Boisseau. Dinwiddie Co. Cameron
Phillip m. 20 Sept., 1790, S. Fleming Bates. Halifax Co. Mar. Recor
Polly m. Jason Meador.
Polly m. Coleman Pitts.
Polly m. Benjamin Perkins.
Polly m. Thomas Lanier.
Ruth m. Giles Brown.
S. m. Edward Nunally.
Sally m. Richard Vawter.
Samuel, b. 1750, Va.; d. 1825, Ky.; m. Mourning Hope, b. 1760, Va.; d. 1842, Ky. DAR Query, March, 1945.
Sarah m. George Wilcox.
Seymour believed m. bef. 1791, Amy Cobb, dau. of Henry, whose will of that date, Southampton Co., names "daughter Amy Vaughan" and "son in-law Seymour Vaughan."
Shadrach m. 19 June, 1770, Mary Merriwether, both in Goochland. Douglas Reg., p. 12.
S. R. m. Robert Wade.
Stanhope m. bef. Dec., 1771, Anne Valentine, dau. of Joseph, whose will recorded on that date, York Co., proves it.
Susannah m. Alex. Andrews.
Susannah m. Stoakley Turner.
Thomas m. bef. 1791, Sarah Long, dau. of Broomfield Long. Proven by Deed of that date, Spotsylvania Co.
Thomas m. 11 Aug., 1767, M. Moody. Halifax Co. Mar. Record.
Thomas m. 9 Dec., 1797, Patsey Tucker. Halifax Co. Mar. Record.
William m. 13 Sept., 1768, Ann Dancy, dau. of John. Charles City Co. Mar. Record.

VAUGHAN (cont.)

William, Capt., m. Jane Seawell, dau. of John and Jane (Boswell). 8W (1)55.

William m. 5 Dec., 1793, Patty Vaughan. Caroline Co. Mar. Record.

William m. 23 Sept., 1781, Patsey Mimms, dau. of Thomas. Sur. James Vaughan. Charlotte Co. Mar. Bond.

William m. 20 Dec., 1791, Lucy LeGrand. Halifax Co. Mar. Record.

VAUGHN

____ m. Sally Harris, dau. of Rebecca (Lanier) Harris, whose will, 1816, Greensville Co., names "daughter Sally Vaughn."

Cornelius m. Nancy Carter, dau. of Job, Sr., and Anne (____). She m. (2) Edward Carter. Boddie-HSF V:257.

James m. 7 Nov., 1796, Betsy Cowling. Isle of Wight Co. Mar. Record.

Martha m. James Shields, Jr.

Mary m. John Whitehead.

Nancy m. Bailey Beech.

Naomi m. William Reames.

Patsy m. William Buckner.

Peggy m. Matthew Garner.

Susan m. David Shelton.

VAUGHOB

Peggy m. Samuel Blare.

VAUGHON

Mary m. William Bourn.

VAUGHTER

____ m. bef. 1788, Agnes Richardson, dau. of John and Mary (Curd), whose wills, 1753 and 1788, Charlotte Co., prove it.

Samuel, d. 1788; m. 1763, Agnes Richardson, d. 1817-8, Charlotte Co., dau. of John and Mary (Curd). 45V201.

VAULX

____ m. ____ Foxhall, sis. of John. Proven by Will of Caleb Butler, 16 Feb., 1708/9, Westmoreland Co.

Elizabeth m. (1) Capt. Richard Craddock; m. (2) Daniel Porten, d. 1717; m. (3) Col. George Eskridge.

Katy m. William Bankhead.

Mary m. James Ball.

Mary (____) m. Alexander Gorges.

Peggy m. John Skinker.

Robert, b. 1651, England; d. 1685, son of Robert and Elizabeth (Burwell); m. Mary Foxall, b. 1665, England; d. Va.; res. Westmoreland Co. She m. (2) Alexander Gorges. 44V66-7; NNHM 3:1:234.

Robert of Westmoreland Co. m. 1 Aug., 1749, Elizabeth (Storke) Washington, widow of Henry. 22V214.

VAUSE

Constance m. William Daniel (1st wife).

John m. 14 June, 1679, Elizabeth Calloway. Christ Church, p. 18.

John m. 19 Jan., 1687, Elizabeth Weekes, both natives. Christ Church, p. 36.

VAWTER

Ann m. Philemon Vawter.

Betsy m. John Wyatt Thornton.

Boulware m. 2 Nov., 1786, Sally Berry. Caroline Co. Mar. Record.

VAWTER (cont.)

David, b. Essex Co.; d. ca 1785, Orange Co.; m. Mary Rucker. 28V79.
Elizabeth m. Thomas Newman.
Elizabeth m. John Hopkins.
Fanny m. Adam Beaseley.
Jenny m. Reuben Dear.
Lucy m. Mark Finks.
Margaret m. Achilles Stapp (or Step).
Margaret m. Ephraim Rucker.
Mary m. Thomas Harvey.
Nancy m. Elijah Wilhoit.
Philemon m. bef. 1803, Ann Vawter, dau. of Richard and Frances (Towles). 13T29.
Richard, will dated 1803; m. Frances Towles, b. 8 May, 1730, dau. of Stokeley and Ann (Vallott). 13T29.
Richard m. 12 July, 1787, Sally Vaughan. Caroline Co. Mar. Record.
Russell m. bef. 1784, Mary Sparks, dau. of Thomas and Mary (Towles). She m. (2) James Smith. 13T28.
Tabitha m. Adam Rouse.
William m. 16 Jan., 1774, Ann Ballard. Orange Co. Mar. Record. She, dau. of Philip and Ann (Johnson). They moved to Monroe Co. Orange III:22.
William, d. 27 Nov., 1823, Boone Co., Ky.; m. 19 June, 1784, Orange Co., Mary Rucker; rem. to Woodford Co., Ky. 28V79.
Winifred m. James Dabony.

VEAL

William m. 28 June, 1787, Jane Skinner. Norfolk Co. Mar. Record.

VEALE

Catherine m. George Webb.
Elizabeth m. John Evans.
Mary m. James Ware.

VEATCH

Lander m. 1787, Peggy Thorpe. Orange Co. Mar. Record.
Susanna m. Aaron Crain (or Crowe).

VEAZEY

Ann m. John Taylor.
Maria m. Lazarus Taylor.

VEECH

George m. 23 Sept., 1793, Alleen Bowman. Shelby Co., Ky. Mar. Record.

VELOTT

Anne m. Stokeley Gales.

VENABLE

Abraham m. 21 Jan., 1790, Amy Hundley. Caroline Co. Mar. Record.
Abraham m. 4 Aug., 1783, Mary Morton, dau. of Samuel. Sur. Bryant Ferguson. Charlotte Co. Mar. Bond. She, b. ca 1763, dau. of Samuel and Ann (Moore). He was a Judge and they moved to Lexington, Ky. 11W(2)212.
Abraham, Jr., b. 22 March, 1700; d. Dec., 1768, son of Abraham of New Kent Co.; m. 1723, Hanover Co., Martha Davis, b. 14 July, 1702; d. 18 Feb., 1765, dau. of Robert and Abadiah (Lewis); rem. to Goochland Co. then to Louisa Co. 36V76; Kegley, p. 113; Venable, pp. 14,

VENABLE (cont.)

20.

Betsy Anne m. Capt. Thomas Watkins.

Charles, b. 1730, Louisa Co.; d. Nov., 1815; m. Elizabeth Smith, dau. of Robert of Port Royal, Va. Venable, p. 21. She was dau. of Charles. 9W(1)44.

Elizabeth m. Josiah Morton.

Elizabeth R. m. John Woodson, Jr.

Elizabeth Woodson m. Capt. William M. Watkins.

Frances m. Stephen Dillard.

Hugh Lewis m. 14 June, 1757, Mary Martin, both in this parish. Douglas Reg., p. 3. She, dau. of William of Albemarle Co. Venable, p. 21; Query 7089(A) Virginia Gazette, 10 April, 1964. Signed Mrs. I. M. McDaniel, 4834 Winfree Drive, Houston, Texas.

Jacob Michaux, son of Abram B. (1725-1778) and Elizabeth (Michaux), m. Mary Venable, dau. of John of Campbell Co. and Agnes (Moorman). 45 V217.

James, b. 1734, Hanover Co.; d. 1814, Shelby Co., Ky.; m. ca 1757, Judith Morton, b. 27 Dec., 1739, Charlotte Co.; d. Shelby Co., Ky., dau. of Joseph and (2) Agnes (Woodson). 9 Ky. Reg. 27:87; DAR No. 75 713.

John, son of Abram B. (1725-1778) and Elizabeth (Michaux), m. Elizabeth Raine. 45V217. She prob. m. (2) John Woodson as 2nd wife. Va. Gene. 5:2:57.

John, Capt., b. 1740, Louisa Co.; d. 1811, Jackson Co., Ga., son of Abraham and Martha (Davis); m. bef. 1778, Agnes Moorman, b. 26 Feb., 1743, dau. of Charles, Jr., and Mary (Adams) of Louisa Co.; rem. to Ga., 1791. Mar. prov. by will of Charles Moorman, 1778, Louisa Co. Lynchburg, p. 82; Venable, p. 22.

Joseph Morton m. 20 Jan., 1791, Elizabeth Watkins, dau. of Francis and Agnes (Woodson) of Prince Edward Co. 46V81.

Josiah, son of Abram B. (1725-1778) and Elizabeth (Michaux), m. Jane Clack Thornton, dau. of Sterling Clack Thornton. 45V217.

Judith m. William Moorman (2nd wife).

Martha m. James Brown.

Martha m. Ralph Banks.

Martha m. Nathaniel Venable.

Mary m. Richard Hayes.

Mary m. (1) Charles Moorman; m. (2) Robert Strange.

Mary m. Jacob Michaux Venable.

Mary m. Robert Martin.

Mary m. Col. Charles Allen.

Nancy m. James Daniel.

Nathaniel m. ____ Carrington, dau. of Paul. Free I:406.

Nathaniel, b. 21 Oct., 1733, Hanover Co.; d. 27 Dec., 1804, at "Slate Hill," Prince Edward Co.; m. 29 March, 1755, Elizabeth Woodson, b. 6 June, 1740; d. 27 or 29 Sept., 1791, dau. of Richard and Anne (Madeline) Michaux. 46V77; DAR No. 28 306; Venable, p. 24.

Nathaniel, son of Abram B. (1725-1778) and Elizabeth (Michaux), m. his cousin, Martha Venable, b. 1765, dau. of Nathaniel and Elizabeth (Woodson). 45V217; 46V79.

Pattie m. James Brown.

VENABLE (cont.)
Polly m. Nathaniel Price.
Richard N. m. May, 1797, Polly Morton by Rev. Archibald Alexander. Charlotte Co. Ministers' Returns. He, b. 16 Jan., 1763, Prince Edward Co.; d. there, 1838, son of Nathaniel and Elizabeth (Woodson); served in Rev. War; m. 5 March, 1797, Mary Morton, b. 1779, Charlotte Co., dau. of Col. William and Susan (Watkins). 46V79; McCullough, p. 253; Venable, pp. 35, 36.
Samuel Woodson, Lieut., b. 19 Sept., 1756, Prince Edward Co.; d. 7 Sept., 1821, Sweet Springs, Va., son of Nathaniel and Elizabeth (Woodson); served in Rev. War; m. 15 Aug., 1781, Charlotte Co., Mary Scott Carrington, b. 21 June, 1758; d. 21 March, 1837, Prince Edward Co., dau. of Judge Paul Carrington and Margaret (Read). 46 V78. She, b. 14 Nov., 1756. Venable, p. 41.
William m. 14 Dec., 1794, Rebecca Hurt. Caroline Co. Mar. Record.

VENBEBBER
Eleaner m. Peter Venbebber.
Peter m. 29 June, 1785, Eleaner Venbebber by Rev. John Alderson, Jr. Rockingham Co. or Greenbrier Co. Ministers' Returns.
Peter m. 22 July, 1785, Sarah Yolkecome by Rev. John Alderson, Jr. Rockingham Co. or Greenbrier Co. Ministers' Returns.
* Verona m. George Dickson.

VENIRIS
David m. 15 Jan., 1788, Jenny Dixon. Prince George Co. Cameron.
Kezia m. Charles Whitehurst.

VENTUS
John m. 27 July, 1799, Mary Fuller. Sur. John Williamson. Norfolk Co. Mar. Bond.

VERELL
John m. 28 Oct., 1754, Susanna Moore, spinster. Sur. Edward Pettway. Sussex Co. Mar. Bond.

VERGITT
Job m. bef. 8 Jan., 1715/6, Elizabeth Shipley, dau. of Alice. Proven by Court Record of that date, Essex Co.

VERMEIL
____ m. Anthony Trabue, Jr.

VERMERE
Joseph m. 24 Sept., 1798, Avy Batten by Rev. Anthony Walke. Princess Anne Co. Ministers' Returns.

VERMILION
Francis m. Aug., 1784, Ann Williams. Norfolk Co. Mar. Record.

VERMILLION
Guy m. 15 May, 1782, Sarah (____) Jacob. Northampton Co. Mar. Record.

VERMINET
Maj. m. Jane Carter, dau. of Edward and Sarah (Champe). Albemarle, p. 163.

VERNER
Christian A. m. 1796, Barbara Ruff. Rockbridge Co. Morton, p. 537.

*VENRICK
Susanna m. Peter Peck.

VERNON
Elizabeth m. John Boyd.
Elizabeth m. Dr. John Strachey.
John m. 1782, Elizabeth Hunter. Rockbridge Co. Morton, p. 537.
John m. 1797, Elizabeth Mathews. Rockbridge Co. Morton, p. 537.
Lydia m. Lawson McCullough.
Thomas, b. 1754, Va.; d. 1841, Tenn.; m. Nannie Hicks. DAR No. 66 887.

VERONEY
Joseph, b. 1755, London, Eng.; d. 1825, Fredericksburg, Va.; m. 1794, Mary Kelley, b. 1759; d. 1823. DAR No. 85 263.

VERREUIL
Moise m. Madeleine Prodhon. She m. (2) Jacob Flournoy. Huguenot 7:227.

VESEY (or VEZEY)
Ann m. John Taylor.
Mary m. Lazarus Taylor.

VEST
James believed m. bef. 1794, ____ Davison, dau. of Edward, whose will, prov. that date, Campbell Co., names son-in-law James Vest.
Sarah m. John LeMaster.

VIA
Elizabeth m. William Smith.
Frances (?Stringer) m. John Edey.
Jane m. Daniel Maupin.
Margaret m. Daniel Maupin.
Micajah m. 14 Jan., 1789, Mary Mills, dau. of Henry. Albemarle Co. Mar. Record.
Wade m. 27 April, 1791, Fanny Maupin. Sur. Daniel Maupin. Albemarle Co. Mar. Bond. She, dau. of Gabriel. Huguenot 7:258.
William III, d. 27 June, 1836, Albemarle Co., son of William, Jr.; served in Rev. War; m. (1) 17 March, 1784, Mary Craig, dau. of Thomas and Jane (Jameson) of Albemarle Co. Pension W6363; 31T276.

VIAL
Claude of Hanover Co. m. 18 Sept., 1786, Rose Lilly Powell. Sur. R. H. Waller. York Co. Mar. Bond. 25V300; 1W(1)55.

VIAS
Littleberry m. 1789, Mary Stratton by James Kenney. Campbell Co. Mar. Record.

VIBERT
Susan m. James Hunter Terrell.

VICARIS
Martha m. William Todd.

VICARS
Margaret m. William Boykin.

VICCANS
John m. 4 Oct., 1792, Esther Clegg, dau. of Clark and Sarah (____). Northampton Co. Mar. Record.

VICE
Abram m. 13 Sept., 1796, Nancy Morgan by Rev. John Stanger. Wythe Co. Ministers' Returns.

VICK
____ m. bef. 1791, Priscilla Porter, dau. of James, whose will of that

VICK (cont.)

date, Southampton Co., names "daughter Priscilla Vick."

____ m. bef. 1791, Edith Porter, dau. of James, whose will of that date, Southampton Co., names "daughter Edith Vick."

____ m. bef. 1758, Ann Joyner, dau. of William, whose will of that date, Southampton Co., names "daughter Ann Vick."

Catey m. Nathaniel Woodroof.

Dorcas m. John Boykin.

Elizabeth m. ____ Pope.

Elizabeth (____) m. ____ Wilson.

Jacob m. bef. 1751, Patience Whitehead, dau. of Arthur III (will, Jan 1750/1, Southampton Co.). 44V361.

James may have mar. Sarah (____) Nicholson, a widow and mother of Parks Nicholson. James Vick's will, dated 1795, Southampton Co., names "wife Sarah Nicholson" and states later "with reversion to my children, Parks Nicholson . . . " Nicholson may have been Sarah maiden name and they had a son Parks Nicholson Vick. Further research is indicated.

Mary m. ____ Pope.

May m. ____ Worrell.

Milly m. Robert Newsom, Jr.

Patience m. Daniel Browne.

Rachel m. James Pennington.

Sarah m. Howell Dugger.

Tabitha m. ____ Vasser.

Thomas m. bef. 1794, Martha Boykin, dau. of John, Sr., whose will of that date, Southampton Co., names "daughter Martha, wife of Thomas Vick."

VIE

Gideon m. 21 March, 1759, Isabel ____, both in Albemarle. Douglas Reg., p. 4.

VIERS

Nancy m. Lieut. David Dille (1st wife).

William m. Martha Moon, dau. of William (d. 1800); rem. to Mason Co., Ky. Albemarle, p. 282.

VILLAIN

Elizabeth "Betty" m. Matthew Woodson.

VINANDES

Nancy m. John Coombs.

VINCENT

____ (____) m. Robert Taylor.

Elynor (____) m. Coleman Brough.

Ezekiel m. 17 Sept., 1779, Elizabeth Cooley, dau. of Jacob. Sur. Jacob Cooley. Pittsylvania Co. Mar. Bond.

Jane m. George Gregg.

Mary m. Richard Hardy.

Rebecca m. Alexander Lowe.

Richard m. 29 April, 1737, Elizabeth Gregg. St. Paul's.

Richard m. 31 Dec., 1730, Grace Cheesman. St. Paul's.

Sally m. George Ridley.

Thomas m. 3 April, 1749, Elizabeth Pennuel. St. Paul's.

William m. 19 June, 1779, Glasey Cooley, dau. of Jacob. Sur. Joseph

VINCENT (cont.)
Aiken. Pittsylvania Co. Mar. Bond.

VINCON
Sarah m. John Hinchman.
Susannah m. William Ligg.

VINE
Hannah m. Thomas Kincaid.

VINES
Ann m. Isaac Collier.
Jane m. Abraham Harnsbarger.
Peter (or Jeter) m. Sarah (____) Toppin Anderson. 31V276.
Thomas m. Mary Hill, dau. of Thomas and Eleanor (Charles). Proven by a Court Suit, 19 Sept., 1726, York Co. 8W(1)256-7.

VINEY
Dinah m. William Lewis.
Leah m. George Lewis.
Rachel m. John Lewis, Jr.
Sarah m. Edward McClung.
Susanna m. John McHenry.

VINEYARD
Elizabeth m. James Bryan.
George m. 1790, Mary Campbell. Rockbridge Co. Morton, p. 537.

VINIGER
Philip m. 7 April, 1796, Peggy Seek by John Stranger, M. G. Wythe Co. Mar. Record.

VINSON
Aaron m. 11 Nov., 1767, Sarah Ogburn, dau. of John, Jr. Sussex Co. Mar. Record.

VINZANT
Joshua m. 1794, Mary Morris. Rockbridge Co. Morton, p. 514.

VIOLETT
____ m. (1) ____ Rogers; m. (2) John Summers.

VIRGETT
Job m. bef. 25 March, 1708, Elizabeth Bendry, widow of William. Proven by Court Record of that date, Essex Co.

VIVANDES
Nancy m. John Coombs.

VIVIAN (or VIVION, VIVIEN)
Diana m. Garrett Minor.
Elizabeth m. Vivion Daniel.
Elizabeth m. Paul Thilman.
Frances m. Philip Bush.
Frances m. William Quarles (2nd wife).
Frances m. Robert Brooking.
Jane m. William Crittenden Webb (1st wife).
Jane m. John Howard.
John m. 23 Feb., 1704, Christian Briscoe. Christ Church, p. 63. He m.(1) Margaret ____. 34V348.
John, b. 10 Aug., 1714, Middlesex Co.; d. 1790-1, Fayette Co., Ky., son of John and Elizabeth (Thacker); m. 12 Aug., 1735, Jane Smith, b. 8 Sept., 1715; d. bef. 1780, dau. of John and Ann (____); res. Orange Co. 34V349, 408; 38V133; 47V56; 5W(2)176-7; Christ Church,

VIVIAN (cont.)

p. 169.

John, b. ca 1655; d. 1705, son of Thomas; m. (1) Margaret Smith, d. bef. 1704, dau. of Capt. John and Margaret (____); m. (2) 23 Feb., 1704, Christian (____) Briscoe, widow of William (will prov. 1700, Middlesex Co.). 36V267; 5W(2)176; 7W(2)280; Mss.

John, b. 28 Aug., 1681; d. 12 Feb., 1721/2, Middlesex Co., son of John and (1) Margaret (Smith); m. 19 June, 1711, Elizabeth Thacker, b. 3 Dec., 1694; d. 12 Jan., 1732, dau. of Henry and Elizabeth (Payne). Christ Church, p. 82 (Mar. Record); 34V348, 408; 46V359; 5W(2)176.

Margaret m. William Ferguson.

Margaret m. James Daniel.

Margaret m. Thomas Pratt.

Mary m. William Walker.

Sally m. Rodes Thompson.

Sarah m. Benjamin Skrine.

Thacker, son of John III (b. 1714) and Jane (Smith); m. Mary Brock; rem. to Ga. 34V349; 5W(2)177.

Thacker Smith m. Mary Brock. A son was born, 1770. 47V63.

Thomas, d. 1761, son of John; m. (1) 2 Jan., 1717, Frances Thacker, b. 19 Dec., 1696, dau. of Henry, Jr., and Elizabeth Payne; m. (2) Mary (____) Paise, widow of Thomas; m. (3) Jane ____. First mar. recorded in Christ Church, p. 162. Second mar. proven by Deed, 3 Oct., 1727, Stafford Co. 46V361; 5W(2)174; 6W(2)147.

Thomas, b. 22 Sept., 1776; d. 11 Oct., 1860, son of John who went from Orange Co. in 1780 to Boone settlement in Ky.; m. (1) 23 Dec., 1798, Nancy Bush, d. 1816; m. (2) 12 Sept., 1816, Ann Davis, b. 25 Jan., 1795; d. 14 Dec., 1865; res. 1850, Clark Co., Ky. 34V350; 47V166.

VOLUME

Elizabeth m. Thomas Stephenson.

VORHEIS

Eleanor m. George King.

VOSDEN

Sallie m. George Wright.

VOSS

____ m. bef. 1660, Anne (____) Wilkins, widow of John of Northampton. Proven by Deed, 30 April, 1660, Northampton Co. 25V404

Catharine m. John Greenhow.

Celia m. Eldridge Harris.

Elizabeth m. Richard Lee.

Harriet m. Alexander McRae.

Nicholas m. 9 May, 1794, Mary Spottswood by Rev. John Woodville. St. Mark's.

VOTAW

Isaac, Jr., m. 22 Jan., 1798, Sarah Yates. Sur. Robert Yates. Harrison Co. Mar. Bond.

VOUGHT

Caty m. Michael Criger.

Henry m. 28 July, 1795, Ester Baugh. Sur. John Montgomery. Wythe Co. Mar. Bond.

VOWEL

Page m. 8 Feb., 1795, Nancy Parrot. Halifax Co. Mar. Record.

VOWELL

John G. m. Mary Jaqueline (Smith) Taylor, b. 12 Feb., 1773, widow of Jesse Taylor of Alexandria and dau. of Augustine and (2) Margaret (Boyd). 4W(1)95.

Lucy m. William Loftis.

Paig m. 21 Jan., 1790, Sarah Holt. Halifax Co. Mar. Record.

VOWLES

Rebecca m. William Berryman.

Richard of St. Mary's Co., Md., m. Ann Walters, dau. of Thomas. Proven by Deed, 7 Aug., 1727, Stafford Co.

VUITE

Mary m. Thomas Wadding.

W

WADDEL(-L)

Alexander, b. 2 Sept., 1734; d. 12 Sept., 1834; m. Eleanour Rouss; rem. from Augusta Co. to Pocahontas Co. to Gallipolis Co., Ohio. DAR Query 15379, Feb., 1935. Signed K. S.

Anne m. Presley Carter.

Elizabeth m. Rev. William Calhoun.

Elizabeth m. James Nelson.

Elizabeth m. Raleigh Taylor.

Frankey m. Joseph Gholston.

Jacob m. 27 Nov., 1788, Drucilla League, dau. of James L. Sur. Beverly Fleming. Amelia Co. Mar. Bond.

James, "the blind preacher," b. July, 1739, Ireland; d. 1805 at Hopewell, near Gordonsville, Va., son of Thomas; m. 1768, in Lancaster Co., Mary Gordon, dau. of Col. James (est. sett., 19 Dec., 1771, Lancaster Co.); rem. to Augusta Co. and after the war to Louisa Co. Albemarle, p. 334; Louisa, p. 187; Peyton, p. 319; Waddell, pp. 329-30.

James m. 16 April, 1792, Mildred T. Lindsay, spinster. Sur. Robert Lindsay. Albemarle Co. Mar. Bond.

James m. 1786, Ann Stephenson. Rockbridge Co. Morton, p. 537.

James Gordon, son of Rev. James, m. (1) Mary T. Lindsay, dau. of Reuben; m. (2) 1797, Orange Co., Lucy Gordon, dau. of John. Albemarle, p. 334.

Jane m. Edward Erwin.

Janetta m. Dr. Archibald Alexander.

John m. 1791, Elizabeth Erwin. Rockbridge Co. Morton, p. 537.

John, b. 1729; d. 1812/3, Ohio Co.; m. in Cumberland Co. Mary Dickey. Hartford C-2288(2), 25 Oct., 1958. Signed J. D. B.

John, son of John (1729-1812), m. ____ Steward. Hartford C-2288(2), 25 Oct., 1958. Signed J. D. B.

Joseph, b. 1778, son of John (1729-1812); m. Jane Brown. Hartford C-2288(2), 25 Oct., 1958. Signed J. D. B.

Margaret m. ____ McConnell.

Mary m. Benjamin Piatt.

Molly m. Aken Armes.

WADDEL(-L) (cont.)

Nathaniel, son of Rev. James, m. 6 June, 1793, by Rev. Mr. Lewis Lunceford to Mary Smith Gordon, b. 17 Sept., 1776, dau. of James and Ann (Payne). Family Bible. 11T42, 43.

Polly m. Thomas Stanfield.

William m. 27 July, 1779, Anne Carter. Halifax Co. Mar. Record.

William m. 2 Dec., 1786, Nancy Avon by Rev. John Buchanan. Henrico Parish. Henrico, p. 230.

WADDEY

Joanna m. Lawrence Pope.

WADDILL

____ m. Nancy Scott, dau. of James, whose will of that date, Lunenburg Co., proves it.

____ m. bef. 1781, Ann Carter, dau. of John, whose will of that date, Halifax Co., proves it. Halifax, p. 274.

Elizabeth m. John Sanders.

Moses m. 14 March, 1800, Elizabeth W. Pleasants. Halifax Co. Mar. Record.

Noel m. 1 March, 1786, Eliza L. Watkins. Petersburg. Cameron.

Noel m. 2 June, 1786, Elizabeth Carter. Halifax Co. Mar. Record.

WADDING

Thomas m. 19 Jan., 1685/6, Mary Vuite. Christ Church, p. 24.

WADDINGTON

____ m. bef. Feb., 1707/8, Frances Gill, dau. of Thomas, whose will of that date, Northumberland Co., mentions "daughter Frances Waddington."

Frances (____) m. Joseph Robinson.

WADDLE

____ m. Elizabeth Pleasants, dau. of Jesse (will 1803). Halifax, p. 326.

James m. 25 Jan., 1786, Anne Robinet. Montgomery Co. Mar. Record.

WADDOW

Samuel m. Christobel Saunders, dau. of John (will prov. 24 Feb., 1700, York Co.). 4W(1)43.

WADDROP

Elizabeth m. Thomas Smith.

John m. Nancy Hunt Cocke. Boddie-Isle, p. 252. She did NOT marry John Waddrop. She m. Gen. James A. Bradley. 4V450.

Lilas m. Rix Lawrence.

Margaret m. William Harwood.

Mary m. Levi Jenkins.

WADDRUP

____ m. Anne Cocke. 5V187.

WADDY

____ m. Robert Osborne.

____ m. Sarah (Harris) Hayne, widow of Anthony. 44V50.

____ m. Jane Spence, b. 1698, dau. of John. Barton I:61.

Anthony m. 10 June, 1799, Elizabeth Smith. Sur. William Smith. Louisa Co. Mar. Bond.

Benjamin, son of James (d. 1772) and Lucy (Chilton) of Northumberland Co., m. 1 Dec., 1766, Lancaster Co., Margaret Payne. 25W(1)264, 266.

Benjamin m. April, 1757, Judith Neal. Northumberland Co. Mar. Record.

WADDY (cont.)

He, b. after 1726; inv. 1782, Northumberland Co., son of Benjamin and Jane (Waddy). She, dau. of Shapleigh and Ann (Jones) Neale. 25 W(1)265.

Elizabeth m. Lieut. Francis Smith.

Elizabeth m. Richard Philips.

Elizabeth m. Joseph Dameron.

Elizabeth m. Lieut. Benjamin Edmundson.

Frances m. William Swift.

Francis, son of James, m. bef. March, 1715, Sarah (Harris) Haynie, will prov. April, 1749, widow of Anthony Haynie and dau. of Maj. John and Grace (____) Harris. 8T46; 21V326; 25W(1)259.

Hannah m. John Street.

Jane m. Capt. William Haynie.

Jemima m. (1) John Spence; m. (2) Lawrence Pope; m. (3) Nicholas Minor.

Jemima m. ____ Renum.

John m. Elizabeth Dameron, dau. of George and Margaret (Taylor). She m. (2) Robert Pinkard. 8T44; Dameron, Chart A and Pt. 1, p. 17-a.

John m. 1748, Rebecca Nelson, b. 1729, dau. of Edward and Mary (Garland). 27T37.

John m. 6 March, 1788, Mary Waddy, dau. of Samuel, who gave consent. Sur. William Philips. Louisa Co. Mar. Bond.

John m. 28 April, 1770, Jane Cobbs. Sur. Waddy Thompson. Louisa Co. Mar. Bond. He, son of Samuel (will prov. 1764, Louisa Co.). She, dau. of Samuel Cobbs. Louisa, p. 256.

Mary m. John Waddy.

Milley m. Richard Anderson.

Shapleigh, b. 14 Sept., 1758; will prov. 10 June, 1805, Northumberland Co., son of Benjamin and Judith (Neale); m. Molly Toulson, dau. of Thomas. 25W(1)265.

Thomas, son of John and Elizabeth (Dameron) of Northumberland Co., m. 1764, his 2nd cousin, Ann Dameron, dau. of Col. Thomas and (3) Ann (Ball). 8T51; 25W(1)265-6; Dameron, Chart A, Pt. 1, p. 14.

Thomas m. 1 Nov., 1788, Adah Carpenter. Northampton Co. Mar. Record.

WADE

____ m. Ann Stokes, b. 11 Oct., 1737, dau. of David and Sarah (Montfort). Free II:330.

____ (____) m. John Morton.

____, physician, m. 15 Sept., 1785, Lucy Davis Green, dau. of Thomas and Lucy (Davis). 7T199.

Allen m. 13 March, 1794, Polly Boxley, dau. of Benjamin and Tabitha (____). Halifax Co. Mar. Record.

Andrew m. 22 Nov., 1790, S. Petty. Halifax Co. Mar. Record.

Anna m. David Jarratt.

Bannister m. 26 May, 1798, Patty Terry. Halifax Co. Mar. Record. He, b. 3 April, 1778, Halifax Co.; d. 21 Jan., 1838, Wadesboro, Calloway Co., Ky. She, b. 10 Oct., 1779, So. Car.; d. 4 Oct., 1871, Farmington, Ky., dau. of Joseph (?d. 1824, Greenville Dist., So. Car.). 15 W(2)314; Hartford C-1681(5), 17 May, 1958. Signed F. L. R.

Betsy m. John Base.

Betsy m. James LeGrand.

Charles m. 6 Feb., 1761, Isabell Boyd. Halifax Co. Mar. Record.

WADE (cont.)

Chidly m. 3 Feb., 1778, Ann Kerby. Sur. William Kerby. York Co. Mar. Bond.

Daniel m. 30 May, 1776, Mary Neves, both in this parish. Douglas Reg., p. 17.

David m. 30 Oct., 1780, Isbella Smith. Halifax Co. Mar. Record.

E. m. Nathaniel Hunt (also given as Elizabeth).

Edmund m. 14 Dec., 1785, Tabitha Wyatt. Halifax Co. Mar. Record.

Edward m. 15 Oct., 1768, Letty Martin, dau. of Abraham. Sur. William Wade. Charlotte Co. Mar. Bond.

Elisha m. 8 Aug., 1787, Mary Ann Stowe, dau. of Susanna Stowe. Sur. John Huntsman. Charlotte Co. Mar. Bond.

Elizabeth m. Henry Heyward.

Elizabeth m. William Scott.

Elizabeth m. Peter Fontaine (2nd wife).

Elizabeth m. ____ Price.

Elizabeth m. William Wright.

Elizabeth m. Nathaniel Hunt.

Elizabeth m. (1) Henry Howard; m. (2) Edmund Sweeney.

Frances m. John Evans.

Frances m. John Robinson, Jr.

Hampton m. 8 Jan., 1785, Elizabeth Green, dau. of Thomas and Lucy (Davis). 7T200.

Hannah m. Peter Leek.

Horatio m. 14 Dec., 1785, Sarah Wyatt. Halifax Co. Mar. Record.

Irene m. John Gwinn.

Jane m. Samuel Perrin.

Jane m. Patrick Boyd.

Jane (____) m. Samuel Perrin.

Jean m. Simon Bowling.

Joanna m. Devreux Jerrat.

John m. bef. 1752, Mary Williams, dau. of Samuel. Proven by Deed of that date. 8W(2)63.

John m. 15 Oct., 1770, Susanna Bowles, both in Goochland. Douglas Reg., p. 12.

John m. 14 Nov., 1793, Patsy East. Halifax Co. Mar. Record.

John Utley m. 21 Oct., 1763, Elles Woodrum, both in this parish. Douglas Reg., p. 7.

Kitty m. Stephen Mitchell.

Letty m. Charles Edwards.

Lucy m. Joseph Barnet.

Luke m. 10 Oct., 1785, Martha Stanley. Halifax Co. Mar. Record.

Margaret m. William Harrison.

Martha m. James Ricket.

Mary m. ____ Hunt.

Mary Willis m. John Strother.

Molley m. Daniel White.

Moses m. 29 Sept., ____, Fanny Ferguson. Henry Co. Mar. Record. 21V280.

Patty m. Paris Green.

Polly m. Thomas Stokes.

Priscilla m. Abraham Gum.

WADE (cont.)

Richard m. 5 Feb., 1755, Eliz. Barker, both in this parish. Douglas Reg., p. 1.

Robert m. 7 Feb., 1771, Rebekah Rowntree, both in Goochland. Douglas Reg., p. 12.

Robert m. 9 May, 1798, E. Bennett. Halifax Co. Mar. Record.

Robert m. 11 Sept., 1800, Nancey Inroughty. Halifax Co. Mar. Record.

Robert m. 8 June, 1786, Salley Boyd. Halifax Co. Mar. Record. She, dau. of George. 11W(2)354.

Robert m. 28 April, 1790, S. R. Vaughan. Halifax Co. Mar. Record.

Robert, Jr., Capt., of Halifax Co., son of Robert, Sr.; m. Ann Stokes. 8W(2)124.

Rosana m. Benjamin Herndon.

S. m. William Stokes.

Sally m. Osborn Williams.

Sally m. Thomas Townes.

Sarah m. William Stokes.

Sarah m. ____ Stokes.

Sarah m. William Martin.

Sarah m. James Brown.

Sarah m. James Baird.

Susannah m. John Bond.

William m. 26 June, 1772, ____ ____. (Mar. bond defaced.) Halifax Co.

WADKINS

Sarah m. Thomas Gardner.

WADLEY

Judith m. Payton Smith.

Sarah m. Peter Walker.

Susannah m. John Leprade.

William m. 15 April, 1768, Mary Womack, both of this parish. Douglas Reg., p. 10. (See 7W(1)103.)

WADLOW

Judith m. Peyton Smith, Jr.

Mary m. John Farrar.

Susanna m. John Laprade.

William (see William Wadley).

WAFFENDELL

Mary m. Benjamin Strother.

WAGENER

Beverley Robinson, b. ca 1771, son of Peter and Sinah (McCarty); m. 1790, Margaret Short Harrison, b. ca 1776, dau. of Capt. Benjamin and Mary (Short). 32T214.

Mary m. William Grayson.

Mary Elizabeth m. Rev. Spence Grayson.

Peter, b. 5 April, 1717, Sisted, Essex Co., England, son of Rev. Peter; m. 5 July, 1739, Katherine Robinson, b. 23 Feb., 1715, dau. of John and Katherine (Beverley). The marriage was announced in The Virginia Gazette, 20 July, 1739. 16V217; 32V123; 33V56. Given as Wagner. 15T448.

Peter m. Sinah McCarty, dau. of Col. Daniel and Sinah (Ball) of Fairfax Co. KCG. Given as Wagoner. 2W(2)129-30.

WAGER

Priscilla m. (1) Ben Harris; m. (2) ____ Moseley.

WAGGENER

Mary m. Ambrose Jones.

Richard, d. Barren Co., Ky., son of James and Ann (Jones); m. 12 Oct., 1773, Orange Co., Caty Gaines, dau. of Rev. Henry of Culpeper Co. and So. Car. 21T129. Given as Waggoner. 20T247.

Thomas, b. 1762; d. 1842; m. 4 Oct., 1786, Mary Garnett, b. 1764; d. 1873. 21T130. Given as Waggoner. 13T30.

WAGGONER

Anne m. ____ Greenhill.

Daniel m. 5 Sept., 1785, Lucy, dau. of Lucy Day. Montgomery Co. Mar. Record.

Dinah m. Erasmus Allen.

Greensby m. 1786, Culpeper Co., Sarah Mitchell. 20T247.

James John, son of James and Ann (Jones), m. bef. 1784, Elizabeth Garnett, dau. of Robert and Lucy (Towles); rem. 1820, to Ky. 20T247, 249. Elizabeth's mother was Lucy Stokeley. 13T30.

John m. Sarah Garnett, dau. of Robert and Lucy (Stokeley). 13T30.

Lucy m. John White.

Margaret m. William Allen.

Mary m. Ambrose Jones.

Mary m. John Evans.

Rebecca m. James Day.

WAGNER

Mary Elizabeth m. Rev. Spence Grayson.

Susie m. Thomas Camp.

WAGONER

____ m. Kate Coleman, dau. of Howard (will prov. 1794, Spotsylvania Co.). Free II:193.

Elizabeth m. John Hardman.

WAGSTAFF

____ m. William Harris.

____ m. Lydia Hansford, dau. of John (d. 1750). 6T57-8.

Mary m. Umphrey Gooch.

Mildred m. George Hutcheson.

WAIGHT

Mary m. Robert Kay.

Richard m. 16 July, 1729, Sarah Blake. Christ Church, p. 166.

WAIL

Nancy m. William Campbell.

WAINHOUSE

Dorothy m. Mitchell Scarburgh.

Rose m. John Michael, Jr.

WAIT

Elizabeth m. Charles Beazley.

Phebe m. George Cowgill.

Richard m. 3 Feb., 1705, Ann Dugless. Christ Church, p. 80.

WAITE

____ m. bef. 1769, Mary Taylor, dau. of Thomas Teackle Taylor, whose will, dated 1769, Newport Co., Rhode Island, filed in Accomac Co., 1772.

WAITE (cont.)

Charity m. John Ingam.

Obed of Winchester, Va., m. ____ Harrison, dau. of Matthew and ____ (Wood). 24V98.

WAITS

Anna m. William Arthur.

Milly m. Fielding Riddle.

WAKE

Ann m. John Gayle Sutton.

Christopher m. 28 Dec., 1789, Sarah Sommers. Christ Church, p. 207.

Flamstead m. 19 Sept., 1798, Mrs. Manning Flamstead Wake. Sur. Henry B. Fitzgerald. Norfolk Co. Mar. Bond.

Joana m. Meacham Wortham.

Johnson m. 4 Dec., 1783, Lucy Harvey. Christ Church, p. 204.

Johnston m. 6 Jan., 1781, Nancy Jackson. Christ Church, p. 171.

Mary m. William Vanhan.

Robert m. 1 Feb., 1788, Ann Elliott. Christ Church, p. 206.

William m. 21 Dec., 1799, Lucy Billups Powel. Christ Church, p. 281.

WAKEFIELD

____ (____) m. Samuel Vancil (2nd wife).

Elizabeth m. Nathaniel Godfrey.

John m. ____ Oliver, youngest dau. of John. A Deed, 1666, proves it. Boddie-Isle, p. 547.

John m. 18 Feb., 1793, Catharine Walmsley. Norfolk Co. Mar. Record.

John m. 22 Nov., 1791, Louise Clark. Halifax Co. Mar. Record.

Peter m. 17 Sept., 1794, Susey Weeks. Northampton Co. Mar. Record.

Samuel m. 14 Jan., 1791, Elizabeth Scates, dau. of William. Sur. George Burrass. Charlotte Co. Mar. Bond.

Sarah m. Phillip Shelley.

Thomas m. 7 Oct., 1731, Betty Gardiner. Christ Church, p. 167.

William m. 2 Aug., 1682, Mary Barnes. Christ Church, p. 21.

WAKELINE (See WARKELIN)

WALCH

Jane m. John Smith.

WALCOM

John of this parish m. 10 July, 1682, Elizabeth Coventry of Petso parish. Christ Church, p. 21.

WALD

Burwell m. 21 Aug., 1796, Prudence Coleman. Sur. Laban Coleman. Amelia Co. Mar. Bond.

WALDEN

Ambrose m. 21 Aug., 1787, Elizabeth Taylor, dau. of Richard. Fauquier Co. Mar. Record. 47V82.

Benjamin m. 21 Feb., 1791, King and Queen Co., Mary Dudley. Christ Church, p. 207.

Benjamin m. 21 Feb., 1793, Mildred Didlake in King and Queen Co. Christ Church, p. 280.

Charles m. 29 Dec., 1791, Mary Ison of King and Queen Co. Christ Church, p. 205.

Drewry m. 1 Aug., 1790, Hannah Scott by H. J. Burgess. Surry Co. Ministers' Returns.

John m. 24 March, 1792, Frances Crittenden of King and Queen Co.

WALDEN (cont.)
Christ Church, p. 257.
Lewis m. 6 Sept., 1788, Judith Kidd. Christ Church, p. 206.
Lewis m. 29 Aug., 1789, in King and Queen Co., Lucy Wallace. Christ Church, p. 207.
Mary m. James Hall.
Mildred m. Thomas Ward.
Richard m. 21 Sept., 1798, Polly Isbell. Caroline Co. Mar. Record.
Richard m. 25 Oct., 1792, in King and Queen Co., Hannah Dudley. Christ Church, p. 280.
Samuel m. 22 Jan., 1756, Rachel Shepherd, both in this parish. Douglas Reg., p. 2.
William m. 2 July, 1795, Milly Rodes. Sur. Horsley Goodman. Albemarle Co. Mar. Bond. Mildred Rodes was dau. of David (d. 1794). Albemarle, p. 306.
William m. 16 Jan., 1794, Dully Buckner. Halifax Co. Mar. Record.
WALDROP(-S)
John m. 1 Jan., 1799, Mary Braxton by Rev. Martin Walton. Louisa Co. Ministers' Returns.
Margaret m. William H. Harwood.
Mary m. Levi Jenkins.
William m. 2 Jan., 1794, Elizabeth Wood by Rev. Martin Walton. Louisa Co. Ministers' Returns.
WALDY
Will. m. 22 Oct., 1781, Ann Baily, both of Fluvanna. Douglas Reg., p. 21.
WALE
Anne m. (1) Thomas Hunton; m. (2) Thomas Carter.
George, a Justice of Lancaster Co., m. bef. Aug., 1678, Mary Jones, sis. of William and dau. of Robert and Martha (____) Jones. Proven by Court Records, May, 1676, and Aug., 1678, Northumberland Co.
George m. Grace (____) Chapman, widow of William. Dau., Sary Wale, m. George Flowers, b. ca 1670. Hartford C-2505(2), 20 Dec., 1958. Signed C. A. R. L.
Joanna m. George Brent.
Letitia m. William Brent (also given as Lisha).
Lettice (____) m. ____ Lawson.
Sary m. George Flowers.
WALES
Ann m. Henry Skipwith.
Ann (see Anne Wale).
Elizabeth m. ____ George.
Johanna m. ____ Doggett.
John m. 23 Jan., 1760, Elizabeth (____) Skelton, widow of Reuben. Sur. Martha Wooll. Goochland Co. Mar. Bond.
John in Charles City m. 26 Jan., 1760, Elizabeth Laumox, both in this parish. Douglas Reg., p. 5.
Judith m. ____ Tucker.
WALKE
____ m. Capt. Arthur Sayer.
Anne McClellan McCauley m. Thomas Williamson.
Anthony of Princess Anne Co., b. 3 Jan., 1726; m. (1) ca 1750, Jane

WALKE (cont.)

Randolph, b. ca 1729, dau. of Richard and Jane (Bolling); m. (2) Mary Mosoley. 5V143; 45V83; 9W(1)182.

Anthony m. 4 April, 1725, Anna Armistead, d. 14 Feb., 1732, dau. of William and Anna (Lee). 25W(1)118.

Anthony m. (1) 11 March, 1712, Mary Sanford; m. (2) Elizabeth Newton; m. (3) Anna Armistead, dau. of Capt. William. 5V141.

Anthony m. Susannah Bedford, dau. of Thomas and Drucilla (Coleman). Halifax, p. 214. See Anthony Walker.

Anthony, minister, m. (1) Anne McClanhan; m. (2) Ann (Newton) Fisher. 5V146.

Elizabeth m. Charles Williamson.

Fanny m. Wright Westcott.

John m. 4 Nov., 1789, Hannah Finney. Sur. James Robertson. Amelia Co. Mar. Bond.

Margaret m. John Thoroughgood.

Margaret m. Dr. Christopher Wright.

Mary m. Dr. Christopher Wright (1st wife).

Mary m. Capt. James Murdaugh.

Mary Ann (____) m. John Phripp.

Nancy m. John Willoughby.

Peggy m. Capt. John Calvert.

Thomas m. Elizabeth Newton, dau. of Lemuel and Anne (Nicholas). 2W(1) 75.

Thomas m. Mary Ann Thoroughgood, dau. of Thomas. 28V175.

Thomas, d. 1761, son of Thomas and Mary (Lawson); m. (1) Margaret Thorowgood, dau. of Capt. John. 2W(1)75.

Thomas from Barbadoes m. 1689, Mary Lawson, dau. of Col. Anthony of Norfolk Co. 5V139; 26V24; 2W(1)75.

William, b. 17 Feb., 1762, son of Anthony and Mary (Moseley); m. 21 Dec., 1782, Mary Calvert, dau. of Cornelius and Elizabeth (Thorowgood) of Princess Anne Co. 5V147, 334; 4W(1)111.

WALKELL

Mary m. John Sandeford.

WALKER

____ m. bef. 1728, Sarah Hancock. 33V317.

____ m. Catherine Rutherford. 34 Ky. Reg. 297.

____ m. by 1797, Esther McCroskey. Rockbridge Co. Morton, p. 539.

____ m. (1) John Bell; m. (2) Edmund W. Rootes; m. (3) Dr. Robert B. Starke.

____ m. Christopher Beverley.

____ m. Mary Weir, dau. of Hugh, who d. 1779. Rockbridge Co. Morton, p. 541.

____ m. Henry Delony.

____ m. ____ Garrett, dau. of William and Ann (Johnson). Louisa, pp. 324-5.

____ m. Sarah Ward, dau. of Joseph (d. 1743, Henrico Co.) and Sarah (____). 27W(1)269-70.

____ m. ____ Taliaferro.

____ m. William Jeffers.

____ m. bef. 8 Oct., 1702, Mary Foster, dau. of Robert, whose will of that date, Westmoreland Co., names "daughter Mary Walker."

WALKER (cont.)

____ m. John Deane.

____ m. bef. Jan., 1655, Mary (____) Sharpe, widow of Robert. She was born ca 1630. Proven by Court Record, 1655, Northumberland Co.

Agnes m. William Jones.

Agnes m. Richard Jones.

Alexander, d. ca 1820, Rockbridge Co.; served in Rev. War from Augusta Co.; m. Sept., 1777, Augusta Co., Jane Stuart, d. 13 Dec., 1843, dau of Alexander and (1) Mary (Patterson). Pension R11040; Waddell, p. 368.

Alexander m. 27 Dec., 1757, Frances Scott. Sur. Edmond Walker. Ameli Co. Mar. Bond.

Alexander m. 1797, Nancy Culton. Rockbridge Co. Morton, p. 480.

Alicia m. Col. John Custis (2nd wife).

Amey m. Thomas Pettus.

Ann m. ____ Payne.

Ann m. Constant Perkins.

Ann m. ____ Stevens.

Ann m. Jesse Deamans.

Ann m. John Bilboa.

Ann m. Frank Clark.

Ann(-e) m. Samuel Hawes.

Ann (____) m. Richard Turnstall.

Anne m. John Payne.

Anne m. (1) John Payne; m. (2) William Daingerfield.

Anne m. Capt. William Taliaferro.

Anne m. George Dejarnet.

Annie m. John S. Clack.

Anthony m. 20 Dec., 1778, Suckey Bedford, dau. of Thomas. Sur. Thomas Bedford, Sr. Charlotte Co. Mar. Bond. See Anthony Walke.

Austin m. 4 Nov., 1797, Martha Scott. Sur. Jesse Wilkerson. Powhatan Co. Mar. Bond.

Banary m. John Boswell.

Barbara m. John Iverson Boswell, Sr. (2nd wife).

Baylor, b. 28 Jan., 1737; d. 7 April, 1773, son of John and ____ (Baylor); m. 25 May, 1759, ____ ____. Old King Wm., p. 107.

Benjamin m. 28 April, 1768, Sarah Hudson, dau. of Thomas. Amelia Co. Mar. Record.

Benjamin m. 1795, Polly Sims. Orange Co. Mar. Record.

Betsy m. ____ Campbell.

Betsy R. m. Josiah Bass.

Catharine m. Samuel Taylor.

Catherine m. John Micou.

Cecelia m. Silvanus Stokes.

Charles m. 1798, Catharine Dyal. Rockbridge Co. Morton, p. 538.

Christopher, Col., m. Catherine (____) Beverley, widow of Robert. SW (1)133.

Clara m. John Allen.

Clara m. Richard Hawes. (Also given as Clary.)

Clara m. William Allen (1st wife).

Connegan m. Thomas Lampkin.

Courtney m. John Norton.

WALKER (cont.)

David m. bef. 1727, Mary Munford of Prince George Co. 14T29. She, dau. of Robert, who d. 1735. 11T175.
David m. 6 April, 1758, Sarah Slaydon, both in this parish. Douglas Reg., p. 3.
David m. 13 Oct., 1770, Elizabeth Gilbert, both in Goochland. Douglas Reg., p. 12.
David m. 31 May, 1786, Mary Elliott. Brunswick Co. Mar. Record.
Delia m. Elisha Taylor.
Dorothy m. Capt. Roger Jones (1st wife).
Drucilla m. Money Gannaway.
Edward m. bef. 18 Oct., 1726, Mary Daniel, dau. of William, who d. ca 1765; res. Culpeper Co. Court Record, 1726, Essex Co.; 12T250.
Edward m. 28 Dec., 1795, Nancy Lored. Charles City Co. Mar. Record.
Elenor m. Joseph Frost.
Elijah m. 1800, Mary M. Dial. Rockbridge Co. Morton, p. 538.
Elizabeth m. Stephen Dewey.
Elizabeth m. George Buckner.
Elizabeth m. Archer Jordan.
Elizabeth m. Francis Kirtley.
Elizabeth m. ____ Thornhill.
Elizabeth m. William Joliffe (2nd wife).
Elizabeth m. John Semple.
Elizabeth m. Thomas Cosby.
Elizabeth m. Isaac Butterworth.
Elizabeth m. John Stuart.
Elizabeth m. Isaac Lacy.
Elizabeth m. Thomas Berry.
Elizabeth m. Rev. Matthew Maury.
Elizabeth m. Rev. Henry Merritt.
Elizabeth m. James McCant.
Elizabeth m. William Taylor.
Elizabeth (____) m. Christopher Beverley.
Fanny m. Samuel Sims.
Frances m. Francis Webb.
Frances m. Col. John Baylor.
Francis, b. 22 June, 1764, Albemarle Co.; d. 1806, son of Dr. Thomas and Mildred (Meriwether); Col. in 88th Reg't.; Representative in Congress; m. 1798, Jane Byrd Nelson, dau. of Gen. Hugh Nelson. Albemarle, p. 336. Francis' mother was Mildred Thornton. Jane's mother was Judith Page. Page, pp. 223, 231.
Freeman, d. bef. 1781; m. bef. 1781, Sarah Minge, dau. of George of Charles City Co., whose will, dated 1781, prov. 1782, Williamsburg, proves it. 2W(2)279.
Freeman m. 14 July, 1789, Polly Toone. Mecklenburg Co. Mar. Record.
Gabriel m. 3 Dec., 1798, Susannah Wheeler, dau. of John, Sr. Sur. John Wheeler. Charlotte Co. Mar. Bond.
George, son of George, m. Ann Keith, dau. of Rev. George, at first a Quaker, but returned to the Episcopal Church. 3T287; 16V79; 9W(1) 127.
George m. 31 July, 1787, Eliza Green. Sur. William x Walker. Goochland Co. Mar. Bond.

WALKER (cont.)

George m. 4 July, 1721, Amey Lyall. Christ Church, p. 163.

George m. Elizabeth Talbot, dau. of John and (2) Mary Mosely. Talbot, p. 31.

Hannah m. Launcelot Macon.

Helen Meade m. William Call, Jr.

Hollen m. William Call.

Henry of Botetourt Co. m. Martha Woods, dau. of Andrew and Martha (Poage). Albemarle, p. 355.

Hester m. Robert Tomlin.

Hope m. Nathaniel Lancaster.

Hugh m. 20 Jan., 1770, Catherine Morgan. Christ Church, p. 304.

Hugh of Gloucester Co. m. Mary Thurston, b. 17 May, 1746, dau. of Col. John and Sarah (Minn). 4W(1)181.

Hugh m. Maria Fry, a relative, dau. of Henry and Susan (Walker). A dau. was born, 1800. Burns, p. X-2.

Humphrey m. 8 Dec., 1794, Nancy Harper. Louisa Co. Mar. Record.

Humphrey, b. 13 Jan., 1762; d. 28 Dec., 1820, son of Baylor; m. Frances ?Temple, d. 9 Feb., 1824. Old King Wm., p. 107.

Isabella m. Robert Reed.

Jacob, son of George, m. Rebecca Servant, dau. of Bertrand; had a son, George, who was two and one-half years old, 27 May, 1697; all died bef. 1698. 9W(1)127.

Jacob m. 6 Nov., 1723, Mrs. Courtney Tucker. Sur. Jno. Tucker. Norfolk Co. Mar. Bond.

James m. 20 May, 1707, Clara Robinson. Christ Church, p. 80. She was dau. of Col. Christopher and (2) Catherine (____) Beverley Robinson. 15T446-7; 8W(1)133.

James m. bet. Oct., 1785, and May, 1786, Rebecca Johnson by Rev. James Shelburne, Baptist. Lunenburg Co. Ministers' Returns.

James m. 9 Sept., 1794, Nancy Mayes. Sur. Frances Jones. Amelia Co. Mar. Bond.

James m. 26 June, 1774, Fanny Cannon, both in Goochland. Douglas Reg., p. 15.

James m. Diana Smith, dau. of William of "Black Rock Run," whose will was made, 1792, Spotsylvania Co. 9W(1)46.

James m. 9 Sept., 1783, Catherine Miller by Rev. John Alderson, Jr. Rockingham Co. or Greenbrier Co. Ministers' Returns.

James, b. 7 March, 1692; m. Ann Hill, b. 1708. (Bible Record.) James was a physician in King and Queen Co. 27V376. Mar. bef. 25 March, 1725, Anne Hill, dau. of Leonard. Proven by Record of that date, Essex Co.

James m. 1773, Margaret Woods. Rockbridge Co. Morton, p. 538.

James m. 1781, Jane Carden. Botetourt Co. Kegley, p. 480.

James m. 4 April, 1798, Culpeper Co., Jemimah Yager, b. 13 Dec., 1765, dau. of Michael and Susanna (Manspeil). 9W(2)186.

Jane m. ____ Moore.

Jane m. John Moore.

Jane m. James Moore.

Jane (or Joan) m. Gabriel Cummings.

Jane m. Andrew McMahan.

Jane m. John Goss.

WALKER (cont.)

Jane m. Samuel Barclay.

Jane m. ____ Rice.

Jane m. William Legwood.

Jane m. John Shaw Foild.

Jane Nolly m. John Caldwell (2nd wife).

Joan m. ____ Reagh.

Joan m. Joseph Patterson.

Joan m. Gabriel Cummings.

Jeremiah m. 1787/8, Mary Mallicoat. Pittsylvania Co. Ministers' Returns, filed 10 Sept., 1788, for preceding year, were found in Pension W6399 folder. The widow res. 1845, Grainger Co., Tenn., and in 1849 in Jackson Co., Ala.

Josiah m. Elijah Lynch.

Jinny m. Samuel Barclay.

Joel m. 13 Jan., 1774, Sarah Bowen, both of Goochland. Douglas Reg., p. 14.

John, b. 29 April, 1711, son of John and Susanna (?Peachey); m. Nov., 1735, ____ Baylor of Essex Co. 4V358; Old King Wm., p. 107; Walker, p. 6. The widow m. (2) Capt. Mariott. Bagby, p. 68.

John, physician of Hanover Co., b. 1726; d. 1777; m. (1) 1756, Sarah Camm, dau. of John and Mary (Bullock). Bible Record. He m. (2) Mary Ann Winston. 35V33; 64V361.

John m. Margaret Corbin. 34V359.

John m. bef. 31 March, 1697, Arbella (____) Cox, widow of John. Proven by Court Record of that date, Essex Co.

John m. 1799, Sally Crawford. Rockbridge Co. Morton, p. 538.

John of St. Stephen's Parish, King and Queen Co., m. bef. 1700, Rachel Croshaw, dau. of Capt. Richard of York Co. 47V138; 2W(1)271; Old King Wm., p. 107; Winston, p. 291.

John of Middlesex Co., son of John of Ashborn-in-the Peak, Derbyshire, England; m. Clara Robinson, b. 11 Oct., 1689, Middlesex Co., dau. of Christopher and Katherine (Beverley). 16V107.

John of King and Queen Co. m. Rachel Croshaw, dau. of Capt. Richard of York Co. Old King Wm., p. 107.

John, Lieut. Col., d. 1665; m. 1661, Sarah (____) Fleet(-e), whose will, prov. 29 Dec., 1679, Old Rappahannock Co., proves it. She was widow of Henry Fleet. 44V345; NNHM 5:1:427, 428.

John m. 2 March, 1769, Lydia Gilbert, both of this parish. Douglas Reg., p. 17.

John, Capt., m. 15 Aug., 1771, Hannah Hunt. Sussex Co. Mar. Record.

John m. 9 May, 1751, Elizabeth Hunter, dau. of John, by Rev. Robert Rose. Albemarle Co. Ministers' Returns.

John m. 1791, Susanna Givens. Botetourt Co. Kegley, p. 481.

John m. 28 Jan., 1786, Mary Kidd. Sur. Edward Herndon. Buckingham Co. Mar. Bond.

John m. 14 Nov., 1798, Catherine Miller by Anderson Weeks. Campbell Co. Mar. Record.

John, b. 13 Feb., 1744, Albemarle Co.; d. 2 Dec., 1809, son of Dr. Thomas and (1) Mildred (Thornton); m. 1764, Elizabeth Moore, dau. of Bernard of King William Co. and Ann Catherine (Spotswood); res. "Belvoir," Albemarle Co. 25V436; Albemarle, p. 336; Page, p. 223; St.

WALKER (cont.)

Mark's, p. 166. (Mildred Meriwether named as his mother. Page, p. 223.)

John m. Mary Moore, dau. of John and Jane (Walker). 34 Ky. Reg. 292.

John, served in Rev. War; m., prob. in Va., ____ Paul; rem. from Rockbridge Co. to Tenn., ca 1808. Son, John Blackburn Walker, b. ca 1801, Va.; d. Lawrence Co., Ala. Hartford B-8856, 25 Feb., 1956. Signed B. L. McC.

John m. Catharine Rutherford. A son, Joseph, b. 1722. Rockbridge Co. Morton, p. 538.

John m. 10 Dec., 1792, Nancy Smith. Louisa, p. 262.

John m. bef. 1736, Sarah Taylor, dau. of Charles, whose will, 1736, Accomac Co., proves it.

John m. 1787, Elizabeth Trotter. Amelia Co. Mar. Record.

John m. bef. 1737, Catherine Yates. 8W(1)133. Mar. 10 May, 1733, by Rev. Em. Jones. Christ Church, p. 168.

John of Derbyshire, Eng., m. Clara Robinson. Winston, p. 127.

John, son of James, m. 1795, prob. Orange Co., Lucy Wood of Madison Co. St. Mark's, p. 78.

Joseph m. 1789, Mary Hayse. Rockbridge Co. Morton, p. 539.

Joseph m. a distant relative, Martha McPheeters, b. ca 1772, dau. of William and Rachel (Moore); rem. to Cynthiana, Ky. 34 Ky. Reg. 286.

Joseph m. 1794, Kitty Kelso. Rockbridge Co. Morton, p. 538.

Joseph, b. 1722, son of John and Catharine (Rutherford); m. 1740, Nancy McClung. Rockbridge Co. Morton, p. 538. He d. 1806, Ky.; served in Rev. War; m. (1) 1749, Nancy McClung, d. 1789. DAR 31 394.

Joseph m. 22 July, 1789, Susannah Willis. Sur. Zach. Alvis. Ellender Willis' letter of consent to daughter's marriage. Goochland Co. Mar. Bond.

Joseph, d. 25 Sept., 1815; m. Jane (or Jean) Moore, dau. of James and Jane (Walker). Rockbridge Co. 34 Ky. Reg. 295; McClung, p. 23; Morton, p. 538.

Joseph m. 22 Feb., 1791, Grizzel McCroskey in Augusta Co. by Rev. John Brown. Ministers' Returns.

Joshua, b. 15 Feb., 1757, Loudoun Co.; d. 16 Jan., 1840; m. Sept., 1800, Grayson Co., Amy Williams by George Keith; res. 1831, Hopkins Co., Tenn. Pension W6403.

Judah m. John Brock.

Judith m. Robert Poor.

Judith m. ____ Bankes.

Lettice m. John Duncan.

Lewis m. 1797, Polly Harris. Orange Co. Mar. Record.

Lucy m. Dr. George Gilmer.

Lucy m. Robert Hobbs.

Lucy m. John Morris.

Lucy C. m. Jacob Cunningham.

Margaret m. James Phrasher (?Thrasher).

Margaret m. Capt. Francis Kirtley.

Margaret m. Robert Anderson.

Margaret m. Thomas Conolly.

Margaret m. Thomas Wythe.

Margaret m. Samuel Houston.

WALKER (cont.)

Martha m. Peter Weaver.
Martha m. Cole Diggos.
Martha m. John Haines.
Martha m. ____ Minerly.
Martha m. John Penix.
Martha m. George Divers.
Martha (____) m. ____ Grimes.
Mary m. Thomas Carrol.
Mary m. ____ More.
Mary m. Garner M. Conico (?McConico).
Mary m. Littleberry Hughes.
Mary m. ____ Graham.
Mary m. Filmer Green.
Mary m. John Harris.
Mary m. Hezekiah Holland.
Mary m. Hugh Kelso.
Mary m. Thomas Masse.
Mary m. Rev. James Maury.
Mary m. Constantine Perkins (2nd wife).
Mary m. Francis Scott.
Mary m. Thomas Wythe.
Mary m. Philip Taylor.
Mary m. Reuben Terrill.
Mary m. George Twyman III.
Mary m. James McDuff.
Mary m. John Hallett.
Mary m. Charles Carter (1st wife).
Mary m. Christopher Wright.
Mary m. ____ Perkins.
Mary m. Thomas Roberts.
Mary m. Nicholas Lewis.
Mary (____) m. James Stuart.
Maryann m. Robert Sampels.
Mary Ann m. Paul Tanner.
Mary Buckner m. Thomas Hayes.
Mary E. m. George Richards Trant.
Mary Peachy m. Dr. George Gilmer.
Merry, d. 1811, Va.; m. Elizabeth Kirtley. Son, Newton, b. 1803, Madison Co.; widow rem. to Fulton Co., Ill., 1835. Fulton, p. 816.
Mildred m. Francis Kinlock.
Mildred m. Thomas Carrol.
Mildred m. Tarleton Goolsby.
Mildred m. Joseph Hornsby. (Also given as Mildred Thornton Walker.)
Millie m. Zachariah Terrell.
Milly m. Richard Johnson.
Moses m. 31 Dec., 1789, Isbell Irvine. Halifax Co. Mar. Record.
Nancy m. James Bibb.
Nancy m. Thomas Moore.
Nancy m. John W. Quarles.
Nancy m. Joseph Maclin.
Nancy m. William Webber.

WALKER (cont.)

Nancy m. James Buford.
Nancy m. Richard Johnston.
Nolly m. John Caldwell.
Oliver m. 1779, Millie Webb. Botetourt Co. Kegley, p. 480.
Olliver m. 23 Nov., 1797, Sarah Allen Parrish by Rev. John Jones, Methodist. Lunenburg Co. Ministers' Returns.
Peachy m. Joshua Fry.
Peter m. 23 Dec., 1756, Elizabeth Harris, both in Cumberland. Douglas Reg., p. 3.
Peter m. 1764, Sarah Harris in Maniken Town. Douglas Reg., p. 7.
Peter m. 6 Nov., 1766, Sarah Wadley, both in this parish. Douglas Reg., p. 9.
Peter m. 8 April, 1783, Elenor Clarke. Sur. Thomas Hodges. Goochland Co. Mar. Bond.
Peter m. 25 Nov., 1785, Elizabeth Ellis. Sur. Richard Johnson. Goochland Co. Mar. Bond.
Peyton m. 1794, Hannah Thompson. Bath, p. 131.
Philip m. 25 Aug., 1763, Agnes Watson, both in this parish. Douglas Reg., p. 7
Philip m. 25 May, 1769, Mary Smith, both in this parish. Douglas Reg., p. 11.
Philip m. 1795, Joan McDaniel. Rockbridge Co. Morton, p. 539. Given as McDonald. Morton, p. 507. (Also given as Jenny.)
Polley m. Julius Johnson.
Polly m. Alexander Stuart.
Polly m. Richard Bernard.
Polly m. Charles Baldwin.
Polly m. Thomas Eakin.
Ralph m. 26 Jan., 1722/3, Sarah Bussey. St. Paul's.
Rebecca m. Rowling Pointer.
Rebecca m. Gideon Macon.
Richard m. 13 Dec., 1793, Mary Johnson by Rev. James Shelburne. Lunenburg Co. Ministers' Returns.
Richard, d. 31 Jan., 1831; served in Rev. War from Culpeper Co.; m. 12 Dec., 1790, Burke Co., No. Car., Anson Swearingen; res. 1818, Bedford Co., Tenn. Pension W1108.
Robert m. 30 April, 1792, Nancy F. Powell, dau. of Wiatt and Sallie (Floyd) of Amherst Co. 30T65.
Robert m. 31 March, 1722, Elizabeth Alford. Christ Church, p. 164.
Robert m. 29 May, 1774, Susanna Harrison. Sur. Nathaniel Harrison. Surry Co. Mar. Bond.
Robert of Dinwiddie Co., Capt. in Rev. War; b. 10 Oct., 1729, Bristol Parish; d. 19 Oct., 1797; m. Elizabeth Stark, d. 23 June, 1828, in the 84th year of her age, dau. of Capt. William and Mary Ann (Bolling). 14T26; 4W(1)271.
Robert m. Rebecca Armistead, b. 22 Feb., 1761, dau. of Edward and (2) Martha (Tompkins). 7W(1)18.
Ruth m. William Cash.
Sally m. James Livingston.
Sally m. Loris Hardwick.
Samuel m. Susanna McDonald, b. 3 Nov., 1765, dau. of Bryan, Jr. Keg-

WALKER (cont.)
ley, p. 504.
Sarah m. Calem Hundley.
Sarah m. John Skip Harris.
Sarah m. Benjamin Whitehead.
Sarah m. Robert Nance.
Sarah m. Robert Sudduth, Jr.
Sarah m. John Baker.
Sarah m. Patrick McMullan.
Sarah m. Robert Page.
Sarah m. Edwin Conway.
Sarah m. Col. Reuben Lindsay (1st wife).
Sarah m. John Paxton.
Sarah m. Thomas Bland, Jr.
Sarah m. William Perkins.
Sarah Everard m. Rolfe Eldridge.
Shadrach m. 21 Jan., 1782, Hannah Shepherd. Sur. Benjamin Johnson. Goochland Co. Mar. Bond.
Solomon, d. 1 April, 1822; served in Rev. War from Hanover Co.; m. July, 1780, Stafford Co., Frances Taylor, b. ca 1760; she res. 1833, Fauquier Co., age 73. Bible record of births of their children is in the Pension W4376 file from which these data have been taken.
Susan m. Thomas Martin.
Susan m. Turner Christian (1st wife).
Susan m. Henry Fry.
Susannah m. Capt. William Fleet, widower.
Susannah m. Rolfe Eldridge.
Susannah m. William McGraw.
Susannah m. Shadrach Woodson.
Tabitha m. William Morriss.
Thomas m. 21 Nov., 1729, Elizabeth Shorter. Christ Church, p. 166.
Thomas m. 2 Dec., 1783, Susanna Johnson by Rev. James Shelburne, Baptist. Lunenburg Co. Ministers' Returns.
Thomas of York Co. m., no date but is listed among those of 1696, Elizabeth Johnson. Elizabeth City Co. 2W(1)211.
Thomas m. Eleanor Stuart, dau. of Alexander and (1) Mary (Patterson). Boddie-HSF V:92.
Thomas, b. 17 March, 1749, Albemarle Co., son of Dr. Thomas and Mildred (Meriwether); served in Rev. War; d. 1798; m. Margaret Hoops. Albemarle, p. 336. He, son of Dr. Thomas and Mildred (Thornton) Meriwether Walker; m. 16 Sept., 1772, Margaret Hoops of Philadelphia, sis. of Maj. Adam Hoops, who founded Olean, N. Y., in 1804. Burns, pages not numbered; Page, p. 228.
Thomas, Capt. in 1707, son of John and Rachel (Croshaw); m. 24 Sept., 1709, Susanna ?Peachey. Old King Wm., p. 107.
Thomas, b. 25 Nov., 1760, Orange Co.; d. there, 2 April, 1834; served in Rev. War; m. Aug., 1783, Orange Co., Messeniah Powell, b. 17 May, 1766. Widow res. 1848, Greene Co., Va. Data from Pension file of the widow.
Thomas m. 21 Feb., 1789, Beckie Pierson Walton by Rev. John Buchanan. Henrico Parish. Henrico, p. 231.
Thomas, physician. (Note: Compilers differed so much on the informa-

WALKER (cont.)

tion given that each reference to Dr. Thomas is given separately, instead of all references being compiled into one paragraph.)

Thomas, b. 1714/5, Castle Hill, Va.; d. there, 1794; m. (1) Mildred Thornton Meriwether. DAR No. 28 056; DAR No. 79 144.

Thomas m. Mildred Merriwether. DAR No. 85 063.

Thomas, b. King and Queen Co., m. (1) Elizabeth (Thornton) Merriwether, widow of Thomas of Louisa; m. (2) Elizabeth Thornton. Louisa, p. 419.

Thomas m. (1) Mildred (____) Meriwether; m. (2) Elizabeth Thornton; res. Albemarle Co. Bagby, p. 71.

Thomas, b. 1715, King and Queen Co., m. Mildred Meriwether, dau. of Nicholas. Albemarle, p. 335.

Thomas, b. 1715; d. 1794; res. Albemarle Co.; m. (1) 1741, Mildred Thornton, b. 1721; d. 1778. DAR No. 41 806.

Thomas of Albemarle m. Elizabeth (Gregory) Willis Thornton, widow 1st of Henry Willis, Jr., and 2nd of Reuben Thornton of Caroline Co., son of Francis, and dau. of Roger and Mildred (Washington) Gregory. She m. (4) Dr. ____ Alcock of the British Army. 4W(1) 159.

Thomas m. Mary (Green) Wilkerson, widow of James and dau. of Thomas and Elizabeth (Filmer). 5T136.

Thomas Belfield, son of Freeman and Frances (Belfield), m. at age 40, Elizabeth Smith of Essex Co. 14T38.

Vincent m. 30 Dec., 1782, Delilah Thrift by Rev. James Shelburne, Baptist. Lunenburg Co. Ministers' Returns.

Walter m. 20 April, 1797, Grissel Buchanan. Wythe Co. Mar. Record.

William m. 23 Nov., 1731, Elizabeth Netherington. St. Paul's.

William m. 23 May, 1744, Elizabeth Monk. OPR.

William m. Mary Vivion. 34V351.

William m. 1795, Elizabeth Casteel. Rockbridge Co. Morton, p. 478.

William m. 5 April, 1796, Milley Anderson by John Lasley. Louisa Co. Ministers' Returns.

William m. 16 Dec., 1793, Elizabeth Jones. Sur. Nicholas Eckson. Albemarle Co. Mar. Bond. William m. Elizabeth (Clayton) Jones, widow of Orlando, who d. 1793, Albemarle Co., and dau. of John Clayton. 13T266.

William m. (date not given) Mary Stowd by Alexander Ross. Montgomery Co. Mar. Record.

William m. Dorothy Strother, dau. of Joseph (b. 1685; d. 1766) and Margaret (Berry). 11T118.

William, b. 1781, son of George who served in Rev. War; m. Sallie Holcomb; res. Albemarle Co. Son, Dr. Algernon S. Walker, b. 1811, Jessamine Co., Ky. Perrin, 1886. Simpson, p. 713.

William, d. 12 Sept., 1718, St. Peter's Parish; m. 19 Jan., 1713, Elizabeth Clopton, dau. of William. She m. (2) Alexander Moss. 14T 239; 30V42; 14W(2)147; St. Peter's, p. 419.

William m. bef. July, 1656, ____ Jeffers, sis. of William. Proven by Court Record of that date, Northumberland Co.

William m. Mary Stuart, dau. of John (b. 1740; d. 1831) of Augusta Co. Waddell, p. 371.

William m. 21 March, 1785, Mary Ann Smith, dau. of John. Sur. John

WALKER (cont.)

Smith. Prince Edward Co. Mar. Bond.

William T. m. 16 Nov., 1781, Frances Williamson, dau. of Jacob. Sur. Hopkins Muse. Amelia Co. Mar. Bond.

William Weymouth m. 7 Aug., 1790, Elizabeth Hudson by Rev. John Buchanan. Henrico Parish. Henrico, p. 232.

Willis m. 10 Feb., 1772, York Co., Sarah Hunter. Sur. Joseph x Hughes. Wit. Thomas Everard, clerk. York Co. Mar. Bond. 1W(1)49.

Wilmoth m. James M. Williams.

Wyatt m. Elizabeth Christian, dau. of William and (1) Elizabeth (Collier). 8W(1)124.

WALKUP

____ m. William Elliott.

____, a dau., m. ____ Stephenson.

____ m. John Graham.

Andrew m. 1795, Agnes Wilson. Rockbridge Co. Morton, p. 543.

Andrew, d. 1817; m. 1795, Nancy Willson. Rockbridge Co. Morton, p. 539.

Arthur, d. 1834; m. 1797, Esther Mackey. Rockbridge Co. Morton, p. 539.

Jane m. Jesse Paxton.

Jean m. David Graham.

John m. Margaret Fulton Blair. A son was born in 1778. Rockbridge Co. Morton, p. 539.

Joseph m. 1794, Eleanor Wilson. Rockbridge Co. Morton, p. 543.

Margaret m. William Gay.

William, son of John and Margaret Fulton (Blair), m. Sarah McCoy. Rockbridge Co. Morton, p. 539.

WALL

____ m. Sarah Gray. 5V201. ____ m. bef. Aug., 1769, Sarah Gray, dau. of Joseph, whose will of that date, Southampton Co., proves it.

____ m. Lucy Holt, dau. of Charles (d. ca 1767) and Elizabeth Presson. 7T281.

____ m. bef. 1803, Rachel Boyd, dau. of George, Sr., whose will of that date, Halifax Co., proves it.

Buckner m. 23 Sept., 1793, Ann Whitlow. Halifax Co. Mar. Record.

Caty m. Richard Clack.

Charles m. 17 Dec., 1762, E. Bates. Halifax Co. Mar. Record.

Charles m. 14 Aug., 1788, Wilmuth Denbery (or Dueberry). Halifax Co. Mar. Record.

Elizabeth m. William Sims.

Elizabeth m. Thomas Gains.

Elizabeth m. John Stanly.

Fanney m. Isham Turner.

George m. 30 Aug., 1789, Nancy Watlington. Halifax Co. Mar. Record.

J. m. 20 Jan., 1763, Ursula Bates. Halifax Co. Mar. Record.

James, Maj., of Greensville Co., m. Sarah Gray, b. 7 Nov., 1739. Family Bible. 30V65.

Jane (____) m. Daniel Dunaway.

J. N. m. 26 Dec., 1799, ____ Oliver. Halifax Co. Mar. Record.

Joel m. 1 April, 1790, Rebecca Gibbons by H. J. Burgess. Surry Co. Ministers' Returns.

WALL (cont.)

John m. 15 Sept., 1754, Greensville Co., Mary Turner, dau. of John and Priscilla Blunt. Will of John Turner, 1796, Greensville Co., proves the marriage. Boddie-SVF I:71.

Judith m. James Douglass.

Lucy m. John Fisher.

Martha m. Frederick Bott.

Martha m. Alex. Madilland.

Mary m. Capt. Thomas Humphries.

Mary m. ____ Grayson.

Mary m. Archilles Jeffie.

Mary m. Archibald Allen.

Mary m. William Stamps.

Michael m. bef. 1794, ____ Jeffries, dau. of Achilles, whose will of that date, Greensville Co., proves it.

Michael m. Mary (____) Harrison, widow of Henry. 34V286.

Molly m. Peter Follis.

Parham m. 26 Dec., 1792, Rachel Boyd. Halifax Co. Mar. Record.

Patsey m. Thomas Tendall.

Patty m. Samuel Clay.

Sally m. Jacobus Early.

Sarah m. George Godby.

Sarah m. Andrew Kelly.

Sucky m. Moses Blackwell.

Susannah m. Josiah Atkinson.

William m. 20 Sept., 1792, Patsey Booker. Halifax Co. Mar. Record.

WALLACE

____, a dau., m. ____ Ballard.

____ m. ____ Maxwell, dau. of David and Nellie (McCullough). Boddie-HSF V:170.

____ m. bef. coming to America, Elizabeth Woods, sis. of Michael of Albemarle Co. Morton, p. 277.

Anderson m. 1796, Margaret Calbreath. Rockbridge Co. Morton, p. 539.

Andrew m. Margaret Woods, b. 1714, Ireland, dau. of Michael (d. 1762, Albemarle Co.) and Mary (Campbell). 51V367. Andrew came to Va. ca 1734; d. 1785, Albemarle Co. Albemarle, p. 336.

Andrew m. Elizabeth Graham. A son was born in 1784. Rockbridge Co. Morton, p. 539.

Anne m. Col. Robert Armistead.

Anne m. George Wray, Jr.

Aphia (____) m. William Haughton.

Caleb, b. 1742, Va.; d. 1814, Woodford Co., Ky., son of Samuel and Esther (Baker); grad. Princeton College; m. (1) 1774, Sarah McDowell; m. (2) 1779, Botetourt Co.,Rosanna Christian, dau. of Capt. Israel of Stanton, Va.; m. (3) Mary (____) Brown of Frankfort, Ky. Kegley, p. 539; 18 Ky. Reg. 53:100,101. He was a minister in Virginia and a lawyer and judge in Kentucky. Kegley, pp. 397, 511.

David m. 12 Oct., 1785, Mary Cartmill, dau. of James. Montgomery Co. Mar. Record.

David m. 22 March, 1798, Nancy Mills. Sur. Larkin Crowder. Mecklenburg Co. Mar. Bond.

Elizabeth m. John Selden.

WALLACE (cont.)

Elizabeth m. William Briscoe.
Elizabeth m. Andrew Willoughby.
Elizabeth m. John Gilmore.
Elizabeth m. John McCrea.
Elizabeth m. Charles Grigsby.
Elizabeth m. Peter Smith.
Elizabeth m. John Carlton.
Elizabeth (____) m. Francis Rice.
Euphan m. (1) Wilson Roscow; m. (2) Capt. William Dandridge (1st wife).
Euphan m. (1) Bailey Washington; m. (2) Daniel Carroll Brent.
Euphan m. Judge William Roscow Wilson Curle (1st wife).
Grace m. Reubin Bonawell.
Hugh, Jr., m. 5 April, 1800, Sally Pully by Rev. John Noblett, Methodist. Lunenburg Co. Ministers' Returns.
James, Capt., son of James, m. Elizabeth Westwood, dau. of William. 32V246; 9W(1)130.
James settled in Augusta Co. in 1748 and d. 1780; m. Elizabeth Campbell, dau. of John and Elizabeth (Walker). Stoddard, p. 245.
James m. ____ Bogan. Rockbridge Co. Morton, p. 474.
James, minister of Elizabeth City Parish, b. 1667, Erroll, Perthshire, Scotland; d. 3 Nov., 1712, "Erroll," Elizabeth City Co.; m. 11 July, 1695, Elizabeth City Co., Anne (Sheppard) Gutherick Wythe, widow 1st of Quintilian Gutherick, 2nd of Thomas Wythe, and dau. of John Sheppard. 2W(1)69, 210; 9W(1)130.
Jean m. Robert Peage.
Jennet m. Thomas Wilson.
Jesse m. 22 Sept., 1792, Phebe Williams. Norfolk Co. Mar. Record.
Joan m. James Macreth.
Joan m. James McNutt.
Joel m. Esther Houston, dau. of John and Sarah (Todd). Rockbridge Co. Morton, p. 493.
John m. 24 Aug., 1785, Margaret Graham by Rev. Edw. Crawford. Her father, Arthur Graham, gave consent. Rockbridge Co. Ministers' Returns.
John, b. 1736, Albemarle Co.; d. 1814, Butler Co., Ohio; m. Mary Whorry. DAR No. 79 476.
John, minister, b. 1754, Va.; d. 1822, Washington Co., Ind.; m. Eleanor Morgan. DAR No. 47 614; DAR No. 51 827.
John, Sr., b. 18 Dec., 1748, Penna., son of Joseph; m. bef. 1779, Jane Finley; prob. res. Loudoun Co. Stoddard, p. 250.
Joseph of Fauquier Co. m. Elizabeth Edmonds. 23V216.
Lucy m. Lewis Walden.
Margaret m. William Ramsay.
Margaret m. John McKenny.
Martha m. Lieut. Samuel Selden.
Martha m. Thomas Tatb.
Martha m. John Smith.
Mary m. Richard Ball.
Mary m. Alexander Henderson.
Mary m. (1) ____ Eakin; m. (2) William Goodwin.
Mary m. Samuel Isaacs.

WALLACE (cont.)
Mary m. Col. James Williams.
Mary m. William Westwood.
Michael m. 21 May, 1795, Agnes Shannon. Shelby Co., Ky. Mar. Record.
Michael m. ____ (____) Wishart, widow of John (d. ca 1774). Proven by Chancery Suit, 1800. 11W(2)118.
Nancy m. Richard Homes.
Nancy (____) m. John Cowden.
Peter m. Elizabeth Woods; rem. from Scotland to Va. ca 1734. Woodford Co., p. 60.
Peter, Jr., to Va. ca 1734; d. 1784; m. Martha Woods, b. 1720, Ireland, dau. of Michael (d. 1762, Albemarle Co.) and Mary (Campbell); res. Rockbridge Co. 51V367; Albemarle, p. 336; Morton, p. 540.
Polly (____) m. Simon Smith.
Rebecca m. James Grigsby.
Rebecca m. ____ Campbell.
Robert m. 1800, Margaret Hughes. Rockbridge Co. Morton, p. 540.
Sallie m. Lieut. Mathew Smith.
Samuel m. 1794, Mary Tate. Rockbridge Co. Morton, p. 540.
Sarah m. William Woods (1st wife).
Selia m. Thomas Casey.
Sukey m. Kemp Galloway.
Susan m. Thomas Collins.
Susanna m. William Woods.
Thomas m. Agnes Chiles, dau. of Walter and Phebe (Carr). 8W(1)106.
William m. 16 Nov., 1794, Sarah Shannon. Shelby Co., Ky. Mar. Record.
William, d. 1809, son of William and Hannah (Woods); m. 1771, Mary Pilson. Albemarle, pp. 297, 337.
William, d. 1779, son of James and Elizabeth (Campbell); m. Jane Hunter, dau. of John and Frances (____). Stoddard, p. 245.
William, to Va. ca 1734, m. Hannah Woods, b. 1710, Ireland, dau. of Michael and Mary (Campbell) of Albemarle Co. 51V367; Albemarle, pp. 335, 351.
William Brown, Capt., b. 1757, Ellerslie, Va.; d. 1833, Lawrenceburg, Ky.; served in Rev. War; m. 22 March, 1787, Barbara Tunstall Fox, b. 1766; d. 1833, dau. of Thomas and (2) Philadelphia (Herndon). 21T 264; DAR No. 68 681.
Wilson C. m. Catherine Cocke (1st husband). 5V73.

WALLAS
Margaret m. ____ Robinson.
Mary m. John Bodgam.

WALLER
____ m. Owen Minor.
____ m. bef. 16 June, 1784, Ann (____) Beverly, widow of Robert. Proven by Deed of that date, Spotsylvania Co.
Absolom, minister, b. 1772; d. 1823, son of Benjamin and Joan (Custis) m. Ciceley Anderson Shelton, dau. of Col. Clough Shelton. Louisa, p 420, Old King Wm., p. 109.
Agnes m. ____ Johnson.
Ann m. Thomas Bailey.
Ann m. (1) Thomas King; m. (2) Thomas C. Morrison.
Ann m. John Beverley Roy.

WALLER (cont.)

Ann m. Thomas Pritchett.

Ann m. James Jones.

Ann (____) m. Thomas Pritchett.

Anne m. James Bullock, Jr.

Anne m. William Ronald.

Benjamin m. bef. Oct., 1791, Elizabeth Lipscomb, dau. of Thomas. Proven by a Deed of Gift of that date.

Benjamin m. 8 May, 1782, Joana Thompson. Caroline Co. Mar. Record.

Benjamin, b. 1749; d. 1835, son of Edmund and Mary (Pendleton); m. Jean Custis. Old King Wm., p. 109. Benjamin, d. 1825. Louisa, p. 420.

Benjamin, b. 1 Oct., 1716; d. 31 May, 1786, son of John and Dorothy (King); m. 2 Jan., 1746, Martha Hall, b. 2 July, 1728; d. 4 Aug., 1780; res. Spotsylvania Co. 59V352; 15W(2)308; Louisa, p. 419; Old King Wm., p. 108; Wilcoxson, p. 416.

Benjamin Carter, b. 24 Dec., 1757, son of Benjamin and Martha (Hall); m. Feb., 1778, Catharine Page, b. 7 Nov., 1758, dau. of Robert and Sarah (Walker) of Hanover Co.; res. James City Co. 59V352; Page, p. 141.

Charles m. bef. 25 March, 1715, Susannah, sis. of Hannah Carber. Proven by Court Record of that date, Essex Co.

Charles m. bef. 17 Dec., 1739, Elizabeth Rowzee, dau. of Edward, dec'd. Proven by Court Record of that date, Essex Co. He, d. 4 Dec., 1749; res. Essex Co. and Stafford Co. She m. (2) John Peyton; m. (3) Benjamin Strothers. 19T226.

Clara m. Edward Travis (2nd wife).

Dabney, b. 20 Feb., 1772; d. 6 June, 1849, aged 77 yrs., 3 mo. and 17 das., son of Thomas and Sarah Ann (Dabney); m. Elizabeth Minor. 36 V382.

Dicey m. Nathaniel Luck.

Dolly m. Henry Tazewell.

Dorothy m. Thomas Goodloe.

Dorothy m. Dr. E. T. Rowzie.

Dorothy m. ____ Quarles.

Dorothy m. Solomon Quarles.

Dorothy m. Aaron Quarles.

Dorothy m. James Haney.

Dorothy Elizabeth m. Henry Tazewell.

Edmund, b. ca 1718; d. 1771, son of Col. John and Dorothy (King); m. 18 Oct., 1740, Mary Pendleton, b. 1720; d. 1808, dau. of Philip, Jr., and Elizabeth (Pollard). Spotsylvania Co. Mar. Record. 43V171, 278; 59V352; Louisa, pp. 419, 420; Old King Wm., p. 109; Wilcoxson, p. 416.

Edmund m. bef. 9 May, 1763, ____ Curtis, dau. of Rice, Sr. Proven by Deed of that date, Spotsylvania Co.

Edmund, b. 1779, son of George and Ann Winston (Carr); m. Maria Duncan. 33T302.

Edward m. Ann Tandy, dau. of Henry (d. 1741) and Frances (____) of King and Queen Co. Br., p. 53.

Elizabeth m. Edmund Eggleston.

Elizabeth m. Jacob McCraw.

WALLER (cont.)

Elizabeth m. John Peyton.

Fanny m. Joseph Graves (2nd wife).

George, Col., b. 1734, Stafford Co.; d. 1814, Henry Co.; m. Mary Ann Winston Carr, dau. of Capt. William and (1) Elizabeth (Winston). 33T302; DAR No. 41 051; DAR No. 51 630.

Hannah m. Edward Webb.

Jane m. John Markham (3rd wife).

Jemima m. Benjamin Stephens.

John m. 4 July, 1751, Mary Mathews. OPR.

John m. 7 March, 1799, Nancy Sears of Gloucester. Christ Church, p. 303.

John, b. ca 1701, King William Co.; d. 1776, Spotsylvania Co., son of John and Dorothy (King); m. 1730, Agnes Carr, b. 1712; d. 1777, dau. of Col. John of "Bear Castle." Louisa, p. 420. She, dau. of Thomas and Mary (Dabney). Boddie-HSF V:133; Wilcoxson, p. 416. Notice: John, Jr., m. bef. 26 Nov., 1731, Agnes Carr, dau. of Thomas of Caroline Co. Proven by a Deed of Gift on that date from Thomas Carr, Spotsylvania Co.

John, minister, b. 23 Dec., 1741; d. 4 July, 1802, Greenwood, So. Car., son of Edmund and Mary (Pendleton); m. (1) Elizabeth Curtis, b. ca 1742, dau. of Col. Rice Curtis, Jr., and (3) Anne (Aylett) Walker Curtis. 59V352; 64V361; DAR No. 56 446.

John, Col., b. 1617, England; d. 1685, Caroline Co.; m. Mary Key; came to New Kent Co., 1635. Boddie-HSF V:133; Louisa, p. 419; Old King Wm., p. 108.

John m. bef. 3 July, 1770, Ann Bowker, dau. of Parmenas and sis. of Ralph. Proven by Deed of that date, Spotsylvania Co. He, b. ca 1714; d. ca 1775, son of William and Ann (Stanard). She m. (2) Thomas Pritchett. 59V351.

John, b. 25 July, 1753, son of Benjamin and Martha (Hall); m. 11 Sept., 1774, Judith Page, b. 15 Oct., 1756, dau. of Robert and Sarah (Walker) of Hanover Co. 59V352; Louisa, p. 420; Old King Wm., p. 108; Page, p. 140.

John, Col., b. 23 Feb., 1673, Newport Pagnell, Buckinghamshire, England; d. 1754, Newport, Spotsylvania Co., son of John and Mary (Pomfrett); came to Va. 28 May, 1696; res. King William Co.; m. ca 1697, Dorothy King, b. 1675; d. 1759, Newport, Va. 59V349; 9W(1)63; Louisa, p. 420; Old King Wm., p. 108; Wilcoxson, p. 416. His mother was Mary (Key) Waller. Boddie-HSF V:133; Louisa, p. 419.

John, b. 1765, son of George and Ann Winston (Carr); m. Polly Cooper. 33T302.

Joseph m. Nancy Minor, dau. of Thomas and Mary (Dabney). 9W(1)180.

Mariah m. Charles Lucas.

Martha m. William Taylor.

Mary m. James Overton.

Mary m. Lieut. John Redd.

Mary m. Thomas Edwards.

Mary m. Col. Zachary Lewis.

Mary m. Joseph Woolfolk.

Mary m. William Wiglesworth.

Mary m. Edward Herndon (record has been interpreted as Kendon).

WALLER (cont.)

Mary m. George Dabney.
Mary m. John Tayloe Corbin.
Mary Winston m. Maj. John Reed.
Nancy m. John Willey.
Patsy m. (1) Montague Williams; m. (2) Joseph H. Travis.
Patty m. Edward Mosby.
Patty m. William Taylor.
Pomfrett, b. 20 Jan., 1747; d. 20 June, 1799, son of John and Agnes (Carr); m. Martha Martin. 59V351; Wilcoxson, p. 416.
Rice m. 5 April, 1792, Elizabeth Lambert by Rev. John Rogers, Methodist. Lunenburg Co. Ministers' Returns.
Robert m. 3 June, 1758, Mazais Wilson. Sur. Sam Boush, Jr. LNCo. 3: 128.
Robert Hall of York Co., b. 7 Jan., 1764; m. Anne Camm, b. 1 Aug., 1770; d. 25 July, 1800, dau. of John and Elizabeth (Hansford). 4W (1)61. He, son of Benjamin and Martha (Hall); m. (2) Martha (Langhorne) Crafford. 59V352.
Sarah m. Clifton Rodes.
Sarah m. John Minor.
Sarah m. John Rodes.
Sarah m. John Smith.
Stephen m. 14 Dec., 1799, Tabitha Prewitt. Shelby Co., Ky. Mar. Record.
Sukey m. James Withers.
Susan m. James Withers.
Susanna m. George Haynes.
Thomas, b. 1705; d. ca 1765, son of Col. John and Dorothy (King); m. ca 1725, Elizabeth Dabney, b. ca 1705; d. 1794. 59V351; Wilcoxson, p. 416.
Thomas, b. 29 July, 1732; d. 10 Feb., 1788, aged 55 yrs. 5 mo. 19 das., son of John and Agnes (Carr); m. 1770, Sarah Dabney, b. 2 Oct., 1740; d. 10 Jan., 1822, aged 81 yrs. 3 mo. 8 das., dau. of John and Sarah Ann (Jennings). 36V381; Boddie-HSF V:133; Wilcoxson, p. 416. Her mother was Sarah A. J. (Harris). 59V351.
William, b. 1775, son of George and Ann Winston (Carr) of Henry Co.; m. Polly Staples. 33T302.
William m. 21 June, 1738, Ann Beverley. Spotsylvania Co. Mar. Record. He, b. 1714; d. 1760, son of Col. John and Dorothy (King); m. 1738, Ann (Standard) Beverly. Wilcoxson, p. 416.
William Edmund, minister, b. 1747; d. 1830, son of Edmund and Mary (Pendleton); m. Mildred Smith, b. 1746; d. 1830. 59V352.

WALLERS

Robert m. 3 June, 1758, Hagar Wilson. Norfolk Co. Mar. Record.

WALLEY

Hannah m. Lovelace Gorsuch (2nd wife).

WALLFORD

Edward m. 10 April, 1708, Rebecca Mason. Christ Church, p. 81.

WALLINGSFORD

Elizabeth m. Michael Hargan.

WALLINGTON

Armistead m. Susannah Coleman, b. 1735, dau. of Thomas and Elizabeth

WALLINGTON (cont.)
(____). Free II:192.

WALLIS
Ann m. Thomas Robey.
Elizabeth m. William Gaines.
John m. Behethland Strother, dau. of Francis (1700-52) and Susannah (Dabney). 11T122.
John m. 11 May, 1780, Jane Miller by Rev. John Alderson, Jr. Rockingham Co. or Greenbrier Co. Ministers' Returns.
Margaret m. Enoch Fauster.
Martha m. Southerd Simmons.
Mary m. Francis Coffley.
Patsy m. William Davenport.
Rebecca m. William Ward.
William m. 11 April, 1726, Betty Davies. Christ Church, p. 165.

WALLS
Mary m. William Taylor.

WALMACK
Nancy m. John Davis.

WALMSLEY
Catharine m. John Wakefield.

WALNE
Richard m. 6 Sept., 1785, Patty Phelps. Halifax Co. Mar. Record.

WALPOLE
Anne m. James Hartley.

WALPOOLE
Dolly R. m. William Barlow.

WALSH
John m. 23 April, 1754, Patience Davis. Norfolk Co. Mar. Record.
John m. 10 Aug., 1790, S. DeGraffenread. Halifax Co. Mar. Record.
Patrick served in Rev. War from Va.; m. 2 Oct., 1786, Catherine May of Baltimore in Philadelphia by Rev. William Rogers. Records of First Baptist Church, Philadelphia, Penna.

WALSTON
James m. bef. 29 Feb., 1743, Ann Poole, dau. of George, whose will of that date, Spotsylvania Co., proves it.

WALTER
____ m. Mary Branch, dau. of Christopher and Ann (Sherman). Farmer, p. 42.
Anne m. Jonathan Stott.
John m. Arabella (Strachey) Cox, widow of John Cox and dau. of William and Elenor (Read) Strachey. 5W(1)6.
John m. Mary Harrison, dau. of William. 23V331.
John m. 8 Dec., 1767, Susanna (____) Stott. Northampton Co. Mar. Record.
Leah m. William Nottingham.
Mary m. Daniel Luke.
Sarah (____) m. Richard Carvey.
Susanna m. Robert Rodgers.

WALTERS
____, a dau., m. ____ Jones.
____ m. Sarah Russell, dau. of William (will, 1775). Halifax, p. 333.

WALTERS (cont.)
____ m. Johannah Mayboo, dau. of William (will, 1758). Halifax, p. 315.
Ann m. Richard Vowlos.
Ann m. Alexander Marshall.
Archer m. 11 March, 1793, Eda Slaton. Halifax Co. Mar. Record.
Betsy m. John Marshall.
Dorcas m. James Taylor.
Frances m. William Smith (or Smyth).
George m. 3 Jan., 1792, Amy Hanks by Alexander Ross. Montgomery Co. Mar. Record.
John m. 28 March, 1782, Mary Madding by Rev. Lazarus Dodson. Pittsylvania Co. Mar. Record.
Joseph m. Joanna Gentry, dau. of Moses (d. 1810). Albemarle, p. 205.
Judith m. Jacob Brown.
Margaret m. George Russell.
Mary m. (1) William Puckett; m. (2) Womack Puckett.
Rosannah m. ____ Farrow.
WALTHALL
Ann m. Lieut. John Robertson.
Anne m. Alexander Marshall.
Bartley m. 17 Feb., 1791, Ann Parkinson. Sur. Richard Walthall. Amelia Co. Mar. Bond.
Christopher m. 6 April, 1796, Sally Sudberry. Sur. John Sudberry. Amelia Co. Mar. Bond.
Clarissa m. Lewis Leath.
Henry m. 27 Feb., 1791, Eliza Eanes. Sur. John Clemons. Amelia Co. Mar. Bond.
Lucy m. John Phelps.
Lucy m. Matthew Wills.
Lucy m. Robert Walthall.
Marley P. m. Thomas Graves.
Martha m. Roland Whitworth.
Mary m. Daniel Hatcher.
Mary m. James Worsham.
Nancy m. William Walthall.
Pheby m. William Perry.
Robert m. 20 Dec., 1777, Lucy Walthall, dau. of Thomas. Sur. William Walthall. Amelia Co. Mar. Bond.
Sarah m. Thomas Branch Willson.
Thomas m. 24 Aug., 1785, Prince George Co., Susannah Peebles. Hinshaw 6:117.
Thomas m. 1 March, 1799, Amelia Co., Elizabeth Bott, b. 23 June, 1755, dau. of William and Susanna (____). Hinshaw 6:101.
Thomas m. 15 Dec., 1789, Kissey Johnson. Amelia Co. Mar. Record.
William m. 6 April, 1752, Anna Elam. Sur. Christopher Walthall. Amelia Co. Mar. Bond.
William m. 18 Feb., 1775, Lucy Willson. Sur. John Willson. Amelia Co. Mar. Bond.
William m. 17 Nov., 1795, Nancy Walthall. Sur. Bartley Walthall. Amelia Co. Mar. Bond.
William m. 7 June, 1781, Sally Perkinson. Sur. William Old. Amelia

WALTHALL (cont.)
Co. Mar. Bond.

WALTHAM

John m. 26 Dec., 1759, Anne (____) Michael. Northampton Co. Mar. Record.

John m. 10 Feb., 1778, Susanna Johnson, dau. of Obediah, dec'd. Northampton Co. Mar. Record.

Susanna m. Charles Carpenter.

William m. 24 Feb., 1780, Sarah Johnson, dau. of Obediah and Pricilla (____). Northampton Co. Mar. Record.

WALTON

____ m. bef. 1785, Frances Carter, dau. of Charles, whose will of that date, Henrico Co., names "daughter Frances Walton."

____ m. bef. Aug., 1801, Elizabeth Moore, dau. of Reuben, whose will of that date, Rockingham Co., proves it. 6T274.

____ m. bef. 25 Oct., 1752, Mary Hughes, dau. of Robert, whose will of that date, Cumberland Co., proves it.

____ m. bef. 25 Oct., 1752, Martha Hughes, dau. of Robert, whose will of that date, Cumberland Co., proves it.

____ m. Elizabeth Moore, dau. of Reuben (will prov. Nov., 1803, Rockingham Co.). Wayland, p. 423.

Agnes m. William Harvey.

Ann m. Charles Cobbs.

Ann m. William Edwards.

Ann m. John Hyde.

Barbara m. Thomas Harvey.

Beckie Pierson m. Thomas Walker.

Benjamin J. m. 21 May, 1828, Elizabeth T. Thorp. Henrico Co. Mar. Record. (This marriage included by error.)

Catharine m. Isaac Coles.

Catherine m. Nathan Harris.

Charlotte m. Anthony Hundley.

Charlotte m. ____ Hundley.

Claiborne m. 14 March, 1796, Milly Warren. Sur. Bartholomew Warren. Louisa Co. Mar. Bond. He, b. 24 Jan., 1774, Henrico Co.; d. Oct., 1822, Barren Co., Ky. She, dau. of Bartholomew. Wilcoxson, p. 417.

Daniel m. 7 Sept., 1793, Sally Webb, dau. of Micajar, who gave consent. Greensville Co. Mar. Record.

David m. 28 Feb., 1788, Rebecca Wyche. Sur. William Wyche. Greensville Co. Mar. Bond.

Drewry m. 26 Sept., 1785, Brunswick Co., Grave Ingram. 3T210.

Edward m. 13 Jan., 1791, Nancy Gentry. Louisa Co. Mar. Record. She, dau. of George (d. 1818). Albemarle, p. 205.

Elizabeth m. Isham Dalton.

Elizabeth m. Henry Wyche.

Elizabeth m. David Lundie.

Elizabeth m. William Walton.

Elizabeth m. David Tinsley.

Fanny m. Braxton Robinson.

Frances m. Richard Calloway.

Frances m. Henry Mullens.

George m. 29 Nov., 1790, Delilah Van Dike Chalmers. Halifax Co. Mar.

WALTON (cont.)

Record. 4T62.

George m. 22 May, 1749, Martha Hughes, spinster. Sur. R. Walton. Cumberland Co. Mar. Bond. 34V356.

George, son of Thomas, m. 25 June, 1759, Margaret Tabb, dau. of Thomas. Sur. Thomas Walton. Cumberland Co. Mar. Bond.

George m. Feb., 1710/11, Sarah Roper. St. Peter's, p. 418.

George, b. Prince Edward Co., coroner of Lunenburg Co., 1775; m. (1) Elizabeth Hughes. DAR No. 135 841.

George m. 30 Jan., 1793, Nancy Sharp. Henrico Co. Mar. Record. He was son of John. Wilcoxson, p. 417.

George, will prov. 1767, Brunswick Co.; m. by 1726, Elizabeth Rowe (or Roe), will prov. 1775, Brunswick Co.

Greshom m. 3 Jan., 1793, Nancy Edlow Watson. Consent of Lewis Grigg and Edith Grigg. Greensville Co. Mar. Record.

Henry, Capt., b. 1753, Brunswick Co.; d. 1813, Greenville, Va.; m. 1775, Rebecca Brewer. DAR No. 79 456.

Isaac R., Jr., m. 24 May, 1800, Rebecca (____) Randolph. Sur. Peter Pelham. Greensville Co. Mar. Record.

Ison m. 4 Jan., 1796, Franky Watson. Sur. John Walton. Albemarle Co. Mar. Bond.

Ison m. ____ Sims, dau. of John (d. 1798). Albemarle, p. 316.

James m. 24 Feb., 1795, Elizabeth Goodman (or Goodwin). Halifax Co. Mar. Record.

John m. 10 Dec., 1792, Nancey Smith. Sur. William Smith. Louisa Co. Mar. Bond.

John m. Martha Gentry, dau. of George (d. 1818). Albemarle, p. 205.

John m. 16 July, 1788, Mary Jenkins, dau. of James. Sur. Matthew Walton. Amelia Co. Mar. Bond.

John, Sr., m. 24 Dec., 1796, Sally Piles. Henrico Co. Mar. Record.

John Leonard, d. Hardy Co., aged 38; will prov. 11 Jan., 1809, son of John; m. Nancy (____) Toler, a widow with seven children. Wilcoxson, p. 417.

Judith m. Tilman Walton.

Littleton m. 21 Dec., 1789, Sally Phillips. Greensville Co. Mar. Record.

Louisa m. Jeremiah Jordan.

Martin, physician, of Louisa, served in Rev. War; m. Elizabeth Hinson, dau. of David. Query in 13T146 by Mrs. W. H. Simmons, 306 7th Ave., Springfield, Tenn.

Martin m. 15 April, 1788, Elizabeth Johnson. Louisa Co. Mar. Record.

Mary m. John Winfrey.

Mary m. Richard Yancy.

Mary m. Absolom Jordan.

Matthew m. 25 Jan., 1791, Frances Watkins. Prince Edward Co. Mar. Record.

Meredith m. 4 June, 1799, Anne Sharp, dau. of William. Louisa Co. Mar. Record.

Mezapina m. Robert Harris.

Molly m. Francis DeGraffenreid.

Moses, Jr., of Woodstock, Va., b. 1740; d. 1782, son of Moses, Sr.; m. Eunice Rogers, d. May, 1822, dau. of Edward and Hannah (Borden); res.

WALTON (cont.)

Frederick Co. She m. (2) 1788, at Crooked Run Meeting, Joseph Allen of Shenandoah Co.; m. (3) 12 June, 1811, in a school house near Smith's Creek, Goldsmith Chandler, b. 1751; d. 1822, son of Benjamin and Mary (____) of Cecil Co., Md. Miller Mss (363a).

Nancy m. Rev. Horace Moore.

Nancy m. William Isbell.

Newil m. 21 March, 1782, Agnes Woolfolk, dau. of Augustine. Louisa Co. Mar. Record. He, b. 13 Dec., 1763, Hanover Co.; d. 1834, So. Car.; served in Rev. War. DAR No. 89 990.

Patsy m. Lewis Davis.

Patsy m. John Sneed.

Patsy m. Edmund Lanier.

Patty m. Woodson Knight.

Polly m. Walter Otey.

Rebecca m. Edward Dromgoole.

Robin Harris m. 7 Nov., 1793, Drusillar Terry. Halifax Co. Mar. Record.

Rubin m. 6 Feb., 1793, Paty Bonner. Halifax Co. Mar. Record.

Sally m. Elisha Betts.

Sally m. John Leftwich.

Sarah m. (1) Thomas Watkins, Jr.; m. (2) Rev. Joshua Morris.

Sarah m. William Fox.

Susanna m. Clayborne Rice.

Susanna m. James Hilton.

Temperance m. Joseph Yarbrough.

Thomas, b. 1704, son of Edward and Elizabeth (Mason); m. bef. 1769, Martha Cox of Cumberland Co., dau. of George and Martha (____). She m. (2) Isaac Hughes. Will of Martha (Cox) Walton Hughes, 1769, proves her marriage. 6W(2)345.

Thomas H. m. 18 March, 1800, Betsy Richardson, dau. of George. Goochland Co. Mar. Record.

Tilman m. 12 April, 1787, Judith Walton. Cumberland Co. Mar. Record.

William m. 30 March, 1797, Elizabeth Terry. Halifax Co. Mar. Record.

William m. 1 Dec., 1758, Elizabeth Tilmon, both of this parish. Douglas Reg.

William, b. 1749; m. 1778, Mary Leftwich, d. 1824, dau. of Lieut. Col. William and Betsy (Haines). DAR No. 65 739; DAR No. 66 427.

William m. 2 March, 1794, Elizabeth Walton. Sur. Jesse Walton. She, dau. of Thomas Walton, who gave consent. Cumberland Co. Mar. Bond.

William m. ca 1795, ____ (____) Lavendar, widow of William of Nelson Co. Proven by Petition, 13 Dec., 1810, Nelson Co.

William m. 31 Dec., 1802, Patsey Warren, dau. of Bartholomew, who was surety. Louisa Co. Mar. Bond. He, b. ca 1778, son of John. Wilcoxson, p. 417.

WALTRIP

Joseph m. 9 March, 1792, Polly McCann. Sur. John Mochen (?). Amelia Co. Mar. Bond.

WAMAACK

____ m. Sarah Owen, dau. of Richard (will, 1753). Halifax, pp. 322-3.

WAMOCK

Eliza m. David Wells.

WAMPLER

Cathrene m. George Kinder.

Christopher m. 25 Aug., 1796, Elizabeth Ketering. Wythe Co. Mar. Record.

WAMSLEY

Mary m. David Hull.

WANDLESS

Ellinor m. John Grieves.

Ralph m. 30 Sept., 1788, Crispy Nicholas by Rev. John Brown. Augusta Co. Ministers' Returns.

WANS

Elizabeth m. Jeremiah Lungate.

WANSLEY

Elizabeth m. Abraham Elliott.

Nathan m. 1 March, 1794, Susanna Watts. Sur. George Taylor. Albemarle Co. Mar. Bond.

WANSLY

Nancy m. John Perry Patterson.

WANT

Sarah m. William Corbin.

WARBURTON

____ m. Frances Booker, dau. of Richard (bapt. 1688) and Margaret (Lowry). 7W(1)50.

William m. 24 Nov., 1785, Nancy Morris by H. J. Burgess. Surry Co. Mar. Record.

WARD

____ m. Martha Worsham. 33V186.

____ m. Catherine Crawley, dau. of William. She m. (2) 1784, Daniel Jones. Eggleston's transcription of Amelia Co. Mar. Bond.

____ m. Col. Seth Ward.

____, Maj., m. Sarah (Clark) Lynch. 32V398.

Agnes m. John Morris.

Ann m. Robert Jones.

Ann m. Christopher Clark.

Ann m. William Armstrong.

Benjamin, will dated May, 1732, Henrico Co., son of Seth; m. Ann Anderson, dau. of Henry (will prov. May, 1734, Henrico Co.) and Prudence (Stratton). 32V388; 24W(1)273; 28W(1)266.

Benjamin of Chesterfield Co. m. 13 Jan., 1779, Mary Eggleston, dau. of Joseph. Sur. Stith Hardaway. Amelia Co. Mar. Bond. He, d. 30 April, 1783. She, b. 1759, dau. of Joseph and Judith (Segar); m. (2) Gen. Everard Meade (2nd wife). Meade, pp. 44, 122, 126.

Caleb m. 15 Dec., 1785, Marian (____) Taylor. Norfolk Co. Mar. Record.

Catharine m. Francis Fitzgerald.

Catherine m. William Brown.

Courtney m. William Shepherd.

Edward m. 20 Dec., 1792, Ann Jones. Sur. Edward Wilkinson. Amelia Co. Mar. Bond.

Edward m. Elizabeth Elam, dau. of Gilbert, Sr.; res. Chesterfield Co. Farmer, p. 17.

Elizabeth m. Edmund Pendleton.

WARD (cont.)

Elizabeth m. Robert Taylor.

Elizabeth m. William Browne Christian.

Elizabeth m. (1) ___ Gaines; m. (2) William Harris.

Elizabeth Crawley m. Richard Jones (1st wife).

Frances m. John Chapman (1st wife).

Frances m. Thomas Kersey.

Francis m. 5 March, 1781, Sarah Webb, dau. of Robert. Sussex Co. Mar. Record.

George, d. Feb., 1791, Randolph Co.; enl. in Rev. War from Hampshire Co.; m. there, 24 Feb., 1783, Margaret Swisicks (also called Thixton), b. 15 Dec., 1757; d. 6 Nov., 1855, Darke Co., Ohio. She m. (2) ca 1793, Hampshire Co., David Riffle; m. (3) John Wintermote of Darke Co. Data from Pension W6550.

Gideon m. 5 March, 1791, Anne Cannon. Princess Anne Co. Mar. Record.

Goldin m. 24 Aug., 1786, Peggy Savage, dau. of Delitha. Northampton Co. Mar. Record.

Henry, son of John and Anne (Chiles), b. 5 April, 1751; d. 12 April, 1823 (tombstone inscription); m. Martha Barbour. 24V180.

Henry, d. 1765, Amelia Co., son of Benjamin and Ann (Anderson) of Henrico Co.; m. Oct., 1746, his cousin, Prudence Jones, b. 19 Feb., 1725, dau. of Col. Richard and Sarah (Stratton) of Amelia Co. 24W (1)273; 27W(1)266; Harllee III:2802.

Henry m. 14 June, 1775, Mary Hankins. St. Paul's.

Jacomine m. Solomon Cason.

James m. 2 July, 1792, Mary (___) Ross. Norfolk Co. Mar. Record.

James, Capt. in Rev. War from Botetourt Co., m. 1749, Phoebe Lockhart. DAR No. 41 303; DAR No. 51 805.

James m. 24 Feb., ___, Mrs. Elizabeth Grogg. Norfolk Co. Mar. Record.

James m. 29 June, 1777, Anne Willis. St. Paul's.

James m. bet. Oct., 1774, and Oct., 1775, Jenny Jennings. King George Co. Mar. Record.

Jane m. Abel Edmonds.

Jane m. John Humphries.

Jane m. John S. Farrish.

Jane (___) m. Edward Winder.

John m. Cleary Ammon. 34V77.

John m. 9 April, 1729, Alice Symonds. Spotsylvania Co. Mar. Record.

John m. 4 Nov., 1786, Savary Harris. Louisa Co. Mar. Record.

John m. 1779, Mary Bennett. Rockbridge Co. Morton, p. 540.

John m. 14 Nov., 1782, Sallie Burton by Rev. James Shelburne, Baptist. Lunenburg Co. Ministers' Returns.

John m. 2 Nov., 1790, Patsey Mason by Charles Cobbs. Campbell Co. Mar. Record.

John m. 1792, Sally Coots. Rockbridge Co. Morton, p. 540.

John m. 18 March, 1783, Sarah Hambleton. Louisa Co. Mar. Record.

John m. 19 April, 1768, M. Smith. Halifax Co. Mar. Record.

John m. (1) Anne Chiles, dau. of Henry; m. (2) 17 Dec., 1766, Sarah (Clark) Lynch, widow of Maj. Charles Lynch and dau. of Christopher and Penelope (___) Clark; res. prob. in Bedford Co. and Albemarle Co. and was taxed, 1767, Pittsylvania Co. 20V106; 23V378; 24V180;

WARD (cont.)

Albemarle, p. 258.

Kesiah m. William Malbone.

Kezia m. David Ledinback.

Lawrence, b. 1753/4; d. 1830, Estill Co., Ky.; m. Dec., 1780, Fairfax Co., Betsy Ford, b. ca 1750. Hartford B-7736(2), 30 April, 1955. Signed L. W. L.

Leland m. 24 Nov., 1752, ___ Jones, dau. of Richard. Amelia Co. Mar. Record.

Leonard m. 26 Sept., 1768, Anne Eggleston, dau. of Richard. Sur. Richard Eggleston. Cumberland Co. Mar. Bond. Leonard's will prov. 1772, Chesterfield Co., son of Joseph and Sarah (___). 27W(1)283.

Levy m. 7 June, 1786, Susan Clarke. Sur. Henry Jones. Amelia Co. Mar. Bond.

Lurena m. Henry Mintee.

Lydia m. William Thompson (2nd wife).

Margaret m. Peter Fore.

Margaret m. Batt Jones.

Margaret m. William Shepherd.

Martha m. Richard Jones, Jr.

Mary m. Micajah Cayce.

Mary m. John Bennett.

Mary m. (1) William Broadnax; m. (2) Richard Gregory.

Mary (___) m. Everard Meade.

Mary (___) m. Nathan Thomas.

Morris J. m. 6 Feb., 1796, Levinia Jones. Halifax Co. Mar. Record.

Nancy m. Hugh Adams.

Prudence m. Lewellyn Jones.

Prudence m. William Munford.

Rhebecah m. Samuel Jamison.

Richard, d. 1724, Henrico Co., son of Richard; m. bef. Oct., 1688, Martha Branch, dau. of Thomas and Elizabeth (___) of Henrico Co.; m. (2) Sept., 1696, Henrico Co., Elizabeth Blackman (transcribed as Blackmoer); m. (3) Mary (___) Jones, widow of Robert. 25W(1)62; 27W(1)194; Farmer, p. 42; Henrico, p. 227. Richard was son of Seth. Farmer, p. 41.

Richard, b. 1694, Va., son of Richard and Sarah (Blackman); m. Frances Stanley; rem. ca 1746 to Carteret Co., No. Car. 9W(2)148.

Rowland m. 10 Nov., 1752, Prudence Jones. Sur. James Claiborne. Amelia Co. Mar. Bond.

Rowland, b. 1730, Henrico Co.; will dated 1800, Amelia Co., son of Benjamin and Ann (Anderson); m. 1752, Rebecca Jones, dau. of Col. Richard and Margaret (___). 27W(1)267; DAR No. 57 899; DAR No. 65 264.

Rowland, Jr., m. 7 April, 1777, Sarah Ward. Sur. Francis Anderson. Amelia Co. Mar. Bond.

Salley m. William Ward.

Sarah m. Samuel Smith.

Sarah m. Rowland Ward, Jr.

Sarah m. Henry Farmer.

Sarah m. ___ Walker.

Sarah m. Joshua Lawrence.

Seth m. 27 Oct., 1796, Peggy Cobbs. Halifax Co. Mar. Record.

WARD (cont.)

Seth m. 30 May, 1793, Mary Hudson by Rev. James Shelburne, Baptist. Lunenburg Co. Ministers' Returns.

Seth of "Sheffield," Henrico Co., later in Chesterfield Co., d. 1735; m. bef. Aug., 1717, Martha Worsham, dau. of John. 32V391; 27W(1)259.

Seth m. Mary Goode, b. 6 April, 1741, dau. of Robert and Mary (Turpin). McCullough, p. 277.

Seth, will dated Sept., 1769, Chesterfield Co., son of Seth and Martha (Worsham); m. ____ Ward, dau. of Benjamin and Ann (Anderson). 27W (1)260.

Seth, b. 1613, son of John (to Va. 1619); m. Katherine Smith; res. Henrico Co. 9W(2)148.

Stephen m. 2 March, 1797, Adah Hickman. Northampton Co. Mar. Record.

Stephen m. 6 June, 1791, Nancy Cook. Northampton Co. Mar. Record.

Stephen m. 2 April, 1774, Elizabeth Harrison, dau. of Salathall. Northampton Co. Mar. Record.

Tahpenez m. Philip Webber.

Thomas, son of John and Anne (Chiles), m. Mildred Walden. 24V180.

Thomas m. 24 Dec., 1795, Amy Levit. Princess Anne Co. Mar. Record.

Wiley m. 23 June, 1787, Martha Mayes. Sur. William Gates. Amelia Co. Mar. Bond.

Wiley m. 28 Feb., 1784, Sally Ford. Sur. John Wynne. Amelia Co. Mar. Bond.

Wiley m. 10 Feb., 1778, Ann Thomas. Sur. John Worsham. Amelia Co. Mar. Bond.

William, b. 1758, Va.; d. 1833, Ind.; m. 1778, Verlinda Harrison, b. 1758; d. 1831. DAR No. 85 112.

William, son of John and Anne (Chiles), m. Mildred Adams, dau. of Robert and Penelope (Lynch). 24V180.

William m. 1800, Rebecca Wallis. Rockbridge Co. Morton, p. 540.

William m. 19 Dec., 1797, Salley Ward. Halifax Co. Mar. Record.

William m. 1787, Catherine McCready. Northampton Co. Mar. Record.

William m. 7 Jan., 1797, Agnes Melvil. Northampton Co. Mar. Record.

William m. 25 Dec., 1753, Elizabeth Jordan. St. Paul's.

William m. 24 Dec., 1741, Margaret Tamian. St. Paul's.

William m. bef. 1798, Nancy Thompson, dau. of William (1722-1798) and (2) Lydia (Ward). Hartford B-8010(2), 16 July, 1955. Signed T. J. C.

William m. 8 Aug., 1786, Elizabeth Johnson. Northampton Co. Mar. Record.

William, Gen., b. ca 1775, Va., son of ____ and Mary (Long); m. 1795, Scott Co., Ky., Sallie Johnson, dau. of Col. Robert and Jemima (Suggett). 15T83.

WARDE

Henry m. 25 Oct., 1746, Prudence Jones. Sur. Henry Anderson. Amelia Co. Mar. Bond.

WARDEN

Arthur m. 19 Jan., 1791, Frances Jones. Princess Anne Co. Mar. Record.

Mary m. Jonas Slack.

Nancy m. Alexander Evans.

Sarah m. Simon Wilson.

WARDLAW

____ believed m. bef. 1784, Mary Coulter, dau. of James, whose will, filed 1784, Rockbridge Co., names "daughter Mary Wardlaw." Mar. Mary Coalter, dau. of James and Margaret (____). Morton, p. 479.
____ m. Elizabeth Coalter, dau. of James (d. 1784) and Margaret (____). Rockbridge Co. Morton, p. 479.
Dr. m. Sarah "Sally" Minor, dau. of James and Mary (Carr). 5V441; 9W (1)181.
Elizabeth m. William McPheeters.
Jenny m. John Temple.
Virginia m. John Stuart.
William m. 11 March, 1795, Sally Minor. Sur. Thomas L. Bell. Albemarle Co. Mar. Bond. She, dau. of James and Mary (Carr). Albemarle, p. 277.

WARE

____ m. Fanny Perkins, b. 1750's, Va., dau. of Abram and Cecily (Turpin). Abram's will, prov. 1793, Caswell Co., No. Car., names "daughter Fanny Ware." 30T285-6.
____ believed m. bef. 1720, Margaret Daniell, dau. of Robert, whose will of that date, Middlesex Co., names "daughter Margaret Ware."
Alse m. Pemberton Proudlove.
Arthur m. 26 Jan., 1733, Jane Daniel. Christ Church, p. 168. Mar. Jean Daniel, dau. of William and Frances (Boseley). 12T206.
Caleb m. March, 1708, Bethinia (____) Douglas, widow. Henrico, p. 228.
Catharine m. John Groom.
Catharine m. Drury Bagwell.
Dudley m. Elizabeth Harris by R. O. Ferguson, minister. (Prob. 1799 or 1800.) Louisa, p. 268.
Edward, Jr., m. 6 May, 1782, Sally Thurmond. 30T60.
Elizabeth m. Oliver Yarrington.
Elizabeth m. John Ellis.
Elizabeth m. Zachariah Crittenden.
Frances m. Thomas Hugget.
Henry m. 15 Aug., 1711, Margaret Daniel. Christ Church, p. 82. She, dau. of Robert and Margaret (Price). 12T208.
Isaac m. 16 March, 177-, Clara Stringer. Christ Church, p. 199.
Jacobb m. 3 Feb., 1690/1, Susana Adams. St. Peter's, p. 418.
James m. 22 July, 1773, Jane Machan. Christ Church, p. 200.
James m. 19 Oct., 1782, Mary Veale, dau. of Carnaby. 30T60.
James, Capt., m. 13 Dec., 1800, Nancy Pendleton, dau. of Reuben and Frances Maria Anna (Garland). 42V269.
James, Jr., physician, b. March, 1741, Va., son of James of Gloucester Co. (d. ca 1795, Ky.); m. 1764 in Va., Catharine Todd, dau. of Dr. James of Gloucester Co. 19 Ky. Reg. 55:46.
John m. 6 Sept., 1780, Margarett Lady. Henry Co. Mar. Record.
John in Maniken Town m. 6 April, 1762, Mary Watson in Henrico. Douglas Reg., p. 6.
John, will dated 24 July, 1703, Westmoreland Co.; m. Elizabeth (____) Morgan, widow of Anthony of Old Rappahannock Co. 25T270.
John m. 25 May, 1756, Ann Harrison, dau. of Andrew. Sur. Will Pryor. James Ware gave consent to his son's marriage. Goochland Co. Mar. Bond. John in Caroline m. 27 May, 1756, Ann Harrison on the Byrd in

WARE (cont.)

this county. Douglas Reg., p. 2.

Judith m. Samuel Jordan.

Judy m. William Banister.

Lucy m. Isaac Webb.

Mary m. Thomas Gunter.

Mary (____) m. Richard Deadman.

Molly m. Maj. John Randall.

Polly m. John Crittenden.

Rachel m. Benjamin Collier.

Robert m. 22 July, 1773, Catherine Machan. Christ Church, p. 200.

Robert m. 2 Jan., 1787, Mary Massie, spinster. Sur. Samuel Bell. Albemarle Co. Mar. Bond. She, dau. of Charles, m. (2) William Lobban. Albemarle, p. 266.

Sarah m. John Smith.

Spencer, d. 1777; m. ca 1769, ____ Digges. Bagby, p. 363.

Tabitha m. William Parks.

Thomas m. 28 Aug., 1788, Sarah Wingo. Sur. D. Cashon. Amelia Co. Mar. Bond.

William m. 29 Dec., 1777, Patty Davis. 30T60.

William, b. March, 1750, Va., son of James of Gloucester Co. (d. ca 1795, Ky.); m. in Va., Sarah Samuels; res. Woodford Co., Ky. 19 Ky. Reg. 55:46.

William m. 15 Feb., 1777, Mary Bolden. Christ Church, p. 201.

WAREN

Michael m. 9 Dec., 1795, Esther Shanklin. Rockingham Co. Wayland, p. 7.

WARFORD

Joseph m. 30 March, 1793, Mary Warford. Shelby Co., Ky. Mar. Record.

Mary m. Joseph Warford.

WARIENT

Edward m. 15 Nov., 1784, Beckey Dabney by Rev. Thomas Sparks. Pittsylvania Co. Ministers' Returns.

WARING

____ m. William Todd.

Ann m. William Latane.

Anna m. Rev. John Smelt.

Catharine Robinson m. John Latane.

Elizabeth "Betty" m. Thomas Todd.

Elizabeth m. Col. Spencer Mottram Ball.

Francis, Col., of Goldsberry, St. Ann's Parish, Essex Co., b. 23 July, 1717; d. 1754, Essex Co., son of Col. Thomas; m. Lucy Cocke, dau. of Secretary William and Elizabeth (Catesby). Jones Gene., p. 135; Old King Wm., p. 76; Winston, p. 166.

Hannah m. Carlile Hance.

Lucy m. James Robb.

Mary "Molly" m. Henry Robinson.

Polly m. David Daniel.

Robert Payne, Jr., of Essex Co., m. 5 July, 1800, Lucy Latane, dau. of William and Ann (Waring). Jones Gene., p. 137.

Susanna m. Dr. John Taliaferro Lewis (2nd wife).

Thomas, Col., m. Lucy Cocke. 5V191.

WARING (cont.)

Thomas m. bef. 20 March, 1715/6, Elizabeth Gouldman, dau. of Thomas and niece of Francis Gouldman, whose Deed of Gift of that date, Essex Co., proves it. Thomas, b. ca 1690; d. Jan., 1754, Essex Co.; came from England to Virginia. Old King Wm., p. 77; Winston, pp. 178-183.

William, Jr., m. bef. 17 Aug., 1778, Sarah Green, dau. of George. Proven by Court Record of that date, Essex Co.

WARKELIN

Matthew, Maj., m. bef. 1698, ____ (____) Purefy, widow of Thomas, Jr. Proven by Court Record of that date, Elizabeth City Co.

WARMAN

Joseph m. 1794, Barbara Smith, dau. of William. Bath, p. 131.

WARMSLEY

Ralph m. Agatha Eltonhead. NNHM 4:1:337.

WARMUCK

Sallie m. Zachariah Taliaferro.

WARN

Martha m. Fleming Jordan.

WARNER

____ m. Lawrence Townley.

____ m. David Cant.

Aetsisah m. Henry Miller.

Augustine, b. 1610, Eng.; d. 24 Dec., 1674, Va.; m. Mary ____; res. Elizabeth City Co. 13 Ky. Reg. 37:80.

Augustine, Col., b. 3 July, 1642, Va.; d. 19 June, 1681, Gloucester Co., son of Capt. Augustine and Mary (____); m. Mildred Reade, dau. of George and Elizabeth (Martian). 1T248; Duke, p. 123; 13 Ky. Reg. 37:80; Old King Wm., p. 74.

Elizabeth m. John Lewis.

Isabella m. John Lewis.

John m. 1775, Ann Walker. Orange Co. Mar. Record.

Margaret m. James Dillon.

Mary m. Jacob Shepherd.

Mary m. Col. John Smith, Jr.

Mary m. James Hipkins.

Mildred m. (1) Lawrence Washington; m. (2) George Gale.

Peter m. Judith Shoemaker, dau. of George. Hartford B-9678(1), 10 Nov., 1956. Signed C. I. L., New York.

Sally m. Robert Fitchett.

Sarah m. Lawrence Townley.

WARON

Eleoner m. ____ Crotzer.

WARREN

____ m. John Hunnicutt.

____ m. John Christian.

____ m. bef. 1794, Martha Booth, dau. of Moses, whose will of that date, Southampton Co., names "daughter Martha Warren."

Agnes m. Thomas Brandon.

Argoll m. 15 Feb., 1709, Elizabeth Marriner. Northampton Co. Mar. Record.

Aylse m. Mathais Marriott.

WARREN (cont.)

Edward m. Jane Christian, dau. of William and (1) Elizabeth (Collier). 8W(1)124.

Eleanor m. John Rucker.

Eleanor Mildred m. John Rucker, Jr.

Elizabeth m. Thomas Jourden.

Elizabeth m. Thomas Clark.

Elizabeth m. ____ Martin.

Elizabeth m. John Hunnicutt.

Elizabeth m. ____ Dupree (or Duprey).

Elizabeth m. ____ Brook.

Elizabeth m. William Steele Fleeman.

Elizabeth m. William Downs.

Elizabeth m. Lothrop Chase.

Elizabeth m. John Smith.

Elizabeth (____) m. William Henry.

Esther m. Daniel Scott.

Faith m. ____ Duprey.

Fanny m. Archibald Christian.

Frances (____) m. James Warren.

Frances (____) m. John Flood.

Hackley m. 2 Nov., 1787, Frances Turner. Halifax Co. Mar. Record.

Hannah m. John Stott.

Hannah m. John Williams.

Henrietta m. Archelaus Rosson.

Henry m. 28 July, 1772, Rose Mary Campbell, dau. of Nicholas. Northampton Co. Mar. Record.

Hezekiah m. 4 Dec., 1794, Adah Kellam. Northampton Co. Mar. Record. He, b. ca 1766; d. 1803, son of Hillary. 8W(2)190.

Hillary, b. 1736; d. 1795, Northampton Co., son of Hillary and Gertrude (____); m. (1) 11 July, 1764, Mary (____) Dixon; m. (2) 11 Dec., 1787, Hannah Rayfield. Both marriage records in Northampton Co. 8W(2)190.

James, d. 1735, son of Robert of Northampton Co.; m. ca 1693, Frances (____) Warren, widow of his brother, Joseph Warren. 8W(2)188.

James m. 6 Oct., 1798, Dolley Stanfield. Halifax Co. Mar. Record.

James m. 23 April, 1792, Mary (____) Word. Norfolk Co. Mar. Record.

James Stuart m. 12 Feb., 1795, Catherine Brandon. Halifax Co. Mar. Record.

Jerry m. 12 Dec., 1786, M. Stanfield. Halifax Co. Mar. Record.

John m. 23 Dec., 1790, Jane Davis. Surry Co. Mar. Record.

John m. 1709, Susanna Spurlock. St. Peter's, p. 418.

John m. 8 Feb., 1791, Sarah Puckett by Rev. Needler Robinson. Chesterfield Co. Ministers' Returns.

Joseph m. Aug., 1707, Martha Lee ____. Northampton Co. Mar. Record.

Lucy m. Joel Madera.

Lucy m. George Gardner.

Maria (____) m. William Cooper.

Martha "Patsey" m. William Walton.

Mary m. ____ Buford.

Mary m. ____ Wilkins.

Mary m. Joseph Curd (1st wife).

WARREN (cont.)

Mary m. Thomas Day, Jr.

Mary (____) m. Robert Williams.

Michael, Sr., b. 1711, near Oystor Bay, Long Island, or at Plymouth, Mass.; d. 1795, Harrisonburg, Va.; res. Penna.; m. Catherine ____, b. 1726; d. 1804; both bur. New Erection Church Cemetery. Hartford C-1679, 10 May, 1958. Not signed.

Mildred m. Claiborne Walton.

Molley m. Thomas Whitlock.

Molly m. Lewis Nolen.

Nathaniel m. 4 Sept., 1788, Lucy Powell. Halifax Co. Mar. Record.

Peter m. 3 Nov., 1774, Rose (____) Johnson. Northampton Co. Mar. Record.

Peter, son of Peter and Rose (Goffigan) Hunt Warren, m. 1780, Mary Waterson. 8W(2)190.

Polly m. George Bean, Jr.

Polly m. William Brown.

Rachel m. ____ Hasken.

Rose m. Edward Smith.

Roxanna m. ____ More.

Sally m. Nicholas Whitlock.

Samuel m. 17 May, 1759, Hannah Inman. Hinshaw 6:113.

Sarah m. Joseph Rambo.

Sarah m. ____ Smith.

Thomas, b. 20 Sept., 1773, Stafford Co.; d. 18 Sept., 1860, Lee Co., son of John and Charity (____); m. ca 1796, Clarkey Hyden, b. 1771, Stafford Co.; d. 12 July, 1844, Lee Co. Orange III:161.

Thomas, mar. agreement, 25 Sept., 1654, with Elizabeth (____) Sheapard, widow of Maj. Robert. Surry Co. Bk. 1, p. 56. Thomas, b. 1621; d. 1668-9; m. Elizabeth (Spencer) Shepherd, dau. of William Spencer. 47V368, 370; 8W(1)152; 27W(1)34; Surry, p. 48.

William m. 3 April, 1789, Elizabeth Davis by Rev. H. J. Burgess. Surry Co. Ministers' Returns.

William m. 26 July, 1788, Anne Wheeler. Northampton Co. Mar. Record.

WARRICK

Benjamin believed m. bef. 1791, Charlotte George, dau. of Benjamin, whose est. sett., 20 Dec., 1791, included widow Catherine and Benjamin Warrick,and est. sett. of Catherine George, 16 Dec., 1793, included "Sharlot Warrick," both in Lancaster Co. records.

Fanny m. John H. Brewer.

Thomas m. 4 Aug., 1711, Mary Jones. Christ Church, p. 82.

WARRIN

Mary m. Joseph Curd.

Rachell m. John Askew.

WARRINER

____ m. bef. Nov., 1772, Ann Truman, dau. of Richard (will dated 3 Nov., 1772, Henrico Co.) and Mary (Woodson). 25W(1)285-6.

James m. March, 1793, Buckingham Co., Betsey Johns, b. ca 1773, dau. of James and Mary (Gannaway). Data from Pension File No. R5593 for James Johns' Virginia service.

James, Sr., son of David, m. in Va. Annie Pollard; rem. to Ky. ca 1810. Cumberland, p. 417.

WARRING
Polly m. David Daniel.

WARRINGTON
___ m. bef. 10 March, 1767, Comfort Taylor, dau. of James, whose will of that date, Accomac Co., proves it.
Rachel m. Richard Brown.
William, b. 1751, Accomac Co.; d. 1850, Delaware Co., Ohio; m. (3) 1803, Nancy Holland, b. 1771; d. 1824. DAR No. 27 253.

WARSON
Alexander m. 14 Oct., 1797, Jane McDowell. Shelby Co., Ky. Mar. Record.

WARWICK
___ m. Stith Thompson.
___ (___) m. Robert Sitlington.
___ (___) m. Andrew Sitlington.
Abraham, b. 1739, Amherst Co.; d. there, 1808; m. Amey Campbell, b. 1743; d. 1843. DAR No. 31 044.
Beverly, minister, b. 1761, Amherst Co.; d. 1794; m. Elizabeth Martin. DAR No. 31 044.
Casandra (___) m. James Meacham.
Elizabeth m. George Goodwin.
Fanny m. John H. Brown.
George m. 30 Jan., 1775, Elizabeth Chowning. Christ Church, p. 201.
Jacob, d. 1826, Bath Co., aged 83; m. ___ Vance, d. 1823, aged 80, dau. of Col. John of No. Car. Waddell, p. 353.
Jane m. John Healey.
Jane m. William Gatewood.
Jean m. James Gay (1st wife).
John m. 1794, Mary Poage. Bath, p. 132.
John m. 8 March (Banns), 1735, Agathee Twyman. Christ Church, p. 169. He, d. 1744; m. Agatha (Beauford) Twyman, b. 13 Aug., 1705, widow of George Twyman and dau. of Thomas, Jr., and Elizabeth (___) Beauford. She m. (3) ___ Lee. Wilcoxson, p. 371.
Margaret m. Adam Soe.
Martha m. John Stevenson.
*Mary m. Sampson Mathews (2nd wife).
Philip m. bef. 1788, Ann Stott, dau. of Thomas, whose will 1786, and est. sett., 1788, Lancaster Co., prove it.
Phillip m. 3 Aug. (Banns), 1735, Cassandra Cheaney. Christ Church, p. 169.
Phillip m. 5 Sept., 1705, Catherine Twyman. Christ Church, p. 79.
Rachel m. Capt. Charles Cameron.
Thomas m. 23 Jan., 1705, Eliza Goodrich. Christ Church, p. 79.
William m. Sarah Barksdale, dau. of William. Albemarle, p. 141.
William from Williamsburg, Va., to Augusta Co. m. Elizabeth Dunlap, dau. of Alexander and Ann (McFarland). She m. (2) Andrew Sitlington. Rockbridge Co. Bath, p. 202; Morton, p. 483.
Winifred m. Joseph Davis.

WASH
Elizabeth m. Thomas Moorman.

*Penelope m. Thomas Mountague.

WASH (cont.)

Heenley m. Thomas Wash.
John m. 2 Aug., 1779, Nancy Frazier Gatewood. Henry Co. Mar. Record.
Lucy m. Zachariah Matlock.
Mary m. ____ Lasly.
Mary m. Cleavers Duke.
Nathan m. 13 Jan., 1791, Mercey Wood, spinster. Sur. Samuel Wood. Albemarle Co. Mar. Bond.
Sarah m. ____ Crank.
Sukey m. ____ Hester.
Susannah m. Ben Moss.
Thomas, son of Thomas and Susannah (____) of Louisa Co., m. 4 Jan., 1785, Susanna Smith Fox, b. 20 Feb., 1767, dau. of Capt. John and Susan (Smith). Louisa, pp. 280, 320, 422-3, 424. She, dau. of John and Grace (Young). 21T238; 26W(1)129.
Thomas m. 12 April, 1784, Heenley Wash. Louisa Co. Mar. Record.
William, b. 4 April, 1752, son of Thomas and Susannah (____); m. 16 Jan., 1770, Anee Lipscomb, b. 1749; d. 7 Sept., 1796. 10W(2)350; Louisa, pp. 422-3.

WASHAM

Charles, b. 1764, Chesterfield Co.; d. 11 March, 1841; m. June, 1787, Polly Ellison (or Allison); family rem. to Amelia Co.; he rem. to Powhatan Co.; res. 1833, Wayne Co., Ky., aged 77. Data from his Pension No. W3057.
William m. ca 1792, Hannah Smith by Rev. Nicholas Reagan, Washington Co. Ministers' Returns.

WASHBAND

Letty m. Calthrop Freeman.

WASHBORN

Susannah m. William Moore.

WASHBOURNE

Mary m. John Noblett.

WASHBURN

John m. 30 Dec., 1799, Betty Jinnet. Halifax Co. Mar. Record.

WASHER

Elias m. 12 May, 1787, Judy Bowman. Halifax Co. Mar. Record.
Peter m. 18 Dec., 1788, Sarah Smith. Halifax Co. Mar. Record.

WASHINGTON

____ m. bef. 1799, ____ Thornton, dau. of John. Proven by Court Record of that date. 11W(2)115, 117.
____ prob. m. Temperance Gerrard (4th husband). NNHM 4:1:331.
____, a dau., m. ____ Berry.
____ (____) m. Griffin Stith.
Agnes (____) m. Thomas Briggs.
Alice Bailey m. Spencer Garner.
Amelia m. James Clayton.
Andrew, son of Joseph and Zilla (Branch), m. Margaret Bridger. Boddie-HSF IV:156.
Ann(-e) m. ____ Robinson.
Ann (-e) m. Burditt Ashton (1st wife).
Ann (-e) m. Maj. Francis Wright.
Ann (-e) m. John Tinsley.

WASHINGTON (cont.)

Anne m. William Thompson.

Anne m. John Stith.

Anne m. Lieut. Thomas Hungerford.

Anne m. John Stevens.

Arthur, b. ca 1795, son of Richard and Elizabeth (Jordan); m. Sarah Tynes, d. 1764. Boddie-SVF I:295. He, b. ca 1681; she, d. Isle of Wight Co. Boddie-HSF IV:157.

Augustine, Capt., b. 1694; d. 12 April, 1743, son of Capt. Lawrence and Mildred (Reade); m. (1) 20 April, 1715, Jane Butler, d. 2 Nov., 1728, dau. of Caleb and Elizabeth (Vaulx); m. (2) 6 March, 1731, Mary Ball, b. 1706; d. 25 Aug., 1789, dau. of Col. Joseph of Lancaster Co. and (2) Mary (Johnson). Boddie-HSF IV:161-2; NNHM 3:1: 196, 235; DAR No. 31 158.

Augustine, Jr., b. 1720, Bridges Creek, Va.; d. 1762, Westmoreland Co.; m. 1743, Ann Aylett, dau. of Capt. William (d. 1744, Essex Co.) and (1) Ann (Ashton). 24T216; 14W(2)163; DAR No. 79 683.

Bailey m. 12 Jan., 1748/9, Catherine Storke. St. Paul's. He, b. 10 Sept., 1731, Stafford Co., son of Capt. Henry and Mary (Bailey); she, b. 17 Dec., 1723, dau. of William and Elizabeth (Hart). 19T 227; 9W(2)176; Mss.

Bailey, b. 12 Dec., 1754, Overwharton Parish, son of Bailey and Catherine (Storke); m. Euphan Wallace, dau. of James of Elizabeth City Co. 22V330.

Betsy m. Nathan Smith.

Betty m. Gen. Fielding Lewis.

Betty m. (2) Thomas Seymour Starke (or Storke).

Buckerton m. 7 Dec., 1795, Ann Syls Smith. Spotsylvania Co. Mar. Record.

Bushrod, Judge, m. Julia Blackburn, dau. of Col. Richard and Alice (Elzey). 4W(1)266.

Catherine m. Col. Fielding Lewis.

Catherine m. Col. John Washington.

Charles, b. 1738; d. 1799, bro. of Pres. George Washington; m. Mildred Thornton, dau. of Francis III and Frances (Gregory). 11T27; 44V280; DAR No. 27 937.

Charlotte (____) m. Charles Neilson.

Corben (or Corbin) m. 1787, Hannah Lee, b. 1766; d. 1801, dau. of Richard Henry Lee and Ann (Aylett) (d. 12 Dec., 1768). 6W(1)125; DAR No. 31 158.

Elizabeth m. Gen. Fielding Lewis (2nd wife).

Elizabeth m. Alexander Spotswood.

Elizabeth m. Richard Reed.

Elizabeth m. (1) Samson Lanier; m. (2) Robert Lanier.

Elizabeth m. (1) Sampson Lanier; m. (2) Cuthbirt Smith.

Elizabeth m. Thomas Berry.

Elizabeth m. John Buckner.

Elizabeth Ann m. Thomas Kendall.

Frances m. Charles Stuart.

Frances m. Burges Ball (2nd wife).

Frances Townshend m. (1) Thornton Washington (2nd wife); m. (2) Griffin Stith.

WASHINGTON (cont.)

George m. 5 Feb., 1781, Lucy Greenhill. Sur. Samuel Greenhill. Amelia Co. Mar. Bond.

George, b. ca 1682; will, 1763, Southampton Co., son of Richard and Elizabeth (Jordan); m. Mary Wright. Boddie-HSF IV:156; Boddie-SVF I: 295.

George, Lieut., b. 1763, Stafford Co.; d. 1793, Fairfax Co.; m. 1785, Frances Bassett, b. 1767. DAR No. 27 937.

George, Pres., m. 6 Jan., 1759, Martha (Dandridge) Custis, b. 2 June, 1731; d. 22 May, 1802, widow of Col. Daniel Parke Custis and dau. of Col. John and Frances (Jones) Dandridge. 13T265; 32V239; 5W(1)35; Boddie-HSF IV:182.

Gray, son of Thomas and Sarah (Gray), m. 23 Dec., 1791, Brunswick Co., Nancy Harrison, dau. of James. 29V509; Boddie-HSF IV:157.

Henry m. 7 Feb., 1775, Ann Hawes, b. 7 Feb., 1758; d. 1 Dec., 1776, dau. of Samuel and (2) Anne (Walker) of Caroline Co. 15W(2)144; Caroline, p. 440.

Henry, b. Sept., 1728, son of John and Catherine (Whiting); m. (1) 9 Jan., 1749, Middlesex Co., Anne Thacker, dau. of Col. William; m. (2) 3 March, 1760, Middlesex Co., Charlotte (____) Montague, who m. (3) Col. Charles Nelson. 4W(1)118; 7W(1)190; Boddie-HSF IV:161.

Henry m. 12 March, 1779, Mildred Pratt. St. Paul's.

Henry, b. 1765; d. 20 May, 1812, son of Lawrence; m. Sarah Ashton, b. Oct., 1768; d. 22 July, 1831, dau. of John and Hannah (____). Family Bible. 22V437.

Henry m. at "Berryhill," Jefferson Co., Ky., Catherine Robinson Bate. 26V418, 420.

Henry, d. 1788, Albemarle Co., son of John; m. 1785, Ann Quarles, dau. of James. She m. (2) 1791, John Tinsley. 22V329; Albemarle, p. 299. Ann Quarles, dau. of Jane (____) Quarles and sis. of Robert. 38V134.

Henry, Jr., bro. of Bailey, m. 18 May, 1743, Elizabeth Storke. St. Paul's. 9W(2)62.

James, b. ca 1693; d. ca 1766, Northampton Co., No. Car., son of Richard and Elizabeth (Jordan); m. ca 1729, Joyce Nicholson, dau. of Robert and Joanna (Joyce) of Surry Co. 12W(2)52; Boddie-HSF IV:158; Boddie-SVF I:295.

Jane m. William Augustine Washington.

Jane m. Col. John Thornton.

Jemima m. Smith Jenkins.

Jessie, son of John (will prov. 1754, Southampton Co.) and Eliza (___), m. Rebecca Wrenn, dau. of Thomas. 7T128; Boddie-HSF IV:157.

John, son of John, m. long before 16 April, 1735, Mary "Polly" Massey, dau. of Dade, Sr. Stafford Co. Bk. M, p. 172; 23V97; 26V418.

John m. 17 Nov., 1749, Betty Massey. St. Paul's.

John m. 24 Dec., 1787, Eleanor Massey. St. Paul's.

John, Col., of "Hylton," King George Co., m. 23 Dec., 1759, Catherine Washington. St. Paul's. 26V417; 33V156. Catherine, b. 13 Jan., 1740, dau. of Capt. John and Mary (Massey); m. her cousin, Col. John Washington (2nd wife), son of Henry. 22V328; 23V98; 26V417, 419; 33 V156; 12W(2)32.

John, Capt., b. 1671, son of Lawrence of Stafford Co.; m. 15 March, 1692, Mary Townshend, dau. of Col. Robert and Mary (____) of Staf-

WASHINGTON (cont.)

ford Co. See Deed, 6 Nov., 1727, Stafford Co. 22V314; 23V97; 26V418; 33V156; Boddie-HSF IV:162.

John, Col., b. 1634; d. 1677, son of Rev. Lawrence Washington of Braxted, England; m. 1 Dec., 1658, Ann(-e) Pope, dau. of Lieut. Col. Nathaniel Pope (will prov. 26 April, 1660, Westmoreland Co.). 3T142; 4T157; 64V365; 24W(1)194; Boddie-HSF IV:160-1. He m. (2) 1669, Anne (____) Brodhurst Brett, widow 1st of Walter Brodhurst (d. 1658, Westmoreland Co.) and 2nd of Henry Brett; m. (3) Frances (Gerrard) Speke Peyton Appleton, widow 1st of Col. Thomas Speke (d. 1659), 2nd of Col. Valentine Peyton and 3rd of Capt. John Appleton. 4T328, 339; 4W(1)36; 18W(2)440.

John, Maj., b. 12 Nov., 1692; d. 1 Sept., 1746, Gloucester Co., son of Lawrence and Mildred (Warner); m. Catherine Whiting, b. 22 May, 1694; d. 7 Feb., 1743, aged 49, dau. of Col. Henry and Elizabeth (____). 32V130; 62V484; 2W(1)157, 225; Boddie-HSF IV:161; Old King Wm., p. 74.

John m. Mary (Flood) Ford Blount, widow 1st of Charles Ford and 2nd of Richard Blount. Hartford C-2219(2), 4 Oct., 1958. Signed R. F. H. Given as widow 1st of ____ Blount, 2nd of Charles Ford. 5V202. She m. (4) Henry Briggs. Boddie-HSF IV:155.

John, will prov. 26 June, 1787, Westmoreland Co., son of Robert; m. Constant ____. 23V99. He m. (1) ____ Sanford; m. (2) Constantia Terrett. 26V419.

John, son of Lawrence and Elizabeth (____), m. Elizabeth "Betsy" Muse, dau. of Nicholas (d. 1779) and (1) Ann (____) Cullum Finch Muse. 53V224.

John, son of Col. John of King George Co., m. ____ Skinker, dau. of Col. Skinker of Prince William Co.; rem. to Ala. 26V418.

John, son of John (will prov. 1754, Southampton Co.), m. Tamar Rickman, dau. of William. 7T128; Boddie-HSF IV:157.

John, b. ca 1740; d. 22 Aug., 1804, son of John and Margaret (Storke) of Stafford Co.; m. 1770, Elizabeth Buckner, d. 15 Oct., 1812, dau. of George, Sr., and Elizabeth (Walker); res. Caroline Co. 22V214; 64V362, 365.

John of Westmoreland and Stafford counties, b. 1661; d. 22 Oct., 1748, son of Col. John and Ann (Pope); m. Anne Wycliffe, sis. of Henry. She m. (2) Col. Charles Ashton. Boddie-HSF IV:161. His will, 1697/8, Westmoreland Co.; her will dated 1698. Washington, pp. 219-223.

John m. 23 Nov., 1738, Margaret Storke. St. Paul's. He, b. ca 1716; d. 1752; res. Stafford Co. She, dau. of William and Elizabeth (Hart), m. (2) Col. Andrew Monroe. 38V185; 64V365.

John Augustine, b. 1735-6; d. 1787, bro. of Pres. George Washington; m. Hannah Bushrod, b. 1738. 33V154; DAR No. 28 903; DAR No. 31 158.

Joseph, d. ca 1803, Southampton Co., son of George and Mary (Wright); m. Zilla Branch. 7T125; Boddie-HSF IV:156.

Joseph, son of Joseph and Zilla (Branch), m. Mary Cheatham, dau. of Frank; rem. to Robertson Co., Tenn. Boddie-HSF:156.

Lawrence, b. 31 March, 1727/8; d. 1804, son of John; m. 31 July, 1751, Elizabeth Dade, dau. of Townshend and (1) Elizabeth (Alexander); res. "Digby," King George Co. 16T164; 23V99; 26V419, 420. Mar. 31 July, 1750. St. Paul's.

WASHINGTON (cont.)

Lawrence m. Ann Fairfax, dau. of William and (1) Sarah (Walker). 15T 6; Fairfax, pp. 12-13.

Lawrence m. 6 Nov., 1797, Winchester, Va., Mary Dorcostrow. 9T284.

Lawrence, b. at Tring, Bedfordshire, England; bapt. 23 Jan., 1635; will prov. 6 Jan., 1667, Va.; m. (1) 26 Jan., 1660, Luton, Eng., Mary Jones, bapt. 10 Oct., 1638, dau. of Edmund and Margaret (____); m. (2) bef. 1671, in Va., Joyce (____) Fleming, widow of Capt. Alexander Fleming; res. Old Rappahannock Co. 23V97; Washington, pp. 134 ff.

Lawrence m. Sarah Lund, dau. of Thomas; res. King George Co. 26V419.

Lawrence m. 5 Oct., 1744, Catherine Foote. St. Paul's. He, b. 14 March, 1740; d. 1799, a twin, son of Townshend. 26V419; 33V156, 160.

Lawrence of Mattox Creek, m. March, 1763, his cousin, Susanna Washington, dau. of Robert. 23V98; 26V418, 419; 33V156.

Lawrence, Maj., b. Sept., 1659; d. age 39; will prov. 1698, Westmoreland Co., son of Col. John and (1) Anne (Pope); m. ca 1686, Mildred Warner, dau. of Col. Augustine and Mildred (Reade) of Gloucester Co. She m. (2) George Gale of Cumberland Co., Eng., and she d. 1700/1, in England. 4W(1)51; Boddie-HSF IV:161; Old King Wm., p. 74; Washington, pp. 224, 229, 243-4.

Louisa m. Thomas Fairfax.

Lucy m. George Clements.

Lucy m. E. C. Williams.

Lund, b. 25 Sept., 1767; d. 4 April, 1853, son of Robert and Alice (Strother); m. 11 Feb., 1793, Susan Monroe Grayson, b. 29 May, 1768; d. 1823, dau. of Rev. Spence Grayson and Mary Elizabeth (Wagener). 5T263; 11T119; 23V100; 33V156; 3W(2)174.

Lund, b. 21 Oct., 1737; d. July, 1796, son of Townshend; m. ca 1782, his cousin, Elizabeth "Betty" Foote. 26V419; 33V156, 160.

Margaret m. Andrew Monroe.

Martha m. Samuel Hayward.

Martha m. ____ Hayward.

Martha m. John Darden.

Mary m. Robert Hart.

Mary m. (1) James Wray; m. (2) Andrew Balmaine.

Mary A. m. Robert Stith.

Mary Townshend m. Col. Robert Stith.

Mary Townshend m. Burdet Ashton.

Mary West m. William James.

Mildred m. (1) Roger Gregory; m. (2) Col. Henry Willis.

Mildred m. Langhorne Dade.

Mildred m. (1) Dr. Walter Williamson; m. (2) John Rose.

Mildred m. (1) Langhorne Dade; m. (2) Dr. Walter Williamson.

Nancy Constantia m. Andrew Balmain.

Nathaniel m. 17 Dec., 1767, Sarah Hooe. St. Paul's.

Nathaniel, b. ca 1691; d. 1718, son of John and Anne (Wycliffe); m. Mary Dade, grdau. of Maj. John Dade; res. Stafford Co. 64V365; Boddie-HSF IV:161.

Nathaniel, son of Col. John and (2) Catherine (Washington), m. ____ Hawkins, grdau. of Mrs. DeButts. 26V418.

Needham Langhorne, d. 1835, son of Lawrence; m. Sarah Ashton Alexander,

WASHINGTON (cont.)

dau. of Gerard Alexander; res. "Waterloo," King George Co. 23V100; 26V420.

Nicholson m. 25 Oct., 1774, Sarah ____. Surry Co. Mar. Record.

Priscilla m. Robert Lanier.

Richard, b. ca 1660; will dated 9 Nov., 1724, son of John and Mary (____) Blunt Ford Washington; m. Elizabeth Jordan, will, 1755, Surry Co., dau. of Arthur (will, 1698) and Elizabeth (Bavinn). 3T142; 4W(1)35; 23W(1)180; 24W(1)44; Boddie-HSF IV:156.

Richard Conway, son of Lawrence and Susannah (____), m. (2) Sophia Roberts of Alexandria; res. Washington, D. C. 26V418.

Robert of St. Paul's Parish m. 16 Dec., 1756, Alice Strother of Overwharton Parish. OPR; St. Paul's. Robert, b. 25 July, 1729, son of Townshend; Alice, dau. of Benjamin and Mary (Mason) Fitzhugh Strother; res. King George Co. 11T119; 23V100; 26V420; 33V156.

Robert, b. 3 Sept., 1700; d. 13 May, 1765, son of John; m. 1 April, 1722, Sarah Fossaker, dau. of Richard. 26V418-9; 33V156.

Sally m. Robert Bolling (3rd wife).

Sally m. Mathew Johnson.

Sally m. (1) Robert Harper; m. (2) Thomas Washington.

Samuel, Col., b. 16 Nov., 1734, at Wakefield, Westmoreland Co.; d. 1781, Harewood, Berkeley Co., bro. of Gen. Washington; m. (1) Jane Champe, d. 1758, dau. of Col. John of Lambs Creek, King George Co., and Jane (____); m. (2) his cousin, Mildred Thornton, dau. of Col. John and Mildred (Gregory) of Caroline Co.; m. (3) Lucy Chapman, dau. of Nathaniel and Constantia (Pearson); m. (4) Ann (Steptoe) Allerton, widow of Willoughby Allerton and dau. of Col. James and Hannah (Ashton) Steptoe of "Hominy Hall," Westmoreland Co.; m. (5) Susanna (Perrin) Holden (or Holding), d. 1783, widow of George Holden and dau. of John Perrin of Gloucester Co. 3T51; 11T27; 25V81; 38V364-5; 39V29; 44V352; 4W(1)161; 5W(1)176; 6W(1)25; Boddie-HSF IV:162; DAR No. 32 163; DAR No. 65 098.

Samuel m. 2 Dec., 1797, Martha Greenhill. Brunswick Co. Mar. Record.

Steptoe, Maj., m. Lucy Payne (1st husband). 25V310.

Susanna m. Lawrence Washington.

Thomas, b. 24 May, 1731; d. 1794, son of Lawrence and Elizabeth (____); m. 3 April, 1766, Ann Muse, b. bef. 1749; d. 16 May, 1817, dau. of Nicholas and (1) Ann (____) Cullum Finch Muse; res. Westmoreland Co. 53V224, 317; DAR No. 66 384. Thomas, son of Townshend; Ann, dau. of Nicholas and Elizabeth (____) of Westmoreland Co. 23V203.

Thomas, d. 1774, Brunswick Co., son of Thomas and Agnes (____); m. Sarah Gray, dau. of Gilbert. 7T129; Boddie-HSF IV:157.

Thomas, son of Thomas and Sarah (Gray), m. 22 Nov., 1784, Janet Love, dau. of Allan; res. Brunswick Co.; rem. to Tenn. Brunswick Co. Mar. Record. 7T129; Boddie-HSF IV:157.

Thomas, b. 5 Sept., 1758; d. 15 June, 1807, age 48 yrs.4mos.10das., son of Robert; m. June, 1788, his cousin, Sally Washington. 26V420.

Thornton Augustine, Ensign, b. 1760, Stafford Co.; d. 1787, Jefferson Co., son of Col. Samuel and Mildred (Thornton); m. (1) 26 Dec., 1779, Charles Co., Md., Mildred Berry, dau. of Thomas and Elizabeth (Dade); m. (2) 2 April, 1786, Frances Townshend Washington, dau. of Lawrence of King George Co. She m. (2) Col. Griffin Stith. St.

WASHINGTON (cont.)

Paul's. 23V99; 25V81; 26V420; 12W(2)32; Boddie-HSF IV:162; DAR No. 47 301. He m. (2) his cousin, Frances Thornton. DAR No. 32 153.

Townshend m. 22 Dec., 1726, Elizabeth Lund. St. Paul's. He, d. 1743, son of John and Mary (Townshend) of Stafford Co.; she, dau. of Thomas Lund. 26V71, 419; 33V156; Boddie-HSF IV:162.

Warner, b. 22 Sept., 1722, son of John and Catherine (Whiting); m. (1) Elizabeth Macon, dau. of Col. William; m. (2)10 May, 1764, Hannah Fairfax, dau. of William of "Belvoir;" res. Gloucester Co. and Clarke Co. 33V155; Boddie-HSF IV:161.

Warner m. Mary Whiting, b. ca 1715, dau. of Col. Francis and Mary (Perrin). 12T260.

William, son of Joseph and Zilla (Branch), m. Margaret Tyler, dau. of Francis. Boddie-HSF IV:156.

William, son of Col. John of King George Co., m. ____ Craycroft, an English lady; res. Alexandria, Va. 26V410.

William, b. 1752, Stafford Co.; d. 1810, Charleston, So. Car., son of Bailey and Catherine (Storke); m. 1782, Jane Reilly Elliott, b. 1763; d. 1830. DAR No. 28 791; DAR No. 68 910; Mss.

William Augustine, b. 25 Nov., 1757; d. 2 Oct., 1810, son of Augustine and Ann (Aylett); m. (1) 25 Sept., 1777, Jane Washington, b. 20 June, 1759, dau. of John Augustine and Hannah (Bushrod); m. (2) 10 July, 1792, Mary Lee, b. 28 July, 1764; d. 2 Nov., 1795, dau. of Richard Henry and Ann (Aylett); m. (3) 11 May, 1799, Sarah Tayloe, "daughter of the late John Tayloe, Esq., of 'Mount Airy.'" His third marriage took place at "Mansfield," the seat of Mann Page, Esq., in the Fredericksburg area and the story appeared in The Virginia Herald, 14 May, 1799. 14T245, 247; 24T216; 30V69; 6W(1)25.

Willis, son of Joseph and Zilla (Branch), m. Lavina Holland. Boddie-HSF IV:156.

WASSLE

George Nailour m. 26 July, 1792, Mary Griffith. St. Paul's.

WASSON

Alexander m. 1791, Elizabeth Pairy. Rockbridge Co. Morton, p. 540.

Mary m. Philip Entsminger.

Sarah m. William Morley.

WASTRIP

Mary m. Joseph Edwards.

WATERFIELD

Ellenor m. Collin Fraser.

Esther m. Major Jones.

Esther (____) m. Elias Dunton.

Jacob m. 21 Feb., 1791, Sarah Joyne. Sur. Elijah Watson. Northampton Co. Mar. Bond.

Jacob m. 11 June, 1748, Susanna Harrison. Northampton Co. Mar. Record.

John m. 12 Feb., 1754, Mary Dunton, dau. of Richard. Northampton Co. Mar. Record.

Mary (____) m. Peter Dickerson.

Meshack m. 14 June, 1785, Jane Salts. Northampton Co. Mar. Record.

Nanny (____) m. Severn Nottingham.

Polly m. John Stott.

WATERFIELD (cont.)

Smart m. Isaac Jones.
Southy m. 27 Dec., 1771, Peggy Wilkins, dau. of William, dec'd. Northampton Co. Mar. Record.
Susanna m. Waterfield Dunton.
William m. 8 June, 1779, Nancy Hunt, dau. of Azariah. Northampton Co. Mar. Record.

WATERMAN

Amy m. Anthony Pool.
Charles m. 15 Jan., 1789, Amey Wright. Princess Anne Co. Mar. Record.
Elkana m. 20 Jan., 1797, Elizabeth Matthias. Princess Anne Co. Mar. Record.
Jacomine m. John Capps.
Joel m. 10 July, 1800, Margaret (____) Douge by Rev. William Morriss, Baptist. Princess Anne Co. Ministers' Returns.
Kedar m. 24 July, 1790, Eliza Whitehurst. Princess Anne Co. Mar. Record.
Kisiah m. Solomon Moore.
Mary m. William Whitehead.

WATERS

____ m. Elizabeth Mary Hack, dau. of Col. Peter and Elizabeth (Fox); res. St. Stephen's Parish. 7T258.
Anne m. Robert Williams.
Asenath m. James Downing.
Dorcas m. James Taylor.
Edward m. Margaret Robins, dau. of John. 1V93.
Edward m. 18 Aug., 1731, Margaret Waters. Northampton Co. Mar. Record.
Edward, Capt., b. 1584; d. 1628; from Eng. to Va., 1609; m. bef. 1622, Grace O'Neil, b. 1603. She m. (2) 1634, Col. Obedience Robins. 1V93; 41V81.
Elizabeth m. William Overton.
Elizabeth m. Charles Ellis, Jr. (1st wife).
Jean m. John Monslow.
John m. 24 May, 1792, Elizabeth Bonney. Princess Anne Co. Mar. Record.
John m. 3 June, 1743, Elizabeth Higgerson. OPR.
John, b. 25 Aug., 1753, Stafford Co.; d. 12 May, 1838; m. Elizabeth Frazier, d. 3 Jan., 1841; both bur. Estill Co., Ky. Ky. Cem., p. 148.
Lydia m. Martin Hardin.
Margaret m. Edward Waters.
Mark m. 20 July, 1756, Ann Harding. OPR. She, b. ca 1724, dau. of Henry of Stafford Co. Ball, p. 304.
Mary m. Charles Blunt.
Mary m. William Overton.
Mary m. William Taylor.
Mary m. John Pettus.
Mary m. George Murrell.
Mary m. John Fitzpatrick.
Mary m. John Shaw.

WATERS (cont.)

Rosanna m. John Farrow (?Farrar).
Sally m. James Smith.
Sarah "Sally" m. David Meade.
Susanna m. Nathaniel Littleton.
Thomas m. 28 Sept., 1738, Catharine Hays. OPR.
Thomas m. 20 April, 1799, Susanna Stringer. Northampton Co. Mar. Record.
Virginia m. Richard Fristoe.
William m. bef. 1696, Isabel Harmanson, dau. of Thomas, Sr., whose will of that date, Northampton Co., proves it. 37V379-80.
William m. 20 March, 1728, Margaret Robins. Northampton Co. Mar. Record.
William m. 10 May, 1739, Rose Harmanson. Northampton Co. Mar. Record.
William m. Sarah Prentis. 32V250.
William m. 6 April, 1751, Jean Cash. OPR.
William m. 1789, Anne Jacob, dau. of Robert Clark Jacob. Northampton Co. Mar. Record.

WATERSON

Comfort m. Thomas Michael.
Elizabeth m. Aron Williamson.
Mary m. Peter Warren.

WATES

Jos. William m. 1773, Rachel Foster. Orange Co. Mar. Record.

WATHAL

Eliza m. Hugh Lyons.

WATHEN

Robert m. Rebecca Hudson, dau. of Charles of Hanover Co. Albemarle, p. 231.

WATKINS

____ m. to Elizabeth Parrish, 10 May, 1773. William Watkins' letter to Thomas Read, County Clerk, consenting to his son's applying for a license to marry. Wit. John Breedlove. Charlotte Co.
____ m. John Samuel Goode.
____ m. bef. 1743, Fortune Maget, dau. of Nicholas, whose will, dated 1743, Surry Co., proves it. Boddie-HSF V:285.
____, a dau., m. ____ English.
____ m. Elizabeth Primo, dau. of Edmund. She m. (2) Robert Ruffin, d. 1693, Surry Co. 24T60.
____ m. ____ Pollard, dau. of Joseph. Bagby, p. 347.
____ m. bef. May, 1743, Katherine Scott, sis. of Robert, whose will of that date, Isle of Wight Co., proves it.
____ m. Littlejohn Morton.
____ m. by 1783, Martha Webb, dau. of William (will prov. 1783, Orange Co.). 5W(2)171.
Ann m. Samuel Southerland.
Benjamin m. 9 Nov., 1757, Phebe Haskins. Cumberland Co. Mar. Record.
Benjamin m. 23 Dec., 1785, Anna Riddle. Sur. John Riddle. Goochland Co. Mar. Bond.
Benjamin, b. 1755, Powhatan Co.; d. 1831; m. 26 Dec., 1774 (or 1775), Agnes Hatcher, dau. of Benjamin. Sur. Benjamin Hatcher. Cumberland Co. Mar. Bond. DAR No. 79 349.

WATKINS (cont.)

Benjamin m. ___ Cary, dau. of Miles. 4V326.

Bessie m. Philip Johnson.

Betsey m. Maj. Nathaniel Massie.

Betsey m. Joseph Morton.

Betsey m. Green Coleman.

Betsey H. m. James Brooks.

Betty m. Edward Woolridge.

Charles m. 23 Dec., 1772, Lucy Curd, in Goochland. Douglas Reg., p. 13. She, dau. of Richard and Sarah (Downer). Curd, p. 4.

Charles m. 25 Dec., 1777, Lucy Curd. Sur. Edmund Curd. Wit. Val. Wood. Richard Curd's consent to Lucy's marriage. Goochland Co. Mar. Bond. 7W(1)105.

Charles m. 28 July, 1785, Peggy Phelps, dau. of Samuel, who gave consent. Cumberland Co. Mar. Record.

Charles m. Elizabeth Crockett of Mecklenburg Co. Huguenot 7:182.

Christopher, b. 1732; d. 6 Nov., 1822, Anson Co., No. Car.; m. Jane Thomas, d. 6 July, 1817, age about 80. Dameron (no page numbers).

Constant m. ___ Woodson.

Edith m. Thomas Riddle.

Edward of King and Queen Co. m. 1723/4, Mary (Taylor) Pendleton, b. 29 June, 1688; d. 1770, Culpeper Co., widow of Henry Pendleton and dau. of James and (2) Mary (Gregory) of King and Queen Co. 39V277; 43V173; 24W(1)256; Essex Co. Records, 1730, 1742, 1752; Page, p. 239; Rhodes, p. 391; Slaughter, p. 148; Taylor, p. 133; Winston, p. 197.

Edward m. bef. 20 June, 1757, Sally Hill, dau. of Thomas; res. Culpeper Co. Crozier-Spts., p. 204.

Edward m. 17 April, 1759, ___ Thompson. Sur. Robert Thompson. Cumberland Co. Mar. Bond.

Eleanor m. Thomas Ingles.

Eliza m. Thomas Cosby (Cosbie).

Eliza m. James Withrow.

Eliza L. m. Noel Waddill.

Elizabeth m. Nathaniel Massie.

Elizabeth m. Elisha Perkins.

Elizabeth m. Isaiah Alley.

Elizabeth m. Stephen Goodwyn.

Elizabeth m. Joseph Adams.

Elizabeth m. Edmund Woolridge.

Elizabeth m. Maj. William Cunningham.

Elizabeth m. John Breedlove.

Elizabeth m. Joseph Morton Venable.

Elizabeth (___) m. Thomas Brewster (alias Sackford).

Elizabeth (___) m. Robert Ruffin.

Elizabeth Willis m. Samuel Wood.

Fannie m. ___ Mackmahany.

Frances m. Matthew Walton.

Frances (___) m. Edward Lloyd (Loyd).

Francis, b. 15 July, 1745, Henrico Co.; d. 1826, Prince Edward Co.; m. 11 June, 1765, Agnes Woodson, b. 4 Oct., 1748; d. July, 1820. 46V77; DAR No. 31 850.

WATKINS (cont.)

Francis m. 4 Aug., 1791, Anna Donnaly by Rev. John Alderson, Jr. Kanawha Co. Wayland, p. 160.

George, will 1782, m. Susannah ___. Halifax, p. 347.

George m. 30 Dec., 1786, Prince Edward Co., Ann Redd, b. ca 1767; d. bef. 1799, dau. of Thomas and (2) ___(Wright). 51V208.

George of Surry Co. m. 1671-3, Elizabeth Prime, dau. of Edmund. She m. (2) 1675, Robert Ruffin of Surry Co. 48V279.

Harriet m. Isaac Thomas.

Henry m. 22 Feb., 1785, Mary Freeman. York Co. King William, p. 56.

Henry m. Elizabeth (Hudson) Clay. 33V395. She, widow of Rev. John and dau. of George and Elizabeth (Jennings). Boddie-HSF IV:113.

Henry m. 28 Jan., 1760, Temperance Hughes. Sur. Robert Hughes. Cumberland Co. Mar. Bond.

Henry m. 22 Feb., 1785, Mary Freeman, spinster. Sur. Thos. Hunt. York Co. Mar. Bond.

Henry A. m. 6 May, 1794, Ann Edmunds. Brunswick Co. Mar. Record.

Humphrey m. 2 Dec., 1770, Elizabeth Thurston. Christ Church, p. 199.

Humphrey m. Nancy Harper by Henry Goodloe, Minister. Louisa Co. Louisa, p. 268.

James, b. 5 Feb., 1728; res. Amelia, Charlotte, Prince Edward counties, Va.; d. 21 Dec., 1800, Wilkes Co., Ga., son of Wm.; m. 20 Nov., 1755, Martha Thompson, b. 10 Dec., 1737, Chesterfield Co.; d. 26 Oct., 1803, Wilkes Co., Ga., dau. of Robert; rem. to Ga., 1796. Free II: 370.

James of Charlotte Co. m. 25 Feb., 1779, Jane Thompson. Sur. William Thompson. Amelia Co. Mar. Bond.

James, Jr., b. 20 Oct., 1758, Prince Edward Co.; d. 10 Oct., 1824, Elbert Co., Ga.; m. 27 Feb., 1779, Jane Thompson, b. 1762; d. 2 Aug., 1815, dau. of Isham and Mary Ann (Oliver). Free II:370.

Jane m. Charles Hundley.

Jane m. Edw. Matthias.

Jane m. William Barber.

Jane (or Jean) m. Thomas Poage.

Jean m. Edward Mathews.

Joel m. 19 Sept., 1781, Barbara O. Harris, dau. of Archilaus. Louisa, p. 264.

Joel m. 15 July, 1752, Rhoda Gresham. Sur. John Pride. Amelia Co. Mar. Bond. Joel, Sr., Capt., of Prince Edward Co., son of Thomas. 49V321.

Joel, Lt. Col., b. 1745, Powhatan Co.; d. 1820, Charlotte Co.; m. Agnes Morton, b. 1747, dau. of Joseph and Agnes (Woodson). DAR No. 68 407. He, son of Thomas. 9 Ky. Reg. 27:87.

John, Lieut., d. 1821, Charlotte Co.; m. Mary Moore. DAR No. 31 022.

John, Capt., m. Mary Hudson, dau. of George and Elizabeth (Jennings). 33V395; Boddie-HSF IV:113.

John m. 12 Jan., 1763, Sarah Turner, both in this parish. Douglas Reg., p. 7.

John, d. 10 March, 1785, aged 53; m. 22 April, 1772, Betty Claiborne, dau. of Philip Whitehead Claiborne. (Tombstone in New Kent Co.) 1V 321; 5W(1)79.

John of Surry Co., d. 1708-9, son of John; m. Elizabeth Spencer, dau.

WATKINS (cont.)
of Capt. Robert. 47V372-3.
John m. prob. bef. Aug. 1762 (date of Indenture between John Watkins of Prince Edward Co. and Daniel Easley), Ann Easley, dau. of Daniel. Halifax, p. 349.
Joseph m. 17 March, 1785, Polly Bushell. Dinwiddie Co. Cameron.
Joseph m. bef. 1789, Mary Boisseau, dau. of James (d. bef. 1789). Proven by Court Suit of that date, Dinwiddie Co. Res. 1787, Charlotte Co., and at sometime in Chesterfield Co. 10T281-2; 22V85; 9W(1)199.
Judith m. Joseph Goode.
Katherine m. Edward Price.
Lewis m. 6 Jan., 1711/2, Margaret Stone. St. Peter's, p. 418.
Lucy m. Stephen Townes.
Lucy m. ___ Perkins.
Lucy m. William Perkins.
Lucy m. Thomas Spencer, Jr. (2nd wife).
Lydia m. John Johnston IV.
Margaret m. Samuel Coates.
Margery m. Thomas Meeke.
Martha m. James Smiley.
Martha m. Lipscomb Ragland.
Martha Hughes m. Sgt. Frederick Nantz.
Mary m. Edward Mumford.
Mary m. Wm. Wills.
Mary m. ___ Welch.
Mary m. William Curd (1st wife).
Mary m. John Pugh.
Mary m. James Clark.
Mary m. William Hudson.
Mary m. Stephen Pankey.
Mary m. Lewis Whithead.
Mary m. Benjamin Breedlove.
Mary (or Milly) m. William Polter.
Mary m. William Trice.
Mary m. William Moseley.
Mary m. Samuel Lucas.
Mary (___) m. Edward Mosby.
Mary Hughes m. Lewis Nuckols.
Mary W. m. Capt. John Dupuy.
Micajah m. 12 Dec., 1764, Mary Boyd. (Dau. by 1st mar. Order by her mother signed Margaret Armstrong.) Halifax Co. Mar. Record. Mar. lic. 12 Jan., 1764. Mary, dau. of Margaret (___) Boyd Armstrong. Halifax, p. 117.
Micajah, Jr., son of Micajah and Mary (Boyd), m. Sarah Williams. Halifax, p. 118.
Moses m. 9 Aug., 1793, Mary Stinson. Sur. Samuel Freeman. Cumberland Co. Mar. Bond.
Nancy m. Smith Blakey.
Nancy m. James Lewis.
Nancy m. John Creely.
Nancy m. James Railey.

WATKINS (cont.)

Paulina m. Lewis Collins.
Peany m. James Landrum.
Phebe m. Silas Watkins.
Polly m. Samuel Puckett.
Polly m. William Wills.
Polly m. Richard Cooke.
Polly m. James Brown.
Poly m. John Wilcher.
Prudence m. William Royster.
Rachel m. Robert Watkins Crockett.
Rebecca m. Nathaniel Mannin.
Rebecca m. Absolom Hall.
Rebecca m. Henry Wright.
Rhoda (____) m. Patterson Bullock.
Richard, b. ca 1730; d. in Tenn., son of Wm.; m. Elizabeth Parish. Free II:369.
Robert m. 8 April, 1790, Hannah Pugh by James Kenney. Campbell Co. Mar. Record.
Robert m. 19 Feb., 1785, Frances Morton, dau. of Wm. and Susan (Watkins). McCullough, p. 252.
Sally m. Thomas Spencer, Jr. (1st wife).
Sally m. John Atkerson.
Sally m. John Clark.
Sally m. John Spencer, Esq.
Sally m. ____ Brown.
Sally m. James Bouldin.
Sally m. John Eley.
Samuel m. 16 Nov., 1787, Eleanor Thompson. Sur. Daniel Marshall. Amelia Co. Mar. Bond.
Samuel m. 26 July, 1773, Elizabeth Goode. Sur. John Goode. Cumberland Co. Mar. Bond.
Samuel V. m. Catherine Scott. Carrington, p. 43.
Sarah m. Robert Furlong.
Sarah m. ____ Dickie.
Sarah m. Richard Yarborough.
Sarah m. Robert Thompson.
Sarah m. Daniel Butler.
Sarah m. James Chalmers.
Sarah m. John Porter.
Shelton C. m. 6 July, 1807, Ky., Nancy (____) Vaughan Daniel, widow 1st of ____ Vaughan, 2nd of Vivion Daniel. 12T245-6.
Silas, son of Joel who gave consent, m. 26 April, 1773, Phebe Watkins. Sur. Edward Watkins. Cumberland Co. Mar. Bond.
Sophia m. Capt. John Worsham.
Stephen m. Judith Trabue, b. ca 1712, dau. of Anthony and Magdelaine (Flournoy). 17 Ky. Reg. 50:49.
Susan m. Jo. Gray.
Susan m. Col. William Morton.
Susanna m. James Roberts.
Susanna m. Shadrack Woodson.
Susannah m. Samuel Hoskins.

WATKINS (cont.)

Susannah m. Martin Merrymoon.

Thomas m. 13 April, 1780, Mary Tuck. Halifax Co. Mar. Record.

Thomas m. 28 Nov., 1775, Magdaline Dupuy, dau. of John. Sur. John B. Dupuy. Amelia Co. Mar. Bond.

Thomas m. 28 Oct., 1793, Mary Marshall Thompson. Sur. Josiah Thompson. Cumberland Co. Mar. Bond.

Thomas, Capt., b. 12 Feb., 1761; d. 1797 at "Oldham," in Prince Edward Co., son of Henry and Temperance (Hughes); served in Rev. War; m. 2 July, 1782, Betsy Ann Venable, b. 11 Nov., 1760, Prince Edward Co.; d. 1826, dau. of Nathaniel and Elizabeth (Woodson). 46V79; Venable, p. 35.

Thomas m. bef. 1772, Sarah Walton, dau. of Robert of Cumberland Co. Proven by Court Record, 1772, Prince Edward Co.

Thomas, Jr., m. Sarah Walton, d. ca 1801; she m. (2) Rev. Joshua Morris b. ca 1753. Johnson, pp. 167, 170, 177, 178.

Thomas, Jr., of "Chickahominy," m. Martha Anderson. McCullough, p. 246

Thompson m. Nancy Taliaferro, dau. of Zachariah (1730-1811) and Mary (Boutwell). 11T19.

William, b. 20 Oct., 1756; d. 28 May, 1832, in Lawrence Co., Ala.; m. 1785, Susan Clark Coleman, b. 1769, Va.; d. 1843, Lawrence Co., Ala. Rem. to Ga. 1790, to Maury Co., Tenn., 1808. Rem. 1819, Madison Co., Ala., 1827 to Lawrence Co., Ala. Free II:370.

William m. 6 Feb., 1795, Elizabeth Clarkson. Sur. George Bruce. Albemarle Co. Mar. Bond.

William B. m. Susan Spencer, dau. of Thomas, Jr. (1751-1806), and (2) Lucy (Watkins) of Charlotte Co. 46V74.

William M., Capt., b. 22 April, 1773; d. 5 Feb., 1865, Charlotte Co.; m. 5 Dec., 1799, Prince Edward Co., Elizabeth Woodson Venable, b. there, 11 May, 1782; d. 7 April, 1858, Charlotte Co. Venable, p. 63.

Winifred m. James Jones.

WATLINGTON

Armistead, b. 27 Dec., 1730, Abingdon Parish; will dated 2 Nov., 1803, son of Paul and Elizabeth (?Armistead); m. Susannah Coleman, b. 16 Jan., 1736, dau. of Thomas and Elizabeth (____); rem. to Halifax Co. and later to Pittsylvania Co. Halifax, pp. 157, 345.

Betsy m. ____ Barksdale.

Edward m. 7 March, 1792, Nancy Boyd. Halifax Co. Mar. Record.

Elizabeth m. Peter Barksdale.

Fanny m. Joshua Boyd.

John, Capt., m. 23 Dec., 1781, Elizabeth Allen. Halifax Co. Mar. Record.

Leah m. William Williams.

Nancy m. George Wall.

Paul, b. 7 May, 1706, Abingdon Parish; d. 8 June, 1752, son of Paul and Elizabeth (Reade); m. Elizabeth ____ (?Armistead). Halifax, p. 157.

Paul, b. May, 1678; res. Abingdon Parish, Gloucester Co.; m. bef. 1706, Elizabeth Reade, dau. of Francis and Jane (Chisman). 3V40; Halifax, p. 157.

Polly m. (1) William Thompson; m. (2) William Terry.

WATLINGTON (cont.)
Rebekah m. Benjamin Shelton.
Susannah m. Creed Haskins.

WATSON
____ m. George Graham (2nd wife).
____ m. bef. 1772, Elizabeth Taylor, dau. of Thomas, Sr., whose will of that date, Mecklenburg Co., proves it.
____ m. David Wood.
____ m. Thomas Williams.
____ m. Sarah Miller, dau. of Simon, whose will, prov. 1806, Culpeper Co., proves it. 12T241.
Abner m. 1786, Elizabeth Dear. Orange Co. Mar. Record.
Abner m. 22 Nov., 1788, Polly Price. Sur. Archibald Wright. Cumberland Co. Mar. Bond.
Agnes m. Philip Walker.
Agnes (____) m. Robert Mosoby.
Amy m. Wood Jones.
Andrew m. 26 Sept., 1742, Mary Moses. OPR.
Ann m. Thomas Eggleston.
Ann m. William Morris.
Ann m. James Lamb.
Ann (____) m. (2) Col. Robert Pitt; m. (3) Col. James Powell.
Anne m. Robert Williams.
Anne m. George Jude.
Anne (____) m. Capt. Henry Pitt.
Arthur, b. 1770, Berkeley Co.; d. 29 Sept., 1827; m. ca 1796, Mason Co., Ky., Temperance Robinson, b. Aug., 1774, Baltimore Co., Md.; d. 11 Sept., 1837; rem. 1825 to Sangamon Co., Ill. Sangamon, pp. 752-3.
Bethmiah m. John Watson.
Betsy Ann m. Robert Standford.
David, Maj., son of Maj. James Watson, m. Sarah "Sally" Minor, b. 1780, dau. of Garrett and Mary O. (Terrell) of "Sunning Hill." 30V232; Louisa, pp. 144, 392.
Drury m. 26 Nov., 1791, Frances Richardson. Sur. Abner Watson. Cumberland Co. Mar. Bond. She was Frances (____) Richardson, widow of Isham (d. ca 1789). 45V201-2.
Edith m. Lewis Grigg.
Elizabeth m. Thomas Williams.
Elizabeth m. Elisha Perkins.
Franky m. Ison Walton.
Hannah m. James Calhoun (2nd wife).
Isabella m. James Boyd.
James m. 22 Dec., 1795, Ann Key. Sur. Walter Watson. Albemarle Co. Mar. Bond.
James, Maj., m. 28 Nov., 1772, Louisa Co., Elizabeth Shelton, dau. of Joseph. Louisa, pp. 144, 255, 281. Mar. 1 Jan., 1773, Eliz. Shilton. Douglas Reg., p. 13.
James m. 8 Sept., 1785, Peggy Wilson by Rev. H. J. Burgess. Surry Co. Ministers' Returns.
James m. 31 Dec., 1798, Jane Conner. Halifax Co. Mar. Record.
Jane m. Thomas Bolling Munford.
Jesse, Capt., b. 1760, Prince Edward Co.; d. 1812, Lunenburg Co.; m.

WATSON (cont.)

1790, Mary Meredith, b. 1769. DAR No. 79 146.

Jesse m. 1789, Milley Ballard. Orange Co. Mar. Record. Milly, b. Orange Co., dau. of Philip and Ann (Johnson) Ballard; m. (2) John Boling; rem. to Monroe Co., then to Ky. Orange III:23.

John m. 27 Feb., 1790, Sarah Addison. St. Paul's.

John m. 12 Feb., 1798, Peggy Bradshaw. Shelby Co., Ky. Mar. Record.

John m. 8 Jan., 1795, Mary Gillum. Sur. James Gillum. Albemarle Co. Mar. Bond.

John m. bef. 1796, Mary Hicks, dau. of Robert and (1) Angelia (____). Proven by will of Robert Hicks of that date, Greensville Co.

John m. Sarah Martin, dau. of James and Elizabeth (____). Albemarle, p. 264.

John m. 31 Dec., 1795, Jane Price. Sur. Thomas Bell. Albemarle Co. Mar. Bond. He moved from Amherst to Albemarle ca 1790; she, dau. of Richard. Albemarle, p. 339.

John m. 24 Oct., 1782, Lurane Polley by Rev. John Bailey. Pittsylvania Co. Ministers' Returns.

John m. 7 Dec., 1763, Mary Smith, spinster. Sur. George Smith. Amelia Co. Mar. Bond.

John m. 12 Nov., 1784, Bethmiah Watson by Rev. Thomas Sparks. Sur. Will Watson. Pittsylvania Co. Mar. Bond.

John, Jr., m. 22 Nov., 1800, Lucy Smith, dau. of George, who gave consent. Sur. Thomas Watson. Pittsylvania Co. Mar. Bond.

Joseph of Henrico Co. m. Anna Stratton, dau. of Edward (1655-1698) and Martha (Shippy) of Henrico Co. 24W(1)276.

Joseph m. Nancy Wood, dau. of William (d. 1820). Albemarle, p. 349.

Josiah m. 22 Feb., 1785, Mary Nelson. Sur. Andrew Nelson. Cumberland Co. Mar. Bond.

Lucy m. Harwood Major (or Major Harwood).

Lucy m. John White Holt.

Lucy m. Thomas Johnson.

Lucy m. James Armstrong.

Margaret m. Oliver Porter.

Mary m. David Wood.

Mary m. John Ware.

Mary m. Phillip Evans.

Mary m. Augustine Edwards.

Matlaid m. James Jones.

Milley (____) m. David Craig.

Moses m. 1 Jan., 1730, Director Twiford. Northampton Co. Mar. Record.

Nancy m. Thomas Cobbs.

Nanny m. Spencer Dalby.

Ninian m. 30 Sept., 1783, Sarah Quissenberry, both of Louisa. Douglas Reg., p. 23.

Peter m. Ann Shepherd, dau. of John (gave Deed, 1696, Accomac Co.) and Elizabeth (Jordan). 10W(2)182.

Priscilla (____) m. Henry Tandy, Jr.

Rachel m. Americus Scarborough II.

Randolph m. 4 Aug., 1788, Lucy Goldsmith by Rev. John Lasly. Louisa Co. Ministers' Returns.

WATSON (cont.)

Rovel m. 15 July, 1794, Nancy Tankard. Northampton Co. Mar. Record.
Robert m. 11 Aug., 1793, Mary Hibble. Christ Church, p. 257.
Sarah m. John Wingate.
Sarah m. William Gillum.
Sarah m. Abel Stott.
Sarah m. William Dabney.
Susan m. Robert Bolling (2nd wife).
Susanna m. William Cole.
Susannah m. Robert Cooke.
Thomas m. 11 April, 1757, Hannah Homus, both in this parish. Douglas Reg., p. 3.
William in Hanover m. 17 Feb., 1767, Martha Pleasants in this parish. Douglas Reg., p. 9. Sur. Richard Pleasants. Goochland Co. Mar. Bond.
William m. Susan Watts, dau. of David (gave them land in 1767). Albemarle, p. 338.
William, physician, b. 19 March, 1798, Prince Edward Co.; d. 20 Nov., 1876; m. Jane T___, b. 15 Jan., 1803; d. 11 March, 1852; both bur. in Henderson Co., Ky. Ky. Cem., p. 204. (This marriage too late to be included here.)
William m. 23 Sept., 1739, Mary Jones. Sur. Samuel Tarry. Amelia Co. Mar. Bond. He m. (2) 10 April, 1767, Prince Edward Co., Jane (Thomson) Baker, b. ca 1726, Sussex Co., Del., widow of Douglas Baker and dau. of John Thomson. 51V402.

WATT

James m. 2 March, 1707, Mason Kendall. Northampton Co. Mar. Record.
John m. 1790, Elizabeth McCormick. Rockbridge Co. Morton, p. 505.
Rebecca m. Richard Mayhew.

WATTERS

David m. 1 June, 1797, Anne Henley by Rev. Anthony Walke. Princess Anne Co. Ministers' Returns.

WATTERSON

Agnes m. Jonathan Chrisman.
Ann m. Jesse Hall.
Elizabeth m. David Stephens.
Mary m. William Taylor.
Nancy m. James Raeburn.
Thomas m. 4 Feb., 1795, Mary Stephens. Sur. David Stephens. Botetourt Co. Mar. Bond.

WATTS

___ m. (1) William Strother; m. (2) John Grant (2nd wife).
___ m. bef. 7 Dec., 1694, Ann Youell, dau. of Thomas, whose will of that date, Westmoreland Co., proves it and names "grandson Youell Watts."
___ m. bef. 1671, Jane (___) Gillott Button, widow 1st of John Gillott, 2nd of Thomas Button; res. Old Rappahannock Co. 33T247.
Agatha m. James George.
Aggey m. John Huckstep.
Ann m. William Daniel.
Ann m. William Robinson.
Ann (___) m. Daniel McPhertain.

WATTS (cont.)

Betty m. ___ Gresham.

Charles m. 17 Nov., 1789, Elizabeth Buckner, spinster. Sur. Hokins Carr. Albemarle Co. Mar. Bond. He, son of David (d. 1817). Albemarle, p. 340.

David, son of David (d. 1817), m. Ruth Twyman, dau. of George. Albemarle, p. 340.

David m. 5 Sept., 1799, Margaret Simpkins. Northampton Co. Mar. Record.

Edward m. 23 Jan., 1772, York Co., Mary Abercrombie. 1W(1)48.

Edward m. 21 Dec., 1787, King and Queen Co., Ann Garrett. Christ Church, p. 206.

Elizabeth m. Stephen Edwards.

Elizabeth m. William Batchelder.

Elizabeth m. Dudley Brown Ellis.

Elizabeth m. Anthony Lunceford (2nd wife).

Frances m. Joseph Edmondson.

Frances m. Spencer Wilson.

Franky m. Nathaniel Terry.

Henry m. bef. May, 1659, ___ (___) Webb, mother of John, Thomas and Francis Webb and widow of Thomas Webb. Proven by Court Record of that date, Northumberland Co. Will of Henry Watts, dated June, 1670, names wife Elizabeth and her three Webb children.

Hugh m. 17 Aug., 1765, Margaret Williamson. Norfolk Co. Mar. Record.

Hugh m. 29 Jan., 1683/4, Johnna Marye by Parson Carr in New Kent Co. Christ Church, p. 22.

Jacob, minister, d. 1821, aged 90; m. Elizabeth Durrett, dau. of Richard, Sr. (d. 1784, Albemarle Co.). Albemarle, p. 340; Br., p. 75.

James m. 7 March, 1793, Elizabeth Durrett, spinster. Sur. John D. Durrett. Albemarle Co. Mar. Bond.

Jane m. (1) Thomas Sanford, Jr.; m. (2) Col. Andrew Monroe (1st wife).

Jane m. Henry Sears.

John, d. 1828, Clark Co., Ky.; served in Rev. War from Va.; m. bef. 1796, Elizabeth Davis, dau. of Leonard. 44V341; 34 Ky. Reg. 402.

John m. 12 April, 1716, Elizabeth Foster. Christ Church, p. 83.

John, b. 1752, Bedford Co.; d. 1830, Appomattox Co.; m. ___ Patterson. DAR No. 68 210.

John m. 24 May, 1792, Betsey Roberts. Halifax Co. Mar. Record.

John m. 17 June, 1714, Elizabeth Worsell. Christ Church, p. 83.

John m. Sarah (Michael) Yeardley (will, 1694, Northampton Co.), widow of Capt. Argall Yeardley and dau. of John Michael, Sr., and Elizabeth (Thorowgood) of Northampton Co. She m. (3) Thomas Maddow. 58V401; Am. Hist. I:344-5.

John Wilkins m. 25 May, 1765, Rachel (___) Fitchett. Northampton Co. Mar. Record.

Johnson m. 1784, Sukey Davis. Orange Co. Mar. Record.

Joseph m. 29 May, 1799, Patsey Canaday. Halifax Co. Mar. Record.

Julius m. 1785, Mary Eve. Orange Co. Mar. Record.

Margaret m. (1) William Strother; m. (2) Capt. John Grant.

Mary m. (1) Col. Henry Ashton (2nd wife); m. (2) Col. Richard Blackburn.

Mary m. William Breedlove.

WATTS (cont.)

Mary m. Daniel Moore (2nd wife).
Mary m. John Ashton.
Mary m. Hezekiah Rodes.
Mary m. William Williams.
Mary (___) m. John Chilton.
Mason m. 18 June, 1793, Deborah Ryker. Shelby Co., Ky. Mar. Record.
Mildred m. Richard Breedlove.
Mildred m. ___ Bruce.
Milly m. John Richards.
Nancy m. William Sims, Jr.
Nancy m. Henry Austin.
Philip, son of David (d. 1817), m. ___ Brown, dau. of John. Albemarle, p. 340.
Polly m. Daniel Jamison.
Polly m. Edward Pines.
Ralph m. 5 Feb., 1711, Elizabeth Mullins. Christ Church, p. 82.
Ralph m. 12 May, 1784, Hanna Dunn. Christ Church, p. 204.
Sarah m. Humphrey Gaines.
Sarah m. John Davis.
Susan m. Carver Thomas.
Susan m. William Watson.
Susanna m. Nathan Wansley.
Susanna m. Francis Turnley.
Susannah m. John Delany.
Thomas m. bef. April, 1690, Frances Norgrave, d. by that date, dau. of Capt. John. Proven by Court Record of that date, Stafford Co.
Thomas m. bef. 8 April, 1767, Mary Kauffman, sis. of George. Proven by Court Record of that date, Essex Co.
William m. 13 May, 1795, Patty Lee. Halifax Co. Mar. Record.
William m. 1778, Elizabeth Beazley. Orange Co. Mar. Record.
Winifred m. Richard Farrell.

WATTSON

Peter m. 8 Feb., 1798, Elizabeth White. Halifax Co. Mar. Record.

WATWOOD

George m. 4 March, 1742, Mary Taylor. Sur. James Robinson. Goochland Co. Mar. Bond.

WAUGH

Abner, minister, m. Philadelphia (Claiborne) Carter. 1V321.
Betty m. Andrew Edwards.
Elizabeth m. Bartley James.
Elizabeth m. John Gregg.
Elizabeth m. George Mason (2nd wife).
George m. 1793, Elizabeth Boston. Orange Co. Mar. Record.
Gowry m. ___ Turberville and had a son, b. 1795. Proven by Chancery Suit, 1800. 11W(2)118.
Gracey m. Elisha Perry.
Hannah m. George Morton.
James, b. 1752, Cumberland Co., Pa.; d. 1816, Fairfax Co.; m. Henrietta Maria Turley, b. 1760; d. 1825. DAR No. 28 844.
James m. 22 Aug., 1740, Betty French. OPR.
John m. 22 April, 1761, Jane Massey. St. Paul's.

WAUGH (cont.)
John m. 4 Nov., 1790, Mary Watts Ashton. St. Paul's.
Joseph of Stafford Co. m. Million Travers, dau. of Gyles. Stoddard, p. 221.
Joseph m. Mary Crosby; res. early 1700's, Stafford Co. 26T281.
Joseph, minister, d. 1726, Stafford Co.; m. (1) Rachel Gowry, dau. of John; m. (2) by 11 June, 1723, Mary (Crosby) Mountjoy Mauzy, widow 1st of Edward Mountjoy (will dated 6 Sept., 1712, Stafford Co.) and 2nd of ?Peter Mauzy. His 2nd mar. proven by Deed, 1723, Stafford Co. 26T101, 104.
Joseph m. 1759, Mary Bronough, dau. of David (will dated 13 Dec., 1773). She m. (2) June, 1772, Elijah Threlkeld. 23V312.
Judith m. Charles Clephon.
Mary m. Alexander Doniphan.
Mary m. Lieut. Robert Howson Hooe.
Mary m. Rev. Musgrove Dawson.
Richard m. 1782, Margaret Brown. Orange Co. Mar. Record.
Solomon m. 13 April, 1748, Betty Chinn. OPR.
William m. 10 Sept., 1738, Margaret Tyler. OPR.
WAUGHOPE
____ m. Elizabeth (Newton) Keene, widow of William Keene (1695-1726) and dau. of Capt. Thomas and Elizabeth (Storke) Newton. 9W(2)176. He was Maj. John Waughope. 33V394; 38V364.
WAUKINS
Peany m. James Landrum.
WAUSON
Robert m. 1790, Elizabeth Brush. Rockbridge Co. Morton, p. 475.
WAWAL
Charles m. 16 Nov., 1751, Mary Hall. OPR.
WAX
Elizabeth m. George Etter.
WAYCOMB
John m. 31 Xmber 1692/3, Eliza Micham. Christ Church, p. 53.
WAYE
Anne m. Thomas Harrison.
WAYFORD
Thomas m. 1 May, 1774, Elizabeth Hodges, both in Goochland. Douglas Reg., p. 15.
WAYLAND
Ann m. Nicholas Yager (or Yeager) (1st wife).
Eleanor m. Matthias Weaver.
John, son of Adam and (1) Elizabeth (Blankenbaker), m. bef. 1776, Rosa (or Rosina) Wilhoit, dau. of John (est. sett. Oct., 1797). 26W(1) 242, 247.
Joshua m. 18 Dec., 1781, Rachel Utz by Rev. George Eve, Baptist. Culpeper Co. Ministers' Returns. He, son of Adam and (1) Elizabeth (Blankenbaker). 26W(1)242.
Mary m. Joshua Yager.
WAYLES
Anne m. Henry Skipwith.
Elizabeth m. Francis Eppes.
John, b. 1715, Lancashire, England; d. after 2 Feb., 1773 (date of

WAYLES (cont.)
last codicil); m. (1) 1746, Henrico Co., Martha (Eppes) Eppes, prob. widow of Col. Littlebury Eppes (d. 1746, Charles City Co.) and dau. of Col. Francis Eppes of Charles City Co.; m. (2) 23 July, 1760, Elizabeth (Lomax) Skelton, widow of Reuben Skelton and dau. of Lunsford Lomax. 6T266; 33V25; 9W(2)213.
Martha m. (1) Bathurst Skelton; m. (2) Thomas Jefferson.
Tabitha m. Henry Skipwith (1st wife).

WAYMAN
Harmon (or Herman) m. (1) bef. 1777, Elizabeth Clore, dau. of Peter (d. 1763) and Barbara (Yager); m. (2) in Culpeper Co., Francis Clore, dau. of John. 26W(1)180; 9W(2)190.
Herman, b. 1752, Germany; d. 1827, Kenton Co., Ky.; served in Rev. War from Va.; m. (2) Adelaide Elizabeth Stansifer. DAR No. 51 002; DAR No. 66 862.

WAYNE
Joseph m. 15 April, 1790, Mary Drinkwater by James Hurt. Campbell Co. Mar. Record.
Milley m. William Driskill.

WAYT
Catharine m. Paschal Garth.
Catharine (____) m. Elijah Garth (2nd wife).
Mary m. Sabrut King.
Tabitha m. ____ Kennerly.
William m. 5 Feb., 1789, Mary Ann Hodges. Caroline Co. Mar. Record. He, son of George of Orange Co., m. ____ Hodges. Peyton, p. 318.

WEAKLEY
____ m. William Pearman.
Anna m. George Scroggin.
Betsey m. Jesse Baker.
Elizabeth m. Moses Threldkeld.
Lilly m. Nathan Scearce.
Mary m. Abraham Dale.
Rebecca m. Henry Scearce.

WEAR
Elizabeth m. John McCutchen.
James m. 29 Sept., 1787, Joice Webb. Norfolk Co. Mar. Record.

WEATHERALL
Elizabeth m. Henry Towles.
John, b. 28 July, 1762; d. 4 Nov., 1824; enlisted in Rev. War from Culpeper Co.; m. 12 June, 1787, Abbeville Dist., So. Car., Elizabeth Jones by Rev. Robert Hall, Presbyterian. She, b. 7 Aug., 1771; d. 21 April, 1843. Birth records of their children are in the application file for Pension R11187.
Mary m. Joseph Towles, Jr.
Sarah m. John Marshall.

WEATHERBY
Thomas m. bef. 1671, Margaret (____) Smith, widow of John (d. 1669). 11W(2)351.

WEATHERFORD
Elizabeth m. Benjamin Evans.
Freeman m. 8 Dec., 1800, Polly Smith, dau. of Buckner, who gave con-

WEATHERFORD (cont.)
sent. Sur. Richard Thompson. Mecklenburg Co. Mar. Bond.
John, physician, m. Martha Sublet, dau. of William and Susannah (Allin). Beddie-HSF IV:74.
Lucy m. Robert Spencer.
Milly m. Josiah Nuckolls.
Molly m. John Robertson.
Obedience m. David Dunn.
William m. 11 June, 1794, Jean Chapman. Sur. Joel Compton. Amelia Co. Mar. Bond.

WEATHERREAD
Patience m. Josiah Wood.

WEATHERRED
James, son of Francis Marcus Weatherred, m. 1799, Polly Bledsoe, dau. of Col. Anthony and Mary (Ramsey). Beddie-HSF IV:3.
John m. 13 April, 1795, Elizabeth Gilmore. Sur. Joseph Gilmore. Albemarle Co. Mar. Bond.

WEATHERS
John m. 3 Oct., 1681, "at my Lady Shipwith's," Margaret Powell. Christ Church, p. 20.
William m. bef. Oct., 1752, Mary Redford. 32V58.

WEATHERSPOON
Mary m. Henry Wood.
Nancy m. William Woolbanks.

WEAVER
Alice m. Thomas Claxton.
Ann m. John Kemper, Jr.
Anna m. John Peters.
Anne m. Nathaniel Whitehurst.
Ben. in Maniken Town m. 27 April, 1758, Mary Woodson in this parish. Douglas Reg., p. 3.
Catherine m. Benjamin Taylor.
Dan. m. 11 Nov., 1756, Sarah Durham, both in Maniken Town. Douglas Reg., p. 2.
Daniel m. ____ Clere, dau. of John and Cafer (____). Wilcoxson, p. 374.
David m. 24 Dec., 1769, Massinbad Shoemaker, both in this parish. Douglas Reg., p. 11.
Dorcas m. William Constant.
Elizabeth m. Bailey Shumate.
Elizabeth m. Josiah Strange.
Elizabeth m. ____ Rainaux.
Elizabeth m. Dempse Anderson.
Eva m. Samuel Porter.
Henrietta m. William Dodd.
James m. 26 Dec., 1791, Vashty Tuck. Halifax Co. Mar. Record.
Jane m. Richard Childrey.
John m. 24 Dec., 1789, Patsy Nichols. Halifax Co. Mar. Record.
Judith m. Herod Reese.
Judith m. Robert Clark.
Katherine m. Francis Frygore.
Margaret m. John Wilhoit.

WEAVER (cont.)

Mary m. Will. Johnson.
Mary m. Herman Hitt.
Mary m. ____ Druine.
Mary m. David Meriwether.
Matthias m. 1791, Eleanor Wayland, prob. dau. of John. 26W(1)243, 245.
Peter m. 1794, Culpeper Co., Martha Walker; rem. 1809, to Indiana. DAR Mag., Aug., 1954, p. 894. Mar. 1797. 26W(1)245.
Peter m. Polly Hepler, dau. of John and ____ (Harness). Rockbridge Co. Morton, p. 492.
Sally m. John Gary.
Sam., widower, m. 19 March, 1755, Eliz. Williams, both in this parish. Douglas Reg., pp. 26-31.
Sarah m. ____ Chowdoin.
Sebinah m. John Collinsworth.
Susanna m. William Marrable.
Thomas m. 29 June, 1715, Judith Strange. St. Peter's, p. 419.
William m. 15 Dec., 1779, Rebecca Whittington, spinster. Sur. John Whittington. Brunswick Co. Mar. Bond.

WEB

Elizabeth (____) m. ____ Thorp.
Is. m. 25 Oct., 1770, Ann Farmer, both in Goochland. Douglas Reg., p. 12.
Jesse m. 31 Dec., 1798, Nancy Boyles. Rockingham Co. Wayland, p. 10.
John m. bet. 1750-1753, ____ ____ in Albemarle. (Illegible) Douglas Reg., p. 31.
Marianne m. Tho. Evans.
Will. m. 25 Nov., 1770, Mary Farmer, both in Goochland. Douglas Reg., p. 12.

WEBB

____ m. bef. 1741, Sarah (____) Floyd, widow of Matthew, Jr. Deed of that date, Northampton Co., proves it.
____ m. bef. 1714, Elizabeth (____) Wornum, widow of John. Proven by Court Record of that date, Northumberland Co.
____ m. Matthew Harrison.
____ (____) m. William Peircifull, Sr.
____ (____) m. Henry Watts.
Anne m. Elijah Perry.
Anne m. William Boulware.
Anne m. Thomas Godin.
Augustine, b. 6 Jan., 1763; d. 9 Oct., 1827, son of William Crittendon and (1) Jane (Vivion); m. 10 April, 1788, Lucy Crittenden, b. 7 Nov., 1762; d. Aug., 1820; tombstones near Somerset, Orange Co. 5W(2)172. He m. 10 April, 1788, Lucy Rogers (same dates as above), dau. of Joseph and Lucy Burgess. 10T170. Mar. Lucy Crittenden, dau. of John and Ann (Rogers). Br., p. 335.
Benjamin m. 2 Aug., 1796, Sarah Hamilton. Rockingham Co. Wayland, p. 8.
Catharine m. Richard Groom.
Catherine m. James Smith.
Catherine m. Samuel Peachey.
Charles m. 7 June, 1791, Sinah Sample. Northampton Co. Mar. Record.

WEBB (cont.)

(Free colored people.)

Conrad of "Hampstead," New Kent Co., m. (1) Lucy Osborne of Chesterfield Co.; m. (2) Georgiana Braxton, grdau. of the Signer. 25V211.

Constance m. Thomas Edmundson.

Edward of Essex Co., will prov. 1750; m. ca 1726/7, Hannah Waller, dau. of Charles and Susanna (___). 14T124-5.

Elizabeth m. James Edmondson.

Elizabeth m. John Goodwin.

Elizabeth m. ___ Wilkinson.

Elizabeth m. Samuel Peachey.

Foster, b. 3 Jan., 1732/3; d. 26 Oct., 1795, son of George and Lucy (Foster); m. 17 June, 1775, Sarah Shore, d. 26 April, 1802, dau. of John of Hanover Co. 25V100.

Foster, Jr., b. 13 Jan., 1756; d. 9 Dec., 1812; m. 22 Sept., 1785, by Rev. John Buchanan to Theodocia Cocke, b. 19 Feb., 1765; d. 28 Oct., 1831, dau. of William Fleming Cocke. 25V211; Henrico, p. 229.

Frances m. Nicholas Fowle.

Frances m. Reuben Sanford.

Francis, b. 1759, Essex Co.; d. 1811, Hancock Co., Ga., son of James, Jr., and Mary (Smith); served in Rev. War in the Va. Navy; m. 1786, Frances Walker, b. 1764; d. 1808, dau. of Freeman and Frances (Belfield); rem. to Hancock Co. in 1810. 7T275-7; 8T52-3; 11T176, 178; 12T145; 14T39; 26W(1)67; DAR No. 32 403; DAR No. 41 202; DAR No. 65 785.

George, son of Conrade Webb of London, England, m. (1) 21 July, 1728, Lucy (Foster) Jones, widow of Josias Jones and dau. of Col. Joseph Foster of New Kent Co. She d. 30 Dec., 1750, in the 54th year of her life. He m. (2) 4 June, 1752, Anne Bickerton, dau. of John of Hanover Co.; res. New Kent Co. 25V99; 29V370; Winston, p. 88.

George m. 3 Nov., 1789, Lucy Gauldin by James Hurt. Campbell Co. Mar. Record.

George m. 19 Oct., 1735, Lucy Hinkston. Spotsylvania Co. Mar. Record.

George in Hanover m. 15 April, 1756, Mrs. Hannah Fleming in this parish. Douglas Reg., p. 2. George, b. 4 July, 1729; d. after 1786, son of George and Lucy (Foster); m. April, 1756, Goochland Co., Hannah Fleming, dau. of Tarleton of "Rock Castle," in Goochland Co. 24V442; 25V100. Given as George, Jr., on Mar. Bond. Sur. Josias Payne, Jr.

George m. 25 June, 1789, Catherine Veale. Norfolk Co. Mar. Record.

George, Jr., d. 9 April, 1803; m. 1785, Judith Fleming, d. aged 83, dau. of Tarleton of Goochland Co.; res. "Rock Castle," Goochland Co. 24V443; 25V211.

George, Jr., b. 1731, New Kent Co.; m. Elizabeth Bickerton, dau. of Philip. 29V371.

Giles m. bef. 1763, Elizabeth (Kirk) Hack, widow of Capt. John. Proven by Lease, 13 April, 1763. 7T258.

Giles m. bef. 2 Sept., 1695, ___ (___) Randolph, widow of Capt. Henry. Proven by Court Record of that date, Henrico Co. Henrico, p. 227.

Giles m. bef. Feb., 1711/2, Elizabeth Spann, dau. of Dorothy (___)

WEBB (cont.)
Spann, whose will of that date, Northumberland Co., proves it.
Giles m. 1762, Elizabeth Shields. Northumberland Co. Mar. Record.
Hannah m. Peter Lanter.
Henry m. Susan Gordon, dau. of Dr. Thomas of Tappahannock, Va. 25V211
Isaac m. 14 Nov., 1710, Winifred Hipkins. Christ Church, p. 82.
Isaac, b. 19 Jan., 1758, son of Isaac and Frances (Barber) of Richmond Co.; m. Lucy Ware, dau. of James of Frederick Co.; rem. to Fayette Co., Ky. 7T196.
Isaac(?) m. bef. 25 March, 1704, Mary Webster, dau. of John Webster, dec'd. Proven by Court Record of that date, Essex Co.
Isaac m. bef. 1758, Frances Barber; res. Richmond Co. 7T196.
James m. Hester Robinson; res. 1811, Hardy Co., when son, John, was born. Ky. Com., p. 149.
James m. 1 March, 1770, Agnes Hughes, both in this parish. Douglas Reg., p. 11.
James m. 24 March, ?1798, Ann Driver. Isle of Wight Co. Mar. Record.
James m. bef. 13 Jan., 1714/5, Sarah (____) Fullerton, widow of James. Proven by Court Record of that date, Essex Co. She was Sarah Pickett, dau. of Henry of Essex Co. 49V81.
James m. 19 Dec., 1680, Frances Herbert. Christ Church, p. 20.
James, b. 1762, son of James and Mary (Smith); m. ca 1790, Dorothy Throckmorton, dau. of Capt. Gabriel and Judith (Edmundson). 7T272; 26W(1)67.
James m. bef. 5 Feb., 1732/3, Mary Edmundson, dau. of Benjamin. Proven by Court Record of that date, Essex Co. James, b. 1705; d. ca 1771, son of James; m. 5 Feb., 1731, Mary Edmundson. 2T198; 7T191, 270; 23V91. James was son of John and Mary (Samford). 11T177.
James; d. 1675; m. Elizabeth Godwin, dau. of Col. Thomas. She m. (2) Joseph Woory; m. (3) Samuel Bridger. Her will prov. 1718, Isle of Wight Co. Boddie-Isle, pp. 427, 462.
James, Jr., m. 9 Nov., 1779, Sarah (____) Shields. Norfolk Co. Mar. Record.
James, Jr., b. 24 Feb., 1734, son of James and Mary (Edmundson); m. 1757, Mary Smith, dau. of Francis and Lucy (Meriweather) of Essex Co. Family Bible. 23V91; 26W(1)67; will, 1760, Essex Co., of Francis Smith.
Jesse m. 1789, Judah Jones. Orange Co. Mar. Record.
Jesse Bennett m. 25 Jan., 1790, Sarah Mason. Orange Co. Mar. Record; 6W(2)63.
John m. 1 Jan., 1694/5, Anne Smith, dau. of Lieut. John Smith. Essex Co. Mar. Record.
John, b. 18 Jan., 1747; m. 1772, Amy Booker, b. 27 Aug., 1752, dau. of James of Essex Co.; rem. to Person Co., No. Car. 8T59-60.
John m. 12 Feb., 1712, Mary Martin. St. Peter's, p. 419.
John believed m. bef. 1775, Hannah Riveer, dau. of John, Sr., whose will, dated 24 Jan., 1775, names "daughter Hannah Woodward" and est. sett. paid to John Webb. Lancaster Co. records.
John, will dated 30 Nov., 1716, son of Giles; m. bef. 1673, Mary Sanford; res. Richmond Co. 7T195; 11T177.
John, son of James, m. bef. 25 March, 1720, Jane Smith, dau. of Lieut. John of Richmond Co. Proven by Court Record of that date, Essex Co.

WEBB (cont.)

7T269.

John, Jr., m. 1790, Mildred Lantor. Orange Co. Mar. Record.

John Crittenden, son of William (d. 1783, Orange Co.), m. by 1754, Mary Singleton, dau. of John and Mary M. (Brockman). 5W(2)171; Br., p. 9.

John Crittenden m. Mary Coke; res. Orange Co. Orange III:112.

John Vivion, b. 11 July, 1765; d. 8 June, 1839, son of William Crittenden and (1) Jane (Vivion) Webb; m. 28 June, 1790, Orange Co., Lucy Woodward; rem. to Lexington, Ky. 35V408; 5W(2)172.

Joice m. James Wear.

Judith m. John Dyke.

Lewis, Capt., b. 14 July, 1759, New Kent Co.; d. 12 July, 1841, Mercer Co., Ky.; served in Rev. War; m. 29 Sept., 1787, Lucy R. Cary, b. 5 April, 1768, of King William Co. Pension W8990. 12T278.

Lewis of New Kent Co., son of George and Lucy (Foster), m. Elizabeth ____ (prob. Bickerton). 25V100.

Lucy m. Francis Dandridge.

Lucy m. Joseph Calvert.

Lucy m. Thomas Dooly.

Martha m. ____ Watkins.

Mary m. Albion Throckmorton.

Mary m. Samuel Smith.

Mary m. Charles Breadlove.

Mary m. (1) ____ Hudnall; m. (2) Edward Saunders.

Mary m. John Patton.

Millie m. Oliver Walker.

Milly m. Thomas Pierce.

Mitchum B., son of John Vivian and Lucy (Woodward) Webb, m. Susan Holmes. 33V408.

Nancy m. Jacob Taylor.

Patience m. ____ Milner.

Polly m. Jacob Lantar.

Sally m. Daniel Walton.

Samuel m. bef. Aug., 1718, Elizabeth (____) Chackalate, widow of Stephen. Proven by Court Record of that date, Northumberland Co.

Sarah m. ____ Dickinson.

Sarah m. (1) Thomas Hobson; m. (2) William Dickinson.

Sarah m. William McClanahan.

Sarah m. Francis Ward.

Southy m. 26 Oct., 1795, Ann Miles. Northampton Co. Mar. Record.

Stephen m. 1785-91, Rosanna Mays. Montgomery Co. Mar. Record.

Susannah m. Israel Patton.

Susannah m. William Humphries.

Susannah m. Thomas Whitlock.

Temperance m. John Cato.

Tilley m. Beverley Deane.

Vivian m. 1790, ____ __ard. Orange Co. Mar. Record.

William, d. 1713, Isle of Wight Co.; m. bef. 1692, Mary Taberer, dau. of Thomas (will dated 14 Jan., 1692, Isle of Wight Co.). 7T193; 7W(1)248.

William, b. 1 May, 1745, Va.; d. 11 April, 1809, Granville Co., No.

WEBB (cont.)

Car.; m. in Essex Co., Frances Young, d. 1810; rem. 1776 to Granville Co. 8T58. He, b. 1 May, 1748; m. 1 May, 1771. 23V91; DAR No. 79 958.

William m. 1798, Margaret Atkins. Orange Co. Mar. Record.

William m. 1785, Sarah Leathers. Orange Co. Mar. Record.

William m. Mary Marshall, b. 10 Nov., 1776, dau. of William (b. Caroline Co.) and Ann (McLeod). 39V268-9.

William, Jr., m. 1797, Patsy Smith. Orange Co. Mar. Record.

William, Sr., b. 21 April, 1741; d. 15 June, 1827; m. 7 Dec., 1769, Mary "Polly" Marshall, b. 14 March, 1749; d. 25 Aug., 1850. 21V330.

William Crittenden, b. 1732; d. 20 Dec., 1815, son of William (will prov. 1783, Orange Co.); m. (1) 23 Feb., 1762, Jane Vivion, b. 1740; d. 25 Feb., 1783, dau. of John III (b. 1714) and Jane (Smith); m. (2) 8 July, 1783, Jane Buckner (Orange Co. Mar. Record); m. (3) 11 July, 1789, Fannie Smith Wortham (Christ Church, p. 207). Family Bible Records. 26V197; 33V408; 47V61; 5W(2)172, 177.

Winnie m. Joseph Norris (1st wife).

WEBBER

Annie m. John Johnson.

Augustine in this parish m. 30 May, 1775, Naomi Jones in Hanover. Douglas Reg., p. 16.

Eleanor m. (1) John Chiles; m. (2) Edwin Hickman.

John in Goochland m. 8 Aug., 1773, Eliz. Wiglesworth in Spotsylvania. Douglas Reg., p. 14.

John m. 3 Oct., 1794, Peggy Porter by Menoah Lesley. Campbell Co. Mar. Record.

Keturah m. Cornelius Harris.

Mary m. Benjamin Bowles.

Mary m. James England.

Mildred m. Ben. Chiles.

Nancy m. John Finch.

Philip m. 4 Feb., 1779, Anne Thomson. Louisa Co. Mar. Record.

Philip m. 14 Oct., 1751, Tahpenez Ward. Douglas Reg., p. 26.

Rachel m. James Hunter.

Seth m. 19 Feb., 1786, Sally White Chapman. Sur. Richard Webber. Amelia Co. Mar. Bond.

Susanna m. Baxter Folkes.

Thomas m. 6 Nov., 1790, Dolly (____) Reynolds. Norfolk Co. Mar. Record.

Will. m. 23 Jan., 1773, Mary Woodford, both in Caroline. Douglas Reg., p. 14.

William m. 15 Nov., 1792, Nancy Walker by Menoah Lesley. Campbell Co. Mar. Record.

WEBER

Barbara m. Andress Zimmerman.

WEBLE

Adam m. 17 Dec., 1795, Jane VanCleve. Shelby Co., Ky. Mar. Record.

WEBSTER

Achilles m. 2 Jan., 1790, Sarah Webster. Caroline Co. Mar. Record.

Aggie m. Will. Woodrum.

Andrew m. 1788, Usilla Smither. Orange Co. Mar. Record.

WEBSTER (cont.)

Anne m. George Reaves.

Anthony m. 30 Jan., 1798, Polly C. Foster. Sur. William Webster. Amelia Co. Mar. Bond.

Barbara m. William Groves.

David m. 10 April, 1770, Judith Carter, both in this parish. Douglas Reg., p. 11.

Edmund m. 20 Nov., 1741, Margery Stanely. OPR.

Edward m. 22 Dec., 1797, Elizabeth Crowder. Sur. Jno. Baldwin. Amelia Co. Mar. Bond.

Edward m. 27 Oct., 1743, Judith Newman alias Jones. St. Peter's, p. 419.

George m. 1793, Mary Highlander. Orange Co. Mar. Record.

Henry m. 8 July, 1784, Anna Richards. Douglas Reg., p. 23.

James m. 26 Nov., 1792, Ann Rison. Sur. Ellery Rison. Amelia Co. Mar. Bond.

Jane m. John Webster, Sr.

John m. 1 Jan., 1695, Anne Smith. Essex Co. Mar. Record.

John m. 23 Dec., 1793, Clarissa Smithers. Sur. Thos. Webster. Amelia Co. Mar. Bond.

John m. 2 April, 1787, Tabitha Robertson. Sur. Thos. Dier. Amelia Co. Mar. Bond.

John m. 1791, Elizabeth Rison. Amelia Co. Mar. Record.

John m. 26 Aug., 1762, Ann Knowline, both in this parish. Douglas Reg., p. 6.

John, Sr., b. ca 1769, Franklin Co.; m. 20 March, 1790, Jane Webster, b. ca 1773. Hartford C-108, 2 March, 1957. Signed Glen V. Barker, P. O. Box 94, Springville, Utah.

Joseph m. 18 July, 1686, Rebecca Baughon. St. Peter's, p. 418.

Joshua m. 25 Dec., 1794, Fanny Lester by Rev. James Shelburne, Baptist. Lunenburg Co. Ministers' Returns.

Mary m. Isaac Webb.

Nanny m. James Mattox.

Peter m. 27 Aug., 1795, Kezza Crittenden. Sur. Jno. Crittenden. Amelia Co. Mar. Bond.

Peter, Jr., m. 27 Oct., 1761, Elizabeth Gibbs. Sur. Thomas Webster. Amelia Co. Mar. Bond.

Peter, Jr., m. 14 Dec., 1796, Mary Hill Johnson. Sur. James Johnson. Amelia Co. Mar. Bond.

Polly m. John Burton.

Rosamond m. Henry Hill.

Roy m. 8 Sept., 1790, Sarah Scanland. Caroline Co. Mar. Record.

Ruth m. Kenneth Sutherland.

Sally m. Jeremiah Coats.

Sarah m. Achilles Webster.

Sarah m. James Knowling.

William m. 30 Nov., 1795, Belle Wright Foster. Sur. Thos. McGlasson. Amelia Co. Mar. Bond.

William m. 10 Jan., 1795, Agnes Jones. Caroline Co. Mar. Record.

WEDDALL

Thomas m. 3 Jan., 1748, Isabel Robe. OPR.

EDDERBURN

____ m. ____ Taliaferro, dau. of William and Elizabeth (Holden). Proven by a Court Suit, 1803. 11W(2)123.

EEDON

Augustine, Jr., b. 1751, Westmoreland Co.; d. 5 May, 1833, Prince William Co., son of Augustine and Rebecca (Baker); served in Rev. War; m. 28 March, 1782, Westmoreland Co., Jane Wroe, b. 16 Feb., 1761; d. March, 1830, Prince William Co., dau. of Richard and Rebecca (Chancellor). 15W(2)188, 196-7; DAR No. 85 395.

Elizabeth m. Rev. Robert McCullock.

George, son of Augustine (d. 1763, Westmoreland Co.) and Rebekah (Baker); served in Rev. War; m. bef. 1 March, 1774, Catherine Gordon, dau. of John (will dated 13 Dec., 1749) and Margret (____) of Spotsylvania Co. Mar. proven by a Deed, 1 March, 1774, Spotsylvania Co. 15W(1)196; Jett, p. 89.

John, d. 1823, Fauquier Co., son of Augustine and Rebecca (Baker) of Westmoreland Co.; m. Lucy Wroe, b. ca 1763, dau. of Richard and Rebecca (Chancellor). 15W(2)190.

Jordon, d. 1716, Westmoreland Co.; m. Martha Sturman, dau. of William and Sarah (Elliott). 13W(2)234.

Mary m. Henry Wroe.

EEKES

Abraham prob. m. Mildred (____) Goodloe. 5V168.

Catharine m. Henry Williamson.

Elizabeth m. John Vause.

Hobbs m. 16 Sept., 1708, Mary Perrott. Christ Church, p. 80. Hobbs, bapt. 21 Jan., 1686; est. sett. 30 June, 1722, son of Francis of Va.; m. Mary Prescott, bur. 10 Sept., 1733, Eng., dau. of Robert of Va. 47V49.

Lettice (____) m. Matthew Lidford.

Margaret m. John Collins.

Mary m. William Faulkener.

EEKS

Benjamin m. bef. 1 April, 1788, Agatha Holladay. Proven by a Deed of that date, Spotsylvania Co.

Betsey m. Daniel Sisco.

Catherine m. (1) Henry Williamson; m. (2) Capt. William Young; m. (3) Thomas Montague.

Comfort m. George Pool.

Elizabeth m. William McCarter.

Richard m. 9 May, 1795, Judith Wilson. Sur. Jesse Case. Amelia Co. Mar. Bond.

Susey m. Peter Wakefield.

EIR

____ m. James Montgomery.

Andrew, d. 1822; m. 1793, Polly Grigsby. Rockbridge Co. Morton, p. 541.

Anne m. Patrick Campbell.

Elizabeth m. ____ McCutchen.

Elizabeth m. James Houston.

Honoria (____) m. George Jones.

Hugh m. Mary McKee, b. 1746, dau. of John and Jane (Logan). Rockbridge

WEIR (cont.)
Co. Morton, p. 508.
James m. 1799, Mary Telford. Rockbridge Co. Morton, p. 541.
James m. by 1785, ___ Montgomery. Rockbridge Co. Morton, p. 541.
James m. bef. 1798, Sarah Marye, sis. of James. Proven by Deed, 31 Dec., 1798, Spotsylvania Co.
James m. by 1777, ___ Campbell. Rockbridge Co. Morton, p. 541.
Jane m. Cornelius Allen.
Jean m. James Cunningham.
John m. 22 June, 1793, Jean Spreil by Rev. John Brown in Augusta Co. Mar. Jane Sprowl. Rockbridge Co. Morton, p. 541.
Margaret m. James Montgomery.
Margaret m. John Cowan.
Mary m. ___ Walker.
Mary m. James Cunningham.
Robert m. 1791, Sarah McCampbell. Rockbridge Co. Morton, p. 541.
Samuel m. ca 1779, Mary Thompson. Rockbridge Co. Morton, p. 536.
Susanna m. ___ Buchanan.
Susanna m. John McCampbell.

WEIRE
Elizabeth m. ___ Gardner.

WEIS
Andrew m. 1793, Polly Grigsby. Rockbridge Co. Morton, p. 489.

WEISIGER
Joseph m. 7 March, 1788, Anna Baird. Prince George Co. Cameron.

WEISMAN
Catherine m. Christian Miller.

WEISS
Adam, b. 1761, son of John Adam Weiss, who came to America ca 1748 from Basil, Switzerland; m. Barbara Pieferin. Hartford B-6167(5), 27 Feb., 1954. Signed W. M. P.

WELBORN
Incy m. Richard H. Ligon.

WELBURN
Elizabeth m. Robert Page.
Lucy m. Drury Peebles.
Thomas m. 23 Oct., 1769, Hannah Lambkin, both in this parish. Douglas Reg., p. 11.

WELCH
___ m. Frances Lester, b. 19 Nov., 1774, dau. of Bryant and Alice (Hooper). Free II:304.
___ m. by 1792, Sarah Grigsby. Rockbridge Co. Morton, p. 542.
Abigail m. Richard Whitaker.
Betty m. Henry Decker.
David m. Frances Mitchell, dau. of John, whose will, dated 7 Feb., 1758, Lancaster Co., and est. sett. prove it.
Elizabeth m. James Edmundson.
Elizabeth m. James Wheeler.
Elizabeth m. Benjamin Darsh.
Elizabeth m. Robert Taylor.
Hannah m. William Dun.
John m. 1799, Sarah Wilson. Rockbridge Co. Morton, p. 541.

WELCH (cont.)

John m. 16 Nov., 1727, Mary Hudson. St. Paul's.
Lucy m. Larkin Clark.
Margaret m. James Bryant.
Margaret m. John Prim.
Margaret (____) m. Robert Thompson.
Mary m. Peter Cooke.
Mary m. James Dudley.
Mary m. John Robinson.
Mary (____) m. Hon. John Robinson.
Melinda m. Will Mallory.
Mildred m. Alexander MacCorkle.
Nancy m. William McCorkle.
Nathaniel, b. 17 Jan., 1755, Orange Co.; d. 1815, Madison Co.; m. 1783, Elizabeth "Betsy" Terrell, b. 2 July, 1763, dau. of John and Ann (Towles). 13T25-6; DAR No. 28 386.
Patrick m. 14 May, 1730, Catherine Redman. Christ Church, p. 167.
Reuben m. bef. 26 March, 1720, Mary (Bathurst) Meriwether, widow of Francis. Proven by Court Record of that date, Essex Co.
Robert m. 1794, Susanna Aps. Rockbridge Co. Morton, p. 542.
Robert m. 12 Aug., 1729, Elizabeth Yates. St. Paul's.
Sarah m. John Bennett.
Sylvester, Jr., will prov. Feb., 1754, Northumberland Co.; m. ca 1720, Ann Spence, dau. of David and Sarah (Downing) Spann Spence. 25W(1)45
Thomas m. Sarah Grigsby, dau. of John (b. 1720). Morton, p. 286.
Thomas m. 19 July, 1787, Jane Edgar. Prince George Co. Cameron.
Thomas m. Mary (Bathurst) Meriwether. 32V127.

WELDAY

Salley m. Daniel Thomas.

WELDEN

Samuel, Maj., J. P. of James City Co., m. Sarah Efford, dau. of Peter. 1W(1)84.

WELDIE

Elizabeth m. Thomas Thomason.

WELDON

Daniel, son of Samuel and Elizabeth (Allen) of Henrico Co., m. 17 Jan., 1753, Elizabeth Eaton, dau. of Col. William of Granville Co., No. Car. Boddie-SVF I:389.
Edith m. Francis Anderson.
Elizabeth m. Silvaney Gardner.
Elizabeth m. Roderick Easley.
Mary m. William Pearman.
Mary m. John Hall.
Priscilla m. John Jones.
Samuel to James City Co., 1675, m. Sarah Efford, dau. of Peter of Middle Plantation. Boddie-SVF I:388. (See Samuel Wolden.)
Samuel of James City Co. m. after 1725, Elizabeth (____) Cobbs, widow of Robert. 5W(1)117.
Samuel, will prov. Aug., 1782, Halifax, No. Car., son of Samuel and Elizabeth (Allen) of Henrico Co.; m. Penelope Short. She m. (2) ____ Simmons. Boddie-SVF I:389.
Susannah m. Heath Gardner.

WELDON (cont.)

William, Maj. in Rev. War from Halifax Co., No. Car., b. ca 1755; will prov. Aug., 1785, Halifax Co., son of Daniel and Elizabeth (Eaton); m. ca 1774, Elizabeth Plummer, dau. of William and Mary (Hayes) of Gloucester Co. Boddie-SVF I:390.

WELDS

Ann (____) m. William Collins.

WELDY

Ann m. Jesse Laury.

WELES

Thomas m. 29 Dec., 1785, Carrie White by Rev. John Brown in Augusta Co. Ministers' Returns.

WELFORD

Beverly R., physician, m. 16 Oct., 1817, Elizabeth Burwell Page. Page Family Bible. 33V87.

Robert, physician, m. Catherine (Yates) Thornton. A son, b. ca 1784. Jett, p. 121.

WELIT

Elizabeth m. John Smith.

WELLBURN

Sarah m. James Page.

WELLER

____ m. Samuel Paxton.

James m. 22 Jan., 1787, Sary Mathes by Rev. Thomas Crymes, Baptist. Lunenburg Co. Ministers' Returns.

WELLINGS

Robert m. 14 Jan., 1786, Sally Wooten by H. J. Burgess. Surry Co. Mar. Record.

WELLONS

Barbary m. Benjamin Oney.

Elizabeth m. Howell Branch.

WELLS

Ancoretta m. Robert Thomas.

Ann m. William Holladay.

Ann m. Robert Greenhow.

Ann m. George House.

Carty m. 28 Sept., 1738, Elizabeth Onsby. OPR.

Charles m. 10 Dec., 1733, Mary Edwards. St. Paul's.

Colin Campbell m. 22 April, 1786, Agatha Dickenson, spinster. Sur. Philip Bidgood. York Co. Mar. Bond.

David m. 3 April, 1790, Eliza Wamock. Petersburg. Cameron.

David, b. 1764, Va.; m. there, 1788, Kittie White, b. 1768; rem. to Cumberland Co., Ky., in 1798. Cumberland, p. 419.

Edmund m. Martha Taylor, d. bef. 1814, dau. of William and Martha (Waller). 14W(2)49.

Edward m. 25 Sept., 1794, Phoebe Paddock. Shelby Co., Ky. Mar. Record.

Elizabeth m. Joseph Calvin.

Elizabeth m. William James.

Fanny Cheeseman m. James Cole.

Freeman m. 19 March, 1798, Martha Combs. Halifax Co. Mar. Record.

Humphrey m. 14 Dec., 1790, Molly Uptegraves. Sur. Samuel Murrell.

WELLS (cont.)

Albemarle Co. Mar. Bond.

Jacob m. 10 June, 1794, Mary Oats by John Stanger, M. G. Wythe Co. Ministers' Returns.

James m. 5 Oct., 1790, Polly Murphy. Halifax Co. Mar. Record.

James m. 1793, Fennetta Reynolds. Orange Co. Mar. Record.

Jane m. Roland Burbridge.

John m. 18 May, 1762, Ann Boyd. Halifax Co. Mar. Record.

John m. 9 Nov., 1791, Lucy Barkley. Louisa, p. 262.

John m. 18 June, 1723, Frances Barnfather. St. Paul's.

John J. m. in Va. Patsy Caroline Flournoy. 4V100.

Joice m. James Johnston.

Martin m. 1797, Sarah Marshall. Orange Co. Mar. Record.

Mary m. Samuel Baldwin.

Mary m. Thomas Neathery.

Mary m. James Farell.

Mary m. ___ Faver.

Mary m. James Douglass.

Mary Ann m. Michael Downing.

Molly m. Richard Napier.

Nancy m. James Grammer.

Reubin m. 8 March, 1797, Tabitha Martin. Halifax Co. Mar. Record.

Robert m. 15 May, 1794, Sally W. Fullilove by Rev. James Shelburne, Baptist. Lunenburg Co. Ministers' Returns.

Salley m. William Swenney.

Samuel, b. 1754, Va.; d. 1835, Missouri; m. (1) 1780, Rebecca Pope. DAR No. 65 053.

Samuel m. 8 July, 1723, Susanna Brandison. St. Paul's.

Susanna m. James Foster Batchellor.

Susanna m. James Foster.

Susanna m. William Davis.

Susannah (____) m. William Davis.

Thomas m. Margaret (____) Porter, widow of Francis, whose inv. they they presented, 4 July, 1680, Lancaster Co.

Thomas m. Nancy Brockman, dau. of William of Albemarle and Elizabeth (____). Orange III:108.

Thomas of Albemarle m. 6 Dec., 1793, Mary Clark, b. 1768, dau. of John and Mary (Towles). Orange Co. Mar. Record; 13T34.

William m. 18 Oct., 1795, Minia Nelson. Wythe Co. Mar. Record.

William m. 1790, Mary Harvey. Orange Co. Mar. Record.

WELSH

____ m. bef. April, 1713, Mary (____) Robards, mother of John. Proven by will of Mary Welsh of that date, Essex Co.

Eliza m. James Scantlin.

Elizabeth m. Robert Taylor.

Mary m. William Buford.

Vienna m. Solomon Boone.

William, b. 1758, Ireland; served in Rev. War from Va.; m. Elizabeth Brower (or Brauer). Hartford B-6006(4), 9 Jan., 1954. Signed Z. S. S.

WELTON

Jesse m. bef. 1805, Mary Hutton, dau. of Moses, whose will of that

WELTON (cont.)
date, Hardy Co., prove it.

WENCE
John m. 1793, Sally McMath. Rockbridge Co. Morton, p. 542.

WENNAN
Thomas m. 14 Aug., 1724, Jane Porterfield. Christ Church, p. 184.

WENNETT
____ m. John Fox.

WERLY
Sally m. Joseph Lee.

WERTENBAKER
Christian, d. 1833; m. Mary Grady, dau. of Joshua; rem. Fluvanna Co. to Albemarle Co. Albemarle, p. 341.

WESLEY
____ m. 23 Feb., 1797, Phebe Bailey. Halifax Co. Mar. Record.
John m. 21 March, 1786, Agatha Powell. Halifax Co. Mar. Record.

WEST
____ m. Mary Cole, dau. of Col. William. She m. (2) Ferdinand Leigh. 1W(1)142.
____ m. Richard Gregory.
____ (____) m. (2) ____ Macon; m. (3) ____ Bigger.
Abigal m. Simon Major.
Abram m. 15 Dec., 1764, Philadelphia Lawson. Sur. Richard Dennis. Amelia Co. Mar. Bond.
Adah m. William Hacker.
Agnes m. William Dandridge.
Agnes m. Richard Gregory.
Amey m. Daniel Kays.
Ann m. Thomas Owsley.
Ann m. Henry Davis.
Ann m. James Ripley.
Anne m. John Baugh.
Anne m. Thomas Sparrow.
Anne m. George Scarburgh.
Anne m. Henry Fox.
Anthony, will prov. 1717, Accomac Co., son of John and Matilda (Scarburgh); m. Elizabeth Rowles. 58V400.
Benjamin m. 19 Oct., 1787, Rebechah Cannifax by James Kenney. Campbell Co. Mar. Record.
Bennony, will prov. 1708/9, Accomac Co., son of John and Matilda (Scarburgh); m. Sarah Snead. 58V400.
Catherine m. Charles Snead.
Catherine m. Maj. John Graves.
Catherine m. Baldwin Dade, Jr.
Charles m. 16 Feb., 1798, Joanna Dunton. Northampton Co. Mar. Record.
Delphy m. Thomas Henkley.
Dorothy m. Lawrence Suddeth.
Easter m. Zachariah Ellitt.
Edward m. 12 July, 1790, Elizabeth (____) Povall. Sur. James Richardson. Henrico Co. Mar. Bond.
Edward m. 6 March, 1726, Martha Vandegrot. Northampton Co. Mar. Rec-

WEST (cont.)

ord.

Edward m. 6 Oct., 1752, Elizabeth Mills. OPR.

Elijah m. 1798, Elizabeth Tennant. Rockbridge Co. Morton, p. 542.

Elizabeth m. Caleb Fisher.

Elizabeth m. ____ Davis.

Elizabeth m. Lieut. James Daniel.

Elizabeth m. William Burton Ellis.

Elizabeth m. Reuben Kelly.

Elizabeth m. ____ Pelham.

Elizabeth m. John Roger.

Elizabeth Claibourne m. Josiah Clay.

Frances m. Abraham Persey.

Frances (____) m. Abraham Piersey.

Francis, Capt., b. 28 Oct., 1586; will dated 17 Dec., 1624; prov. 28 April, 1634, in England, son of Thomas, second Lord De La Ware and Anne (Knollys); m. (1) bef. 1626, Margaret (____) Powell Blaney, widow 1st of Capt. William Powell and 2nd of Edward Blaney; m. (2) 1627, Temperance (Flowerdew) Yeardley, widow of Gov. George (d. Nov., 1627); m. (3) Jane Davye, dau. of Sir Henry. 6T118; 31T87; 25V123; Boddie-HSF V:50; Winston, p. 272.

Francis, Capt., m. Jane (Cole) Claiborne Bingham, widow 1st of Nathaniel Claiborne (d. ca 1756) and 2nd of Stephen Bingham and dau. of William Cole of Warwick River. 1W(1)142; King William, p. 6; Louisa, p. 428; Winston, p. 281.

George m. 16 July, 1761, Mary Sarah (____) Robinson, widow of William. Sur. Richard Davis. Middlesex Co. Mar. Bond.

George m. 28 Aug., 1779, Winney Shelton. Christ Church, p. 202.

George m. 20 July, 1788, Frances Barrick. Christ Church, p. 206.

George m. Anne Fowke Dade, b. 13 Dec., 1737, dau. of Townshend and Parthenia (Alexander) Massey Dade. 16T165. He m. (2) Penelope Payne, b. 7 Dec., 1751; d. 2 Aug., 1785, dau. of William, Jr., and Susan (Clarke). Col. West d. 1786, Fairfax Co. 36V374; 2 Ky. Reg. 5:54.

George m. Ann Alexander, dau. of John and Susanna (Pearson). 9W(1)55.

Hannah m. John Ashton (2nd wife).

Harriot m. Isaac Bignall.

Hugh, will prov. 1754, Fairfax Co., son of Hugh; m. Sybil Harrison, will prov. 1787, Fairfax Co., dau. of William and Sarah (Hawley). 23V331; 36V374.

James H. m. 29 Aug., 1794, Susannah Harlow. Sur. Thomas West. Albemarle Co. Mar. Bond.

John, d. 1818, son of Col. John and Elizabeth (Seaton); m. Anne Cornick; res. Norfolk, Va. Louisa, p. 428.

John m. 1791, Sally Coots. Rockbridge Co. Morton, p. 542.

John m. 2 Oct., 1788, Rachel Spencer. Halifax Co. Mar. Record.

John m. 12 Aug., 1790, Sarah DeGraffenread. Halifax Co. Mar. Record.

John m. 5 (or 15) April, 1786, Rebecca Willcox. Charles City Co. Mar. Record.

John m. 4 Nov., 1790, Elizabeth Mitchell Jones. Prince George Co. Cameron.

John, Lieut. Col., son of Anthony and Anne (____), m. 1660-1, Matilda Scarborough, dau. of Col. Edmund and Mary (____). 34V374; 58V399.

WEST (cont.)

John, Col., son of Thomas, m. Elizabeth Seaton, b. 28 March, 1741, dau. of George and Elizabeth (Hill) of King William Co. Louisa, p. 428; Seaton, p. 108; Winston, p. 281.

John, Col., b. 1632; d. ca 1691, son of Hon. John; m. ca 1667, Unity Croshaw, dau. of Maj. Joseph, who patented 1750 acres in York Co. 1T240; Boddie-SVF K:398; Louisa, p. 427. Given as Ursula. 1V424; Old King Wm., p. 111.

John, Col. of New Kent Co., m. 15 Oct., 1695, Elizabeth City Co., Judith (or Judah) Armistead, dau. of Anthony. 2W(1)211; Winston, p. 278. He m. (2) Mrs. Jno. Butts. Louisa, p. 427.

John, b. 14 Dec., 1590; d. prob. 1659, son of Thomas, second Lord De La Ware and Anne (Knolly); m. Ann ____. Winston, p. 275.

John, Jr., Capt., d. 1777; m. Catherine Colville. 16T171.

John, Jr., d. 1718; m. 1702, Frances Yeardley, b. 1679; d. 1716, dau. of Argoll II and Sarah (Michael). 31T90-1; Squires, p. 233.

John, Jr., m. Margaret (Pearson) Terrett, b. 5 March, 1720; d. 1798, widow of William Henry Terrett. 32V309; Orange III:88, 90, 92.

Jonathan m. Ann Smith, dau. of Isaac (d. 1760) and Sarah (West). Am. Hist. I:366.

Joseph m. 13 July, 1786, Anne Lawson. Halifax Co. Mar. Record.

Joseph m. 17 Feb., 1781, Agnes Carpenter by Rev. John Alderson, Jr. Rockingham Co. or Greenbrier Co. Ministers' Returns.

Joseph m. 1 Sept., 1766, Anne (____) Johnson. Northampton Co. Mar. Record.

Joseph m. 13 March, 1781, Catherine Snead. Northampton Co. Mar. Record.

Lemuel m. 13 Jan., 1791, Margaret Woodhouse. Princess Anne Co. LNCo. 2:20.

Letty m. William Perrin.

Lewis m. 23 Aug., 1790, Elizabeth Dabney Whitlock in Charlotte Co. Query in Va. Gen. No. 223, signed H. H. West, 640 West Main St., Gallatin, Tenn.

Littleton m. 6 Feb., 1781, Elinor Galloway by Rev. John Alderson, Jr. Rockingham Co. or Greenbrier Co. Ministers' Returns.

Luke m. 9 Nov., 1784, Rosey Acars by Rev. John Alderson, Jr. Rockingham Co. or Greenbrier Co. Ministers' Returns.

Margaret m. David Shaw.

Martha m. Orlando Jones.

Martha m. Col. James Poindexter.

Mary m. Arthur Arrington.

Mary m. Isaac Avery.

Mary m. ____ Dickenson.

Mary m. Robert Snead.

Mary m. William Green.

Mary m. Solomon Turpin.

Matilda m. John Wise.

Miles m. 12 July, 1794, Lucy Parker. Halifax Co. Mar. Record.

Miranda m. Sgt. James Clark.

Molly m. Joseph Meacham.

Nancy m. Thomas Barlow.

Nathaniel, b. 30 Nov., 1592, son of Thomas, second Lord De La Ware

WEST (cont.)

and Ann (Knollys); d. in Va. between April, 1623 and Feb., 1624; m. Frances ___. Winston, p. 276.

Nathaniel m. Frances Hinton, dau. of Sir. Thomas. She m. (2) Abraham Poirsey; m. (3) Col. Samuel Mathews. 2T115; 6T118.

Nathaniel, Capt., son of John and Unity (Croshaw), m. Martha (Woodward) Macon, widow of Gideon Macon of New Kent Co. and dau. of William Woodward. 6T119; 31V343; Boddie-SVF I:399; Louisa, p. 427; Old King Wm., pp. 7, 110.

Nathaniel m. Jane Cole, dau. of Col. William. She m. (2) Stephen Bingham; m. (3) Col. Francis West. 1W(1)142. Jane m. (1) Nathaniel Claiborne of "Sweet Hall," not Nathaniel West. 5W(1)179.

Nathaniel, son of Col. John, m. (1) 1699, ___ ___, aged 15. She m. (2) 1724/5, ___ Macon; m. (3) 1727, ___ Bigger. 5W(1)140.

Nolly m. James Calhoun.

Penelope m. John Bonney.

Penelope m. Mitchel Porter.

Ralph m. 20 June, 1774, Frances King. Isle of Wight Co. Mar. Record.

Richard m. bef. 25 March, 1693, Elizabeth Page, dau. of Thomas, dec'd. Proven by Court Record of that date, Essex Co.

Robert, Col., son of William (b. 1735) and Letitia (Martin), m. Elizabeth Carter McKean. 3W(2)263. He m. (2) Mary Beverly. Louisa, p. 428.

Sarah m. Col. Tully Robinson.

Sarah m. Isaac Smith.

Sarah m. John Ogle.

Sarah Yeardley m. Americus Scarborough.

Susanna m. (1) West Gregory; m. (2) Col. Holt Richeson (1st wife).

Susanna m. William Giddin.

Talitha m. William Kinder.

Temperance m. Sir John Yeardley.

Thomas m. 26 Oct., 1788, Margaret Willoughby by Rev. A. Emmerson. Norfolk Co. Ministers' Returns.

Thomas of King William Co., son of John and Unity (___), m. Frances ___. Winston, pp. 280, 281.

Sir Thomas, second Lord De La Ware, b. 1555; d. 1603; m. Mary Cary, a cousin of Queen Elizabeth. He was never in Va. but was the progenitor of the family there. Louisa, pp. 427-8.

Thomas, b. 14 April, 1774, son of William and Letitia (Martin); m. Ann Thornton of Gloucester; rem. from Va. to Mo. and to Calif. Louisa, p. 429.

Thomas, Capt., m. 31 Jan., 1779, Anna Payne, b. 4 July, 1757; d. 5 May, 1788, dau. of William, Jr., and Susan (Clarke). 2 Ky. Reg. 5:54.

Thomas m. Martha Macon, dau. of Gideon of New Kent Co. She m. (2) 31 Jan., 1703, Orlando Jones. 13T265.

Thomas, Maj., son of Col. John and Elizabeth (Seaton), m. Elizabeth Blair Bolling of Campbell Co. Louisa, p. 428.

Thomas m. Martha Cole, dau. of William and Mary (Roscoe). She m. (2) Ferdinando Leigh. Old King Wm., p. 23. Given as Mary Cole. Louisa, p. 428.

Thorowgood m. 14 Jan., 1786, Susanna Eshom. Northampton Co. Mar.

WEST (cont.)
Record.

Unity m. Hon. William Dandridge (2nd wife).

William m. 19 Dec., 1793, Elizabeth Stone. Princess Anne Co. Mar. Record.

William m. 14 Dec., 1790, Mary Shelton. Louisa, p. 266.

William m. 1796, Jenny Carson. Rockbridge Co. Morton, p. 542.

William, will, 1708; m. (1) Rebecca Braswell, dau. of Rev. Robert of Isle of Wight Co.; m. (2) Martha ____. Boddie-Isle, p. 263; Boddie-SVF I:85, 88, 89.

William, b. 25 Oct., 1735, son of Capt. Francis; m. Letitia Martin, dau. of George of King and Queen Co. 3W(2)263; Old King Wm., p. 78. He, son of Col. John and Elizabeth (Seaton). Louisa, p. 428.

William m. Mary Ellzey, dau. of Lewis (will, 1786, Fairfax Co.). Stoddard-Sudduth, p. 220.

WESTBROOK

Hellen m. ____ Speed.

James m. 9 Jan., 1697, Eliza Puckett. Henrico, p. 227. Mar. License, 6 Jan. Puckett, p. 6.

Temperance m. William Smith.

WESTCOAT

Edmund m. 19 May, 1796, Polly Dunton. Northampton Co. Mar. Record.

WESTCOTE

John m. 25 April, 1774, Esther (____) Floyd. Northampton Co. Mar. Record.

Joshua m. 14 Sept., 1771, Mary Pitts, dau. of Major Pitts, dec'd. Northampton Co. Mar. Record.

Littleton m. 1 Sept., 1766, Mary Jacob, dau. of Philip, dec'd. Northampton Co. Mar. Record.

WESTCOTT

Wright m. Fanny Walke, dau. of Thomas and Margaret (Thorowgood). 2W (1)75.

WESTERHOUSE

Adah m. John Widgeon.

Anne (____) m. Jonathan Smith.

Bridget m. Thomas Mapp.

Bridget m. Coventon Simpkins.

Catherine m. Robert Thurmer.

Keziah m. John Dolby.

Reuben m. 11 Nov., 1766, Sarah Scott, dau. of William, dec'd. Northampton Co. Mar. Record.

Susanna m. Levin Davis.

William m. 23 July, 1745, Margaret (____) White. Northampton Co. Mar. Record.

William m. 20 Dec., 1764, Ann Jacob, dau. of Abraham, dec'd. Northampton Co. Mar. Record.

William m. 13 March, 1759, Leah (____) Mapp. Northampton Co. Mar. Record.

WESTERLY

____ believed m. bef. Nov., 1758, ____ Scott, dau. of Elizabeth Scott, whose will of that date, Isle of Wight Co., recorded in Southampton Co., names "grandson Jesse Westerly."

WESTFALL
Christiana m. Simon Harris.
Mary m. James Bodkin.
Sarah m. William Briggs.

WESTFIELD
Mary m. (1) ___ Holloway; m. (2) Maj. Robert Lide.

WESTGATE
Elizabeth m. Col. Anthony Lawson.

WESTMORE
Joseph m. 9 July, 1786, Elizabeth Baird. Prince George Co. Cameron.

WESTMORELAND
Edmund m. 30 Dec., 1789, Sally Hawkins by Rev. James Shelburne, Baptist. Lunenburg Co. Ministers' Returns.
John, b. 25 May, 1768; d. 11 Oct., 1827; m. 13 Jan., 1791, Rachel Ford, b. 28 Sept., 1773; d. 5 May, 1847; rem. Va. to So. Car. Br., pp. 407-8.

WESTON
___ m. Ann Smith, dau. of William, whose will, 1705, named her. Boddie-Isle, p. 254.
John m. 30 Dec., 1725, Elizabeth Wright. Christ Church, p. 165.

WESTRAY
Levi m. 6 Feb., 1792, Sarah Tomlin. Isle of Wight Co. Mar. Record.
Sally m. Samuel Powell.

WESTRIP
Mary (___) m. John Edwards.

WESTWOOD
___ m. bef. 1695, Elizabeth Naylor, dau. of William, whose will of that date, Elizabeth City Co., names "daughter Elizabeth Westwood" and "grdau. Mary Westwood."
Eliza m. Charles Jennings, Jr.
Elizabeth m. (1) Capt. James Wallace; m. (2) Hon. Thomas Mason.
Elizabeth m. Col. Anthony Armistead (2nd wife).
John Stith, son of William and Ann (Stith), m. (1) ___ ___; m. (2) ___ ___; m. (3) Elizabeth Stanworth. 9W(1)131.
Louisa m. Robert Armistead.
Mary m. Col. Robert Armistead.
Mary Tucker m. Anthony Armistead.
Rachel m. Henry King.
William m. Mary Wallace, dau. of Rev. James Wallace of "Erroll," Elizabeth City Co. Will of James Wallace, prov. 8 June, 1770. 32V246; 9W(1)130.
William, Jr., will, prov. 1782, son of William and Mary (?Wallace); m. Ann Stith. 32V246; 9W(1)131.
Worlich m. Elizabeth Naylor, dau. of William. She m. (2) 1702, Charles Jennings, Jr. 9W(1)131.

WESTWRAY
William, d. bef. 8 May, 1666; m. Elizabeth (___) Marshall. Boddie-Isle, p. 544.

WETHERALL
Eleanor m. Thomas Brown.

WETHERBURN
Henry m. 11 July, 1751, Ann (Marot) Inglis Shields, widow 1st of James

WETHERBURN (cont.)

Inglis, 2nd of James Shields, and dau. of Joan Marot, Huguenot of Williamsburg, who d. 1717. Data from John Blair's Diary. 5W(1)112; 7W(1)151.

WETHERSPOON

Mary m. William Page.

Patty m. John Thurston.

WETTNER

Mary m. ____ Henop.

WETZELL

Susanna m. Peter Heiskell.

WEYBOLE

Barbary m. Jonathan Stanly.

WEYTON

Susannah m. James Williamson.

WHALEBONE

Duke m. 3 Dec., 1745, Elizabeth Powell. OPR.

WHALEY

Barbara m. Harry Talbott.

Edward, b. 18 Feb., 1773; m. 15 April, 1794, Nancy Haynie, b. 25 July, 1777. Family Record Book of Matthew Thomson, who m. 1801. 23V92, 93.

James, d. ca 1782, Loudoun Co.; m. (1) Lydia Anne Remy; m. (2) ca 1758-9, Barbara Remy, b. 1738; d. 1828, Ky. 10W(2)344.

James, merchant and lawyer of York Co., son of Thomas (Maj. in Bacon's Rebellion), m. Mary Page, niece of Col. John Page. 1T253.

Joshua m. 25 Nov., 1778, Leah Wheeler. Northampton Co. Mar. Record.

Mary m. Benjamin Talbott.

Susanna (____) m. Presly Cockarell.

Theophilus m. Elizabeth Mills, b. bef. 1665; res. Va. during Indian Wars; rem. to R. I., where he d. 1719. 66V77-9.

WHARTON

____ m. Jane Sparks. Orange III:94.

____ m. Phoebe (Neill) Chandler, widow of ____ Chandler and dau. of John and Anne (Hollingsworth). Joliffe, p. 184.

Abraham m. 7 Jan., 1724, Mary Humpheries. Christ Church, p. 165.

Ann m. ____ Conners.

Elizabeth m. William Markham.

Elizabeth m. Thomas Settle.

Jesse, physician, m. Elizabeth Sewell, dau. of Henry and Jane (Lowe) both of England. She m. (2) William Digges. 1W(1)213.

Joseph m. bef. 1745, Ann Edmunds, dau. of Elias, whose will, dated 24 April, 1745, Lancaster Co., mentions "daughter Ann Wharton" and appoints "son-in-law Joseph Wharton" as one of the extrs.

Mary m. John Browne.

Mary m. John Deagle.

Patty m. William Johnson.

Polly m. Abraham Perry.

Sam. m. 8 March, 1786, Lotty Hutchison, both in Spotsylvania. Douglas Reg., p. 24.

Samuel m. 6 Xber, 1737, Ann Williams. Spotsylvania Co. Mar. Record.

Samuel, Capt., b. 13 Sept., 1740, Fredericksburg, Va.; served in Rev. War; m. 10 June, 1771, Maudeline Sullivan of Va. in Charleston, So.

WHARTON (cont.)
Car.; res. Laurens Dist., So. Car. Puckett, p. 135.
Sarah m. Gregory Grant.
Sarah m. William Clark, Jr.
Thomas, d. ca 1748, Orange Co.; m. Jane Sparks, dau. of John. She m. (2) Stokeley Towles. 13T24.
Zacheus m. 1790, Sally Young. Orange Co. Mar. Record.

WHATELY
John m. 23 May, 1708, Mary Hurford. Christ Church, p. 80.

WHEADON
Phillip m. Sarah (Jennings) Luck, widow of ____ Luck and sis. of John Jennings. Beddie-Isle, p. 258.

WHEALY
James m. 8 July, 1738, Hannah Higgerson. OPR.

WHEAT
____ m. Edith Chastain, dau. of John, Sr.,(will prov. 1807, Bedford Co.). Huguenot 6:162-3.
Levi m. Patience Buster, dau. of John. Albemarle, p. 158.

WHEATHERSTONE
Margaret m. William Chelton.

WHEATLEY
George m. 3 Xber, 1729, Mary Henry. Spotsylvania Co. Mar. Record.
George m. bef. 1764, Sarah Williams, sis. of Jonas, Jr. 4T254.
Leah m. ____ Owing.
Mary Martin m. Gideon Brown (2nd wife).

WHEELBARGER
Caty m. John Keplinger.
Elizabeth m. George Ruebush.

WHEELBERGER
Susanna m. John Roller.

WHEELER
____ m. Ann Emperour, dau. of Tully (will prov. 6 Feb., 1722/3, Princess Anne Co.). 23V439.
____ m. Micajah Spradling.
____, father of Francis, m. Eleanor (____) Comins, widow of Nicholas (d. ca 1656). 5W(1)123.
____ m. Manus Burgher.
Ann m. Hezekiah Collins.
Ann m. Giles Thomas.
Anne m. William Warren.
Anne m. John Mazret(?).
Benjamin W. m. Damaris Brown, dau. of Andrew (d. 1804). Albemarle, pp. 153-4.
Betsey m. William Sumptor.
Betty m. Thomas Maslin.
Eleanor m. William Edwards.
Elizabeth m. John Old, Jr.
Elizabeth m. Benjamin Woods.
Elizabeth m. Graves Harris.
Francis m. after 1656, Eleanor (____) Comins, widow of Nicholas (will prov. 1656, York Co.). Will of Eleanor Wheeler, dated 1660. 1T244-5; 15T196.

WHEELER (cont.)

Franky m. William Moore.

Jacob m. 13 Oct., 1791, Nancy English. Isle of Wight Co. Mar. Record.

James m. 20 June, 1786, Elizabeth Welch. Sur. John Welch. Buckingham Co. Mar. Bond.

James m. 3 Sept., 1781, Elizabeth Saals. Northampton Co. Mar. Record.

James m. 8 Dec., 1778, Elizabeth Rippin, dau. of John. Northampton Co. Mar. Record.

John m. 24 Nov., 1778, Margaret Garret, dau. of Amos. Northampton Co. Mar. Record.

John m. 14 July, 1772, Edith Luke, dau. of Daniel. Northampton Co. Mar. Record.

John m. 13 June, 1774, Anne (____) Scott. Northampton Co. Mar. Record.

John m. 24 April, 1782, Kesiah Snale. Northampton Co. Mar. Record.

Leah m. Joshua Whaley.

Lettice m. Anthony Garton.

Martha m. William Howard.

Mary m. John Cox.

Mary m. Thomas Spady.

Mary m. George James.

Micajah, d. 1836, son of Micajah (d. 1809); m. Mary Emerson. Albemarl p. 342. Mar. 24 Nov., 1786. Sur. Joshua Martin Wheeler. Albemarle Co. Mar. Bond.

Micajah, d. ca 1832, son of Benjamin (patent, 1734); m. bef. 18 June, 1779, Susannah Woodson, dau. of John, whose will of that date, Albemarle Co., proves it. Albemarle, pp. 342, 357.

Micajah m. Julia Martin, dau. of Benjamin and Catherine (____). Albemarle, p. 264.

Polly m. David Allegree Reynolds.

Sally m. John Adcock.

Sally m. George Bartley.

Sally m. George Berkeley.

Sarah m. Obadiah Britt.

Sarah m. William Taylor.

Sarah m. Capt. Jonathan Drowne.

Susannah m. Gabriel Walker.

Thomas of Old Rappahannock Co. and Essex Co. m. bef. 25 March, 1693, Elizabeth Gregory, dau. of John, dec'd. Proven by Court Record of that date, Essex Co. Winston, p. 240.

William m. 9 May, 1711, Elizabeth Begerley. Christ Church, p. 82.

WHEELIN

Richard m. 14 Feb., 1791, Rebecca Goodwin by Rev. John Buchanan. Henrico Co. Ministers' Returns.

WHEELIS (?WHEELER)

____ believed m. bef. 1779, Martha Burn, dau. of David, whose will of that date, Southampton Co., names "daughter Martha Wheelis." WB III p. 291.

WHEELOR

Peggy m. Thomas Johnson.

WHELAN

Elizabeth m. William Harris.

WHELLING

Eliza m. Thomas Spencer.

WHERRY

Martha m. Stephen Willis.

WHETLOE

Obedience m. Pleasants Atkinson.

WHETSTONE

Susanah m. Abraham Eyman.

WHICKLIFF

Robert m. 18 June, 1759, Mary Harden. Sur. Martin Harden. Fauquier Co. Mar. Bond.

WHIDDON

John m. 14 Feb., 1758, Mary Corprew. Norfolk Co. Mar. Record.
John m. 22 May, 1729, Mrs. Abigail Cawson. Sur. Christopher Cawson. Norfolk Co. Mar. Bond.

WHIRLEY

Rebecca m. William Carr.

WHISLER

Mary m. Daniel Funkhouser.

WHIT

____ m. bef. 15 Nov., 1734, Elizabeth Liptrot, dau. of Edmond, whose will of that date, Henrico Co., proves it.

WHITAKER

Acquilla m. 5 Feb., 1795, Drucey Price. Shelby Co., Ky. Mar. Record.
Ann m. Abraham Haff.
Anthony m. Elizabeth Camm, dau. of John, Pres. of William and Mary College. 4W(1)278.
Betty m. John Baptist.
Charity m. John Williamson.
Charles m. 30 June, 1785, Elizabeth Stevens. Christ Church, p. 204.
Charles m. 21 Jan., 1795, Sarah James. Shelby Co., Ky. Mar. Record.
Dudley m. 22 April, 1742, Polly Wills. Isle of Wight Co. Mar. Record.
Edward m. 13 Feb., 1725, Elizabeth Hill. Christ Church, p. 165.
Elizabeth m. John Best.
Joseph m. Phebe Chiles, dau. of Walter and Phebe (Carr). 8W(1)106.
Mary m. Lieut. Burwell Boykin.
Mary m. James Anderson.
Richard of Middlesex, England, m. bef. 24 Feb., 1735/6, Abigail Welch. Proven by Court Record of that date, Essex Co.
Thomas m. 20 Aug., 1724, Rebecca Hues. Christ Church, p. 164.
William of Warwick Co. m. Katherine Gorsuch. Winston, p. 110.
William of Warwick Co. m. bef. 1704, Sarah Collier, sis. of Charles (d. 1704). She, dau. of Isaac, Sr., and Mary (Lockey), m. (2) James Dowling. 6T56; 10T52; 8W(1)203.

WHITBY

Mary m. William Starke.

WHITCOMB

John m. 24 Nov., 1743, Elizabeth Simpson. OPR.

WHITCRAFT

John m. 25 Sept., 1711, Mary Magdelene Delore. St. Paul's.

WHITE

____ m. Thomas Parks (1st wife).

____ m. John Campbell.

____ m. Lawrence Balthrop.

____ m. James Gaines (1st wife).

____ m. John Meador.

____ (____) m. Richard Cocke (2nd wife).

____ (____) m. William Corker.

____ m. bef. Nov., 1794, Ann Jackson, dau. of Thomas, whose will of that date, Louisa Co., proves it.

____ believed m. bef. 1791, Rosannah Dearing, dau. of Edward, whose will, prov. 1791, Campbell Co., names daughter Rosannah White.

____ m. Rebecca Harris, dau. of ____ and Rebecca (Lanier). Will of Rebecca Harris, 1816, Greensville Co., names "daughter Rebecca White."

____ m. bef. 1765, Elizabeth Sorsby, dau. of Thomas, whose will, of that date, Surry Co., names "daughter Elizabeth White." Boddie-HSF V:284.

____ m. Sophia Drummond, dau. of John, whose Pension application S8376, proves the marriage and shows that they lived in Accomac Co. in 1851.

Abigail m. Abraham White.

Abraham m. Franky Sanders, dau. of William, whose will, 1779, Lancaster Co., proves it.

Abraham m. 11 Sept., 1800, Abigail White. Shelby Co., Ky. Mar. Record.

Agnes m. William Chiles.

Alexander, Minister, d. 1775; m. Elizabeth Camm, dau. of John of King and Queen Co. Old King Wm., p. 32.

Alexander, d. 1804, aged 66; b. Rappahannock Co., son of Dr. Robert and Margaret (Hoge); m. Elizabeth Wood. 23V195.

Alexander m. 30 April, 1775, Priscilla Flower. St. Paul's.

Anderson m. 14 Oct., 1794, Mary Branner. St. Paul's.

Ann m. Alec Mandle.

Ann m. Isaac Hall.

Ann m. Richard Hobday.

Ann m. Thomas Higgason.

Anne m. George Nash.

Arabella m. ?Randall Bird.

Archibald m. 15 April, 1786, Hannah Low. Montgomery Co. Mar. Record.

Barrett m. 4 Feb., 1754, Elizabeth Starke, b. 3 April, 1736, dau. of John and Anne (Wyatt). 5W(1)257.

Bartlett m. 2 March, 1792, Elizabeth Mardus. St. Paul's.

Behethland m. Samuel Kelly.

Betty m. Parmenas Taylor.

Betty m. William Scott.

Caleb m. 14 Nov., 1798, Ann Seay. Sur. James Hillsman. Amelia Co. Mar. Bond.

Caleb m. 23 Feb., 1785, Susanna Stern. Sur. James Anderson. Cumberland Co. Mar. Bond.

Camilla m. Elijah Carmine.

Carrie m. Thomas Weles.

Carter m. between Nov., 1790, and May, 1791, Betsey Winn Cockerham by Rev. James Shelburn. Lunenburg Co. Ministers' Returns.

WHITE (cont.)

Carter, Jr., m. 30 Jan., 1794, Betty Wood by Rev. John Williams, Baptist. Lunenburg Co. Ministers' Returns.

Catherine m. George Ernest.

Cathrine m. Thomas Wiles.

Catie m. George Earnest.

Caty m. William Magee.

Charles, b. 1761, Westmoreland Co.; d. 1854, Greenfield, Ohio; m. 1794, Charlotte Downs, b. 1771; d. 1847. DAR No. 65 071.

Chilson m. Ann Fox of King William Co. 25V175.

Christopher m. 24 Feb., 1789, Martha Church. Halifax Co. Mar. Record.

Crenshaw, son of Conyers, m. Sarah Austin; rem. ca 1825 to Missouri. Albemarle, p. 343.

Daniel m. 7 Oct., 1778, Molley Wade. Sur. John White. Pittsylvania Co. Mar. Bond.

Daniel m. 12 Jan., 1775, Elizabeth MacGhee. Louisa Co. Mar. Record.

Edward m. bef. Sept., 1684, Mary, dau. of Mrs. Mary Thomas. Proven by Court Record of that date, Northumberland Co.

Edward m. between 20 Oct., 1777, and 20 Oct., 1778, Pamela Singleton. Gloucester Co. Mar. Record.

Elias m. 1 March, 1790, N. Flyn. Halifax Co. Mar. Record.

Elijah m. 1 Dec., 1789, Susannah Brame. Caroline Co. Mar. Record.

Elizabeth m. James Bartlet.

Elizabeth m. William Howell.

Elizabeth m. Capt. Robert Spencer (2nd wife).

Elizabeth m. Ambrose Lee.

Elizabeth m. John Jones.

Elizabeth m. Peter Wattson.

Elizabeth m. John Meadors, Sr.

Elizabeth m. Phil B. Johnson.

Elizabeth m. Thomas Outland.

Elizabeth m. Robert Dudley.

Elizabeth m. George Johnston.

Elizabeth m. John Queen.

Elizabeth m. Josiah Willis.

Elizabeth m. George Tomlinson.

Elizabeth m. Benjamin Cave.

Elizabeth m. Robert Harrison.

Elizabeth m. Webb Kidd.

Elizabeth (____) m. Col. William White.

Epaphroditus m. 9 Jan., 1767, Tabby Spraggins. Halifax Co. Mar. Record.

Felicia m. Absalom Graves.

Frances m. Joseph Gray.

Frances m. George Davis.

Francis reported m. 16 Feb., 1788, to Mary Simmons of Virginia. He was of No. Car. Hinshaw 6:121.

Franky m. Benjamin Zachary.

Garrett, Magistrate in 1806, m. Elizabeth Piper, dau. of John. Albemarle, p. 344.

George m. 4 Aug., 1743, Anne Doniphan. OPR. She, dau. of Mott and Rosannah (Anderson). 26T285.

WHITE (cont.)

George m. May, 1772, Suckey Drake. King George Co. Mar. Record.
George m. 25 Dec., 1799, Sarah Cooper. Spotsylvania Co. Mar. Record.
George m. 21 Oct., 1792, Anne Jeter. Caroline Co. Mar. Record.
Goring m. 18 Jan., 1789, Fauquier Co., Leanna Duncan, dau. of John, Jr., and Diana (Bradford); rem. to Russellville, Ky. 27T139.
Hampton m. 5 Dec., 1788, Elizabeth Mullins. Halifax Co. Mar. Record.
Hannah m. Henry Howard.
Henry m. bef. 1661, Mary Croshaw, dau. of Joseph. 2W(1)271.
Isaac m. by 1754, ____ Campbell. Rockbridge Co. Morton, p. 542.
Jacob, b. 13 Nov., 1766, Orange Co., son of James, who served in Rev. War; m. Sarah Stevens, dau. of John and Elizabeth (DeBow). DAR Mag., Nov., 1951, p. 994.
James m. 2 May, 1797, Anne Glenn. Shelby Co., Ky. Mar. Record.
James m. 26 Dec., 1798, Elizabeth Green. Caroline Co. Mar. Record.
James m. 5 Aug., 1788, Anne Nimmo. Princess Anne Co. LNCo. 2:17.
James m. 1787, Lucy Wood. Orange Co. Mar. Record.
Jane m. Henry Crafford.
Jane m. William Clark.
Jane (____) m. ____ Paice.
Jeremiah m. Jane Shelton, dau. of Henry. Albemarle, p. 343.
Jessie m. 1792, Elizabeth Martin. Orange Co. Mar. Record.
Joel m. 1784, Franky Rucker. Orange Co. Mar. Record.
John m. 25 Dec., 1783, Ann Jackson, both of Louisa. Douglas Reg., p. 23. She, dau. of Thomas (will, 1796). Louisa, pp. 373-4.
John m. 3 Jan., 1790, Dolly Peed. St. Paul's.
John m. Mary Ellet. 25V174.
John m. 15 Sept., 1735, Elizabeth Pace. Christ Church, p. 169.
John, Lieut. in Rev. War, b. 1715, Ireland; d. 1799, Fayette Co., Ky.; in 7th Va. Regiment; m. 1744, Catherine Evans, b. 1715; d. 1803. DAR No. 85 390. Rockbridge Co. Morton, p. 542.
John m. 12 Nov., 1730, Elizabeth Smith. St. Paul's.
John of King and Queen Co., son of Rev. Alexander and Elizabeth (Camm); m. 11 Dec., 1779, Judith Braxton, dau. of Carter, Sr. Old King Wm., p. 32.
John m. 25 March, 1790, Culpeper Co., Lucy Waggoner. 20T247.
John m. 28 Jan., 1768, Ann Clements, widow of William. Sur. Ed Tabb. Amelia Co. Mar. Bond.
John m. 3 Aug., 1762, Hannah Pickett, dau. of Henry. Sur. Alex. Walker. Cumberland Co. Mar. Bond.
John m. 3 Feb., 1773, Martha MacGhee. Louisa, p. 255.
John m. 2 Dec., 1769, Frances Gardner. Louisa, p. 266.
John m. Sarah Gambell; res. prob. Isle of Wight Co. Hartford C-305, 20 April, 1957. Signed J. V. S.
John m. 31 Dec., 1793, Margaret McClelland. Shelby Co., Ky. Mar. Record.
John m. bef. 1708, Elizabeth Johnson, dau. of Obedience, whose will of that date, Northampton Co., proves it.
John m. 23 Jan., 1794, Phebe Clark. Halifax Co. Mar. Record.
John m. 21 Jan., 1790, Jeanie Crank, both in Louisa. Douglas Reg., p. 25.
John m. 29 Jan., 1789, Sarah (____) Deale. Northampton Co. Mar. Rec-

WHITE (cont.)

ord.

John of No. Car. m. Mourning Cornwall. Report made 17 Nov., 1787. Hinshaw 6:105.

John m. 22 Feb., 1775, Ann Cornwell, dau. of Samuel, dec'd., of Sussex Co. Hinshaw 6:105.

John m. Martha Key, dau. of Martin (d. 1791). Albemarle, p. 245.

John of Isle of Wight Co. m. bef. 23 April, 1664, Eady Llewellin, dau. of Thomas, formerly of Isle of Wight Co. Boddie-Isle, p. 536.

John of Isle of Wight Co. m. (1) Rachel ___ (a son, b. 1696); m. (2) Elizabeth ___. 31V360.

John, d. s. p. 1807; m. 19 Aug., 1789, Mourning Shelton. Sur. John White, Sr. Albemarle Co. Mar. Bond. She, dau. of Henry. Albemarle, p. 343.

John, Jr., m. 18 Dec., 1784, Frances Terry. Louisa, p. 258.

Jonathan m. 1776, Nancy Martin. Orange Co. Mar. Record.

Jonathan m. 1786, Elizabeth Townsend. Orange Co. Mar. Record.

Joseph m. 10 Jan., 1775, Peggy Jacob, dau. of Hancock. Northampton Co. Mar. Record.

Joseph m. 13 Nov., 1788, Rose Jacobs. Princess Anne Co. Mar. Record.

Joseph m. 31 Jan., 1749, Elizabeth Gill. OPR.

Joshua m. 15 Jan., 1749/50, Mary Cornwell. Hinshaw 6:45.

Joshua m. 15 April, 1760, Lydia White. Norfolk Co. Mar. Record.

Kary m. James Moorman.

Kittie m. David Wells.

Lovel m. 14 Dec., 1749, Sarah Thomas. St. Paul's.

Lucy m. William Corker.

Lydia m. James Haynes.

Lydia m. Joshua White.

Margaret m. Thomas Jackson.

Margaret m. James McMillan.

Margaret (___) m. William Westerhouse.

Martha m. Thomas Paxton.

Mary m. Robert Snodgrass.

Mary m. John Pearce.

Mary m. Thomas Martin.

Mary m. James Fisher.

Mary m. Henry Burge.

Mary m. Sgt. Valentine Leach.

Mary m. Abner Totty.

Mary m. William Smith.

Mary m. Robert Harris.

Mary m. William Keeling.

Mary m. Zachariah Bailey.

Mary m. Edward Millen.

Mary m. Thomas Brown.

Mary m. Francis Giddin.

Mary m. Capt. John Price.

Mary m. James Burton.

Mary m. William Thomas.

Mary Ann m. Thomas Martin.

Mary McConnell m. (1) Dr. Francis May; m. (2) John Overton.

WHITE (cont.)

Matthew m. 7 Oct., 1783, Martha Hayes. Sur. Richard Hayes. Amelia Co. Mar. Bond.

Mildred m. John Tomlinson.

Molly m. Lieut. William Kinchloe.

Moses m. 26 Jan., 1797, Nancy Isabel by Rev. Martin Walton. Louisa Co. Ministers' Returns.

Nancy m. Overton Garland.

Nancy m. Will Harwood.

Nancy m. Caleb Olliver.

Nancy m. John Roberts.

Nathaniel, son of John and Katharine (Evans), m. Margaret McFarland. Rockbridge Co. Morton, p. 542.

Nathan Skipwith m. 15 April, 1759, Mary Burgess. St. Paul's.

Phebe Carter m. Marion Coy Smithson.

Philip of Hanover Co., d. 1822; m. 31 March, 1786, Lucy Mills, dau. of Capt. David and Lucy (Wyatt). 15T49.

Polly m. William Hardaway, Jr.

Polly m. John Polly.

Polly m. Abner Martin.

Polly m. William Barnhart.

Rachel m. James Sleet (2nd wife).

Rachel m. William Outland.

Rawley m. 19 March, 1771, Maacah Spraggins. Halifax Co. Mar. Record.

Rebecca m. William McFarland.

Rebecca m. Samuel Cecil.

Rebecca m. John Blick.

Reuben m. Mary Harper, dau. of Castleton (d. 1799). Albemarle, p. 218

*Richard m. 10 June, 1782, Mary Merriwether, dau. of Thomas. Louisa, p. 265.

Richard m. 1783, Catey Oliver. Orange Co. Mar. Record.

Richard m. 1771, Lucy Richardson. Louisa, p. 255.

Richard m. 27 Dec., 1784, Jenny Compton, dau. of Elizabeth. Sur. John White. Amelia Co. Mar. Bond.

Richard m. 8 Feb., 1768, Peggy Donald. Sur. John Rowland. Pittsylvania Co. Mar. Bond.

Richard m. 10 Feb., 1767, Margaret Donald. Sur. John Cox. Pittsylvania Co. Mar. Bond.

Robert, Physician, m. ____ Hoge, dau. of William; res. Frederick Co. Joliffe, p. 65. Mar. Margaret Hoge. A son, b. ca 1738. 23V195.

Robert m. 17 March, 1800, Nancy Perry. Shelby Co., Ky. Mar. Record.

Sally m. John Page.

Sally m. Edward Carter.

Samuel, d. bef. Sept., 1816, Green Co., Ky.; m. Jane Roy (Coleman) Duke, widow of John Garland Duke. 62V343.

Samuel m. 7 June, 1786, Clary ____ by H. J. Burgess. Surry Co. Mar. Record.

Samuel, b. 16 March, 1759; d. 29 Oct., 1841; m. 1780, Jane Stuart; served in Rev. War; rem. to Ohio, 1805. DAR Query 13 574, Nov., 1930.

* Rhoda m. Joseph Grayson.

WHITE (cont.)

Samuel m. Sarah Cary, d. 20 Jan., 1800, aged 28; tombstone in St. John's Churchyard, Richmond, Va., dau. of William and Mary (____) of Boston, Mass. Henrico, p. 519.

Samuel m. 24 June, 1789, Rhoda Spencer by Rev. John Buchanan, Henrico Parish. Henrico, p. 231.

Sarah m. John Leatherer.

Sarah m. George Arnold.

Sarah m. Edward Garland Sydnor.

Sarah m. Byares Thomason.

Sarah m. Jacob Castleman.

Susanna m. Cuthbert Williamson.

Susannah m. James Callaway.

Susannah m. Mosos Willis (2nd wife).

Tabitha m. William Vasser.

Teackle m. 28 May, 1789, Elizabeth (____) Pitts, widow of George. Northampton Co. Mar. Record.

Thomas m. Anne Moore, dau. of George (d. 1714) and Jane (Bancroft). Boddie-HSF V:63.

Thomas, b. 1753; m. 1775, Sarah Shelton, b. 1759, dau. of Thomas and Sallie (Farrar) of Louisa Co. DAR No. 76 395.

Thomas m. 10 Dec., 1785, Sally Davis. Sur. William Mahone. York Co. Mar. Bond.

Thomas m. 4 Nov., 1745, Esther (____) Cowdry. Northampton Co. Mar. Record.

Thomas m. 1788, Elizabeth Long. Orange Co. Mar. Record.

Thomas, son of John of Isle of Wight Co., m. 13 Aug., 1719, Rachel Jordan, dau. of Joshua. Hinsahw 6:31, 37.

Unity m. Ralph Graves.

William m. Ann, dau. of Margaret (____) Grymes, who m. previously ____ Attawell and prob. ____ Rhotan (or Raughton). The will of Margaret Grymes, prov. 30 March, 1659, Lancaster Co., gives information for this statement. 5V430.

William m. 17 Oct., 1771, Rachel Jacob. Northampton Co. Mar. Record.

William m. 12 Sept., 1782, Mary Brockman, in Orange. Douglas Reg., p. 22.

William m. 16 Feb., 1662, Mary Moore. Hungars Parish Record. Northampton Co.

William, b. 15 March, 1751; m. Catherine ____, b. 9 June, 1762. 31V258.

William, Major, m. Jane Meriwether. She m. (2) Henry Hartwell. 11T 171-2.

William m. 22 May, 1790, Eliza Durrett. Caroline Co. Mar. Record.

William m. 21 Dec., 1769, Ann Overstreet, both of this parish. Douglas Reg., p. 11.

William m. 30 Oct., 1800, Polly Voden (or Vaden) Jackson. Lunenburg Co. Cameron.

William, Col., of Louisa, m. 18 July, 1787, Elizabeth (____) White of Hanover. Announced in The Virginia Gazette, 19 July, 1787.

William, Sr., m. 9 May, 1782, Susannah Davis, both in Louisa. Douglas Reg., p. 22; Louisa, pp. 265, 281.

WHITEBY

Phebe m. Minor Wilkes.

WHITECHURCH

Charity (____) m. John Rudder.

WHITECOTTON

Bridget m. William McConchie.

WHITEFIELD

____ m. Mary Hancock. 33V419.

Will. m. 14 Dec., 1772, Mary Towler, both in Goochland. Douglas Reg., p. 13.

WHITEHALL

Margaret m. Capt. Robert Craig (1st wife).

WHITEHARD

William m. 31 Aug., 1797, Mary Waterman by Rev. Anthony Walke of Princess Anne Co. LNCo. 2:51.

William, Jr., m. 18 Nov., ____, Keziah Moore in Princess Anne Co. LNCo. 2:17.

WHITEHEAD

____ m. Stephen Horsfield.

____ m. bef. 1720, Mary Godwin, dau. of William, whose will, prov. 1720, Isle of Wight Co., proves it. 7W(1)264.

Abia m. Nathan Munden.

Abia m. Arthur Frizzle.

Alexander m. 10 Nov., 1799, Nancy Moseley. Sur. Hillary Moseley. Norfolk Co. Mar. Bond.

Allen m. 13 Sept., 1792, Bridget Brown. Halifax Co. Mar. Record.

Benjamin m. 4 May, 1789, Sarah Walker. Sur. Saymer Wright. Cumberland Co. Mar. Bond.

Dudley m. 2 Dec., 1795, Polly Morris. Princess Anne Co. Mar. Record.

Dudley m. 14 Feb., 1794, Elizabeth Lovit. Princess Anne Co. Mar. Record.

E. m. B. Dickson.

Elizabeth m. Moses Wright.

Elizabeth m. Capt. William Claibourne.

Isabel m. James Allen Bridger.

James m. 1790, Aphia Cappy by Rev. Joshua Lawrence. Princess Anne Co. Ministers' Returns.

John m. 11 May, 1790, Sucky Smith, dau. of James. Northampton Co. Mar. Record.

John m. 1789, Juleance Mackie by Rev. Joshua Lawrence. Princess Anne Co. Ministers' Returns.

Lewis m. 20 Jan., 1745/6, Mary Watkins. Hinshaw 6:46.

Mary m. Benjamin Denson.

Mary m. Richard Cocke.

Nancy m. Francis Powell.

Nancy m. David Stovall.

Nancy m. Michael Scott.

Patience m. Jacob Vick.

Rebeckah m. George Stovall.

Susanna m. William Dennis.

Susannah m. Richard Milner.

William m. bef. 1697, Elizabeth (____) Loughland, admx. and widow of Dorman, Jr. Proven by Court Record of that date, Northampton Co.

William m. 6 Aug., 1789, Lucretia Spady. Northampton Co. Mar. Record.

WHITEHEAD (cont.)

William, b. 1740, Southampton Co.; d. there, 1796, son of Arthur IV; m. (1) Patience Boykin, dau. of William (d. 1789, Isle of Wight Co.); m. (2) 30 Nov., 1790, Clarissa Lamb in Petersburg by Rev. Cameron. She was Clarissa (Boswell) Lamb, d. 1814, widow of Col. Richard Lamb and dau. of Joseph and Elizabeth (Elliott) Boswell of Gloucester Co. 21V206; 44V362; Cameron; FreeII:171; DAR No. 64 776.

WHITEHORN

____ believed m. bef. 1797, Sally Meglamore, dau. of John, whose will of that date, Southampton Co., names "daughter Sally Whitehorn with reversion to her children."

Sarah m. Abel Israel.

WHITEHOUSE

Sarah m. Martin Coffman.

WHITEHURST

Amey m. John Munden.

Anna m. Gideon Land.

Anne m. John Parsons, Jr.

Batson m. 1787, Elizabeth Smith by Rev. Joshua Lawrence. Princess Anne Co. Ministers' Returns.

Batson m. 12 Feb., 1790, Phoeby Eaton. Princess Anne Co. Mar. Record.

Batson m. 6 June, 1790, Mary Timons. Princess Anne Co. Mar. Record.

Betts m. Andrew Smith.

Cader m. 24 Nov., 1797, Frances Wright. Princess Anne Co. Mar. Record.

Cason m. 3 Dec., 1791, Jacamine Capps. Princess Anne Co. Mar. Record.

Charles m. 27 March, 1790, Kezia Ventris. Norfolk Co. Mar. Record. Mar. 1 April, 1790, Kesiah Fentress. Princess Anne Co. LNCo. 2:20.

David m. 10 May, 1792, Anne Williamson. Princess Anne Co. Mar. Record.

David m. 25 July, 1799, Frances Whitehurst by Rev. Anthony Walke. Princess Anne Co. Ministers' Returns.

Dinah m. Jeremiah Hosier.

Dorcas m. William McCoy.

Elisabeth m. Willis Morris.

Eliza m. Kedar Waterman.

Elizabeth m. Hillary Moseley (2nd wife).

Elizabeth m. Joseph Vanholt.

Elizabeth m. Nathan Bonney.

Elizabeth m. John Prichart.

Fanney m. Neil Jamison.

Fanny m. Francis Wright.

Frances m. David Whitehurst.

George m. 6 April, 1798, Margaret Calloway by Rev. Anthony Walke. Princess Anne Co. Ministers' Returns.

Hillary m. 18 Aug., 1798, Lydia Simmons by Rev. William Morriss, Baptist of London Bridge, Princess Anne Co. LNCo. 2:77.

Jacomine m. William Dauge.

James m. 19 Dec., 1794, Amy Kincey. Princess Anne Co. Mar. Record.

James m. 2 April, 1795, Sally Brinson. Princess Anne Co. Mar. Record.

Jane m. William Nimmo Dyson.

John m. 26 Jan., 1797, Francis Davis by Rev. Anthony Walke. Princess Anne Co. Ministers' Returns.

WHITEHURST (cont.)

John m. 28 Jan., 1790, Dinah Matthias. Princess Anne Co. Mar. Record.

John m. 1789, Kesia Smith by Rev. Joshua Lawrence. Princess Anne Co. Ministers' Returns.

John m. 4 Dec., 1789, Elizabeth Ashby. Princess Anne Co. Mar. Record.

John m. 25 July, 1799, Elizabeth Chapple by Rev. William Morriss, Baptist of London Bridge. Princess Anne Co. Ministers' Returns.

John m. 5 Feb., 1795, Jacoma Barnes. Princess Anne Co. Mar. Record.

Jonathan m. 13 June, 1789, Priscilla Willeroy. Princess Anne Co. Mar. Record.

Julia m. Charles Capps.

Kesia m. William Kinsey.

Kesiah m. Nathan Fentress.

Lydia m. Edward Petty.

Lydia m. Reuben Brown.

Malachi m. 1 Nov., 1796, Anne Matthias. Princess Anne Co. Mar. Record.

Martha m. Malachi Carril.

Martha m. William Moseley.

Mary m. Gasking Brock.

Mary m. Henry Edwards.

Mary m. Christopher Etheredge.

Mary m. Henry Fountain.

Mary m. Moses Eaton.

Moses m. 31 Aug., 1791, Sarah Robinson. Princess Anne Co. Mar. Record.

Nancy m. William Dyer.

Nathaniel m. 4 April, 1789, Anne Weaver. Princess Anne Co. Mar. Record.

Rewben m. June, 1786, Mary Smith by Rev. Joshua Lawrence, Baptist. Princess Anne Co. Ministers' Returns.

Sally m. Hillary Williamson.

Sally m. Jesse Capps.

Samuel m. 2 July, 1797, Mary Edmonds by Rev. Anthony Walke. Princess Anne Co. Ministers' Returns.

Sarah m. John Hunter.

Sarah m. Jonathan Fentress.

Sarah m. Caleb Moore.

Sarah m. Cornelius Brinson.

Tully m. 18 March, 1790, Chloe Franklin. Princess Anne Co. Mar. Record.

Tully m. 4 April, 1797, Elizabeth Bromley by Rev. Anthony Walke. Princess Anne Co. Ministers' Returns.

Willoughby m. 24 Oct., 1793, Martha Edmonds. Princess Anne Co. Mar. Record.

Willoughby m. 22 Sept., 1796, Frances Shipp. Princess Anne Co. Mar. Record.

Willoughby m. 9 March, 1797, Margaret Matthias by Rev. Anthony Walke. Princess Anne Co. Ministers' Returns.

WHITELEY
____ m. bef. 1810, Franky Lee, dau. of William, whose will, prov. that date, Russell Co., names "daughter Franky Whiteley."

WHITELY
John m. 25 Dec., 1787, Sally Saunders. Christ Church, p. 206.

WHITEMAN
Elizabeth m. Matthew McDonald.
Hannah m. William McDonald.
Nancy m. William McDonnel.
Rachel m. Samuel Paxton.

WHITESEL
____ m. Mary Tutwiler, dau. of Leonard (will, dated 25 June, 1804, Rockingham Co.). Wayland, pp. 435-6.

WHITESIDE
James m. by 1796, Polly Dougherty. Rockbridge Co. Morton, p. 542.
John m. 29 July, 1788, Jean Hopkins by Rev. William Graham. Rockbridge Co. Ministers' Returns.
Mary m. Ephraim Lewis.
Moses m. 1797, Margaret Paxton. Rockbridge Co. Morton, p. 542.
William m. 18 Feb., 1764, Augusta Co., Anne (____) Thompson. Kegley, p. 304.

WHITESIDES
____ m. bef. 1795, Nancy Kinney, dau. of William. Albemarle, p. 287.
Catherine m. James Usher.
Isaac m. 17 April, 1799, Elinor Ellis. Shelby Co., Ky. Mar. Record.
Isabel m. Isom Tolley.
Letitia m. Henry Kemper.
Sarah m. Jacob Kemper.

WHITEWORTH
____ m. Elizabeth Wills, dau. of Filmer and Rebecca (Green). 5T137.
Rebecca m. Isaac Stone.

WHITFIELD
Copeland m. 19 Feb., 1791, Catharine Howard. Isle of Wight Co. Mar. Record.
Edith m. Samuel Smith.
Elizabeth m. ____ Crenshaw.
Louisa m. Samuel S. Luffingwell.
Margaret m. Jesse Ladd.
Mary m. Jacob Dickinson.
Mary m. ____ Hargrave.
Matthew of Nansemond Co. m. bef. 1708, Priscilla Lawrence, dau. of John, dec'd. Proven by Deed of that date, Isle of Wight Co.
Priscilla m. Joseph Driver.
Sarah m. ____ Revell.

WHITHEAD
____ m. Fleming Brown.

WHITHURST
Tully m. Polly Coyle, d. bef. 1797, dau. of Benjamin. Proven by Deed of that date, Spotsylvania Co.

WHITING
____ m. Thomas Beverley Whiting.
____ m. Elizabeth Woodside, dau. of John of Norfolk, whose will, dated

WHITING (cont.)
2 Dec., 1800, Williamsburg, Va., proves it.
Ann m. Dolphin Drew.
Ann m. Humphrey Brooke.
Anne m. (1) John Pryor; m. (2) M. Fremont.
Anne m. John Beattie.
Anne Beverley m. (1) Maj. John Prosser; m. (2) ____ Fremont.
Beverley, Col., b. 1707; d. 1755, son of Maj. Henry and Anne (Beverley); m. 22 Aug., 1733, Mary Skaife, b. ca 1715, King and Queen Co., dau. of Rev. John and Ann (Lewis); m. (2) Elizabeth ____. 12T260; 32V130; 62V484.
Catherine m. Maj. John Washington.
Elizabeth m. John Clayton.
Elizabeth m. Mordecai Cooke.
Elizabeth Thurston m. John Thurston.
Francis, Col., m. 24 Jan., 1747, Frances Willis. 5W(1)174.
Francis, Col., sheriff, 1718, Ware Parish, Gloucester Co.; m. Mary Perrin, b. 1684; d. 1731/2, dau. of Thomas. 12T260; 32V130.
Francis, son of Maj. Henry and Anne (Beverley), m. 24 Jan., 1747, Gloucester Co., Frances Perrin, dau. of John and Elizabeth (Throckmorton) rem. to Frederick Co. or Berkeley Co. 12T260; 32V130; 6W(1)28.
Francis of "Eaton Hill," Gloucester Co., m. there, 6 Dec., 1788, Mary Hartwell Fox, dau. of Capt. John and Ann (Macon). 21T229.
Harriet m. John Linger.
Harriet m. Edmund Brooke.
Harry Ann m. Gwyn Reade.
Henry, Maj., d. 1728, son of Dr. Henry; m. Ann(-e) Beverley, dau. of Peter of Gloucester Co. 12T260; 32V130; 55V256.
Henry, b. 1730, Gloucester Co.; d. 1797, Prince William Co.; m. Humphrey Ann Frances Toye. DAR No. 31 432.
Henry, physician, of Gloucester Co., m. bef. 1670, Apphia (____) Bushrod, widow of Richard; m. (2) Elizabeth ____, surviving in 1729. 12T260; 32V130; 1W(1)91.
Henry, Col., will prov. 1765, Middlesex Co., son of Maj. Henry; m. Joyce ____, will prov. 1771. 32V130.
Henry, son of Francis, m. (1) 1777, Anne Fairfax Carlyle, dau. of John and Sarah (Fairfax); m. (2) 16 Nov., 1780, Elizabeth Braxton, dau. of George. 32V131.
Horatio Gates, son of Thomas and prob. (3) Elizabeth (Seawell), m. 1799, Hannah Armistead Cary, b. 1778; d. 1821, dau. of John and Susanna (Armistead). 12T261.
Jane m. Charles Grymes.
John, Capt., son of Beverley and Mary (Skaife), m. Mary Perrin, b. 1738; d. 1787, dau. of John and Mary (Booth); rem. to King and Queen Co. 32V131; 62V485.
John, son of Col. Francis, is said to have married ____ Perrin. 32V131
John m. 26 Dec., 1788, Mildred Jones. St. Paul's.
John m. 10 Aug., 1791, Mary McLean. St. Paul's.
John m. 25 Oct., 1785, Nancy Gouldie. St. Paul's.
Kennon of Hampton, Va., m. Anne Wythe Mallory, dau. of Johnson and Anne Wythe (Boush). 35V77.
Lawrence m. 29 Aug., 1744, Jane Kelly. St. Paul's.

WHITING (cont.)

Leonard m. 1719-20, Elizabeth City Co., Easter Minson. 1W(1)157.
Martha m. Daniel Fingleston.
Martha m. Benjamin Derrick.
Mary m. John Stephens.
Mary m. George Boyle.
Mary m. Gregory Baylor.
Mary m. Warner Washington.
Mary Robinson m. William Curtis.
Matthew, Jr., m. 31 March, 1763, Elizabeth Robinson, spinster. Sur. John Robinson. Middlesex Co. Mar. Bond. She, dau. of John Robinson (will prov. 1787, Williamsburg, Va.)
Maxfield m. 3 Feb., 1753, Lettice Johnson. St. Paul's.
Molly m. James Hubard.
Molly m. Archibald Blair.
Peter, Maj., of Gloucester Co., son of Maj. Henry and Anne (Beverley), m. Anne Cary, b. 1706, dau. of Miles Cary and (2) Mary (Wilson). 12 T260; 32V130; 15W(2)257.
Peter Beverley of Ware Parish, son of Beverley and Mary (Skaife), m. Elizabeth Burwell, b. 1739; d. 1803, dau. of Lewis of "Carter's Creek," Gloucester Co. 32V131; 62V485.
Samuel m. 5 Oct., 1750, Sarah Hall. St. Paul's.
Sarah m. Capt. Robert Cowne.
Sarah m. Lovell Massey.
Sarah m. Thomas Duncomb.
Susanna m. (1) Gibson Cluverius; m. (2) John Lowry.
Susanna m. John Thurston.
Thomas of Hampton, Va., b. bef. 1749, son of Thomas and (?)(1) Elizabeth (Beverley); m. (1) ___ Whiting; m. (2) bef. 1798, Elizabeth (Kennon) Perrin, widow of John. 12T261; 32V131.
Thomas of Petsworth Parish, Gloucester Co., son of Dr. Henry, prob. m. ___ Kemp, dau. of Matthew. 32V130.
Thomas, Col., of Gloucester Co., b. 1712; d. 1781, son of Maj. Henry; m. (1) Elizabeth Beverley, d. 1749; m. (2) Elizabeth Thurston, b. 27 April, 1740, dau. of Col. John and Sarah (Minn); m. (3) Elizabeth Seawell, dau. of John and Jane (Boswell). Family Record. 32V130-1; 4W(1)181; 7W(1)194. Elizabeth (Seawell) m. (2) Maj. Samuel Cary.

WHITINGTON

Nancy m. John Davis.

WHITLEDGE

___ m. William Coppedge.
Jane m. James Browning.
John of Hamilton Parish m. 15 Sept., 1733, Elizabeth Overall of this parish. St. Paul's.
Lydia m. Thomas Green.

WHITLER

Isabella m. William Herndon.
Margaret m. Edward Herndon.
Martha m. Lewis Atkinson.

WHITLEY

Ann m. Thomas Boggs.
Betsey m. James Casey.

WHITLEY (cont.)

Elizabeth m. John Reynolds.

Isabelle m. Philip Allen Sublet.

Jean m. John Brooks.

Jonathan m. 1773, Sarah Cunningham. Rockbridge Co. Morton, p. 542.

Mary m. Josiah Wynne.

Samuel m. 29 Aug., 1786, Sarah Baggs by Rev. James McConnell. Her mother, Sarah Baggs, gave consent. Rockbridge Co. Ministers' Returns.

Sarah m. James Fallen.

Susanna m. Henry Taylor, Sr.

Thomas m. bef. 6 Jan., 1719/20, Susannah Fulgham, dau. of Nicholas, whose will of that date, Isle of Wight Co., proves it. 7W(1)265.

William, Col., b. 14 Aug., 1749, Augusta Co. (or Rockbridge Co.); killed 1813; m. ca 1770, Esther Fuller; rem. to Ky., 1775. Morton, pp. 226, 485; Waddell, p. 322. Mar. Sarah Fuller. Morton, p. 542.

William m. 29 March, 1786, Elizabeth Strutton, dau. of Solomon. Sur. Solomon Strutton. Montgomery Co. Mar. Bond.

WHITLOCK

____ m. Thomas Pollard.

____ m. Judith Slaughter, dau. of Martin (will dated 1732). Proven by Court Suit, 1737. Barton II:251.

____ (____) m. Edward Rowzie.

Ann m. John Minson.

Benjamin m. 19 May, 1793, Polly Richeson. Caroline Co. Mar. Record.

Betsy m. William Reynolds.

Charles m. 29 Jan., 1793, Polly Davis by Daniel Lockett. Wythe Co. Mar. Record.

Dorthy m. William Turner.

E. m. Daniel Malone.

Elizabeth m. James Woodson.

Elizabeth Dabney m. Lewis West.

Gilley m. Thomas Lipscomb.

John m. 6 Oct., 1754, Ann Logan, both in this parish. Douglas Reg., p. 1.

John m. Sary Wilbourne, dau. of Lewis, whose will, 1799, proves it. Halifax, p. 350.

John m. 2 Feb., 1797, Nancy Shepherdson by Rev. John Lasley. Louisa Co. Ministers' Returns.

John m. 12 Jan., 1786, Christian Bosely by Rev. Thomas Crymes, Baptist. Lunenburg Co. Ministers' Returns.

Lucy m. Amos Worril.

Mary m. David Lewis.

Nancy m. Robert Barton.

Nancy m. David Sims.

Nathan m. 7 Sept., 1756, Diana Hicks, both in this parish. Douglas Reg., p. 2.

Nicholas m. 22 Jan., 1798 or 1799, Sally Warren by Rev. Richard O. Ferguson. Louisa Co. Ministers' Returns.

Sarah m. James Hunt.

Temperance m. James Bartlett.

Thomas m. 28 Nov., 1788, Susannah Webb. Halifax Co. Mar. Record.

WHITLOCK (cont.)
Mar. 1 Dec., 1788, by Rev. James Hurt. Campbell Co. Ministers' Returns.
Thomas m. 15 Dec., 1793, Judith Carter. Halifax Co. Mar. Record.
Thomas m. 9 June, 1776, Sally Henderson, both of this parish. Douglas Reg., p. 17.
Thomas m. 10 Sept., 1792, Hannah Richardson. Louisa Co. Mar. Record.
Thomas m. 12 Oct., 1797, Molley Warren, by Rev. John Lasley. Louisa Co. Ministers' Returns.
William m. 22 Dec., 1767, Mary Rowntree, both in this parish. Douglas Reg., p. 10.

WHITLOE
Obedience m. Pleasants Atkinson.

WHITLOW
Ann m. Buckner Wall.
Ann m. John Cannon.
E. m. Owen London.
Henry m. 21 Dec., 1786, Judith Parker. Halifax Co. Mar. Record.
Henry m. 3 Dec., 1767, Martha Radford, both in this parish. Douglas Reg., p. 10.
Jean m. John Crow.
Judith m. James Perkins.
Lucy m. Thomas Jones.
Milly m. William Bailey.
Polly m. James B. Owen.
Rebeckah m. John Thompson.

WHITLY
David m. Mary (____) Bridges Pope Nicholas. 7W(1)62. See also 44V 179 and 24W(1)94.

WHITMAN
____ m. 1745, Catherine Carlock, dau. of David. Widow res. 1782, Rockbridge Co. 33T202.
____ m. Sarah Paxton, dau. of Thomas and (2) Martha (White). Rockbridge Co. Morton, p. 520.
Paul m. Mary Doswell, dau. of Thomas. 22V90.
Sarah, Jr., m. John Christian Carlock.

WHITMORE
Betsey m. Michael Stultz.
William m. 5 Jan., 1781, Molly Carver. St. Paul's.

WHITNEY
____ m. bef. 25 Oct., 1760, Margaret Jones, dau. of Joseph, whose will of that date, Southampton Co., names "daughter Margaret Whitney."
Francis m. 10 Dec., 1790, Elizabeth Woodside. Norfolk Co. Mar. Record.
Thomas, Col., m. Elizabeth Seawell. 32V130-1.

WHITSELL
Mary m. John Long.

WHITSETT
Elizabeth m. William Breathitt.
William, Sr., b. 20 Aug., 1731, Ireland; d. 1805, Logan Co., Ky.; served in Rev. War; rem. to Albemarle Co. with his father ca 1741; m. bef. 1765, Ellen (or Eleanor) Menees in Amherst Co.; rem. to Hen-

WHITSETT (cont.)
ry Co.; 1790 to Nashville, Tenn.; 1800 to Logan Co., Ky. Am. Hist. 9:382.

WHITSON
Elizabeth m. Benjamin MacCullough.
John m. bef. 7 April, 1671, Ann Spenser, d. bef. 5 Sept., 1671. Court Records of those dates, Surry Co., prove it.
Margaret m. Nicholas George.
Mary m. William George.
Mary (____) m. Michael Judd.
Sarah m. John Nelson.

WHITT
Jesse m. 1785-1791, Ruth Whitt. Montgomery Co. Mar. Record.
Mary m. Gutrich Jones.
Rachel m. Abraham Henderson.
Ruth m. Jesse Whitt.

WHITTEKER
Robert m. 1 Oct., 1705, Esther Francis. Christ Church, p. 79.

WHITTEN
____ m. Polly Pendleton, dau. of John. Slaughter, p. 151.
Jeremiah m. Mary Pendleton, dau. of William (1720-1779) and Elizabeth (Tinsley). 42V183.
Nelly m. William Whitten.
William m. 19 July, 1784, Nelly Whitten. Sur. William Burdett. Pittsylvania Co. Mar. Bond.

WHITTERS
Precilla m. John Chowning.

WHITTICOR
Charles m. 21 Dec., 1776, Mary Herrin. Christ Church, p. 201.

WHITTINGTON
Littleton, b. Va., bro. of William (b. 1759); m. bef. 1800, Sarah Hearn; res. bef. 1810, Woodford Co., Ky. 18 Ky. Reg. 54:60; Woodford Co., p. 93.
Rebecca m. William Weaver.
William, b. 1759, Va.; d. 1824, Woodford Co., Ky.; m. 1791, in Ky., Lucy Long, b. 1775; d. 1861, dau. of John, Sr., and Mary (Haynes). Lucy was in Bryan's Station during the siege. 18 Ky. Reg. 54:59; Woodford Co., p. 92.
William prob. m. bef. 1717, Elizabeth Taylor, dau. of Elias, whose will dated 19 April, 1717, Accomac Co., names "my daughter Elizabeth Whittington" and appoints "my son-in-law William Whittington executor."

WHITTLE
Fortescue, from Ireland, m. Mary Ann Davies, dau. of William and Mary (Murray). Yesterday, p. 289.

WHITWELL
Capt. m. at York, 5 Oct., 1751, ____ ____. From John Blair's Diary. 7W(1)152.

WHITWORTH
____ m. 15 Aug., 1782, S. Cunningham. Halifax Co. Mar. Record.
Ann m. David Walker Pettus (1st wife).
John m. 18 Dec., 1787, Elizabeth Worley. Halifax Co. Mar. Record.
Mary m. (1) Charles Collier; m. (2) Benjamin Collier.

WHITWORTH (cont.)

Mary m. George Overton.

Nancy m. John Worsham.

Roland m. 21 Jan., 1790, Martha Walthall, dau. of Daniel W. Amelia Co. Mar. Record.

Sarah m. Benjamin Puckett.

Thomas m. Eliza Goodwin, dau. of Peterson Goodwin of Petersburg, Va. Family Records. 21V444.

WHITZEL

Abraham m. 5 Nov., 1797, Magdalin Keller. Rockingham Co. Wayland, p. 9.

WHORRY

Mary m. John Wallace.

WHORTON

Mary m. John Brown.

Thomas, Jr., m. 29th 7ber, 1709, Honor Harrison. St. Peter's, p. 418.

WIAT

John m. 3 June, 1775, Sarah Charles. Christ Church, p. 201.

Richard m. 16 April, 1713, Charity Beamont. Christ Church, p. 83.

WIATT

____ m. Sary Tomlinson, dau. of Benjamin (will prov. 1789, Lunenburg Co.). Bell, p. 295.

____ m. 14 Nov., 1799, ____ ____. Christ Church, p. 303.

Catherine m. William Hall.

Eliza Maria m. Walker Jones.

James m. 10 Oct., 1798, Fanny Curtis. Christ Church, p. 302. She was Frances Curtis, dau. of Christopher of Gloucester Co. Proven by Court Suit, 1799, Middlesex Co.

Nathan m. 23 May, 1773, Sarah Smith by Rev. John Alderson, Jr. Rockingham Co. or Greenbrier Co. Ministers' Returns.

Pitman m. 1 June, 1782, Martha Fuller of King and Queen Co. Christ Church, p. 203.

Thomas m. 2 July (prob. 1785), Catharine Robinson of Gloucester Co. Christ Church, p. 204.

William, d. 16 April, 1800, age 47, son of William Wiatt, mariner; m. 11 Jan., 1776, Catherine Julian by Rev. James Marye. She, d. 27 May, 1792, in her 36th year, dau. of Charles Julian. Family Bible. 10T 12, 13, 14.

WIBLIN

William m. bef. 19 Aug., 1778, Hannah (____) Doggett, mother of Reuben, whose will of that date and Court Record, 20 April, 1790, both in Lancaster Co., prove it.

WICK

Ann m. Jeremiah Fentress.

James m. 19 Dec., 1774, Sally Nicholson. Surry Co. Mar. Record.

WICKENS

Sally m. Adam Lockhart.

WICKERSHAM

Mary m. William Davis.

WICKHAM

Edmund Fanning, son of John and Mary Smith (Fanning), m. Lucy Carter, dau. of Robert of "Shirley." 30V294.

WICKHAM (cont.)

John, d. 22 Jan., 1839, age 76; m. 24 Dec., 1791, Mary Smith Fanning, b. 25 Sept., 1775; d. 1 Feb., 1799, dau. of Rev. William and Mary (Tazewell); m. (2) Elizabeth Selden Maclurg. 30V65, 294.

Mary m. Capt. Daniel Shelor.

William Fanning, son of John and Mary Smith (Fanning), m. Anne Carter, dau. of Robert of "Shirley." 30V294.

WICKINGS

Corprew m. 6 Nov., 1799, Nelley Woodard by Rev. William Sory, Baptist. Princess Anne Co. Ministers' Returns.

Pegg m. Tulley Phillips.

WICKLIFF(-E)

____ m. William Stokes.

Ann m. Capt. John Washington, Jr.

Charles m. Lydia Hardin, sis. of Col. John. A son, Robert, b. 16 Jan. 1775, in Penna. while parents on way from Va. to Ky. Biog. Enc. Ky., p. 25.

David, b. Md.; m. Mary (Sisson) Nicholas. 31V170.

Mary m. John Kincheloe, Jr.

Nancy m. Studley Middleton.

Robert m. 18 June, 1759, Mary Harden. Sur. Martin Harden. Fauquier Co. Mar. Bond.

Robert m. ____ Howard, dau. of John and Mary (Preston). 33V37.

Sarah m. William Rousseau Combs.

WIDGEON

Adah m. William Evans.

John m. 22 Aug., 1772, Esther (____) Ellegood. Northampton Co. Mar. Record.

John m. 24 March, 1770, Anne Floyd, dau. of Matthew, dec'd. Northampton Co. Mar. Record.

John m. 8 May, 1765, Adah Westerhouse, dau. of Thomas. Northampton Co. Mar. Record.

John m. 19 Jan., 1792, Bridget Robins. Northampton Co. Mar. Record.

Joseph m. 11 Dec., 1787, Peggy Russel. Northampton Co. Mar. Record.

Levin m. 13 Sept., 1777, Susanna Wilson, dau. of William, dec'd. Northampton Co. Mar. Record.

Mary m. John Tyson.

Sally m. Westerhouse Widgeon.

Severn m. 30 April, 1791, Molly Knight. Northampton Co. Mar. Record.

Severn m. 25 Nov., 1778, Rachel Willis, dau. of Isaiah. Northampton Co. Mar. Record.

Susanna (____) m. John Dennis.

Thomas m. 3 March, 1759, Anne (____) Stockley. Northampton Co. Mar. Record.

Westerhouse m. 5 Aug., 1789, Nancy Fitchett, dau. of Daniel. Northampton Co. Mar. Record.

Westerhouse m. 3 March, 1798, Nancy Costin. Northampton Co. Mar. Record.

Westerhouse m. 11 July, 1796, Sally Widgeon. Northampton Co. Mar. Record.

William m. 18 April, 1761, Rachel Pitts. Northampton Co. Mar. Record.

WIER (or WEAR)

Samuel, b. ca 1750; served in Battle of King's Mountain; m. Mary Thompson. Morton, p. 404.

WIGEON

Edward m. 18 Jan., 1797, Sarah Boush by Rev. Anthony Walke. Princess Anne Co. Ministers' Returns.

WIGGINGTON

____ m. Frances Johnson. 33V300.

James m. Sarah Anne Pendleton, b. 17 Dec., 1774; d. 21 Aug., 1804, dau. of William and (1) Elizabeth (Fargeson) of Essex, Culpeper and Berkeley Cos. 40V297.

John m. 25 March, 1795, Mary M. Bell at Capt. J. Slaughter's by Rev. John Woodville. Culpeper Co. Ministers' Returns.

WIGGINS

Elizabeth m. James (?) Rogers.

Elizabeth m. Benjamin Mehorner.

WIGGINTON

Ann m. John Mitchell.

Anne m. John Conner.

Benjamin, b. bef. 1766, son of James and Sarah (Botts); m. ____ ____ and had a dau., Elizabeth. 33T253.

Benjamin, son of John (d. 1825) and Elizabeth (Botts) of Culpeper Co., m. Harriet Scott; rem. to Bedford Co. 33T253.

Elizabeth m. Richard Wright.

James of Loudoun Co., d. 1766; m. Sarah Botts, b. ca 1739, dau. of Seth and Sabina (____) of Overwharton Parish, Stafford Co. 31T44. Mar. 9 Feb., 1756. OPR. (Given as Wiggonton.)

James, Jr., Capt., d. 1847, son of James and Sarah (Botts); m. Sarah Ann Pendleton, dau. of William. Rhodes, p. 372.

Jane m. Gabriel Jones III.

John m. bef. 1775, ____ Young, dau. of Robert, whose will of that date, Culpeper Co., names as legatees John Wigington and grandson Richard Young Wigington.

Mary m. Samuel Thornberry.

Nancy m. John Mitchell.

Richard Young, d. 1807, Culpeper Co., son of John and Elizabeth (Botts); m. Mary Jones, dau. of Gabriel and Martha (Slaughter). 33 T253.

Sarah m. James Wigginton Thornberry.

Susan m. William Pendleton.

WIGGONTON

Henry m. 12 Nov., 1750, Margaret Bridwell. OPR.

Jane m. Moses Bland.

Jean m. Thomas Barton.

Peter m. 13 Oct., 1746, Winefred Eaves. OPR.

WIGGS

Elizabeth m. Francis Braise (or Bressie).

Henry, d. 1711; m. 3 Dec., 1674, Nansemond Co., Katherine Yarrett, will prov. 24 Nov., 1729, dau. of William and Margaret (____); res. Isle of Wight Co. Harllee III:2674; Hinshaw 6:37.

William m. 5 June, 1742, Lidia Sebrell. Hinshaw 6:46.

WIGLESWORTH (or WIGGLESWORTH)

___ m. bef. 1768, Sarah Duerson, dau. of Thomas, whose will of that date, Spotsylvania Co., proves it.

Elizabeth m. John Webber.

John of Spotsylvania Co. m. Philadelphia Fox, b. ca 1754, dau. of Thomas and Philadelphia (Claiborne). 2T258.

Sarah m. Thomas Duerson.

Thomas m. bef. 1793, ___ Johnston, dau. of Henry. Proven by Deed, 24 Sept., 1793, Spotsylvania Co.

William m. bef. 24 Jan., 1761, Mary Waller, dau. of Edmund. Proven by Deed of Gift of that date, Spotsylvania Co. She, dau. of Edmund (ca 1718-1771) and Mary (Pendleton). 59V352.

WIGLEY

Elizabeth m. John Trimble.

WILBERTON

Ann m. Richard Howell.

WILBON

Simon m. 23 Dec., 1789, Elizabeth Writtin. Norfolk Co. Mar. Record.

WILBOUR

Letitia m. Thomas Simmons.

WILBOURN

Thomas m. 22 Aug., 1799, Susannah Ligon. Halifax Co. Mar. Record.

William m. 13 July, 1791, Hannh Shelton. Halifax Co. Mar. Record.

WILBUR

Sally m. John Carril.

WILBURN

Frances m. Edward Harrison.

Margret m. Paul Phillpotts.

Robert m. 9 Oct., 1755, Ann Mims, both in this parish. Douglas Reg., p. 2.

Thomas m. 22 Oct., 1759, Christian Page, both of this parish. Douglas Reg., p. 4.

WILCHER

John m. Poly Watkins, dau. of John, who served in Rev. War. Rockbridge Co. Morton, p. 404.

Mary m. John Linsey.

WILCOX

Frances m. Col. Philip Rootes.

George m. 22 July, 1784, Sarah Vaughan. Halifax Co. Mar. Record.

Hamlin of Charles City Co. m. Susannah (Shields) Allen, dau. of Col. James and Susannah (Page) Shields. 5W(1)118.

John of Northampton Co. m. Ann (Custis) Yeardley, widow of Col. Argall Yeardley and dau. of John and Joane (___), residents of Rotterdam. Am. Hist. I:341-2.

John m. 1791, Shelby Co., Ky., Sarah Boone, dau. of Squire, Jr., and Jane (VanCleve). Shelby Co., p. 179.

Margaret m. William Congleton.

Martha m. Reuben Layton.

Nancy m. Alexander Anderson.

Rebecca m. John West.

WILCOXSON

Daniel m. 1780, Bryant's Station, Va. (later Ky.), Sarah Faulconer,

WILCOXSON (cont.)
dau. of John and Joyce (Craig). Wilcoxson, p. 390.

WILD
____ m. Tabitha Taylor, b. 2 March, 1713, dau. of James and Martha (Thompson). Taylor, p. 133.
Daniel m. Margaret (____) Stephens, widow of William. She d. 12 Feb., 1675. They res. 1655, York Co. 4W(1)4.
Margaret m. Capt. Philip Chesley.
Thomas m. Tabitha Taylor. 30V387.

WILDAIR
Eliza m. Millerson Wrighton.
Sarah (____) m. Hezekiah Taylor.

WILDER
Mary (____) m. James Simmons.
Sarah m. William George.
Sarah m. Joseph Sawyer.

WILDEY
Elizabeth m. Henry Fleet.
Jane m. Alexander Morehead, Jr.
Nathaniel m. Sarah Phillips, dau. of William; so stated in will of Nathaniel Wildey, dated 10 June, 1730, Lancaster Co.
William m. bef. 1706, Elizabeth Mottley, dau. of John. Proven by Deed, 13 Dec., 1706, Northumberland Co.

WILDMAN
Phebe m. Benjamin Yates.

WILDON
Sarah m. Joseph Hill.

WILDS
Ann (____) m. William Collins.

WILDY
Judith m. John Anderson.
Nathaniel m. Sarah Phillips. See Nathaniel Wildey.
Sylvania m. John Robertson.

WILES
Dinah m. Matthias Price.
John, minister, of Culford Parish, Suffolk Co., England, m. Elizabeth Ludlow, dau. of Thomas (d. 1660). 1T236.
Thomas m. 6 Dec., 1785, Cathrine White by Rev. John Brown. Rockbridge Co. Ministers' Returns.
William m. 28 June, 1792, Anne Grymes. Princess Anne Co. Mar. Record.

WILEY
____ m. Margaret Reardon, dau. of John (inv. 1778, Fairfax Co.) and Ann (Thompson) Mason Reardon. 13W(2)59.
Bartlett m. 5 April, 1792, Elizabeth Perrow by Menoah Lesley. Campbell Co. Mar. Record.
Elizabeth m. Charles Lattimore.
Elizabeth m. David Boyd.
Elizabeth m. James Crowders.
George, son of William, m. Frances Stanfield, dau. of Thomas (d. ca 1796, Halifax Co.) and Elizabeth (____); rem. ca 1800 to Ga. Hartford B-8788(4), 25 Feb., 1956. Signed B. L. McC.

WILEY (cont.)

Hugh m. Jan., 1793, Polly Holcombe. Consent of John Holcombe. Sur. Philemon Holcombe. Cumberland Co. Mar. Bond.

Jennet m. Ralph G. Yates (given as Ralph Gyates).

John m. 1791, Mary Cooper. Rockbridge Co. Morton, p. 542.

John m. March, 1770, Jane Johnson. Louisa Co. Mar. Record.

John m. 28 Feb., 1775, Jane Johnson. Louisa Co. Mar. Record.

John m. 22 May, 1782, Sally Munford, dau. of Thomas. Sur. John C. Cobbs. Amelia Co. Mar. Bond.

Joseph m. 1791, Mary McCampbell. Rockbridge Co. Morton, p. 542.

Mary m. Absalom Yager (or Yeager).

Mary m. John Lockhart.

Robert m. 1794, Martha Cooper. Rockbridge Co. Morton, p. 542.

William m. 2 Feb., 1797, Mary Nicholus by Rev. John Alderson, Jr. Rockingham Co. or Greenbrier Co. Ministers' Returns.

William m. 24 May, 1784, Karanhapouch Gatliff by Rev. John Alderson, Jr. Rockingham Co. or Greenbrier Co. Ministers' Returns.

WILHITE

Maria m. Wilhelm Zimmerman.

WILHOIT

Aaron, son of John and (1) ____ (Smith), m. bef. 1786, Mary Yager, dau. of John and Mary (Wilhoit). 26W(1)193; 9W(2)192.

Elijah m. bef. 1803, Nancy Vawter, dau. of Richard and Frances (Towles). 13T29.

Jeremiah, b. 4 May, 1774; d. 4 April, 1824, son of Michael; m. 20 Dec., 1796, Madison Co., Susanna Yager, b. 9 Oct., 1778; d. 2 June, 1853, dau. of Nicholas and Susanna (Wilhoit). 9W(2)195.

John, est. sett. Oct., 1797, son of Michael; m. prob. in late 1730's, Margaret Weaver. 26W(1)243, 247.

John, b. ca 1750; served in Rev. War; m. Lucy Stopp; rem. to Ky. bef. 1794. 26W(1)247.

Margaret m. Joseph Yager.

Margaret m. John W. Yager.

Mary m. John Yager.

Nancy m. Elisha Embree.

Rosa m. John Wayland.

Susan m. Nicholas Yager.

Tobias, b. 15 Oct., 1750; d. 7 Feb., 1839; served in Rev. War; m. Mary Shirley, b. 1 April, 1755; d. 21 Jan., 1844. 26W(1)248.

William, son of Tobias, m. bef. 1782, Elizabeth Shirley. 26W(1)246.

WILHOUT

____ m. ____ Step, dau. of Joshua, whose will, prov. 27 March, 1783, Orange Co., proves it.

WILKENSON

Elizabeth m. John Outland.

WILKERSON

Ageia m. William Owen.

Anthony m. 11 June, 1788, Elizabeth Ellington. Sur. Henry Fergusson. Amelia Co. Mar. Bond.

Edward m. 29 Jan., 1759, Mary Ogilsby, widow. Sur. William Archer. Amelia Co. Mar. Bond.

Edward m. 5 Nov., 1794, Mary "Milley" Bruce. Halifax Co. Mar. Record.

WILKERSON (cont.)
Elizabeth m. Peter Jones.
Elizabeth m. Henry Mickelborough.
Elizabeth m. John Page.
George m. 7 June, 1788, Martha Dickerson by Rev. John Waller. Louisa Co. Ministers' Returns.
Gerard m. 9 May, 1774, Ann Perkins, both in Goochland. Douglas Reg., p. 15.
Henry m. 21 Feb., 1793, Polly Bruce. Halifax Co. Mar. Record.
James m. Mary Green, dau. of Thomas and Elizabeth (Filmer). 5T136.
James m. 26 Feb., 1798, S. Hambleton. Halifax Co. Mar. Record.
Joseph m. Feb., 1700/1, Priscilla (Branch) Skerme, widow of Edward. 45V90.
Joseph m. 11 Oct., 1792, Charity Strong. Louisa, p. 260.
Mary m. James Jones.
Mary m. Will. Scot.
Mary m. Joel Owen.
Nelly m. Thomas Markham.
Sally m. Jeremiah Godwin (4th wife).
Sarah m. Jacob Cornwell.
Will. m. bet. 1750-1753, Lorana Perkins in Goochland. Douglas Reg., p. 31.
Will. m. 11 July, 1761, Sarah Franklin, both in this parish. Douglas Reg., p. 6.
Wyat m. 26 Dec., 1765, Mary Britt, both in this parish. Douglas Reg., p. 8.

WILKES
Burwell m. 1 Dec., 1787, Eliza Gunn. Sur. William Gunn. Amelia Co. Mar. Bond.
Elizabeth m. Col. William Claiborne.
Joseph, b. Va.; d. Ky.; served in Rev. War; m. Amelia Mills; rem. to Maysville, Ky., bef. 1790. Hancock Co., p. 409; Rhodes, p. 409.
Joseph, son of Joseph (will, 1784, Brunswick Co.), m. Delphia W. Clay. Hartford C-756, 31 Aug., 1957. Signed C. M. K.
Judith m. Thomas Barrett.
Luke m. Hannah Stovall, dau. of Bartholomew and Ann (Burton). Scarborough, p. 287.
Minor m. Phebe White by Rev. William Ellis, Baptist. Lunenburg Co. Ministers' Returns, Oct., 1791, for six months previous.
Polly m. Berry Cockerham.
Samuel m. 12 Dec., 1798, Barbara Mattox. Shelby Co., Ky. Mar. Record.
Thomas m. 30 Jan., 1794, Sally Gunn. Nottoway Co. Cameron.

WILKESON
Ralph m. 25 July, 1690, the widow Richans. Christ Church, p. 37.

WILKINES
John m. 31 Aug., 1788, Lucy Gibson. Christ Church, p. 206.

WILKINS
____ m. Mary Warren, dau. of Argoll (d. 1727, Northampton Co.). 8W (2)188.
____ m. bef. 1711, Mary Stockley, dau. of John, whose will of that date, Northampton Co., proves it.

WILKINS (cont.)

____ m. Betsy Jones, b. ca 1760, dau. of John and Elizabeth (Binns). 5T140.

____ m. Elizabeth Limbry, dau. of Philip (d. bef. 1667). Boddie-HSF V:73.

____ (____), widow of John, m. Rev. Thomas Higby.

Anne m. Thomas Rippin.

Anne m. Thomas Kendall.

Anne (____) m. ____ Voss.

Benjamin m. 26 July, 1775, Elishe Willis, dau. of Josias. Northampton Co. Mar. Record.

Charles m. 13 Sept., 1764, Mary Thompson. Norfolk Co. Mar. Record.

Eleazer m. 17 June, 1772, Rachel Griffith, dau. of Nathan. Northampton Co. Mar. Record.

Elizabeth m. John Randle.

Elizabeth m. John Speakman.

Elizabeth m. John S. Wilkins.

Elizabeth m. Josiah Bristow.

Elizabeth m. William Hackney.

Elizabeth m. Richard Nottingham.

Elizabeth m. Jacob Moor.

Esther m. John Ellegood.

Frances m. John McCaul.

Joanna m. Laban Pettitt.

John m. 15 Nov., 1786, Susanna Carpenter. Northampton Co. Mar. Record.

John m. 30 Dec., 1769, Sarah Hunt, dau. of Thomas, dec'd. Northampton Co. Mar. Record.

John m. 31 March, 1794, Elizabeth Ellet. Northampton Co. Mar. Record.

John, a blacksmith, m. 10 Jan., 1764, Smart Stockley, dau. of Woodman. Northampton Co. Mar. Record.

John, Jr., m. 18 May, 1752, Susanna Stratton, dau. of Susanna. Northampton Co. Mar. Record.

John, Jr., m. 13 June, 1769, Mary (____) Pettitt. Northampton Co. Mar. Record.

John, Jr., m. 7 Sept., 1748, Catherine (____) Custis. Northampton Co. Mar. Record.

John S. m. 10 Nov., 1795, Elizabeth Wilkins, dau. of William. Northampton Co. Mar. Record.

Judith m. Nathaniel Tyson.

Lucy m. John Layton, Jr.

Major m. 1778, Mary (____) Guy. Northampton Co. Mar. Record.

Major m. 22 July, 1769, Adah Fathery. Northampton Co. Mar. Record.

Margaret m. Josiah Tannehill.

Margaret m. John Holland.

Nancy m. Joshua Thornton.

Nancy m. William Jarvis, Jr.

Nancy m. Jonathan Herbert.

Nathaniel m. 21 Dec., 1779, Susanna Wilkins, dau. of William, Sr. Northampton Co. Mar. Record.

Peggy m. Matthew Moore.

WILKINS (cont.)

Peggy m. Southy Waterfield.
Peggy m. John Stratton.
Peter m. 19 Sept., 1795, Elishe Collins. Northampton Co. Mar. Record.
Rachel m. John Stringer.
Robert m. 4 Nov., 1793, Elizabeth Harmanson, dau. of Henry. Northampton Co. Mar. Record.
Robert m. 19 Nov., 1730, Elizabeth Miller. Christ Church, p. 167.
Robert m. 6 Jan., 1792, Ann Stratton, orphan of Nathaniel. Northampton Co. Mar. Record.
Robert of Prince George Co., d. 1738; m. Mary Limbrey, dau. of John and Elizabeth (____). 49V183.
Smart m. Stockley Wilson.
Susanna m. Daniel R. Hall.
Susanna m. Nathaniel Wilkins.
Susanna (____) m. John Ellegood.
Thomas m. 30 March, 1786, York Co., Elizabeth Mitchell. 25V300.
William, b. 1746; d. 1807; rem. Va. to So. Car.; m. bef. 1769, Elizabeth Terrell and had 17 children who are listed in this reference. DAR Answer 11756.
William m. 9 Nov., 1758, Agnes Stratton, dau. of John, dec'd. Northampton Co. Mar. Record.
William m. 11 Aug., 1773, Elizabeth (____) Johnson. Northampton Co. Mar. Record.
William m. 11 Jan., 1790, Peggy Scott, dau. of William. Northampton Co. Mar. Record.
William m. 5 March, 1793, Margaret Speakman. Northampton Co. Mar. Record.

WILKINSON

____ m. Sarah Dudley, sis. of Capt. John. She m. (2) William Southall, 1784, Charles City Co. 45V280.
____ m. bef. 1718, Elizabeth Webb, dau. of James and Elizabeth (Godwin). Proven by Will of her mother, who, at death, was Mrs. Elizabeth Bridger. Boddie-Isle, p. 462.
____ m. ____ Taliaferro, 5th dau. of Col. Richard. 5V75.
____ m. Martha Cocke. 4V95.
____ m. Mary Worsham, dau. of John and Agnes (Osborne). 33V186.
Adaline Amelia m. ____ Godwin.
Amelia m. Joseph Godwin.
Angelica m. Peterfield Trent.
Ann (____) m. ____ Goodall.
Ann (____) m. Benjamin Lanier (3rd wife).
Anthony m. 13 Sept., 1792, Margaret Jones. Halifax Co. Mar. Record.
Benjamin, b. 23 Sept., 1748; m. Ann (Ray, Gibson or Sweeney); prob. res. Pittsylvania Co., Va.; later in Wilkes Co., Ga., or his son was there. Hartford B-6814(4), 14 Aug., 1954. Signed L. L. D.
Carter m. Sarah Langhorne, dau. of Maj. Maurice and Elizabeth (Trotter). 13T263.
Daniel m. 2 July, 1782, Ann Powell. Sur. Robert Powell. Amelia Co. Mar. Bond.
Daniel, b. 1660; m. bef. 1693, Rebekah Parke, b. ca 1665, dau. of

WILKINSON (cont.)

Daniel and Rebekah (Evelyn) Knipe Parke; res. New Kent Co. 11W (2)256. He, son of Thomas II and Ann (Izard); she, b. ca 1665. 8W(2)142. Daniel, bapt. 17 Oct., 1703, St. Peter's Parish. 49V356.

Easter m. Anthony Holladay.

Edward of Henrico and Chesterfield counties, son of Joseph and Priscilla (Branch) Skerme Wilkins (d. after 1750); m. ____ Epes, dau. of Lewellin of Charles City Co. 25W(1)111-2; Baskerville, 1917, pp. 140-1.

Elizabeth m. Richard Gregory.

Frances m. James Snoddy.

Frederick m. 12 Aug., 1789, Patsey McDowell. Prince George Co. Cameron.

James m. 3 Oct., 1792, Charity Stanley by Richard Pope, Minister. Louisa Co. Ministers' Returns.

John m. Sarah Royall. 32V412.

John m. 13 Nov., 1730, Sarah Ross. St. Paul's.

John m. 14 Aug., 1743, Katherine Copley. St. Paul's.

Joseph m. 7 Feb., 1700/1, Henrico Co., Priscilla (Branch) Skerme, widow of Edward Skerme and dau. of John and Martha (____) Branch. 25W(1)111, 115. He, d. 1750, Chesterfield Co. Her mother was Martha (Jones) Branch. Baskerville, 1917, pp. 140-1.

Joyce m. William Clopton, Jr.

Judith m. Robert Clark.

Lucy m. Francis Smith.

Lucy m. Moses Fuzzil.

Martha m. James McKennee.

Mary (____) m. ____ Mason.

Mary Asson m. Benjamin Robinson.

Nathaniel m. 26 Jan., 1758, Elizabeth Willson. Sur. Daniel Willson. Amelia Co. Mar. Bond.

Patsey m. John Baxter.

Priscilla m. Henry Embry, Jr.

Rebecca m. Peter Hord.

Richard m. 2 Feb., 1707, Martha Cox. Henrico, p. 228.

Sally m. Jeremiah Godwin.

Samuel m. 9 Dec., 1734, Mary Cotes. St. Paul's.

Sarah m. Thomas Henderson.

Stephen m. 5 March, 1784, Tabitha Morgan. Sur. John Morgan. Amelia Co. Mar. Bond.

Stephen m. 3 Feb., 1790, Anne (____) Speakman. Northampton Co. Mar. Record.

William m. 31 July, 1793, Lucy Moseley. Sur. George Rowlett. Amelia Co. Mar. Bond.

William of James City Co. m. Sarah Taliaferro, dau. of Richard and Rebecca (Cocke). 20W(1)269.

William m. 21 Aug., 1740, Sarah Heffernet. OPR.

William of James City m. Elizabeth Thornton (1st husband). 5V74.

William m. 20 July, 1779, Sally Dix. Sur. John Dix. Pittsylvania Co. Mar. Bond.

William m. Huldah Godwin, dau. of Jonathan and Charity (Holladay). Boddie-Isle, p. 466.

WILKINSON (cont.)
William m. 21 Sept., 1723, Rebecca Powell, dau. of William of Isle of Wight Co. William, son of Henry, dec'd., of Nansemond Co. Hinshaw 6:34, 37.
Winnie m. William Morris.
WILKISON
____ m. Malachi Cooper.
WILKS
Ann m. Allen Melton.
Elizabeth m. Wilks Daniel.
Frances m. William Guttery.
Minor m. betw. Oct., 1785, and May, 1796, Susanna Hazlewood by Rev. James Shelburne, Baptist. Lunenburg Co. Ministers' Returns.
Thomas, b. 1759, Charlotte Co.; m. Frances Leicester. DAR No. 65 127; DAR No. 79 454.
WILL
Catherine m. Lawrence Pitman.
John m. bef. 1774, Susanna Schierman (or Sherman), dau. of Adam, whose will dated 1797, Shenandoah Co., names "daughter Susanna Will." They had a dau., b. 1774. 32T240-1.
WILLARD
____ m. Lissey Counts, dau. of John, Sr. (will, 1802, Russell Co.). 25V193.
John m. bef. 11 Aug., 1705, Sarah Brown, dau. of William, dec'd. Proven by Court Record of that date, Essex Co.
John m. 18 May, 1756, Martha Edwards, dau. of Simon, who gave consent. Sur. Thomas Turpin. Prince Edward Co. Mar. Bond.
Polley m. Benjamin Purkins.
WILLBORE
Jacomo m. William Duffe.
WILLCOCKS
____ m. bef. 1790, Winney Caffrey, dau. of John, whose will, filed 1790, Campbell Co., names "daughter Winney Willcocks."
Elizabeth m. John Gibson.
WILLCOX
Rebecca m. John West
WILLEROY
Priscilla m. Jonathan Whitehurst.
Sally m. Kedar Moore.
WILLET
David m. 1799, Polly Baughan. Orange Co. Mar. Record.
Douglas m. 13 Jan., 1796, Betsy Savage, dau. of Abel. Northampton Co. Mar. Record.
WILLETT
Elizabeth m. Southy Nelson.
WILLEX
Ann m. (1) Robert Roscoe; m. (2) Hon. James Blount; m. (3) Hon. Seth Sothell; m. (4) Hon. John Lear.
WILLEY
John m. 18 March, 1789, Nancy Waller. Norfolk Co. Mar. Record.
Margaret m. Capt. John Gassoway.

WILLFRED
Charles m. 15 May, 1686, Sarah Ells. St. Peter's, p. 418.
WILLHEIT
Eva m. Nicolaus Hold.
WILLIAM
Annas m. Nathaniel Corley.
Sarah m. John Twisdell.
WILLIAMS
____ believed m. bef. Nov., 1758, Elizabeth Scott, dau. of Elizabeth Scott, whose will of that date, Isle of Wight Co., recorded in Southampton Co., names "daughter Elizabeth Williams."
____ m. bef. March, 1754, Mary Trueman, dau. of Richard, Sr., whose will of that date, Henrico Co., names "daughter Mary Williams."
____ m. Mary Pope, dau. of Henry (will dated 1728, Isle of Wight Co.). 27W(1)63.
____ m. bef. 1758, Mary Womack, dau. of William, whose will of that date, Goochland Co., names "daughter Mary Williams."
____ m. Sabina (Stuart) Wilson, dau. of David Stuart (d. 1767, Augusta Co.). Waddell, p. 370.
____ m. bef. Jan., 1760, Anne Carter, dau. of Joseph, whose will of that date, Prince George Co., proves it.
____ m. William Daniel.
____ m. Martha Eley, dau. of Robert III (will prov. 1739) and Martha (Daughtie). Boddie-SVF I:91.
____ m. Joel Taliaferro.
____, Gen., of Culpeper Co., m. Elizabeth Bruce. 34V71.
____ m. Sarah Lawson, dau. of Thomas, whose will, rec. 1795, Hampshire Co., names "daughter Sarah Williams."
____ m. Mildred Durrett, dau. of Bartholomew. Albemarle, p. 183.
____ believed m. bef. 1794, Elizabeth Edwards, dau. of William, whose will, dated 1794, Southampton Co., names "daughter Elizabeth Williams."
____ m. Anthony Sale.
____ m. bef. 1733, Elizabeth Curd, dau. of Edward. She m. (2) bef. 1749, Samuel Allen. 45V401; Curd, pp. 2, 3. Will of Edward Curd, 1739/40, Henrico Co., proves her 1st marriage.
____ m. ____ Moore, dau. of George, d. 1714, and Jane (Bancroft). Boddie-HSF V:63.
____ m. Mildred (____) Bennett, widow of William, whose est. inv. 1761. Boddie-Isle, p. 297.
____ believed m. bef. 1779, Ann Grizard, dau. of William, whose will, dated 1779, Southampton Co., names "daughter Ann Williams." WB III, p. 268.
____ (____) m. Charles Garner.
Abia m. James Batton.
Abigail m. David Stoops.
Abraham m. 25 Dec., 1798, Polly Hudson by Rev. John Neblett, Methodist. Lunenburg Co. Ministers' Returns.
Absalom m. 4 Aug., 1796, Joan Taylor by Rev. John Neblett, Methodist. Lunenburg Co. Ministers' Returns.
Agatha m. Lieut. Robert Burton.
Agnes m. William Clark.

WILLIAMS (cont.)

Agnes m. Robert Spoor.
Agnes m. Daniel Tiller.
Alex. Leonard m. 25 Nov., 1800, Nancy Smith by Rev. James Shelburne, Baptist. Lunenburg Co. Ministers' Returns.
Amy m. Joshua Walker.
Anderson, son of Samuel, m. 18 Dec., 1786, Mildred Shepard, dau. of William and Mary (Booker). Sur. Samuel Williams. Cumberland Co. Mar. Bond. 12W(2)40; Va. Gene. V:173.
Ann m. John Wright, Jr.
Ann m. Samuel Wharton.
Ann m. Richard Lattimore.
Ann m. John Wright.
Ann m. John Mosely.
Ann m. William Moseley.
Ann m. William Irby.
Ann m. John Hardy.
Ann m. John Freeman.
Ann m. Richard Pope.
Ann m. Isaac Bryant.
Ann m. Francis Vermilion.
Ann m. Alexander Scott.
Anna Hughs m. George Carrington.
Annas m. Nathaniel Corley. (Also spelled William.)
Anne m. James Crossfield.
Anne m. Thomas Downs.
Anne m. John Bateman.
Anne m. Sam Schooler.
Anne m. Francis Parke.
Anne m. Benjamin Davis.
Azariah m. 4 Aug., 1787, Anne Costin. Northampton Co. Mar. Record.
Bazel m. 27 Feb., 1798, Nancy Koes. Shelby Co., Ky. Mar. Record.
Benjamin m. 25 Feb., 1778, Esther Smith. Christ Church, p. 201.
Betsey m. William Bonham.
Betsey m. Wm. Tompkins Collier.
Betsy m. James Knight.
Betsy m. Benj. Alexander.
Brazine (or Brazure) m. 16 June, 1762, Agatha (____) Johnson, widow. Charles City Co. Mar. Record.
Bridget m. William Woodard.
Burnett m. 1771, Eliza Correl. Orange Co. Mar. Record. (Spelled William.)
Catherine m. John Rowley.
Catherine m. Richard Routt.
Caty m. Elias Sudduth.
Charles m. 21 April, 1783, Sarah Dix. Sur. Peter Witson. Pittsylvania Co. Mar. Bond.
Charles m. 3 March, 1770, Ann Wilson. Sur. Peter Wilson. Pittsylvania Co. Mar. Bond.
Christine m. William Robertson.
David m. 21 Aug., 1722, Mary Ingram. Christ Church, p. 164.
David m. 15 Dec., 1787, Mary Peebles. Sussex Co. Cameron.

WILLIAMS (cont.)

David m. 1793, Elizabeth McNutt. Rockbridge Co. Morton, p. 542.

Dinah m. Joseph Roach.

E. C. m. Lucy Washington, dau. of Joseph and Zilla (Branch). Boddie-HSF IV:156.

Ede m. Joseph Heath.

Edward, d. 1800, Franklin Co.; served in Rev. War, Maryland; m. (2) 1781, Margaret Linn. DAR No. 89 550.

Edward m. 7 Aug., 1778, Sarah Saunders, dau. of Richard. Northampton Co. Mar. Record.

Eleazer m. Francis Nickols.

Elias m. 10 March, 1757, Agatha Mosely, both in this parish. Douglas Reg., p. 3.

Elisha, b. 1735, Md.; d. 24 Nov., 1812, Bath Co.; m. Ann Swearingen; rem. ca 1779, Montgomery Co., Md., to Frederick Co., Va.; rem. 1800 to Bath Co., Va. 32T316-20.

Elisha, b. Bedford Co.; d. Williamson Co., Tenn.; m. ____ ____. DAR No. 79 380.

Elisesha m. ____ Grantham.

Eliz. m. Abram. Perkins.

Eliz. m. Sam. Weaver.

Eliz. m. Thomas Taberer.

Eliza. m. George Priestnall.

Elizabeth m. Richard Reynolds.

Elizabeth m. Abner Thurstain.

Elizabeth m. Lewis Dillard Collins.

Elizabeth m. John Gill.

Elizabeth m. Rev. John Kerr.

Elizabeth m. Elijah Pruett.

Elizabeth m. ____ Settle.

Elizabeth m. ____ Haines.

Elizabeth m. ____ Darden.

Elizabeth m. George Douglass.

Elizabeth m. Jeremiah Cooper.

Elizabeth m. John Cary.

Elizabeth m. Samuel Henderson.

Elizabeth m. Richard Reynolds, Jr.

Elizabeth m. Maston Clay.

Elizabeth m. Jesse Lee.

Elizabeth m. Reason Nichols.

Elizabeth m. James Taylor.

Elizabeth m. Benedick Alsie.

Elizabeth m. John Conway.

Elizabeth m. Col. William Marshall.

Elizabeth m. Spence Smith.

Ellen m. Nimrod Long.

Eva m. James Glass.

Fanny m. John Man.

Fanny m. William Shaw.

Florandin m. ?Abraham Marshall.

Frances m. Allen Hines.

Frances m. Paul Sweeny.

WILLIAMS (cont.)

Frances m. Lieut. Abram Davenport, Jr.
Frances m. Thomas Hall.
Frances m. Wm. Robinson.
Frances m. Saymer Wright.
Francis m. 1775, Nanny Harvie. Orange Co. Mar. Record.
Francis m. 1795, Sally Rogers. Orange Co. Mar. Record.
George m. 24 Feb., 1781, Ann Chowning. Christ Church, p. 171.
George m. 31 Dec., 1734, Alice Fowler of Brunswick Parish. St. Paul's.
George m. 9 May, 1786, Elizabeth Hill. Sur. Colin C. Willis. York Co. Mar. Bond.
Grace m. Benjamin Cheatham.
Hannah m. Augustin (or Augustine) Jennings.
Hannah m. David Murphy.
Henrietta m. William Thompson.
Henry, Rev. soldier of Wheeling, W. Va., m. Hannah Davey Morrison, Rev. War nurse, d. age 103, Athens Co., Ohio. DAR Mag., April, 1943, p. 240.
Hester m. Isaac Brown.
Hithy m. John Keen.
Howard m. 23 March, 1769, Elizabeth Montague. Christ Church, p. 198.
Hugh m. 18 Jan., 1791, Jane Bell by Rev. John Alderson, Jr. Rockingham Co. or Greenbrier Co. Ministers' Returns.
Jacob m. 3 Dec., 1747, Elizabeth Miller. St. Paul's.
Jacob m. 1786, Mary Delaney. Orange Co. Mar. Record.
Jacob m. 16 Dec., 1795, Jane Galbraith. Shelby Co., Ky. Mar. Record.
Jael (____) m. Richard Johnson.
James m. 1787, Margaret Johnson. Northampton Co. Mar. Record.
James, Col., b. 1740, Hanover Co.; d. 1780, in Battle of King's Mountain; m. Mary Wallace. DAR No. 66 332. Mar. 1762. DAR No. 79 378.
James m. 24 April, 1782, Molly Price. St. Paul's.
James m. 1795, Elizabeth Bruce. Orange Co. Mar. Record. He was Capt. in Continental Army and Maj. Gen. in War of 1812. She was dau. of Charles (d. 1792). Halifax, pp. 119-20.
James m. 21 May, 1787, Rachall Roberts. Sur. Richard Hansford. York Co. Mar. Bond.
James m. 16 Dec., 1777, Elizabeth Mullins, dau. of John. Sur. John Page. Goochland Co. Mar. Bond.
James m. 18 Sept., 1799, Salley Crews. Halifax Co. Mar. Record.
James m. 18 Feb., 1781, Catherine Nicholus by Rev. John Alderson, Jr. Rockingham Co. or Greenbrier Co. Ministers' Returns.
James m. 25 Aug., 1785, Patsey Fewqua. Prince George Co. Cameron.
James m. bef. 17 Dec., 1763, Elizabeth, dau. of Robert Brooke, dec'd. Proven by Court Record of that date, Essex Co.
James, Gen., son of Wm., m. Eleanor Green, dau. of Moses and Mary (Blackwell) of Culpeper Co. 23V101.
James m. 24 Nov., 1785, Jemimah Gunn. Sur. George Hightower. Amelia Co. Mar. Bond.
James m. 9 May, 1780, Sibna Wilson by Rev. John Alderson, Jr. Rockingham Co. or Greenbrier Co. Ministers' Returns.
James M. m. 15 Nov., 1784, Wilmoth Walker. Sur. John Corbin. Pittsylvania Co. Mar. Bond.

WILLIAMS (cont.)

Jane m. Jno. Fussell.
Jane m. John Erwin.
Jane m. George Carr.
Janet m. ___ Story.
Jemimah m. Thomas Brockwell.
Jenney m. Charles Parrish.
John m. 14 July, 1779, Hannah Warren, age 21, dau. of Mary Warren. Norfolk Co. Mar. Record.
John m. 27 Dec., 1767, Frances Hughes, dau. of Robert, dec'd., of Cumberland Co. Consent of Joseph Williams for marriage of son, John. Sur. John Woodson. Cumberland Co. Mar. Bond.
John m. 30 May, 1736, Susanna Brookes. Christ Church, p. 169.
John m. 11 Aug., 1775, Edith Nottingham, dau. of Thomas. Northampton Co. Mar. Record.
John m. 12 June, 1793, Margaret Goffigon. Northampton Co. Mar. Record.
John m. 21 Dec., 1754, Courtney Thelaball. Sur. Philip Dison. Norfolk Co. Mar. Bond.
John m. 1778, Elizabeth Rumsey. Orange Co. Mar. Record.
John m. 17 Feb., 1708, Anne Shurley. Christ Church, p. 81.
John m. 16 Nov., 1797, Agnes Simpson. Spotsylvania Co. Mar. Record.
John m. 22 Aug., 1717, Michall Curles. Christ Church, p. 162.
John m. 24 June, 1733, Catherine Davis. Christ Church, p. 168.
John m. 17 July, 1728, Catherine Perrott. Christ Church, p. 166.
John of Oxfordshire m. 10 Oct., 1686, Mary Cordwell of Shropshire in England. Christ Church, pp. 29, 33.
John, Col., b. 1745, Hanover Co.; d. 1799, Orange Co., No. Car.; m. 1766, Elizabeth Williamson, b. 1744; d. 1831. DAR No. 65 145; DAR No. 85 401.
John, Capt., m. ca 1754, Winifred (Dameron) Downing, b. 1719, widow of Samuel Downing, Jr., and dau. of Col. Thomas and Winifred (Conway). 8T51; 25W(1)96.
John m. 17 Aug., 1787, Margaret Glanville. Northampton Co. Mar. Record.
John m. 29 Jan., 1778, Alice Banks. Sur. Randolph Moss. York Co. Mar. Bond.
John m. 10 April, 1792, Martha Ambrose by Rev. John Noblett, Methodist. Lunenburg Co. Ministers' Returns.
John m. bef. 1787, Mary (___) Williams, widow of Benjamin. Proven by report on est., 1787, Southampton Co.
John m. bef. 23 Feb., 1713/4, Elizabeth, dau. of Margaret Lemon. Proven by Court Record of that date, Essex Co.
John of this parish m. 12 Jan., 1775, Susannah Ellis in Henrico. Douglas Reg., p. 16.
John m. Amye (or Amey) Tomlinson, dau. of Benjamin (his will prov. 1789, Lunenburg Co.) Bell, p. 294.
John m. Mary Pendleton, dau. of Nathaniel. Slaughter, p. 154.
John m. 26 Feb., 1793, Sarah Bryant by Charles Hardy. Wythe Co. Mar. Record.
John m. 30 Dec., 1781, Winifred Howard. Sur. Leroy Howard. Richmond Co. Mar. Bond.

WILLIAMS (cont.)

John m. bef. 25 March, 1693, Elizabeth Dawson. Proven by Court Record of that date, Essex Co.

John m. 7 Sept., 1793, Elizabeth Tawney, dau. of George. Botetourt Co. Kegley, p. 597.

John m. 11 Jan., 1791, Martha McMillen by Rev. John Alderson, Jr. Rockingham Co. or Greenbrier Co. Ministers' Returns.

John, son of Joseph who gives consent, of Lunenburg Co., m. 27 Dec., 1767, Frances Hughes. Sur. John Woodson. Cumberland Co. Mar. Bond.

Jonathan m. 7 Feb., 1798, Annis Lovitt by Rev. Wm. Morriss, Baptist. Princess Anne Co. Ministers' Returns.

Joseph m. 9 Feb., 1741, Mary Mallaken. OPR.

Joseph m. 1766, Oxford, No. Car., Sarah Lanier, dau. of Thomas. 3T139.

Joseph, Col., b. 1748, Hanover Co.; d. 1827, Surry Co., No. Car.; m. Rebekah Lanier, b. 27 Jan., 1757, dau. of Thomas and Elizabeth (Hicks). 3T138; DAR No. 31 905; DAR No. 65 371.

Joseph m. 10 Dec., 1791, Rosamond Simms. Sur. William Sims. Albemarle Co. Mar. Bond. She, dau. of Capt. William (d. 1797). Br., p. 41; Albemarle, p. 315.

Joseph m. 21 Aug., 1797, Easter Hambleton. Shelby Co., Ky. Mar. Record.

Joseph m. 27 Nov., 1783, Elisabeth Raulston by Rev. John Alderson, Jr. Rockingham Co. or Greenbrier Co. Ministers' Returns.

Joseph m. 25 Dec., 1797, Nancy Hallam Smith by Rev. Thomas Hardie. Chesterfield Co. Ministers' Returns.

Joseph m. 3 Sept., 1787, Ann (____) Strong. Norfolk Co. Mar. Record.

Josiah m. 24 May, 1785, Judith Elmore. Sur. Thos. Elmore. Amelia Co. Mar. Bond.

Judith m. Nathaniel Tyson.

Leroy m. 24 Dec., 1794, Amey Mills. Sur. George Baker. Consent of her mother, Susannah Stubbs. Mecklenburg Co. Mar. Bond.

Letia m. Joseph Goodwin.

Lettisher m. Thomas Elmore.

Lodwick m. 28 Dec., 1797, Deally Heays. Princess Anne Co. Mar. Record.

Lucy m. Robert Call.

Lucy m. Drury Christian.

Lucy m. Robert Adams.

Lucy m. William Green.

Luke m. 15 June, 1795, Mary Parr. Halifax Co. Mar. Record.

Margaret m. John Ball.

Margaret m. Joseph Lemon.

Margaret m. John Henry.

Margaret m. Martin Sutton.

Margarett m. John Maxkemett.

Martha m. James Moore.

Martha m. Simon Carson.

Martha m. Joshua Temple.

Martha m. John Henry.

Martha m. Thomas Scott.

Martha m. Jo. Holland.

WILLIAMS (cont.)

Martha m. William Gainer.
Martha m. Joseph Hollowell.
Martha m. Shepherd Davis.
Martha m. William Nutt.
Martha G. m. Richard Epes.
Mary m. ___ Seward.
Mary m. Richard Attford.
Mary m. Willis Biggs.
Mary m. Thomas Williams.
Mary m. Lemuel Clark.
Mary m. Lieut. Matthew Clay.
Mary m. James Crook.
Mary m. Orlando Jones (2nd wife).
Mary m. Wm. Farrar.
Mary m. Willoughby Frizzle.
Mary m. Thomas Massie.
Mary m. Nathaniel Parish.
Mary m. Benj. Perkins.
Mary m. John Slaughter.
Mary m. John Stotts.
Mary m. John Tod.
Mary m. David Trowe.
Mary m. John Winn.
Mary m. John Wade.
Mary m. Peter Sherman.
Mary (___) m. John Williams.
Mary Ann m. Thomas Smith.
Molly m. Godfrey Shelton.
Molly m. William Tebbs.
Montague m. Patsy Waller, dau. of John of Enfield. She m. (2) Joseph H. Travis, son of Edward and (2) Clara (Waller). 5W(1)16.
Nancy m. John Pratt.
Nancy m. Jno. Hudson.
Nancy m. John Tofel.
Nancy m. ___ Sandefur.
Nancy m. Archibald Nance.
Nancy m. John Gregory.
Nancy m. John Sudduth.
Nancy m. Maj. John Wimbish.
Nathan m. 21 Dec., 1775, Sarah Brown in Henrico. Douglas Reg., p. 16.
Nathaniel, b. 1741, Hanover Co.; d. 1805, Guilford Co., No. Car.; m. Mary Ann Williamson. DAR No. 66 337.
Nicholas m. 24 Oct., 1782, Alse Aumon (Almond?) Love, by Rev. James Shelburne, Baptist. Lunenburg Co. Ministers' Returns.
Notley m. ___ Taylor, dau. of Henry, Sr., (d. 1770, Loudoun Co.) and Susanna Whitcley. 71V(2)219.
Osborn, b. 1775, Va.; d. 1854, son of Garrod (1755, Va. - 1827, Ky.); m. 1797, Sally Wade; rem. ca 1799 to Cumberland Co., Ky. Cumberland, p. 421.
Patty m. David W. Collier.
Peggy m. Nathaniel Frost.

ILLIAMS (cont.)

Peggy m. George Colly.
Peter m. 14 June, 1791, Elishe Dixon. Northampton Co. Mar. Record.
Peter m. bef. 1760, Sarah(?) Carter, dau. of Joseph, whose will of that date, Prince George Co., proves it.
Phebe m. Jesse Wallace.
Polly m. John Stevens.
Polly m. Michael Robertson.
Polly m. John Covington.
Prudence m. Hezekiah Holliday.
Rachel m. William Blake.
Rawling, b. 1754, Culpeper Co.; d. 1827, Ky.; m. Rebecca Luttrell. DAR No. 65 867; DAR No. 68 057.
Rebeccah m. George Marable.
Richard m. 1797, Sarah Beazley. Orange Co. Mar. Record.
Richard m. 1788, Nancy Rogers. Orange Co. Mar. Record.
Richard, b. 1759, Prince George Co.; d. 1819, Petersburg, Va.; m. Susan Eppes Harrison. DAR No. 85 247.
Richard m. after 1750, Martha (____) Wills, widow of Thomas. Boddie-Isle, p. 264.
Robert m. 6 May, 1737, Mary Brookes. Christ Church, p. 169.
Robert m. 18 Nov., 1800, Polly Eubank by Rev. Edward Almond. Lunenburg Co. Ministers' Returns.
Robert m. 1 April, 1771, Anne Watson. Sur. Paul Carrington. Charlotte Co. Mar. Bond.
Robert m. 10 Oct., 1774, Sarah (Lanier) Williams, dau. of Thomas Lanier and widow of Joseph. Robert rem. to Pittsylvania Co.; served in Rev. War as colonel. Mar. Bond, Oxford, No. Car. 3T139.
Robert, b. 1740, Hanover Co.; d. 1834, Suffolk, Va.; m. Sarah Lanier, b. 1748. DAR No. 79 216.
Robert m. bef. 20 Aug., 1710, ____, widow of ____ Ballenger. Proven by Court Record of that date, Essex Co.
Robert m. 24 March, 1785, Anne Waters. Norfolk Co. Mar. Record.
Robert m. 20 May, 1790, Mary (____) Warren. Norfolk Co. Mar. Record.
Robt. m. 1703, Eliza Buckskin. Henrico, p. 228.
Ruddy m. 25 May, 1796, Sarah Fisher. Shelby Co., Ky. Mar. Record.
Ruth m. John Canterbury.
S. m. James Hill.
Sacience m. John Ragsdale.
Sally m. Young Phillips.
Sally m. William Griffeth.
Sally m. Wm. Ussery.
Sally m. John Chapman.
Samuel m. 25 Sept., 1795, Sally Buster. Wythe Co. Mar. Record.
Samuel, b. 25 Nov., 1725; m. (1) 7 Nov., 1753, Sarah Haggoman, b. 23 Jan., 1732, dau. of John and Sarah (Powell); m. (2) 4 Dec., 1764, Sarah Dunton, dau. of Levin. Sur. Levin Dunton. Mar. (3) 12 Dec., 1772, Margaret Nottingham, dau. of Thomas. Sur. Thomas Nottingham. Northampton Co. Mar. Bonds. Bible Record. 31T92-3.
Samuel m. 20 Dec., 1762, Susan Ligon. Sur. Richard Jones. Amelia Co. Mar. Bond.

WILLIAMS (cont.)

Sarah m. Bryant Handley.
Sarah m. William Tyler.
Sarah m. Charles Floyd.
Sarah m. ____ Twisdale.
Sarah m. Thomas Woodlief.
Sarah m. James Chalmers.
Sarah m. George Wheatley.
Sarah m. John Twisdell. (Spelled William.)
Sarah m. James Tench.
Sarah m. Nicholas Crutchfield.
Sarah m. Reuben Lee.
Sarah m. Micajah Watkins, Jr.
Sarah G. m. Francis Epes.
Solomon m. 11 Feb., 1778, Lucy Holland, aged 21, 6 Dec., 1779. Sur. James Williams. John Holland's letter of consent to daughter's marriage. Wit. by John Massie and Thomas Haden. Goochland Co. Mar. Bond.
Sterling m. 13 Aug., 1779, Elizabeth Morgan. Sur. Peter Ellington. Amelia Co. Mar. Bond.
Steward m. 11 Dec., 1768, Sarah Roan. Christ Church, p. 198.
Susana m. Peter Lee.
Susanna m. William Major.
Susanna m. John Boulware.
Susannah m. John Nicholson.
Susannah m. Will. Brocks.
Tabitha m. Thomas McClanahan (2nd wife).
Thaddeus m. bef. 1787, Catharine Corrie, dau. of John and Catharine (Tyler) of Essex Co., whose will, prov. 1787, proves it.
Thomas m. 23 Dec., 1744, Anne Floyd. St. Paul's.
Thomas m. 13 Nov., 1744, Janet Johnson. St. Paul's.
Thomas m. 4 Sept., 17[illegible]3, Helen Murphy. St. Paul's.
Thomas m. 19 Jan., 1685/6, Isabella Roberts. Christ Church, p. 23.
Thomas, b. 1702, St. James Parish, London, England; m. 28 Aug., 1735, Rachel Freeman, b. 15 April, 1718; d. 23 July, 1746, dau. of John and Mary (____) of Willesy, Gloucester, England; bur. Old Blandford Churchyard, Petersburg, Va. 43V61; 5W(1)239; Old King William, p. 56.
Thomas m. 27 Nov., 1746, Lucy Boisseau, b. 8 Feb., 1730; d. 25 July, 1747, tombstone at Old Blandford Churchyard, near Petersburg, Va., dau. of James. 5W(1)238.
Thomas m. 14 Feb., 1791, Mary Williams. Surry Co. Mar. Record.
Thomas m. 12 Oct., 1786, Jane Charlton by Rev. John Buchanan, Henrico Parish. Henrico, p. 230.
Thomas m. 20 Dec., 1762, Elizabeth Watson. Sur. Richard Jones. Amelia Co. Mar. Bond.
Thomas m. 6 May, 1786, Elizabeth Nickolus by Rev. John Alderson, Jr. Rockingham Co. or Greenbrier Co. Ministers' Returns.
Ursula m. Richard Oldham.
William m. 8 Dec., 1743, Mildred Duncomb. St. Paul's.
William m. 10 Sept., 1789, Betty Anderson. Prince George Co. Cameron.
William m. 3 Aug., 1795, Lear Goffigon. Northampton Co. Mar. Record.

WILLIAMS (cont.)

William m. 5 Jan., 1788, Martha Reese. Prince George Co. Cameron.

William m. 21 May, 1795, Mary Watts by Rev. John Alderson, Jr. Rockingham Co. or Greenbrier Co. Ministers' Returns.

William m. 30 Dec., 1762, Elizabeth Comber, both of this parish. Douglas Reg., p. 7.

William m. bef. 8 May, 1704, Jael, dau. of James Harrison. Proven by Court Record of that date, Essex Co.

William m. Lucy Clayton. 23V103.

William m. 31 Oct., 1795, Polly Moody by Rev. John Neblett, Methodist. Lunenburg Co. Ministers' Returns.

William m. 17 Nov., 1791, Dorathea Traynham. Halifax Co. Mar. Record.

William m. 25 Nov., 1755, Lucy Terry. Halifax Co. Mar. Record.

William m. 1789, Lilly Teller. Rockbridge Co. Morton, p. 543.

William m. 11 July, 1788, Mary Jordan. Sur. Philip Greenhill. Amelia Co. Mar. Bond.

William m. 26 Oct., 1785, Canadace Meeks. Sur. William Vineset. Goochland Co. Mar. Bond.

William m. 2 July, 1784, Mary Lewis, dau. of John. Sur. Robert Lewis. Pittsylvania Co. Mar. Bond.

William m. 2 May, 1792, Leah Watlington. Norfolk Co. Mar. Record.

William m. ___ Taylor, dau. of Henry, Sr., (d. 1770, Loudoun Co.) and Susanna (Whiteley). 7W(2)219.

William L., Capt., m. Mary Gannaway, dau. of William and Elizabeth (Wright) of Buckingham Co.; res. there bef. 1793. 6W(2)246-7.

Zach. m. 20 Nov., 1755, Mary Poor, both in this parish. Douglas Reg., p. 2.

Zachariah m. 17 March, 1795, Frances Haygood. Halifax Co. Mar. Record.

WILLIAMSON

___ m. Frankie Young, dau. of Edward and Kerenhappuch (Hardaway). 8W(1) Supplement, p. 137.

___ m. Elizabeth Curd, dau. of Edward of Henrico. Proven by Deed, July, 1733, Goochland Co. 22V315.

___ m. Barnaby Godwin.

___ m. Olive Exum, dau. of Francis, whose wife's will, prov. 1752. Boddie-Isle, p. 452.

___ m. Jacob Darden.

___ thought to have m. Rebecca Jones, dau. of Thomas of Southampton Co., whose will, dated 1799, prov. 1800, Williamsburg, Va., names "daughter Rebecca Williamson."

___ m. Capt. William Ball.

___, Lt. Col., b. 1735, Bedford Co.; d. 1795, Wilkes Co., Ga.; m. Sarah Gilliam. DAR No. 51 059.

___ (___) m. John Ruffin.

Alexander of Northampton Co. m. 1642, Anne (___) Wyatt, widow of Thomas of Gloucester Co. 26T119.

Amy m. ___ Murphy.

Andrew, Brig. Gen., served in Rev. War from So. Car., believed m. Betty Tyler, dau. of John and (2) Ann (Graves) of Essex Co. 14T54.

Ann m. George Williamson.

WILLIAMSON (cont.)

Ann m. James Holley.

Anne m. David Whitehurst.

Arabella m. Capt. Thomas Carter, Jr.

Aron m. 7 June, 1683, Elizabeth Waterton. Christ Church, p. 22.

Arthur m. bef. June, 1749, Ann Exum, dau. of Mary. Proven by Wills of Mary Exum (1749) and Ann (Exum) Williamson (1752), both in Isle of Wight Co., and Will of Francis Exum (1753), Southampton Co.

Benjamin m. 9 June 17__, Amey (Clay) Green. Mar. Bond, Amelia Co., states "Amey Green." Will of William Green, rec. 1747, Amelia Co. Will of Henry Clay, Chesterfield Co., names "daughter Amey Williamson."

Benjamin m. 26 April, 1770, Mildred Hutton. Christ Church, p. 199.

Catherine m. Edward Thomas.

Catherine m. Richard Tyler (1st wife).

Charles, Capt., m. 13 Sept., 1792, Frances Henley. Princess Anne Co. Mar. Record.

Charles, Capt., m. bef. 1760, Elizabeth Walke, dau. of Thomas and Margaret (Thorowgood). 26V412; 2W(1)75.

Clara m. John Daniel.

Cornelius m. 1790, prob. Hampshire Co., Rhoda Stone, b. 1774, Culpeper Co.; res. Hampshire Co. Hartford B-9468(1), 8 Sept., 1956. Signed G. C. K.

Cuthbert, son of John and Rebecca (Chamberlayne), m. Elizabeth Allen. Free II:377.

Cuthbert, b. 1752, Charlotte Co.; d. there, 1812, son of Cuthbert and Elizabeth (Allen); m. (1) ____ Price; m. (2) 7 Sept., 1772, Charlotte Co., Susanna White. DAR No. 68 204; Free II:378.

Deborix m. 12 Dec., 1791, Patsey Roberts by Menoah Lesley. Campbell Co. Mar. Record.

Dorcas m. Solomon Butt.

Elinor m. James Brewster.

Elizabeth m. John Moseley.

Elizabeth m. ____ Joyner.

Elizabeth m. ____ Pursell.

Elizabeth m. Thomas Meriwether.

Elizabeth m. John Williams.

Elizabeth m. Edward McBride.

Elizabeth m. Rev. Wright Tucker (2nd wife).

Elizabeth m. John Adams.

Ellianor m. Augale Cummins.

Fanny (____) m. Lewis Dey.

Frances m. John Alding.

Frances m. (?)Randall Bird.

Frances m. John Macfarlan.

Frances m. William T. Walker.

Frances m. John Bryant.

Francis m. 18 Sept., 1758, Martha Mathias. Sur. John Williamson. Norfolk Co. Mar. Bond.

George, will prov. 1723, son of Dr. Robert of Isle of Wight and Joan (or Jane) (Allen); m. Hester Bridger, dau. of Col. Joseph and Hester (Pitt). Boddie-Isle, p. 426.

WILLIAMSON (cont.)

George, son of George and Hester (Bridger); rem. to Henrico Co.; m. bef. 1721, Frances Davis, dau. of Thomas, whose will of that date proves it. Boddie-Isle, p. 427.

George m. 31 Oct., 1769, Ann Williamson, dau. of Jacob. Sur. Jacob Williamson. Amelia Co. Mar. Bond.

George, physician, m. bef. 1800, Molly Temple, dau. of Benjamin and Mollie Brooke (Baylor). Proven by will of Benjamin, prov. 27 Sept., 1802. Dr. George d. by 1806. Old King Wm., p. 59. Mar. 23 March, 1797. 14W(2)55.

Gideon m. 8 Dec., 1790, Nancy Dudley. Princess Anne Co. Mar. Record.

Gracey m. Aaron Campbell.

Hannah m. Col. Richard Fox.

Henry m. bef. 25 March, 1693, Catherine Weeks (or Wooks), dau. of Abraham, dec'd., of Middlesex Co.; res. 1688, Middlesex Co. 5V168, 433. He, b. 1643; d. 1699; m. (2) Catherine Weeks. She m. (2) Capt. William Young; m. (3) Thomas Montague. 14T49.

Hester m. William Bidgood.

Hillary m. 24 Oct., 1789, Sally Whitehurst. Princess Anne Co. Mar. Record.

Jacob m. 25 Dec., 1794, Sally Ragsdale by Rev. James Shelburne, Baptist. Lunenburg Co. Ministers' Returns.

James m. 4 Nov., 1756, Susannah Weyton. OPR.

James m. 15 Jan., 1795, Kezia Thomas. Rockingham Co. Wayland, p. 7.

James m. Mary Underwood, dau. of Col. William. Dameron Part 1, p. 51-e.

James, d. bef. 8 Dec., 1656, Rappahannock Co.; a doctor, formerly res. Isle of Wight; m. Ann(-e) Underwood, dau. of Col. William and Margaret (____). 7T190; 30T84; 5V433; 7W(1)220-1; Boddie-HSF V:257; Boddie-Isle, p. 110. Her mother was Margaret (____) Underwood Upton Lucas. 40V94; 20W(1)133.

Jane (or Joan) (____) m. Robert Burnett.

Jesse m. 25 Oct., 1758, Mary Person, dau. of Thomas who gave consent. Sur. Thomas Person. Brunswick Co. Mar. Bond.

John m. 5 Nov., 1786, Martha Davis by Rev. Thomas Crymes, Baptist. Lunenburg Co. Ministers' Returns.

John, b. 1687; d. 1757; m. Rebecca Chamberlayne of New Kent Co. A son was born in 1708. Free II:375-6.

John, b. 1733; d. 1806; res. 1754, Henrico Parish; m. 1754, Sarah Price. Free II:376.

John m. 26 Nov., 1796, Dorcas Edmonds. Princess Anne Co. Mar. Record.

John m. 17 Jan., 1736, Prudence Cox. Sur. Charles Turnbull. Goochland Co. Mar. Bond. Prudence was dau. of William Cox. Proven by Deed, 3 April, 1747, Henrico Co.

John m. 19 Aug., 1795, Charity Whitaker. Shelby Co., Ky. Mar. Record.

John m. 3 Dec., 1760, Prudence Wilson. Norfolk Co. Mar. Record.

John m. Hannah Stone, b. 1779, dau. of Sgt. Benjamin and Anna (Asbury). Hartford B-9468(1), 8 Sept., 1956. Signed G. C. K.

John m. Mary Finney, dau. of Rev. William. Proven by Deed, 17 May, 1743, Goochland Co. 22V317.

WILLIAMSON (cont.)

John, Jr., m. 1 April, 1755, Mary (____) Mathias. Sur. John Williamson. Norfolk Co. Mar. Bond.
Joseph m. 7 July, 1700, Priscilla Skerme. Henrico, p. 227.
Katharine m. Henery Follwell.
Katherine m. William Young.
Lewelling m. 23 Aug., 1764, Sarah Lewis. Sur. Lewellen Jones. Amelia Co. Mar. Bond.
Malachi m. 7 March, 1793, Sarah Carol. Princess Anne Co. Mar. Record.
Margaret m. Capt. William Ball.
Margaret m. William Robinson.
Margaret m. Hugh Watts.
Mary m. Daniel Saunders.
Mary m. Thomas Stapleton.
Mary m. Henry Quarles.
Mary m. Craddock Vaughan.
Mary m. John Rozier.
Mary m. Edward Nash.
Mary Ann m. Nathaniel Williams.
Nancy m. John Skelton.
Nathan m. 1799, Elizabeth Johnson by Samuel Mitchell. Campbell Co. Mar. Record.
Patience m. Robert Exum.
Patsey m. John Roach.
Polly m. William Applewaite.
R. m. 5 Sept., 1790, Caty Pendleton. Prob. Orange Co. St. Mark's, p. 78.
Rebecca m. William Mosby.
Rebecca m. Ezekiel Cloyd.
Rebecca m. Ezekiel Rogers.
Rebecca (____) m. Buckner Lanier.
Rhoda m. Archibald Meadows.
Robert m. 13 Feb., 1726, Elizabeth Mickleburrough. Christ Church, p. 165.
Robert m. 27 Feb., 1681/2, Katherine Lewis. Christ Church, p. 20.
Robert m. 21 Dec., 1716, Elizabeth Minor. Christ Church, p. 162.
Robert m. 18 Sept., 1793, Nancy Cox. Henry Co. Mar. Record.
Robert, b. 15 Feb., 1735, son of Thomas and Judith (Fleming); m. Susannah Williamson, b. 28 Aug., 1733. Free II:377.
Robert m. 16 June, 1782, Martha Smith. Sur. Philip Smith. Chesterfield Co. Mar. Bond.
Robert m. 1781, Elizabeth Caldwell, b. 1765, dau. of James and Elizabeth (Alexander) of Ohio Co., Va.-W. Va. DAR No. 76 741.
Robert, physician, of Isle of Wight Co., m. bef. 1669, Joan (or Jane) Allen, dau. of Arthur and Alice (Tucker) of Surry Co. Proven by will of Dr. Robert Williamson, 1669, Isle of Wight Co., and deed of Arthur Allen II to his sister, Joan Proctor. She m. (2) Robert Burnett; m. (3) Reuben Proctor. Boddie-Isle, p. 426; Boddie-SVF I:1; Hines Mss., Vol. 18.
Salley m. Nathaniel Collier.
Sarah m. (1) ____ Ruffin; m. (2) John Taylor (2nd wife).
Sarah m. Thomas Gilham.

WILLIAMSON (cont.)

Susanna m. Charles Smith.

Susannah m. Robert Williamson.

Thomas, son of George and Hester (Bridger), m. Olive Exum, sister of Francis. Isle of Wight Co. Will and Deed Book 5, p. 451. Boddie-Isle, p. 427. Mar. 1749-53, Olive (Exum) Pryor. Proven by will of her mother, Mary Exum, 1749, Isle of Wight Co., and will of Francis Exum, 1753, Southampton Co.

Thomas m. 18 Feb., 1762, Afarillah Corley, both in this parish. Douglas Reg., p. 6.

Thomas, son of Arthur, dec'd., m. 17 Sept., 1785, Martha Graves, dau. of Solomon, dec'd. Sussex Co. Mar. Record. She was dau. of Sarah Graves (will, June, 1801, Sussex Co.).

Thomas m. bef. 1770, ____ McKenny, dau. of John, whose will of that date, Culpeper Co., proves it.

Thomas m. 1796, Milly Bledsoe. Orange Co. Mar. Record.

Thomas of Middlesex Co. m. bef. March, 1695, Mary (____) Dudley, widow of Thomas. Proven by Deed of that date, Middlesex Co. 5V433; 23V149.

Thomas, b. 1708, son of John and Rebecca (Chamberlayne); m. 1730, Judith Fleming, dau. of Tarleton of New Kent Co. Free II:376.

Thomas m. 20 Nov., 1766, Margaret Wilson. Norfolk Co. Mar. Record.

Thomas, b. 22 May, 1777; d. 1846; res. Norfolk, son of John and Sarah (Price); m. (1) 24 May, 1800, Elizabeth Galt, b. 7 May, 1779; d. 5 April, 1807; m. (2) Anne McClellan McCauley Walke. Free II:376.

Thomas m. 3 Dec., 1768, Mary Talbutt. Norfolk Co. Mar. Record.

Thomas Jasher m. 22 Sept., 1785, ____ McGraw. Halifax Co. Mar. Record.

Tully m. July, 1786, Tamer Sharwood by Rev. Joshua Lawrence, Baptist. Princess Anne Co. Ministers' Returns.

Walter, physician, m. 1 March, 1755, Mildred Dade. St. Paul's. She was Mildred (Washington) Dade, dau. of John Washington and widow of Langhorne Dade, whom she had married in 1743. 23V97.

William m. 23 Aug., 1686, Sarah Danger. Christ Church, p. 29.

William m. 14 Dec., 1798, Elizabeth Fentress by Rev. Anthony Walke. Princess Anne Co. Ministers' Returns.

William m. 25 Oct., 1763, Ann Mayo, both in this parish. Douglas Reg., p. 7.

William, son of George and Frances (Davis), m. 13 July, 1750, Martha Green, in Amelia Co., dau. of William and Amey (Clay). Sur. William Booker. Amelia Co. Mar. Bond. 6T42; Hines Mss., Vol. 18.

William m. Feb., 1800, Mary Smith, b. 18 Sept., 1783, Essex Co.; d. 21 March, 1814, dau. of Samuel and Mary (Webb). Family Records. 2T196.

WILLIARD

William, b. 1755, Loudoun Co.; d. 1846, McDonough Co., Ill.; m. Jane Cook. DAR No. 85 382.

WILLIFORD

____ believed m. bef. 1795, ____ Brock, dau. of Thomas, whose will of that date, Northampton Co., names "granddaughter Susanna Williford" and devises to "Belah Williford's four children, Josiah, Samuel, Susanna and William when twenty-one." Bila, son of William and

WILLIFORD (cont.)

Mary (Johnson) of Southampton Co., m. (1) Patience Brock, dau. of Thomas and Lucy (____) of the same county; m. (2) 8 Jan., 1796, Elizabeth Parker. Sur. John Tillott. Surry Co. Mar. Bond. Wilford, pp. 59-60.

Charles m. 19 March, 1799, Peggy Williford. Sur. Jesse Williford. Southampton Co. Mar. Bond.

Jesse, in Rev. War, m. (1) 11 Sept., 1783, Susanna Rowe of Southampton Co. Wilford, p. 97.

Johnson, son of William and Mary (Johnson), m. 23 April, 1785, Molley Jenkins of Southampton, dau. of Spencer, whose will, 1788, proves it. Wilford, p. 61.

Jordan, b. 30 May, 1759; d. ca 1855, Rutherford Co., Tenn., son of William and Mary (Johnson) of Southampton Co.; m. Feb., 1783, Charity Holloman of Surry Co.; rem. to Guilford Co., No. Car., and, in 1804, to Rutherford Co., Tenn. Wilford, pp. 60-61.

Mildred m. (1) ____ Kerlew; m. (2) David Crewes.

Peggy m. Charles Willeford.

William, son of John and Mary (____) of Southampton Co., m. bef. 1757, Mary Johnson, dau. of Robert of Isle of Wight Co., whose will (Book 6, p. 304) proves it.

WILLING

Maria (or Mary) m. William Byrd (2nd wife).

WILLINGHAM

Fanny m. Joshua Powell.

George m. 13 Oct., 1800, Anne Utterback, b. ca 1756, Germantown, Va., dau. of Henry and Anna (____). Utterback, p. 36.

Jarrell m. 13 Jan., 1790, Nancy Roberts, dau. of Peter (will dated 30 April, 1801). Halifax Co. Mar. Record. Halifax, p. 331.

Jeremiah m. 17 May, 1790, Tabitha Powell. Halifax Co. Mar. Record.

Jerrald m. 15 July, 1793, Rachel Boyd. Halifax Co. Mar. Record.

Mary m. Royal Daniel.

Rebeckah m. William Finch.

WILLIS

____ m. Bettie Landon, dau. of Thomas and Mary (____) of Hereford, England. She m. (2) Robert Carter. Jones, p. 160.

____ m. John Clayton.

____ m. Elizabeth Edwards, dau. of Col. Nathaniel (will dated 29 April, 1771). 28V163.

Ann m. Thomas Maclin.

Ann (or Anna) m. (1) Seth Sewell (Sethel?); m. (2) Col. John Lear (3rd wife).

Ann Rich m. Nathaniel Burwell.

Anne m. James Ward.

Alexander, Col., m. 25 Feb., 1800, Elizabeth Montague Twyman, b. 17 Aug., 1782; d. 1844, dau. of William, Jr., and Elizabeth (Garnett). She m. (2) Col. Joshua Fry. Cowherd, p. 268.

Augustine m. 28 Dec., 1772, Anne (____) Heath, widow of John. Sur. Allen Cocke. Surry Co. Mar. Bond.

Comfort m. Jacob Mills.

David m. 12 Dec., 1791, Drusilla Bragg. Halifax Co. Mar. Record.

David m. 7 April, 1791, Sarah Stapleton. Botetourt Co. Kegley, p.

WILLIS (cont.)

596.

Edmund m. 18 Jan., 1787, Frances Towles, dau. of Joseph and Sarah (Terrell). (Incorrectly transcribed as "Edward" on Culpeper Co. marriage record.) 13T28.

Edward m. 30 June, 1765, Calis Barker, both of this parish. Douglas Reg., p. 3.

Edward m. 18 Dec., 1788, Susanna Smith. Sur. George Payne. Goochland Co. Mar. Bond.

*Eleanor m. (1) Robert Allden; m. (2) ___ Kemp.

Elizabeth m. Thomas Cocke. * Elisho m. Benjamin Wilkins.

Elizabeth m. Reuben Thornton.

Elizabeth m. ___ McKain.

Elizabeth m. John Clayton.

Elizabeth m. Lawrence Duff.

Elizabeth m. Dr. John Sale.

Elizabeth Carter m. Henry Hiort.

Frances m. William Camp.

Frances m. Francis Whiting.

Frances m. Daniel James.

Frances m. (1) Thomas Marston; m. (2) ___ Camp.

Francis, Col., b. 1690, Ware Parish, Gloucester Co.; living in 1729; m. 1715, Anne Rich, b. 1696; d. 10 June, 1727, Gloucester Co., dau. of Edward. 32V63, 136; 5W(1)172.

Francis, son of Francis and Anne (Rich), m. 30 Sept., 1742, Elizabeth Carter. Abingdon Parish Register. 5W(1)172.

Francis, son of Francis and Elizabeth (Carter); of "Whitehall;" b. 20 Oct., 1744; d. 28 July, 1791; m. Elizaboth Perrin, b. 1 Aug., 1751; d. 5 Dec., 1791. 5W(1)172; 6W(1)27.

Henry, b. ca 1690; d. 1740; m. (1) 2 Nov., 1714, Anne (Alexander) Smith, widow of John Purton Smith and dau. of David Alexander of Gloucester Co.; m. (2) 30 Oct., 1726, Mildred (Howell) Brown, widow of Dr. John Brown and dau. of John Howell; m. (3) 5 Jan., 1733/4 (date of marriage contract regarding land, Spotsylvania Co.), Mildred (Washington) Gregory, d. 5 Sept., 1747, widow of Roger Gregory and dau. of Lawrence and Mildred (Reade) Washington. 32V136; 56V48; Boddie-HSF IV:161.

Henry, Jr., of Spotsylvania Co., m. 29 April, 1743, Elizabeth Gregory. Spotsylvania Co. Mar. Record. He, son of Col. Henry and (3) Mildred (Washington) Gregory; she, dau. of Roger and Mildred (Washington), m. (2) Reuben Thornton; m. (3) Dr. Thomas Walker; m. (4) Col. Alcock. 5V163; 2W(2)134; Old King Wm., p. 58.

Jacobina m. Hamilton Jones.

Jemima m. David Lykins.

Jemima m. John Woodhal.

John, b. 17 Aug., 1724, son of Col. Harry of "Willis Hall," near Fredericksburg, Va.; m. Elizabeth Madison; b. 1725; d. 1773, dau. of Ambrose. She m. (2) Richard Beale. 4V463; 8W(1)98; Br., p. 8; Winston, p. 232. She, dau. of Col. James. 4V463.

John, will prov. 26 Jan., 1769, Brunswick Co., son of Francis; m. 26 Jan., 1743, Mildred Smith, b. 22 Sept, 1719; will prov. 27 Feb., 1769, Brunswick Co., dau. of Augustine and Sarah (Carver) of "Shoot-

WILLIS (cont.)
er's Hill," Middlesex Co. 4W(1)49; 6W(1)28; 25W(1)187; Harllee III: 2651.
John of Richmond Co. m. bef. 10 Aug., 1699, Mary Coghill, dau. of James. Proven by Court Record of that date, Essex Co.
John m. Matilda Thacker. Mar. agreement, 22 July, 1693, Richmond Co.
John, b. 24 Oct., 1774, son of Francis and Elizabeth (Perrin); m. Nelly C. Madison. 6W(1)27.
John m. 27 April, 1772, Sally Thomas. Orange Co. Mar. Record.
John, d. 1762, Orange Co., son of William and Sarah (____) of Richmond Co. and King George Co.; m. 17 Jan., 1734/5, Elizabeth Plunkett of Hanover Parish. Orange III:98; St. Paul's.
Josiah m. 18 Feb., 1788, Elizabeth White, dau. of Lovin. Northampton Co. Mar. Record.
Judith m. William Marshall.
Lewis of Fredericksburg, Va., served as Lieut.-Col. in Rev. War; m. (1) Mary Champe, dau. of Col. John and Jane (____) of King George Co.; m. (2) 1775, Ann (Carter) Champe, widow of John, Jr., and dau. of Charles Carter of "Cleve;" m. (3) ____ ____. 24T217-8; 31V58; 38V365.
Lewis, son of John and Elizabeth (Plunkett), m. Edna Tilman; res. 1816, Ga. Orange III:100.
Lucy m. Jesse Clark.
Margaret m. Edmund Terrill.
Margaret Ann m. Gen. John Cowper Cohoon.
Marrat m. 23 April, 1790, Sally Freshwater. Northampton Co. Mar. Record.
Mary m. Col. William Daingerfield.
Mary m. John Redd.
Mary m. Capt. James Cole.
Mary m. Richard Price.
Mary m. Lewis Burwell.
Mary m. Hancock Lee.
Mary (____) m. Matthew Bentley.
Mildred m. Landon Carter.
Moses m. 1781, Elizabeth Thomas. Orange Co. Mar. Record. He d. 1806, son of John and Elizabeth (Plunkett); m. (2) Susannah White. Orange III:100.
Nancy m. Nathaniel Burwell (2nd wife).
Nancy m. Daniel Maddox.
Parker m. 15 Dec., 1795, Sarah Goffigon. Northampton Co. Mar. Record.
Parker m. 27 July, 1797, Elishe Costin. Northampton Co. Mar. Record.
Peggy m. Edmund Terrill.
Pleasants m. 10 Dec., 1774, Sally Read, both in Henrico. Douglas Reg., p. 15.
Priscilla m. (1) Col. William Kennon; m. (2) David Flower.
Rachel m. Severn Widgeon.
Reuben m. 1776, Ann Garnett. Orange Co. Mar. Record. He, son of John and Elizabeth (Plunkett); she, dau. of Robert and Lucy (Stokeley); res. 1815, Orange Co. 13T30; Orange III:98. Given in one reference as Ann Garrett.

WILLIS (cont.)

Richard, inv. 1700, Middlesex Co., son of Thomas; m. (1) Dorothy ____; m. (2) Ann (____) Griggs, widow of Michael; m. (3) Betty Landon, dau. of Thomas of Middlesex Co. 5V251.

Sallie m. John Freeman.

Sally m. Thomas Aldridge Sikes.

Sarah m. Walter Shropshire.

Sarting m. 26 April, 1779, Sarah Payne, dau. of William. Sur. Jos. Akin. Pittsylvania Co. Mar. Bond.

Stephen, b. 1760, Va.; d. 1820, Ohio, son of Stephen; m. 1782, Martha Wherry, b. 1761, Va.; d. 1846, Ill. DAR Query 14209(a).

Stephen m. Anna (Lewis) Terrell, b. 1733; d. 1835, Rutherford Co., No. Car., widow of Joel Terrell and dau. of David Lewis. Jones, p. 189.

Sterling. See Sarting.

Susannah m. Andrew Douglass.

Susannah m. Joseph Walker.

Susannah m. Moses Crawford.

Thomas m. 1 Sept., 1792, Anne Knight. Northampton Co. Mar. Record.

Thomas m. 11 Aug., 1794, Elishe Groves, dau. of Peter. Northampton Co. Mar. Record.

Thomas m. 3 May, 1777, Mary Blake. Christ Church, p. 201.

William m. 1 Sept., 1775, Margaret Ellegood. Northampton Co. Mar. Record.

William of Westmoreland Co. m. bef. Jan., 1711/2, Mary Kirk, dau. of Thomas (d. bef. 1711). Proven by Deed of that date, Essex Co.

William m. Elizabeth Garnett, d. 4 Jan., 1835, age 90, dau. of Anthony and Elizabeth (____). Orange III:49.

William, b. 22 Feb., 1742, son of John and Elizabeth (Plunkett); m. ____ ____; res. Ky., 1816, when will of his bro., Benjamin Willis, was probated. Orange III:100.

William m. 3 Jan., 1788, Smart Dunton, dau. of Elias, dec'd. Northampton Co. Mar. Record.

William m. 23 June, 1685, Bridget Robinson. Christ Church, p. 23.

William Champe of Orange Co. m. Lucy Taliaferro, dau. of Richard (d. 1747) and Jane (Bankhead). 11T27; 9W(2)311.

WILLISON

James m. 25 Nov., 1777, Mary Janson. Sur. William Short. Surry Co. Mar. Bond. James, b. 15 Feb., 1751, Glasgow, Scotland; d. 1786, Surry Co.; m. Mary I'Anson, dau. of John and Lucy (Cocke) of Surry Co. 28V67; Boddie-SVF I:150.

John, b. 22 Oct., 1778, son of James, the immigrant; m. 26 Aug., 1805, Mary Burridge Dandridge, dau. of Bartholomew Dandridge of New Kent Co, 28V67.

Margaret Dunbar m. Colin Campbell.

WILLISTON

Annie m. Matthew Talbot.

Mary m. Matthew Talbot (1st wife).

WILLITT

Douglas m. 21 June, 1760, Henrietta Johnson, dau. of John, dec'd. Northampton Co. Mar. Record.

WILLMORE

John m. 19 July, 1794, Patty Taylor. Caroline Co. Mar. Record.

Judith m. Paul Michaux.

WILLMUT

Fanny m. John Belsher.

WILLOUGHBY

____ m. Rev. Moses Robertson.

Andrew, b. 1717; one of the founders of Abingdon, Va.; m. Elizabeth Wallace (or Wallis), b. 1729. DAR Query 15498, Oct., 1935.

Elizabeth m. Henry Edwards.

Elizabeth m. (1) Simon Oversee (2nd wife); m. (2) Maj. George Colclough.

Elizabeth m. John Breckenridge.

Hanform m. 2 July, 1794, Julian Kinsey. Princess Anne Co. Mar. Record.

Henry, d. bef. March, 1674/5; m. Joane (____) Hitchcock Henly, widow 1st of Robert Hitchcock, 2nd of Edward Henly. Proven by Court Record of that date, Northumberland Co.

John, Maj., m. 21 April, 1756, Sarah Abyvon. Sur. George Abyvon. Norfolk Co. Mar. Bond.

John m. 26 Dec., 1743, Mary Hutchings. Sur. Lemuel Willoughby. Norfolk Co. Mar. Bond.

John m. 1787, Sarah Mansfield by Rev. Joshua Lawrence. Princess Anne Co. Ministers' Returns.

John m. Nancy Walke, dau. of Thomas and Margaret (Thorowgood). 2W(1) 75.

Lem m. 18 Sept., 1751, Martha Sweeny. Norfolk Co. Mar. Record.

Lemuel m. 23 June, 1791, Elizabeth Wells. Norfolk Co. Mar. Record.

Margaret m. Thomas West.

Margaret m. John Porter.

Margaret m. Jesse Newcomb.

Mary m. Rev. Moses Robertson.

Sally m. James Cash.

Thomas, Col., b. 25 Dec., 1632, Va.; d. 1672, son of Capt. Thomas; m. ca 1660, Sarah Thompson, b. bef. 1649, dau. of Richard and Ursula (Bissho). Proven by Deed, 1661, Westmoreland Co. 9T266; 1 V448; 34V287.

Thomas of Lower Norfolk m. Margaret Herbert. 1V449.

Thomas, Capt., m. bef. 1744, Ann Mason, dau. of Thomas. 4V85; 5V182.

Thomas m. 11 Dec., 1755, Mary Portlock. Sur. Lemuel Willoughby. Norfolk Co. Mar. Bond.

Thomas m. 1790, Fanney Wright by Rev. Joshua Lawrence. Princess Anne Co. Ministers' Returns.

Thomas, Jr., m. 1788, Anne Sillivant by Rev. Joshua Lawrence. Princess Anne Co. Ministers' Returns.

WILLS

____ m. Sarah Hope, b. 25 July, 1777. Family Bible. 8W(1)258.

____ m. Peachy (Davenport) Purdie Holt, widow 1st of Alexander Purdie, 2nd of William Holt and dau. of Joseph Davenport of Williamsburg, Va. 7W(1)17.

____ m. Polly Pendleton, dau. of Reuben. She m. (2) ____ Seay; m. (3) ____ Nowlin. Slaughter, p. 151.

WILLS (cont.)

Ann m. William Moseley.

Ann Whitlock m. John Minor.

Barshaba m. Thomas Darden.

Betty m. Thomas Cobbs.

Elijah m. 1798, Elizabeth Ragsdale by Rev. Matthew Dance. Lunenburg Co. Ministers' Returns.

Elizabeth m. Joel Mann. (?Elizabeth Mills)

Elizabeth m. ___ Whiteworth.

Elizabeth m. Lemuel Willoughby.

Emanuel from Bristol, England, m. Elizabeth Cary, dau. of Col. Miles Cary, emigrant from Bristol. 25T55.

Filmer m. 24 May, 1755, Elizabeth Rebecca Green. Sur. Abr. Green. Amelia Co. Mar. Bond. She, prob. dau. of Abram and Elizabeth (Cowles). 5T137.

Hannah m. Col. Brewer Godwin.

John m. 10 Nov., 1791, Lucy W. Barclay by Rev. John Waller. Louisa Co. Ministers' Returns.

John m. bef. 1711, Eliza (___) Harwood, widow of Thomas. Proven by Court Suit of that date, York Co. 1W(1)96.

John B. m. 4 Feb., 1797, Susanna Howard. Shelby Co., Ky. Mar. Record.

Josiah m. 11 Dec., 1797, Patsey Uzzell. Isle of Wight Co. Mar. Record.

Katy m. John Drinkwater.

Martha m. Col. Thomas Marston Green.

Martha (___) m. Richard Williams.

Mary m. John Cole.

Mary m. James Cole.

Mary Ann m. Robert Greenhow.

Matthew m. 20 May, 1795, Elizabeth Cousins. Sur. Jas. Worsham. Amelia Co. Mar. Bond.

Matthew m. 12 Dec., 1788, Martha "Patsy" Daniel, dau. of Abraham, who gave consent. Sur. Leonard Daniel. Cumberland Co. Mar. Bond.

Matthew m. 15 March, 1793, Lucy Walthall. Sur. Abraham Green. Amelia Co. Mar. Bond.

Matthew of Warwick Co. m. Lucy Jones, dau. of Allen (d. after 1787) and Lucy (Moss). 6T52.

Matthew of Warwick Co. m. Mary (Armistead) Tabb, widow of Thomas Tabb. She m. (3) ca 1762, Robert Armistead of Elizabeth City Co. 7W(1)47.

Miles, Capt., of Warwick Co., son of Emmanuel and Elizabeth (Cary) of Bristol, England; m. ca 1692, Hannah Scarsbrook, dau. of Lt.-Col. John and Elizabeth (___) Bushrod Scarsbrook. 24W(1)200.

Mina Ann m. Caleb Cobbs.

Moses m. 15 Feb., 1723, Patience Chapman, dau. of John and Frances (Ward). Boddie-Isle, p. 280.

Nancey m. Josiah Barry.

Nancy m. William Bentley.

Nathaniel m. 18 Aug., 1791, Mary Podin. Isle of Wight Co. Mar. Record.

Nathaniel m. 28 Feb., 1786, Mildred Comer by H. J. Burgess. Surry Co. Mar. Record.

WILLS (cont.)
Polly m. Dudley Whitaker.
Prudence m. John Harvey.
Rebecca m. ____ Cole.
Sally Goodwin m. James Gray.
Thomas m. 5 Nov., 1793, Anne Gray. Isle of Wight Co. Mar. Record.
Thomas, Capt., b. 1738, Warwick Co.; d. 1802, Va.; m. Angelica Cary. DAR No. 68 650.
Thomas m. 25 Sept., 1773, Sarah Dean. Christ Church, p. 200.
Thomas Tabb m. 14 June, 1774, Elizabeth Ridley Morgan, dau. of Samuel. Sur. John Morgan. Amelia Co. Mar. Bond.
William m. 13 Jan., 1785, Mary Watkins. Dinwiddie Co. Cameron. He, son of Filmer and Rebecca (Green). 5T137.
Willis m. 10 Feb., 1774, Constant Harrison. Isle of Wight Co. Mar. Record.

WILLSON
Ann m. John Sinclair.
Ann (____) m. John Moseley, Jr.
Daniel, Jr., m. 28 Feb., 1776, Ann Finney. Sur. T. B. Willson. Ameli Co. Mar. Bond.
Elizabeth m. Nathaniel Wilkinson.
Fenelson R., b. 14 Feb., 1768, England; d. 1838; m. 14 April, 1794, Elizabeth Trabue, b. 29 Feb., 1768; d. 6 Aug., 1835, dau. of John James Trabue and Olympe (Dupuy). 17 Ky. Reg. 50:58.
Frances m. John Beevers.
James m. Caty Collins, dau. of Thomas, Jr. (d. 1781, Caroline Co.). Collins, pp. 16, 26.
John m. Oct., 1794, Sally French. Amelia Co. Mar. Record.
Lucy m. William Walthall.
Nancy m. Andrew Walkup.
Peter m. 2 May, 1796, Patsy Tanner. Sur. William W. Hall. Amelia Co. Mar. Bond.
Thomas Branch m. 28 Feb., 1760, Eliza Finney. Sur. Daniel Willson. Amelia Co. Mar. Bond.
Thomas Branch m. 1 April, 1782, Sarah Walthall. Sur. John T. Peachey. Amelia Co. Mar. Bond.
William m. Lucinda Collins, d. bef. 1797, dau. of John and Mary (Carr) of Caroline Co. Collins, p. 21.
William m. 11 Feb., 1795, Delphia Foster. Caroline Co. Mar. Record.
William m. 28 April, 1769 (or 1767), Frances Cousins. Sur. John Cousins. Amelia Co. Mar. Bond.

WILLY
Henry m. 2 Jan., 1790, Elizabeth Tinsley. Caroline Co. Mar. Record. (?Henry Wiley)

WILMANS
Lewis m. 27 Feb., 1798, Mrs. Sally Young. Sur. George Haynes. Norfolk Co. Mar. Bond.

WILMORE
Judith m. John Paul Michaux.

WILSON
____ m. ____ Mahan, dau. of Patrick. Ky. Papers, p. 259.
____ m. George Brent.

WILSON (cont.)

____ m. (1) Lazarus Sweny; m. (2) Maximilian Boush.

____ m. Jean Wallace, dau. of Andrew and Margaret (Woods). Albemarle, p. 336.

____ m. bef. 1803, Sarah Corprew, dau. of George Durant Corprew. 2W (1)76.

____ m. by 1771, Eleanor Mitchell. Rockbridge Co. Morton, p. 545.

____ m. Elizabeth Patton, dau. of James (d. 1814). Rockbridge Co. Morton, p. 517.

____ m. Susanna Pendleton, dau. of Nathaniel. Slaughter, p. 154.

____ m. Nancy Caruthers, b. 1779; d. 1857, dau. of William and Ann (____). Rockbridge Co. Morton, p. 478.

____ m. bef. 1777, Agnes Kirkpatrick. Rockbridge Co. Morton, p. 545.

____ m. by 1787, Katron Reid. Rockbridge Co. Morton, p. 545.

____ m. Tabitha Mason, dau. of Col. Lemuel and Ann (Seawell). Hartford B-8420, 19 Nov., 1955. Signed W. M.

____ m. Samuel Eakin.

____ m. Alexander McKinley.

____ m. bef. 1798, Elizabeth (____) Vick, widow of Joshua. Proven by Court Record of that date, Southampton Co.

____ m. Sabina Stuart, dau. of David (d. ca 1767, Augusta Co.). She m. (2) ____ Williams. Waddell, p. 370.

____ m. Ann (Kennedy). She m. (2) 1760, William Poage (d. 1778, Ky.); m. (3) Joseph Lindsey; m. (4) James McGinty. 11 Ky. Reg. 31:101; Waddell, p. 324.

____ (____) m. Capt. John Moon.

Abraham, b. 1759, Spotsylvania Co.; d. there, 10 Aug., 1841; served in Rev. War from Culpeper Co.; m. 10 Nov., 1794, Spotsylvania Co., Elizabeth Stears by Rev. Alexander Boggs, Episcopal. Sur. John Stears. Elizabeth, b. ca 1766; d. 9 May, 1849. Pension W6532, Va.

Affiah m. George Newton.

Agnes m. Col. Peter Perkins.

Agnes m. Col. Ralph Humphreys.

Agnes m. Andrew Walkup.

Alexander m. 16 Oct., 1799, Mary Cunningham. Sur. Robert Barron. Norfolk Co. Mar. Bond.

Alexander m. 8 Nov., 1787, Mary Dickson by Rev. John Alderson, Jr. Rockingham Co. or Greenbrier Co. Ministers' Returns.

Andrew m. 1789, Lottie Porter, Rockbridge Co. Morton, p. 543.

Andrew m. 24 Feb., 1791, Janey Hutchison by Rev. John Alderson, Jr. Rockingham Co. or Greenbrier Co. Ministers' Returns.

Ann m. Charles Williams.

Ann m. Thomas Estes.

Ann m. Thomas Harvey.

Ann m. Andrew Taylor.

Ann m. William Morris.

Anna m. John Swann.

Anne m. John Groves.

Aphia m. George Newton.

Benjamin m. 27 Feb., 1757, Alinda McDonald. St. Paul's.

Benjamin m. 25 March, 1754, Mary Ann(-e) Seay, dau. of James, whose consent was dated 20 Dec., 1754. Sur. Thomas Tabb. Cumberland Co.

WILSON (cont.)

Mar. Bond. Benjamin, b. 26 Dec., 1733, at estate of his grandfather, Benjamin Goodrich; d. 27 Oct., 1814, son of Willis; m. Anne Seay, d. 26 April, 1814, dau. of James, a Huguenot, near York River. 25V200.

Benjamin, Col., b. 1747, Shenandoah Co.; d. 1827, Harrison Co.; m. 1795, Phoebe Davisson, b. 1777; d. 1849. DAR No. 66 499. Phoebe Ann Davison, dau. of Ensign Hezekiah and Ann (___), was 2nd wife of Benjamin Wilson. DAR No. 85 708.

Betsey m. Henry Fitchew.

Betty m. Samuel Hight (Hite).

Bridgett m. Thomas Newman, Jr.

Buddy m. Michael Sullivan.

Caleb m. 1738, Mrs. Ann Church. Sur. Willis Wilson, Jr. Norfolk Co. Mar. Bond.

Catherine m. Aaron Owens.

Charles m. 16 June, 1780, Rachel Clarke. Sur. John Wilson. Amelia Co. Mar. Bond.

Christian m. Elizabeth Hansford (1st husband), dau. of John of York Co. 7T278; 5V452.

David, b. 1761; d. 1831; m. Eleanor McClure, dau. of Andrew. Wilson and McClure families res. in Augusta Co. She d. 25 March, 1843; both bur. John Gilmore graveyard on Edward West farm, Jessamine Co., Ky. Ky. Cem. 1:240.

David m. 1799, Betsy Patton. Rockbridge Co. Morton, p. 543.

David m. 19 May, 1791, Sarah Steel by Rev. John Brown. Augusta Co. Ministers' Returns.

Eleanor m. (1) ____ Dedman; m. (2) David Walker Pettus.

Eleanor m. Joseph Walkup.

Elias m. after 1700, Mary (Lane) Mountjoy, widow of Alvin and dau. of William Lane. She m. (3) Dr. Joseph Belfield. Barton II:121.

Elishe (____) m. Thomas Owen.

Eliza m. Lazarus Sweeny.

Elizabeth m. Isaac Luke.

Elizabeth m. Jonathan Clark.

Elizabeth m. James Blain.

Elizabeth m. Maj. William Crocker.

Elizabeth m. Benjamin McReynolds.

Elizabeth m. James Blair.

Elizabeth m. William Paxton.

Elizabeth m. Edward Mosby.

Elizabeth m. John Carson.

Elizabeth m. Solomon Smith.

Elizabeth m. John Lindsay.

Elizabeth m. Henry Tregany.

Elizabeth m. John Griffin.

Elizabeth m. William Campbell.

Elizabeth m. William Nusum (or Newsom) (3rd wife).

Elizabeth m. James Smith.

Ellender m. Samuel Martin.

Esther m. Robert Tart.

Euphan m. John Corprew.

Euphan m. John Hunter (1st wife).

WILSON (cont.)

Frances m. Joshua Matthias.
Frances (____) m. John Woodley.
Frances G. m. Joel Hickman.
George m. 19 March, 1789, Mary Ann Banister. Petersburg. Cameron.
George m. 17 Oct., 1789, Dinny Browder. Prince George Co. Cameron.
Hagar m. Robert Wallers.
Hannah m. Dr. Charles Clay.
Hannah m. Matthews Potter.
Henry m. 1782, Ky., Frances Faulconer, b. 1763, dau. of John and Joyce (Craig). Wilcoxson, p. 390.
Hugh m. 1792, Elizabeth Miller. Rockbridge Co. Morton, p. 543.
Hugh m. 1793, Sarah Finley. Rockbridge Co. Morton, p. 485.
Isaac m. 18 Aug., 1785, Susanna Mathews. Halifax Co. Mar. Record.
James m. 16 Oct., 1786, Agnes Pickett. Caroline Co. Mar. Record.
James, b. 1715, Augusta Co.; d. 1809, Adams Co., Ohio; m. Rebekah Wilson, b. 1728; d. 1820. DAR No. 79 040.
James m. 10 Aug., 1770, Mary Wilson. Norfolk Co. Mar. Record.
James m. bef. 1793, Margaret Pharr, dau. of Edward and Rachel (Board) of Bedford Co., Va., No. Car., and Ga. Pharr, p. 238.
James m. 26 Dec., 1766, Sarah Gray. Sur. Benjamin Dingly Gray. Princess Anne Co. Mar. Bond.
James m. 26 Aug., 1788, Agnes McKee by Rev. William Graham. Rockbridge Co. Ministers' Returns.
James m. 21 Feb., 1786, Loucresta Sturgen by Rev. John Alderson, Jr. Rockingham Co. or Greenbrier Co. Ministers' Returns.
James m. 11 Feb., 1781, Susannah Pendleton, dau. of Nathaniel and Elizabeth (Clayton) Anderson Pendleton of Culpeper Co. 40V295.
James m. 20 Aug., 1725, Dinah Nickason. Sur. Solomon Wilson. Norfolk Co. Mar. Bond.
James, Sr., m. 20 July, 1724, Grace Phillips. Sur. Willis Wilson. Norfolk Co. Mar. Bond.
James, Jr., m. 16 Dec., 1743, Grace Duke. Willis Wilson, bro. of James, Jr., certified as to age of Grace Duke. Norfolk Co. Mar. Record.
James, Jr., b. Jan., 1693; m. bef. 25 April, 1728, Sarah Nock, dau. of Thomas and Jane (Eyre). 19T422.
Jane m. Cornelius Vanosdale.
Jane m. Col. Nicholas Curle.
Jane m. (1) Nicholas Curle; m. (2) James Ricketts; m. (3) Merritt Sweeney.
Jane m. Richard Gross.
Jane m. George Humphrey (1st wife).
Jane "Jenny" m. John Paxton.
Jenny m. William Caruthers.
Jeremiah, b. 1762, Albemarle Co.; m. Rhoda Sutton; rem. to Ky. DAR Query 13573(b), Nov., 1930.
Joane m. Peter Garland.
John, d. 1754; m. Anna Adair. Rockbridge Co. Morton, p. 544.
John m. ca 1756, Sarah Alexander. Morton, p. 544.
John m. 16 Aug., 1748, Ann Asberry. OPR.
John m. 7 Feb., 1752, Sarah Brooks. OPR.

WILSON (cont.)

John m. 21 May, 1799, Mrs. Mary Brown. Sur. John Trimble. Norfolk Co. Mar. Bond.

John m. 1796, Ann E. Davidson. Rockbridge Co. Morton, p. 481.

John m. 11 Oct., 1792, Lucy French. Sur. Thomas Wilson. Amelia Co. Mar. Bond.

John m. 28 Oct., 1759, Anne Lambert. St. Paul's.

John m. bef. 1740, Pittsylvania Co., Mary Lumpkin. DAR No. 85 158.

John m. 1792, Elizabeth Miller. Rockbridge Co. Morton, p. 544.

John m. 1795, Sally Miller. Rockbridge Co. Morton, p. 544.

John m. 18 Sept., 1780, Elizabeth Moore, dau. of John, who gave consent. Sur. Andrew Baker. Prince Edward Co. Mar. Bond.

John m. 1793, Prudence Munro. Shelby, p. 239.

John, b. 30 Nov., 1750, Md.; enlisted in Rev. War from Albemarle Co.; m. 9 April, 1812, Pulaski Co., Ky., Elizabeth Snead, d. after 1853. Data from Pension W2391.

John m. 14 Feb., 1772, Priscilla Tront, dau. of Henry, who gave consent. Sur. Benjamin Wilson. Cumberland Co. Mar. Bond.

John m. 6 April, 1786, Rachel Wilson. Augusta Co. Mar. Record.

John m. 12 Feb., 1750/1, Jane Wood. St. Paul's.

John m. 2 Aug., 1784, Mary Wormington, dau. of Abram. Norfolk Co. Mar. Record.

John Buckner, b. 28 May, 1776, Augusta Co.; m. Elizabeth Patterson of Penna. Hartford B-7389, 22 Jan., 1955. Signed W. F. A.

John M. m. Sally Moore, dau. of Andrew (d. 1791). Rockbridge Co. Morton, p. 512.

Joshua, b. 1759, Westmoreland Co.; d. 1822, Clarke Co., Ala.; m. Barbara ____, d. 1848. DAR No. 89 298.

Josiah m. 14 Feb., 1796, Elizabeth Matthias. Princess Anne Co. Mar. Record.

Judith m. Richard Weeks.

Judy m. Thomas Link.

Lemuel m. 1789, Abiah Alderson by Rev. Joshua Lawrence. Princess Anne Co. Ministers' Returns.

Lemuel. Admx. was Dinah (____), who later m. William Trevethan. Proven by Court Record, 12 Jan., 1713, Princess Anne Co. 26V415.

Lucy m. John Hood.

Lydia m. John Bailey.

Margaret m. Joseph Bennett Bradford (2nd wife).

Margaret m. George Daniel.

Margaret m. James Russell.

Margaret m. Thomas Williamson.

Margaret (____) m. Richard Sparrow.

Margret m. William Asten.

Margrett m. John Hill.

Martha m. John Buchanan.

Martha m. William Reynolds.

Martha m. Thomas Board.

Mary m. James Wilson.

Mary m. Charles Smith.

Mary m. Thomas Smith.

Mary m. James Meggs.

WILSON (cont.)

Mary m. Gilbert McNary.
Mary m. (1) William Roscow; m. (2) Col. Miles Cary; m. (3) Archibald Blair.
Mary m. Thomas Munford.
Mary (____) m. Paul Phaben.
Mazais m. Robert Waller.
Moses m. 29 April, 1790, Martha Rickey by Rev. John Alderson, Jr. Rockingham Co. or Greenbrier Co. Ministers' Returns.
Nancy m. Matthew Floyd.
Nathaniel m. 19 May, 1793, Susannah Stephens. Henry Co. Mar. Record.
Nelly m. William Lord.
Nice m. Jacob Wingate.
Nicholas m. bef. 9 April, 1689, Margaret Sampson, dau. of James, whose will prov. on that date, Isle of Wight Co., proves it. He m. (1) bef. 1678, ____ (____) Tooker, widow of William of Surry Co. Wilson, p. 3.
Patsey m. Robert Jones.
Patsy m. James Cannon.
Peggy m. James Watson.
Peggy m. Thomas Goffigon.
Peter in Pittsylvania m. 18 April, 1775, Sally Ellis in Henrico. Douglas Reg., p. 16.
Phebe m. ____ Snead.
Polly m. James Myers.
Polly m. Stephen Smith.
Polly m. John Lucas.
Prudence m. Solomon Smith.
Prudence m. John Williamson.
Prudence m. Nathaniel Tatum.
Rachel m. John Wilson.
Rachel m. Capt. Thomas Petty.
Randolph m. 4 Aug., 1788, Lucy Goldsmith. Louisa, p. 259.
Rebecca m. Simon Smith.
Rebekah m. James Wilson.
Richard m. 12 April, 1781, Mary Rogers by Rev. John Alderson, Jr. Rockingham Co. or Greenbrier Co. Ministers' Returns.
Richard m. 31 Oct., 1722, Anne Smith. St. Paul's.
Richard m. Ellen Douglas Ruffin. 5V202.
Robert m. 8 Oct., 1786, Betty Payne. Christ Church, p. 205.
Robert m. bef. March, 1705/6, ____ (____) Oliver, widow of John. Proven by Court Record of that date, Northumberland Co.
Robert m. 21 May, 1789, Sarah Tolbert. Halifax Co. Mar. Record.
Robert m. 19 April, 1787, Patience Cumbo. Halifax Co. Mar. Record.
Sally m. Charles Gee.
Sally m. John Hall.
Sally m. Mathias Swink.
Samuel m. ca 1790, Eleanor Alexander. Rockbridge Co. Morton, p. 545.
Samuel m. Priscilla Fleming, dau. of Col. William (d. 1795) and ____ (Christian) of Augusta and Botetourt counties. Waddell, p. 182.
Samuel m. Rebecca Burk, dau. of James and 1st wife. Kegley, pp. 195, 620.

WILSON (cont.)

Samuel m. 25 March, 1760, Peggy Custis, dau. of Ann Tompkins. Northampton Co. Mar. Record.

Samuel, d. ca 1710, Norfolk Co.; m. ___ Mason. 25V199.

Sarah m. John T. Howard.

Sarah m. James Patton.

Sarah m. Jonathan Neall.

Sarah m. Andrew Taylor.

Sarah m. John Welch.

Sarah m. John Logan.

Sarah m. Benjamin J. Brice.

Sarah m. Capt. Robert Hatton.

Sarah m. Stockley Wilson.

Sary m. Arthur Ferguson.

Sibna m. James Williams.

Simon m. 16 Aug., 1792, Sarah Warden. Norfolk Co. Mar. Record.

Soloman m. 1787, Isle of Wight Co., Ann Riddick. 40V169.

Spencer m. 22 Sept., 1774, Frances Watts, dau. of Thomas, dec'd. Northampton Co. Mar. Record.

Spencer m. 17 May, 1788, Nancy Stott, dau. of Thomas, dec'd. Northampton Co. Mar. Record.

Spicer m. Jane Clark, b. 1764; d. 1821, dau. of William and Sarah (Wharton). 13T34.

Stephen m. bef. 1796, Jane Dinwiddie, dau. of Robert, whose will of that date, Bath Co., proves it.

Stockley m. 21 Sept., 1785, Sarah Wilson. Northampton Co. Mar. Record.

Stockley m. 19 April, 1787, Smart Wilkins. Northampton Co. Mar. Record.

Susan m. Lieut. William Jones.

Susanna m. Levin Widgeon.

Tabitha m. Obadiah Smith.

Tabitha m. William Freeman.

Theadocia m. Benjamin Johnston.

Thomas m. 27 April, 1679, Mary Seers. Christ Church, p. 18.

Thomas m. 15 Aug., 1798, Anne Dinwiddie by Rev. Archibald McRoberts. Campbell Co. Ministers' Returns.

Thomas m. 3 Aug., 1786, Jennet Wallace by Rev. Edw. Crawford. She, dau. of Peter Wallace, dec'd. John Wallace gave consent. Rockbridge Co. Ministers' Returns.

Thomas, b. 1766, Va.; d. 24 Jan., 1826; m. Mary "Polly" Poage, dau. of Thomas; res. Monongalia Co. Dames, p. lxxviii; Waddell, p. 260.

Warren m. Mary Price; rem. to Ky. A son, b. 1782. 41V255.

William m. bef. 1800, Ann Parks. Augusta Co. Mar. Record.

William m. 10 Feb., 1795, Molly Spady, dau. of Abraham. Northampton Co. Mar. Record.

William, b. 1722; m. 1746, in Shenandoah Valley, Margaret Blackburn. 27V369.

William, Col., m. Jane ___. Winston, p. 339.

William m. 16 Sept., 1698, Jane Davis. Elizabeth City Co. Mar. Record.

William, minister, m. Elizabeth Poage, dau. of Thomas and Polly (McClanahan); res. Augusta Co. Waddell, p. 260.

WILSON (cont.)

William m. 7 Feb., 1787, Caty Jett Hardwick. Halifax Co. Mar. Record.

William m. 7 Jan., 1796, Jane Griffen. Halifax Co. Mar. Record.

William m. 1791, Eleanor Lackey. Rockbridge Co. Morton, p. 545.

William m. 14 April, 1788, Elizabeth Robinson. Louisa Co. Mar. Record.

William m. 22 June, 1780, Mary Dix, dau. of James. Sur. Hezekiah Smith. Pittsylvania Co. Mar. Bond.

William, Jr., m. 18 Nov., 1797, Adah Pratt. Northampton Co. Mar. Record.

William Bishop m. 17 May, 1790, Nancy Freshwater. Northampton Co. Mar. Record.

William W. m. 14 Jan., 1795, Peggy Custis Tompkins. Northampton Co. Mar. Record.

Willis of Princess Anne Co., Master of a merchant ship, d. 1740; m. ca 1732, Elizabeth Goodrich, dau. of Benjamin of James City Co. 25V200; 32V61; 39V136. Mar. 7 June, 1728. Sur. Solomon Wilson. Norfolk Co. Mar. Bond.

Willis of Surry Co. m. bef. 1758, Sarah Bland of Isle of Wight Co. 7W(1)260; Boddie-Isle, p. 217.

Willis m. Jane Lane, dau. of John. 29V520.

WILTON

Mary m. Robert Doniphan.

Mary m. Carnaby Peyton.

WILTSHIRE

Benjamin m. 21 Dec., 1797, Sally Jones. Spotsylvania Co. Mar. Record.

William m. bef. Nov., 1715, Catherine (____) Dawson, widow of Henry. Proven by Court Record of that date, Northumberland Co.

WILY

Elizabeth m. John Ravenscroft Fisher.

John m. 21 Jan., 1731, Elizabeth Clark. Christ Church, p. 167.

John m. bef. 1742, Elizabeth Fleming, grdau. of William, whose will of that date, Hanover Co., proves it. She was prob. dau. of Robert Fleming. 34 Ky. Reg. 98.

Mary m. Michael Heathcote.

WIMBISH

Ann m. Lieut. John Pannill.

Elizabeth (____) m. Dudley Barksdale.

James m. 26 Jan., 1789, Lucy Hunt. Halifax Co. Mar. Record.

John m. 12 Dec., 1796, N. Wolliams. Halifax Co. Mar. Record. Mar. Nancy Williams. Halifax, p. 258.

John m. 18 Sept., 1766, M. Brady. Halifax Co. Mar. Record.

John m. 22 Aug., 1780, Sarah McCraw. Halifax Co. Mar. Record.

Mary m. Samuel Pryor.

WIMBROUGH

Sally m. Ezekiel Bloxom.

WIMER

Barbara m. Valantine Smathers.

Charles m. 9 Jan., 1782, Lottis Hannah by Rev. John Alderson, Jr. Rockingham Co. or Greenbrier Co. Ministers' Returns.

WIMER (cont.)

John, Jr., m. bef. 21 May, 1748, Eleanor Byrom, dau. of James. Proven by Court Record of that date, Essex Co.

WIN

Elizabeth m. John Harris.

WINBORN

Mary m. Elijah Johnson.

WINBUSH

Sarah m. Bryant Lester.

WINCH

William, merchant in New Kent Co., m. Fanny Parke Custis, dau. of Hon. John Custis. Va. Gazette, 29 June, 1739.

WINCHESTER

Arthur m. 21 Jan., 1704/5, Mary Butler. St. Peter's, p. 418.

WINDER

____ m. bef. March, 1698/9, Elizabeth Brereton, sis. of Capt. Thomas. Proven by Court Record of that date, Northumberland Co.

Edward, merchant, m. Feb., 1790, Jane (____) Ward, relict of Capt. James. Announced in The Virginia Herald. 30V68.

Elizabeth m. Richard Kenner.

Thomas, Capt., m. Elizabeth Brereton, dau. of Col. Thomas and Jane (Claiborne). 9W(1)186.

WINDERS

Ep. m. 29 June, 1789, Fany Chambers. Halifax Co. Mar. Record.

Reform m. Henry Boyd.

WINDHAM

John m. bef. 1799, Sally Clark, dau. of Peter, whose will of that date, Greensville Co., proves it.

Moses m. 14 April, 1796, Ester Hosier. Princess Anne Co. Mar. Record.

Reuben m. 3 Dec., 1785, Jane Clements by H. J. Burgess. Surry Co. Mar. Record.

WINDLE

Catharine m. James Dryden.

WINDOWS

Adam m. 6 Dec., 1788, Mary Douglass. Halifax Co. Mar. Record.

WINE

Richard m. 23 July, 1738, Anne Harvie. OPR.

WINFIELD

Ann m. John Parham.

Elizabeth m. Daniel Mason.

Elizabeth m. Thomas Scott.

Ephraim, b. 24 Oct., 1769, son of William, Jr., and Elizabeth (____); m. 31 Oct., 1792, Nancy Tucker by Rev. George Parkham. Sur. Thomas Eppes. Boddie-HSF IV:166.

Lucretia m. Seth Pettypool.

Martha m. William Faison.

Porter, Jr., m. 6 Jan., 1783, Elizabeth Tucker, b. 16 April, 1764, dau. of Joel and Judith (____). She was ward of David Thweatt. Boddie-HSF V:297.

Sarah m. Thomas Eppes.

William, b. 29 April, 1762, son of William, Jr., and Elizabeth (____); m. 6 Jan., 1783, Elizabeth Tucker, ward of David Thweatt. Sur.

WINFIELD (cont.)

Peter Cain. Bristol Parish Reg. Prince George Co. Boddie-HSF IV: 166. (See Porter Winfield, Jr., above.)

WINFREE

John m. 27 April, 1752, Mary Walton. Sur. Isaac Hughes. Cumberland Co. Mar. Bond.

Reuben, b. and d. Chesterfield Co.; m. Ann Scott. DAR No. 79 349.

Robert m. 26 Nov., 1781, Susan Crowder. Sur. Robert Crowder. Amelia Co. Mar. Bond.

Valentine I, d. 1795, Chesterfield Co.; m. Martha Graves, d. 1814, dau. of William and Sarah (Cox). Farmer, p. 55.

Valentine II, b. 15 June, 1762; d. 8 April, 1824, son of Valentine I and Martha (Graves); m. 3 Jan., 1783, Lucy Cheatham, b. 26 March, 1764; d. 1836; res. Chesterfield Co. Farmer, p. 55.

William m. Sarah Cox. Farmer, p. 55.

WINFREY

____ m. Ned Tuck.

____ m. Mary Graves, dau. of William. 2W(1)271.

Elizabeth m. John Fearne.

Isaac m. 6 Oct., 1775, Mary Graves. York Co. Mar. Record.

Jacob m. 3 Nov., 1698, Elizabeth Alford. St. Peter's, p. 418.

John m. 27 April, 1752, Mary Walton. Sur. Isaac Hughes. Cumberland Co. Mar. Bond.

Mary Ann m. Capt. Dionysius Oliver.

Mary Ann m. James Oliver (1st wife).

Polly m. Robert Hubbard.

Sarah m. Ira Meador.

Susannah m. Jacob Amonett.

William m. 5 April, 1780 (or 1785) Ann Chappell. Sur. Miles Chappell. Amelia Co. Mar. Bond.

WINFRY

Nancy m. James Overstreet.

WINGATE

Elishe Parks m. William Nottingham.

George m. 22 June, 1786, Mary Miller. Northampton Co. Mar. Record.

Jacob m. 11 March, 1796, Nice Wilson. Northampton Co. Mar. Record.

John m. 27 Feb., 1760, Sarah Watson, dau. of Robert. Northampton Co. Mar. Record.

Roger m. bef. 21 July, 1648, Dorothy (____) Burwell, mother of Lewis Burwell. Proven by Court Record of that date, York Co. She was Dorothy Bedell, dau. of William of Catworth, Huntingdonshire, England. 1W(1)84.

Thomas m. 1 Aug., 1789, Arady Deare, dau. of William. Northampton Co. Mar. Record.

WINGER

Thomas m. 15 July, 1688, Ann Doss. Christ Church, p. 37.

WINGFIELD

Ann m. John Harrison.

Ann m. James Garland, Jr.

Barbara m. Dr. Frederick Sims.

Benjamin m. 2 Feb., 1795, Susannah Wingfield. Sur. Francis Wingfield. Albemarle Co. Mar. Bond.

WINGFIELD (cont.)
Charles m. 28 Jan., 1790, Elizabeth Day, spinster. Sur. John Day. Albemarle Co. Mar. Bond.
Charles, Jr., d. 1819, son of Charles; m. 1783, Mary (Lewis) Lewis, dau. of Charles, Jr., and widow of Col. Charles Lewis of Rev. War and Mary (Randolph). Albemarle, pp. 251, 253, 345.
Edward m. 27 Dec., 1790, Nancy Hazelrig. Sur. Richard Hazelrig. Albemarle Co. Mar. Bond. Edward, d. 1806. Albemarle, p. 346.
Elizabeth m. Edward Butler.
Elizabeth m. Walter Leake.
Elizabeth m. Charles Cosby.
Elizabeth m. Isaac Robinson.
Elizabeth m. Henley Hamner.
Frances m. William Terrell.
Frances m. Lieut. David Meriwether.
Garland m. his cousin, Sarah Garland (Wingfield) Poullain, widow of Dr. Antoine Poullain and dau. of Thomas and Elizabeth (Terrell). 60V314.
Jemima m. Samuel Barksdale.
John m. 4 Nov., 1777, Rebecca Carles. Brunswick Co. Mar. Record.
John m. Ann Buster, dau. of John. Albemarle, p. 158.
John, b. 23 Feb., 1757; d. 28 March, 1828, son of Thomas and Elizabeth (Terrell); m. 1 Feb., 1781, Hanover Co., Rebecca Nelson, b. 1759, dau. of James and Keziah (Harris). 27T37; 60V314.
John, b. ca 1695; d. bef. Nov., 1759, son of Thomas and (1) Mary (____); m. Mary Hudson, dau. of Charles. 60V317-8; Albemarle, pp. 200, 344; Bell, p. 233.
Joseph m. 28 Aug., 1789, Mary Tool. Sur. John Wingfield, Jr. Albemarle Co. Mar. Bond.
Martha m. Lieut. Harden Foster.
Mary m. Richard Worsham.
Mary m. John Cosby.
Mary m. Peter Terrell.
Mary m. John Hamner.
Mary m. Robert Gentry.
Mathew m. 21 Dec., 1775, Sarah Hinds, both in Hanover. Douglas Reg., p. 17.
Matthew m. Martha Buster, dau. of John. Albemarle, p. 158.
Mildred m. John Sims.
Nancy m. George Eubanks.
Owen m. 26 Nov., 1748, Mary Hurst. OPR.
Robert m. 11 June, 1765, Frances Jordan, both of this parish. Douglas Reg., p. 8.
Sarah m. ____ Martin.
Sarah m. John Martin.
Sarah m. Stephen Pettus.
Sarah Garland m. (1) Dr. Antoine Poullain; m. (2) Garland Wingfield.
Susanna m. John Cosby.
Susannah m. Benjamin Wingfield.
Thomas, physician, son of Thomas and Elizabeth (Terrell), m. Sidney Mounger and had a dau., b. 1801. 60V315.
Thomas, b. 17 Sept., 1745, Va.; d. 24 July, 1797, Wilkes Co., Ga.,

WINGFIELD (cont.)
son of John and Frances Oliver (Buck); served in Rev. War; m. 9 Dec., 1768, Hanover Co., Elizabeth Nelson, b. 1749; d. 1802, 60V311.
Thomas, b. ca 1733; will prov. 1806, Wilkes Co., Ga., son of Thomas and Sarah (Garland); m. ca 1754, Elizabeth Terrell, dau. of Joel and Sarah Elizabeth (Oxford). 60V312.

WINGHAM
Sarah m. Nathan Yancy.

WINGO
Abner m. 22 May, 1788, Elizabeth Seay. Sur. Waller Ford. Amelia Co. Mar. Bond.
Churchill m. 17 Dec., 1788, Mary Seay. Sur. Rawley Fossett. Amelia Co. Mar. Bond.
John m. 9 Dec., 1786, Mary Seay. Sur. William Wingo. Amelia Co. Mar. Bond.
John m. 18 May, 1780, Frances Seay. Sur. Archer Cheatham. Amelia Co. Mar. Bond.
John, Jr., m. 12 Sept., 1791, Elizabeth Smith. Sur. Thomas Burnett. Mecklenburg Co. Mar. Bond.
Obadiah m. 7 Sept., 1784, Oney Seay, dau. of Jesse. Sur. Larkin Ferguson. Amelia Co. Mar. Bond.
Sarah m. Thomas Ware.
Uraney (____) m. James Arnold.
William m. 23 Nov., 1783, Mary Holt, dau. of Mary. Sur. John Foster. Amelia Co. Mar. Bond.
William m. 12 Dec., 1786, Lurany Loving. Sur. John Wingo. Amelia Co. Mar. Bond.
William m. 9 Dec., 1786, S. Seay. Amelia Co. Mar. Record.

WINKFIELD
Cynthia m. Rev. William Shropshire (3rd wife).

WINKLEFIELD
Mary m. Wilford Martin.

WINLOCK
Anne m. Joseph Carter.

WINN
____ m. Margaret ____, dau. of Margaret Connor, whose will, prov. 1751, Culpeper Co., names "daughter Margaret Winn."
Catharine m. Jesse Laffoon.
Elizabeth m. George Brown.
Elizabeth m. John Harris.
Elizabeth P. m. Samuel T. Mosby.
Fanny m. John Courts.
Horatio m. 4 Jan., 1800, Pattey B. Pettipool by Rev. James Shelburne, Baptist. Lunenburg Co. Ministers' Returns.
Jemima m. Daniel Gunn.
Jerusha m. Daniel Gunney.
John m. 1 Nov., 1783, Mary Williams. Sur. Wood Jones. Amelia Co. Mar. Bond.
Keturah m. Thomas Ford.
Major m. Sally (Godwin) Godwin, widow of Thomas. Boddie-Isle, p. 484.
Mary m. Walker Dalton.
Mourning m. James Glenn.

WINN (cont.)

Nancy m. Samuel Clay.

Ollive m. William Haley.

Richard m. bef. 1734/5, Phebe (____) Phleger. Proven by Court Record of that date, Hanover Co.

Richard m. 12 April, 1779, Jane Pincham. Sur. Charles Irby. Amelia Co. Mar. Bond.

Richard m. 28 May, 1711, Anne Cocke. Christ Church, p. 82.

Robert m. 11 Feb., 1796, Susanna Jordan by Rev. John Neblett, Methodist. Lunenburg Co. Ministers' Returns.

Sarah m. David Powell, Jr.

Sarah B. m. Robert Hayes.

Susanna P. m. John G. Newbill.

Susannah m. William H. Robertson.

WINNARD(?)

John m. 14 Dec., 1787, Myrtile Minor by Rev. Thomas Crymes, Baptist. Lunenburg Co. Ministers' Returns.

WINNING

Niels m. 24 Dec., 1787, Ann Miller. Christ Church, p. 206.

WINSLOW

Agatha Beverley m. John Nelson.

Benjamin of Essex Co. m. 22 Nov., 1726, Susanna Beverley, dau. of Capt. Harry. Spotsylvania Co. Mar. Record. 35V33.

Elizabeth m. William Meriwether.

Fortunatus(?) m. 5 Feb., 1796, Polly Alcocke. St. Mark's, p. 78.

Susanna m. William Parker.

Thomas m. 15 April, 1694, Anne Parker, dau. of Thomas. Essex Co. Mar. Record.

William m. Margaret "Peggy" Mills, b. May, 1776; d. 24 June, 1816, dau. of William and Peggy (Swift). 15T43-4.

WINST

John m. 1793, Sally V. McMath. Rockbridge Co. Morton, p. 509.

WINSTON

____, a dau., m. ____ Price.

____, a dau., m. ____ Schenck.

____, a dau., m. ____ Dabney.

____ m. Benjamin Pollard.

____ m. bef. Jan., 1715/6, Martha Gouldman, sis. of Francis, whose will of that date, Essex Co., mentions "my sister Martha Winston."

____ m. Dorothea Spottswood Henry, b. 2 Aug., 1778, at "Red Hill," in Va.; d. 17 June, 1854, Memphis, Tenn., dau. of Patrick Henry. 35V299.

____ m. Isaac Davis.

Alecy Ann m. Henry Pendleton (1st wife).

Alice m. Judge Edmund Winston.

Alice m. Frederick Cabell.

Ann m. Benjamin Mosby.

Anthony m. 7 March, 1776, Uphans Tate. Sur. Joseph Street. Louisa Co. Mar. Bond. Anthony m. 14 Dec., 1794, Mary Barret, dau. of Charles, who gave consent. Sur. John Poay. Louisa Co. Mar. Bond. Uphans Tate was sis. of Zedekiah Winston, whose will, dated May, 1784, Louisa Co., proves it. Anthony, b. ca 1750; will prov. 1834,

WINSTON (cont.)

son of Samuel; served in Rev. War; m. (1) Uphans Tate; m. (2) Mary Barret. Louisa, p. 436.

Anthony, Capt., b. 1750, Hanover Co.; d. 1828, Ala.; m. Keziah Jones. DAR No. 28 005.

Anthony, b. 29 Sept., 1723; d. 29 Feb., 1747/8; m. 27 Feb., 1747, Alice Thornton Taylor, b. 21 May, 1730, dau. of James and Alice (Thornton) Catlett Taylor. 4W(1)281; Huguenot 7:197; Taylor, p. 133; Winston, p. 20.

Barbara m. ___ Barrett.

Barbara m. Capt. Thomas Price.

Barbara Overton m. (1) Paul Thilman.

Bickerton, b. 28 June, 1768; m. (1) Mary Lyle Smelt; m. (2) Mary Smith. (Deed, 1818, Louisa Co., proves it.) Winston, p. 40.

Catherine Overton m. Henry S. Shore.

Catherine Robinson m. Henry Smith Shore (2nd wife).

Dorothy m. William Barrett.

Edmund, Judge, b. 1745, Hanover Co.; d. 1818, son of William and Sarah (Dabney); m. (1) Alice Winston, b. 20 March, 1753; d. 1784, dau. of Anthony and Alice (Taylor); m. (2) ___ (___) Henry, widow of Patrick Henry. 5V206; Taylor, p. 133.

Edmund, b. 1778; d. 1864, son of Edmund; m. Caroline Wyatt. 5V206.

Elizabeth m. Dr. Bennett W. Moseley.

Elizabeth m. Edward Curd.

Elizabeth m. Col. John Johns.

Elizabeth m. Hezekiah Mosby.

Geddes m. Mary Jordan. 3T179.

George of Henrico Co., son of Nathaniel, m. Mary Harris, dau. of James. Louisa, p. 348.

George, son of Edmund, m. his step-sister, Dorothea Henry, dau. of Patrick. 5V206.

Henry Robinson, b. 2 Jan., 1782; m. (1) Elizabeth Buckner; m. (2) Jane (Deswell) DeJarnette. Winston, p. 45.

Is. m. 2 June, 1770, Lucy Cole, both in Hanover. Douglas Reg., p. 12.

Isaac, d. 1766, son of Isaac (d. 1760, Hanover Co.); m. Mary Ann Fontaine, dau. of Rev. Peter. Free I:58; Winston, p. 20.

Isaac of Hanover, d. 1760; m. Mary Dabney, dau. of John Dabney, Huguenot refugee to Hanover Co. NOT dau. of Cornelius, Sr. Huguenot 6:182; Winston, p. 20.

James, Capt., b. 12 March, 1752/3; d. 17 July, 1826, Louisa Co., son of John, Jr., and Alice (Bickerton); m. 25 Dec., 1782, Albemarle Co., Sarah Marks, d. 1829, dau. of Hastings (will dated 5 Nov., 1761). 31V350; Louisa, p. 432; Winston, p. 41.

James m. 15 Nov., 1790, Rebecca John. Louisa Co. Mar. Record.

James, b. ca 1725, son of John and Barbara (Overton); m. Anne Farrell. Beddie-HSF V:129.

John m. 7 Dec., 1780, Mary Johnson, both in Louisa. Douglas Reg., p. 20. He, b. 14 Oct., 1757; d. ca 1800, son of John and Alice (Bickerton); she, d. ca 1823, dau. of Thomas Johnson, Jr. Louisa, pp. 264, 435.

John, Capt. in Rev. War, son of William and Polly (Overton), m. Nancy Overton, dau. of William and Jemima (Harris). Beddie-HSF V:132;

WINSTON (cont.)

Louisa, p. 397.

John m. 1706, Barbara Overton, b. 5 Feb., 1690; d. 30 Oct., 1766, dau. of William and Elizabeth (Waters). Boddie-HSF V:129.

John, b. 9 June, 1724, Hanover Co.; d. there, 23 Jan., 1772, son of John and Barbara (Overton); m. 3 Feb., 1746, Alice Bickerton, dau. of John and Mary (Todd). Boddie-HSF V:129. He, son of William and Barbara (Overton). Winston, p. 39.

Joseph m. 15 Nov., 1790, Rebecca Johnson, dau. of Thomas, Jr., who gave consent. Sur. Harry Lawrence. Louisa Co. Mar. Bond. Joseph, b. 2 April, 1763, son of John and Alice (Bickerton); Rebecca, b. 2 June, 1773, dau. of Thomas and Elizabeth (Merriwether). 26V105; Louisa, pp. 265, 383, 435.

Joseph, Col., m. Betty Hicks Lanier, b. 29 Sept., 1750, dau. of Thomas and Elizabeth (Hicks). 3T138.

Lucy m. (1) William Dabney; m. (2) William Coles.

Lucy m. Alexander Murray.

Lucy m. Thomas Rose.

Lucy m. Robert F. Storey.

Margaret m. Dr. John Adams.

Martha m. William Terrell.

Martha m. Capt. William Overton Callis (1st wife).

Martha Lowry m. Laney Jones.

Mary m. (1) ____ Phillips; m. (2) Garland Carr.

Mary m. Augustine Seaton.

Mary m. Col. John Johns.

Mary m. (1) Charles Woodson; m. (2) Peter Fore, Jr.

Mary Ann m. Francis Irwin.

Mary Ann m. John Coles.

Mary Todd m. Benjamin Pollard.

Nathan m. 14 Jan., 1796, Ann Yarbrough. Caroline Co. Mar. Record.

Nathaniel, son of Anthony of Hanover Co., m. 15 Aug., 1749, Jemima Bell, dau. of George of the same county. Henrico Monthly Meeting, 1699-1756.

Patsy m. William Terrell.

Peter m. ____ Jones, dau. of John and Elizabeth (Crawley). Orange III:83.

Pleasant m. Jane Quarles, dau. of Roger (b. 1720) and Mary (Goodloe). 38V361-2.

Rebecca m. William Radford.

Rebecca m. Cornelius Schenk.

Sally m. Samuel Teler.

Sally m. Thomas Falconer.

Sarah m. (1) Col. John Syme; m. (2) Col. John Henry.

Sarah m. Thomas Rutherford.

Sarah m. Col. John Littlepage (1st wife).

Sarah m. Dr. John Woodson.

Sarah m. John Quarles.

Sarah m. Dr. George Cabell.

Susanna m. Lawrence Slaughter (2nd wife).

Susanna m. John Pettus.

William, d. 1727-8, son of William of St. Peter's Parish; m. (1) 1701,

WINSTON (cont.)

Sarah (Jennings) Dabney, widow of John Dabney of New Kent Co.; m. (2) Martha (Tomlin) Gouldman (Court Record, June, 1714, Essex Co., proves it); m. (3) Barbara Overton; res. King William Co.; rem. to Hanover Co. by 1725. 20T101; 49V357; Louisa, p. 431; Winston, p. 172.

William, son of Isaac (d. 1760) of Hanover Co., m. Sarah Dabney. Winston, p. 20.

William of Hanover Co. m. 1769, Mary Ann Curd, b. ca 1750, dau. of Edward and Mary (Morris). Curd, p. 7.

William m. Polly Overton. 5V442.

William Chamberlayne, b. 22 Nov., 1802; m. Sarah S. Pollard. Winston, p. 45.

William Overton, b. 6 Nov., 1747, Hanover Co.; d. 1815, son of John and Alice (Bickerton); m. (1) 27 Dec., 1770, Joanna Robinson, dau. of Henry of Hanover Co.; m. (2) Anne Kidley (Chamberlayne) Posey. Louisa, p. 431; Winston, pp. 43-4.

William R. "Bobby" m. 1800, Anne "Nancy" Meriwether, b. 13 July, 1763, dau. of James and Elizabeth (Pollard). 7W(2)224; Louisa, p. 388.

WINTER

____ m. bet. 1711 and 1722, Margaret (Taylor) Dameron, widow of George and dau. of Lazarus Taylor, whose will, 1711, and codicil, 1722, Northumberland Co., prove it.

Elizabeth m. Daniel Payne.

Hannah m. Henry Miller.

James m. Harriet Parker, dau. of Harry. Hartford B-8845, 26 Nov., 1955. Signed C. B. S.

Katherine m. Thomas Ingram.

Susanna m. John Green.

Thomas m. Margaret (Taylor) Dameron, widow of George (d. 1720) and dau. of Lazarus. (Also given as Winters.) 8T44; Dameron, Chart A.

WINTERS

Mary m. Northrup Fuller.

William of "Efton Hills," Md., m. Catherine Taliaferro Hooe, dau. of Richard and Anne (Ireland). Mar. 1 Nov., 1781, Caty Hooe. St. Paul's. 2W(1)88.

WIRT

William m. 23 May, 1795, Mildrod Gilmer. Sur. Charles Meriwether. Albemarle Co. Mar. Bond. Mildred, dau. of George and Lucy (Walker). Albemarle, p. 207.

WISDOM

____ m. bef. 1757, Ann Collins, dau. of Joseph, whose will of that date, Spotsylvania Co., names "daughter Ann Wisdom."

Ann m. Richard Allen.

Clary m. Samuel Ham.

Fanny m. Joseph Griffey.

Frances m. Edward Atkins.

John m. Ann Collins, dau. of Capt. Joseph and Susannah (Lewis). Orange III:33.

Joseph m. 1773, Sarah Gardner. Orange Co. Mar. Record.

Sally m. Rev. Joseph Craig.

WISE

____ m. Scarburgh Robinson.

____ m. Rebecca Massie, dau. of Joseph (will, dated 19 Aug., 1760, Brunswick Co.). 28V162.

Abraham, b. 1767, Romney, Va., son of Abraham; m. Dorothy Day; rem. to Mason Co., Ky. Hartford B-6167(1), 27 Feb., 1954. Signed W. M. P.

Ann (____) m. Edward Magee.

Anne m. Thomas Parsons.

Christine Elizabeth m. John Stephens.

Elizabeth m. Noah Belotte.

Elizabeth m. Maj. Thomas Whittington Custis.

Elizabeth m. Patrick Roath.

Frances m. Thomas Frayser.

Hugh m. 1797, Polly McCroskey. Rockbridge Co. Morton, p. 545.

Johannes m. 23 Jan., 1799, Peggy Dunton. Northampton Co. Mar. Record.

John of Accomac m. bef. 1801, ____ Henry, dau. of James of Northumberland Co., whose will of that date, prov. 1805, Williamsburg, Va., proves it.

John m. Matilda West, dau. of John (will prov. 1703, Accomac Co.) and Matilda (Scarbrough). 58V401.

John m. 2 Jan., 1765, Sarah (____) Batson. Northampton Co. Mar. Record.

Sarah (____) m. John Stott.

Tabitha m. Thomas Custis (3rd wife).

Tobias m. 4 Sept., 1795, Mary Griggsby. Shelby Co., Ky. Mar. Record.

Tully R. m. 7 Dec., 1797, Mary Fisher. Northampton Co. Mar. Record.

WISEHART

Nancy m. John Miller.

WISEKOP

Abraham m. 19 Feb., 1799, Macdelane Wisler. Rockingham Co. Wayland, p. 10.

WISEMAN

Caty m. Jesse Courtney.

Mary m. John McKenney.

Rachel m. Frederick Coniker.

Samuel m. 10 May, 1797, Polly Bowaer. Rockingham Co. Wayland, p. 9.

WISER

Mary m. Elias Shovelbarger.

WISHARD

John m. 13 Sept., 1732, Joyce (____) Thelaball, widow of Lemuel, dec'd. Sur. James Hunter. Princess Anne Co. Mar. Bond.

WISHART

____, a dau., m. ____ Taliaferro.

____ m. bef. Feb., 1801, Anne Singleton, sis. of Arthur Sayer Singleton. Proven by Deed of that date, Princess Anne Co.

____ (____) m. (2) Michael Wallace.

Dinah m. Cornelius Calvert, Jr.

Wilhelmina m. James Garnett Taliaferro.

William m. 31 Dec., 1766, Mary Haynes. Sur. John Konline. Princess Anne Co. Mar. Bond.

WISLER

Macdolano m. Abraham Wisokop.

WISMAN

John m. 29 Nov., 1796, Mary Coponhagor by J. Finloy. Wytho Co. Mar. Rocord.

Philip m. 17 Fob., 1795, Elizaboth Koppohoffor. Wytho Co. Mar. Rocord.

WIT

Susan m. Jamos Batos.

WITCHARD

Sarah m. Tully Brown.

WITCHER

Elizaboth m. Abraham Razor.

Jamos m. 1 Nov., 1781, Mary Colloy by Rov. Lowis Sholton. Pittsylvania Co. Ministors' Roturns.

William, Capt., d. 1808, Pittsylvania Co.; m. ____ Majors. DAR No. 68 311.

William m. 1 April, 1782, Molloy Dalton by Rov. John Bailoy. Pittsylvania Co. Ministors' Roturns.

WITH

Mary m. Samuol Baldwin.

WITHAM

Elizaboth m. Joshua Gowor.

WITHER

John m. 21 Fob., 1755, Eliz. Barnot. Douglas Rog., p. 1.

WITHERS

____, a dau., m. ____ Roovos.

Alcy m. John Ball.

Ann m. Honry Mauzy (1st wifo).

Bonjamin of Stafford Co. m. by 1795, Anno Markham, dau. of John and (1) Alico (Millor); ros. Fauquior, whon dau. Alico was born. 31T 186; Porrin, 1882, p. 481.

Bridgott m. William Allon.

Ed. m. Mary DoJarnotto. Collins, p. 133.

Edmond m. ca 1777, Mary Wronn, dau. of John and Mary (Chappoll) of Sussox Co. 10W(2)265.

* Enoch Koano, b. 1760, Va.; d. thoro, 1818; m. Janot Chinn. DAR No. 47 642.

Francos m. Richard Fossakor.

Jamos m. 7 Doc., 1757, Sukoy Wallor. OPR. Jamos, b. 29 Aug., 1736, Stafford Co., son of John and Hannah (Allon); Susan, dau. of Charlos Wallor. Emison, Sup. p. 133.

Jamos, d. 1808; bur. at Dolraino, Va.; m. Sarah Pickott. DAR No. 28 173.

Jamos, b. ca 1680; d. 1746, Stafford Co., son of William III and Mary (Littlojohn); m. ca 1701, Elizaboth Koono, d. 26 July, 1769, dau. of Matthow and Bridgot (____). Emison, Sup. p. 133.

Jamos, b. 9 Aug., 1762; d. 28 Nov., 1812, Ky., son of John and Hannah (Routt) of Stafford Co.; m. 18 Sopt., 1792, Mary Pennick, b. 25 Jan., 1767; d. 12 April, 1837, dau. of Joromiah. Emison, Sup. 133.

* Elizaboth m. Androw Edwards.

WITHERS (cont.)

James m. 12 Nov., 1792, Frances "Frankie" Morgan, dau. of William, whose will, 1797, Ky., names "James Withers, husband of my daughter Frances Withers." Fauquier Co. Mar. Record. 25T274.

John m. 27 Oct., ____, Elizabeth Smith by Rev. John Alderson, Jr. Rockingham Co. or Greenbrier Co. Ministers' Returns.

John m. Mary Herbert Jones. 1V320.

John, b. 15 Dec., 1738, Stafford Co.; d. 12 June, 1818, Ky.; m. Hannah Routt, b. 31 Jan., 1740; d. 9 Oct., 1774, dau. of Peter and Martha (____); rem. ca 1803 to Jessamine Co., Ky. Emison, Sup. p. 133.

John, b. 1708; d. Oct., 1828, son of James and Susan (Waller); m. ca 1787, Sarah Speake, dau. of Thomas (d. 1766) and Agnes (Ward); res. 1811, Ky. Emison, Sup. p. 133.

John, Capt., d. 1698; m. Frances (Townshend) Dade, widow of Francis, Jr., and dau. of Col. Robert and Mary (Langhorne) Townshend. She m. (3) Col. Rice Hooe. 16T160.

Keene m. 21 Dec., 1747, Elizabeth Cave. OPR.

Mary m. John Cloyd.

Ollie m. Lewis Payne.

Priscilla m. John Grammer.

Sarah m. ____ Conway.

Sucky m. Henry Field.

WITHERSPOON

John m. 1774, Mary Boston. Orange Co. Mar. Record.

Mary Edris m. Rev. Wm. Shropshire (2nd wife).

WITHROW

James m. Eliza Watkins, dau. of John. Rockbridge Co. Morton, p. 404.

Sarah m. James McDowell.

WITMON

Andrew m. 2 Dec., ____, Elizabeth Stevens. Frederick Co. Mar. Record.

WITT

Benjamin m. Mary Chastain. 32V396.

Celia m. Jesse Oglesby.

Elizabeth m. James Luttrell.

Elizabeth C. m. William Luttrell.

Jesse m. Alice Brown; res. Bedford Co., 1801, when son, Rev. Daniel Witt, was born. Prince Edward, p. 343.

Jesse m. Martha Cheatham, dau. of Benjamin. Farmer, p. 43.

Judah m. John Madlock.

Mary m. Robert Mitchell.

Mary Ann m. Rolley Crouch.

Miles m. Jane Dawson; res. Bedford Co., when son, Richmond T. Witt, was born. Perrin, 1886, Simpson, p. 718.

Polly m. Tandy Wood.

Rebecca m. John Graham.

Rowland m. 31 Jan., 1793, Sally Duvall by Joseph Drury. Campbell Co. Mar. Record.

Sarah m. Joseph Crouch.

Siller m. Elisha Barton.

Suckey m. Claibourne Creasy.

WITT (cont.)
Tabitha m. William Dillon.
WITTE
Agathy m. John Key.
WITTEN
Rebecca m. John Graham.
WITTY
Elizabeth m. Benjamin Dillon, Jr.
WITZEL
Elizabeth m. Michael Pickle.
WODROP
John m. 12 Jan., 1769, Mary Clarke. Charles City Co. Mar. Record.
WOFFENDALL
____ m. Tabitha Payde, d. 1790. She m. (2) George Strother. 11T117.
Mary m. Benjamin Strother.
William m. bef. 1730, Jane (____) Tyler, widow of Charles (d. bef. 1723). Proven by Court Suit, 25 Feb., 1730, Westmoreland Co. 21W (1)22.
WOLDEN
William m. 23 Jan., 1794, Polley Burner. Halifax Co. Mar. Record.
WOLEN
Mahitable (or Esther) m. Moses Russell.
WOLF
Barbary m. Henry Lambert.
Lawrence m. 17 Dec., 1795, Elizabeth Sanders by Leonard Straw. Wythe Co. Mar. Record.
Polly m. George Terrell.
WOLFE
Elizabeth m. Lewis Stephens.
George m. 16 April, 1798, Catharine Armontrout. Rockingham Co. Wayland, p. 9.
Keaty m. John Cole.
WOLFENBERGER
Hannah m. John Gillock.
WOLLAND
Hannah (____) m. James Goodwin.
WOLLIAMS
N. m. John Wimbish.
WOMACK
____ m. Froderick Reams.
Abram m. 21 Oct., 1785, Tabitha Hudson. Halifax Co. Mar. Record.
Abraham m. 4 May, 1787, Susan Jolley by Rev. John Buchanan. Henrico, p. 230.
Abraham m. 18 Oct., 1788, Joanna Levisay. Prince George Co. Cameron.
Allen m. 12 March, 1789, Sally Womack. Halifax Co. Mar. Rocord.
Ann m. Thomas Livesay.
Betsey m. Baker Davidson.
Elizabeth m. Thomas Harris.
Elizabeth m. Henry Buckner, Jr.
Elizabeth m. Timothy Harris.
Henry m. 31 July, 1778, Mary Terry in Louisa. Douglas Reg., p. 18.
Jesse, b. 1739, Va.; d. 1815, Madison Co., Ga.; m. Dorothy Prior.

WOMACK (cont.)
DAR No. 66 894.
Judith m. John Clarkson.
Martha m. ___ Roberts.
Martha m. ___ Nichols.
Martha m. (1) John Mosby; m. (2) James Humbleton.
Mary m. ___ Williams.
Mary m. William Wadley.
Mary m. Thomas Puckett.
Mary m. Presley Britt.
Nancy m. Thomas Powell.
Polly m. Samuel Baldwin.
Richard m. bef. 29 May, 1679, ___ Puckett, dau. of John, whose est. sett. of that date, Henrico Co., proves it. Richard, Jr., b. ca 1657; d. ca 1684; m. Mary Puckett, dau. of John and Anne (___). She m. (2) John Granger. Puckett, pp. 1, 2.
Sally m. Allen Womack.
Sarah m. ___ Rise.
Susannah m. Duncan Young.
William m. 9 June, 1791, Elizabeth Perkinson. Chesterfield Co. Cameron.
William m. 15 Aug., 1792, Mary Logan. Halifax Co. Mar. Record.
William m. 17 Oct., 1762, M. Allen. Halifax Co. Mar. Record.
William W. m. 22 Feb., 1798, N. Dismukes. Halifax Co. Mar. Record.

WOMAX
Rody m. Jacob Mayberry.

WOMBELL
Joyce m. Henry Reynolds.

WOMBLE
___ m. Frederick Taylor.
Charlotte m. Thomas Derr.
Elizabeth m. Edmond Bailey.
Jeremiah m. 28 Dec., 1792, Nancy Mountford. Isle of Wight Co. Mar. Record.
Temperance m. Samuel Jefferson.

WOMBRELL
Thomas m. 27 Feb., 1799, Sally Scott by Nathaniel Benimon. Surry Co. Ministers' Returns.

WOMBWELL
Chasey m. James Hancock.

WOMECK
Susanna (___) m. Daniel Nunnally.

WOMMACK
Peter m. 9 Nov., 1786, Christina Utterback, b. ca 1752, Germantown, Va. Utterback, p. 36.
William m. 4 Feb., 1790, Margaret Ellis by Rev. James Shelburne, Baptist. Lunenburg Co. Ministers' Returns.

WOMOCK
Eliza m. Tim Harris.
Mary m. William Wadlow.

WOOD (See WOODS)
___ believed m. bef. 1798, Mary Pond, dau. of Mary (___) Pond, Sr.,

WOOD (cont.)

whose will of that date, Southampton Co., names "daughter Mary Wood."

___ believed m. bef. 1805, Polly Medley, dau. of James, whose will of that date, Halifax Co., names "daughter Polly Wood."

___ m. Mary Michie, dau. of John, who d. 1777. Albemarle, p. 272.

___ m. Matthew Harrison.

___ m. bef. 1729, Martha Worsham, dau. of John, whose will of that date, Henrico Co., names "daughter Martha Wood."

___ m. bef. 1751, Hannah ___, dau. of Margaret (___) Conner, whose will prov. that date, Culpeper Co., names "daughter Hannah Wood."

___ believed m. bef. March, 1784, Lucy Henry, dau. of Sarah (___) Henry, whose will of that date, Amherst Co., mentions "my daughter Lucy Wood."

Alexander m. 4 June, 1799, Catherine Goodloe. Spotsylvania Co. Mar. Record.

Alexander m. 1789, Anne Poague. Rockbridge Co. Morton, p. 521.

Andrew, Colonel of Romney, Va. (now W. Va.), m. ___ Harrison, dau. of Matthew and ___ (Wood). 24V98.

Ann m. Richard Quinn.

Ann m. Barnet Smith.

Ann m. James Brooks.

Anne m. Ezekiel Thacker.

Archer S. m. 14 Nov., 1793, Sally Petty. Halifax Co. Mar. Record.

B. m. ___ Porter, prob. 1791 in Orange Co. St. Mark's, p. 78.

Bartholomew m. bef. 31 Oct., 1724, Charity ___, dau. of Elizabeth Tapp of Spotsylvania Co. Proven by a Deed of that date, Spotsylvania Co.

Basil m. 15 Jan., 1791, Peggy Richardson by Rev. Benjamin Blagrove, Henrico Parish. Henrico, p. 232.

Betty m. Carter White, Jr.

Caldwell m. 1785, Charlotte Co., Nancy Sublett, dau. of Abraham and Marte (Martain). Gazette Query 6263 (A), 19 Jan., 1962. Signed Lt. Col. Kenneth P. Darling, 5704 Nebraska Ave., N. W., Washington 15, D. C.

Catherine m. Thos. Lenard.

Catherine m. James Broun.

Catie m. John Blackwell.

Charles m. 22 Sept., 1712, Mary Catherine ___. Sur. Hugh Daniel. Norfolk Co. Mar. Record. (This is not complete in the reference but may be in the Court House.)

Charles m. 29 Oct., 1732, Mary Baldwin. Christ Church, p. 168.

Christopher m. Sarah Michie, dau. of John (d. 1777). Albemarle, p. 274.

David, d. 1813; rem. in 1774 from Louisa Co. to Albemarle Co.; m. ___ Watson. Albemarle, p. 350.

David, b. 1737, Va.; d. 1813, Albemarle Co.; m. 1756, Louisa Co., Mary Watson. Wilcoxson, p. 411.

David, son of Josiah, who had a Patent in 1741; d. 1816; m. 1781, Mildred Lewis, dau. of Col. Nicholas. Albemarle, p. 348.

Delilah m. William Pentecost.

Dianah m. Shelton Smith.

WOOD (cont.)

Drury, d. 1841, son of David (d. 1813); m. Malinda Carr, dau. of John. Albemarle, p. 350.

Drury m. 12 Feb., 1794, Caroline Matilda Carr. Sur. Elijah D. Gillum. Albemarle Co. Mar. Bond.

E. m. John Moore.

E. m. Thomas Puckett.

Edmund m. 1788, Jane Franklin by James Kenney. Campbell Co. Mar. Record.

Elijah m. 20 June, 1722, Jane Powell. St. Paul's.

Elizabeth m. Matthew Bowen.

Elizabeth m. John Clack.

Elizabeth m. Robert Lewis.

Elizabeth m. William Roper.

Elizabeth m. Micajah Carr.

Elizabeth m. Thomas Puckett.

Elizabeth m. Richard Jennings.

Elizabeth m. William Waldrops.

Elizabeth m. John Brown.

Elizabeth m. Alexander White.

Ellet m. 1775, Mary Conner. Orange Co. Mar. Record.

Elmira m. (1) Joseph Field; m. (2) John Robinson.

Frances m. William Hill.

Frances (____) m. William Cox.

George m. 14 Dec., 1786, Polly Wood. Halifax Co. Mar. Record.

George m. 1791, Jenny Curry. Rockbridge Co. Morton, p. 546.

Harrison m. 9 Aug., 1792, Mary Simmonds, spinster. Sur. Ephraim Simmonds. Albemarle Co. Mar. Bond.

Henrietta m. James Jeffries.

Henry m. Sarah (____) Willis, widow of William. She m. (3) Rush Hudson; m. (4) Edward Turberville (2nd wife). Orange III:98.

Henry m. 1780, Mary Weatherspoon. Orange Co. Mar. Record.

Henry, prob. b. 1690, London; to Yorktown, Va., 1713; rem. to Henrico Co.; m. ca 1713, Henrico Co., Martha Cocke, dau. of William of "Bremo." 5V78; 32V391. Henry, b. 8 July, 1696, London, Eng.; d. 2 May, 1757, Goochland Co., son of Valentine and Rachel (____); m. 13 Oct., 1723, Martha Cocke (or Cox), dau. of William and Sarah (____) of Henrico Co. 44V150; 53V64; 2W(2)138.

Hopewell m. 1793, Willy Terman. Orange Co. Mar. Record.

Isaac, son of William, m. Susan Grayson, dau. of Capt. William. Albemarle, p. 349.

James m. Sarah Martin, dau. of John and Ann (Tooley). Albemarle, p. 264.

James m. 9 Sept., 1783, Ann Lipscomb. Louisa Co. Mar. Record. Mar. 12 Oct., 1785. Douglas Reg., p. 23.

James, General and Governor of Virginia, m. Jean Moncure, dau. of Rev. John. Huguenot 7:266.

James m. 18 Jan., 1788, Sarah Johnson by John Lasly, minister. Louisa Co. Ministers' Returns.

James m. Mary Garland, dau. of James and Mary (Rice); rem. to Ky.; in Garrard Co., Ky., in 1797. Albemarle, p. 199; Bell, p. 235.

James m. 11 Oct., 1792, Elizabeth Carr. Sur. Gideon Carr. Albe-

WOOD (cont.)

marle Co. Mar. Bond.
Jane m. Matthew Dyall.
Jane m. John Wilson.
Jess, d. 1824, son of William; m. Mildred Terrell, dau. of Reuben. Albemarle Co. Mar. Record.
Jesse m. Mildred (____) Terrell, widow of Reuben (d. 1776). Albemarle, p. 325.
Jesse, Jr., d. 1829, son of Jesse; m. Lucy Wood. She m. (2) Hudson Oaks. Albemarle, p. 349.
John m. 2 April, 1788, Nancy Longest. Christ Church, p. 206.
John m. 25 Dec., 1788, Caroline M. Smith. Halifax Co. Mar. Record.
John m. 18 March, 1783, Sarah Hambleton. Louisa Co. Mar. Record.
John, d. ca 1792; m. bef. 1783, Eleanor Israel, dau. of Solomon. Albemarle, pp. 349, 359.
John m. 3 Feb., 1788, Elizabeth Yancey, spinster. Sur. Charles Yancy. Albemarle Co. Mar. Bond. She, dau. of Jeremiah (d. 1789). Albemarle, p. 358.
John m. 12 April, 1793, Keziah Franklin by Menoah Lesley. Campbell Co. Mar. Record.
John, b. England; d. 1781, Stafford Co.; m. Frances Carter. DAR No. 27 846; DAR No. 28 232.
John m. 19 April, 1791, Jeen Shirly. Sur. William Wood, Jr. Albemarle Co. Mar. Bond.
John, son of David and Mildred (Lewis), m. Amelia Harris; rem. to Richmond, Va. Albemarle, p. 348.
John m. bef. 1 April, 1788, Elizabeth Holladay, dau. of John. Proven by a Deed of that date, Spotsylvania Co. John, d. 1794, son of William and Ann (Crane); Elizabeth, d. 1832, dau. of John and Mildred (____) Thomas Holloday. Mss.
John m. 27 Dec., 1785, Lucy Rice. Sur. Lucia Brecken. Goochland Co. Mar. Bond.
John m. 9 Oct., 1788, Mary Terrell, spinster. Sur. William Wood. Albemarle Co. Mar. Bond. He, d. 1843, son of Isaac and Susan (Grayson); she, dau. of Reuben. Albemarle, p. 349.
John m. Margaret ____. She m. (2) Thomas Taberer. Hinshaw 6:37.
John m. bef. 9 April, 1698, Frances, dau. of ____ Hill, prob. Richard. Proven by Court Record of that date, Essex Co.
John, b. 1776, son of Valentine (1724-1781) and Lucy (Henry); m. Gertrude Spencer, dau. of Charles of Albemarle Co. 53V67; 6W(2)135.
John m. Elizabeth Thomas, dau. of Cornelius Thomas, who was son of James Nevill and Lucy (Thomas) but took his mother's surname. See Chancery Suit, Nevill, Williamsburg, Va. 36V74.
John Henry m. Elizabeth Spencer. 5V79. He, son of Valentine and Lucy (Henry); she, dau. of Charles. Albemarle, p. 347.
Johnson m. 30 Sept., 1784, Fanney Thompson by Rev. David Ellington, Baptist. Lunenburg Co. Ministers' Returns.
Joseph m. 1781, Margaret Bell. Orange Co. Mar. Record.
Joseph, Capt., m. Elizabeth Scott, b. ca 1739, dau. of Capt. John and Elizabeth (____). Cowherd, p. 327.
Josiah m. 8 May, 1787, Patience Weatherread, spinster. Sur. Samuel Wood. Albemarle Co. Mar. Bond.

WOOD (cont.)

Judith m. William Drew.
Lucy m. Edward Carter (2nd wife).
Lucy m. (1) Jesse Wood, Jr.; m. (2) Hudson Oaks.
Lucy m. Elisha Dickinson Gillum (or Gilliam).
Lucy m. James White.
Lydia m. Joseph Green.
Magdalene m. John McDowell.
Margaret m. Capt. Peter Jones.
Margaret m. William Moor.
Margaret (____) m. Thomas Taberer.
Margaret Caldwell m. Henry Barnes.
Maria m. James Clarkson.
Martha m. Francis Smithson.
Martha m. Thomas Moore.
Martha m. (1) Maj. Stephen Southall; m. (2) George F. Stras.
Martha m. William Meriwether.
Martha m. Nathaniel Thomason.
Martha (____) m. ____ Boyd.
Martha (____) m. Henry Turner.
Martha Cocke m. William Meriwether.
Mary m. Nathan Hall.
Mary m. John Sandidge (or Sandridge).
Mary m. Judge Peter Johnston.
Mary m. William Jordan.
Mary m. Peter Jones, Sr.
Mary m. Edward Bowman.
Mary m. John Garland.
Mary m. Thomas Chamberlayne.
Mary m. Malcolm McIntosh.
Mary Ann m. Reuben Woody.
Mary Virginia m. James Edwin Crockett.
Mercey m. Nathan Wash.
Mildred m. James Lester.
Mildred m. Reuben Mitchell.
Mildred m. Ralph Field.
Mildred m. Jechonias Yancey.
Moses m. 3 June, 1709, Mary Cox, dau. of Bartholomew. Henrico, p. 228.
Moses m. betw. Oct., 1688, and Oct., 1689, Eliza Ferguson. Court Orders, Henrico Co., prove it.
Nancy m. Joseph Watson.
Nancy m. Meekins Carr.
Nancy m. John Parker.
Nancy m. Newbill Puckett.
Nancy m. Rawser Spicer.
Nancy Elizabeth m. George Mathes.
Patsey m. H. Cox.
Patsey m. Adler Arrington.
Patsy m. Henry Coke.
Pattey m. Job Meador.
Patty m. Col. William Meriwether.

WOOD (cont.)

Patty m. John Ellis.
Peggy m. Thomas Ryan.
Polly m. George Wood.
Polly m. Thomas Jones.
Rebecca m. Capt. John Earle (2nd wife).
Rebecka m. William Evans.
Rice, son of William (d. 1820); m. Elizabeth Burgher, dau. of David; rem. to Missouri. Albemarle, p. 349.
Richard m. bef. 10 Jan., 1694, Alice (Davis) Lee, widow of Henry Lee (d. 1693) and dau. of William Davis. 24W(1)48.
Robert m. 21 Oct., 1711, Mary Alford. St. Peter's, p. 418.
Robert, d. 1839, son of David and Mildred (Lewis); m. Mary Ann Miller. Albemarle, p. 348.
Robert, b. Va.; m. Mary Kester. Their 10th child, Keziah Wood, b. 1814, Harrison Co., Ohio. Fulton, p. 934.
Sallie m. John Goff.
Sally m. Jac. Clark.
Sally m. Johny Manspoile.
Sally m. William Jordan.
Sally m. George Scott.
Samuel m. 19 Jan., 1769, Sarah Durham. Christ Church, p. 198.
Samuel m. 8 May, 1787, Elizabeth Willis Watkins, spinster. Sur. Josiah Wood. Albemarle Co. Mar. Bond.
Samuel m. 23 Dec., 1762, Elizabeth Merian, both in this parish. Douglas Reg., p. 7.
Sarah m. Francis Baleman.
Sarah m. William Palmer.
Sarah m. ____ Gooch.
Sarah m. John Field.
Sarah m. Elias Houghland.
Sarah m. Moses Hubbard.
Sarah m. Samuel Blake.
Sarah m. John Fulin.
Sarah m. William Pryor.
Sarah m. Henry Salmon.
Sarah m. Charles Crawford.
Sarah (____) m. ____ Wooten.
Sary m. Aaron Brooke.
Stephen m. 4 June, 1765, Anne Smith. Halifax Co. Mar. Record.
Susan m. William Gidden.
Susan m. Jonathan Bolling.
Susan m. Robert Cowan.
Susan m. John Adams.
Susanna m. Daniel Miller.
Susanna m. James Stiffe.
Susanna (____) m. Edward Digges.
Susannah m. Jesse Posey.
Susannah m. Philemon Richards.
Tandy m. 11 Feb., 1785, Polly Witt. Fluvanna Co. Mar. Record.
Thomas m. 3 March, 1789, Mary Pulliam, spinster. Sur. Barnabas Pulliam. Albemarle Co. Mar. Bond.

WOOD (cont.)

Thomas m. 1792, Rebecka Porter. Orange Co. Mar. Record.

Thomas m. 27 Aug., 1759, Sarah Buchanan, spinster. Sur. Joseph Buchanan. Wit. Humphrey Brooks. Fauquier Co. Mar. Bond.

Thomas m. 14 July, 1791, Lucy Gehee. Sur. William Gehee and/or William Campbell. Albemarle Co. Mar. Bond.

Thomas m. 19 March, 1781, Helender Johnson in Goochland. Douglas Reg., p. 21.

Thomas W., d. 1831, son of David and Mildred (Lewis); m. Susan Irvin, dau. of Joseph H. She m. (2) John Fray. Albemarle, p. 348.

Usley m. Jonathan Clifton.

Valentine, Col., b. 2 Sept., 1724; d. 13 March, 1781, Goochland Co., son of Henry and Martha (Cox) of Henrico Co.; m. 3 Jan., 1764, Hanover Co., Lucy Henry, b. there, 29 March, 1743; d. 14 July, 1826, Fluvanna Co., dau. of Col. John and Sarah (Winston); res. Goochland Co. 5V79; 32V391; 53V65; 6W(2)134-5; Albemarle, p. 347; Prince Edward, p. 330.

William m. 12 Jan., 1786, Rebecca Scott. Northampton Co. Mar. Record.

William m. 25 Jan., 1787, Susan Overstreet, dau. of Thomas. Sur. Robert Crute. Amelia Co. Mar. Bond.

William m. 11 Nov., 1784, Sarah Hall. Louisa, p. 257.

William m. 10 April, 1729, Elizabeth Brown. Christ Church, p. 166.

William m. 10 Feb., 1791, Fanny Jones. Christ Church, p. 207.

William m. 4 Dec., 1774, Fanny Blake. Christ Church, p. 201.

William m. 9 Nov., 1716, Susanna Dinely. Christ Church, p. 162.

William m. 24 Jan., 1792, Mary Martin. Sur. John Wood. Albemarle Co. Mar. Bond. She, dau. of James and Elizabeth (____). Albemarle, p. 264.

William m. 27 Oct., 1799, Martha Evans by Rev. James Shelburne, Baptist. Lunenburg Co. Ministers' Returns.

William, son of David and Mildred (Lewis), m. Pamela Dickerson, dau. of John; rem. to Missouri. Albemarle, p. 348.

William, d. 1833, son of Jesse; m. Nancy Field, dau. of Robert (d. 1824). Albemarle, p. 194.

William m. bef. 1773, Ann Crane, dau. of John Scandland Crane. Proven by Will of John Crane, dated 4 June, 1773, Spotsylvania Co., and by Deeds there, 1777 and 1779.

William, Jr., m. 4 July, 1788, Jane Stern Jeter, dau. of Ambrose. Sur. William Crowder. Amelia Co. Mar. Bond.

William Johnson m. 15 Sept., 1795, Elizabeth "Betty" Twyman, dau. of George III and Mary (Walker). Albemarle Co. Mar. Record. Wilcoxson, p. 415.

Zachariah m. 23 April, 1794, Lucy Seamonds. Sur. Harrison Wood. Albemarle Co. Mar. Bond.

WOODAL

John m. 10 Oct., 1794, Sarah Foster. Louisa Co. Mar. Record.

WOODALL

Jacob m. 20 Dec., 1787, Rebecah Covington. Halifax Co. Mar. Record.

John m. 27 Jan., 1786, Susanna Stovall. Halifax Co. Mar. Record.

John m. 9 Sept., 1797, Nancey Tombs (or Tunes). Halifax Co. Mar. Record.

WOODALL (cont.)

Mary m. Howell Heathcock.

Patsy m. William Thomas.

Suckey m. Martin Covington.

William m. 13 Feb., 1793, Martha Talbert. Halifax Co. Mar. Record.

William m. 14 March, 1797, Sarah Thomasson by Rev. John Lasley. Louisa Co. Ministers' Returns.

WOODARD

William of Ware River m. 14 Aug., 1684, Bridget Williams of this parish. Christ Church, p. 23.

WOODBRIDGE

Elizabeth m. Morris McCathlin.

John m. ____ Keene, dau. of William and Elizabeth (Rogers) of Northumberland Co. 8W(1)45-6.

WOODCOCK

John Shearman m. 1759, Frances Rust. Northumberland Co. Mar. Record.

WOODE

Mary m. John Reynolds.

WOODFIELD

John m. 15 Feb., 1800, Sally Sargent. Shelby Co., Ky. Mar. Record.

Mary m. Maj. James Brenton.

WOODFIN

Sarah m. Edward Haymond.

WOODFOLK

____ m. Mary Harris, dau. of William (d. 1788) and Mary (Netherland). Albemarle, p. 219.

Frances m. Thomas Burnet.

Joseph m. 6 July, 1786, Betsy Barnet, both of Louisa. Douglas Reg., p. 24.

WOODFORD

____ m. ____ Thornton, dau. of Francis of Caroline Co. 4W(1)158.

____ m. bef. 1799, Mary Thornton, dau. of John. Proven by Court Suit of that date. 11W(2)115.

Catesby, b. 19 June, 1738, Caroline Co.; d. Oct., 1791, Augusta Co., son of Maj. William and Ann (Cocke); m. 1771, Mary Buckner of Williamsburg, Va. 5V191; 33V34; 9W(2)337; Jones, p. 132.

Elizabeth m. James Dunn.

John Thornton, b. 29 July, 1763; d. 31 Jan., 1845, Ky., son of Gen. William and Mary (Thornton); m. Mary Turner Taliaferro, b. 13 March, 1772; d. 1 March, 1828, Ky. Jones, p. 133.

Mary m. Will. Webber.

Mary (____) m. Richard Mason.

William m. 6 Nov., 1795, Hannah Mass. Rockingham Co. Wayland, p. 7.

William, Maj., of "Windsor," Caroline Co., m. Anne Skelton. 26V178.

William m. 3 Aug., 1732, Elizabeth Cock. Spotsylvania Co. Mar. Record.

William, Maj., d. 1780, prob. son of William and Elizabeth (____) Battaile Woodford; m. 2 or 3 Sept., 1732, Ann Cocke, b. June, 1704, dau. of Dr. William and Elizabeth (Catesby) Cocke of Williamsburg, Va.; res. "Windsor," Caroline Co. 5V191; 33V34; 41V359; Jones, p. 131. Mar. 2 Sept., 1722. Caroline, p. 184.

William m. bef. 11 Nov., 1708, Elizabeth (____) Battaile, widow of

WOODFORD (cont.)

John, the immigrant. 41V359.

William, Gen., m. bef. 1777, Mary Thornton, dau. of John (d. 1777). Proven by Chancery Suit, 1799. 11W(2)117. William, b. 6 Oct., 1734; d. 13 Nov., 1780, son of Maj. William and Ann (Cocke); a prisoner of war in Rev.; m. 1763, Mary Thornton, dau. of John and Mildred (Gregory). 5V191; 33V34; 41V359; Jones, p. 132; DAR No. 31 155.

William Catesby, b. 1768; d. 1820, Caroline Co., son of Gen. William and Mary (Thornton); m. 1793, Elizabeth Battaile, dau. of Lawrence and Sarah (Robinson); res. "White Hall," Caroline Co. 5V191; 41V 359; Jones, p. 133.

WOODFORK

Patsy m. James Allen.

Thomas m. 27 Oct., 1788, Mary Cole, spinster. Sur. Robert Clark. Albemarle Co. Mar. Bond.

WOODGAR

Martha m. Richard Worsdall.

WOODHAL

Elizabeth m. John Foster Taylor.

John m. 13 Oct., 1757, Jemima Willis, both in this parish. Douglas Reg., p. 3.

WOODHALL

Ann m. Thomas Fielder.

Charles m. 1 Oct., 1765, Elizabeth Black, both of this parish. Douglas Reg., p. 8.

Elizabeth m. Thomas Harris.

John m. 12 Aug., 1756, Dorothy Pledge, both in this parish. Douglas Reg., p. 2.

William, widower, m. 3 Dec., 1758, Marianne Hancock, both in this parish. Douglas Reg., p. 4.

William m. 12 April, 1759, Mary Fielder, both of this parish. Douglas Reg., p. 4.

WOODHOUSE

Anna m. Jonathan Bonney.

Elizabeth m. Thomas Ewell.

Elizabeth m. Maj. Nicholas Merriweather.

Josiah m. 24 Feb., 1791, Eliza Smith. Princess Anne Co. Mar. Record.

Margaret m. Lemuel West.

Mary or Mary (____) m. Bagwell Moore.

Pembrook m. Gisbon Pallet.

Sally or Sally (____) m. Tully Otterson.

Sarah m. Maximilian Boush (1st wife).

William m. 18 Dec., 1788, Elizabeth Rainey. Princess Anne Co. Mar. Record.

William, Jr., Col., had wife "Betty" in 1776. 5V144.

William D. m. 20 Dec., 1791, Frances Keeling. Princess Anne Co. Mar. Record.

WOODHOUST

Pemme m. Moses Brock.

WOODIE

Jane m. Dan Johnson.

WOODING
John m. 24 Nov., 1774, Sucky Hill. Halifax Co. Mar. Record.
M. m. James Taylor.
Martha m. James Chappell.
WOODLAND
___ m. Sarah Eaton, dau. of John (will, 1717, York Co.). 6T123.
WOODLEIF
Anne m. Jesse Herring.
Rebecca m. John Nelson (2nd wife).
Sarah m. Austin Heath.
WOODLEY
___, a dau., m. ___ Copeland.
Andrew, b. 27 April, 1769, son of John and Catherine (Bryant); m. 9 Nov., 1797, his cousin, Elizabeth Hill Harrison, dau. of John and Elizabeth (Hill). Boddie-Isle, p. 265; Woodley, p. 9. She was dau. of John and Frances (Hill). Woodley, p. 35. Mar. 7 Nov., 1797. Isle of Wight Co. Mar. Record.
Frances m. Joseph Hill.
John, son of Andrew (will prov. 1720), m. Frances (___) Wilson, widow of John. Woodley, p. 28.
John m. 19 Jan., 1789, Mary Jefferson. Christ Church, p. 207.
Mary m. Joseph Copeland.
WOODLIEF
George m. 24 Sept., 1787, Katherine Clayton. Brunswick Co. Mar. Record.
Peter m. Ann P. (Bland) Morrison, widow of John and dau. of Richard and Mary (Bolling). Pocahontas, p. 36.
Sarah m. ___ Pace.
Thomas m. 19 Dec., 1788, Sarah Williams. Amelia Co. Mar. Record.
Thomas m. Martha Taylor, dau. of Thomas and Lucy (___) of Southampton Co. 23V219.
WOODLOOK
Elizabeth m. Samuel Hicks.
WOODNOTT
Rebecca m. William Hudson.
WOODROO
Rachel m. Abraham Neill.
WOODROOF
David, Jr., Capt., b. 1730-5; d. 1817, Amherst Co.; served in Rev. War; m. ca 1759, Clary Powell, b. 1739; d. 22 Feb., 1825, Amherst Co., dau. of Richard and Elizabeth (___). 30T65; 36V78-9.
Ely m. James Nicholson, Jr.
Nathaniel m. 22 Dec., 1779, Catey Vick. Sur. Howel Vick. John Vick, her father, gave consent. Brunswick Co. Mar. Bond.
Sarah m. Thomas Hackney.
WOODRUFF
Jenny m. Samuel Avent.
Jesse, b. 20 May, 1757, Spotsylvania Co.; d. 13 Oct., 1825, Fayetteville, Lincoln Co., Tenn.; m. 21 March, 1783, in Washington Co., Esther Buchanan, b. 1 June, 1763; d. after 1848. DAR Query K-48(a), Nov., 1948. He, b. 1757, Loudoun Co.; d. 1800, Lincoln Co., Tenn. DAR No. 79 852.

WOODRUFF (cont.)
Patsy m. Sterling Harris.

WOODRUFFE
Job m. 12 June, 1769, Mary Clarke. Consent of Benjamin Cocke, guardian. Charles City Co. Mar. Record.

WOODRUM
David m. 22 Sept., 1765, Susannah Barnet, both in this parish. Douglas Reg., p. 8.
Elles m. John Utley Wade.
John m. 15 Nov., 1761, Mary Baze, both in this parish. Douglas Reg., p. 6.
Lucy m. John Childres.
Sarah m. John Snead.
Susanna m. Robert Smith.
William m. 16 Dec., 1782, Aggie Webster, both of Goochland. Douglas Reg., p. 22.

WOODS (See WOOD)
____ m. Elizabeth Campbell, dau. of Gilbert. Kegley, p. 157; Morton, p. 476.
____ m. 17 Dec., 1785, Elizabeth Brooks. Christ Church, p. 205.
____ m. bef. 2 July, 1779, Joanna Shepherd, dau. of Christopher, whose will of that date, Albemarle Co., proves it.
____ m. Frances "Frankie" Sublett, dau. of William (1735/6-1783) of Charlotte Co. 62V490.
____ m. Martha Poage, dau. of Robert (will, 1774). Kegley, p. 554.
Amelia m. John Lauderdale.
Andrew, b. 1722, Ireland; will prov. 9 Aug., 1781, Botetourt Co., son of Michael and Mary (Campbell); m. Martha Poage, dau. of Robert of Augusta Co. 4V459; 51V367; Albemarle, p. 355; Kegley, p. 419.
Andrew, Jr., son of Andrew and Martha (Poage), m. Mary McCullock; res. in part now W. Va. Kegley, p. 419.
Archibald, Maj., of Botetourt Co.; d. 1846, Ohio Co., son of Andrew and Martha (Poage); m. 5 March, 1789, Ann Poage, his cousin, dau. of Thomas and Polly (McClanahan) of Augusta Co. 4V461; Albemarle, p. 355; Kegley, p. 419; Waddell, p. 260.
Archibald m. Mourning Shelton, dau. of William (d. 1815). Albemarle, p. 315.
Barbara m. George Martin.
Benjamin m. 16 Nov., 1713, Elizabeth Wheeler. Christ Church, p. 83.
Elizabeth m. David Cloyd, Jr.
Elizabeth m. ____ Wallace.
Elizabeth m. Peter Wallace.
Elizabeth m. John Buster (1st wife).
Elizabeth m. William B. Harris.
Elizabeth m. James Brooks.
George m. 17 Feb., 1778, Fanny Mason. Henry Co. Mar. Record.
Hannah m. James Hatton.
Hannah m. William Wallace.
Hugh m. 5 Aug., 1779, Sarah Ann George. Henry Co. Mar. Record.
Isbell m. John Dickinson.
James, Col., b. 1748, Albemarle Co.; d. 1822, Garrard Co., Ky., son of Michael and Esther (Carothers); officer in Rev. War; m. 1779,

WOODS (cont.)

Mary Garland, b. 1760; d. 1835, dau. of James of North Garden and Mary (Rice). Albemarle, p. 352; DAR No. 68 186; DAR No. 76 152.

James m. Abigail Estill, b. 22 Nov., 1752, dau. of Wallace and (3) Mary Ann (Campbell); rem. to Tenn. Kegley, p. 372.

James, son of Andrew and Martha (Poage), m. Nancy Rayburn (or Raeburn), dau. of Joseph Raeburn. Kegley, pp. 419, 618.

Jane m. Joseph Montgomery.

John m. 10 April, 1782, Lucy Hawkins. Henry Co. Mar. Record.

John m. by 1750, Elizabeth Campbell. Rockbridge Co. Morton, p. 546.

John m. 30 April, 1778, Abigail Estel by Rev. John Alderson, Jr. Rockingham Co. or Greenbrier Co. Ministers' Returns.

John, b. 19 Feb., 1712, prob. Ireland; d. 14 Oct., 1791, son of Michael and Mary (Campbell); m. Susanna Anderson, dau. of Rev. James of Pennsylvania. 51V367; Albemarle, p. 352.

Magdalene m. (1) John McDowell; m. (2) Benjamin Borden (or Burden), Jr.; m. (3) John Bowyer.

Margaret m. Richard Netherland.

Margaret m. James Walker.

Margaret m. Andrew Wallace.

Martha m. Henry Walker.

Martha m. Peter Wallace.

Mary m. George Davidson.

Mary m. James Poage.

Mary m. Hugh Barclay.

Mary m. Benjamin Harris.

Michael, b. 1684, North of Ireland; d. 1762, Albemarle Co.; res. 1st in Lancaster Co., Penna.; crossed the Blue Ridge mountains in 1734; m. Mary Campbell. 4V459; 51V366-7; 10W(2)92; Albemarle, p. 351.

Michael, son of John and Susanna (Anderson), m. 1795, Esther Caruthers of Rockbridge Co. Albemarle, p. 352; Morton, p. 546.

Micajah of Albemarle Co. m. Sarah Harris (Rodes) Davenport, b. 3 July, 1777; d. 25 Jan., 1880, dau. of John and Sarah (Harris) and widow of William Davenport. Albemarle, p. 307; Am. Hist. 9:184.

Peter m. 25 April, 1782, Jael Kavanaugh by Rev. John Alderson, Jr. Rockingham Co. or Greenbrier Co. Ministers' Returns.

Rachel m. John Federa.

Rebecca m. Isaac Kelly.

Rebecca m. Alexander Culton.

Rebecca Berry m. John Earle.

Richard, Col., d. 1801, son of James (d. 1784); m. (1) Margaret ____; m. (2) Elizabeth Ann Stuart, sis. of Col. John of Greenbrier Co. and dau. of David (d. ca 1767, Augusta Co.). Albemarle, p. 356; Kegley, pp. 562, 572; Waddell, p. 370.

Robert, son of Andrew and Martha (Poage), m. (1) Lovely Caldwell; m. (2) Elizabeth Eoff. Kegley, p. 419.

Samuel, Lieut., b. 1735, Albemarle Co.; d. there, 1826; m. bef. 22 June, 1769, Margaret (____) Robinson. Kegley, pp. 316, 335; DAR No. 79 216.

Samuel, son of Michael and Esther (Carothers), m. Sarah Rodes, dau. of John; rem. to Marion Co., Mo. Albemarle, p. 352.

Sarah m. ____ Shirkey.

WOODS (cont.)
Sarah m. Joseph Lapsley
Sarah m. Nicholas Shirkey.
Searight m. 1797, Ann McCoskey. Rockbridge Co. Morton, p. 546.
Susan m. Nathaniel Massie.
Susan m. Robert Cowan.
Susanna m. John Trimble.
William, b. 1706-7, Ireland, son of Michael and Mary (Campbell); m. Susanna Wallace, sis. of William; res. 1774, Fincastle Co. 51V367; Albemarle, p. 353.
William m. 25 Nov., 1797, Ruth Beaser. Rockingham Co. Wayland, p. 9.
William, d. 1819, son of Michael (d. 1777, Botetourt Co.); m. Joanna Shepherd, dau. of Christopher. Albemarle, p. 354.
William, d. 1829, son of William (d. 1836); m. Mary Jarman, dau. of William. Albemarle, p. 353.
William, d. 1836, age 92, son of William and Susanna (Wallace); m. (1) his cousin, Sarah Wallace; m. (2) his cousin, Ann Reid; m. (3) Nancy (____) Richardson. Albemarle, p. 353.
William M., son of Michael and Esther (Carothers), m. (1) Louisa Dabney, dau. of William S., Sr.; m. (2) Martha Scott, dau. of Charles A. Albemarle, p. 352.

WOODSIDE
____ m. John Shockency.
Elizabeth m. ____ Whiting.
Elizabeth m. Francis Whitney.
John of Fauquier Co., son of John (d. on or bef. 1787); m. ____ ____; rem. bef. 1800 to Shelby Co., Ky. 34 Ky. Reg. 100.

WOODSON
____ m. bef. 23 Feb., 1781, Elizabeth Payne, dau. of George, whose will of that date, Goochland Co., proves it.
____ m. bef. 28 July, 1743, Constant Watkins, dau. of John, whose will of that date, Henrico Co., proves it.
____ m. bef. 24 July, 1755, Rebecca Pryor, dau. of John, whose will of that date, Goochland Co., proves it.
____ m. Frances Thompson, dau. of Joseph (d. 1765). Albemarle, p. 328.
____ m. bef. 1724, Elizabeth Murry, dau. of John (will, 1724, Isle of Wight Co.). 7W(1)265.
____ m. Mary DeGraffenreid, dau. of Tscharner and (1) Mary (Baker). Free II:206.
____ m. bef. 4 May, 1757, Susanna (____) Bates, mother of several Bates children whom she names in her will of that date. Goochland Co.
____ m. bef. 25 Oct., 1752, Sarah Hughes, dau. of Robert, whose will of that date, Cumberland Co., proves it.
____ m. Nancy Pleasants, dau. of Jesse (will, 1803). Halifax, p. 325.
____ m. Jos. Passon.
____ m. Polly Harris, dau. of John (will prov. 1800, Powhatan Co.). Louisa, p. 333.
____ (____) m. Col. Joseph Crockett.
Agatha m. Pleasant Turner.

WOODSON (cont.)

Agnes m. Francis Watkins.
Agnes m. Joseph Morton.
Agnes m. Samuel Spencer.
Agnes m. Pleasant Turner.
Anderson m. 3 July, 1780, Julia Lacklin. Sur. John Coleman. Charlotte Co. Mar. Bond.
Ann m. John Stephen Woodson.
Ann m. Capt. William Pope.
Augustine m. Ann Martin, dau. of Benjamin and Catharine (____). Albemarle, p. 264.
Ben. m. 14 March, 1779, Sally Johnson, both in Goochland. Douglas Reg., p. 18.
Benjamin, b. ca 1666; d. 1723, Henrico Co., son of Col. Robert and Elizabeth (Ferris) of Prince George Co.; m. 12 da 5 Mo 1700, Sarah Porter, dau. of William, Jr. Society of Friends, Henrico. 45V313-4; Mss.
Booker m. 7 Oct., 1789, Elizabeth Hylson. Sur. John Seay. Cumberland Co. Mar. Bond.
Caroline Matilda m. Thomas Fleming Bates.
Charles m. 5 da 1 mo 1737, Mary Pleasants, dau. of John. Society of Friends, Henrico Co. Charles, son of Tarlton and Ursula (Fleming); m. (1) Mary Pleasants, dau. of John (Deed of Gift, 12 Dec., 1752, Cumberland Co.); m. (2) 16 da 12 mo 1744, Agness Richarson. Society of Friends, Henrico Co. She was Agnes (Parsons) Richardson, widow of Samuel and dau. of Joseph Parsons. 9W(1)256; Henrico, p. 228.
Charles, son of Drury, who gave consent, m. 23 Sept., 1780, Judith Leake, dau. of Josiah. Sur. George Christian. Goochland Co. Mar. Bond. Charles of Cumberland Co., Capt. in Rev. War; Judith, dau. of Josiah and Ann (Fenton). 6W(2)350.
Charles m. Mary Winston. She m. (2) Peter Fore, Jr. Huguenot 7:197.
Charles, Jr., m. 5 da 3 mo 1768, Ann Trotter. Society of Friends, Henrico. 24W(1)196.
Drury of Cumberland Co. m. 3 March, 1800, Sally Stovall, dau. of Jesse, who gave consent. Sur. Jesse Stovall. Powhatan Co. Mar. Bond.
Elizabeth m. William Wright.
Elizabeth m. Alexander Trent.
Elizabeth m. Abraham Salloe (or Salley).
Elizabeth m. Samuel Ridgeway.
Elizabeth m. Joseph Pleasants.
Elizabeth m. William Lewis.
Elizabeth m. Nathaniel Venable.
Elizabeth m. John Pleasants.
Elizabeth m. Capt. James Daniel.
Elizabeth m. Patrick Napier.
Elizabeth m. Shadrach Mims.
Elizabeth m. William Johnson.
Elizabeth m. Lieut. John Kennon.
Elizabeth m. John Morton.
Elizabeth m. William Jordan.
Elizabeth m. Josiah Woodson.

WOODSON (cont.)

Elizabeth m. Jesse Hughes.

Fanny m. Robert Farrar.

Jacob m. 13 June, 1791, Dorathea Pears, dau. of Anderson, who gave consent. Sur. William Powell. Goochland Co. Mar. Bond.

Jacob, Capt., m. 1773, Elizabeth Morton, b. 28 Nov., 1754, dau. of Capt. John and Mary (Anderson). 11W(2)216.

James m. 23 July, 1754, Elizabeth Whitlock, both in this parish. Douglas Reg., p. 1.

Jane m. Joseph Woodson.

Jane m. ____ Pleasants.

Jane m. Archibald Pleasants.

Jane m. Robert Lewis.

Jane m. Lilburn Lewis.

Joan m. Richard Clough.

John, physician, b. 1586, England; killed by Indians, 1644, at Fleur de Hundred on the James River; m. in England, Sara Winston; came to Virginia in 1619. 44V167; Mss.

John m. 18 March, 1760, Mary Mimms, dau. of David. Sur. Charles Christian. Goochland Co. Mar. Bond.

John m. 8 Oct., 1751, Dorothea Randolph. Sur. Tarleton Woodson, Jr. Goochland Co. Mar. Bond. John, b. ca 1730, Va.; d. 1789, Goochland Co., son of Josiah; Dorothea, b. 1732; d. 2 Feb., 1794, dau. of Isham and Jane (Rogers). 45V82; 24W(1)282; DAR No. 65 142.

John m. 5 Nov., 1772, Anne Davenport, dau. of Thomas, Jr., who gave consent. Sur. Norvel Dunivant. Cumberland Co. Mar. Bond.

John, d. 1715, Henrico Co., son of Robert and Elizabeth (Ferris); m. Judith Tarleton, dau. of Stephen of New Kent Co. 22V48; 49V177; 9W(1)255; 24W(1)282; Br., p. 389; McCullough, p. 242.

John m. Frances Garland, dau. of Nathaniel. Albemarle, p. 200.

John m. 26 May, 1794, N. Pleasants. Halifax Co. Mar. Record.

John, b. 1695; d. 21 May, 1754; m. Susannah (Fleming) Bates, widow of John Bates of York Co. and dau. of Charles Fleming; res. 1724, Henrico Co.; rem. to Goochland Co., where he was Sheriff in 1732. 23V325; 33V36; 36V76.

John m. 24 Dec., 1754, Elizabeth Bailey, both in this parish. Douglas Reg., p. 1.

John of Goochland Co., b. 1705; d. 1791, son of Benjamin and Sarah (Porter); m. 10 Aug., 1731, Mary Miller, dau. of William of Lancaster Co. A dau., Sarah, m. 1756. A son, John, b. ca 1747, Cumberland Co. 45V313; Va. Gene. 5:2:57; DAR No. 65 790; DAR No. 82 510. Mar. 1731. 8W(2)312.

John, Jr., of Cumberland Co., d. there, 1798, son of John and Mary (Miller); m. (1) Joanna Booker, b. ca 1750; d. ca 1780, dau. of James; m. (2) Elizabeth (Raine) Venable, widow of John. Va. Gene. 5:2:56; DAR No. 65 790.

John, Jr., d. 1700, son of John (ca 1632-1688) of Henrico Co.; m. bef. 20 Aug., 1681, ____ Tucker. Proven by Deed, 1681, Henrico Co. Mar. Mary Tucker, dau. of Samuel and Jane (Larcome) Tucker. Jane m. (2) John Pleasants, whose will of 27 Sept., 1690, proves the marriage of Mary Tucker. 24W(1)283; Hartford B-8019(6), 23 July, 1955. Signed H. K. B.

WOODSON (cont.)

John Stephen m. 9 Oct., 1777, Anna Woodson. Sur. Joseph Woodson. Letters of consent from Matthew Woodson, father of John Stephen and Col. John Woodson, father of Anna. Goochland Co. Mar. Bond. He, b. 17 Aug., 1757, son of Matthew and Elizabeth (LeVillian). Huguenot 7:253.

Joseph, son of Robert and Elizabeth (Ferris) of Henrico Co., m. 6 April, 1701, Jane Woodson, dau. of John and Mary (Tucker). Society of Friends, Henrico Co. 24W(1)281.

Joseph m. 18 Sept., 1798, Sarah Ford. Shelby Co., Ky. Mar. Record.

Joseph m. 11 Sept., 1706/7, Mary Sanborn, dau. of Daniel. Hinshaw 6:37.

Joseph in Goochland m. 24 Nov., 1779, Sarah Hughes in Cumberland. Douglas Reg., p. 19.

Joseph, Jr., m. 30 Dec., 1769, Mildred Redford, dau. of William, dec'd. Consent of Joseph Woodson to his son's marriage and consent of Stoakes McCaul to his ward's marriage. Sur. David Maddox. Goochland Co. Mar. Bond. Mar. 2 Jan., 1770. Douglas Reg., p. 11.

Josiah m. Mary Royall (1st husband). 33V104.

Josiah, Maj., b. 1758, Va.; d. 1817, Mason Co., Ky., son of John and Dorothy (Randolph); m. 22 Nov., 1778, Goochland Co., Elizabeth Woodson, b. 12 May, 1759, dau. of Matthew and Elizabeth (LeVillian). Goochland Co. Mar. Record. 7W(1)198; Douglas Reg., p. 18; Huguenot 7:253; DAR No. 65 142.

Judith m. Joseph Michaux.

Judith m. ____ Railey.

Judith m. Enoch Ward Ellington.

Judith m. Orlando Jones (1st wife).

Judith m. William Railey.

Judith m. Jacob Michaux.

Judith m. Jonathan Knight.

Judith m. William Cannon.

Judith m. Stephen Cox.

Judith m. Thomas Cheadle.

Lucy m. James Chappel.

Martha m. ____ Railey.

Martha m. Thomas Railey.

Martha m. John Gannaway.

Mary m. John Pleasants.

Mary m. George Payne.

Mary m. Richard Truman.

Mary m. ____ Pleasants.

Mary m. Jesse Redd.

Mary m. Nathaniel G. Morris.

Mary m. Poindexter Mosby.

Mary m. Ben. Weaver.

Mary m. Aires Lane.

Mary Ann Elizabeth Miller m. Jacob Michaux.

Mary R. m. William Porter.

Mary R. m. Nathaniel Gorsdean Morris.

Matthew m. 22 Nov., 1753, Elizabeth LeVillian, dau. of John, who gave consent. Sur. Jacob Woodson. Cumberland Co. Mar. Bond.

WOODSON (cont.)

Mar. 28 Nov. Douglas Reg., p. 1. Rev. Matthew, b. 1731, Goochland Co.; d. there, 1800; Elizabeth, b. 28 Nov., 1737; d. 1804, dau. of John (will, 1765, Cumberland Co.). 24V423; Huguenot 7:253; DAR No. 55 142; DAR No. 85 003.

Miller, b. 1745; d. 1823, son of John and Mary (Miller); m. 1769, Mary de Graffenreidt, dau. of Tcharner. Court Record, 20 Dec., 1796, Cumberland Co. 45V313.

Murray m. 15 Jan., 1795, Susanna Railey. Sur. Edmond Toney. Powhatan Co. Mar. Bond.

Nancy m. Archer Pledge.

Patty m. John Gannaway.

Rene in Albemarle m. 2 Feb., 1775, Martha Johnson in Louisa. Douglas Reg., p. 16.

Richard, Jr., of "Poplar Hill," Prince Edward Co., b. ca 1706, Henrico Co.; will prov. Jan., 1744, Prince Edward Co., son of Richard and Ann (____); m. Anne Madelin Michaux, b. ca 1710; d. 1796, age 86, dau. of Abraham and Susanna (Rochet); rem. to Amelia Co. 44V368; 45V104-5; 45V419.

Robert, b. 1634 at Flower de Hundred, Prince George Co.; d. after 1707, son of Dr. John and Sarah (Winston); m. Elizabeth Ferris, dau. of Richard of "Curles," Henrico Co. 44V167; 45V314; 48V35-6; 24W(1)280; 11 W(2)261; Br., p. 389, McCullough, p. 242; Mss.

Robert, Jr., b. ca 1660 at "Curles," Henrico Co.; d. there 1729, son of Robert and Elizabeth (Ferris); m. (1) 1691-2, Sarah Lewis; m. (2) Rachel Watkins. 44V167; Henrico, p. 226.

Samuel m. 19 June, 1777, Elizabeth Payne, both of this parish. Douglas Reg., p. 18.

Sanburn said to have m. Elizabeth Michaux, dau. of Abraham (1672-1717) and Susanna (Rochet). 45V104, 107.

Sarah m. Joseph Parson.

Sarah m. Turner Rowntree.

Sarah m. Edward Mosby.

Sarah m. Frederick Hatcher.

Sarah m. Thomas Overton.

Sarah m. ____ Terrill.

Sarah m. John Everett.

Sarah m. Edward Moseley.

Sarah m. Enoch Word Ellington.

Sarah m. Henry Terrell (2nd wife).

Sarah m. Jesse Ellis.

Sarah m. Gen. Thomas Overton (1st wife).

Shadrach in Buckingham m. 14 Aug., 1766, Susannah Walker in this parish. Douglas Reg., p. 9.

Shadrack m. bef. 4 Aug., 1772, Susanna Watkins, dau. of David, Jr., whose will of that date, Henrico Co., proves it.

Susan m. Beverley Langhorne.

Susan m. Joseph Morris.

Susanna m. Perrin Redford.

Susanna m. Isham Randolph Railey.

Susanna m. ____ Shores.

Susanna m. ____ Pleasants.

WOODSON (cont.)

Susanna m. John Pleasants.

Susanna m. Micajah Wheeler.

Tarleton, b. ca 1681, Henrico Co.; will, 1761, Chesterfield Co.; son of John; m. 3 April, 1710, his cousin, Ursula Fleming, dau. of Charles of New Kent Co. Minutes of Society of Friends, 1710. 35V 437; 9W(1)256; Br., p. 389; Hartford B-8205(5), 17 Sept., 1955. Signed H. K. B.

Tarleton, son of Tarleton and Ursula (Fleming), m. in New York, Anne Van der Veer; res. Prince Edward Co. 9W(1)256.

Thomas of Goochland m. 20 July, 1798, Elizabeth Redford, dau. of John. Sur. John Redford. Henrico Co. Mar. Bond.

Thomas m. 15 Feb., 1796, Sally Saunders, dau. of Robert, who gave consent. Sur. Robert Saunders. Goochland Co. Mar. Bond.

Tscharner de Graffenreidt, d. Oct., 1829, son of Miller; m. 8 Sept., 1788, Mecklenburg Co., Lucy Michaux, dau. of Jacob and Sally (Neville). Sur. William Hendrick. Joseph Michaux, guardian of Lucy, gave consent. 45V312.

Tucker m. 18 March, 1741, Sarah Hughes. Sur. John Cannon. Consent given by Stephen Woodson, guardian to Tucker, and Robert Hughes, father of Sarah. Goochland Co. Mar. Bond.

Tucker of Goochland Co. m. 22 Feb., 1762, Mary Netherland. Sur. Wade Netherland. Cumberland Co. Mar. Bond. Deed of Gift, 1762, Goochland Co., and will of Wade Netherland, dated 11 Aug., 1765, Cumberland Co., prove Wade was father of Mary.

Tucker, d. 1779, son of Tucker and Sarah (Hughes); m. Elizabeth Moore, dau. of John (d. 1785); res. 1769, Albemarle Co. She m. (2) 1782, Maj. Joseph Crockett; rem. to Ky. Albemarle, pp. 284, 356-7.

Tucker Moore, son of Tucker and Elizabeth (Moore), m. 11 March, 1799, Martha Eppes Hudson, dau. of Charles, who gave consent. Sur. Matthew Henderson. They moved to Jessamine Co., Ky. Albemarle Co. Mar. Bond. Albemarle, p. 357.

Unita m. John Redford.

Ursley m. William Pledge.

WOODVILLE

John, minister, b. 1763, White Haven, Cumberland Co., England; to America, 1787; Rector of St. Mark's Parish, Culpeper Co.; d. 1834; m. Sarah Stevenson, dau. of Rev. James. Jett, pp. 123-4.

WOODWARD

Ann m. William Spencer.

Anne m. Capt. Thomas Spencer.

James m. Jane "Jenny" Hyden, dau. of Henry and Lydia (____); res. Stafford Co. 24T134; Orange III:161.

Jesse, d. 1820, Lee Co.; m. Mary Hyden, b. 12 May, 1765, Stafford Co.; d. 20 Aug., 1855, Lee Co., dau. of Henry and Lydia (____). 24T134; Orange III:161.

Jesse m. 20 July, 1779, Martha Maves. Sur. Samuel Morgan. Amelia Co. Mar. Bond.

John m. 12 June, 1708, Rebecca Chandler. Northampton Co. Mar. Record.

Launcelot of Charles City Co. m. 1708, Elizabeth Cocke, dau. of William. 4V78. Mar. bef. 1705. Proven by Deed of that date, Henrico

WOODWARD (cont.)
Co.
Lucy m. John Vivian Webb.
Martha m. (1) Gideon Macon; m. (2) Capt. Nathaniel West; m. (3) ___ Bigger.
Mary m. Ambrose Hailey.
Nelley m. Corprew Wickings.
Philarite m. John Giles.
Philip m. Elizabeth Brockenbrough. 5V449.
Rebekah m. William Hawthorn.
Sally m. John Marchant.
Samuel of Charles City Co. m. Sarah Hallam, dau. of Robert of Henrico Co. (Patent, 1636). She m. (2) John Sturdivant of Charles City Co. 5V212; 24W(1)128.
William m. 12 Oct., 1784, Sarah Hall. Louisa, p. 281.
Wittha m. Mathew Fathery.

WOODY
Elizabeth m. William Nichols.
Martha m. Ashley Johnson.
Mourning m. Alexander Ross.
Reuben m. Mary Ann Wood, dau. of John and Eleanor (Israel). Albemarle, p. 349.
Samuel m. 8 Sept., 1785, Elizabeth Denie by Rev. John Buchanan. Henrico, p. 229.

WOODYARD
Katherine m. William Dess.

WOOLAMS
Sarah m. Deamon Harris.

WOOLBANKS
Polly m. Francis Blankenship.
William m. 29 Dec., 1778, Nancy Weatherspoon. Louisa Co. Mar. Record.

WOOLDRIDGE
___ m. Jane Roberts, dau. of John (will dated 5 Nov., 1774). Halifax, p. 331.
Edmund m. 22 Aug., 1774, Elizabeth Watkins. Sur. Samuel Watkins. Cumberland Co. Mar. Bond.
Robert of Powhatan Co., d. 1800; m. Susanna Major, dau. of John and Elizabeth (Redd). She m. (2) 1802, Ritchie Boulware in Franklin Co., Ky. 3 Ky. Reg. 96.
Thomas m. 25 April, 1774, Anne Povall. Sur. Arthur Moseley. Cumberland Co. Mar. Bond.

WOOLEY
Mary prob. m. Capt. Augustine Moore.

WOOLF
Mary m. George Bush.

WOOLFOLK
___ m. Sallie Minor, dau. of Thomas and Mary (Dabney). 9W(1)180.
___ m. Mary Cole, dau. of William and Susannah Digges. 5W(1)180.
___ m. Anne (___) Harris, widow of Henry (d. 1744, Caroline Co.). Louisa, p. 339.
Aggathy m. Taylor Noel.

WOOLFOLK (cont.)

Agnes m. Newil Walton.

Augustine m. 6 March, 1789, Sarah Brown by Rev. Charles Hopkins. Louisa Co. Ministers' Returns.

Augustine m. 1777, Franky Thomas. Orange Co. Mar. Record.

Christian (____) m. Samuel Brockman (2nd wife).

Eleanor m. Edward Spencer.

Elizabeth m. William Thomas.

Elizabeth m. ____ Thomas.

Frances m. Reuben Cowherd.

Francis m. 14 Dec., 1793, Eliza Taylor. Bristol Parish, Sussex Co. Recorded in Cumberland Parish, Lunenburg Co. Cameron.

John, Sr., m. bef. 1792, Sarah (____) Partlow, widow of John, Sr. Proven by a Deed of 13 July, 1792, Spotsylvania Co.

Joseph m. 3 July, 1786, Betsy Barnet. Louisa Co. Mar. Record.

Joseph m. Mary Waller, b. 26 Feb., 1761; d. 1850, dau. of Thomas and Sarah Ann (Dabney). 36V381.

Patsey m. James Allen.

Patty m. John Scott.

WOOLIN

William m. Elizabeth Stone, b. 18 May, 1736, dau. of William and Frances (Taylor). 5W(2)201.

WOOLINGTON

Susan m. Archibald Nichols.

WOOLINS

Joseph m. bef. 1777, Elizabeth Stone, dau. of William, whose will dated 5 Sept., 1777, Fluvanna Co., proves it.

WOOLLAMS

John m. Dec., 1711, Sarah Henderson. St. Peter's, p. 419.

WOOLRIDGE

Daniel m. 25 July, 1791, Agnes Osborne. Sur. Abraham Marshall. Amelia Co. Mar. Bond.

Edmund (or Edward) m. 22 Aug., 1774, Elizabeth Watkins. Sur. Samuel Watkins. Cumberland Co. Mar. Bond.

Elizabeth Branch m. Moses Morris.

Josiah m. Martha "Patsy" Trabue, b. 1762, dau. of John James Trabue and Olympe (Dupuy). 17 Ky. Reg. 50:54.

Thomas m. 25 April, 1774, Anne Powell. Cumberland Co. Mar. Record.

WOORY

____ (____) m. Samuel Bridger.

Joseph, d. 1692; m. Elizabeth (Godwin) Webb, widow of James Webb (d. 1675). She m. (3) Col. Samuel Bridger and her will was recorded, 1718, Isle of Wight Co. Boddie-Isle, pp. 427, 462.

WOOSHOM

Amelia m. Perrin Cardwell.

WOOSLEY

Thomas m. 18 April, 1786, Dianna Tribble. Halifax Co. Mar. Record.

WOOTEN

____ m. Sarah (____) Wood, widow of Arthur. Proven by a Deed, 1669, Isle of Wight Co.

Benjamin m. Elizabeth Rousseau, dau. of Hilliare and Elizabeth (____) of Stafford and Westmoreland counties; rem. to Halifax Co., No. Car.

WOOTEN (cont.)
27W(1)105.
Nancy m. James Taylor.
Nancy m. Jacob Puckett.
Priscilla m. Burwell Pope.
Sally m. Robert Willings.
Thomas m. 4 Oct., 1785, Mary Tomlinson by H. J. Burgess. Surry Co. Mar. Record.

WOOTON
____ m. bef. 1792, Elizabeth Cobb, dau. of John of Southampton Co., whose will, prov. 1792, Williamsburg, proves it.

WORD
Benjamin m. 2 June, 1791, Elizabeth Edwards. Halifax Co. Mar. Record.
Elizabeth m. Richard Hooper.
Mary (____) m. James Warren.
Salley m. William Word.
Sarah m. Moses Hubbard.
Thomas, b. 1756, Va.; d. 1838, So. Car.; m. Fanny Dickinson. DAR No. 65 588.
William m. 24 Dec., 1797, Salley Word. Halifax Co. Mar. Record.

WORKMAN
Abraham m. 24 Sept., 1785, Margaret Lirner, dau. of Mathias. Montgomery Co. Mar. Record.
Samuel m. 30 June, 1785, Martha Rhea by Rev. John Brown. Archibald Rhea, father of Martha, gave consent. Rockbridge Co. Ministers' Returns.

WORLEY
____ m. bef. 1760, Mary Taylor, dau. of Samuel, whose will of that date, Frederick Co., proves it.
Caleb m. Rebekah Allen, dau. of Malcolm. Kegley, p. 484.
Elizabeth m. John Whitworth.
Frederick m. 7 March, 1797, Sally Fry. Wythe Co. Mar. Record.
Mary m. James Smith.
Moses m. 10 June, 1789, Rhoda Worley by Joshua Worley. Campbell Co. Mar. Record.
Rhoda m. Moses Worley.
Sarah m. John Shotwell.

WORLY
____ d. bef. Dec., 1704; m. Mary Keisiel, dau. of George, who d. bef. 1704. Proven by Court Record, of that date, Essex Co.
Valentine m. 13 July, 1793, Barbara Spreger. Wythe Co. Mar. Record.

WORMELEY (See WORMLEY)
____ m. Beverley Randolph.
Agatha m. Beverley Randolph.
Catherine m. Gawin Corbin.
Christopher, Col., of Middlesex Co., m. (1) bef. 1654, Frances (Armistead) Alymer Elliot, d. 25 May, 1685. (See Deed, 2 Nov., 1686, Old Rappahannock Co.) He m. (2) Elizabeth (Travers) Carter, widow of Col. John, Jr., and dau. of Capt. Raleigh Travers; m. (3) Margaret (____). 19T60, 61; 5V429; 6W(1)32; 8W(1)186; Winston, p. 153.
Elizabeth m. John Lomax.

WORMELEY (cont.)
Elizabeth m. Landon Carter.
Elizabeth m. Dudley Digges (2nd wife).
Elizabeth m. (1) Richard Kemp; m. (2) Sir Thomas Lunsford; m. (3) Maj. Gen. Robert Smith.
Elizabeth (____) m. William Churchill.
Frances m. Nathaniel Burwell.
James, Capt., m. in England Arianna Randolph, dau. of John and Arianna (Jennings). 8W(1)265.
Jane m. Carter Beverley.
Judith m. (1) Corbin Griffin; m. (2) William Beverley; m. (3) Christopher Robinson.
Judith m. Philip Ludwell Grymes.
Judith m. Mann Page (1st wife).
Judith m. George Lee.
Katherine m. Gawin Corbin (1st wife).
Mary (____) m. Capt. William Brocas.
Ralph, Capt., m. Agatha Eltonhead, dau. of Richard of Lancashire, England. She m. (2) ca 1652, Sir Henry Chicheley. 17T145.
Ralph of York Co. mar. contract 2 July, 1645, with Agatha (____) Stubbins, widow of Luke of Northampton Co. 1W(1)155.
Ralph, Esq., m. Eleanor Tayloe. 25V191.
Ralph, Esq., will dated 2 Feb., 1700; m. 16 Feb., 1687, Elizabeth Armistead, dau. of John and Judith (____) of Gloucester Co. She m. (2) William Churchill. Christ Church, p. 36; 25W(1)118.
Ralph, d. 1786; m. (1) Sarah Berkeley; m. (2) ____ Bowles. 1V221.
Ralph, Esq., d. 17 May, 1685, Middlesex Co.; m. ca 1672, Catherine (Lunsford) Jennings, widow of Capt. Peter Jennings and dau. of Sir Thomas Lunsford and (3) Elizabeth (____). 1V115; 25V379; 32V64; 8W(1)185.
Sarah m. Christopher Robinson (2nd wife).
WORMINGTON
Mary m. John Wilson.
William m. 24 July, 1784, Mary Silvester. Norfolk Co. Mar. Record.
WORMLEY (See WORMELEY)
Agatha (____) m. Sir Henry Chicheley.
Elizabeth m. John Carter.
Elizabeth m. William Diggs.
John m. Ann Tayloe, dau. of William, whose will, dated 1767, Lancaster Co., names them and their daughter and son-in-law.
Ralph m. (1) Katherine (Lunsford) Jennings; m. (2) Elizabeth Armistead. 16V82; 36V291.
Ralph, d. 19 Jan., 1806; m. 19 Nov., 1772, Eleanor Tayloe, b. 16 Oct., 1756; d. 23 Feb., 1815, dau. of John and Rebecca (Plater). Bible Record. 14T245.
WORNNELL
Sucky m. Thomas Pittman.
WORNOM
Betty m. John Thomas.
WORNUM
Elizabeth (____) m. ____ Webb.

WORRELL

____ m. bef. 1795, May Vick, dau. of James, whose will of that date, Southampton Co., names "daughter May Worrell."

Eliza m. John Lowry.

Priscilla m. John Peacock.

WORRIL

Amos m. 8 Oct., 1780, Lucy Whitlock. Halifax Co. Mar. Record.

WORSDALL

Richard m. 26 Sept., 1680, Martha Woodgar. Christ Church, p. 20.

WORSELL

Elizabeth m. John Watts.

WORSHAM

____ m. Anne Mitchell, b. prob. 1750's, dau. of Walter and Rachel (Appling). 60V179.

____ m. William Eppes.

____, a dau., m. ____ Eppes.

____ m. Judith Archer. She m. (2) Edward Booker. Bell, p. 113.

Ann m. Edward Osborne.

Ann m. ____ Dison.

Anne m. ____ Osborn.

Archer m. 10 Feb., 1790, Nancy Smith. Sur. Alexander Fowler, Jr. Goochland Co. Mar. Bond.

Charles of Henrico Co., d. 1735; m. Elizabeth ____. 33V185.

Daniel m. Judith Archer, dau. of John of Bermuda Hundred who d. 1718. She m. (2) Col. Edward Booker. 33V104; Meade, p. 111.

Elizabeth m. Thomas Liggon.

Elizabeth m. Col. Richard Kennon.

Elizabeth m. John Royall.

Elizabeth m. ____ Marshall.

Elizabeth m. Perrin Cardwell.

Elizabeth m. David Meredith.

Elizabeth (____) m. Col. Francis Eppes.

Ellen m. Benjamin Lawson.

Essex, will dated 8 Nov., 1758, Chesterfield Co., named wife Anne. 33V186.

Essex m. 28 Dec., 1786, Elizabeth Dunnavant, dau. of Hodges. Sur. Hodges Dunnavant. Amelia Co. Mar. Bond.

Frances m. ____ Rowlett.

Frances m. William Rowlett.

George, son of George, m. Sarah Irby, dau. of Joshua; res. 1746, Henrico Co. 33V185.

George, son of Capt. George (b. 1648), m. Mary Pigott, dau. of John; res. Henrico Co. 33V185.

James m. 11 March, 1786, Mary Walthall. Sur. Charles Worsham. Amelia Co. Mar. Bond.

Jeremiah m. 19 March, 1782, Ann McDowell by Rev. John Bailey. Pittsylvania Co. Ministers' Returns.

John m. 2 Jan., 1800, Betsey Bennett. Halifax Co. Mar. Record.

John, Capt., b. 1731; d. 1779, Hanover Co.; m. Sophia Watkins, b. 1735; d. 1780, dau. of William and Martha (Herndon). 60V314.

John m. 20 April, 1794, Nancy Whitworth. Sur. Charles Worsham. Amelia Co. Mar. Bond.

WORSHAM (cont.)

John m. Mary Wynne, b. bef. Dec., 1696, dau. of Maj. Joshua and Mary (Jones). Boddie-SVF 1:221.

John of Henrico Co., d. 1745, son of Capt. John; m. Agnes (____) Osborne. 33V186.

Martha m. James Sanderson.

Martha m. ____ Wood.

Martha m. Seth Ward.

Martha m. ____ Ward.

Mary m. John Hester.

Mary m. Richard Lygon (or Liggon).

Mary m. Benjamin Hubbard.

Mary m. ____ Robertson.

Mary m. ____ Wilkinson.

Obedience m. ____ Howson.

Phebe m. ____ Harper.

Richard, b. 1756; d. 17 Feb., 1826, son of Capt. John and Sophia (Watkins); m. Mary Wingfield, b. ca 1764, dau. of Thomas and Elizabeth (Terrell). 60V314.

Sally m. Nathan McCoy (?McLoy).

Sarah m. (1) Archibald Baugh; m. (2) Chastain Clark.

Thomas m. 23 Oct., 1788, Prudence Gooch. Sur. William B. Giles. Amelia Co. Mar. Bond.

William, d. bef. 1661; m. Elizabeth ____. 33V185.

William m. Elizabeth Littlepage. 32V411.

WORSLEY

Elizabeth m. Roderick McCulloch.

John m. 31 Jan., 1781, Susanna Thomson. Hanover Co. Mar. Record.

WORTER

John m. ____ (____) Salsbury, widow of John. Proven by will of Gov. Richard Bennett, 1676, Nansemond Co. Boddie-Isle, pp. 287-8.

WORTH

Anne m. William Davis.

WORTHAM

____ m. Mary Berryman Taliaferro, b. 6 Oct., 1745, dau. of Capt. Richard and Rose (Berryman). 11T20.

Ann m. Cary Smith.

Ann m. Samuel Wortham.

Ann m. Edmund Cowles.

Ann (____) m. William Jones.

Anne (____) m. Joseph Stephens.

Elizabeth m. Richard Daniel.

Fannie Smith m. William Crittenden Webb.

James m. 4 Jan., 1778, Franky Smith. Christ Church, p. 201.

John m. 2 Nov., 1732, Judith Stewart. Christ Church, p. 168.

John m. 26 Feb., 1687, Mrs. Prudence Needham. Christ Church, p. 36.

Katy m. Thomas Gaines.

Lucy m. John Angus.

Mary m. John Bagot.

Meacham m. 14 Nov., 1795, Joana Wake. Christ Church, p. 302.

Samuel m. 14 July, 1763, Ann Wortham, dau. of George, dec'd. Middlesex Co. Mar. Record.

WORTHAM (cont.)
Sarah m. John Fearn.

WORTHINGTON
____ m. ____ Bordon, dau. of Benjamin. She m. (2) bef. 1796, ____ Pritchard. 11W(2)112.
____ m. Abigail Bordon, dau. of Benjamin. Proven by Deed Book 10, p. 326, Augusta Co. She m. (2) bef. 1 June, 1761, James Pritchard. Kegley, p. 253; Morton, p. 474.
Christina m. Samuel Hawkins.
Jacob, d. ca 1749; m. Abigail Bordon, dau. of Benjamin, Sr., and Zeruiah (Winter). She m. (2) James Pritchard and rem. to Orange Co., No. Car. 11W(2)327; Morton, p. 24.
James m. 8 Dec., 1797, Hannah Perkins. Shelby Co., Ky. Mar. Record.
James m. 12 March, 1798, Milly Sorrels. Shelby Co., Ky. Mar. Record.
N. m. Lewis Hancock.
Polley m. William Thompson.

WORTLEY
Catherine m. Thomas Bristow.

WOSHER
Caty m. James Smith.

WOTTEN
Susannah m. William Griffith.

WRAY
Anne m. John Stith.
George, Jr., m. Anne Wallace, dau. of James. 9W(1)130.
Helen m. Charles Stuart.
Jacob m. 13 May, 1761, Mary Ashton. St. Paul's. She, dau. of Burdett. 14W(2)158.
James m. Mary Washington (1st husband). 26V419.
Thomas m. 23 April, 1795, Louisa Howell. Sur. John Hendricks. Amelia Co. Mar. Bond.

WREEN
John m. bet. Oct., 1785, and May, 1786, Martha Estes by Rev. James Shelburne, Baptist. Lunenburg Co. Ministers' Returns.

WREN
James m. 27 March, 1753, Catharine Brent. OPR.
John m. Ann Turner. She m. (2) by 1752, Alexander Hansford of King George Co. 26T285.
Sarah m. Bartley Tackett.
William, d. 1766; m. Mary Strother, dau. of Joseph and Margaret (Berry) 11T118.

WRENIE
Jesse m. 22 Dec., 1785, Mary Hall. Sussex Co. Cameron.

WRENN
Betty m. Thomas George.
Francis, Jr., m. 8 Jan., 1774, Martha Harrison. Isle of Wight Co. Mar. Record.
James A. m. 14 Jan., 1795, Lucy Gwaltney. Isle of Wight Co. Mar. Record.
Mary m. Edmond Withers.
Polly m. Richard Pierce.
Polly m. John Barlow.

WRENN (cont.)
Rebecca m. Jessie Washington.
Richard m. 30 Dec., 1797, Rebecca Smith. Sur. William Cross. Sussex Co. Mar. Bond.
Richard m. 23 Aug., 1790, Sarah "Charity" Smith. Sur. Nicholas Presson. Sussex Co. Mar. Bond.
Sarah m. Edward Pettypool.

WRESSELL
Charles m. bef. 1688, Mary (____) Loughland, widow of Dorman (will prov. Feb., 1687, Northampton Co.). Proven by est. sett. 26 Sept., 1688. She m. (3) Walter Mannington, with whom she had difficulty. Proven by Court Orders, 1692-3, Northampton Co. Book XVII:224.

WRICH
Samuel m. 1773, Jane Bruce. Orange Co. Mar. Record.

WRIGHT
____ believed m. bef. 1800, Mary Bracy, whose will, dated 1800, Southampton Co., names "brother Francis Bracy and sister Mary Wright" among her legatees.
____ m. Jourden Jackson.
____ m. by 1771, Mary Mitchell. Rockbridge Co. Morton, p. 546.
____ m. bef. 1778, Molly Fitzpatrick, dau. of Joseph, whose will, dated 17 Aug., 1778, Fluvanna Co., proves it.
____ m. bef. 1717, ____ Prime, dau. of Edmund, prob. of Isle of Wight Co. 48V279.
____ m. bef. May, 1786, Margaret Yarbough, dau. of Alsup (dec'd. in 1786). Proven by Court Record of that date, Hanover Co., at which time it seems that ____ Wright had died.
Aconath m. Adam Sill.
Agathy m. William Furlong Calvin.
Amey m. Charles Waterman.
Ann m. William Arnold.
Ann m. Henry Cox.
Ann m. Robert Deputy.
Ann m. Samuel Coleman.
Ann m. Thomas Griffin.
Ann m. William Duff.
Ann m. George Nicholas Hack (or Hacke).
Ann m. John Tatem, Sr. (1st wife).
Anna m. Benjamin Page.
Anna m. Asa Bennett.
Archibald m. Elizabeth Sheppard, sis. of Samuel of Gloucester Co. and dau. of Samuel and Mary (Kavanagh). Had a dau., b. 1724. 7W (2)175.
Asa m. 17 Sept., 1799, Phebe Martin. Shelby Co., Ky. Mar. Record.
Athaliah Kessia m. (1) Thomas Hunt; m. (2) David Tucker.
Benjamin m. 1792, Ann Herndon. Orange Co. Mar. Record.
Betsy m. John Farmer.
Betsy m. Nathan Underwood.
Bledsoe m. 1791, Sarah Beasley. Orange Co. Mar. Record.
Catherine m. ____ Bailey.
Charles m. 22 Dec., 1791, Nancey Wright by Rev. John Rogers, Methodist. Lunenburg Co. Ministers' Returns.

WRIGHT (cont.)

Christopher, physician, m. Margaret Walke. 5V141. Mar. 12 Sept., Mary Walke; m. (2) 25 Oct., 1764, Elizabeth (___) Thorowgood Hunter, widow 1st of Argill Thorowgood, Sr., and 2nd of William Hunter. Her bro., Capt. William Keeling, was extr. with her of will of Argill Thorowgood, Sr. LNCo. 1:127.

Christopher m. 12 Sept., 1753, Mary Walker. Norfolk Co. Mar. Record.

Daniel m. 1799, Peggy David. Rockbridge Co. Morton, p. 546.

David, son of Nathaniel, m. Mary Armistead, dau. of William and Sarah (Jordan); res. in Nansemond Co. 7W(1)184.

Dolly m. James Dismang.

E. m. William Mullins.

Elizabeth m. Thomas Dawss.

Elizabeth m. Joseph Sandage.

Elizabeth m. Isaiah Harrison (1st wife).

Elizabeth m. Taliaferro Stribling.

Elizabeth m. Robert Jones.

Elizabeth m. Alexander Sproul.

Elizabeth m. John Campbell.

Elizabeth m. Jonathan Payne.

Elizabeth prob. m. William Houston.

Elizabeth m. William Glenn.

Elizabeth m. John Weston.

Elizabeth m. William Sawyer.

Elizabeth m. (1) William Gannaway; m. (2) John Newland.

Elizabeth m. John Herndon.

Elizabeth m. Nathaniel Tatem.

Elizabeth m. James Sandidge.

Fanney m. Thomas Willoughby.

Frances m. John Sleet.

Frances m. Larkin Miller.

Frances m. Nimrod Ashby.

Frances m. John Hall.

Frances m. Cader Whitehurst.

Frances m. Nicholas Spencer.

Frances (____) m. Edwin Young.

Francis, Major, d. 1713, age about 53; m. (1) ca 1680, Anne Washington, b. ca 1662; d. 1698, dau. of Col. John and Ann (Pope); m. (2) Martha ____. 4T156-7; Boddie-HSF IV:161.

Francis m. 18 Feb., 1797, Fanny Whitehurst. Princess Anne Co. Mar. Record.

Francis m. 7 Dec., 1737, Anne Massey. St. Paul's.

Francis m. 1 June, 1770, Ann Godfrey Tatem. Norfolk Co. Mar. Record.

Francis m. Dec., 1737, Anne Massey, b. 19 March, 1719, dau. of Dade, Jr., and Elizabeth (____). 12W(2)34. (See above.)

Gabriel m. 26 Dec., 1785, Catherine Ransone (or Ransom), dau. of Thomas, who gave consent. Sur. Creed Taylor. Cumberland Co. Mar. Bond.

George, b. 1761, Frederick Co.; d. 1836, Ky.; res. 1832, Hopkins Co., Ky.; m. 1785, Sallie Vosden, b. 1767; d. 1859. DAR No. 79 485.

George m. 30 Nov., 1799, Sarah McCall. Rockingham Co. Wayland, p. 11.

WRIGHT (cont.)

Hannah m. Thomas Hawes.
Henry m. 1 Feb., 1796, Rebecca Watkins. Isle of Wight Co. Mar. Record.
Hester m. ____ Jackson.
Isaac m. Susannah Ellis, dau. of Charles and Susannah (Harding). Orange III:44.
Jacamine m. Cader Flanakin.
James m. 14 July, 1790, Elizabeth Gooch. Louisa Co. Mar. Record.
James, b. 1754, Botetourt Co.; d. 2 June, 1825, Bourbon Co., Ky.; m. 29 Feb., 1776, Martha Hamilton, dau. of Andrew. He was son of Peter, Jr., and Jane (Hughart) of Oyster Bay, Long Island and Augusta Co., Va.; rem. to Ky., 1794. Calhoun, p. 202.
James, b. 1762, Culpeper Co.; d. 1845, Morgan Co., Ill.; m. Frances Finney. DAR No. 31 347.
James, son of John, m. 8 Dec., 1763, Mary Duncan. Fauquier Co. Mar. Record.
Jane m. Walis Estel.
Jane m. Richard Nowland.
Jennie m. Wallace Estill, Jr.
Jenny m. John Parker.
Jeremiah, Lieut. in Rev. War, b. 1762, Va.; d. 1833, Crawford Co., Ind.; m. Mary Cunningham. DAR No. 51 703; DAR No. 68 986.
Jo. m. 5 Feb., 1783, Fannie Thomason. Louisa, p. 281.
John m. 1797, Elizabeth Sebree. Orange Co. Mar. Record.
John m. 1789, Susanna Grasty. Orange Co. Mar. Record.
John m. 1783, Margaret Jones. Orange Co. Mar. Record.
John m. 28 June, 1781, Avey Hardin by Rev. John Bailey. Pittsylvania Co. Ministers' Returns.
John m. 14 Jan., 1796, Elizabeth Durrett. Caroline Co. Mar. Record.
John m. 21 May, 1795, Mary Cox, spinster. Sur. E. Reade. Wit. William Waller. York Co. Mar. Bond.
John, Jr., son of John, m. bef. 1748, Ann Williams, sis. of Jonas, Jr. 4T229. She was dau. of Jonas, Sr., and Honor (____). Proven by Chancery Suit, Fauquier Co., Session of 24 March, 1763. He rem. to Surry (now Yadkin) Co., No. Car. 1T183-4.
John Lee m. 8 Aug., 1751, Mary Kitchen. St. Paul's.
John Lee, Jr., d. 1815, Prince William Co.; m. 5 Dec., 1767, Elizabeth Coppage, will prov. 1839, Prince William Co. Mar. in Fauquier Co. 4T224.
Jonathan m. 16 Jan., 1783, Hannah Ridgway. Frederick Co. Mar. Record.
Joseph m. 1790, Elizabeth Douch. Louisa, p. 281.
Larkin m. 1799, Lucy James. Orange Co. Mar. Record.
Letostino m. 1799, Mary Lindsey. Orange Co. Mar. Record.
Letty m. Hickman Mitchell.
Lucy m. Robert Boston.
Lucy m. Richard Rhodes.
Lucy m. Isaac Smith.
Margaret m. Abraham Hollingsworth.
Martha m. William Estill.
Martha m. ____ Connor.

WRIGHT (cont.)

Martha (___) m. John Howell
Mary m. Reubon M. Dunnington.
Mary m. George Washington.
Mary m. Thomas Mims.
Mary m. ___ Russell.
Mary (or Nancy) m. Nathaniel Taylor.
Mary m. Henry Lancaster.
Mary m. Isaac Stevens.
Mary (___) m. Andrew Smith.
Mattrom m. Ruth Griggs, dau. of Robert. They had a dau., b. 1685/6. Jones, p. 182. (See Mottrom, below.)
Methany m. Joseph Robison.
Moses, b. Amherst Co.; d. there; m. Elizabeth Whitehead. DAR No. 47 092.
Mottrom, son of Richard and Anne (Mottrom), m. bef. 12 March, 1684, Ruth (Griggs) Mottrom, widow of John Mottrom, Jr., and dau. of Robert Griggs of Lancaster Co.; res. Richmond Co. and Lancaster Co. 11T166; 12T141; Washington, p. 335.
Nancey m. Charles Wright.
Nancy m. William Davis.
Nancy m. Jehu Meador.
Nancy m. James Asberry.
Nancy m. Edward Lewis.
Nancy m. George Rhodes.
Nannie m. John Holman.
Patience m. William Porter (2nd wife).
Penelope m. ___ Read (or Reed).
Peter, Jr., b. Oyster Bay, Long Island; d. 1793, Augusta Co., son of Adam; m. Jane Hughart, dau. of James and Agnes (Jordan); rem. 1746 to Augusta Co. Calhoun, p. 202.
Pleasant m. 23 Jan., 1800, Sally Mayes. Sur. Claiborne Foster. Amelia Co. Mar. Bond.
Polly m. William McGlasson.
Polly m. Lewis Martin.
Rachel m. George Shinn.
Rachel m. Capt. James Estill.
Rachel m. Richard Scrugs.
Reuben m. Elizabeth Collins, dau. of John and Mary (Carr) of Caroline Co. Proved by Chancery Papers. Collins, p. 20.
Reuben m. 23 July, 1789, Polly Foster, granddaughter of William Wood. Sur. William Wood, Jr. Amelia Co. Mar. Bond.
Richard, b. ca 1633, of London; to Va. ca 1655; d. by 10 Dec., 1663; m. Ann(-e) Mottrom, d. 1707, dau. of Col. John. She m. (2) David Fox; m. (3) Col. St. Leger Codd. Mar. is proved by Court Record, Dec., 1663, Northumberland Co. 7T254; 11T164; Washington, pp. 306, 334.
Richard m. ca 1730, Elizabeth Wigginton, dau. of William and Frances (Johnson) of Westmoreland Co. She m. (2) Dr. Thomas McFarlane (will prov. Nov., 1755, Westmoreland Co.). 21W(1)264; Washington, p. 393.
Richard m. 5 June, 1799, Ann Smith by Rev. William Mason, Baptist. Culpeper Co. Ministers' Returns.

WRIGHT (cont.)

Robert m. 21 Feb., 1798, Frances Staples by Rev. William Flowers. Campbell Co. Ministers' Returns.

Robert m. 27 Oct., 1798, Ann Doss by Rev. William Flowers. Campbell Co. Ministers' Returns.

Robert m. 6 Nov., 1791, Rachel Paxton by Rev. William Dameron. Campbell Co. Ministers' Returns.

Robert m. 3 April, 1775, Molly Mosby. Sur. Joseph Carrington. Cumberland Co. Mar. Bond.

Ruth (____) m. Robert Gibson.

S. m. William Flynn.

Sally m. William Conselvo.

Samuel m. 27 Jan., 1794, Patience C. Glenn. Sur. William Glenn. Cumberland Co. Mar. Bond.

Sarah m. Thomas Edwards.

Sarah m. Lieut. James Steele.

Sarah m. Paulser Kimberling.

Sarah m. Thomas Gwin.

Sarah m. William Mitchell.

Sarah m. James Libby.

Saymer m. 11 Aug., 1788, Frances Williams. Sur. William Wright. Cumberland Co. Mar. Bond. Saymour, son of John and Nancy (Dodson). 38V84. Spelled Seymour. 10W(2)180.

Stephen m. 13 Aug., 1724, Kathrine ____ (illegible). Sur. Solomon Wilson. Norfolk Co. Mar. Bond.

Stephen, Ensign in Rev. War, b. 1763, Norfolk Va.; d. there, 1851; m. Abby Conner. DAR No. 32 112.

Stephen m. 1 Nov., 1784, Peggy Brooks. Sur. Peter Ford. Buckingham Co. Mar. Bond.

Stephen m. 4 Jan., 1728/9, Mrs. Mary Thorowgood. Sur. Charles Sayer. Wit. Charles Burrough, Charles Sayer, Jr. Princess Anne Co. Mar. Bond.

Sukey m. Reuben Reeve (or Rowe).

Susannah m. Isaac Hollingsworth.

Susannah m. Joseph Rennolds.

Thomas m. 30 Nov., 1761, Edith Hawkins. Sur. Benjamin Hawkins. Amelia Co. Mar. Bond.

Thomas m. 9 March, 1792, Orphy (____) Taylor. Norfolk Co. Mar. Record.

Tolliver m. 1797, Elizabeth Rhea. Bath, p. 131.

William m. 23 Dec., 1781, Martha Jackson, spinster. Charles City Co. Mar. Record.

William m. 26 May, 1791, Nancy Levitt. Princess Anne Co. LNCo. 2:21.

William, b. 1761, London, Eng.; d. 1837, Pulaski Co., Mo.; m. Milly Malone; served in Rev. War from Virginia. DAR No. 47 793.

William m. 7 Jan., 1789, Fanny Riddle. Caroline Co. Mar. Record.

William m. 30 Oct., 1785, Elizabeth Wade. Sur. Samuel Williams. Cumberland Co. Mar. Bond.

William m. bef. 1787, Ann Blount, dau. of William, Sr., whose will, prov. 13 Sept., 1787, Southampton Co. 5V202.

William m. 1787, Rachel Perry. Orange Co. Mar. Record.

William m. 18 Oct., 1753, Mary Brent. OPR.

WRIGHT (cont.)
William m. 30 March, 1783, Mary Bowers of King and Queen Co. Christ Church, p. 209.
William m. 30 Oct., 1793, Molly (___) Thompson. Norfolk Co. Mar. Bond.
William m. 30 March, 1793, Elizabeth Woodson, dau. of John, who gave consent. Sur. Seymour Wright. Cumberland Co. Mar. Bond.
Willis m. 2 Jan., 1790, Leah Howlett. Caroline Co. Mar. Record.
WRIGHTON
Millerson m. 9 June, 1784, Eliza Wildair. Norfolk Co. Mar. Record.
WRITESMAN
Christine m. Henry Lower.
WRITSON
John m. bef. 4 Sept., 1672, Anne Spencer, dau. of Capt. Robert. Proven by Court Suit of that date, Surry Co.
WRITTIN
Elizabeth m. Simon Wilbon.
WROE
Anjalottah m. Capt. Joseph Fox.
Bunce m. Elizabeth Monroe, dau. of Andrew (res. 1652, Westmoreland Co.). 13W(2)234.
Elizabeth m. ___ Scott.
Elizabeth m. Isaac Stephens.
Henry, d. 1725, son of Bunce; m. Mary Weedon, dau. of George and Susannah (Monroe). 13W(2)234.
Jane m. Sgt. Augustine Weedon.
Lucy m. John Weedon.
Susannah m. John Edwards.
WROW
Frances m. Thomas William Clark.
WYAND
Christina m. Adam Steele.
WYANT
Jacob m. 9 Feb., 1798, Mary Gay. Rockingham Co. Wayland, p. 9.
John m. 1793, Sally McMath. Rockbridge Co. Morton, p. 546.
WYATE
Thomas m. 14 Sept., 1784, Rachel Burnside by Rev. John Alderson, Jr. Rockingham Co. or Greenbrier Co. Ministers' Returns.
WYATT
___ m. ___ Smith, dau. of Thomas Ballard Smith. Proven by Deed, Spotsylvania Co., 5 Jan., 1786.
___ m. John Collins.
Anne m. John Stark(-e).
Anne (___) m. Alexander Williamson.
Barbara m. Nelson Harris.
Barbary m. Robert Jones.
Conque m. 22 April, 1795, Fanney Hunt. Halifax Co. Mar. Record.
Dorothy m. John Coleman.
Edward m. Margaret Buchanan Cocke. 5V186.
Elizabeth m. Col. Cornelius Collier.
Elizabeth m. James Nicholls.
Francis m. 23 Dec., 1799, Fanny Austin. Caroline Co. Mar. Record.

WYATT (cont.)

Francis, b. 1588; knighted 7 July, 1618; Gov. of Virginia, Nov., 1621-26 Aug., 1625, and Nov., 1626-Feb., 1641; bur. Boxley, Eng.; m. 1618, Margaret Sandys, dau. of Sir Samuel. 31V243.

Hannah m. Ralph Gresham.

Henry of Prince George Co. m. bef. 1727, Mary ____. She was prob. Mary Hill, dau. of Edward of Charles City Co. Proven by Deed, 13 Feb., 1727, Prince George Co. Henry Wyatt and wife, Mary, convey slave, devised by will from Edward Hill to Mary. 29V100.

Hubbard m. 23 July, 1767, Tabitha Mingo, dau. of George. Charles City Co. Mar. Record.

James m. 25 Aug., 1790, Milly Compton. Halifax Co. Mar. Record.

James m. 30 Nov., 1785, Lucy Martin. Halifax Co. Mar. Record.

John, b. 1755; d. 2 May, 1814, Charlotte Co.; served in Rev. War; m. 19 Feb., 1783, Lunenburg Co., Mary "Polly" Tomlinson, dau. of Maj. Benjamin of Lunenburg Co. Data from her Pension W6595. 38V173.

John, b. 1755; will recorded in Charlotte Co., son of Richard and Ann (Garrett); m. Mary Tree. 38V83.

John, b. 1748; d. 1833, Ind., son of John and Martha (____); served in Rev. War; m. ca 1768, Susan Summit, b. 1754; d. 1823; res. Gloucester Co., Botetourt Co., Mercer Co., Ky., 1794, Harrison Co., Ky., 1825, Rush Co., Ind. Mss.

John m. 20 Feb., 1790, Leah Younger. Halifax Co. Mar. Record.

John m. Mary Todd. 25V315.

John, res. near Harper's Ferry, m. May Tremble. DAR 31 184.

John m. bef. 25 March, 1693, Anne Jones, dau. of Rice. Proven by Court Record of that date, Essex Co. He, b. ca 1637, son of Maj. William of Gloucester Co. 26T120.

Joseph m. bef. 25 March, 1693, Sarah (____) Coker, widow of William. Proven by Court Record of that date, Essex Co.

Joseph m. 23 Jan., 1783, Elizabeth Turner. Middlesex Co. Mar. Bond. Christ Church, p. 203.

Lettice m. David Hamrick.

Lucy m. David Mills.

Major m. 23 Jan., 1793, Jane Faulkner. Halifax Co. Mar. Record.

Overstreet, b. ca 1753; d. 11 Sept., 1826, son of Richard and Anne (Garrett) of King and Queen, Lunenburg and Charlotte counties; m. Sarah Tomlinson, dau. of Maj. Benjamin of Lunenburg Co. 38V173.

Peter m. 2 Oct., 1790, King and Queen Co., Josie Shepherd. Christ Church, p. 207.

Rachel m. Thomas Moore.

Ralph m. Alice (____) Savidge Button. 33V311.

Rebecca m. Jacob Luster (or Lester).

Richard of Gloucester Co., son of Richard (b. 1650) and Sallie (Peyton), m. Sarah Overstreet. 38V173.

Richard, b. 1650, son of George of Middle Plantation; m. Sallie Peyton. 38V173.

Richard, b. ca 1730; d. 1782, Charlotte Co., son of Richard and Sarah (Overstreet) of Gloucester Co.; m. bef. 1755, Ann(-e) Garrett, dau. of Humphrey, Sr. The wills of both are recorded in Charlotte Co. 26T119; 38V83, 173.

Richard, son of Maj. William, m. Catherine (Long) Tunstall, widow of

WYATT (cont.)

Edmund Tunstall and dau. of John (d. bef. 1671) and Katherine (Morris) Pettis Long. 21T241; 26T120; Gillmore, p. 97.

S. m. Horatio Wade.

Sally m. (1) William Bibb (2nd wife); m. (2) William Barnett.

Sarah m. (1) Matthew Thomson; m. (2) Augustine McGehee.

Susannah m. (1) Solomon Day; m. (2) Thomas Davis.

Tabitha m. Edmund Wade.

Thomas m. 1747, Sukey Edmonson. Orange III:1.

Vincent m. 23 Feb., 1787, E. Simpson. Halifax Co. Mar. Record.

William m. bef. 12 Feb., 1692/3, Ann Jones, sis. of John. Proven by Court Record of that date, Essex Co.

William m. 15 June, 1790, Susan Jones. Sur. Peter Jones. Amelia Co. Mar. Bond.

William of Caroline Co. m. Elizabeth Eggleston, dau. of Joseph (d. 1730) and (2) Anne (Pettus) (1702-1738) of James City Co. 29T141; Duke, p. 339.

William, Jr., of King and Queen Co., m. Rachel Smith, dau. of Alexander of Middlesex Co., whose will was prov. there, 6 April, 1696. 26T119; 9W(1)46.

William E., b. 1762; d. 26 Sept., 1802, son of John and Mary (Todd); m. 8 Feb., 1781, Mary Graham, dau. of John and Elizabeth (____). 25V315.

WYCHE

____ m. bef. 1767, Leah Maclin, dau. of James, whose will, dated 18 March, 1767, Brunswick Co., proves it.

Abigail m. ____ Brewer.

Anna m. Col. Thomas Taylor.

Benjamin m. 20 May, 1758, Elizabeth Peete, dau. of Samuel. Sur. Thomas Peters. Letter of consent from Samuel Peete. Sussex Co. Mar. Bond.

Benjamin m. Elizabeth Mason, dau. of John, Sr. (will 1802). 34V213.

Elinor m. Francis Mayberry.

Frances m. Fred Raines.

George m. 15 Oct., 1761, Margaret ____. Sur. Nathaniel Dobie. Sussex Co. Mar. Bond.

Hannah m. William Howell.

Henry m. 9 June, 1800, Elizabeth Walton. Sur. Isaac Rowe Walton, Jr. Greensville Co. Mar. Bond.

James of Sussex Co. m. 29 Jan., 1755, Leah Maclin of Brunswick Co. Sur. Nicholas Edmunds. Brunswick Co. Mar. Bond. 23 Jan. Mar. Bond in Lunenburg Co. 7W(1)37. Given as 21 Jan., 1755, Sarah Maclin. 28V167.

Leah (____) m. Capt. James Jones.

Rebecca m. ____ Dupree.

Rebecca m. David Walton.

Winnie m. William Maclin.

WYCKE

Benjamin m. 24 July, 1788, Elizabeth Mason. Sussex Co. Cameron. (See Wyche.)

WYCOFF

Williampy m. Abel Stout.

WYE

Anne m. Lavey Derey.

WYETT

Elizabeth m. Zachariah Groom.

WYGEL

Bostch m. 14 Feb., 1785, Elenor Collins. Montgomery Co. Mar. Record.

WYLIE

Frances m. Col. Edward Hack Moseley (2nd wife). Also given as Wyllie.
Elizabeth m. James Collins.

WYNKOOP

Anne m. Isaac VanMeter.

WYNN

John m. 27 Dec., 1764, Mary Lewis. Sur. Jesse Lunsford. Amelia Co. Mar. Bond.
Lucretia m. Joseph Tucker.
Martha m. Henry Dixon.

WYNNE

____ m. Martha Jefferson, sis. of Peter. Yesterday, p. 51.
Angelica m. William Raines.
Christiana m. John Cobbs.
Elizabeth m. Higginson Lee.
Green m. bef. 1794, Hannah Tyus, dau. of Lewis, Sr., whose will of that date, Greensville Co., proves it.
John m. July, 1795, Polly St. John by Charles Cobbs. Campbell Co. Mar. Record.
Joshua, son of Col. Robert (d. 1678, Charles City Co.), m. Mary Jones, dau. of Peter and Margaret (Wood). 12T175.
Joshua m. 9 Dec., 1784, Mary Todd. Dinwiddie Co. Cameron.
Josiah, son of William, m. March, 1786, Mary Whitley, dau. of Robert. Montgomery Co. Mar. Record.
Lavina m. John Dill.
Lucretia m. Joseph Tucker.
Lucy m. John Lee.
Martha m. Mathew Parham.
Mary m. John Worsham.
Mourning m. Solomon Stepp.
Peter, son of Maj. Joshua, m. Frances (Anderson) Herbert, widow of John Herbert (d. 1704) and dau. of John Anderson. Her will recorded, 1727, Prince George Co. 12T175-6; 8W(1)147.
Robert of Surry Co., son of Soloman (will prov. 1760, Sussex Co.), m. 9 Aug., 1753, Brunswick Co., Mary Phillipson. Brunswick Co. Mar. Record. 12T176; 28V168; 29V509.
Robert, from Kent in England, res. 1658, Charles City Co.; will, 1678; m. Mary (____) Poythress, widow of Capt. Francis Poythress. 12T173.
Sarah m. Levi Marshall.
William m. bef. 1805, Ann Cary. Proven by will of Elizabeth Cary, who names "sister Ann Wynne and bro.-in-law William Wynne." Found in Williamsburg Wills, but Elizabeth res. in Warwick Co.

WYTHE

Ann m. Charles Sweney.
Anne m. William Mallory.

WYTHE (cont.)

Anne m. Charles Mallory.
Anne (____) m. Thomas Harwood (2nd wife).
Anne (____) m. James Wallace.
Constance m. John Tomer.
George, b. 1726; d. 1806; m. (1) 26 Dec., 1747, Anne Lewis, b. 1726; d. 2 Aug., 1748, dau. of Zachary and Mary (Waller) of Spotsylvania Co.; m. (2) bef. 1779, Elizabeth Taliaferro, dau. of Richard and Eliza (Eggleston) of James City. Spotsylvania Co. Mar. Record. Will of Richard Taliaferro, 1779, Williamsburg, Va. 11T13; 59V350; 9W(1)128.
John, physician, d. bef. 1713; m. Diana Howard, dau. of Henry (d. 22 Dec., 1711). She m. (2) Benjamin Moss. 6T50.
Thomas, son of Thomas and Anne (Sheppard), m. 1719-20, Margaret Walker, dau. of George and ____ (Keith). 3T287; 1W(1)157; 2W(1)69.
Thomas, son of Thomas, m. Anne (Sheppard) Gutherick, widow of Quintilian Gutherick and grdau. of John Sheppard. She m. (3) Rev. James Wallace of Elizabeth City Parish. 2W(1)69; 9W(1)130.

Y

YAGER

Absalom, son of Nicholas and Susan (Wilhoit), m. Jan., 1786, Lincoln Co., Ky., Mary Wiley. 26W(1)194.
Barbara m. Asa Smith.
Diana m. William Downing Smith.
Elijah, b. 1769; d. 12 Dec., 1844, son of Nicholas and Susanna (Wilhoit); m. 19 Feb., 1800, Madison Co., Jemima Stansifer, b. 20 Nov., 1774; d. 14 June, 1863, dau. of John and Jemima (Clore). 26W(1)194; 9W(2)194.
Elijah, b. 15 Feb., 1782, son of Adam; m. Nancy Snyder, b. 5 Oct., 1784, dau. of Adam. 26W(1)188.
Ephraim, son of Godfrey and (1) ____ (Klug), m. 20 Jan., 1791, Culpeper Co., Sarah Rodoheifer. 26W(1)195; 9W(2)188.
Hannah m. John Yager.
Jemima m. (1) Nicholas Yeager (2nd wife); m. (2) John Smith.
Joel, b. 1786; d. 1852, son of Adam and Juriah (Berry); m. 20 Feb., 1800, Madison Co., Frances Tinsley (or Tousley). 26W(1)195; 9W(2)197
John, b. 15 Sept., 1732; d. 17 Aug., 1826, son of Adam and Susanna (Kobler); m. Mary Wilhoit, d. bef. 1800, dau. of John (est. sett. Oct., 1797). 26W(1)192, 247; 9W(2)187.
John m. 19 Dec., 1786, Culpeper Co., Hannah Yager, b. 1 Dec., 1770, dau. of Michael and Elizabeth (Manspiel). 9W(2)186.
John W., b. 12 Nov., 1773; d. 18 April, 1851, son of John and Mary (Wilhoit); m. 3 Nov., 1791, Culpeper Co., Margaret Wilhoit, b. 25 Sept., 1774; d. 25 Jan., 1849, dau. of George. 26W(1)193; 9W(2)191.
Joseph, son of John and Mary (Wilhoit), m. Margaret Wilhoit, dau. of Nicholas; rem. to Boyle Co., Ky. 26W(1)192; 9W(2)191.
Joshua, d. 1838, Mercer Co., Ky., son of John and Mary (Wilhoit); m. ca 1783, Mary Wayland, dau. of John and Catharine (Broyles). 26W(1)192; 9W(2)190.
Mary m. Aaron Wilhoit.

YAGER (cont.)

Nicholas, b. 1735; d. 1781, son of Adam and Susanna (Kobler); m. Susan Wilhoit, dau. of John (est. sett. Oct., 1797). 26W(1)193, 248; 9W(2)187.

Nicholas, son of Nicholas (b. 1735), m. Jemimah Yager, dau. of Adam and Joriah (Berry). She m. (2) bef. 1799, John Smith. 26W(1)195.

Nicholas, will prov. 1793, son of Nicholas and Susan (Wilhoit); m. (1) 1785, Ann Wayland, d. 1786; m. (2) 16 March, 1790, Jemima Yager, dau. of Adam. 26W(1)194.

Rosanna m. Michael Smith.

Rosina m. Michael Schmidt.

Susan m. Nicholas Smith (or Nicolaus Schmidt).

Susanna m. Jeremiah Wilhoit.

YAMONS

Betty m. Levi Gathry.

YANCEY

____ m. Charles Lewis.

____ m. ____ Coleman, dau. of Robert of Culpeper Co. Caroline, p. 418.

____ m. bef. 1805, Agatha Benson, dau. of Charles, whose will, 23 Sept., 1805, Culpeper Co. Book 7, p. 443, proves it.

____ m. Winifred Kavanaugh, dau. of Philemon, whose will, 1744, Orange Co., proves it.

____ m. Cadwalader Slaughter (1st wife).

Archilaus m. 27 Jan., 1789, Henrietta Nuckols by Rev. John Waller. Louisa Co. Ministers' Returns.

Augustus m. 20 June, 1787, Elizabeth Cole. Louisa Co. Mar. Record.

Charles m. Mary Crawford. They had a child, b. 13 Oct., 1784. Douglas Reg., p. 439.

Charles m. 8 June, 1786, Sarah Field. Sur. John Miller. Albemarle Co. Mar. Bond. He, son of Robert of Buckingham Co.; she, dau. of Robert Field of Albemarle Co. Charles m. (2) Jane Alexander. Albemarle, pp. 194, 358.

Charles m. Frances Slaughter, dau. of Col. Thomas and Sarah (Thornton). 21V428.

Eleanor m. Edward Stubblefield.

Elizabeth m. John Wood.

Elizabeth m. Robert Kimbrough.

Elizabeth m. Joseph Kimbrough.

Elizabeth m. William Smith.

Jane C. m. Shelton Smith.

Jechonias m. 14 Oct., 1793, Mildred Wood. Sur. John Wood. Albemarle Co. Mar. Bond. He, son of Jeremiah (d. 1789). Albemarle, p. 358.

Jemima m. James Cosby.

Joel, son of Jeremiah (d. 1789), m. Martha Rodes, dau. of David; rem. 1811 to Barren Co., Ky. Albemarle, p. 358.

Joel m. Elizabeth Brown, dau. of Andrew (d. 1804). Albemarle, pp. 153-4.

Joel m. 11 Nov., 1777, Barbara Smith. Louisa Co. Mar. Record.

Joseph m. 25 June, 1783, Elizabeth Cosbie. Louisa, p. 439.

Judith m. Hon. Daniel Field.

Judith m. Varter Chandler.

YANCEY (cont.)

Keziah m. George D. Freeman.

Layton, Col. in Rev. War, of Rockingham Co., m. 17 Dec., 1786, Augusta Co., Frances Lewis, b. 1769; d. 1845, dau. of Thomas and Jane (Strother). Peyton, p. 289.

Lewis Davis m. bef. April, 1743, Winifred Cavanaugh, dau. of Philemon, whose will of that date, Orange Co., proves it.

Mary m. David Rodes.

Polly m. James Gardner.

Rebecca m. Spenser Atkins.

Richard, Capt., m. Judith Field, dau. of Abraham, whose will, prov. 1775, Culpeper Co., names "daughter Judith Yancey." Field II:1103.

Richard m. 1 Jan., 1797, Mary Walton by Rev. James Walker. Louisa Co. Ministers' Returns.

Robert m. 9 Dec., 1795, Phebe Rosel. Sur. Daniel Maupin. Albemarle Co. Mar. Bond.

Sally m. Capt. Joseph Kimbrough.

Samuel m. 8 Oct., 1779, Jane Bond, dau. of Thomas. Louisa Co. Mar. Record.

Sarah m. Richard Lane.

Stephen m. 12 Oct., 1779, Jean Bond. Louisa, p. 438.

Thomas, physician, m. Nancy Minor, dau. of James and Mary (Carr). 5V441; Albemarle, p. 277.

Tyree m. 9 Jan., 1775, Sarah Jennings. Louisa Co. Mar. Record.

Wiley m. 20 Sept., 1797, Judith Ligon. Halifax Co. Mar. Record.

William m. 3 Jan., 1792, Nancey Sandford. Halifax Co. Mar. Record.

YANCY

Nathan m. 7 June, 1774, Sarah Wingham. Sur. Thomas Mallicote. York Co. Mar. Bond.

YANKEY

Jacob m. 19 Dec., 1796, Mary Shrum. Rockingham Co. Wayland, p. 8.

YANT

Liddie (____) m. Alexander Rede.

YARBOROUGH

Grigg m. 27 June, 1735, Elizabeth Lewis. Christ Church, p. 169.

John m. 19 July, 1785, Mary Dickason. Louisa Co. Mar. Record.

Joseph m. Temperance Walton, dau. of George (will prov. 1798). Proven by Court Suit, 1820. 11W(2)128.

Richard m. 24 Jan., 1775, Sarah Watkins. Surry Co. Mar. Record.

William m. 26 June, 1792, Leanus Andrews by Rev. James Shelburne, Baptist. Lunenburg Co. Ministers' Returns.

William, son of William and Mary (Mitchell) Randall Yarborough, m. Hannah Mitchell, dau. of John (d. 1770). Boddie-HSF V:58-9.

William, b. 1763, Va.; d. 1831, Fairfield Co., So. Car.; served in Rev. War; m. 1782, Charlotte Burnes. DAR No. 79 961.

YARBOUGH

Margaret m. ____ Wright.

YARBROUGH

Ann m. Nathan Winston.

Elizabeth m. Reubin Graves.

Jane m. Elijah Camall.

Joseph m. 9 Dec., 1785, Temperance Walton. Prince Edward Co. Mar.

YARBROUGH (cont.)
Record.
Priscilla m. Edward Thacker.
Sara m. ___ Pollard.

YARBRUGH
John m. 21 Oct., 1762, Bershaba Harris, dau. of William. Sur. William Meriwether. Thomas Gregg Yarbrugh gave consent to son's marriage. Goochland Co. Mar. Bond.

YARDLEY (See YEARDLEY)
Frances m. Adam Thorowgood.
Francis, Col., m. Dec., 1647, Sarah (Offley) Thorowgood Gookin, d. 1657, widow 1st of Capt. Adam Thorowgood (d. 1640), 2nd of Capt. John Gookin (d. bef. Dec., 1647). 4W(1)170. See Francis Yeardley.
George, d. 1627, Va.; m. Temperance Flowerdew. She m. (2) Capt. Francis West. 2T115; 6T118. See George Yeardley.
Richard m. 12 Jan., 1790, Hannah Jameson, spinster. Sur. Alexander Jameson. Albemarle Co. Mar. Bond.
Rose m. Thomas Ryding.

YARNELL
Mordecai I m. (1) ___ ___; m. (2) Mary Roberts. Joliffe, p. 93.
Mordecai II, son of Mordecai and (2) Mary (Roberts), m. 5 April, 1775, Phoeby Joliffe, b. 12 Feb., 1758, Frederick Co., dau. of William and Lydia (Hollingsworth); rem. to Wheeling, Va., after 8 March, 1780. Joliffe, p. 93.

YARRATT
Adam m. bef. Aug., 1678, Rachel Rhodes, sis. of Augustine. Proven by Court Record of that date, Northumberland Co.

YARRET
Peter m. 25 Nov., 1756, Mary Perrue, both in Manikentown. Douglas Reg., p. 2.

YARRETT
Elizabeth m. John Murry.
Katherine m. Henry Wiggs.

YARRINGTON
Frances m. James Burton.
John m. 23 July, 1752, Mary Bryant. Sur. Benjamin Rhodes. Middlesex Co. Mar. Bond.
Judith m. James Brown.
Massey m. 13 Sept., 1720, Anne Chowning. Christ Church, p. 163.
Oliver m. 15 July, 1785, Elizabeth Ware. Christ Church, p. 204.
Vincent m. 5 Nov., 1795, Elizabeth B. Stiffe. Christ Church, p. 302.

YARROW
Mary m. Edmund Day.

YATES
___ m. John Robinson (1st wife).
Abner m. 31 Dec., 1795, Clara Smith by Rev. William Mason, Baptist. Culpeper Co. Ministers' Returns.
Anne m. Robert Spratt.
Bartholomew m. 11 May, 1769, Anne Daniel. Christ Church, p. 198. She, dau. of Robert and Lucy (Daniel). 12T209.
Bartholomew m. bef. 1808, Sally Catlett, dau. of John of Gloucester Co., whose will, prov. 4 July, 1808, mentioned "Bartholomew Yates,

YATES (cont.)

husband of my daughter Sally."

Bartholomew, minister, m. 14 Sept., 1704, Sarah Mickleburrough. Christ Church, p. 63. He, b. 1676; d. 26 July, 1734. Free II:381. He m. Sarah (Stanard) Mickelborough, b. 12 Sept., 1680, widow of Tobias. 13T194.

Bartholomew m. 9 Sept., 1741, Elizabeth Stanard. Sur. John Reade. Middlesex Co. Mar. Bond.

Benjamin reported m. to Phebe Wildman, Fairfax Monthly Meeting; rem. to Ohio, 1805. Prewitt, p. 84.

Catharine m. John Mountague.

Catharine m. (1) ____ Thornton; m. (2) Dr. Robert Wellford.

Catherine m. John Thornton.

Catherine m. John Walker.

Deborah m. Benjamin Smith.

Edward Randolph, under age, m. 20 Sept., 1783, Elizabeth Murray, dau. of John. Mecklenburg Co. Mar. Record. Yesterday, p. 290.

Elizabeth m. Rev. William Bland.

Elizabeth m. Samuel Klug.

Elizabeth m. Elisha Taylor.

Elizabeth m. Robert Welch.

Elizabeth Stanard m. John Quarles.

Else m. William Smith.

Frances m. Rev. John Reade.

George W. m. 25 Dec., 1800, Mary Wade Browning, b. 9 May, 1776, dau. of John and Elizabeth (Strother). 11T197.

Harry Beverley m. 19 May, 1779, Lucy Murray, dau. of Rachel, who gave consent. Middlesex Co. Mar. Record. Mar. 23 May. Christ Church, p. 202.

Harry Beverley m. 27 Feb., 1783, Jane Montague. Christ Church, p. 208.

James of Sittenbourne Parish m. 19 Nov., 1745, Mary Green of Washington Parish. St. Paul's.

James m. 1799, Sally Hansford. Orange Co. Mar. Record.

John of Culpeper Co. m. ca 1772, Elizabeth Gaines; rem. ca 1810 to Adair Co., Ky. DAR Query 14317, May, 1933.

Mary m. William Garde.

Mary Ann m. Anthony Collings.

Molly m. Thomas Shirley.

Nancy m. Esau Coles.

Phillis m. Jesse Toler.

Phillis m. Jesse Fowler.

Polly m. Thomas Hall.

Rebecca m. Roger Prichard.

Robert m. 17 Feb., 1750/1, Elizabeth Dade. St. Paul's. She, dau. of Henry and Elizabeth (Massey). 16T161.

Robert m. 11 April, 1777, Jane Dade. St. Paul's. She, dau. of Baldwin and (2) Verlinda (____). 16T171.

Robert, minister, b. 8 Jan., 1715, son of Rev. Bartholomew and Sarah (Mickleburrough); m. Mary Randolph, dau. of Capt. Edward (d. 1690) and ____ (Groves). 45V84; Free II:381.

Robert m. betw. 20 Oct., 1777, and 20 Oct., 1778, Mary Tomkies. Gloucester Co. Mar. Record.

YATES (cont.)

Sarah m. John Chinn.

Sarah m. Richard Meador.

Sarah m. Isaac Votaw, Jr.

William, minister, b. 10 Dec., 1720; Pres. of William and Mary College; m. Elizabeth Randolph, dau. of Capt. Edward (b. 1690) and ____ (Groves). She m. (2) Col. Theodorick Bland. 45V84; Free II:381-2.

William m. 13 Feb., 1786, Isabella Gaines, b. ca 1761, dau. of Benjamin and Elizabeth (____) of Culpeper Co. 31T49.

William, Col., served in Rev. War; m. 2 June, 1777, Anne Isham Poythress. 33V32.

William m. 1 Oct., 1790, Nelley Trammel. Halifax Co. Mar. Record.

YEAGER

Absalom, b. Va., son of Nicholas and Susanna (Wilhoit); served in Rev. War from Ky.; m. 9 Jan., 1786, Lincoln Co., Ky., Mary Wiley. 9W(2) 193.

Godfrey m. bef. 1775, ____ Klugg, dau. of Rev. Samuel Klugg, whose est. sett. of that date, Culpeper Co., proves it.

Nicholas, will dated 1792, Culpeper Co., son of Nicholas and Susanna (Wilhoit); m. (1) 22 Dec., 1785, Culpeper Co., Ann Wayland, d. 1786; m. (2) 16 March, 1790, Culpeper Co., Jemima Yager, b. 15 Nov., 1772; d. 17 Dec., 1824, dau. of Adam and Juriah (Berry). She m. (2) John Smith. 9W(2)194.

Samuel E. m. 11 April, 1791, Mary Hill. Louisa Co. Mar. Record.

YEARDLEY (See YARDLEY)

Argall, Col., b. 1605; d. ca 1670, son of George; m. Sarah Custis, dau. of John of Northampton Co. 1V85.

Argall, Col., b. 1621, Jamestown, Va.; d. 1655, Northampton Co., son of Sir George and Temperance (West); m. (1) ca 1640, ____ ____, d. 1648; m. (2) 1649, in Holland, Ann Custis, dau. of John and Joane (Powell) of Rotterdam. She m. (2) John Wilcox of Northampton Co. Am. Hist. I:341-2. His mother was Temperance (Flowerdew) Yeardley. 58V402. He d. 1682. Squires, p. 233.

Argall, Capt., b. 1650; d. 1682, son of Col. Argall (d. 1655) and Ann (Custis); m. 23 Jan., 1678, Sarah Michael (will, 1694, Northampton Co.), dau. of John, Sr., and Elizabeth (Thorowgood) of Northampton Co. She m. (2) John Watts; m. (3) Thomas Maddox. 31T90; Am. Hist. I:344-5; Squires, p. 233.

Elizabeth m. George Harmonson.

Frances m. John West, Jr.

Frances m. Lt. Col. Adam Thorogood.

Francis, Col., son of Sir George and Temperance (West), m. Sarah (Offley) Thoroughgood Gookin. 17T109; 31T87-8; 1V86; 5V330; Am. Hist. I:343-4. See Francis Yardley for more details.

George, Knight, b. 1580, England; d. 1627, Va.; m. Temperance Flowerdieu, b. ca 1597, England, dau. of Anthony and Martha (____) of Hethersett, Norfolk Co., England. 25V208; 28V322; 50V75; Squires, p. 234. See George Yardley for more details.

George, Gov., m. Sarah (Offley) Thoroughgood Gookin. 5V435.

John, Knight, b. 1577-1580; m. ca 1618, Temperance West, d. bef. Feb., 1628/9. Am. Hist. I:101, 340.

Rose m. (1) Thomas Ryding; m. (2) Robert Peale.

YEARDLEY (cont.)
Sarah m. John Powell.
Sarah (____) m. John Watts.
Temperance (____) m. (2) Francis West.

YEATES
John, b. 1751, Culpeper Co.; d. 14 Jan., 1847; served in Rev. War from Halifax Co.; m. 1780, Elizabeth Chandler. Wilcoxson, p. 418.
Rachel Murray Beverley m. Thomas Cooke.
Susanna m. Gabriel Smith.
Susannah m. John Bohannon.

YEATMAN
John m. 15 Dec., 1792, Lucy Patty. Caroline Co. Mar. Record.

YEGER
Samuel m. 12 April, 1791, Mary Hill by Rev. John Lasly. Louisa Co. Mar. Record.

YELTON
James m. 13 Nov., 1743, Isabell Hinson. OPR.

YEO
George m. 1719/20, Ellinor Boswell. Elizabeth City Co. Mar. Record. George, Jr., d. ca 1745; m. 1719/20, Elinor (____) Brough Boswell, widow 1st of Coleman Brough, 2nd of Capt. William Boswell. 9W(1)125. Also given as Elizabeth. 9W(1)125.
Leonard, Col., m. Rebecca (____) Moryson, widow of Col. Charles. Winston, p. 325.
Rebecca (____) m. (2) Charles Moryson; m. (3) Col. John Lear (2nd wife).

YERBY
____ m. Elijah Perciful.
Capt. of Frederick Co. m. Margaret Fauntleroy, dau. of Griffin Murdock and Ann (Belfield) Fauntleroy. Jones, p. 174.
Betty m. ____ Harris.
Betty Woodbridge m. ____ Steptoe.
Caty m. ____ Meredith.
George m. (2) May, 1790, Elizabeth Rust. 11W(2)120.
George m. bef. 1784, Elizabeth Meredith, dau. of John, whose will, dated 27 March, 1784, and est. sett. May, 1784, both in Lancaster Co., prove it.
George m. bef. 1789, Elizabeth Pinckard, dau. of Robert, bro. of James Pinckard, whose will, dated 9 Nov., 1789, Lancaster Co., proves the marriage.
George, Jr., m. bef. 1762, Sally Gibson, dau. of William, whose will, dated 6 March, 1752, and est. sett., 17 Sept., 1762, both in Lancaster Co., prove the marriage.
Hannah m. ____ Edwards.
Hannah m. John Edwards.
Joannah m. Charles Purcill.
John m. bef. 1758, Sarah Simmons, dau. of John, whose est. sett. of that date, Lancaster Co., proves it.
John m. bef. 1760, Mary Hutchings, dau. of William, whose est. sett. of that date, and will of William Hutchings, Jr., 1770, both in Lancaster Co., prove the marriage.
Judith m. William Parrott (or Parrett).
Judith m. ____ Kirk.

YERBY (cont.)

Mary m. George Phillips.
Mary m. ____ Hubbard.
Peggy m. John Carter.
Richard believed m. bef. 1791, Judith George, dau. of Benjamin, whose est. sett. of that date, and est. sett., 1793, of his widow, Catherine George, both in Lancaster Co., prove the marriage.
Sarah m. William Boatman.
Thomas m. bef. 1723, Hannah Doggett, dau. of Benjamin, whose will of that date, Lancaster Co., proves it.
William m. Frances McTire, dau. of Robert, whose will, dated 27 Jan., 1775, Lancaster Co., proves it.
William m. 23 Nov., 1782, Mary Satchell. Northampton Co. Mar. Record.

YOCOME

William m. 17 April, 1787, Jane Smith by Rev. Charles Cummings. Washington Co. Ministers' Returns.

YOCUM

____ m. Malinda King, b. ca 1768, Va.; d. 12 Oct., 1854, Lincoln Co., Ky., dau. of Nimrod and Sidney (____). 57 Ky. Reg. 270.

YOLKECOME

Sarah m. Peter Vonbebber.

YOPP

____ m. James Nutt.
____ m. William Hubbard.
Ann m. Thomas Hubbard.
Judith m. William Hubbard.
Samuel m. bef. 1774, Mary Simmons, dau. of John and Elizabeth (____). Proven by will of Elizabeth Simmons, widow, 1774, Lancaster Co.
Samuel, Jr., m. bef. 1789, Mary Doggett, dau. of Coleman (d. 1783). Proven by his est. sett., 16 Feb., 1789, and orphans' acct. recorded 19 Oct., 1788, both in Lancaster Co.

YOUEL

Jennet m. Oliver Miller.

YOUELL

____, a dau., m. ____ Watts.
____, a dau., m. ____ Spence.
Ann m. ____ Watts.
Dorcas m. (1) Patrick Spence; m. (2) John Jordan.
Thomas, Capt., of Nominy, Westmoreland Co., m. bef. 1693, Anne Lee, dau. of Col. Richard of Essex Co. Proven by Deed of that date, Westmoreland Co.
Winifred m. ____ English.

YOULEKEM

Elisabeth m. John Shoumaker.

YOUNG

____ m. James Martin.
____ m. Mary Cary, dau. of John of Surry Co. and London. She m. (2) Nathaniel Harrison, b. 1677; d. 1727. 31V277; Surry, p. 87. Her mother was Jane (Flood) Cary. Boddie-HSF V:72.
____ m. Lucy Ragsdale, dau. of John (will, prov. 1795, Lunenburg Co.).

YOUNG (cont.)

Bell, p. 278.

____ m. bef. 19 May, 1759, Tamar Samuel, dau. of James. Proven by Court Record of that date, Essex Co.

Alice m. John Jackson.

Alice (____) m. ____ Marmaduke.

Andrew m. 1799, Jenny McBride. Rockbridge Co. Morton, p. 545.

Ann m. Christopher Haines.

Ann m. Richard Covington.

Ann m. Sydnor Belfield.

Ann (____) m. John Peyton.

Ann Drucilla m. James Cowherd.

Anne m. John Bagwell.

Anne m. Christopher Haynes.

Barbara m. Henry Geerhart.

Catherine (____) m. Thomas Montague.

Clement m. 18 Dec., 1799, Amy Landrum by Rev. John Neblett, Methodist. Lunenburg Co. Ministers' Returns.

David, b. 18 June, 1772; d. Oct., 1847, son of William and Elizabeth (Huff); m. Elizabeth Vance. Hartford C-2337(1), 1 Nov., 1958. Signed L. J. B. Answer, 27 Dec., 1958. Signed E. H. B.

Duncan m. 7 July, 1784, Susannah Womack. Dinwiddie Co. Cameron.

Duncan m. 21 Aug., 1787, Mary Moore. Petersburg. Cameron.

Edward, son of Edward and Kerenhappuch (Hardaway), m. Fanny Dabney. 8W(1)Supp.137.

Edward m. Kerenhappuch Hardaway, b. 27 June, 1741, Dinwiddie Co., dau. of John, who received Land Grant, 1755. 8W(1)Supp.136-7.

Edward m. 15 April, 1794, Susanna McCartney. Shelby Co., Ky. Mar. Record.

Edwin m. 1784, Frances (____) Wright. Orange Co. Mar. Record.

Elijah m. 28 Dec., 1794, Anna Farler (?Farley) by Rev. James Shelburne, Baptist. Lunenburg Co. Ministers' Returns.

Elizabeth m. William Smith.

Elizabeth m. Benjamin Thomas.

Elizabeth m. (1) Joel Hitt; m. (2) Edward Tyler.

Elizabeth m. (1) ____ Ramsey; m. (2) Henry Nance; m. (3) Samuel Morris.

Evan m. 28 Dec., 1792, Mary Cumbo. Halifax Co. Mar. Record.

Frances m. William Webb.

Frances m. Israel Tully.

Frances m. Henry Mead.

Frances m. Edmund Mason.

Francis m. Elizabeth Bennett, bef. Rev. War. Boddie-Isle, p. 298.

Francis, b. 5 Sept., 1731, Brunswick Co.; d. 31 Dec., 1794, Isle of Wight Co., son of Michael Cadet and Temperance (Sadler) Young; served in Rev. War; m. Feb., 1754, Elizabeth Bennett, dau. of James and Elizabeth (Peyton). Young Chart.

Frankie m. ____ Williamson.

Grace m. Capt. John Fox.

Hannah m. Benjamin Burson.

Hannah m. William Cosby.

Hardaway, son of Edward and Kerenhapouch (Hardaway), m. Angeline Goodwin. 8W(1)Supp.137.

YOUNG (cont.)

Henry, son of Edward and Kerenhappuch (Hardaway), m. Winnie Tucker Goodwin. 8W(1)Supp.137. Mar. 25 Dec., 1786, Winney Tucker Goodwyn. Dinwiddie Co. Cameron.

Jacob, b. 18 May, 1774, prob. Essex Co., son of William and Elizabeth (Huff); m. Mary Boren of Robertson Co., Tenn. Hartford C-2337(1), 1 Nov., 1958. Signed L. J. B. Answer, 27 Dec., 1958. Signed E. H. B.

James m. (1) Martha Goodwin, dau. of James of Dinwiddie Co.; m. (2) Judith Goodwin, dau. of James of Dinwiddie Co. 8W(1)Supp.136.

James m. 13 April, 1791, Lucy Feason. Isle of Wight Co. Mar. Record.

James m. Elizabeth Johnson, dau. of Richard and Susan (Garrett). Louisa, p. 385.

James m. 5 Aug., 1800, Nancy Booker. Shelby Co., Ky. Mar. Record.

James m. 15 Dec., 1792, Sally Jeter. Caroline Co. Mar. Record.

James, mar. contract 1753, with Sarah (____) McMurtry, in Scotch manner; apparently Augusta Co. Kegley, p. 79.

James m. bef. 29 Feb., 1743, Joanna Poole, dau. of George, whose will of that date, Spotsylvania Co., prov. 5 Feb., 1744, proves it.

Jane m. William Cook.

Jean m. William Allison.

Jeanette m. Capt. Joseph Haynes.

Jo. m. 8 Aug., 1781, Sarah Martin. Louisa, p. 281.

John, b. 25 June, 1778; d. May, 1835; m. Matilda Gibson. Hartford C-2337(1), 1 Nov., 1958. Signed L. J. B. Answer, 27 Dec., 1958. Signed E. H. B.

John, b. 1757, Northumberland Co.; d. 1850, Kanawha Co., Va.-W. Va.; m. 1787, Keziah Tackett, b. 1769. DAR No. 79 390.

John m. 1719-20, Elizabeth Ryland. Elizabeth City Co. Mar. Record.

John m. 7 Aug., 1781, Sarah Martin. Louisa Co. Mar. Record.

John m. 1795, Franky Grady. Orange Co. Mar. Record.

John m. 1788, Sarah Rogers. Orange Co. Mar. Record.

Joseph m. 4 April, 1798, Polly Darkes. Shelby Co., Ky. Mar. Record.

Josiah m. 18 Oct., 1791, Eliza Terrell. Halifax Co. Mar. Record.

Judith m. Carter Chandler.

Kitty m. Tho. Gray.

Leonard m. 7 Dec., 1786, Mary Nance. Sur. Giles Nance. Amelia Co. Mar. Bond.

Leonard, b. ca 1745; m. (1) 11 Sept., 1765, Caroline Co., Mary Ann "Mollie" Higgins, b. there, 10 Nov., 1744; d. 24 June, 1813, Fayette Co., Ky.; m. (2) 13 Sept., 1813, Fayette Co., Ky., Elizabeth Doggett. Cowherd, p. 329.

Lewis m. 27 Sept., 1781, Elizabeth Smith. Louisa, p. 281.

Lucy m. John Heath.

Lurania m. (1) ____ Taylor; m. (2) ____ Featress; m. (3) Thomas Hudson; m. (4) Robert Miller.

Margaret m. John Glasscock.

Margaret m. Robert Anderson.

Margaret m. John Humphreys, Jr.

Mary m. ____ Rives.

Mary m. Thomas Doyle, Sr.

Mary m. (1) Arthur Fox; m. (2) Henry Lee.

YOUNG (cont.)

Mary m. Peter Coutanceau.
Mary m. Martin Depoy.
Mary m. Elliott Steveman.
Mary m. Robert Campbell.
Mary Chlosantha m. Zachariah Thomas.
Matthew m. Agnes Lusk, dau. of Nathan (d. 1748). Rockbridge Co. Morton, p. 499.
Michael Cadet, d. 1769, son of Francis of England; m. Temperance Sadler; res. Brunswick Co. Young Chart.
Nancy m. Joel Sturdivant.
Nancy m. Hezekiah Proctor.
Naomi m. ____ Douglas.
Polly m. James Allen.
Polly m. George Dickenson.
Polly m. Joel Puckett.
Rebeccah m. William Heth.
Richard m. 27 Dec., 1746, Elizabeth Green. OPR.
Richard m. Mary Paul, sis. of William (d. 1774, Spotsylvania Co.). She m. (2) Mark Lowdon. 15T216.
Richard, b. Fauquier Co.; d. 1815, Woodford Co., Ky.; m. Mary Moore, b. Va.; sett. in Fayette Co., Ky., 1783. Woodford Co., pp. 69-70; 4 Ky. Reg. 67; 18 Ky. Reg. 54:35-6.
Robert m. 1795, Elizabeth Hatton. Rockbridge Co. Morton, p. 491.
Robert m. 1795, Isabella Hutton. Rockbridge Co. Morton, p. 546.
Robert, killed by Indians, bur. Mason Co., Ky.; m. Judith Tebbs, b. Jan., 1757, Va.; d. May, 1849, aged 92; dau. Margaret, b. 1788, in Va. Ky. Com., p. 303.
Sally m. Zacheus Wharton.
Sally (____) m. Lewis Wilmans.
Samuel m. 3 Aug., 1798, Sophira Rollings. Shelby Co., Ky. Mar. Record.
Sarah m. John Humphreys.
Sarah m. Spencer Mottram.
Susannah m. John Potterfield.
Thomas, b. 1732, Brunswick Co.; d. 1829, Iredell Co., No. Car.; m. (1) Judith Johnston. DAR No. 31 288; DAR No. 51 034. Mar. (2) Lucy Ragsdale. 15T214; DAR No. 66 291.
Thomas, Capt., m. bef. 1789, ____ Brent, sis. of Hugh; mig. 1789 to Ky. with Hugh Brent; res. 1789-92, Lexington, 1792-1824, Paris, Ky. Perrin, 1882, p. 445. Mar. Margaret Brent. 34V379.
Thomas m. 25 Feb., 1789, Elizabeth Nance, dau. of Mary Scales. Sur. Robert Crute. Amelia Co. Mar. Bond.
Thomas, Jr., m. ca 1750, Mary Tatum, dau. of John and Mary (Eppes); res. Albemarle Parish, Surry Co. Boddie-SVF I:103.
William m. Patience St. Clair; res. Essex Co. Son, William, b. 15 April, 1755. Hartford C-2337(1), 1 Nov., 1958. Signed L. J. B. Answer, 27 Dec., 1958. Signed E. H. B. Mar. 23 July, 1744, Patience Sinclair. OPR.
William, b. 15 April, 1755, son of William and Patience (St. Clair); m. 25 March, 1770, Elizabeth Huff, b. 27 Oct., 1754; d. 22 May, 1810. Hartford C-2337(1), 1 Nov., 1958. Signed L. J. B. Answer,

YOUNG (cont.)

27 Dec., 1958. Signed E. H. B.

William, Capt., d. 1719, Essex Co.; m. bef. 1702, Catherine (Weeks) Williamson, widow of Henry and dau. of Abraham and Millicent (____) Weeks. She m. (3) Thomas Montague. 14T49. See Essex Co. records 1699 and 1707.

William m. 8 April, 1773, Jane Mickelborough, dau. of Henry. 13T194. Spelled Mickelburrough. Christ Church, p. 200.

William m. bef. 1760, Elizabeth Smith, dau. of Francis, whose will of that date, proves it. Her mother was Lucy (Meriwether). 25W(1)173. Mar. 30 Nov., 1755. 12W(2)41.

William m. 21 Jan., 1748, Mary Darby, dau. of John. Northampton Co. Mar. Record.

William m. bef. 20 Feb., 1707/8, Catherine (____) Thomas, widow of Edward. Proven by Court Record of that date, Essex Co.

William m. bef. 1 Jan., 1756, Elizabeth, sis. of Col. Meriwether Smith. Proven by Court Record of that date, Essex Co.

William m. 1795, ____ Hillis. Rockbridge Co. Morton, p. 546.

William m. 20 Jan., 1788, Eleanor Healy. Petersburg. Cameron.

William m. 29 Aug., 1746, Elizabeth Griggs. St. Paul's.

William m. 1781, Mildred Duglass. Orange Co. Mar. Record.

YOUNGER

Ann m. John Price.

Betsy m. Aaron Boyd.

Betsy m. Armstead Bomar.

Catey m. Martin Brown.

Dolly m. William Light.

Elizabeth m. Richard Fulcher.

Elizabeth m. John Legrand.

Jesse m. 23 Jan., 1783, Temperance Brown. Halifax Co. Mar. Record.

John m. 12 Dec., 1799, Polly Owen. Halifax Co. Mar. Record.

John m. 1796, Mary Dearing, dau. of Robert and Agatha (Twyman); res. 1843, Shelby Co., Ky. Wilcoxson, p. 380.

John, b. prob. King and Queen Co.; d. 1817, Halifax Co.; m. Lucy Hart. Hartford B-9178(5), 16 June, 1956. Signed I. B. Y.

John m. 1757-60, Ann Moss, dau. of Alexander and Ann (Thurmond) of Goochland Co. Moss, p. 1.

Joseph m. 6 Dec., 1788, Sally Brown. Halifax Co. Mar. Record.

Keziah m. John Ellis Bentley.

Leah m. John Wyatt.

Mary m. Jesse Grubs.

Mary m. George Estes.

Rebecha m. John Frankling.

Sally m. John Thomas.

YOUNGHUSBAND

____ m. bef. Aug., 1783, Mary Pleasants, dau. of Mary Pleasants, whose will, prov. that date, Goochland Co., names "daughter Mary Younghusband."

YOUST

Charles m. 5 July, 1796, Polly Brock. Rockingham Co. Wayland, p. 8.

YOWELL

Anne "Nancy" m. Edward W. Gaines.

YOWELL (cont.)

James, b. 20 Aug., 1755, Va.; m. 23 May, 1779, Nancy Shirley, dau. of James and Judith (Garriott). 35V298.

Samuel m. Mildred Clore, dau. of John (will prov. June, 1785). 26W (1)180; Wilcoxson, p. 374.

YUILLE

Susannah m. Don McNichol.

YULAND

Thomas m. 28 June, 1790, ____ ____. Halifax Co. Mar. Record.

YUNT

Elizabeth m. John Cline.

Joseph m. 23 (or 30) Feb., 1798, Elizabeth Bowman. Rockingham Co. Wayland, pp. 9, 10.

Z

ZACHARY

Benjamin m. 1775, Franky White. Orange Co. Mar. Record.

Jonathan m. 11 Dec., 1787, Jane Allen Gordan by Rev. Thomas Crymes, Baptist. Lunenburg Co. Ministers' Returns.

Joshua m. Elizabeth Stokes by Rev. William Ellis, Baptist. Lunenburg Co. Ministers' Returns of Oct., 1791.

Mary m. Capt. Ellison Ellis.

Thomas m. 20 April, 1760, Anne Griffin. St. Paul's.

ZANE

Ebenezer, b. 1747, Berkeley Co.; d. 1811/12, Wheeling, Va.-W. Va.; m. Elizabeth McCulloch. DAR No. 27 315; DAR No. 51 774. He, b. Oct., 1747, Augusta Co. Peyton, p. 349.

Elizabeth m. ____ McFarlane.

ZANES

____ (____) m. Ralph Jones.

ZEIGHLER

____ m. Barbara Zimmerman, dau. of Christopher (will, 1748, Orange Co.). Wayland, p. 548.

ZELLS

Ann (____) m. Joseph Renn.

ZEMEE

Mary m. William P. Thompson.

ZIGLER

Elizabeth m. Reuben Zimmerman.

ZIMMERMAN

____ m. William Slaughter.

____ m. Judith Bourn, dau. of Andrew, whose will, prov. 1790, Culpeper Co., proves it.

Andrew m. ca 1751, Barbara Weber, dau. of Peter, Sr. 26W(1)244.

Barbara m. ____ Zeiglar.

Ceny m. Daniel Bowman.

Christopher, d. 4 Feb., 1813, age 56; m. bef. 1781, Margaretta Reinhardten, d. 3 June, 1821, age 78. Wayland, pp. 359-60.

Christopher, b. ca 1745, Orange Co.; d. 1832, Boone Co., Ky., son of John; m. 1786, Culpeper Co., Maria Tanner, d. 1824, Ky. Hartford B-6095(6), 6 Feb., 1954. Signed N. E. N. Answer, 3 April, 1954.

ZIMMERMAN (cont.)

Signed C. W. R.

Frederick, Maj. in Rev. War, m. in Culpeper Co., Judith Bourne, dau. of Andrew (d. 1790) and Jane (Morton). Gillmore, p. 91.

John m. 31 Jan., 1805, Jemima (Camp) Rubicam, widow of Jacob, who rem. from Penna. to Shenandoah Valley of Va. 20T113; 63V82.

Reuben m. 1785, Culpeper Co., Elizabeth Zigler. 26W(1)238.

Rosanna m. Moses Samuel.

Wilhelm m. bef. 1757, Maria Wilhite, dau. of Adam. 26W(1)237.

ZYILLE

Margaret m. John Sinclair.

ERRATA

p.41. "Harloo" should be "Harlloo."
p.45. "Handell" should be "Randell."
p.52. "Joh" should be "John."
p.79. "Bagley" should be "Bagby."
p.117. "of Rev." should be "by Rev."

INDEX